LANGUAGE
its structure and use
Second Edition

EDWARD FINEGAN
University of Southern California

Harcourt Brace College Publishers

Fort Worth   Philadelphia   San Diego   New York   Orlando   Austin   San Antonio
Toronto   Montreal   London   Sydney   Tokyo

Publisher	**Ted Buchholz**
Acquisitions Editor	**Bill McLane, Stephen T. Jordan**
Developmental Editor	**Karl Yambert**
Senior Project Editor	**Kay Kaylor**
Associate Project Editor	**Deanna M. Johnson**
Senior Production Manager	**Kathleen Ferguson**
Art Director	**Sue Hart**

Copyright © 1994, 1989 by Harcourt Brace & Company

All rights reserved. No part of this publication may be reproduced or transmitted in any form or by any means, electronic or mechanical, including photocopy, recording, or any information storage and retrieval system, without permission in writing from the publisher.

Requests for permission to make copies of any part of the work should be mailed to: Permissions Department, Harcourt Brace & Company, 8th Floor, Orlando Florida 32887

COPYRIGHT AND ACKNOWLEDGMENT
Pages 190–191: Dictionary entries for ''husky'' and ''junior'': Copyright © 1981 by Houghton Mifflin Company. Reprinted by permission from *The American Heritage Dictionary of the English Language.*

Address for Editorial Correspondence: Harcourt Brace College Publishers, 301 Commerce Street, Suite 3700, Fort Worth, Texas 76102.

Address for Orders: Harcourt Brace & Company, Publishers, 6277 Sea Harbor Drive, Orlando, Florida 32887; 1-800-782-4479 or 1-800-433-0001 (in Florida).

ISBN: 0–15–500122–1

Library of Congress Catalog Card Number: 93–78400

Printed in the United States of America

4 5 6 7 8 9 0 1 2 016 9 8 7 6 5 4 3 2

PREFACE

For more than two millennia, philosophers, rhetoricians, and grammarians have analyzed and described the structures of human languages and the uses to which they have been put in the high and low affairs of women and men. In the twentieth century, linguists have built on past observation and reflection and broadened our understanding of languages and of language use. As physicists have recast our understanding of atoms and as space explorers have revised our images of the satellites of Uranus, so linguists have contributed to a burst of new insight into the nature of language. In *Language: Its Structure and Use,* Second Edition, you will find a glimpse of language as it is understood at the close of the twentieth century.

Despite the pace at which researchers have gained insight into the nature of language, many questions remain unanswered; indeed, the realization that today's insights replace those of yesterday serves as a reminder that tomorrow's insights will replace today's. Far more is to be learned about languages than we currently know, and much exciting and important work remains for future generations. You are invited to participate in advancing our knowledge of language, the single most important and powerful tool of human endeavor and one, remarkably, that is available to all human beings equally.

A Word to Students

Throughout this book you will find words in **boldface** type. When an important concept is first discussed (not necessarily when it is first mentioned), the term used to identify it is set in **boldface** type, thus highlighting its importance and indicating that it is defined in the Glossary (beginning on page 503) whenever you need a reminder of its meaning. For ease of reference as you read the chapters and do the exercises, there are also tables of English vowel and consonant symbols on the inside front cover and a table of most consonant symbols used in the book on the inside back cover. For any topic you wish to learn more about than is offered in this book, the Suggestions for Further Reading at the end of each chapter will steer you in a useful direction.

A Word to Instructors

This book includes more topics than can normally be covered in a one-semester course. Probably most instructors cover the first six chapters and select from among the remaining ones according to their own interests and the needs of their students. Experience indicates that students benefit from regular use of the Glossary, and from time to time you may wish to call attention to its availability. At the suggestion of some instructors, the Second Edition has an accompanying workbook, which students may find useful in reviewing basic concepts and in applying them to a range of languages.

The Second Edition differs from the first in many respects. Most apparent are the addition of a chapter on "Language Acquisition" and the elimination of the chapter on "Language Standards and Language Attitudes," whose contents have now largely been incorporated in other chapters. Virtually every chapter has been extensively revised, with material updated where desirable, clarity improved where needed, and coverage expanded where recommended. At the request of some instructors, the chapter on dialects includes linguistic features and dialect maps representing greater geographical breadth than in the first edition, and the discussion of native American languages is also expanded. The chapters treating "The Historical Development of Languages" and "The Historical Development of English" have been placed side by side for greater coherence, while the chapter on "Registers" now precedes the chapter on "Dialects" in order to introduce language variation in less sensitive circumstances than social dialects often represent. The chapter on "Writing" falls at the end of the book so as to permit a sustained discussion of language use in earlier chapters, without having to turn attention to the representation of speech in writing, a subject that intrigues many instructors and students alike but that not all syllabi have time to include.

The publisher and author sincerely invite comments and suggestions from you, and from your students, concerning any aspect of the book that could be changed to benefit future users on either side of the desk. We are eager to hear about materials that prove particularly useful or valuable and about discussion and exercises that prove perplexing or of doubtful benefit. Letters may be sent through the publisher or directly to the author.

Acknowledgments

In writing this book, I have drawn on the work of countless scholars whose analysis and writing provide more than a footing from which to address the questions taken up here. The References at the end of each chapter give only a hint of the range of scholarship relied on, but my indebtedness is no less to those who are not cited than to those whose work is recommended to readers. Many colleagues and student readers have offered helpful comments about parts of this book, and to each of them (and any whose name may be inadvertently omitted) goes special appreciation: John Algeo, Joseph Aoun, Douglas Biber, Dede Boden, Larry Bouton, Leger Brosnahan, William Brown, Paul Bruthiaux, Allan Casson, Bernard Comrie, Jeff Connor-Linton, Marianne Cooley, Carlo Coppola, David Dineen, Alessandro Duranti, Paul Frommer, John Hedgcock, Kaoru Horie, José Hualde, Larry M. Hyman, Yamuna Kachru, Audrey Li, Ronald K. S. Macaulay and his students, Erica McClure, Joseph L. Malone, James Nattinger, John Oller, Douglas Pulleyblank, La Vergne Rosow, Harold F. Schiffman, Trevor Shanklin, Gunnel Tottie, Robert R. van Oirsouw, Rebecca Wheeler, Roger Woodard, and

Anthony Woodbury, and several anonymous readers whose views were solicited by the publisher. In addition, the book has benefitted from data contributed by Zeina el-Imad Aoun, Liou Hsien-Chin, Yeon-Hee Choi, Du Tsai-Chwun, Eric Du, Jin Hong Gang, José Hualde, Yong-Jin Kim, Won-Pyo Lee, Mohammed Moham-med, Phil Morrow, Masagara Ndinzi, Charles Paus, Minako Seki, Don Stilo, and Bob Wu. Paul Bruthiaux and Min-Kyong Ju deserve thanks for their careful compi-lation of the indexes. To Bill McLane, Stephen T. Jordan, Karl Yambert, Kay Kaylor, Deanna Johnson, Kathy Ferguson, and Sue Hart at Harcourt Brace goes much appreciation for intelligent editorial supervision and attentive production.

Edward Finegan

CONTENTS IN BRIEF

CONTENTS IN DETAIL

PART II   LANGUAGE USE

1

Languages and Linguistics

IDEAL LANGUAGES AND REAL LANGUAGES

Students of linguistics sometimes ask whether there are any ideal languages, and wonder what one would look like. Indeed, from time to time idealists of various sorts—linguists, philosophers, and science fiction writers among them—have imagined various kinds of ideal languages. One common expectation is that an ideal language would provide a one-to-one correspondence between what you wanted to say and how you said it—between content and expression. Every single thought would have a unique expression, and each expression would represent just one meaning. We can think of this ideal as represented in the following schema.

Content	Ideal Language	Expression
Content A	⟷	Expression "A"
Content B	⟷	Expression "B"
Content C	⟷	Expression "C"

In a language that managed such an extraordinary one-to-one mapping between content and expression, no ambiguity would exist and no synonymy. Communication would be consistently accurate and reliable for all speakers. This one-to-one matching, a favorite of logicians, would certainly be an ideal communication system, though only in certain respects. On the negative side, such a language system would make the artful use of ambiguity and synonymy impossible—in jokes and poetry, for example—and that would be a massive disadvantage; double entendres and all other word play would vanish from speech forever (and be sorely missed by some of us).

Another popular ideal language differs radically from the first one. In this second ideal communication system, there would be only one expression for everything—irrespective of what you wanted to say. That single utterance would convey any content you intended to convey. The sole expression needed in this ideal language would be "uh," a simple *uh!* And by voicing it, the content of your intended communication would be clearly and directly conveyed to your addressee. We can think of this system as represented in the following diagram.

Content	Ideal Language	Expression
Content A		
Content B	⟵	"uh"
Content C		

As with the first idealization, no communicative misfiring could occur in this ideal language either. To take a tempting example, your linguistics instructor would be refreshingly brief each day, walking into the classroom, perhaps raising a hand, and, with due solemnity, uttering "uh." (What breathtaking simplicity!) Then you and your classmates would leave the lecture hall, knowing exactly what your instructor had intended to convey by the lecture (and he or she would rush off to the library to prepare the next day's lecture).

We need not tease this imaginary scene out any further, but you might find it provocative to think about what form your final exam questions would take, what your answers and those of your classmates would be like, and whether or not everyone would receive the same evaluation. You might even wish to contemplate how large the library would be, whether all instructors would be equally clear and equally appreciated as lecturers, and so on.[1]

Of these two ideal languages, the first, the logician's favorite, appears at first glance to be theoretically within human reach, although no natural language actu-

---

[1] As envisioned in this ideal language, your final exam would comprise questions solely of the form "uh" (there being no other utterances in this language). All your answers would likewise be "uh," of course. Disappointingly, however, evaluations would not be the same for everyone, simply because some students' utterances of "uh" could represent better answers than those of other students (depending on what other lectures or discussions had been experienced, how good one's memory was, and so on). Naturally, the instructor would be in a position to discriminate among answers because, in this ideal language, content would be communicated independently of expression.

ally could achieve a one-to-one correspondence between content and e.
In actuality, however, it is not a practical language. For, unfortunately,
take days (at least) to utter even simple thoughts in a one-to-one systen.
second ideal—a favorite of infants and intimates—would constitute an extrad
narily *efficient* language and be breathtakingly fast, but it too is impossible .
attainment; it would depend upon a degree of mental telepathy that lies entirely
beyond human ability—much to the chagrin not only of infants but of adults
stranded in a culture whose language is unfamiliar. So much, then, for ideal languages: at both ends of the spectrum such ideals lie beyond human capacities.

Competing Forces in a Tug-of-War

The varieties of natural language that social groups do in fact use daily in the
real world fall somewhere along the continuum between the ideal languages just
described. In the circumstances of human communication, our ideal systems represent competing poles between a need for explicitness and a drive toward efficiency. For the advantage of *hearers* and *readers,* the need for adequately explicit
communication tugs language in the direction of full and unique expression. But
for the ease of *speakers* and *writers,* efficiency tugs in the direction of minimal
(and therefore similar) expression for all content, towards "uh"! (You know what
I mean?)

It's a simple matter: The more explicit *you* are in *your* expression (at least
within limits), the easier it is for *me* to grasp your meaning. On the other hand,
as a speaker, the less *I* need to say in order to communicate *my* meaning to you,
the easier *my* task will be. It's as if expression were governed by competing forces:
a centrifugal force teasing it out and a centripetal force tending to compress it. The
centrifugal force, by promoting explicitness, supports hearers and interpreters; the
centripetal force, slighting hearers and addressees, is a boon to speakers.

When Samuel Johnson, the first great English dictionary maker, alleged that
"tongues, like governments, have a natural tendency to degeneration," he was
referring to the centripetal force that tends to collapse expression. It is the inevitable result of a natural tendency to communicate economically in accordance with
a principle of cooperation that speakers rely upon. For the sake of efficiency, we
abbreviate sentences, blend words together, use homonyms *(break* and *brake)*
and structurally ambiguous sentences *(Visiting relatives can be a disaster),* convert nouns to verbs ("*water* the lawn," "*smoke* a cigar," "*view* a film") and
verbs to nouns ("a good *read,*" "a vigorous *swim,*" "a disdainful *look*"), use the
same word *(they, her,* and *it)* for countless references, and run sounds together
or skip them altogether. *Said 'e'd be 'ere* (He said that he would be here) and
J'eat yet? (Did you eat yet?) are the workaday products of efficient communication
in English, while *shaypa* (*Je ne sais pas* 'I don't know') is one of its French
manifestations.

In face-to-face communication between people who know one another well,
the tolerance for abbreviated expression tends to be affordably great. Contractions
like *don't, gonna,* and *j'eat yet* are most frequent in face-to-face conversation
but decrease in frequency as the degree of shared context between interlocutors

diminishes (as you'll see in detail in Chapter 12). In less contextualized circumstances, linguistic expression must be fuller if communication is to succeed. In some kinds of speech and especially in certain types of writing, a good deal must be made explicit that could remain implicit in conversation between people of similar background and shared assumptions. (Y'understand?)

The two forces—one to compress, the other to elaborate—are fairly well balanced simply because the need to be understood serves as a check on the urge to economize. Teachers and editorial-page writers often fret that the telegraphic expression resulting from centripetal efficiency will overpower the need for articulated expression, especially in writing. They recognize that insufficient explicitness can be corrected with a question in the course of conversation, but a reader has no ready opportunity to solicit clarification or elaboration from a writer other than that already provided by the text. As a result, writers tend to heed the need for explicitness and clarity more than speakers do.

What Is Human Language?

Languages—both ideal and real—have been a focus of people's curiosity and intellectual probing for millennia. Like other inquiries central to human experience, questions about language and how it functions are not new to the twentieth century. As old as speculation on any subject, inquiry into the nature of language occupied not only Plato and Aristotle, but other Greek and Indian philosopher-grammarians as well. In some areas of grammatical analysis, the ancients made contributions that have remained useful for two thousand years.

In the nineteenth and twentieth centuries, the field of linguistics emerged to address these questions: What is language and what are its structures? How do its structures function and how are they acquired? In what ways can they change and develop? This book provides a modern context for asking and addressing those questions. Ensuing chapters will provide views of language as it has come to be understood toward the end of the twentieth century. Still, it is useful here to make some general observations about the nature of language and to offer a framework for a journey through the various aspects of its structures, development, and use.

Two Sides of a Coin or Three Faces of a Triangle   One basic observation about language is that it seems to face in two directions, for the fundamental function of every language is to link expression to content—to provide words and sentences for the expression of thought and feeling. A language can be viewed as a coin whose two sides are *expression* and *content*.

But languages have a third face, critically important for communicating and interpreting meaning. Consider the question, "Is there a state income tax in Connecticut?" Among the replies that this question is likely to elicit are "Yes," "No," and "I don't know." The question could be taken as a request for a piece of information that the inquirer wishes to have. Now consider the equally straightforward inquiry made by a guest at a holiday meal: "Is there any salt on the table?" In this instance, a host who earnestly replied "Yes," "No," or "I don't know," and let it go at that would raise eyebrows, at the very least. The form of the holiday question resembles the form of the question about Connecticut income tax, but the expected responses could hardly differ more. In the context of a dinner, a guest would have every reason to expect the host to recognize that it is not information about salt that is lacking but salt itself! And a host who ignored the *context* of the question and took it literally as a request for information would be regarded as dull indeed (or perhaps a tease). In a related context—for example, where the host is standing in the kitchen with sugar bowl and pepper shaker in hand and asking a guest who has just emerged from the dining room, "Is there any salt on the table?"—the host is likely to be understood as seeking information even though *the form of the question* is identical to that asked by the guest at the table. And in this instance a reply of "Yes" or "No" would be altogether appropriate. In fact, if the guest returned to the table to fetch the salt and deliver it to the host in the kitchen, the likely upshot would be consternation.

Besides content and expression, then, there is a third aspect to language, and it is the *use* to which expression and content are put *in particular contexts.* Language is better viewed as a figure with three sides: *expression, content,* and *context,* as represented in the triangle below.

The Three Faces of Language

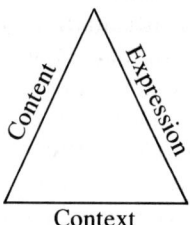

Context

In the case of the question, "Is there any salt on the table?" the meaning of the words *(salt, table)* and phrases (for example, *on the table*), as well as of the entire sentence, is the same in both contexts. But the intended *use* of this utterance differs in the two contexts, and speakers expect addressees to interpret words and sentences within their context. All utterances are embedded in a context, and their interpretation relies on familiarity with that context.

All language users must distinguish among expression, content, and context of use. **Expression** refers to the words, phrases, and sentences. **Content** refers to the meaning of the words, phrases, and sentences. **Context** refers to the social situations in which words, phrases, and sentences are uttered. The code that links content and expression is *grammar.* The system that links grammar and interpretation is *grammar in use,* and grammar in use is *language.* Without attention to grammar and context, no one can adequately understand language and how it functions.

Real and Ideal Languages As we saw in our discussion of ideal languages, neither the one-to-one nor the "uh" ideals are possible as human communication systems. In reality, though, each variety of every language falls somewhere along the continuum of expression between these extremes. For effective communication, varieties that can presume relatively little shared context between interlocutors fall toward the one-to-one end—they tease out expression and rely less on shared context. By contrast, varieties supported by a great deal of shared information and background and shared communicative situation fall toward the other end, toward "uh," leaving unsaid as much as context can be expected to provide. For this reason, varieties falling toward the "uh" end of the continuum are characteristic of intimate, face-to-face communication between interlocutors who share a great deal of information and background, as in dinnertime conversation among family members.

Language: Mental and Social   Traditionally, language has been viewed as a vehicle of thought, a system of expression that mediates the transfer of thought from one person to another, and this certainly is one of its important tasks. To view language solely this way, however, is to confine oneself to a narrow perspective. In everyday life, from birth through old age, language serves social and affective functions as well as cognitive ones, and these are equally important tasks.

The notion of thought is a familiar one. "I was just thinking . . . ," we say, or "I think I'll skip lunch today." Such statements, frequent as they are in conversation, pass unnoticed with respect to the verb *think*. Language and thought are so intimately entwined that we tend to equate them. Still, as speakers and writers striving to find words to match our thoughts, we tacitly acknowledge that thought and language are distinct. From time to time, all of us recognize better and worse "fits" between our thoughts and the words we use to express them—better fits between content and expression in particular contexts of use.

Content encompasses what you are attempting to say; expression encompasses the way you articulate the content; and grammar is the mental code that links the two. To enhance students' ability to find an adequate and suitable fit between written expression and various kinds of content—narrative, description, argument, and especially exposition—colleges traditionally require writing courses, whose aims are essentially utilitarian. Courses in linguistics are less traditional and not so practical. While they too tend to focus on the expressive side of language, they do so as an inquiry into the organization of language and the uses to which its forms are put in speaking, writing, and signing, rather than to provide a practical tool for discovering and conveying thoughts.

Linguistics addresses language in two foundational arenas of human experience: the *mental* and the *social*. Linguists are interested in models of how language is organized in the mind and in how the social structures of human communities shape languages to their own purposes, reflecting those social structures in linguistic expression and linguistic interpretation. To be sure, knowledge of how languages are organized and put to use can be helpful in your interactions with members of your own and other societies, but the main goal of this book is to provide an understanding of how languages are structured and of how they function in social interaction. In that goal, linguistics provides an essential element in a liberal arts education, for language is at the heart of all intellectual and social activities. It is at the core of being human.

Signs and Symbols

Signs   We often use the word *sign* in everyday conversation. We talk about signs of trouble with the economy, no sign of a train coming into a railway station, someone's vital signs at the scene of an accident, and so forth. A sign is an indicator of something; in the cases we've specified, the indicator is inherently related to the thing that is indicated—it is a *nonarbitrary* indicator. That is to say, there is a direct, usually causal relationship between the indicator and the thing indicated. Smoke is a *sign* of fire, and clouds are a *sign* of impending rain. **Signs,** then, are nonarbitrary indicators of the things they signal, the things they are signs of.

Symbols   In thinking about language, it is crucial to distinguish nonarbitrary signs from indicators that are partly or wholly arbitrary. *Arbitrary* indicators of anything are called **symbols,** and common symbols in the workaday world include traffic lights, railroad crossing indicators, flashing red or blue lights on police vehicles, wedding rings, and national flags. With these, there is no inherent connection between the symbols and the things they symbolize. For example, no property of the color red is inherently associated with stopping, yet red lights are used *conventionally* in traffic codes to indicate that cars must stop. Being arbitrary, a strictly symbolic indicator can be present without the thing indicated (as with a wedding band worn by a bachelor). There is nothing causal in the relationship between a symbol and what it symbolizes. Nor is there anything in the nature of an arbitrary symbol that makes it inherently better (or worse) than other potential representations for the same thing. Societies are free to select any symbol to represent a particular notion. If, for example, a national transportation department decided to use the color blue as a signal for traffic to stop, nothing would prevent that from happening. Being only conventional representations, symbols can be changed. By contrast, it is impossible to change the relationship between smoke and fire or clouds and rain, because they are not arbitrary relationships.

Iconic Symbols   Some essentially arbitrary symbols are not entirely arbitrary, of course. Sometimes a symbol directly suggests its meaning to some degree. Such symbols as a skull and crossbones to indicate poison, or ☼ to refer to the sun, or the Roman numeral III to refer to the number three are not entirely arbitrary. But there is no inherent connection between the symbol and the symbolized even in these cases; the symbol can be present without the symbolized, and vice versa. Such basically arbitrary but partly related symbols are called **representational** (or *iconic*) symbols. Linguistic examples of iconic symbols might include the words *meow* and *trickle,* for it is commonly supposed that these words have some nonarbitrary relation to the things they symbolize. (Iconicity, or representational symbolization, has played a role in the development of writing; see Chapter 15.)

Besides the kind of iconicity captured in words—as when the sound of the word *meow* echoes the sound of a kitten—iconic expression appears spontaneously in ordinary speech. I once telephoned the home of a friend and had a brief conversation with her four-year-old son. I was trying to reach the boy's mother, but he reported that she was showering just then. As the matter was of some urgency,

I told the boy that I would call back in a few minutes but he indicated that calling back soon would do no good. His explanation was this:

My mother is taking a *long, loong, looong* shower.

By repeating the word *long* and by increasing its length—making the expression longer to mirror the content—the boy illustrated the potential for iconicity in human language. **Iconic** language is expression that in any fashion mimics or directly suggests its content. By repeating words and by lengthening sounds, the boy stretched out the expression itself in order to underscore the salient part of the content of his message.

Similarly, certain aspects of grammar also appear to be influenced by iconic principles. English, for example, has two ways of expressing conditional sentences:

If you behave, I'll bring you some candy.
I'll bring you some candy if you behave.

In other words, we have a choice between placing the conditioning part *(if you behave)* before or after the consequence of the condition *(I'll bring you some candy)*. Though contextual factors sometimes influence the choice of alternatives, speakers and writers show a strong preference for the first pattern (condition followed by consequence). This preference, also found in many other languages, is most apparent in speech. Why might the first pattern be preferred to the second pattern? The answer has to do with the order of occurrence of events described by conditional clauses. In this example, the hearer must first behave, and then the speaker will bring the candy. So the events described by the preceding sentences are ordered in time, and this order is reflected in the preferred linguistic order of condition first, consequence second. There is thus an iconic explanation for preferring the condition-consequence order over the opposite one: With the order condition-consequence, the expression side iconically reflects the sequencing of events in the content side. In some languages, only the condition-consequence pattern is allowed; but there is no language, as far as we know, in which conditional sentences can be expressed only with the noniconic order consequence-condition.

Arbitrary Symbols   Despite such occasional iconic characteristics, human language is *not* fundamentally representational. It is essentially arbitrary. The form of expression is generally independent of its content except for the meanings that have been established by social convention. The fundamental arbitrariness of human language is unaltered by the fact that certain symbols come to be so closely associated with what they represent that reaction to the symbol—the expression—can be as strong as reaction to what it represents—the content. Burning a flag, for example, has in some cases provoked reactions nearly as strong as would betraying one's country. Though the important difference between arbitrary and nonarbitrary representations is sometimes overlooked in common parlance, we reserve the word *symbol* for representations whose meaning is assigned in a partly or wholly arbitrary manner.

We can illustrate the arbitrary nature of linguistic symbols with an example. Imagine a parent cooking dinner and trying to catch a few minutes of the televised evening news. Suddenly a strong aroma of burning rice wafts into the TV room. This aroma, an unmistakable *sign* that the rice is burning, will send the parent scurrying to salvage dinner. Compare this nonarbitrary sign with the words of a youngster in the kitchen who sees the smoke and shouts, *The rice is burning!* Like the aroma, this utterance is likely to send a parent scurrying, but there is a world of difference between the two modes of communication. The aroma—directly caused by the burning rice—will convey its message to speakers of any language. There is nothing conventionalized about the aroma; it is thus a *sign*. The words of the child, on the other hand, are arbitrary. It is a fact about English—agreed to conventionally by generations of English speakers—and not a fact about burning rice that enables the utterance to do the work intended by the child: alerting the parent to the situation. The utterance is thus a *symbol*.

Other languages convey the same message differently: Korean by the utterance *pap tʰanda,* Swahili by *wali inaunguwu,* Arabic by *yaḥtaqiru alruzzu,* and so on. The forms of these utterances have nothing to do with rice or its chemistry, or with the manner in which it is cooking, or with anything inherent in the situation; they are not iconic. Instead, they have to do solely with the nature of the systems of symbolic expression that we call Korean, Swahili, and Arabic.

Hence the utterances, unlike the aroma, can and do differ from culture to culture. Moreover, they can be uttered—and convey their message—whether or not rice is in fact burning. Pranksters contriving an opportunity to switch channels to a favorite program, or looking for attention from a busy parent, or being jocular or cantankerous, might use the same utterance regardless of the situation in the kitchen. Signs, on the other hand, are not arbitrary and do not exist independently of their causes. Only by an elaborate ruse could a *sign* of burning rice be devised independently of an actual occurrence.

Because the relationship between symbols and what they stand for is arbitrary, the meaning of a given symbol can differ from culture to culture, and different cultures typically evolve different symbols to represent the same thing. Even words that mimic natural noises are cross-linguistically distinct. Cats don't *meow* in all languages (compare Korean *yaong,* for instance).

To repeat, a central fact about language is that the connection between the things signified and the words used to signify them—between signified and signifier, or symbolized and symbol—is arbitrary. In English, we refer to the stuff that bakers make as *bread.* The French call it *pain,* the Russians *xleb.* In Chinese, the word is *miànbāo;* in Fijian, *madrai.* Not only can one and the same thing be symbolized differently in different languages, but even in a single language several symbols can represent the same entity or notion. We purchase *a dozen* or *twelve* bagels for the same price. We can write 12 or XII for the same concept, as well as *TWELVE, twelve,* or *Twelve.* Thus, to represent even a straightforward numerical concept, English permits several alternative symbols. For more complex content, the variety of possible expressions in phrases and sentences seems limitless.

Languages as Rule-Governed Systems

Precisely because the relationship between linguistic symbols and the things they represent is arbitrary, languages must be highly organized systems if they are to function as reliable vehicles of expression and communication. If there were no pattern to the way we voiced our thoughts and feelings, listeners would face an insuperable task in determining what we meant. If languages were not highly organized and patterned systems, listeners would find it impossible to unravel their arbitrary symbols for the content they encode. It is not surprising, then, that languages have evolved over centuries into such extraordinarily complex systems that an entire field of inquiry has arisen to investigate their basic properties.

We have said that language is rule governed. It follows observable patterns that obey certain inherent "rules." Such rules are not imposed from the outside, and they do not specify how something *should* be done. Instead, they are merely the regularities that we can observe being followed when people use language. In other words, the linguistic rules described in this book are based on nothing more than the observed regularities of language behavior and of the underlying systems that we can infer from such language behavior. Linguistic rules are more like the patterns describing how the digestive tract or the circulatory system works than like traffic regulations or the kinds of rules that prescribe how to behave when visiting a dignitary.

A language is a set of elements and a system of rules for combining those elements to form patterned sentences that can be used to do specific jobs in specific contexts: Utterances report something, greet someone, invite a friend to lunch, request the time of day, make a wisecrack, poke fun at someone, argue for a particular course of action, make inquiries, express admiration, propose marriage, create fictional (and science-fictional) worlds, and so on in an endless list. And languages do this using a finite system of elements and rules that a child normally masters in a few short years. The mental capacity that enables speakers to form grammatical sentences such as *My mother is taking a long shower* rather than *A taking long my shower is mother* (or literally thousands of other conceivable ill-formed strings of exactly the same words) is called **grammatical competence.**

Speech as Rule-Governed Language Use

There is much more to the ability to speak than grammatical competence. Knowing the elements of a language and the patterns for putting them together into well-formed, or grammatical, sentences falls far short of knowing how to accomplish the work that speakers accomplish with language; it falls short of native-speaker fluency. To be fluent in a language requires not only mastery of its grammatical rules but also competence in the appropriate use of the sentences that are structured by those rules. Fluency requires knowledge of how to put sentences together in conversations, for example, and of how to rely on nonlinguistic context and previous linguistic context in shaping utterances appropriately, and in interpreting them. The point is that fluency presumes two kinds of competence: knowledge of how to form sentences and knowledge of what those sentences are capable of doing and of when and how to use them appropriately (as well as how to interpret them in context).

The capacity that enables us to use language appropriately is called **communicative competence.** It enables language users to weave utterances together into conversations, apologies, requests, directions, descriptions, sermons, scoldings, or jokes and to do the myriad things we do with language when it is appropriate to do them. When asked by a curious visitor the whereabouts of the campus bookstore, a student who replied *There's a great show on channel 4 tonight about California condors* would certainly be greeted with raised eyebrows, though no one could point to ungrammatical English as the culprit. We would say that the student's grammatical competence was fine, but his or her communicative competence was sorely lacking. Knowing a language—being a fluent speaker—presumes both communicative competence and grammatical competence. Neither one is sufficient by itself to constitute fluency in the ordinary sense of the word—in the sense that encompasses both structure and use. To be fluent, grammatical competence and communicative competence are jointly needed.

We can summarize by saying that grammatical competence is the language user's implicit knowledge of vocabulary, pronunciation, sentence structure, and meaning, while communicative competence is the implicit knowledge that underlies the appropriate use of grammatical competence in the various situations of language use. The rules that govern the appropriate use of language differ from one speech community to the next, so even a shared grammatical competence may not be adequate to make you a fluent speaker in another community, at least in some situations. Joke telling is not the same cross-culturally: Members of one culture may find jokes about other people's misadventures funny, whereas members of another culture may find such jokes offensive. In fact, the very concept of telling jokes (as distinct from telling "funny stories") seems not to exist in certain societies. Likewise, even within the English-speaking world, what is considered impolite in one place might be routine interaction elsewhere. Differences in the rules for speaking to strangers explain why some visitors to the Big Apple think New Yorkers are brusque or impolite when giving directions, though the same utterance that provokes an unfavorable judgment in an outsider will be interpreted by a native New Yorker as routinely polite.

VIEWS OF THE ORIGIN OF LANGUAGE

A good many people in all parts of the world share a belief that the origin of language can be traced to a Garden of Eden, where the first woman and the first man spoke the language originally bestowed upon them by their creator. Even among people who may give little credence to that story, many are persuaded that language originated in a paradise where its pristine form was perfectly logical and perfectly grammatical. The belief is widespread that languages, once pure, are becoming progressively contaminated with illogicalities, ungrammaticalities, and assorted impurities. English speakers and French speakers seem particularly inclined to worry over linguistic pollution, but they are far from alone.

As examples of *impurities,* subscribers to this view might cite such borrowed words as American *okay* and French *disco,* which have spread into many other languages. Alleged *illogicalities* come in many shapes, with double negatives being a commonly cited English example. The claim is that as two negatives yield a positive in algebra or logic (*It is **not untrue*** means 'It **is** true'), so *I don't want **none*** should logically mean 'I **do** want some' and *He **never** did **nothing*** should mean 'He **did** do something.' Of course they don't. Alleged *ungrammaticalities* also come in many shapes. Commonly cited is the use of the personal pronoun *I* as the object of a preposition, as in *just between you and I,* or the use of *him* and *me* as subjects, as in *Him and me were friends in the army.* The argument is offered that objects of a preposition *must* be in the objective case (thus, *just between you and me*) and that subjects of a sentence *must* be in the subjective case (thus, *He and I were friends in the army*). Of course, millions of English speakers all around the globe use these allegedly ungrammatical expressions. And the sun continues to rise over them each morning and set each evening, and the moon continues to orbit around the earth. More to the point, no greater or more frequent misunderstanding arises among people using these expressions than among people using expressions claimed by some to be more "grammatical" or more "logical." The "laws" of language and the "laws" of logic are not the same, and language symbols are essentially arbitrary.

Language Diversity from Babel to Babble

As to why languages differ from one another and why they change, people have different ways of explaining the facts. The Old Testament relates that before the Tower of Babel all men and women spoke the same language and could understand one another without difficulty; human haughtiness eventually provoked God into punishing people by confounding their language and introducing mutually unintelligible tongues. Given this story, language differences among people can be seen as a penalty for sinful behavior. Similarly, Moslems believe that God spoke to Mohammed in a form of Arabic that was by definition pure and perfect. The Koran is viewed as the exemplar of pure and grammatically perfect Arabic, while the many varieties of present-day Arabic spoken in the Gulf, North Africa, and elsewhere are seen as having arisen through the subsequent weakness and culpability of their speakers.

Professional linguists take a different approach. They see the multiplicity of languages as the product of natural historical change, the inevitable result of people shaping and reshaping their languages to meet changing social and intellectual needs, and as a reflection of contact with peoples speaking still other languages. When groups of people move to different places and mix with people who speak different tongues or settle previously uninhabited areas with unfamiliar flora and fauna, their language must adapt to new circumstances. Meeting people with new artifacts and different views of the world and confronting unfamiliar aspects of nature invite accommodation and linguistic adaptation. As a result, individual languages have evolved quite differently around the globe. Remarkably, however, as increasing numbers of languages have been examined and as the tools of linguistic analysis have been sharpened, what is even more striking about the world's languages than their differences is the extraordinary extent of their similarities.

But this insight should not be so surprising! Given that all languages must conform to the constraints imposed by the structure of the human brain, only so much variation is possible. Of the many conceivable kinds of language and language structure, only a relatively narrow band can in fact be found among the world's repertoire of languages.

As you recognized the first time you heard a foreign tongue, there is marked variation from language to language. Not only does Japanese sound vastly different from French, but French differs from Spanish, Italian, Romanian, and Portuguese, its close relatives. Even speaking the same language, different social groups speak it differently, and every social group controls a range of language varieties for use in different social situations. Whatever the ultimate explanation of the origins of language and whatever one's faith, language appears to be *inherently* variable: It marks different social groups, and it marks different speech situations. Given our nature, human beings show a powerful tendency toward language diversification, with some language varieties marking groups of *users* (Burmese and Brooklynese, for example) and others marking situations of *use* (such as legalese and motherese). Each language variety marks something of the social identity of those who speak it and reflects the uses to which it is put. Among the remarkable things about these subtle and not so subtle differences across language varieties is that they all fall within a very narrow range of conceivable languages.

From the point of view of the discipline of linguistics, there is no basis for preferring the structure of one language variety over another. Judgments like "illogical" and "impure" are notions imported from outside the realm of language; they represent attitudes to language varieties or to particular forms of expression within particular language varieties; often, too, they represent judgments of speakers rather than speech. As to the notion of "ungrammatical," we use it throughout this book, but only to characterize utterances that are not said and cannot be said by native speakers of a language. In this book we will not call an expression like *just between you and I* "ungrammatical," and the simple reason is that it is in fact said (and sometimes written) by too many English speakers to count. We will limit the term "ungrammatical" to an utterance like *Book the ingread am I right now* (compare *I am reading the book right now*), because it is an utterance that will not be found in the speech of those who know English anywhere in the world (except, of course, as examples of ill-formed sentences crafted by linguists for use in textbooks).

WHAT IS LINGUISTICS?

With this background we can ask, What is linguistics? Linguistics can be defined as the scientific inquiry into human language—into its structures and uses and the relationship between them, as well as into the development and acquisition of language. The scope of linguistics as discussed in this book includes both language structure (and the grammatical competence underlying it) and language use (and its underlying communicative competence).

Linguists acknowledge that, despite significant strides in our understanding in recent years, not enough is known to provide a complete understanding of language. Linguistics is best regarded as an enterprise whose principal objective is to provide an increasingly adequate understanding of particular facets of languages, thereby gradually building our understanding of the nature of language itself.

In many discussions of the subject, language is defined as an arbitrary vocal system used by human beings to communicate with one another. This common definition is useful as far as it goes, but it downplays one important element that philosophers have brought to the forefront of current thinking. Speech is more than communication; it is *action*. A language is a communication system that has work to perform, a system that speakers exploit purposefully. Language is used to *do* things, not merely to *report* them or talk about them. *That color looks terrific on you!* is not likely to be a mere report (whereas *Halloween falls on a Tuesday next year* might well be)—rather, it compliments the addressee. *Out!* is a mere conjecture when shouted by a fan at a baseball game, but it is a call (a ruling, if you will) when uttered by the umpire—it can end an inning or a game.

As mentioned earlier, people have been interested in language structure and language use for millennia. Plato and Aristotle discussed language in the fourth and third centuries B.C., and we have inherited several central categories of grammatical analysis from them. Nouns and verbs were identified by the Greek philosophers, whom we also credit with establishing the grammatical genders of masculine and feminine, as well as neuter (that is, 'neither'), and with recognizing that verbs have tenses, such as present and past. More than a century before Plato and Aristotle, grammatical analysis was underway in India, where a sage named Pāṇini wrote a description of Sanskrit that some scholars regard as one of the finest grammars ever produced for any language. Both the Greeks and the Indians were concerned with the relationship between symbols and the things they signify—an issue that still warrants attention, as we have seen.

Today, the empirical and scientific study of language has taken on additional importance in an age where communication is so critical to social, intellectual, political, economic, and moral concerns. Linguistics—now augmented by insights from psychology, sociology, anthropology, philosophy, and rhetoric as well as from communications engineering and other sciences—has become a prominent academic discipline in universities throughout the world, alongside departments of cognitive science and of language and literature.

Branches of Linguistics

There are many branches of linguistics, and new ones continue to arise. Historically, the central branch has been grammar, and many linguists today are engaged in the study of grammatical systems—of sentence formation, of human speech sounds, of word structure, and of meaning. Some are interested in the description of particular languages, others in uncovering the patterns across languages and explaining universal patterns in psychological or social terms.

Other linguists focus on language variation both across speech communities and within a single community, across time, and across different situations of use—conversational structure and sports announcer talk, for example. Like grammarians, linguists interested in variation seek two kinds of explanation: those that are psychological and have to do with constraints on the human language-processing capacities and those that are social and have to do with the organization of societies and the interaction of people. Ultimately, much of what is found will be explained by a combination of social and psychological approaches.

A third group of linguists applies the findings of the discipline to real-world problems. In *educational* matters they apply their knowledge to understanding the acquisition of literate aspects of language (reading and writing) and the acquisition of second languages and foreign languages, and in *clinical* matters they work toward understanding aspects of Alzheimer's disease and aphasia. Further, in *forensic* settings they analyze conversation to uncover conspiracy, threats, defamation, and other matters of law; interpret contracts of all sorts (from insurance policies to rental agreements); clarify public safety instructions (like medical labels and dosage directions); and identify such things as voice and authorship. Other applied linguists address problems in language policy at national and local levels: what languages to allow for use in the schools, the courts, the voting booth, and so on; what kind of writing system to aim for; what regulation of existing language is needed, as in the rise of the Plain English movement in the United States or in the development and production of the tools of standardization, such as dictionaries and grammars. As the world shrinks and different cultures mix together, linguists are also applying the tools of their trade to the challenges of cross-cultural communication, as well.

MODES OF LINGUISTIC COMMUNICATION

All of us have at our disposal several different ways of communicating. We can communicate our feelings and moods with gestures, as dancers and mimes do professionally. We can also draw sequences of figures, as on a cryptic treasure map. We can convey moods and emotions through painting or music. These channels of artistic communication do not rely on language but belong instead to the realm of nonlinguistic communication and lie beyond the scope of this book.

In linguistic communication, by contrast, meaning is conveyed chiefly through the channels of language. There are three basic **modes** of linguistic communication, corresponding to different modes of perception: oral communication, which relies on the use of speech and hearing organs; writing, a visual representation that was invented about five thousand years ago; and signing, another visual (or sometimes tactile) representation, which many hearing-impaired and speech-impaired people (and their friends) rely on for communication. In this section we briefly review some of the characteristics of these three modes of linguistic communication.

Speaking

To observe a group of human beings engaged in a conversation is to witness several kinds of communication. There is first of all the voice, with all its complexity and richness of intonation and other modulation. There is also a tapestry of gestures, including hand waving of various sorts, body stance, gaze, and other facial movements. These combine to communicate intentions—not only the seemingly obvious ones encoded in utterances themselves, but also more subtle ones like the participants' wish to speak or to let someone else speak.

The ordinary vehicle of linguistic communication is the voice, and speech is a primary *mode* of human language. That this is so is hardly surprising, for speech has several advantages over other potential vehicles of human communication. It is extremely valuable to have a vehicle whose use interferes minimally with other life-sustaining activities. Because speech does not need to be seen, it can do its work as effectively in darkness as in light, around corners, and in other visually inaccessible spots. Although in its natural state it cannot span time, its physical reach is far greater than arm's length. Unlike signing, speech leaves the eyes and the hands free for other work. We can talk and listen while looking at things besides our interlocutors. In the development of speech in the human species, when hands and eyes were occupied in hunting, fishing, food gathering, and other manual activities of work and play, speech was free to carry out other tasks: to report, point, ask for and give directions, explain, promise, bargain, warn, flirt, threaten, and deceive. Eating is one thing that people can't do well while talking, but even eating doesn't preclude speech—as the lunchtime din in any college cafeteria will demonstrate.

Speaking has still other advantages. For one thing, the human voice is a complex vehicle with many channels. It has variable volume, pitch, stress, and speed: It is capable of wide-ranging modulation. Take a simple sentence like *Isn't that sad?* and consider the various utterances created by different voice modulations. With different modulations, we can express irony, suggesting that it isn't sad at all, or sarcasm, or humor. We can make an assertion, ask a question, poke fun, be teasing, or express sympathy in a relatively straightforward way. This variation in expressive power through modulations of the voice occurs at the level of language that is called phonology.

We also have other linguistic channels, including vocabulary and sentence structure, which subsequent chapters will cover in detail. Speech is not a single-channel mode. It has intonation and stress, as well as the more familiar grammatical levels. Besides a set of sounds, speech takes advantage of the organization of those sounds—of their sequencing into words and sentences. Like writing and signing, speech can take advantage of word choice and word order. In many ways, speech is even more versatile than writing. Intonation, stress, and volume are more fully privileges of the spoken mode than of the written or signed modes.

Writing

Long before the invention of writing, people had been painting stories on cave walls or exploiting other kinds of visual symbols to record events and other matters. Such *pictograms* were independent of language—a kind of cartoon world, in which anyone with knowledge of the lives of people but without specifically linguistic knowledge could come along and reconstruct the depicted story or event. Pictograms are language independent. When shown to adult speakers of different languages, the depicted stories can be told in Japanese, Arabic, English, Swahili, Mohawk, Indonesian, or any other language. Pictograms tell a story or provide information that can be understood in any language: they are a direct, nonlinguistic symbolization, like a silent film or like the road signs used internationally to indicate a curved roadway ahead or the availability of food and lodging.

If we decide to associate such drawings not with the objects they represent but with the *words* that refer to the objects they represent, then we have a more sophisticated system. The system of representation becomes *linguistic* because it relies on language for its organization and communication. There is ample evidence that writing was invented about five thousand years ago by some ingenious souls who chanced upon an occasion or a need to use pictograms to represent spoken words instead of the objects that they customarily represented. For example, while it is very difficult to express with pictograms a message containing reference to abstract objects (hunger or danger, for instance), the task becomes possible if the graphic symbols represent existing words. Once someone recognized—at least implicitly—that a written symbol could serve to represent a spoken (linguistic) symbol, the first step in the development of writing had been taken. People came to realize that the possibilities of the new mode of linguistic communication were immense.

It should be clear that speech and writing are related in different ways to the world they symbolize. Speech, which preceded writing by a very long time in human history, is a symbolic system that represents entities in the physical and mental world—things like sun, moon, fish, grain, running, height, and truth. Writing, on the other hand, does not directly represent this same world. A written sentence like *John caught a fish* is a secondary symbolization in which the written symbols represent the spoken words, not the entities themselves. (Various types of writing are investigated in Chapter 15; the relationship between speech and writing is discussed in Chapter 12.)

Signing

The third mode of linguistic communication is *signing,* the exclusive use of gestures to communicate messages. Of course, speakers use gestures and facial expressions to convey some meaning as well. But these gestures differ from signing because they serve only to support oral communication and would not be adequate by themselves for communication. Signing, in contrast, can be used as the sole means of conveying messages and accomplishing the work of language.

Two kinds of signing are possible. One consists of spelling out words by "drawing" with the hands the shape of written symbols (such as letters) that are used in writing to represent sounds. Like writing itself, this method depends on the prior existence of a spoken language, and it requires a form of written representation. Thus, any signing system that relies on the modeling of letters (such as the one used by the deaf and blind Helen Keller) is two steps removed from the linguistic system that hearing and seeing children acquire.

The other kind of signing is independent of the spoken word and could be used cross-linguistically, provided users understood the code. In this type of signing, particular gestures stand for particular words. The fact that these words may be pronounced differently from one language to another does not matter because the gesture does not make any reference to the sound of the word in any language. Such a system was traditionally in use among certain American Indian nations in the western United States and among certain Australian Aborigine nations. It is also what underlies certain signing systems in use today for the hearing impaired.

Like writing, signing may be seen as a secondary symbolic system whose signed symbols represent words, which in turn are symbols for objects, concepts, and feelings. Signing differs from writing in that its users must be in full sight of one another for it to function successfully, and in this sense signing is more similar to speaking than to writing.

Speaking, Writing, Signing: Modes of Linguistic Communication

Speaking, writing, and signing are the three primary modes of linguistic communication, each with advantages and limitations. For example, speech is the only mode of linguistic communication possible when visibility is hindered. It is also the only mode in which the communicator's hands and eyes are left free to do other things. People signing to one another must be in view of one another and, in effect, facing one another. Speech has limitations, too, some of which are shared by signing. Both speech and signing have an evanescent character and vanish upon being uttered. Neither spoken nor signed utterances can be retrieved after they have been uttered unless they were taperecorded or filmed. Writing, on the other hand, has evolved to meet other needs. It can be preserved for thousands of years, as with the words of Homer, Plato, Aristotle, and Jesus—all of whom were public speakers whose words were written down by others. Writing has another advantage over speech and signing in that it can transcend space. One can send a written message anywhere on earth. With technology, of course, this advantage of writing over speaking and signing is decreasing.

In this book we focus on language as it is represented in spoken and written communication. It is important to keep in mind that, historically and developmentally, writing is a secondary mode of linguistic communication. This can be a challenge to students, whose principal focus and principal context for discussing language heretofore has been written language, and for all literate people, who are familiar with the extraordinary power and influence of the written word.

SUMMARY

We can imagine two kinds of ideal languages. One would require maximally simple expression and be forced to rely on telepathy; the other would leave nothing implicit but would be impossible to master or use in ordinary time frames. All varieties of all human languages operate between these two extremes. Some favor more economical expression, others more explicit expression, depending on the degree of shared context.

Human language is thought by some people to have originated in a paradise where it was perfectly grammatical and altogether logical but to have become contaminated over the centuries with impurities and illogicalities. By contrast, linguists see the changes that affect every language every day as the product of an inevitable and natural process of historical development, and they view every language as being as logical (or illogical) as every other.

In part, language is a system of grammatical rules that structure the organization of expression. Equally important is the role of language as a tool that we use to accomplish tasks with one another. Structure and use go hand in hand and correspond to the dual function of language as an integral component of our mental functions and as a tool in the regulation of social interaction.

Human language is a system primarily of arbitrary symbols, although certain symbols are representational. Communication that involves language can take place in any of three modes: speaking, writing, or signing.

EXERCISES

1. In the course of reading this chapter, you were faced on a couple of occasions with parenthetical questions such as *You know what I mean?* and *Y'understand?* Decide whether you judge those questions to be appropriate to the written mode, and justify your decision. Then determine in which ideal language they fit better—the one-to-one or the one-to-many content/expression ideal, and explain your judgment.

2. Listen to a radio program or watch a television show and make a list of examples of various types in which the language used is iconic. (*Hint:* It may be easier to find examples of iconic language in programs for children or programs featuring children.)

3. In what sense can computer "languages" be compared to natural languages? Is there any similarity in the way that computer languages are learned and natural human languages are acquired? What about computer languages and foreign languages? Can you think of any similarities in the ways that computer languages and human languages evolve? Any differences?

4. Below is a list of characteristics that describe linguistic communication through speaking, writing, and signing. Decide which characteristics apply to the three modes of linguistic communication, and provide examples to illustrate your claim. Pay particular attention to the different types of spoken, written, and signed communication, for some of these characteristics might apply to some but not others. Also note the impact that modern communication technology has had on these characteristics.

   (1) A linguistic message is ephemeral—that is, it cannot be made to endure.
   (2) A linguistic message can be revised once it has been produced.
   (3) A linguistic message has the potential of reaching large audiences.
   (4) A linguistic message can be transmitted over great distances.
   (5) A linguistic message can rely on the context in which it is produced; the producer can refer to the time and place in which the message is produced without fearing misunderstanding.
   (6) A linguistic message relies on the senses of hearing, touching, and seeing.
   (7) The ability to produce linguistic messages is innate; it does not have to be learned consciously.
   (8) A linguistic message must be planned carefully before it is produced.
   (9) The production of a linguistic message can be accomplished simultaneously with another activity.

5. Consider the following quotation from *A Pronouncing Dictionary of American English* (John S. Kenyon and Thomas A. Knott, Springfield, MA: Merriam, 1953, p. vi).

> As in all trustworthy dictionaries, the editors have endeavored to base the pronunciations on actual cultivated usage. No other standard has, in point of fact, ever finally settled pronunciation. This book can be taken as a safe guide to pronunciation only insofar as we have succeeded in doing this. According to this standard, no words are, as often said, "almost universally mispronounced," for that is self-contradictory. For an editor the temptation is often strong to prefer what he thinks "ought to be" the right pronunciation; but it has to be resisted.

    a. Provide two arguments to support the view that editors should resist the temptation to record their own personal pronunciation preferences in a dictionary. Do your arguments also apply to editors' expressing personal preferences for other aspects of language such as spelling or usage? Explain your view.

    b. In what sense is it accurate to say that the phrase "almost universally mispronounced" is self-contradictory?

    c. What do you understand by the phrase "cultivated usage"? How would a dictionary editor determine whose usage is "cultivated"? Whose usage do you think a dictionary should set out to describe? Explain your view.

6. Consider the following quotation from John Simon's *Paradigms Lost* (New York: Penguin, 1980, pp. 58–59) concerning Edwin Newman's book *A Civil Tongue:*

> With demonic acumen, Newman adduces 196 pages' worth of grammatical errors. Clichés, jargon, malapropisms, mixed metaphors, monstrous neologisms, unholy ambiguities, and parasitic redundancies, interspersed with his own mocking comments . . . and exhortations to do better. The examples are mostly true horrors, very funny and even more distressing. . . . Worse than a nation of shop-keepers, we have become a nation of wordmongers or word-butchers, and abuse of language whether from ignorance or obfuscation, leads, as Newman persuasively argues, to a deterioration of moral values and standards of living.

    a. Which types of "grammatical errors" that Simon refers to (clichés, jargon, and so on) can legitimately be called errors of grammar? What are the others?

    b. Cite some errors of grammar that you have heard from nonnative speakers of English. Have you heard similar errors from native speakers? What do you judge to be the reason for your findings about native speakers?

    c. The point that Newman and Simon make about "abuse of language" leading to a deterioration of moral values and standards of living is a common claim of language guardians. What kinds of abuse does Simon seem to have in mind when he makes that claim? Is he correct in claiming that such abuses lead to a deterioration of moral values? Could it be the other way around? What stake could anyone have in advancing the Newman/Simon claim? (Who are the winners and losers if their view is accepted?)

    d. Do you think that actual grammatical errors (such as nonnative speakers make) could also lead to a deterioration of moral values? Explain your position.

7. Writing and gesture are visual modes of linguistic communication. What is the relationship between writing and Braille (the writing system used for blind readers)? Is Braille

a mode of linguistic communication? How many modes of linguistic communication are there?

8. When there is a choice between linguistic modes, as in telephoning a distant friend or sending a letter, what are the advantages and disadvantages of each mode? List some of the circumstances in which each mode of linguistic communication would be preferred over the others.

SUGGESTIONS FOR FURTHER READING

Certain topics covered in this chapter are treated clearly and concisely in Clark and Clark (1977) and Slobin (1979). For sources on particular aspects of language as a system of rules and as a communicative tool, consult the "Suggestions for Further Reading" in later chapters. For a discussion of the relationship between signs and symbols consult Part I of de Saussure (1959). The papers in Haiman (1985) touch on the still little understood iconic elements in syntax and intonation. For sources on speaking and writing, refer to the "Suggestions for Further Reading" in Chapters 11 (page 362) and 15 (page 500) of this book. For additional information on American Sign Language and other sign languages, see Stokoe (1970), and for a survey of sign languages among American Indians and Australian Aborigines, see Umiker-Sebeok and Sebeok (1978). On the origins of language, see Lieberman (1975, 1984). For various approaches to linguistics, see Sampson (1980). Sapir (1921) and Bloomfield (1933) are both classics of twentieth-century linguistics, both readable and worth the time.

REFERENCES

Bloomfield, Leonard. 1933. *Language* (New York: Holt, Rinehart and Winston).

Clark, Herbert, and Eve Clark. 1977. *Psychology and Language: An Introduction to Psycholinguistics* (New York: Harcourt Brace Jovanovich).

de Saussure, Ferdinand. 1959. *Course in General Linguistics,* translated from 1917 French edition by Wade Baskin (New York: The Philosophical Library).

Haiman, John, ed. 1985. *Iconicity in Syntax* (Amsterdam: Benjamins).

Lieberman, Philip. 1975. *On the Origins of Language: An Introduction to the Evolution of Human Speech* (New York: Macmillan).

————. 1984. *The Biology and Evolution of Language* (Cambridge: Harvard University Press).

Sampson, Geoffrey. 1980. *Schools of Linguistics* (Stanford: Stanford University Press).

Sapir, Edward. 1921. *Language: An Introduction to the Study of Speech* (New York: Harcourt).

Slobin, Dan I. 1979. *Psycholinguistics,* 2nd ed. (Glenview, IL: Scott Foresman).

Stokoe, William C., Jr. 1970. *Semiotics and Human Sign Languages* (The Hague: Mouton).

Umiker-Sebeok, Jean D., and Thomas A. Sebeok, eds. 1978. *Aboriginal Sign Languages of the Americas and Australia,* 2 vols. (New York: Plenum).

LANGUAGE STRUCTURE

2

Phonetics: The Sounds of Languages

SOUNDS AND SPELLINGS

As a reader of English, you are accustomed to seeing language written down as a series of words set off by spaces, with each word consisting of a sequence of separate letters likewise separated by spaces. You readily recognize that words exist as separate entities made up of a relatively small number of discrete sounds. The words *banana* and *cement,* for example, are readily judged by English speakers to have six sounds each, while *adult* has five, *post* four, and *set* three. Somewhat less obvious perhaps is the number of sounds that occur in the words *speakers, series, letters,* and *phone,* which do not have an exact correspondence between numbers of sounds and numbers of letters. This lack of correspondence is common in English. *Cough* has three sounds, though it is spelled with five letters; *freight* has only four sounds despite its seven letters. *Through* with seven letters and *thru* with four are alternative spellings for a word with three sounds. *Phone* and *laugh* have three sounds each, represented by five letters. *Delicacy,* which has an equal number of sounds and letters, uses the letter ⟨c⟩ to represent two sounds, a *k*-like sound and an *s*-like sound.

FIGURE 2-1
Same Spelling, Different Sounds

Because of the close association between writing and speaking in the minds of most literate people, it is important to stress that in this chapter we are interested in the *sounds* of spoken language, not in the letters of the alphabet that are used to represent those sounds. For this reason we begin with a discussion of English spelling, hoping to clarify the differences between the sound system of a language and its representation in the ordinary writing system.

Same Spelling, Different Pronunciations

Observe the variety of pronunciations represented by the same letter or series of letters in different words. Consider the pronunciations of the following words, all of which are represented in part by the letters ⟨ough⟩.

cough	"koff"
tough	"tuff"
bough	"bow"
through	"thru"
though	"tho"
thoroughfare	"thurafare"

Though the precise sounds of these words may vary somewhat among English speakers, still the lesson of the distant relationship between sounds and letters will not be lost on any of you. Orthographic ⟨ough⟩ represents at least six different sounds in English, as indicated in Figure 2-1.

Same Pronunciation, Different Spellings

Other sets of English words are pronounced alike but spelled differently, as school children learn when they are taught sets of homophones (or homonyms) like *led/lead, bear/bare,* and *to/two/too.*

Consider the set of words in Figure 2-2, where twelve different spellings represent the same sounds, as in the word *see*. Still other, though rarer, spellings for

see/senile/sea/seize/scenic/siege/ceiling/cedar/cease/juicy/glossy/sexy

FIGURE 2-2
Different Spellings, Same Sound

the sounds of the word *see* could be cited, including *situ* and *cee* (the name of the letter). Notice that the letter ⟨x⟩, as in *sexy,* actually stands for the two sounds [k] and [s]; thus the phenomenon of identical pronunciations represented by different spellings applies not only to groups of letters but to single letters as well.

If you compare the sound and spelling of the words *woman* and *women,* you will note that the difference in the written vowels ⟨a⟩ and ⟨e⟩ does not represent a difference in pronunciation—the second syllables of these words are pronounced alike. On the other hand, the vowel letter that does not change (the ⟨o⟩) represents two different sounds (the vowel sound of *wood* in *woman* and of *win* in *women*). The pair *Satan* and *satin* illustrates the same point—the constant written vowel ⟨a⟩ represents different sounds, while the varying written vowels ⟨a⟩ and ⟨i⟩ represent the same vowel sound.

Playwright George Bernard Shaw, a keen advocate of spelling reform, pointed up the problems in establishing correspondences between sounds and spelling in English when he alleged that *ghoti* could be pronounced "fish": the ⟨gh⟩ as in *cough,* the ⟨o⟩ as in *women,* and the ⟨ti⟩ as in *nation.* Despite the efforts of Shaw and other reformers, English spelling has remained relatively fixed. You can see some very modest success at simplification in such isolated spellings as *thru, nite,* and *foto*—though not even these few examples have been widely adopted to replace the more traditional *through, night,* and *photo.*

Whys and Wherefores of Sound/Spelling Discrepancies

There are five principal reasons for the discrepancy between the written representations of many English words and their actual pronunciation.

1. English orthography has diverse origins with different spelling conventions.

    a. The system that had evolved in Wessex before the Norman Invasion of 1066 gave us such spellings as *ee* for the sound in words like *deed* and *seen.*

    b. The system that was overlaid on the Old English system by the Normans, with their French orthographic customs, gave us such spellings as *queen* (for the earlier *cween*) and *thief* (for earlier *theef*).

    c. A Dutch influence from Caxton, the first English printer, who was born in England but lived in Holland for thirty years, gave us such spellings as *ghost* (which replaced *gost*) and *ghastly* (which replaced *gastlic*).

    d. During the Renaissance, an attempt to reform spelling along etymological (that is, historically earlier) lines gave us *debt* for earlier *det* or *dette* and *salmon* for earlier *samon.*

2. A spelling system established several hundred years ago is still used for a language that continues to change its spoken form. Thus the initial ⟨k⟩ in *knock, knot, know, knee,* and certain other words was once pronounced, as was the ⟨gh⟩ in *knight* and *thought,* among others. As to vowels, change in progress when the system was developing and yet further change in pronunciation have led to such matched spellings for mismatched pronunciations as *beat/great* and *food/foot.*

3. English is spoken differently in different countries throughout the world (and in different regions within a country), despite a relatively uniform standard for the written orthography. Though this orthographic uniformity certainly facilitates international communication, it also increases the disparity between the way English is written and spoken in any given place.

4. Word parts alter their pronunciation depending on the adjacent sounds and stress patterns. For example, in *electric* the second ⟨c⟩ represents the sound [k] as in *kiss,* but in *electricity* it represents [s] as in *silly.* Compare also the pronunciations of ⟨i⟩ in *senile* (like the ⟨I⟩ of *I'll*) and *senility* (like the ⟨i⟩ of *ill*).

5. Spoken forms differ from one set of circumstances to another—in formal and informal situations for example. While some degree of variation is incorporated into the written system *(do not/don't; it was/'twas),* there is relatively little tolerance for such spellings as *gonna* (going to), *wanna* (want to), *gotcha* (got you), and *j'eat?* (did you eat?). Such variable spellings would force readers to determine the pronunciation of the represented speech before arriving at meaning, instead of reading directly for meaning, as adult readers normally do, without the necessity of silent pronunciation.

Advantages of Fixed Spellings   While the disadvantages of an irregular set of sound-spelling correspondences are obvious, there are nevertheless some advantages. Consider Chinese, in which many written characters have little or no reference to sounds but instead symbolize meanings directly—much as numerals such as ⟨3⟩ and ⟨7⟩ and miscellaneous other symbols like ⟨+⟩ and ⟨%⟩ do for European languages. With such characters, groups of people whose spoken languages are so dissimilar that mutual intelligibility is difficult can nevertheless communicate well in writing, as is the case between speakers of Cantonese and Mandarin Chinese. Thus the symbol ⟨7⟩ has a uniform meaning across the various European languages, even though the word for the concept for which it stands is pronounced and spelled differently in different speech communities: *seven* in English, *sept* in French, *sette* in Italian, *sieben* in German, and so on. Similarly, then, the fact that English orthography is somewhat removed from pronunciation is not altogether unfavorable for a language that has such exceptionally varied dialects, from New Zealand to Jamaica to India—to say nothing of pronunciations in hundreds of places where it is used in official capacities alongside indigenous native tongues or as a second language for scientific and other international enterprises. Despite diverse pronunciations around the globe, a uniform written symbol is associated with a single meaning in English. Moreover, in a language with different pronunciations for the same element of meaning, stable spellings can contribute to reading comprehensibility—as in *musical/musician, electrical/electricity,* and even the ⟨s⟩ of *judges, cats,* and *dogs.*

Independence of Script and Speech   The untidy relationship between sound and spelling is not limited to English; it is found in other languages whose orthographic systems are centuries old but whose speech continuously renews itself in everyday use. It is therefore important to distinguish between the sounds of a language and the way those sounds are customarily represented in the orthography.

To underscore the independence of sounds and orthographies, bear in mind that some languages are represented by different writing systems. For instance, Hindi-Urdu is written by Hindus living in India in Devanāgarī, an Indic script that derives from Sanskrit. The same language is written with Arabic script by Moslems living in Pakistan and parts of India. Sometimes, too, people adopt a new orthography. In the early part of this century, the government of Turkey switched from Arabic script to the Roman alphabet to represent Turkish.

Sometimes languages have different scripts for different purposes. Imagine how an international telegram is sent in a language that uses a script other than the Roman alphabet—in Japanese, Korean, Greek, Russian, Persian, Thai, or Arabic, for example. Rather than using their customary orthographies, speakers of these languages use the Roman alphabet for sending telegrams internationally. Even within a country, an alternative to the customary orthography may be needed. In China, for example, a numeric system is used for sending telegrams: Each character has a four-digit numeral assigned to it, and it is these numerals that are sent telegraphically and then "translated" back into Chinese characters. Sometimes a language uses more than one orthography for different aspects. Written Japanese draws upon three different kinds of orthography: *kanji,* based on the Chinese character system, in which a symbol represents a word independent of its pronunciation; and two syllabaries, orthographic systems in which each symbol represents a syllable. Thus, throughout the world, wherever languages are written down, there are disparities between sounds as they are spoken and as they are represented in writing.

In Chapter 15 we return to the relationship between sound and orthographic representation. Now, we focus on the sounds of spoken language and not the letters of the alphabet. The rest of this chapter examines the human vocal apparatus and the sounds it can produce; Chapter 3 will examine the nature of the sound systems of human language.

PHONETICS

Phonetics, the study of the sounds made in the production of human speech, has three principal branches. *Articulatory phonetics* focuses on the human vocal apparatus and describes sounds in terms of their articulation in the vocal tract; it has been central to the discipline of linguistics. *Acoustic phonetics* uses the tools of physics to study the nature of sound waves produced in human language; it is playing an increasingly larger role in linguistics as attempts are made to use machines for interpreting speech patterns in voice identification and automatic voice-initiated mechanical operations. The third branch of phonetics studies the perception of sounds by the brain through the human ear; *auditory phonetics,* as this branch is called, has played only a minor role in linguistics to date, but it too can be expected to play a larger role in the future. Our discussion will be limited almost exclusively to *articulatory phonetics*—to the nature of human sounds as produced by the vocal apparatus.

Phonetic Alphabets

In discussing the sounds of human language from the point of view of their articulation, phoneticians have evolved descriptive techniques to allow comparison across languages and to avoid the difficulties inherent in describing sounds in terms of standard orthographic practices. You now know that it is not possible to use customary orthographic representations to analyze sound structure. Even within one language, some sounds correspond to more than one letter while some letters correspond to more than one sound. And, of course, a single letter can be used to represent different sounds in different languages. As a result, we need a completely separate system to represent the actual sounds of human languages.

In scientific discussion, the requisite characteristics of symbols to represent sounds are clarity and consistency. The best tool is a phonetic alphabet, and the one most widely used is the International Phonetic Alphabet (IPA). The IPA is an attempt to provide a unique written representation of each sound in the languages of the world, one that is independent of the orthographies of particular languages. Most dictionaries do not use the IPA, preferring systems of their own devising. Linguists, too, mix and match from different systems to suit specific purposes. In keeping with customary practice in American books, we use a modified version of the IPA, substituting more traditional and more transparent orthographic symbols (sometimes with diacritics such as ˇ) for a few of the IPA symbols.

A list of the symbols used to represent the consonant sounds of English is given in Table 2-1. The table shows the phonetic symbol for each sound, alongside representative words that have the relevant parts emphasized. In the few instances in which our symbols differ from those of the IPA, the IPA symbol is shown in parentheses. The words illustrate word-initial, word-medial, and word-final occurrences of the sounds.

The Vocal Tract

Human beings have no organs that are used *only* for speech. The organs that produce speech sounds have evolved principally to serve the life-sustaining processes of breathing and eating. Speech is a secondary function of the human "vocal apparatus" and in that sense is sometimes said to be parasitic on these organs.

Each speech sound is produced in a different way by our vocal apparatus. Every speech sound sounds different from every other speech sound because of some unique combination of features in the way that you shape your mouth and tongue and move parts of the vocal apparatus when you make that speech sound. Figure 2-3 is a simplified drawing of the vocal tract. In this section we will look at the different parts of the human vocal tract and show how these parts work together to produce different sounds.

How are speech sounds made? First, air coming from the lungs passes through the vocal tract, which shapes it into different speech sounds. The air then exits the vocal tract through the mouth or nose or both. The processes that the vocal tract uses in creating a multitude of sounds are similar to those of wind instruments and organ pipes, which produce different musical sounds by varying the shape, size, and acoustic character of the cavities through which air passes.

TABLE 2-1
English Consonants Arranged by Position in Word
(Alternative phonetic symbols in parentheses)

Phonetic Symbol	Initial	Medial	Final
p	pill	caper	tap
b	bill	labor	tab
t	till	petunia	bat
d	dill	seduce	pad
k	kill	sicker	lick
g	gill	dagger	bag
f	fill	beefy	chief
v	villa	saving	grave
θ	thin	author	breath
ð	then	leather	breathe
s	silly	mason	kiss
z	zebra	deposit	bruise
š (ʃ)	shell	rashes	rush
ž (ʒ)	_____	measure	rouge
č (tʃ)	chill	kitchen	pitch
ǰ (dʒ)	jelly	bludgeon	fudge
m	mill	dummy	broom
n	nil	sunny	spoon
ŋ	_____	singer	sing
h	hill	ahoy	_____
y (j)	yes	beyond	toy
r (ɹ)	rent	berry	deer
l	lily	silly	mill
w	will	away	cow

No language takes advantage of all the possibilities for forming different sounds, and there are striking differences in the sounds that occur in different languages. For example, Japanese and Thai lack the [v] sound of English *van,* and Japanese lacks the [f] sound of *fat.* Thai lacks the sounds represented by ⟨g⟩ in *gill,* ⟨z⟩ in *zebra,* ⟨sh⟩ in *shell,* ⟨s⟩ in *measure,* and ⟨j⟩ and ⟨dg⟩ in *judge.* French, Japanese, and Thai lack the quite different ⟨th⟩ sounds in *either* and *ether.* Just as these languages lack sounds that English has, many languages possess sounds that English lacks. You are probably aware that English lacks the rolled *r* that exists in Spanish and Italian and that Arabic has several sounds that do not occur in English. You recognize that German has a sound at the end of words like *Bach* 'stream' and *hoch* 'high' that does not occur among the inventory of English sounds. Arabic has a sound similar to the German ⟨ch⟩ of *Bach,* but in Arabic it can occur word initially. A similar (but not identical) sound occurring finally in the German word *ich* does occur in English (for those dialects that pronounce the ⟨h⟩) in the initial sound of *human* and *huge.* Still, it can be tough for English speakers learning German to pronounce the sound in a word like *ich* because English doesn't permit that sound to occur word finally.

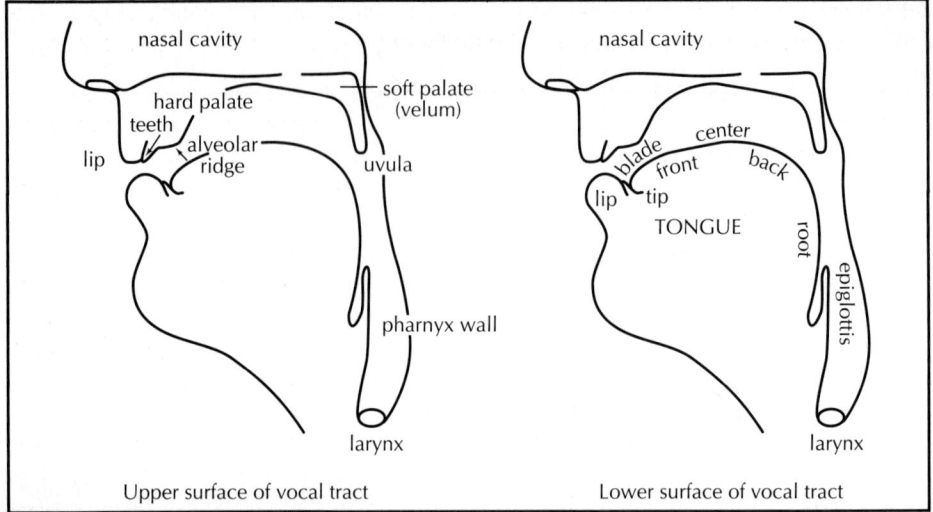

FIGURE 2-3
The Vocal Tract

Adapted from Ladefoged, 1993.

Describing Sounds

As we explore the inventory of sounds, you should produce with your vocal tract the sounds that are described. Pronounce the sounds aloud, noting the shape of your mouth and the position of your tongue as each sound is produced. Such first-hand experience will familiarize you with the reference points of phonetics, make the discussion easier to follow, and give you confidence in your ability to master articulatory phonetics.

In our early discussion, we will continue to use square brackets to enclose the symbols representing sounds. Thus [t] will symbolize the initial sound of *tickle,* the initial and final sounds in *tot,* and the final sound of *boat,* [d] the initial and final sounds in *did,* and [z] the initial sound in *zebra,* the medial consonant in *busy,* and the final sound of *buzz.*

Different speech sounds can be identified in terms of their *articulatory* properties—that is, by *where* (in the mouth) and *how* they are produced. Some of the sounds we have mentioned so far would be described as

[f]	voiceless	labio-dental	fricative
[v]	voiced	labio-dental	fricative
[t]	voiceless	alveolar	stop
[d]	voiced	alveolar	stop
[z]	voiced	alveolar	fricative

Notice that each description includes reference to three features of articulatory phonetics: **voicing** (voiced or voiceless); **place of articulation** (for example, labio-dental or alveolar); and **manner of articulation** (such as fricative or stop). This kind of descriptive analysis can be extended to all the consonants of any language.

Voicing   Begin by distinguishing between [s] (as in *bus* or *sip*) and [z] (as in *buzz* or *zip*). When you pronounce a long, continuous [zzzzz] and alternate it with a long, continuous [sssss], you will notice that the position of your lips and the position of your tongue within your mouth remain the same for [s] and [z], even though these sounds are noticeably different.[1]

Some English words (like *peace* and *peas, bus* and *buzz, sip* and *zip, sane* and *Zane*) are distinguished solely on the basis of the contrast between [s] and [z]. If you touch your **larynx** (Adam's apple) while alternately saying [zzzzz sssss zzzzz], you will feel the difference between [s] and [z]. The vibration that you feel from your larynx when you utter [zzzzz] but not [sssss] is called *voicing;* it is the result of air being forced through a narrow aperture (called the *glottis*) between two folds of muscle (the vocal cords) in the larynx, much like the leaf with a slit in it that children use to make a vibrating noise by blowing air through it. When the vocal cords are held together, the air forced through them from the lungs causes them to vibrate. It is precisely this vibration, or "voicing," that distinguishes [z] from [s] and enables speakers to differentiate between two otherwise identical sounds.[2] Using these very similar but distinct sounds enables us to create words that differ by only a single feature of voicing on a single sound but carry quite different meanings, as in *bus* and *buzz* or *sip* and *zip*.

Not only [s] and [z] but other consonants—in English and many other languages—are characterized by a voiced versus voiceless contrast. Consider [f] and [v], as in *fine* and *vine:* Both sounds are produced with air being forced through a narrow aperture between the upper teeth and the lower lip; they are therefore labio-dental fricatives, [f] being voiceless, [v] voiced. Other voiceless/voiced pairs include [p] and [b] as in *pet* and *bet* and [t] and [d] as in *ten* and *den*. Most, perhaps all, languages have some pairs of consonants that are phonetically different only in that one is voiced and the other voiceless—though this difference is not necessarily significant in all languages, as you will see in the case of Korean in Chapter 3.

Manner of Articulation   Besides having a voicing feature, [s] and [z] can be further characterized as to their manner of articulation. In pronouncing them, air is continuously forced through a narrow opening at a place behind the upper teeth known as the *alveolar ridge* (see Figure 2-3). Compare the pronunciation of [s] and [z] with the sounds [t] and [d]. Unlike [s] and [z], [t] and [d] do not permit a continuous stream of air to pass through the mouth. Rather the air is completely stopped behind and above the upper teeth at the alveolar ridge and then released

[1] You can perceive the difference between voiced and voiceless consonants by alternating between the pronunciations of [f] and [v] or [s] and [z] while holding your hands clapped over your ears. You may also find it helpful to see whether you can tell from pronouncing the words *tall, talent, bid, dead,* and *dilemma* whether [t] or [d] is voiced; take care not to confuse their voicing with the voicing that is part of the pronunciation of the vowels that follow them. In English, vowels are always voiced (unless they are whispered). Check your conclusions against Table 2-7 on page 46.

[2] The vocal cords offer an illustration of the "parasitic" nature of speech: the primary function of these two muscle flaps is to keep food from going down the wrong tube and entering the lungs.

(or exploded) in a small burst of air. For this reason, [t] and [d] are called **stops;** because the air is released through the mouth (and not the nose), they can also be called oral stops. Sounds like [s] and [z] that are made by a continuous stream of air passing through a narrowed passage in the vocal tract are called **fricatives.** It may be helpful for you to check the sounds [p], [b], [f], and [v] to see which are stops and which are fricatives.

Place of Articulation   Of the consonant sounds we have analyzed so far, [s] and [t] are voiceless, while [z] and [d] are voiced. All four of them are pronounced with the point of greatest closure right behind the upper teeth at the *alveolar ridge.* Pronounce *ten* and *den* aloud; feel where the tip of your tongue touches the top of your mouth for the consonants. Both words start (and finish) at the alveolar ridge. Because the three consonants [t], [d], and [n] are all articulated at the alveolar ridge, they are called **alveolars.** [s] and [z] are also articulated at the alveolar ridge, as you will notice by pronouncing the words *sin* and *zen.* (Of course, as to *manner* of articulation, [s] and [z] are fricatives, whereas [t] and [d] are stops.)

There are three major places of articulation for English stop consonants. One is the alveolar ridge. The others are the lips and the soft palate (or *velum*). If you say the words *pin* and *bin,* you will notice that for the initial sound in each word air is built up behind the two lips and then released. Thus the point of greatest closure is at the lips; [p] and [b] are therefore called **bilabial** stops. If you compare your pronunciations of [p] and [t], you will see that both are voiceless and that the sole difference between them is in the place of articulation.

If you attend to the pronunciation of the first sound of *kin,* you will notice that [k], like [p] in *pill* and [t] in *till,* is a voiceless stop, but it differs from them in its place of articulation: [k] is pronounced with the tongue touching the roof of the mouth at the velum and is therefore called a **velar;** [k] is thus a voiceless velar stop.

Corresponding to the three voiceless stops [p], [t], and [k], English has three parallel voiced stops: [b] as in *bib* is a voiced bilabial stop; [d] as in *did* is a voiced alveolar stop; and [g] as in *gig* is a voiced velar stop. Thus English has six stops, three pairs each containing one voiceless and one voiced sound—one pair pronounced at the lips, another at the alveolar ridge, and the third at the velum.

Besides these three articulators, English takes advantage of other places of articulation for other sounds. The ⟨th⟩ of *thin* (the Greek letter theta [θ] serves as the phonetic symbol) is a fricative pronounced with the tongue between the teeth; it is described as a voiceless **interdental** fricative. [š] (represented by ⟨sh⟩ in *shoot* and *wish*) and [ž] (the final sound in *beige* and the medial consonant in *measure*) are pronounced with near closure at a place in the mouth between the alveolar ridge and the velum (or palate); sounds produced there are called **palato-alveolars.** [š] is a voiceless palato-alveolar fricative; [ž] is a voiced palato-alveolar fricative.

CONSONANTS, VOWELS, AND DIPHTHONGS

Consonants

Consonants are sounds produced by partially or completely blocking air in its passage from the lungs through the vocal tract. If you review the inventory of

English consonants given in Table 2-1 and pronounce the sounds aloud while concentrating on the place and manner of articulation, you will perceive how the rest of the table represents the distribution of English consonants according to their voicing, their place of articulation, and their manner of articulation. We will now describe these consonants, grouped here according to their manner of articulation and described in terms of their voicing and their place of articulation. While concentrating on the consonant sounds of English, we shall also mention selected consonants from other languages as a help to understanding.

Stops   The principal *stops* of English are [p], [b], [t], [d], [k], [g]. By pronouncing words with these sounds in them (see Table 2-1), you can recognize that [p] and [b] are bilabial stops, [t] and [d] are alveolar stops, and [k] and [g] are velar stops.

Voicing	Place of Articulation			
	Bilabial	*Alveolar*	*Velar*	*Glottal*
Voiceless	p	t	k	ʔ
Voiced	b	d	g	

In addition, many languages have a glottal stop, which is pronounced by briefly and completely blocking air from passing in the throat with the glottis (and is therefore voiceless by definition). The glottal stop is represented phonetically as [ʔ]. In English, the glottal stop occurs only as a marginal sound—between the two parts of the exclamation *Oh oh!* in American English and in Cockney English as the medial consonant of words like *butter* and *bottle*. In languages like Hawaiian, the glottal stop is a full-fledged consonant that can distinguish two different words; compare Hawaiian *paʔu* 'smudge' and *pau* 'finished.' There can be no voiced equivalent of the voiceless glottal stop [ʔ].

Fricatives   To pronounce the alveolar fricatives [s] and [z], air is forced through a narrow opening between the tip of the tongue and the alveolar ridge. English has a large inventory of fricatives, some of them articulated in front of [s] and [z] in the mouth, others behind them. All are characterized by a similar forcing of air in a continuous stream through a narrow opening. In pronouncing the first sound in the words *thin, three,* and *theta* and the final sound in *teeth* and *bath,* notice that the tongue tip is placed between the upper and lower teeth, where the air stream is most constrained and makes its articulation. Represented by the phonetic symbol [θ], the sound in these words is a voiceless interdental fricative. The voiced counterpart is the initial sound in the words *there* and *then* and the medial consonant in *either.* Notice that in English the spelling ⟨th⟩ is used for two distinct sounds: [θ] as in *ether* and [ð] as in *either* or *feather.*

If you pronounce the following words, you will discover other fricatives and become aware of their common properties as well as their different places of articulation.

fine/vine [f] [v]: labio-dental fricatives

thigh/thy; ether/either [θ] [ð]: interdental fricatives

sink/zinc [s] [z]: alveolar fricatives

rush/rouge; fishin'/vision [š] [ž]: palato-alveolar fricatives

here/ahoy [h]: glottal fricative

The complete set of English fricatives is [f v θ ð s z š ž h].

Voicing	Place of Articulation				
	Labio-dental	*Interdental*	*Alveolar*	*Palato-alveolar*	*Glottal*
Voiceless	f	θ	s	š	h
Voiced	v	ð	z	ž	

Some languages have other fricatives articulated in different parts of the vocal tract. Spanish, for example, has a voiced bilabial fricative (represented by the phonetic symbol [β]), as in *cabo* 'end.' Japanese has a voiceless bilabial fricative represented by the phonetic symbol [Φ] and pronounced somewhat like [f] but by bringing together both lips instead of the lower lip and the upper front teeth. The West African language Ewe has both a voiced [β] and a voiceless [Φ]. Spanish has a voiceless velar fricative [x], which also exists in many other languages, and a voiced velar fricative [ɣ], which is less common. Pronounce [x] as if you were gently clearing your throat. The sound occurs in the Spanish word *joya* 'jewel' and in the personal name *José* (when they are borrowed into English, these words are pronounced with an [h], the closest sound to [x] that English has). [ɣ] is represented by ⟨g⟩ in Spanish *lago* 'lake.' German, Irish, and Mandarin Chinese have a voiceless palatal fricative [ç], as in the German word *Reich* 'empire.'

Notice that in English the physical distance in the mouth between the places of articulation for the fricatives is not as great as the distance for the different stops. The bilabial, alveolar, and velar places of articulation for the stop consonants are spaced farther apart than are the labio-dental, interdental, alveolar, and palato-alveolar articulations of the fricatives. The tighter packing of the fricatives in the mouth can cause difficulty in perceiving them as distinct, especially when any interference is present. If you ask a friend to identify the fricative sounds either over the telephone or when you pronounce them while facing away, you'll discover that they're tougher to distinguish from one another than you might have thought. The acoustic differences may be especially difficult to perceive for speakers of languages that have fewer fricatives than English does or have them better spaced. Because French does not have the interdental fricatives [θ] and [ð], some French speakers tend to perceive (and pronounce) English words like *thin* and *this* as though they were *sin* and *zis*.

Affricates   Two consonant sounds in English are a little more complex to describe than stops and fricatives but are closely related to them. These are the sounds that occur initially in the words *chin* and *gin* and finally in the words *batch* and *badge*. If you pronounce these sounds slowly enough, you can recognize that they are stop-fricatives. We refer to stop-fricatives as *affricates*. In the pronunciation of an **affricate,** air is built up by a complete closure of the oral tract at some place of articulation, then released (something like a stop) and continued (like a fricative). The sound in *chin,* for example, is a combination of the stop [t] and the fricative [š]; we represent it as [č]. The sound at the beginning and end of *judge* is a combination of the stop [d] and the fricative [ž]; we represent it as [ǰ]. English has just two affricates: voiceless [č] and voiced [ǰ], both of which are palato-alveolar affricates.

Other affricates occur in other languages. The most common are the alveolar affricates [ts] and [dz], which occur at the beginning of the Italian words *zucchero* 'sugar' and *zona* 'zone' respectively.

The complete set of English affricates is [č ǰ].

Voicing	Place of Articulation
	Palato-alveolar
Voiceless	č
Voiced	ǰ

Obstruents   Because *stops, fricatives,* and *affricates* share the phonetic property of impeding the air flow by constricting the vocal passage, these three sets of sounds are together referred to as **obstruents.**

Approximants   English has four sounds that are known as **approximants** because they are produced by two articulators approaching one another as for fricatives but not coming close enough to produce audible friction. The English approximants are [y], [r], [l], and [w]. [y] is a palatal approximant as in *you;* the word *cute* begins with the consonant cluster [ky]. As to [r] and [l], among the languages of the world it is not so common as English speakers might expect for them to be distinctive sounds by which words can be contrasted, as in English *rid/lid* or *fear/feel.* The difference between [r] and [l] is that [r] is pronounced by channeling air through the central part of the mouth, [l] by channeling it on each side of the tongue. [r] is therefore called a central approximant, [l] a lateral approximant. To distinguish them from the other approximants, [r] and [l] are sometimes called *liquids.* The difference between the two is not always easy to master, and even some native English speakers have difficulty with them. As you will see in the next chapter, in some Asian languages, [r] and [l] are not distinctive sounds, so native speakers of these languages find it challenging to distinguish them when speaking English.

In the pronunciation of the approximant [w], the lips are rounded, as in *wild.* For certain dialects, in some words [h] precedes [w] as in *which* or *whether.* When [w] is the second element of a cluster (as in *twine* or *quiet*) the initial sound ([t] or [k]) is rounded in anticipation of the [w].

One approximant that does not occur in English but is familiar to English speakers is the French voiced uvular *r* (as in such words as *Paris* or *rue* 'street'), which is made farther back in the mouth and is represented by the phonetic symbol [ʁ].

Voicing	Place of Articulation			
	Bilabial	*Alveolar*	*Palatal*	*Uvular*
Voiced (central)	w	r	y	ʁ
Voiced (lateral)		l		

Nasals   **Nasal** consonants are pronounced by lowering the velum, thus allowing the stream of air to pass out through the nasal cavity instead of through the oral cavity. English has three nasal stops: [m] as in *mad, cram, drummer;* [n] as in *new, ten, sinner;* and a third, symbolized by [ŋ] and pronounced as in the words *sing* and *singer.*

Place of Articulation		
Bilabial	*Alveolar*	*Velar*
m	n	ŋ

[ŋ] does not occur word initially in English. Because of the way we spell it, English speakers sometimes think of [ŋ] as a combination of [n] and [g], but it is actually a single sound, as you can see by comparing your pronunciation of the words *singer* and *finger*. Leaving aside the initial sounds [s] and [f], if your pronunciation of these words differs (for some speakers of English it does not), then you have [ŋ] in *singer* and [ŋg] (not [ng]) in *finger*. Most American English speakers have a three-way contrast among *simmer, sinner,* and *singer* solely according to whether the medial consonant is [m], [n], or [ŋ]. By noticing where the tongue touches the upper part of the mouth in the articulation of these nasal consonants (and by comparing their place of articulation with other sounds identified above), you will be able to determine that [m] is a bilabial nasal, [n] an alveolar nasal, and [ŋ] a velar nasal. If, while you are saying [mmmmm], you cut off the air stream passing through the nose by pinching it closed (as a clothespin would), the sound stops abruptly; this demonstrates that nasal stops are produced by passing air through the nose. Compare cutting off the air passing through your nose while saying [nnnnn] and [sssss], and you will get a clear sense of the use of the nasal and oral cavities in sound production. You will see that when you cut off the air passing through the nose for oral consonants there is virtually no difference in the quality of the sound, but when you cut off the air passing through the nose for a nasal consonant no sound at all is made.

If you have successfully identified the places of articulation for the nasals and understood why they fit in their particular slots in the consonant table, you will have noticed that English has three sets of consonants articulated in the same places though differing in their manner of articulation: the oral stops [p] and [b] and the nasal stop [m] are articulated at the two lips and are known as bilabials; the oral stops [t] and [d] and the nasal stop [n] are articulated at the alveolar ridge and are called alveolars; [k], [g], and [ŋ] are articulated at the velum and are called velars.

The nasal consonants of English are: [m], [n], [ŋ]. Other languages have other nasals. French, Spanish, and Italian, for instance, all have a palatal nasal [ɲ]; examples include the French word *mignon* 'cute' (which English has borrowed in the phrase *filet mignon*), the Spanish words *señor* and *cañón* (the latter borrowed into English as *canyon*), and the Italian *bagno* 'bath' and *lasagna* (also borrowed into English).

Clicks, Flaps, Trills   Some languages have consonants that belong to the same classes we have discussed but are strikingly different from those in European languages. Several languages of southern Africa, for instance, have among their stop consonants certain **click** sounds as an integral part of their sound system. One example is the lateral click made on the side of the tongue; it occurs in English when we urge a horse to move on, for example, but it is not part of the inventory of English speech sounds; it is represented by the IPA symbol [‖]. Another click sound that occurs in some of these languages can be represented in English writing by the reproach *tsk-tsk*. This last click is not a lateral but a dental—IPA [∣]—or alveolar—IPA [!]—made with the tip of the tongue at the teeth or the alveolar ridge.

A few consonant sounds are not stops, fricatives, affricates, approximants, or nasals. The medial consonant of the word *butter* is commonly pronounced in American English as an alveolar **flap,** produced by throwing the tongue against the alveolar ridge. We represent this flap (which will be discussed in Chapter 3) with the symbol [D] (IPA [ɾ]). Spanish, Italian, and Fijian have an alveolar **trill** *r,* as in Spanish *correr* 'to run,' represented by the symbol [r̄] (IPA [r]).

Vowels

Vowel sounds differ from consonant sounds in that they are produced not by blocking air in its passage from the lungs but by passing air through different shapes of the mouth and different positions of the tongue and lips unobstructed by narrow passages (except at the glottis). Some languages have as few as three distinct vowels in their sound systems; others have more than a dozen. Many people think of English as having only five vowels; but this is a reflection of the orthography rather than the spoken language (and is a clear example of the influence of writing on our thinking about language). In pronouncing the following words, you will realize that English has many more than five vowels: *peat, pit, pet, pate, pat, put, putt, poke, pot, part,* and *port.*

Vowel Height and Frontness   Unlike consonants, which are described by place and manner of articulation, vowels are characterized by the position of the tongue and the lips, in particular by the relative height and relative frontness or backness

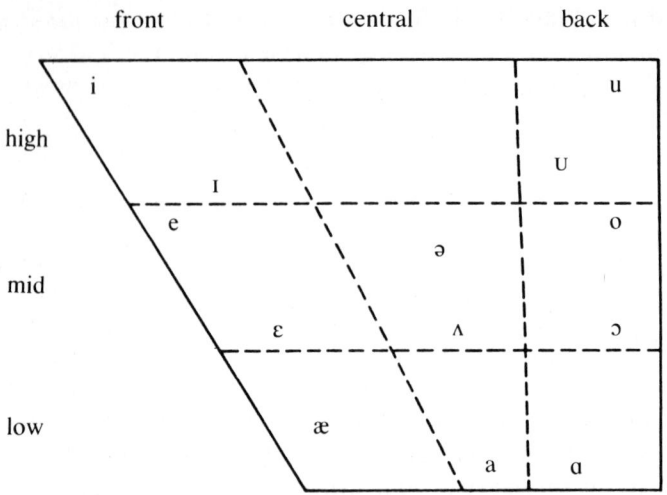

FIGURE 2-4
The Vowels of English

of the tongue and the relative rounding of the lips. We refer to vowels as being high or low and front or back; we also consider whether the lips are rounded (as for *pool*) or nonrounded (as for *pill*). You can get a feel for these descriptors by alternately saying *feed* and *food,* the first of which contains a front vowel, the second a back vowel. To get a feel for tongue height, alternate saying *feet* and *fat*. If you fail to feel the difference between high and low vowels with this pair of sounds, look at yourself in the mirror (or at a classmate saying them); you'll see that because the tongue is lower, the mouth is open much wider for the vowel of *fat* than for the vowel of *feet*.

Figure 2-4 indicates the relationship of the English vowels to one another and the approximate positions of the tongue during their articulation.

Here are English words for each of the vowel symbols shown in the figure.

i	Pete, beat			u	pool, boot
ɪ	pit, bit			ʊ	put, foot
e	late, bait	ə	*a*bout, sof*a*	o	poke, boat
ɛ	pet, bet	ʌ	putt, but	ɔ	port, bought
æ	pat, bat	a	park (in Boston)	ɑ	pot, father

The symbols [ə], often called *schwa*, and [ʌ], an inverted v called *caret* or *wedge,* stand for sounds that are very much alike. They both occur in the word *above* [əbʌv]. In this book we use [ə] to represent a mid central vowel in unstressed syllables, as in *buses* [bʌsəz] and *capable* [kepəbəl]. We also use it before [r] in the same syllable whether stressed, as in *person* [pərsən] and *sir* [sər], or unstressed, as in *pertain* [pərten] and *tender* [tɛndər]. We use [ʌ] to represent mid central vowels in other stressed syllables, such as *flooded* [flʌDəd] and *suds* [sʌdz].[3]

Diphthongs There are also three **diphthongs** in English, represented by pairs of symbols to capture the fact that a diphthong is a vowel sound for which the tongue starts in one place in the mouth and moves to another: [ay] (as in *bite*); [aw] (as in *pout, bout*); [ɔy] (as in *soy, toy*). Diphthongs change in quality while being pronounced, as you can notice by pronouncing these words slowly: *buy, boy, bough*. Thus American English dialects have up to thirteen distinctive vowel sounds (plus three diphthongs), not the five vowels that are commonly said to exist by people who forget to distinguish between sounds and letters. In England and certain parts of the United States, including metropolitan New York City, sixteen distinct vowels and diphthongs exist. In some parts of the United States, including Pittsburgh and surrounding areas, fewer distinct vowel and diphthong sounds exist, because no distinction is made between the vowels of *caught* and *cot*.

Other Articulatory Features of Vowels

Languages have other possibilities besides tongue height and backness for creating differences among vowels. Five other features of vowel quality that languages can exploit to add to their inventory of distinctive vowels are tenseness, rounding, lengthening, nasalization, and tone.

Tenseness Many languages make a distinction between tense and lax vowels. Tense vowels are produced with greater overall muscular tension in the mouth; lax vowels are pronounced with less tension and tend to be shorter. In English the contrast between [i] of *peat* and [ɪ] of *pit* is in part a tense/lax contrast; likewise for *bait/bet* and *cooed/could*.

Rounding Whereas in English high front vowels tend automatically to be unrounded (and high back vowels to be rounded), some languages have both rounded and unrounded front vowels. To cite two examples, French and German have high front and mid front rounded vowels as well as unrounded ones. French has a high front unrounded [i] in words such as *dire* 'to say' and *dix* 'ten' and a high front rounded vowel [ü], as in *rue* 'street'; it also has a contrast between upper mid front unrounded [e] (as in *fée* 'fairy') and upper mid front rounded [ø] (*feu* 'fire'); and between lower mid front unrounded [ɛ] (*serre* 'hothouse') and lower mid front rounded [œ] (*soeur* 'sister'). German has similar contrasts (see Table 2-4, p. 44).

Length German has two of each vowel type—one long, the other short. The pronunciation of long vowels is held longer than that of short vowels. Long vowels are commonly represented with a colon after them in phonetic transcriptions or by the vowel symbol doubled (in dictionaries and some orthographic systems, a

---

[3] Other books commonly use [ɚ] to represent a mid central vowel with r-coloring. In systems using the [ɚ] notation, *person* would be transcribed [pɚsən], *sir* [sɚ], and *pertain* [pɚten].

macron (ˉ) is sometimes used above the vowel symbol). Thus, in addition to the short vowels [i] and [ü], as in *bitten* 'to request' and *müssen* 'must,' German has words with high front long vowels, such as unrounded [i:] in *bieten* 'to wish' and rounded [ü:] in *Mühle* 'mill.' From these German examples, we see that languages can multiply differences among vowels by exploiting long and short varieties of the same vowel. English, too, has vowels of differing length, although it does not exploit length to create different words (see Chapter 3). To sense differences in the duration of vowels, pronounce these English words: *beat, bead, bit.* You should be able to hear that the vowel of *bead* is longer than that of *beat,* and that both are longer than that of *bit.*

Nasalization   All vowel types can also be nasalized. This is done by pronouncing the vowels while passing air through the nose (as for nasal stops) as well as through the mouth. Nasal vowels are indicated by a tilde (˜) above the vowel symbol. One well-known example of a language with nasal vowels is French, which has several nasal vowels paralleling the oral vowels. Thus French has a contrast between *lin* [lɛ̃] 'flax' and *lait* [lɛ] 'milk,' between *ment* [mã] '(he) is lying' and *ma* [ma] 'my' (feminine), and between *honte* [ɔ̃t] 'shame' and *hotte* [ɔt] 'hutch.' Other languages with nasal vowels include Irish, Hindi, and many American Indian languages, such as Delaware, Mixtec, Navaho, and Seneca. English also has some nasal vowels, but they are not significant (see Chapter 3).

Tone   In many languages of Asia, Africa, and North America, a vowel may be pronounced on several pitches and be perceived by the native speakers of these languages as different sounds. Typically, a vowel pronounced on a low pitch contrasts with the same vowel pronounced on a higher pitch. An example of such a two-tone language is Hausa, spoken in West Africa. In Hausa, the word *górà* 'bamboo,' in which the first vowel is pronounced with a high tone (´) and the second vowel with a low tone (`), contrasts with the word *gòrá* 'large gourd,' in which the tones are reversed. Other tone languages have more complex systems. The Beijing (Peking) dialect of Chinese has four tones: a high level tone (symbolized with (ˉ); a rising tone (´); a falling-rising tone (ˇ), in which the pitch begins to fall and then rises sharply; and a falling tone (`), in which the pitch falls sharply. Thus there is a four-way contrast among the following four vowels pronounced on different tones; these vowels happen to be words by themselves, with separate meanings.[4]

ī	(high level)	'one'
í	(rising)	'proper'
ǐ	(falling-rising)	'already'
ì	(falling)	'thought'

---

[4] Note that a given diacritic mark can be used to represent different tones in different languages. Thus, [´] represents a high tone in Hausa but a rising tone in Chinese; [`] represents a low tone in Hausa but a falling tone in Chinese.

TABLE 2-2
French Vowels with Illustrative Words

	Front Unrounded	Front Rounded	Central Unrounded	Back Rounded
Oral Vowels				
high	i	ü		u
upper mid	e	ø		o
mid			ə	
lower mid	ɛ	œ		ɔ
low			a	
Nasal Vowels				
lower mid	ɛ̃	œ̃		ɔ̃
low				ã

Examples

i	gr<u>i</u>s 'grey'	ü	m<u>û</u>r 'ripe'	u	f<u>ou</u> 'crazy'
e	ferm<u>é</u> 'shut'	ø	j<u>eû</u>ne 'fasts'	o	m<u>o</u>t 'word'
ɛ	fr<u>ai</u>s 'fresh'	œ	j<u>eu</u>ne 'young'	ɔ	f<u>o</u>rt 'strong'
ɛ̃	br<u>in</u> 'sprig'	ə	ch<u>e</u>min 'path'	ɔ̃	f<u>on</u>d 'bottom'
		a	p<u>a</u>r 'by'	ã	f<u>aon</u> 'fawn'
		œ̃	br<u>un</u> 'brown'		

Some languages have even more complex tone systems: Thai has five tones; the standard dialect of Vietnamese has six tones; and the Guangzhou (Canton) dialect of Chinese has nine different tones. Tone is thus not only a widespread phenomenon, but a diverse one.

Tables 2-2 through 2-5 are vowel charts illustrating the sound patterns of four of the world's major languages—French, Spanish, German, and Japanese.

TABLE 2-3
Spanish Vowels with Illustrative Words

	Front Unrounded	Central Unrounded	Back Rounded
high	i		u
mid	e		o
low		a	

Examples

i	ch<u>i</u>ste 'joke'	a	m<u>a</u>r 'sea'	u	s<u>u</u>r 'south'
e	f<u>e</u> 'faith'			o	b<u>o</u>ca 'mouth'

TABLE 2-4
German Vowels with Illustrative Words

	Front Unrounded	Front Rounded	Central Unrounded	Back Rounded
high				
long	i:	ü:		u:
short	i	ü		u
upper mid				
long	e:	ø:		o:
short	e			o
mid				
short			ə	
lower mid				
long	ɛ:			
short		œ		
low				
long			a:	
short			a	

Examples

i: bieten 'to wish'
i bitten 'to request'
e: wen 'whom'
e wenn 'when'
ɛ: Käse 'cheese'

ü: Mühle 'mill'
ü müssen 'must'
ø: ölig 'oily'
œ röntgen 'X-ray'

ə liebe 'dear'
a: Rabe 'crow'
a Ratte 'rat'

u: Huhn 'hen'
u Mutter 'mother'
o: Ofen 'oven'
o Ochs 'ox'

TABLE 2-5
Japanese Vowels with Illustrative Words

	Front Unrounded	Central Unrounded	Back Unrounded	Back Rounded
high	i		ɯ	
mid	ɛ			ɔ
low		a		

Examples

i ima 'now'
ɛ sensei 'teacher'

a aki 'autumn'

ɯ buji 'safe'

ɔ yoru 'to approach'

SUMMARY

Sounds must be distinguished from letters and other visual representations of language. Phonetic alphabets represent sounds in a way that is consistent and comparable across different languages; each sound is assigned a distinct representation, independently of the customary orthography used to represent the language in which the sound occurs. The phonetic alphabet used in this book is very similar to the International Phonetic Alphabet (IPA).

All languages contain two basic kinds of sounds: consonants and vowels. Consonants are produced by obstructing the flow of air as it passes from the lungs through the vocal tract and out through the mouth or nose. In the production of fricative consonants, air is forced through a narrow opening in the passage to form a continuous noise, as in the initial and final sounds of the words *says* and *five*. For stop consonants the air passage is completely blocked and then released, as in the initial and final sounds of the words *tap* and *cat*. Affricates are produced by combining a stop and a fricative, as in the final sound of the word *peach* or the initial and final sounds of *judge*. Together, fricatives, stops, and affricates are called obstruents. When one articulator approaches another but the vocal tract is not sufficiently narrowed to create the audible friction of a consonant, an approximant is produced, as in the initial sounds of *west, yes, rest, left;* liquid is a cover term for [r] and [l] sounds. Vowels are produced by positioning the tongue and mouth to form differently shaped passages. Oral vowels are released through the mouth, and nasal vowels are released through the nose, as well as through the mouth.

Consonant sounds can be characterized by specifying a combination of articulatory features: voicing, place of articulation, and manner of articulation. For example, [t] is a voiceless alveolar stop; [v] is a voiced labio-dental fricative. Vowels are described by citing the relative height and frontness of the tongue: thus [æ] is a low front vowel; [u] is a high back vowel. Sometimes secondary features of vowel production—such as tenseness, nasality, lengthening, or rounding—are specified. Finally, in many languages vowels can be pronounced on different pitches, or tones.

Different languages have different numbers of speech sounds in their inventories. Tables 2-6 and 2-7 summarize all the vowels and consonants introduced in this chapter.

EXERCISES

1. Give a phonetic description of the following sounds. For consonants, include voicing and place and manner of articulation. For vowels, include height, a frontness/backness dimension, and where needed a tense/lax distinction. *Examples:* [s] voiceless alveolar fricative; [i] high front tense vowel.

    Consonants: [z] [t] [b] [n] [ŋ] [r] [j] [š] [θ] [Φ]
    Vowels: [ɛ] [æ] [ɔ] [ɪ] [ʊ] [o] [ə] [a] [e] [ay]

2. A minimal pair is a set of two words that have the same sounds in the same order, except that one sound differs: pit [pɪt]/bit [bɪt]; *bell* [bɛl]/bill [bɪl]; and *either* [iðər]/ *ether* [iθər].

TABLE 2-6
Vowels Discussed in Chapter 2
(All vowels can be nasalized and either short or long.)

	Front Unrounded	Front Rounded	Central Unrounded	Back Unrounded	Back Rounded
high					
tense	i	ü		ɯ	u
lax	ɪ				ʊ
upper mid	e	ø			o
mid			ə		
lower mid	ɛ	œ	ʌ		ɔ
low	æ		a	ɑ	

TABLE 2-7
Consonants Discussed in Chapter 2

Manner of Articulation and Voicing	Place of Articulation								
	Bilabial	*Labio-dental*	*Interdental*	*Alveolar*	*Palato-alveolar*	*Palatal*	*Velar*	*Uvular*	*Glottal*
Stops									
voiceless	p			t			k		ʔ
voiced	b			d			g		
Nasals									
	m			n		ɲ	ŋ		
Fricatives									
voiceless	Φ	f	θ	s	š (ʃ)	ç	x		h
voiced	β	v	ð	z	ž (ʒ)		ɣ		
Affricates									
voiceless				ts	č (tʃ)				
voiced				dz	ǰ (dʒ)				
Approximants									
voiced central	w			r (ɹ)		y (j)		ʁ	
voiced lateral				l					
Others									
voiced trill				r̃ (r)					
voiced flap				D (ɾ)					

a. For each of the following pairs of English consonants, provide minimal pairs that illustrate their occurrence in initial, medial, and final position. (Examples are given for the first pair.)

		Initial	**Medial**	**Final**
[s]	[z]	sue/zoo	buses/buzzes	peace/peas
[k]	[b]			
[t]	[b]			
[s]	[t]			
[r]	[l]			
[m]	[n]			

b. For each of these pairs of vowels, cite a minimal pair of words illustrating the contrast. *Example:* [u] [æ] boot/bat.

[i] [ɪ]; [ɔy] [ay]; [u] [ʊ]; [æ] [ɛ]

3. Write out in standard orthography the words represented by the following transcriptions. *Examples:* [pɛn] pen; [smok] smoke; [bənænə] banana

[læŋgwəj]	[træpt]	[spawts]
[θwɔrt]	[ðiz]	[ðɪs]
[lʌvd]	[plɛžər]	[kwɪkli]
[mənatənəs]	[ɛntərprayzɪŋ]	[frənɛtək]

4. Transcribe each of the following words as you say them in casual speech. (Do not be misled by the orthography.) *Examples:* bed [bɛd]; rancid [rænsəd]; shnook [šnʊk]

changes	mostly	very	friend	teacher
semantics	system	ready	more	musician
crackers	peanuts	palm	music	photographer
pneumonia	attitude	psalm	fuel	photograph

5. The following transcription represents one person's reading of a passage about love potions (adapted from *The Encyclopedia of Things That Never Were*, p. 159). Write out the passage using ordinary English orthography. (Periods mark the end of sentences.)

[æz ðə nem ɪndəkets ðiz pošənz ɑr kampawndəd spəsɪfəkli tu ətrækt ə sʌbjɛkt hu ɪz rilʌktənt tu sərɛndər tə wʌnz kɑrnəl dəzayərz. ðə pošən me bi hæd æt ə prays frəm ɛni ælkəmɪst ɔr ʌðər pərsən skɪld ɪn ðə prɛpərešən əv mayn čɛnjɪŋ kampawnz. wɪčəz wɪzərdz ən sɔrsərərz hu ɑr jɛnrəli nat ɪntərɛstəd ɪn lʌv ɑr sʌmtaymz ənwɪlɪŋ tə mænyəfækšər ðə pošənz. ðə pərčəsərz onli prablǝm me bi ðæt əv pərswedɪŋ ði abjɛkt əv hɪz ɔr hər dəzayər tu swalo ɛni əv ðə pošən. ə risənt rɛsəpi fɔr ə lʌv pošən ɪnkludəd jɪnjər sɪnəmən drayd ən grawnd grep sidz ɔystərz ɛlk æntlər ən tel her frəm ə mel ænəməl ænd ɛni sutəbəl abjɛkt frəm ðə pərsən sʌč æz hɪz ɔr hər nel klɪpɪŋz.]

6. Examine the following list of consonants as they are represented in three popular desk dictionaries, and compare the dictionary symbols with the phonetic symbols used in this book. (WNNCD stands for *Webster's Ninth New Collegiate Dictionary*; WNWD for *Webster's New World Dictionary*, 3rd college ed.; AHD for *The American Heritage Dictionary*, 2nd college ed.)

Phonetic Symbol	*WNNCD*	*WNWD*	*AHD*
p	p	p	p
k	k	k	k
θ	th	th	th
ð	<u>th</u>	*th*	*th*
s	s	s	s
š	sh	sh	sh
ž	zh	zh	zh
č	ch	ch	ch
ǰ	j	j	j
ŋ	ŋ	ŋ	ŋ
h	h	h	h
y	y	y	y

Note that some of the symbols used by these dictionaries are the same as those used in this book, but not all. Choose three sounds for which one or more of the dictionaries use a different symbol than the one used in this book, and discuss why that different symbol might have been chosen.

7. Examine the following list of vowels as they are represented in three dictionaries; compare the dictionary symbols with the phonetic symbols used in this book. (See exercise 6 for identification of the dictionaries.)

Phonetic Symbol	Words	*WNNCD*	*WNWD*	*AHD*
i	peat, feet	ē	ē	ē
ɪ	pit, bit	i	i	ĭ
ɛ	pet, bet	e	e	ĕ
e	wait, late	ā	ā	ā
æ	pat, bat	a	a	ă
ə	<u>a</u>bove, sod<u>a</u>	ə	ə	ə
ʌ	but, love	ə	u	ŭ
u	pool, boot	ü	o͞o	o͞o
ʊ	push, put	u̇	oo	oo
o	boat, sold	ō	ō	ō
ɔ	port, or	ȯ	ô	ô
ɑ	pot, bottle	ä	ä	ŏ
aw	cow, pout	au̇	ou	ou
ay	buy, tight	ī	ī	ī
ɔy	boy, toil	ȯi	oi	oi

In contrast to their practice with consonants, the desk dictionaries differ from one another and from our representation in their transcription of vowels. Cite three instances of a difference from our transcription; discuss the advantages and disadvantages of the dictionary's representation as compared to ours.

8.   George Bernard Shaw's tongue-in-cheek claim that English spelling is so chaotic that *ghoti* could be pronounced [fɪš] 'fish' has been called misleading. That judgment is based on observations like these: ⟨gh⟩ can occur word initially in only a few words (for example, *ghost* and *ghastly*), and then it is always pronounced [g]; only following a vowel in the same syllable (as in *cough* and *tough*) can ⟨gh⟩ be pronounced as [f]; thus, *ghoti* could not be pronounced with an initial [f]. What other generalizations about the English spelling patterns of ⟨gh⟩, ⟨o⟩, and ⟨ti⟩ can be used to argue that Shaw's claim is at least exaggerated?

SUGGESTIONS FOR FURTHER READING

MacKay (1987) is the most complete elementary treatment of all aspects of phonetics; it is accessible and has excellent illustrations. Ladefoged (1993) is an excellent introduction to the production mechanisms of speech and to the variety of sounds in the languages of the world. Pullum and Ladusaw (1986) covers the various symbols used in the International Phonetic Alphabet (IPA) and by other writers in their treatments of phonetics and phonology; this book is arranged like a dictionary, with each symbol clearly illustrated. Maddieson (1984) inventories the sounds of a representative sample of the world's languages; the inventories vary from a low of 11 sounds to a high of 141. Crystal (1991) is an excellent source of information about the meanings of terms used in phonetics and all other fields of linguistics. Stubbs (1980) has an excellent discussion of the relationship between sounds and spelling in English and other languages and offers insights into the problems facing spelling reform. Denes and Pinson (1973) is an accessible account of the physics of language sounds and acoustic phonetics.

REFERENCES

Crystal, David. 1991. *A Dictionary of Linguistics and Phonetics,* 3rd ed. (Oxford: Blackwell).

Denes, Peter, and E. N. Pinson. 1973. *The Speech Chain* (Garden City, NY: Anchor).

Ladefoged, Peter. 1993. *A Course in Phonetics,* 3rd ed. (Fort Worth: Harcourt).

MacKay, Ian R. A. 1987. *Phonetics: The Science of Speech Production*, 2nd ed. (Boston: Little Brown).

Maddieson, Ian. 1984. *Patterns of Sound* (Cambridge: Cambridge University Press).

Pullum, Geoffrey K., and William A. Ladusaw. 1986. *Phonetic Symbol Guide* (Chicago: University of Chicago Press).

Stubbs, Michael. 1980. *Language and Literacy: The Sociolinguistics of Reading and Writing* (London: Routledge).

3

Phonology: The Sound Systems of Language

INTRODUCTION

This chapter focuses on the systematic structuring of sounds in languages: on which phonetic distinctions are significant in the sense that they can signal differences in meaning; on the relationship between how sounds are pronounced and how they are stored in the mental lexicon; and on the ways sounds are organized within words.

It may be useful to approach our task from the point of view of children acquiring their native language. Children acquire different parts of their language at different stages, but all of them learn a great deal about speaking before they learn even the most rudimentary things about the visual representation of speech in writing. To repeat a point stressed earlier, we are interested in sound systems as such—independently of their representation in writing.

Try to imagine the task of an infant listening to utterances made by its parents, siblings, and others. From the barrage of utterances that it faces in early life, a child must decipher the code of its language and learn to speak a mother tongue. Although caretakers in some cultures sometimes use the slow and careful speech of baby talk in addressing children, they do not do so consistently; and the utterances that children hear are often incomplete, interrupted, or flawed in other ways.

In Chapter 2 you learned to distinguish the number of letters in a written word from the number of sounds in its pronunciation. You know, for example, that *set* has an equal number of sounds and letters, while *brick* does not. In our discussion, we have taken for granted that words have a specific number of sounds. Children hearing language in their earliest months, however, have no ready access to that simple fact. It would be instructive to listen to a conversation in a language you do not know; if you attempt to gauge the number of words in a sample of even a few seconds' duration, you will discover that most words are run together with no separation between them. This is true of all languages and all dialects.

Itisasifthesentencesonthispagewereprintedwithoutspacesb

etweenwordsitwouldbeverydifficulttofigureoutwouldntit?

As you recognize, it would be tough to sort out the individual words. Yet the task of sorting out the continuous noise of utterances into separate words is part of the challenge that every child faces in acquiring a language.

Actually, the task is even more difficult than is suggested by the run-together words in the printed sentence above. The reason is simple: whereas the letters in the run-together sentence are distinct and separated from one another, the individual sounds in a spoken word are not separated but blend together into a continuous noise stream. To take our writing analogy a step further, imagine attempting to spot the beginning and end points of each letter in a handwritten sample: this would more closely capture the challenge that infants face in deciphering the code of distinct sounds in their language. Consider the following:

In cursive writing, the letters of each word are joined.

Although anyone who knows English and is able to decipher this handwriting can count the letters in each word, there is no clear separation in their visual representation. Each word is written continuously, with the letters blending into one another. No beginning or end can be pinpointed (except for the initiation of the first letter and the termination of the last letter in each word). The same is true of the speech that infants hear; there is no separation between the individual sounds of a word, no beginning or end for the individual sounds in the speech stream. Children nevertheless learn the words of their language quickly and efficiently, a feat all the more remarkable considering how much else they have to learn in their earliest years.

If you examine a physical "picture" of a word as made by a sound spectrogram, you will see that there is no separation between the sounds. (The seeming gap in the sound spectrogram of Figure 3-1 represents the complete closure of the vocal tract for the stop consonant [b].) One reason for this is that a particular sound's

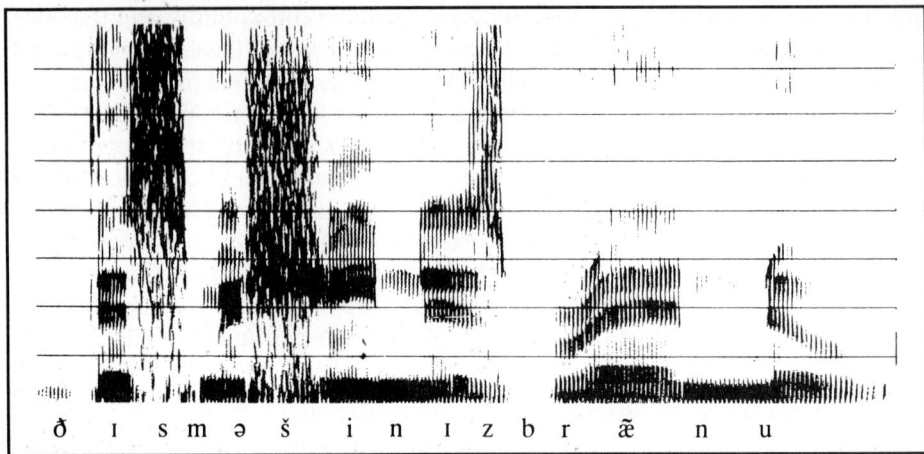

FIGURE 3-1
Sound Spectrogram of a Casual Utterance

various phonetic features—voicing, nasalization, and so on—do not all begin or end at the same time. For example, the voicing of a particular sound may be discontinued in anticipation of a following voiceless sound—as in *imp*, in which the tail end of [m] is devoiced in anticipation of the following voiceless [p]. Figure 3–1 is a spectrogram that illustrates how the simple utterance *This machine is brand new* appears acoustically. There is not only no separation between one sound and another within a word but no physical separation between one word and the next. In the same way, the acoustic signal that an infant's ears picks up is continuous, and part of the task of acquiring a language is to sort out words within sentences and sounds within words. The language system that every child acquires must eventually contain words as separate units and sounds as separate units within a word.

You may wonder, then: What must a child understand in order to know a word of its language? At the most obvious level, it is clear that to know a word is to know its meaning and its sounds—that is, both content and expression. Children pass through several stages in learning the words of their language, and there is some disagreement about how they succeed at this task. Some children appear to take up the phrases and clauses of utterances as whole units and later to dissect them into their word parts (a gestalt approach). Others seem to manage a more analytic approach from the start, taking up words directly and constructing phrases and clauses from them as necessary. All children eventually sort utterances into distinct units of meaning that are stored in the brain. It is this internalized diction-ary, called the **lexicon,** that stores units of meaning as they are acquired.

Focusing attention on one crucial ingredient in the acquisition of words, we can ask what kind of information a child must learn about the sounds of a word. What is required to be able merely to recognize a word? One not terribly obvious thing is that we must recognize pronunciations of a given word by different people as the same word, whether it is uttered by a woman or a man, a teenager or an octogenarian, a sniffler with a cold, or anyone else. To identify words—to understand language—it is essential to disregard certain voice characteristics and certain particularities of volume, speed, and pitch.

A child must observe a word's sounds and the order in which they occur. When learning the word *bad,* for example, a child must recognize that it contains the three sounds [b], [æ], and [d] and contains them in exactly that order. After all, *bad* and *dab* are not the same word, though they have the same sounds.

PHONEMES AND ALLOPHONES

Eventually every child also learns that certain sounds are pronounced one way in one context and another way in another context; thus the "same sound" can have more than one pronunciation. Two examples will help reconcile this seeming contradiction.

Although English speakers aren't generally aware of the fact, the words *cop* [kɑp] and *keep* [kip] begin with somewhat different [k] sounds, as you can notice if you alternately pronounce the two words. Don't just *listen* for the difference, which is very difficult for English speakers to hear; instead, notice where the tongue touches the roof of your mouth at the start of each word. You will discover that the tongue touches the velum farther back for *cop* than for *keep.* The reason for this difference is easy enough to understand: in anticipation of pronouncing the back vowel [ɑ], you pronounce the [k] in *cop* farther back in the mouth than you do for the [k] that precedes the front vowel [i] of *keep.*

If pronouncing these words aloud while attending to the position of the back of your tongue as it touches the roof of the mouth does not reveal the difference, try this: position your tongue as if you were about to say *keep;* then, when your tongue is in position for the initial sound of *keep,* say *cop* instead. You will discover that you must reposition your tongue in order to pronounce *cop;* if you say *cop* from the *keep* position, it will sound peculiar or foreign. The need to reposition the back of your tongue to achieve a natural pronunciation demonstrates that the two [k] sounds are not identical, though speakers of English think of them as the same.[1]

For the second example, you should readily be able to identify differences in the sounds represented by ⟨p⟩ in the first and second words of the pairs *pot/spot* and *poke/spoke.* If you hold the back of your hand (or a small piece of paper) up to your mouth when saying these word pairs, you should feel (or see) a considerable difference in the puff of air that accompanies the sounds represented by ⟨p⟩. The sound that ⟨p⟩ represents in *pot* and *poke* is strong enough to blow out a lighted match held in front of the mouth; it is an **aspirated** stop, represented as [pʰ]. The sound following ⟨s⟩ in *spot* and *spoke* is not aspirated (and will not blow out a match); we represent it as [p].

---

[1] In some languages—Basque, Malay, and Vietnamese, for example—these two [k] sounds function as distinct sounds. In fact, the IPA assigns different symbols to them. The voiceless velar stop of *cop* is represented by IPA [k], and the voiceless stop of *keep,* pronounced in the palatal region, is represented by IPA [c].

In discussing these two *p* sounds, we have noted that they occur in different positions within words. Examine the following list of words to identify the positions in which unaspirated [p] and aspirated [pʰ] occur.

pill   [pʰɪl]
poker   [pʰokər]
plate   [pʰlet]
sprint [sprɪnt]
spine   [spayn]

You'll notice that aspirated [pʰ] occurs at the beginning of words (as in *pill, poker,* and *plate*), whereas unaspirated [p] occurs after [s] (as in *sprint* and *spine*). When different sounds do not occur in the same position in words but only in different positions, we say they occur in **complementary distribution.** Complementary distribution simply means that where one sound occurs, the other does not occur.

In the words just listed, aspirated [pʰ] occurs only word initially, while unaspirated [p] occurs only after [s]; thus, [pʰ] and [p] occur in complementary distribution. Because they occur in complementary distribution they could never occur in the same position in a word and therefore could not serve to distinguish words from one another. Thus [pʰ] and [p] are not distinctive sounds in English words but constitute a single unit of the English sound system; as such they are called *allophones* of a single *phoneme*—in this case allophones of the phoneme /p/. **Allophones** are variants of a single structural element, or **phoneme,** in the sound system of a language. Allophones of a given phoneme cannot serve to create different words, and we say they are noncontrastive. To native speakers they seem to be the same sound despite their physical difference. Given that aspirated [pʰ] and unaspirated [p] are allophones of the phoneme /p/ in English, there can be no pair of contrasting words such as [pʰit]/[pit]. Likewise the two [k] sounds of *cop* and *keep* are allophones of the phoneme /k/ in English and cannot serve to make contrasting words.[2]

Besides the aspirated and unaspirated allophones of /p/, there is a third voiceless bilabial stop in English, also represented orthographically by ⟨p⟩, as in the word *mop.* This allophone of /p/ occurs sometimes at the end of a word that is pronounced at the end of an utterance: *Where's the mop?* In this utterance position, the lips can stay closed so that the sound represented by ⟨p⟩ is *unreleased;* we represent this allophone as [p˺]. In this case, however, we do not have complementary distribution because both unaspirated [p] and unreleased [p˺] can occur word finally. When two sounds can occur in the same position in a word without contrasting—that is, without creating different words—those sounds are said to occur in **free variation.** At the end of an utterance, English speakers can pronounce the word *lip* as [lɪp] or as [lɪp˺]. Thus, both the unaspirated and unreleased voiceless bilabial stops are allophones of the phoneme /p/, and /p/ therefore has three allo-

---

[2] We have now started using slanted lines / / to enclose phonemes and square brackets [ ] to enclose allophones (that is, sounds). We will continue this practice from now on, though sometimes we will have to choose one representation or the other when either would serve as well.

phones: aspirated [pʰ], unaspirated [p], and unreleased [p˺]. To repeat, the allophones of a phoneme occur in complementary distribution or in free variation; allophones of a phoneme can never signal a difference of meaning.

Distribution of Allophones

One way to differentiate phonemes from allophones is to view a phoneme as an abstract structural element in the sound system of a language—a unit of sound that lacks a fully specified pronunciation but can be pronounced in different ways depending on where in a word and an utterance it occurs. For example, while all allophones of the phoneme /p/ are voiceless bilabial stops, one is aspirated, another unaspirated, and a third unreleased. The pronunciation of the phoneme /p/ cannot be fully specified unless its position in a word (or utterance) is known; only then can its characteristic aspiration and release be determined.

We have just seen that particular allophones are determined by where they occur in a word. If you examine the sets of words in Table 3-1, you will see that the picture is still a bit more complicated than that. In these words the acute accent mark ´ above a vowel is used to indicate primary stress on that syllable (as in *rídicule* versus *ridículous*).

All the words have /p/ in syllable-initial position. The words in column A have primary stress on the first syllable, with [pʰ] as the initial sound. Those in column B also have aspirated [pʰ] word initially, though primary stress occurs on the second syllable. The words in columns A and B demonstrate that /p/ is aspirated word initially in stressed and unstressed syllables. In column C aspirated [pʰ] introduces the second syllable, which carries primary stress in each case. Thus aspirated [pʰ] occurs not only word initially but word internally, introducing a stressed syllable. The words in column D demonstrate that unaspirated [p] occurs word internally introducing unstressed syllables. In summary, the phoneme /p/ is aspirated word initially in stressed and unstressed syllables, but word internally it is aspirated only when initiating a stressed syllable.

Given these observations, we must refine our description of the distribution of the allophones of /p/ to account for the stress patterns of a word. A description of the distribution of these allophones of /p/ is shown in Table 3-2.

Contrast these facts about [pʰ] and [p] with the facts about /p/ and /s/. If a child attempting to learn the word *sat* said *pat* instead, it would have failed to make

TABLE 3-1
Allophones of /p/ in English Words

A	B	C	D
[pʰ]	[pʰ]	[pʰ]	[p]
pédigree	petúnia	empórium	rápid
pérsonal	patérnal	compúter	émpathy
pérsecute	península	rapídograph	competítion
pílgrimage	pecúliar	compétitive	computátional

TABLE 3-2
Two Allophones of English /p/

Phoneme	Allophones	Distribution
/p/ → [pʰ]		in syllable-initial position in a stressed syllable and in word-initial position
/p/ → [p]		elsewhere (as in a consonant cluster following /s/ and in word-final position)

one of the significant differences in English pronunciation: /p/ and /s/ are distinct phonemes and can serve to distinguish words, as in these word pairs.

A		B		C		D	
[pʰɪt]	pit	[pʰʌn]	pun	[læpt]	lapped	[sip]	seep
[sɪt]	sit	[sʌn]	sun	[læst]	last	[sis]	cease

The words in each pair have different meanings and differ by only a single sound. Two words that differ by only a single sound constitute a **minimal pair.** (Note that the distinction depends on sounds, not spelling.) Minimal pairs are valuable in identifying the significant sounds—the phonemes—of a language. Each minimal pair above demonstrates that /s/ and /p/ are distinct phonemes of English and not allophones of the same phoneme. Articulatory descriptions of /s/ and /p/ show that these two phonemes differ in both place and manner of articulation.

	/s/	**/p/**
Voicing	voiceless	voiceless
Place of articulation	alveolar	bilabial
Manner of articulation	fricative	stop

To take another example, /s/ and /b/ differ from one another not only in place and manner of articulation but also in voicing.

	/s/	**/b/**
Voicing	voiceless	voiced
Place of articulation	alveolar	bilabial
Manner of articulation	fricative	stop

/s/ is a voiceless alveolar fricative, /b/ a voiced bilabial stop. The fact that /s/ and /b/ contrast (as in the minimal pair *sat/bat*) provides definitive evidence that they are significantly different sounds—that they belong to distinct phonemes.

Sounds (allophones) that belong to a single phoneme share certain phonetic features but differ in one or more other features—such as voiced/voiceless, stop/ fricative, dental/alveolar, or aspirated/unaspirated. When analyzing the sound system of a language, it is important to take particular note of the distributions of sounds that have similar phonetic descriptions. Consider this list of English words:

[pʰæt]   pat
[bæt]   bat
[tʰæp]   tap
[tʰæb]   tab
[spæt]   spat

[pʰ] and [b] are both bilabial stops; they share those two features. On the other hand, [pʰ] is voiceless and aspirated, while [b] is voiced and unaspirated. Are they distinct phonemes or are they allophones of a single phoneme? You cannot answer that question by examining the phonetic descriptions alone. But, because there is at least one minimal pair above, we know that [pʰ] and [b] contrast. That is, *pat/bat* demonstrates that [pʰ] and [b] are members of different phonemes. Since there are no examples in English in which aspirated [pʰ] and unaspirated [p] contrast (in fact, they occur in complementary distribution), [pʰ] and [p] are allophones of a single phoneme. From the minimal pair *tap/tab* above, we know that unaspirated [p] contrasts with [b]; thus aspirated [pʰ] and unaspirated [p]—both voiceless bilabial stops—contrast with the voiced bilabial stop [b].

The phonemes /p/ and /b/ contrast in both word-initial and word-final position, as we saw. Sometimes, however, two sounds contrast in some positions but not all. Nevertheless, two sounds remain distinctive if they contrast in *any* one position. Consider, for example, the position following /s/ as in the word s__at: there are no two words of English like *sbat* and *spat* that carry different meanings. Thus, even though /p/ and /b/ are different phonemes in English, the contrast between them is not exploited in the position following /s/.

Now consider the very different situation in Korean. Like English, Korean has the three bilabial stops [pʰ], [p], and [b]. The following list of words illustrates their typical occurrence.

[pʰul]   'grass'
[pul]   'fire'
[pap]   'law'
[mubap]   'lawlessness'

The minimal pair [pʰul] and [pul] demonstrates that in Korean [p] and [pʰ] contrast. On the other hand, even with a much larger sample of words you could find no minimal pair in which [p] contrasts with [b]; Korean [p] and [b] are in complementary distribution, with [b] occurring only between vowels and other voiced segments, as in [mubap], but [p] never occurring in that environment. This demonstrates that while [p] and [pʰ] are distinct phonemes in Korean, [p] and [b] are allophones of a single phoneme.

TABLE 3-3
Three Sounds of English and Korean Compared

English Phonemes	Sounds: English and Korean	Korean Phonemes

The diagram in Table 3-3 represents the difference in the phonological systems of English and Korean with respect to these three sounds. It is important to underscore that although the same three sounds occur in both languages, their systematic role in those languages is altogether different. In English, [pʰ] and [p] are not functionally different; rather, they are noncontrastive allophones of a single phoneme and therefore cannot signal a difference of meaning. In Korean, [pʰ] and [p] are significantly different sounds; that is, they are separate phonemes and can distinguish one word from another (as in [pʰul] and [pul]). In terms of articulatory properties, voicing is phonemic in English; the *voiced* bilabial stop [b] is distinct from the *voiceless* bilabial stop [p]. Aspiration, however, is not phonemic in English, for no two English phonemes are different solely because one is aspirated and the other is not. In Korean, on the other hand, the voiced bilabial stop [b] is an allophone of /p/ occurring between voiced sounds; hence [b] and [p] cannot be used to distinguish Korean words. We can summarize by saying that voicing is not contrastive in Korean but aspiration is, while aspiration is not contrastive in English but voicing is.

PHONOLOGICAL RULES AND THEIR STRUCTURE

You are probably aware that French has nasal vowels and you may conclude that English lacks nasal vowels. In fact, however, English has nasal vowels, and it is instructive to look closely at them. In Table 3-4, the words in column B have

TABLE 3-4
Oral and Nasal Vowels in English

A	B
sit	sin
pet	pen
light	lime
brute	broom
sitter	singer

nasalized vowels (vowels pronounced through the nose, in addition to the mouth), while those in column A have oral vowels (pronounced through the mouth).[3]

If you search out nasal vowels in English words, you will discover that *all* of them precede one of the nasal consonants /m n ŋ/. The distribution of nasal vowels in English is regular and predictable: before a nasal consonant a vowel is nasalized. Since the distribution is predictable in English, the occurrence of nasal vowels cannot signal a meaning distinction (although it can in French and other languages where its distribution is not predictable). Two sounds whose distribution with respect to one another is *predictable* constitute allophones of a single phoneme; their distribution is describable by a general rule.

Regular **phonological rules** have this general form:

$$A \longrightarrow B / C\_\_\_D$$

Such a rule can be expressed as ''A becomes B in the environment following C and preceding D.'' Often the phrase ''in the environment'' is omitted, thus ''A becomes B following C and preceding D.'' A, B, C, and D are generally specified in terms of phonological features, although in this book rules will be presented in more informal terms. In cases where it is unnecessary to specify both C and D, one of them will be missing. For example, the phonological process of nasalization in English can be represented by the following rule statement:

Nazalization Rule

vowel $\longrightarrow$ nasal / ____ nasal

(vowels become nasalized preceding nasal sounds)

As noted in the introduction to this chapter, in acquiring a word a child must learn the number of phonemes in the word, what those phonemes are, and in what order they occur. As the English *cop/keep* alternation shows for the allophones of /k/ and the *poke/spoke* alternation shows for the allophones of /p/, a child must also learn to pronounce particular allophones of a phoneme depending on the phoneme's position in a word and the character of nearby sounds. This is done *not* by memorizing the sounds in each individual word but by acquiring rules that apply to all words, as with the nasalization rule above.

The situation for a child acquiring Korean [p] and [b] is parallel to that of an English-speaking child acquiring nasal vowels. Since [p] and [b] never contrast, they are allophones of a single phoneme; thus only one form is needed to represent them in the lexicon (along with a phonological rule that specifies the distribution of [b] between vowels and [p] elsewhere). The alternative to having a single representation in the lexicon for [p] and [b] in Korean would involve considerable

---

[3] To discover that the vowels in column B are nasalized, pinch your nose closed while saying the words in each column. For the words in column A, it will make no perceptible difference in the pronunciation; for those in column B, it will make a striking difference. This demonstrates that when you pronounce the words of column B, air from the lungs exits through the nasal passage; hence when that passage is blocked the sound of the vowel changes perceptibly.

inefficiency. It would require a specific differentiation between these sounds in every word that contains either of them. For example, *pap* 'law' and *mubap* 'lawlessness' would have different specifications for [p] and [b]. To speakers of English (which does not have a predictable distribution of [p] and [b]), this differentiation seems natural and necessary. But to have different forms for [p] and [b] in the lexicon of a Korean speaker would be equivalent to an English speaker's having different representations in the lexicon for the different /k/ sounds of *cop* and *keep,* for the different /p/ sounds of *poke* and *spoke,* or for the different /ɪ/ sounds of *sit* and *sin.* Moreover, unless there were consistent different spellings assigned to each allophone, a reader coming across the preceding word pairs for the first time would be unable to know their pronunciations. However, each phoneme is represented in the lexicon by only a single underlying form. Native speakers internalize the phonological rules specifying the distribution of allophones and automatically apply these rules wherever the phoneme appears.[4]

Since the distribution of the allophones of every phoneme is regular, a great deal of memory in the mental dictionary is saved by specifying only the phonemes in a word; a few general phonological rules can then specify the correct allophone for each occurrence of the phoneme. To see how this process works, imagine the brain as a computer with a very large but finite memory. Every redundant piece of information that is stored in a computer makes valuable memory space unavailable for other uses. Linguists think that a significant degree of "space" in the brain is saved by specifying only the distinctive features of each phoneme (thus, "voiceless bilabial stop" for /p/) and leaving the specification of allophonic features (such as "aspiration" or "release") to a few general rules that apply to tens of thousands of words and to all new words as they enter a person's lexicon.

Generalizing Phonological Rules

Until now we have been considering phonological rules as though they were formulated to apply to particular sounds; in fact, they are more general. Consider the aspiration that accompanies the production of initial /p/ in English words like *pillow* and *pot;* it can be represented by the following rule:

1. voiceless
    bilabial $\longrightarrow$ aspirated   /   word initially and initially in stressed syllables
    stop

---

[4] One indication, incidentally, that such information as the differences between allophones is not in fact stored in the lexicon can be found in pronunciations of a nonnative language. Consider a native speaker of English who knows no French and has been introduced by a speaker of French to a friend named Pierre. Unlike English, French does not aspirate initial /p/, so the French speaker introducing Pierre will pronounce his name without aspiration. English speakers—despite the fact that they have not heard aspiration in the pronunciation of *Pierre*—will nevertheless tend to pronounce *Pierre* with an aspirated [pʰ]. This reformulation of Pierre's name to conform to the phonological rules of English indicates that English speakers have a general rule that aspirates initial /p/ (even when attempting to speak French). The subconscious application of the phonological rules of one's native tongue to a foreign language contributes to a foreign accent and marks one as a nonnative speaker.

This representation says that a voiceless bilabial stop is aspirated in specific environments.

If you examine other English words with stop consonants, you will discover that it is not only /p/ that has aspiration when syllable initial but also /t/ and /k/. Since /p t k/ have parallel distributions of these allophones, English would appear to need two additional rules like the one in 1. These are given as 2 and 3:

2. For /t/:
   voiceless
   alveolar $\longrightarrow$ aspirated / word initially and initially in stressed syllables
   stop

3. For /k/:
   voiceless
   velar $\longrightarrow$ aspirated / word initially and initially in stressed syllables
   stop

Because these three rules exhaust the list of voiceless stops in English, they can be collapsed into a single rule of greater generality as follows:

4. For /p/, /t/, and /k/:
   voiceless
   stop $\longrightarrow$ aspirated / word initially and initially in stressed syllables

Notice in 4 that the combination of the phonetic features "voiceless" and "stop" leaves the place of articulation unspecified. In the absence of any specification, a phonological rule like 4 will apply to all voiceless stops irrespective of place of articulation; it will apply to bilabial, alveolar, and velar voiceless stops.

The more general a rule is, the simpler it is to state using phonetic feature notation. Moreover, many linguists see considerable evidence that the brain's lexicon seeks similar simplicity. It appears that internalized phonological rules are specified not in terms of allophones such as [p] and [pʰ], or in terms of phonemes such as /p/, /t/, and /k/, but in terms of *classes* of sounds specified by sets of phonetic features such as "voiceless" and "stop."

Natural Classes of Sounds

A set of phonemes, such as /p t k/, that can be described using fewer features than would be necessary to describe each sound individually is called a **natural class** of sounds. A natural class of sounds contains all the sounds that share one or more features. Thus /p t k/ constitute the natural class of "voiceless stops" in English. /p t k/ share the two features "voiceless" and "stop," and there are no other sounds in English that have both of those features.

Now consider the set /p t k b d g/. This is the natural class of "stops." There are no other stops in English, and all the sounds in the set share the feature "stop."

The set of sounds /p t k b d/ would *not* constitute a natural class. To be sure, the five sounds share the feature "stop"—but so does /g/, which is not included.

Whatever feature we use to describe this set would also describe /g/. Notice too that the set /p t k m/ does not constitute a natural class, because any feature we introduce to specify /m/ also belongs to other sounds. Adding the feature "nasal" to the description in order to accommodate /m/ would entail including /n/ and /ŋ/, because these too are nasals. Notice, however, that in order to specify the set /p t k m n ŋ/ we would need an either/or description: either "voiceless stop" or "nasal." There is no combination of features that would uniquely specify just those six sounds; hence /p t k m n ŋ/ is not a natural class of sounds.

Underlying Forms

Thanks to internalized rules that yield the correct allophones for every phoneme in a given word, children eventually can produce entries in their lexicons like those in Table 3-5. Such forms are called **underlying forms;** we will represent them between slanted lines, using the same notation we have used for phonemes. The **surface form,** which characterizes a word's actual pronunciation, results from the application of the phonological rules of English to the underlying forms. In some cases the surface form is the same as the underlying form simply because there are no applicable phonological rules.

Rule Ordering

One additional phonological rule will illustrate a point about the organization of phonological rules in the internalized grammar. Consider the following words:

A	B
write	ride
neat	need
rope	robe
lop	lob
lock	log
tap	tab
pick	pig
recruit	recrewed

TABLE 3-5
Underlying and Surface Forms for Six English Words

Underlying Form	Rule	Surface Form	Written Form
/kʌlər/	aspiration	[kʰʌlər]	color
/bʊk/	none	[bʊk]	book
/bit/	none	[bit]	beat
/ʌp/	none	[ʌp]	up
/spɪn/	nasalization	[spɪ̃n]	spin
/pɪn/	aspiration/nasalization	[pʰɪ̃n]	pin

If you listen carefully while pronouncing these words, you may notice that the vowels in column B have a longer duration than those in the corresponding words of column A. In phonetic symbols, we represent long vowels with a colon after them as in [a:]. Since in English there is no minimal pair such as [pit]/[pi:t] or [bæt]/[bæ:t], we know that vowel length is noncontrastive, nonphonemic. In English, vowel length is predictable and can be specified by a general phonological rule. What environment in the listed words causes vowel lengthening? If you look past the spelling, you will see that all the words of column A end with a voiceless consonant, while the words of column B end in a voiced consonant. In fact, there is a general process of English phonology that lengthens vowels preceding voiced consonants. We can state the rule as follows (V stands for vowel, C for consonant):

Lengthening Rule

$$V \longrightarrow V: / \underline{\hspace{1cm}} \underset{\text{voiced}}{C}$$

(vowels are lengthened preceding voiced consonants)

As a result of this rule, the following processes take place in English:

$$i \longrightarrow i: / \underline{\hspace{1cm}} /d/ \text{ (as in } seed \text{ versus } seat)$$
$$o \longrightarrow o: / \underline{\hspace{1cm}} /g/ \text{ (as in } brogue \text{ versus } broke)$$
$$ay \longrightarrow a:y / \underline{\hspace{1cm}} /d/ \text{ (as in } slide \text{ versus } slight)$$

(Note that this rule applies to diphthongs like /ay/.) Because vowel length is predictable in English, it can be specified by rule and need not be learned for every word individually. In many other languages, vowel length is not predictable, not specifiable by a rule, and must be learned word by word. In Fijian, for example, there is a minimal pair *oya* 'he, she' and *oyaa* 'that [thing].' *Dredre* means 'to laugh'; *dreedree* means 'difficult.' *Vakariri* means 'to boil'; *vakaririi* means 'speedily.' Thus in Fijian, vowel length cannot be assigned by a phonological rule, and vowel length is therefore contrastive, significant, phonemic in that language.

Now consider the following pairs of words, attending to how the pronunciations of the words in column A differ from those in column B. Notice that the difference is not the one represented by the spelling difference of ⟨t⟩ and ⟨d⟩; instead, it is a difference of vowel length. For most dialects of American English, the first vowels in the words of column B are longer than those of column A.

A	B
writer	rider
liter	leader
seater	seeder
rooter	ruder

The reason the medial consonants do not differ in pronunciation is that Americans tend to "flap" /t/ and /d/ between vowels in these words. A flap is a sound produced when one articulator rapidly touches another articulator a single time (see Chapter 2). In the pronunciation of /t/ or /d/ in the words above, the tip of the tongue rapidly flaps against the alveolar ridge. Because the flap allophones of /t/ and /d/ are identical (represented here by the symbol [D], in IPA by [ɾ]), the difference of pronunciation that might have resulted from the *t/d* distinction is lost, or **neutralized.** Notice that the distinction is not lost in the words *write* [rayt]/*ride* [ra:yd]. The flapping rule for American English is specified as follows (V = vowel):

Flapping Rule

$$\text{alveolar stop} \longrightarrow \text{voiced flap} \Big/ \text{V} \underline{\quad\quad} \underset{\text{unstressed}}{\text{V}}$$

(/t/, /d/ become [D] between two vowels, the second of which is unstressed)

Even though the *t/d* (voiceless/voiced) distinction is lost in this environment by the flapping rule, many Americans pronounce the column B words differently from those in column A. By combining the flapping rule and the lengthening rule, they pronounce the words in column B with a vowel of longer duration, despite the fact that there is no difference in the pronunciation of the medial consonant. It's useful to examine why.

We have now specified two rules of English that can operate on the same words, and we want to see how they interact in producing a pronounceable surface form. Consider the pair of words *writer* and *rider*. Assume that the underlying forms in the lexicon are /raytər/ for *writer* and /raydər/ for *rider*. We can then represent the derivation of the surface forms as in Table 3-6. (When the form of a word does not meet the requirements of a rule, that rule does not apply, and we write DNA.) From the underlying forms and the application of the two rules in the order shown (lengthening first, flapping second), the surface forms [rayDər] and [ra:yDər] are produced. This is in fact the correct output—the correct pronunciations of these words for some speakers—call them speakers of dialect A.

TABLE 3-6
Derivation of *Writer* and *Rider* in Dialect A

	Writer	Rider	
Underlying form	/raytər/	/raydər/	(input)
Lengthening rule	DNA	↓	
Derived form	[raytər]	[ra:ydər]	(output/input)
Flapping rule	↓	↓	
Surface form	[rayDər]	[ra:yDər]	(output)

TABLE 3-7
Derivation of *Writer* and *Rider* in Dialect B

	Writer	Rider	
Underlying form	/raytər/	/raydər/	(input)
Flapping rule	↓	↓	
Derived form	[rayDər]	[rayDər]	(output/input)
Lengthening rule	↓	↓	
Surface form	[ra:yDər]	[ra:yDər]	(output)

If we apply the same two rules in the reverse order (flapping first and lengthening second), the results will be different because the flapped sound is voiced; therefore the vowel preceding it would be lengthened in both words. As Table 3-7 shows, this is precisely what happens for speakers of another variety of English—call it dialect B.

The two identical surface forms [ra:yDər] and [ra:yDər] that are derived by applying the flapping rule prior to the lengthening rule would not be correct for dialect A. In that dialect (the more common one), *writer* and *rider* are not pronounced alike; instead, *rider* has a longer vowel than *writer*. Thus, given the same underlying forms, we see that the same pair of phonological rules if applied in one order produces surface forms that are correct in a given dialect; if applied in the other order, however, the rules produce incorrect forms for that dialect. Evidence such as this has led researchers to hypothesize that rule ordering is an essential part of the organization of phonological rules.

Note that the forms resulting from the second derivation (Table 3-7), though incorrect in dialect A, are correct in dialect B. This illustrates how speakers of different dialects can share the same underlying forms and the same rules but apply them in different sequences to produce different surface forms. Dialects that apply the lengthening rule before the flapping rule will have distinct forms of *writer* and *rider*. Dialects that apply flapping before lengthening will produce identical forms, both with a long vowel. Different orderings of the same rules are thus one mechanism to explain pronunciation differences among dialects.

SYLLABLES AND SYLLABLE STRUCTURE

Syllables

We have said little so far about how sounds are organized sequentially within words (although our analyses have presumed a certain organization, as you will see). It may seem obvious that sounds occur in words as a simple sequence *abcdef*, but that isn't entirely correct. Instead, sounds are organized into syllables, and syllables are organized into words. Thus each word consists of one or more syllables (and each syllable consists of one or more sounds), as indicated here.

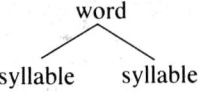

Syllable is not a tough notion for speakers to grasp intuitively, and there is considerable agreement in counting syllables. But technical definitions have proven challenging, especially in terms of articulatory or acoustic phonetics. Still, there is agreement that a **syllable** is a phonological unit consisting of one or more sounds and that syllables can be divided into two parts—a rhyme and an onset. The *rhyme* consists of a *peak* (also called a *nucleus*) and any consonants following it. The peak is usually a vowel, although a class of consonants called *sonorants* can also function as syllable peaks. **Sonorants** include nasals like [n] and a class called *liquids* like [r] and [l]. Consider the words *button, butter,* and *bottle.* In this book, we have represented the second syllable of each as [əC] (C meaning consonant), with [ə] as the vowel. These same words are represented in other books as [bʌtn̩], [bʌDṛ], and [bɑDl̩], where the diacritic under the sonorant indicates that the sonorant is functioning as the peak of a syllable. Consonants that precede the rhyme in a syllable constitute the *onset.* Any consonants following the peak as part of the rhyme are called the *coda.*

The chart below represents the structure of a syllable as just described.

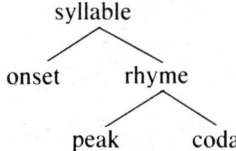

The only essential element of a syllable is the peak. Thus, not every syllable has an onset, nor every rhyme a coda. Consequently, a single sound can constitute a syllable, and a single syllable can constitute a word, both of which are illustrated in the phrase *a book.* Table 3-8 gives some English words with one, two, three, and four syllables.

TABLE 3-8
English Words Divided into Syllables

1 Syllable	2 Syllables	3 Syllables	4 Syllables
ton /tʌn/	even /i-vən/	loveliest /lʌv-li-əst/	anybody /ɛ-ni-bɑ-di/
spin /spɪn/	although /ɔl-ðo/	anyone /ɛ-ni-wən/	respectively /ri-spɛk-təv-li/
through /θru/	consists /kən-sɪsts/	computer /kəm-pyu-tər/	algebraic /æl-ǰə-bre-ək/
sail /sel/	writer /ray-tər/	syllable /sɪ-lə-bəl/	definition /dɛ-fə-nɪ-šən/

Phonotactic Constraints

The sequences of sounds that can make up a syllable differ from language to language and are strictly limited within each language. If you examine the four words of the following phrase, you will notice that English syllables allow several patterns of consonants and vowels. (As in the transcriptions above, we use hyphens to separate syllables within a word.)

in a pre-vi-ous chap-ter

/ɪn ə pri-vi-əs čǽp-tər/

VC V CCV-CV-VC CVC-CVC

From this example, you can see that English permits the following syllable types: VC, V, CCV, CV, and CVC. Some other permissible syllable types can be seen in monosyllabic words like *past* (CVCC), *queen* (CCVC), *churned* (CVCCC), and *squirts* (CCCVCCC).

Not every language allows so wide a variety of syllable types as English does. In fact, the preferred syllable type among the world's languages is a single consonant followed by a single vowel: CV. Another very common type is CVC, and a third is simply V. (All three of these occur in the illustrative phrase above.) Polynesian languages such as Samoan, Tahitian, and Hawaiian have CV and V syllables only. Similarly, Japanese allows syllables basically of the forms CV, V, and (if the last consonant is a nasal) CVC. Korean permits V, CV, and CVC syllables. Mandarin permits syllables of the forms V, CV, and (if the second consonant is [n] or [ŋ]) CVC.

It is not very common in the languages of the world to have onset consonant clusters—CC—as in the English words *try, twin,* and *stop,* and it is very uncommon to have onset consonant clusters of more than two consonants—CCC—as in *scream, sprint,* and *stress.* Even in English there is a limited range of consonants that can occur in each of the positions C_1 and C_2 of a two-consonant onset cluster (C_1C_2) and an extremely narrow range of consonants in each of the positions $C_1C_2C_3$ of a three-consonant onset cluster. (It is no coincidence that all three illustrations of initial CCC begin with /s/.) Likewise, English three-consonant onset clusters have different constraints from those clusters that constitute the coda.

The rules that characterize permissible syllable structures in a language are called **phonotactic constraints,** and they determine what constitutes a possible syllable. As a result of such constraints, there are thousands of words that may not exist in a given language but *could,* and thousands upon thousands that *could not* exist because their syllable structures are not permissible sequences of consonants and vowels in that language. The following would be impossible words in Hawaiian and Japanese because they violate the phonotactic constraints of those languages: "pat" (CVC), "pleat" (CCVC), and "stew" (CCV).

Sniglets

Comedian Rich Hall has compiled lists of "sniglets"—words that do not appear in a dictionary but should. Here are a few of Hall's sniglets and proposed definitions.

charp   'the green mutant potato chip found in every bag'

elbonics   'the actions of two people maneuvering for one armrest in a theater'

glarpo   'the juncture of the ear and skull where pencils are stored'

hozone   'the place where one sock in every laundry disappears to'

spibble   'the metal barrier on a rotary telephone that prevents you from dialing past O'

Notice that these sniglets conform to the phonotactic constraints of English. On the other hand, the following violate the phonotactic constraints of English and therefore could not serve as sniglets: "ptlin," "brkow," "tsmtot," "ngang."

Facing foreign languages whose syllable structures differ from those of their native tongue, speakers tend to impose the phonotactic constraints of their native syllable structures on the foreign words. For example, neither Spanish nor Persian permits onset clusters such as /st/ and /sp/, so it is not uncommon for speakers of those languages to pronounce the English words *study* and *speech* as /ɛs-tʌdi/ and /ɛs-pič/, which conform to their native phonotactic constraints. Similarly, the words *baseball* and *strike* have been borrowed by Japanese speakers as *beesubooro* and *suturaiko,* in which forms they obey the phonotactic constraints of Japanese.

STRESS

A shopworn aphorism among American linguists points out that "Not every white house is the White House, and not every black bird is a blackbird." The point is simply that stress patterns on words can be significant. In pronouncing the phrase *every white house,* relatively strong stress is given to both *white* and *house: whíte hóuse.* In referring to the official residence of the American president, relatively strong stress is assigned to *White* but only secondary stress to *House: Whíte Hòuse.* The stress pattern assigned to the name of the president's residence matches that in the word *téachèr: Whíte Hòuse.* The stress pattern of the same words in the phrase *(every) whíte hóuse* does not. Given that stress can vary and that the meanings of the two expressions differ, we know that stress can be contrastive in English. Below is a list of several other English word pairs. The pairs of column A are distinct words—they constitute noun phrases, comprising an adjective and a noun (as well as an article); the stress patterns of the pairs of column B match the pattern of *téachèr*—they constitute compound nouns.

A	B
a bláck bóard	a bláckbòard
a blúe bírd	a blúebìrd
a hígh cháir	a híghchàir
a réd néck	a rédnèck
a jét pláne	a jétstrèam
an íced téa	an íce crèam
a yéllow jácket (clothing)	a yéllow jàcket (a kind of wasp)

English thus has variable, rather than fixed, stress. The same is also true of German and some other languages, but many languages have fixed stress. In such languages, stress is assigned to a particular syllable in words. For example, Polish and Swahili words typically have stress on the next to last (penultimate) syllable, while Czech words carry stress on the first syllable and French usually on the last. Obviously, in languages that have a fixed word stress, contrastive stress cannot normally occur.

SYLLABLES AND STRESS IN PHONOLOGICAL PROCESSES

We saw earlier in this chapter that certain important phonological rules depend for their formulation on the syllable or on stress or on both. As we formulated it, the aspiration of voiceless stops (/p/, /t/, /k/) in English occurs "word initially and initially in stressed syllables" (page 61). Such a formulation assumes that words are organized into syllables. That, in turn, means that children must have some grasp of how words are organized into syllables. Likewise, the flapping rule that produces [rayDǝr], [mɛDǝl], and so on relies on stress, and you can probably guess now that our flapping rule could be reformulated in terms of syllables and their parts, instead of vowel segments as we formulated it on page 64.

As the investigation of phonological systems has unfolded in the last two decades, there has been increasing interest in the role of syllables in phonological processes and in the ways in which words are structured phonologically. No longer viewing words as comprising only sound segments in sequence, current phonological models of words comprise multiple tiers to accommodate such phonologically significant levels as segments, syllables, and stress.

SUMMARY

Chapter 3 examines linguistic sound systems. A *phoneme* is a unit in the phonological system of a language; it is an abstract element, a set of phonetic features having several possible manifestations, called *allophones,* in speech. Two words can differ minimally by virtue of having a single pair of different phonemes (as in *pin/bin*).

Each phoneme comprises a set of allophones, each allophone being the particular realization of the phoneme in a particular linguistic environment. The allophones of a phoneme occur in complementary distribution or in free variation; they never contrast. Allophones of a single phoneme cannot signal a difference in meaning in a minimal pair of words.

Different languages can have the same sounds and yet structure them differently in their sound systems. Both Korean and English have the three sounds [p], [pʰ], and [b] in their inventories. In English, unaspirated [p] and aspirated [pʰ] are allophones of one phoneme, while [b] belongs to a different phoneme. In Korean, on the other hand, aspirated [pʰ] and unaspirated [p] contrast and are therefore distinct phonemes, while [b] is merely the allophone of the phoneme /p/ that occurs between voiced sounds.

Each simple word in a speaker's internalized lexicon consists of a sequence of phonemes that constitutes the abstract underlying phonological representation of the word. *Underlying forms* differ from pronunciations; they are abstract and must be inferred because they cannot generally be directly observed in speech. From the underlying form of a word, the phonological rules of a language specify the allophonic features of its phonemes in accordance with their linguistic environment.

One fundamental task of children in acquiring a language is to uncover its phonological rules and to infer efficient, economical underlying forms for word units. From these abstract underlying forms, the phonological rules of a language will specify the rule-governed features of the *surface form.*

Phonological rules may be ordered with respect to one another. The first applicable rule applies to the underlying form to produce a derived form; the subsequent rules apply in turn to successive derived forms until the last applicable rule produces a surface form. The surface form is the basis of a word's pronunciation. Two dialects of a language may contain some of the same rules but apply them in a different order, thereby producing different surface forms for different pronunciations.

Words are made up of groups of sounds called *syllables,* not of sounds themselves. Different languages have different phonotactic constraints on the structure of permissible syllable types and on the occurrence of particular consonants and vowels within syllable types. CV is the most common syllable type in the world's languages. English has an unusually large range of syllable types, including consonant clusters of two and three consonants, although the consonants that can appear in any position are constrained. Stress is contrastive in English, as captured in the aphorism, "Not every white house is the White House." Phonological processes (for example, aspiration and flapping in English) can depend on syllable structure and stress, as well as on a sequence of sound segments.

EXERCISES

1. Consider the following words of English with respect to how the sound represented by ⟨t⟩ is pronounced. For each column, specify the phonetic character of the allophone. (For instance, how it is pronounced: aspirated? flapped?) Then, as was done in this chapter for the allophones of English /p/, describe the allophones of /t/ and specify their distribution.

A	B	C	D
tougher	standing	later	petunia
talker	still	data	potato
teller	story	petal	return

2. Fijian has prenasalized stops among its inventory of phonemes. The prenasalized stop [ⁿd] consists of a nasal pronounced immediately before the stop, with which it forms a single sound unit. Consider the following Fijian words as pronounced in fast speech:

vi^{n}di	'to spring up'	dina	'true'
ke^{n}da	'we'	dalo	'taro plant'
tiko	'to stay'	vu^{n}di	'plantain banana'
tutu	'grandfather'	ma^{n}da	'first'
viti	'Fiji'	tina	'mother'
dovu	'sugarcane'	mata	'eye'
do^{n}do	'to stretch out one's hand'	mokiti	'round'
		veve^{n}du	(a type of plant)

On the basis of these data, determine for Fijian whether [d], [^{n}d], and [t] are allophones of a single phoneme or whether they constitute two or three distinct phonemes. If you find that two of them (or all of them) are allophones of a single phoneme, give the rule that describes the distribution of each allophone. If you analyze all three as distinct phonemes, justify your answer. (*Note:* In Fijian all syllables end in a vowel.)

3. Examine the following words of Tongan, a Polynesian language. (*Note:* In Tongan all syllables end in a vowel.)

tauhi	'to take care'	sino	'body'
sisi	'garland'	totonu	'correct'
motu	'island'	pasi	'to clap'
mosimosi	'to drizzle'	fata	'shelf'
motomoto	'unripe'	movete	'to come apart'
fesi	'to break'	misi	'to dream'

a. On the basis of these data, determine whether [s] and [t] are allophones of a single phoneme in Tongan or are distinct phonemes. If you find that they are allophones of the same phoneme, state the rule that describes where each allophone occurs. If you conclude that they are different phonemes, justify your answer.

b. In each of the following Tongan words, one sound has been replaced by a blank. This sound is either [s] or [t]. Without more knowledge of Tongan than you could figure out from (a), is it possible to make an educated guess as to which of these two sounds fits in the blank? If so, provide the sound; if not, explain why.

__ili	'fishing net'	fe__e	'lump'
__uku	'to place'	lama__i	'to ambush'

c. In the course of this century, Tongan has borrowed many words from English and has adapted them to fit the phonological structure of its words.

kaasete	'gazette'	suu	'shoe'
tisi	'dish'	koniseti	'concert'
sosaieti	'society'	pata	'butter'
salati	'salad'	suka	'sugar'
maasolo	'marshall'	sikaa	'cigar'
sekoni	'second'	taimani	'diamond'

How does the phonemic status of [s] and [t] differ in borrowed words and in native Tongan words? In other words, is the situation the same in these borrowed words? Write an integrated statement about the status of [s] and [t] in Tongan. (*Hint:* Your statement will have to include information about which area of the Tongan vocabulary each part of the rule applies to.)

4. The distribution of the sounds [s] and [z] in colloquial Spanish is represented by the following examples in phonetic transcription:

izla	'island'	čiste	'joke'
fuersa	'force'	eski	'ski'
peskado	'fish'	riezgo	'risk'
muskulo	'muscle'	fiskal	'fiscal'
sin	'without'	rezvalar	'to slip'
rasko	'I scratch'	dezde	'since'
resto	'remainder'	razgo	'feature'
mizmo	'same'	beizbɔl	'baseball'
espalda	'back'	mas	'more'

Are [s] and [z] distinct phonemes of Spanish or allophones of a single phoneme? If they are distinct phonemes, support your answer; if they are allophones of the same phoneme, specify their distribution.

5. Consider the following Russian words. On the basis of this limited list, where does Russian appear to have a contrast between [t] and [d] and where does it appear not to have one? (*Note:* An apostrophe marks a palatalized consonant.)

pərʌxot	'steamboat'	t'ɛlə	'body'
gʌz'ɛtə	'newspaper'	pot	'perspiration'
zapət	'west'	dərʌgoy	'dear'
rat	'glad'	d'ɛlə	'business'
zdan'iyə	'building'	štat	'state'
most	'bridge'	pot	'under'

6. In Samoan, words may have two forms, one called 'bad speech' (used in formal oratory and when addressing peers or kin), the other called 'good speech' (used in literacy and religious situations and with chiefs and strangers). (The Samoan words for 'good' and 'bad' do not carry the same connotations in this case as the English words.) The difference between the two forms can be described by phonological rules.

"bad"	"good"	
taatou	kaakou	'us all'
teine	keiŋe	'girl'
taŋata	kaŋaka	'man'
ŋaŋana	ŋaŋaŋa	'language'
totoŋi	kokoŋi	'price'
nofo	ŋofo	'to stay'
ŋaalue	ŋaalue	'to work'
fono	foŋo	'meeting'

a. Describe the phonological difference between the ''bad'' and ''good'' forms. Which form is more basic—the ''good'' form or the ''bad'' form? (In other words, which one can serve as the underlying form for both forms?)

b. Wherever possible, fill in the blanks in the following table. If it is impossible to know the form of a missing word, say why.

''bad''	**''good''**	
manu		'bird'
mate		'dead'
	maŋoo	'shark'
	kili	'fishing net'
tonu		'correct'
	kaŋi	'to cry'

7. In German, the sequence of letters ⟨ch⟩ can represent (among other things) either of two sounds: [ç] (a voiceless palatal fricative) or [x] (a voiceless velar fricative). On the basis of the following data, determine whether these two sounds are distinct phonemes in German or allophones of a single phoneme.

kɛlç	*Kelch*	'cup'
fɪçtə	*Fichte*	'fir tree'
knœçl	*Knöchel*	'knuckle'
kɔx	*Koch*	'cook'
tsurɛçt	*zurecht*	'in good order'
vʊxt	*Wucht*	'weight'
çɪrʊrk	*Chirurg*	'surgeon'
nüçtərn	*nüchtern*	'sober'
bux	*Buch*	'book'
bɛrayç	*Bereich*	'scope'
hɛkçan	*Häkchen*	'apostrophe'
bax	*Bach*	'Bach'

If [ç] and [x] are distinct phonemes, justify your answer; if they are allophones of the same phoneme, specify their distribution.

8. Using the monosyllabic English words below, provide a list of fifteen ordered pairs whose stress patterns indicate they constitute a compound. It will be helpful to mark the stress pattern on the vowel of each element, using ´ to represent primary stress and ` for secondary stress. *Examples:* tíme zòne, shów hòrse

ball	beam	court	face	fall	free	gear	hand	hat
heart	hold	horse	house	kick	lance	land	life	light
paint	port	rein	ride	road	show	style	table	throw
tide	time	way	weight	year	zone			

9. We think the following words do not exist in English. Some of them are candidates for ''sniglets'' (they *could* exist); others could not be sniglets because they violate the phonotactic constraints of English. Identify the potential sniglets, and explain

why the others are not permitted. For the potential sniglets, provide an appropriate spelling in the standard orthography.

pɛtribɑr	twɪnč	rizənənt
læktomæŋgyulešən	pʌpkəss	blɪbyulə
pæŋgəkd	spret	spwent

10. Provide a list of all the consonants that can fill each slot in a word-initial three-consonant cluster in English words such as *spleen* ($C_1C_2C_3$). Examine the list that you have made for each consonant slot to decide whether it constitutes a natural class or not and, if it does, provide the name.

11. Although English makes a contrast between /p/ and /b/ (*pill* versus *bill*), it doesn't exploit the contrast in the environment following /s/ (as in *spell* and *spin*). Hence, there is no pair of words such as /sbɪn/ and /spɪn/. When a language exploits a distinction in some environments but not all, there is a tendency for the potential contrast to be neutralized where it isn't exploited. As a consequence, the /p/ of *pill* differs more from the /b/ of *bill* than does the /p/ of *spin* (try distinguishing "spin" from "sbin"). For one thing, the /p/ of *spin* (but not the /p/ of *pill*) lacks aspiration, like the /b/ of *bill*. Thus at least one feature that distinguishes /p/ and /b/ elsewhere is not exploited following /s/.

Below are two sets of words containing a contrast that is exploited in the environment in column I but neutralized in the environment in column II.

   a. Identify the segment which is likely to prompt different transcriptions and specify what those transcriptions would be.

   b. Characterize the environment that supports the neutralization.

   c. Based on your knowledge of English phonology (such as its phonotactic constraints) provide reasons for preferring one of the transcriptions over the other.

I		II
bit	beat	here, beer, peer (contrast *mill*/*meal*)
sit	seat	sing, ring, fing(er)
hat	hate	hang, sang, rang
tad	dad	sting, star, study
cad	gad	skill, score, scam

12. In light of our discussions in this chapter and your experience with some of the preceding exercises, discuss the following quote from Halle and Clements (1983).

> The perception of intelligible speech is . . . determined only in part by the physical signal that strikes our ears. Of equal significance . . . is the contribution made by the perceiver's knowledge of the language in which the utterance is framed. Acts of perception that heavily depend on active contributions from the perceiver's mind are often described as illusions, and the perception of intelligible speech seems . . . to qualify for this description. A central problem of phonetics and phonology is . . . to provide a scientific characterization of this illusion which is at the heart of all human existence.

SUGGESTIONS FOR FURTHER READING

Wolfram and Johnson (1982) is a good basic introduction to the phonological analysis of English, with many illustrations and examples. Giegerich (1992) is a clear, but more advanced, treatment of English phonetics and phonology. Sloat, Taylor, and Hoard (1978) is usually clear and accessible in both phonetics and phonology and treats a range of languages; Clark and Yallop (1990) is more advanced. The "problem book" by Halle and Clements (1983) has separate chapters on complementary distribution, natural classes, phonological rules, and systems of rules. Anderson (1974) and Hyman (1975) pay attention to the development of phonological theory. Dell (1980), first published in 1973, is a valuable treatment—with examples from French—of the kind of phonology made popular in Chomsky and Halle's (1968) classic book. More recent treatments of phonology include Kenstowicz and Kisseberth (1979), Lass (1984), and Hawkins (1984). Kaye (1989) is a lively and provocative, mostly accessible, follow-up to this chapter. A more specialized treatment is available in Hogg and McCully (1987).

REFERENCES

Anderson, Stephen. 1974. *The Organization of Phonology* (New York: Seminar).

Chomsky, Noam, and Morris Halle. 1968. *The Sound Pattern of English* (New York: Harper & Row).

Clark, John, and Colin Yallop. 1990. *An Introduction to Phonetics and Phonology* (New York: Blackwell).

Dell, François. 1980. *Generative Phonology*, translated from 1973 French edition by Catherine Cullen (Cambridge: Cambridge University Press).

Giegerich, Heinz J. 1992. *English Phonology: An Introduction* (Cambridge: Cambridge University Press).

Hall, Rich. 1984. *Sniglets* (New York: Collier).

Halle, Morris, and G. N. Clements. 1983. *Problem Book in Phonology* (Cambridge, MA: MIT Press).

Hawkins, Peter. 1984. *Introducing Phonology* (London: Hutchinson).

Hogg, Richard, and C. B. McCully. 1987. *Metrical Phonology: A Coursebook* (Cambridge: Cambridge University Press).

Hyman, Larry M. 1975. *Phonology: Theory and Analysis* (New York: Holt, Rinehart and Winston).

Kaye, Jonathan. 1989. *Phonology: A Cognitive View* (Hillsdale, NJ: Erlbaum).

Kenstowicz, Michael, and Charles Kisseberth. 1979. *Generative Phonology: Description and Theory* (New York: Academic).

Lass, Roger. 1984. *Phonology* (Cambridge: Cambridge University Press).

Sloat, Clarence, Sharon Henderson Taylor, and James E. Hoard. 1978. *Introduction to Phonology* (Englewood Cliffs, NJ: Prentice-Hall).

Wolfram, Walt, and Robert Johnson. 1982. *Phonological Analysis: Focus on American English* (Washington, DC: Center for Applied Linguistics and Harcourt Brace Jovanovich).

4

Morphology and Lexicon: Structured Meaning in Words

WORDS AND THEIR PARTS

For most people, the most basic and most tangible elements of a language are certainly its words. "There's no such word," you've heard people say. Or, "What does the word *futharc* mean?" Or, from someone doing a crossword puzzle, "What's a three-letter word for 'excessively'?" We say that one person always uses "two-bit" words, while someone else exhibits a preference for "four-letter" words. Intuitively, people seem to have clear notions of what a word is.

When it comes to identifying meaningful units smaller than a word, our intuitions are not so clear. Though we readily intuit that *car, walk, sing,* and *tall* have a single meaningful element each and that *bookstore, gameshow,* and *sidestep* have two each, our intuitions are less certain about the number of meaningful elements in words such as *bookkeeper, sneakers, women's, impracticality, fenced, resumed,* and *presumption.* This chapter examines the segmentation of words into their meaningful elements, the principles that govern the composition of words from meaningful elements, and the functions of words and word parts in sentences. We describe what it means to know a word and the ways in which a language can expand its stock of words.

What It Means to Know a Word

Consider what a child must know when it knows a word in its language. A child able to utter a sentence like *My new dolls can cry* knows much more about the word *doll* than the kind of toy it refers to. The child knows what sounds make up *doll* and in what sequence they occur, as well as how to use *doll* in a sentence. The child also knows that *doll* is a common noun (and hence can be preceded by the possessive pronoun *my,* as here, or by an article like *a* plus an adjective); that *doll* is a count noun (that is, it can be followed by a plural marker *-s,* in contrast to mass nouns like *milk* and *sugar,* which do not take *-s*); and that the plural of *doll* is formed regularly and is not an irregular plural like *teeth* or *deer.*

Thus, knowing a word requires having at least four kinds of information:

1. Phonological: what sounds the word contains and their sequencing (as discussed in Chapter 3)

2. Semantic: the meanings of the word (to be discussed in Chapter 6)

3. Syntactic: what category (noun, verb, etc.) the word belongs to and how to use it in a sentence (to be discussed in this chapter and further in Chapter 5)

4. Morphological: how related words, including plurals (for nouns) and past tenses (for verbs), are formed (a topic of this chapter)

Knowing even the simplest word requires that phonological, morphological, syntactic, and semantic information be stored in the mind's dictionary (the *lexicon*) as part of that word's mental representation.

There are certain parallels between the kinds of information stored in the lexicon and the information that can be found in an ordinary desk dictionary. In a desk dictionary, basic phonological, semantic, morphological, and syntactic information is found along with information that neither children nor adult speakers need to possess in order to speak a language—information, for example, about a word's orthographic representation or about its etymology (the history of its phonological development and of the semantic path it followed in getting to its current meaning). In addition, dictionaries sometimes provide illustrative sentences for words or actual citations from well-known sources. Obviously children will not normally have any orthographic, etymological, or illustrative information in their lexicon.

LEXICAL CATEGORIES (PARTS OF SPEECH)

We said above that small children implicitly know the category (part of speech) of all the words they use, though of course they can't name categories like "noun" or "verb." The ability to use a word in a sentence requires knowledge of its part of speech, or *lexical category*. In this section we describe four major lexical categories (verbs, nouns, adpositions, and adjectives) and briefly touch upon three others (determiners, pronouns, adverbs). All seven are familiar to you, although ''adpositions'' may be an unfamiliar term: it is the name of a more general category that includes the category of prepositions.

There are two basic ways to discuss lexical categories. The first focuses on the word itself and involves identifying the different forms that a set of words can take (for example, compare the possible forms of *bright, tall, big, green, tidy,* and other adjectives with *fast/faster/fastest*). The second involves identifying those lexical categories that can be combined to form phrases (such as *a faster race* and *those very big, green apples*). The composition of words is the concern of morphology, the subject of this chapter. The composition of phrases is the concern of syntax, which is the subject of the following chapter although our discussion of morphology will anticipate certain aspects of syntax because morphology and syntax are interrelated.

Verbs

English-speaking children know that words in the category of **verbs** can have past tense forms *(talked)*, forms in *-ing (talking)*, and third person singular forms (the *-s* of *it talks*). The articulation of this knowledge does not come easily even when it is taught in ''grammar'' school, but English-speaking children know it implicitly, and know it from an early age.

Subcategorization   Another important kind of information that a child must learn for each verb is what kind of sentence structure it allows. (This is part of the knowledge about each word that children must learn and store in their mental lexicon, and it is convenient to address it here, although it falls within the realm of syntax.) Consider the following sentences:

1. Sarah purchased a book.

2. Sarah laughed at the joke.

3. *Sarah purchased.

4. Sarah laughed.

5. *Sarah laughed the joke.

6. *Sarah laughed a book.

The asterisks in front of sentences 3, 5, and 6 indicate that they are ill formed—that is, they are not permissible English sentences. Examine sentences 1 through 6 and you will notice that the verbs *purchased* and *laughed* require different sentence structures. A sentence with *purchase* requires a noun phrase after it and will be ill formed if it lacks one, as 3 demonstrates. But not all verbs require a noun phrase to follow, as 4 illustrates. The verb *laugh* does not need a noun phrase; in fact, it doesn't permit one, as 5 and 6 illustrate. *Laugh* does permit other structures to follow it—for example, a prepositional phrase *(at Fred)*—but typically not a noun phrase. Other verbs, like *sing,* permit a following noun phrase but don't require one, as sentences 7 and 8 demonstrate.

7. The diva sang.

8. The diva sang the aria.

The examples in 1 through 8 illustrate an important point about words like *purchase, laugh,* and *sing.* All belong to the *category* verb, but there are different *subcategories,* according to the different sentence structures that they permit. Verbs that take noun phrases after them are called **transitive verbs,** while verbs that do not require noun phrases are called **intransitive verbs.** Sentences 1 and 8 above contain transitive verbs; sentences 2, 4, and 7 contain intransitive verbs.

The kinds of structures that verbs permit differ considerably from one another. As the following sentences illustrate, the verb *proclaim* permits a sentence to come after it, but it cannot be used intransitively, as in the ill-formed 3 below, or with a noun phrase, as in 2, though it does permit two noun phrases after it, as in 4.

1. Sarah proclaimed that Fred is funny.

2. *Sarah proclaimed Fred.

3. *Sarah proclaimed.

4. Sarah proclaimed Fred the winner.

Thus, besides being categorized as a verb in a speaker's lexicon, each verb is *subcategorized* as transitive or intransitive. (Because a verb like *proclaim* permits two noun phrases, but not one, it is marked as *ditransitive.*)

Nouns

Nouns constitute another important lexical category, and as such they share certain properties.

Number   In many languages, nouns have the grammatical category of **number.** In English, virtually all nouns have distinct forms for singular and plural number, as in *cat/cats* and *child/children.* (A few exceptions like *deer/deer* have identical singular and plural forms).

Case   Besides a common form *(summer, Rex, runner),* English nouns also have a possessive form, as in *summer's day, Rex's biscuits,* and *runner's shoes.* In many other languages, there are several forms of the noun depending on its grammatical role in the sentence, and these forms represent different cases. **Case** corresponds to—and marks—such categories as subject, direct object, indirect object, and object of a preposition. Languages have several ways of marking case, one of which is variant forms of the noun. Besides the common and possessive case forms of its nouns, English has an additional case distinction in its pronouns. Alongside the common forms *I, we, he, she,* and *they* and their possessive forms (for example, *my* and *their*), the objective forms *me, us, him, her,* and *them* also exist.

Gender   In many languages, nouns occur in different classes, each class having its own case markers, number markers, and other forms. Traditionally, such noun classes are called **genders,** but bear in mind that grammatical genders are distinct from natural (biological) gender and may have little to do with the sex of the object referred to.[1] In French, for example, with its two genders, *mur* 'wall' is masculine, and *mer* 'sea' is feminine, although there is no clue to gender in the words or their referents. When referring to 'a wall' with a pronoun, however, speakers of French use the masculine pronoun *il* 'he,' and when referring to 'the sea' they use the feminine pronoun *elle* 'she.' In German, *Bleistift* 'pencil' is masculine, *Wand* 'wall' is feminine, and *Mädchen* 'girl' is neuter. German articles and adjectives in a noun phrase are marked with the same gender as the noun, as you'll see in the following discussion. In some languages, notably the Bantu languages of Africa, there are numerous noun classes—far more than the two or three genders found in European languages. English is an example of a language whose nouns lack grammatical gender.

Adjectives

Words like *fast* and *beautiful,* which serve to specify the attributes of nouns (in traditional terminology, to "modify" nouns), are members of the category **adjective.** As we saw above, some English adjectives can take on three forms—*fast, faster, fastest*—while others cannot be inflected, although they can be combined with *more* and *most* into phrases.

Degrees of Comparison   Adjectives can be marked for two **degrees:** *comparative* (*younger, grungier*) and *superlative* (*youngest, grungiest*). These particular markers cannot be used with all English adjectives (we say the markers are not entirely "productive") in that adjectives of more than two syllables require *more* and *most* instead of *-er* and *-est* to mark comparative and superlative degrees: **beautifuller* and **beautifullest* are not well-formed English words (hence they are starred). Some adjectives can mark comparative and superlative degrees in either way; they can add *-er* and *-est* (*cleverer, cleverest*) or be combined with *more* or *most* (*more clever, most clever*). Unmarked adjectives (*tall, clever, beautiful*) are said to be in the *positive* or absolute degree.

Agreement   In some languages (including Spanish, French, German, and Russian, but not English), adjectives *agree* in form with the nouns they modify. In languages that have **agreement** between nouns and adjectives, an adjective carries markers for certain grammatical categories (typically gender, number, and case) that also mark the agreeing noun. Thus, an adjective modifying a masculine singular noun in the objective case will itself carry markers for masculine *gender,* singular *number,* and objective *case;* we say such an adjective *agrees* with the noun

---

[1] In the fifth century B.C., Protagoras first recognized three genders for Greek: masculine, feminine, and "things." Seeing that many "things" were *grammatically* masculine or feminine, Aristotle proposed "intermediate" as the third gender. Later the genders were called masculine, feminine, and "neither." *Neuter* is English for Latin 'neither.' Gender does not originally have anything to do with sex but is a much more general term (related to *genus*) meaning 'kind' or 'class.'

it modifies in gender, number, and case. For example, the German adjectives *gut* 'good,' *schwer* 'hard,' and *kalt* 'cold' are marked differently depending on the gender of the noun they modify: *guter Wein* 'good wine' (*gut* carries the masculine *-er* affix because *Wein* is a masculine noun), *schwere Arbeit* 'hard work' (*schwer* carries the feminine *-e* affix because *Arbeit* is a feminine noun), and *kaltes Wasser* 'cold water' (*kalt* carries a neuter *-es* affix to agree with *Wasser,* which is a grammatically neuter noun). In French one says *le petit garçon* 'the little boy' but *la petite maison* 'the little house.' Because *maison* is *grammatically* feminine (irrespective of its biological neutrality), the adjective modifying it gets marked as feminine (orthographically by the affix *-e,* in speech by pronouncing the second /t/), whereas the same adjective modifying the masculine singular noun *garçon* carries no such marker. Similarly, *petits garçons* (whose pronunciation is identical to the singular despite the orthographic difference) means 'little boys.' Notice that the French definite article also varies in form, being *le* [lə] with the masculine class of nouns and *la* [la] with the feminine class. Like nouns, then, adjectives can be marked for gender, number, and case. But unlike nouns, adjectives have no inherent gender; instead, the gender marked on an adjective is determined by, or agrees with, the gender of the noun it modifies, as are its number and case.

Attributive and Predicative Adjectives   Although word order and phrase structure are syntactic matters, it is useful here to mention two terms that are associated with adjectives. When an adjective is part of a noun phrase *(the tall dancers)*, it is said to be an **attributive** adjective. An adjective that complements a verb and is not part of a noun phrase *(She looks tall; The room is tidy)* is said to be a **predicative** adjective. Agreement between nouns and adjectives generally affects both attributive and predicative adjectives.

Adpositions

Adpositions constitute a class of words that is typically few in number and generally "closed" in the sense that it is a class to which new words are rarely added. Adpositions typically indicate a semantic relationship between two other entities. There are two types of adposition—prepositions and postpositions.

Prepositions   Prepositions are adpositions that precede the noun phrase that complements them: *at home, on Tuesday.* Like other adpositions, the English words *on, to, for,* and *before* indicate a semantic relationship between other entities. *The book is on/under/near the table* indicates location of one thing with respect to another. *Sarah rode to/from Athens* (indicates direction) *with/without Fred* (indicates accompaniment) *at/near/by her side* (indicates location of Fred with respect to Sarah). (Although it is not very common in English, prepositions can occur without complements, as in the sentence, *The doctor isn't in* [the office].)

Postpositions   In many languages, adpositions follow their complement nouns instead of preceding them and are called **postpositions.** Japanese has postpositions, and as the Japanese-English pairs below illustrate, prepositions and postpositions function similarly.

Japanese Postpositions	English Prepositions
Taroo *no*	*of* Taro
hasi *de*	*with* chopsticks
Tookyoo *e*	*to* Tokyo

The term *adposition* is a cover term for both prepositions and postpositions. It is useful to recognize that the position of ''pre''positions, which seems so natural to speakers of English (as well as French, Spanish, Russian, and many other languages), would seem unnatural to speakers of Japanese, Turkish, Hindi, and the many other languages that postpose rather than prepose their adpositions.

Determiners

Determiners constitute another word class that can occur with nouns as part of a noun phrase: *a book, an orchestra, the players, this problem, those guys.* Determiners fall into several subcategories, including definite and indefinite articles *(the* and *a/an)* and demonstratives *(this/that/these/those).*

Pronouns

Like adpositions, pronouns constitute a closed class. This lexical category includes several subcategories, the most familiar of which is personal pronouns, such as the English words *I, you, she, her,* and *them.* Such pronouns are often said to take the place of nouns or noun phrases. Demonstrative pronouns constitute another class of pronouns, including *this* and *those (This is like the one I bought; Those are mine).* There are also interrogative pronouns, like *who* in *Who is that young man?* and *what* in *You told him what?* Still another pronominal category is relative pronouns, like *who* in *Ellen's a doctor who specializes in gerontology* and *that* in *No, ''60 Minutes'' is the one that took most of the awards.*

Adverbs

As adjectives serve to modify nouns, adverbs serve to modify certain word classes. In the following examples, the italicized adverbs modify verbs (sentences with comparable adjectives are provided in parentheses).

Adverbs Modifying Verbs

He talked *loudly*. (Cf. He was a *loud* talker.)
She slept *soundly*. (Cf. She was a *sound* sleeper.)
She thought *quickly*. (Cf. She was a *quick* thinker.)
They studied *diligently*. (Cf. They were *diligent* students.)

The English adverbs above (and many other adverbs) are formed by adding *-ly* to an adjective stem, but not all adverbs are formed that way and not all adverbs have related adjectives, as demonstrated in the examples that follow (where ill-formed sentences with comparable adjectives are shown in parentheses):

Adverbs Modifying Verbs

She spoke *often*. (Cf. *She was an often speaker.)
She studied *here*. (Cf. *She was a here student.)
They'll arrive *soon*. (Cf. *They will have a soon arrival.)
She believes it *now*. (Cf. *She has a now belief.)

Besides modifying verbs, adverbs can modify adjectives, other adverbs, and sentences, as in these examples.

Adverbs Modifying Adjectives	**Adverbs Modifying Adverbs**
a *very* tall tree	*very* soon
a *truly* splendid evening	*truly* unbelievably fast
a *bitterly* cold winter	*unbelievably* quickly

Adverbs Modifying Sentences

Surprisingly, they were late.
Miraculously, she wasn't hurt.
Sadly, it sank.

Semantically, then, adverbs indicate when, where, how, or to what degree, and they can modify verbs, adjectives, adverbs, or sentences.

MORPHEMES: THE MEANING-BEARING CONSTITUENTS OF WORDS

We now turn to the smallest units of language that can be associated with meaning or grammatical categories. As it happens, those units need not be words.

English speakers are aware that words like *girl, ask, tall, father, uncle,* and *orange* cannot be divided into smaller meaningful units. *Orange,* for example, is not made up of *o* + *range* or *or* + *ange* or *ora* + *nge*. Nor is *father* made up of, say, *fath* and *er*. But many words do have more than one meaningful part. *Oranges, fathers, grandmother, asks, asked, asking, homemade, taller,* and *tallest* have two elements each. Other words having more than one element that contributes to their overall meaning include *beautiful, churches, supermarkets, book-shelves,* and *television*. A set of words can be built up by adding certain elements to a core element. For example, built up around the core element *true* is the following set of words:

truer	untrue	truthfully
truest	truth	untruthfully
truly	truthful	untruthfulness

Speakers of English recognize that these words share a stem whose meaning or lexical category has been modified or changed by the addition of other elements.

The *meaningful* elements of a word are called **morphemes.** Thus, *true* is a single morpheme; *untrue* and *truly* contain two morphemes each; and *untruthfulness* contains five (UN + TRUE + TH + FUL + NESS). *Truer,* with the two elements TRUE and -ER ('more'), means 'more true.' The morphemes in *truest* are TRUE and -EST ('most'); in *truly,* TRUE and -LY; in *untrue,* TRUE and UN-; in *truthful,* TRUE + -TH + -FUL.

We have been using the word "meaningful" somewhat loosely, for it is only by stretching the use of that word a bit that we can call *-er* in *truer* and *-ed* in *looked* meaningful elements. Morphemes can indeed have meaning, as with *true* and *look,* but they can also represent a grammatical category, such as comparative degree or past tense.

Morphemes cannot be equated with syllables. On the one hand, a single morpheme can have two or more syllables, as in *harvest, grammar, river, gorilla, hippopotamus,* and *Connecticut.* On the other hand, there are sometimes two or more morphemes in a single syllable, as in *judged* (JUDGE + 'PAST TENSE'), *dogs* (DOG +'PLURAL'), and *men* (MAN + 'PLURAL'), with two morphemes each, and *men's,* with three morphemes (MAN + 'PLURAL' + 'POSSESSIVE').

Free and Bound Morphemes

Some morphemes like TRUE, MOTHER, and ORANGE can stand alone as words. Others cannot stand alone: UN-, TELE-, -NESS, and -ER, for example, function *only* as parts of words. Morphemes that can stand alone as words are called **free morphemes;** those that function only as parts of words are called **bound morphemes.**

Derivational Morphemes

Certain bound morphemes (like the underscored parts of the following words) have the effect of changing the lexical category of the word to which they are affixed: *truthful, establishment, darken, frighten,* and *teacher.* When added to the noun *truth,* -FUL yields the adjective *truthful;* -MENT added to the verb *establish* yields the noun *establishment; dark* is an adjective, *darken* a verb; *fright* a noun, *frighten* a verb; *teach* a verb, *teacher* a noun. In English (though not in all languages) such morphemes tend to be added to the end of words as suffixes. We can represent these relationships as in the following rules:

Noun + -FUL ⟶ Adjective (*doubtful, beautiful*)
Adjective + -LY ⟶ Adverb (*beautifully, truly*)
Verb + -MENT ⟶ Noun (*establishment, amazement*)
Verb + -ER ⟶ Noun (*teacher, rider, thriller*)
Adjective + -EN ⟶ Verb (*sweeten, brighten, harden*)
Noun + -EN ⟶ Verb (*frighten, hasten, christen*)

Similar processes of **derivation**—processes whereby one word is transformed into a word with a related meaning but belonging to a different lexical class—are common in the languages of the world. We illustrate with these Persian words:

dærd	'pain'	dærdnak	'painful'
næm	'dampness'	næmnak	'damp'
xætær	'danger'	xætærnak	'dangerous'

The suffix -*nak* can be added to certain nouns to form adjectives. Thus Persian has the following rule of derivational morphology:

Noun A + -NAK ⟶ Adjective 'the quality of being or having A'

Another derivational suffix of Persian creates abstract nouns from adjectives, as illustrated in the word pairs below.

| gærm | 'warm' | gærma | 'heat' |
| pæhn | 'wide' | pæhna | 'width' |

This process of derivational morphology can be expressed by this rule:

Adjective + -A ⟶ Noun

Of course, whether a particular word belonging to the appropriate lexical category can undergo a given derivational process in any language is a matter that must be specified for each word in the lexicon. In English, the nouns *doubt* and *beauty* can take the suffix -*ful*, but the nouns *love* and *book* cannot. Unless words are marked for particular derivational processes, the ungrammatical forms **loveful* and **bookful* would result instead of the grammatical *loving* and *bookish*.

In Fijian VAKA-, meaning 'in the manner of,' is a derivational morpheme that can be prefixed to adjectives and nouns to derive adverbs according to these two rules:

VAKA- + Adjective ⟶ Adverb
VAKA- + Noun ⟶ Adverb

The following adverbs exhibit the morpheme VAKA-: *vaka-Viti* 'in the Fijian fashion' (from *Viti* 'Fijian'), *vakatotolo* 'in a rapid manner, rapidly' (from *totolo* 'fast, rapid'). To illustrate the derivation from a noun, consider *vakamaarama* 'ladylike' (formed by prefixing *vaka-* to *maarama* 'lady').

Not all bound morphemes serve to change the lexical category of words. Adding other bound morphemes like English DIS-, RE-, and UN- (*disappear, repaint, unfavorable*) to a word changes its meaning without altering its lexical category. For example, *appear* and *disappear* are both verbs, as are *paint* and *repaint; favorable* and *unfavorable* are both adjectives. There is a notable tendency in English for morphemes that change meaning without altering lexical category to be added to the front of words as prefixes, though this is not universal across all languages (and in fact some languages lack prefixes altogether, as Turkish does).

The two types of morphemes we have just examined are called **derivational morphemes.** To recapitulate, derivational morphemes can produce new words from existing words in two ways. First, they can change the meaning of a word: *true* and *untrue* have opposite meanings; *paint* and *repaint* have different meanings. Second, they can change the lexical category of a word, thereby permitting it to function differently in a sentence: *true* is an adjective, *truly* an adverb, *truth* a noun.

Inflectional Morphemes

Another type of bound morpheme is illustrated in the underscored parts of the words *cats, collected, sleeps,* and *louder*. These morphemes behave differently from derivational morphemes: they alter the form of a word without changing either its lexical category or its central meaning. These **inflectional morphemes** create variant forms of a word to conform to different functional roles in a sentence or in discourse. On nouns and pronouns, for example, inflectional morphemes serve to mark grammatical categories like gender and case or semantic notions like number. On verbs, they can mark such things as tense or number, while on adjectives they serve to indicate degree or, as in Old English, gender, number, and case.

Sometimes inflectional morphemes serve merely to integrate a word into its sentence, redundantly indicating on a verb, for example, that the subject of the sentence is third person, as in *She sleeps to dream.* Only in a very limited sense can inflectional morphemes be said to change meaning. To be sure, *cigar* and *cigars* don't mean exactly the same thing, but *cigars* means simply 'more than one cigar.' *Collect* and *collected* can be thought of as meaning the same thing but orienting listeners (or readers) to different time frames. Many languages have large inventories of inflectional morphemes, as did older forms of English. Russian and German have maintained fairly elaborate inflectional systems over the centuries, while English has shed inflections until today it has only eight remaining: two on nouns, four on verbs, and two on adjectives, as shown in Table 4-1. Compare this inflectional system of English with the examples from the Russian noun *žena* 'wife' and verb *pišat'* 'to write' in Tables 4-2 and 4-3. For the moment, the chief point is merely that Russian nouns and verbs have many more inflections than

TABLE 4-1
Inflectional Morphemes of English

Lexical Category	Grammatical Category	Examples
Noun	Plural	cars, churches
	Possessive	car's, children's
Verb	Third person	(she) swims, (it) seems
	Past tense	wanted, showed
	Past participle	wanted, shown (or showed)
	Present participle	wanting, showing
Adjective	Comparative	taller, sweeter
	Superlative	tallest, sweetest

TABLE 4-2
Russian Noun Inflections: *žena* 'wife'

	Singular	Plural
Nominative	žena	žĕny
Accusative	ženu	žĕn
Genitive	ženu	žĕn
Dative	žene	žĕnam
Instrumental	ženoy	žĕnami
After some prepositions	žene	žĕnax

English ones; the meanings of the various inflectional cases (nominative, accusative, and so on) are discussed later in the chapter (on page 93).

The eight inflectional morphemes of English are fully productive. That is, when new nouns, verbs, and adjectives are added to the language they are extremely likely to be inflected like the examples just listed. A child hearing a noun (like *pool* or *tooth*) or a verb (like *talk* or *speak*) for the first time will automatically inflect it for plural and past tense in the regular, rule-governed way. Children at first produce not only the correct *pools* and *talked* but the incorrect *tooths* and *speaked.

The system of English pronouns gives some hint of an earlier inflectional morphology that also affected nouns. Except for *you,* English pronouns, like nouns, have distinct singular and plural forms (*I* and *we; he/she/it* and *they*). Unlike nouns, however, pronouns exhibit distinct forms for use in other than subject functions (*I* and *me; we* and *us; he* and *him; she* and *her; they* and *them); you* and *it* are exceptions.

He saw Luke	*Him saw Luke.
Luke saw him.	*Luke saw he.
Luke saw it.	It saw Luke.
Luke saw you.	You saw Luke.

In Old English, nouns had inflected forms not only for number, as they do today, but for several cases besides subject and object (see Table 10-1 in Chapter 10). In addition, Old English pronouns had a dual number in addition to singular and

TABLE 4-3
Russian Present-Tense Verb Inflections: *pišat'* 'write'

Person	Singular	Plural
First person	pišu	pišem
Second person	pišeš	pišete
Third person	pišet	pišut

plural. It had singular and plural pronouns for first, second, and third persons, as well as a distinct form in the first and second persons to refer to just two people: 'we two' and 'you two.'

We have mentioned the category of person in incidental ways above; **person** refers simply to the person or persons *speaking* (the first person: *I* or *we*), the person(s) *spoken to* (the second person: *you*), or the person(s) or other entities *spoken about* (the third person: *he, she, it, they*).

LINEAR AND HIERARCHICAL ORGANIZATION OF MORPHEMES IN WORDS

Linear Ordering of Morphemes

The morphemes in a word are not arranged randomly, as all readers of this book know implicitly. Rather, they have a strict linear sequence.

Affixes   Some morphemes, called **suffixes,** always follow the stems they attach to, like 'PLURAL' in *boys* and -MENT in *commitment:* both *sboy and *mentcommit are ill formed. Languages can also have **prefixes,** which attach to the front of another morpheme, as in the words *untrue, disappear,* and *repaint.* (Compare *true + un, *appear + dis, and *paint + re; and, of course, English does not permit *NESS + FUL + TRUTH + UN or any arrangement other than *untruth-fulness.*)

In English, all *inflectional* morphemes are suffixes. *Derivational* morphemes, on the other hand, can be either prefixes (<u>un</u>*happy*, <u>dis</u>*appear*) or suffixes (*happi-<u>ness</u>*, *appear<u>ance</u>*). Generally, inflectional morphemes are added to the outermost parts of words: they precede derivational prefixes or follow derivational suffixes.

Besides prefixes and suffixes, some languages have *infixes.* An **infix** is a morpheme that is inserted *within* another morpheme instead of being affixed to an end of it. If English had morphemes TTH meaning 'tooth' and GSE meaning 'goose' (which it doesn't!), then we could say that -OO- was an infix meaning 'singular' and -EE- an infix meaning 'plural.' English speakers find any interpretation calling for singular and plural infixes in words like *tooth/teeth* and *goose/geese* to be counterintuitive, but other languages do exploit this morphological possibility. In Tagalog (the most widely spoken language of the Philippines), infixing does exist. The word *gulay* meaning 'greenish vegetables' can take the infix -IN-, creating the word *ginulay,* meaning 'greenish blue.' Compared to prefixes and suffixes, infixes are relatively rare in the languages of the world.

Some languages also combine a prefix and a suffix in a single morpheme called **circumfix**—a morpheme that occurs in two parts, on both sides of another morpheme. In Samoan, for example, the morpheme FE-/-AʔI, meaning 'reciprocal,' exists. Thus the verb 'to quarrel' is *finau;* the verb meaning 'to quarrel with each other' is *fefinauaʔi.* Taken together, suffixes, prefixes, infixes, and circumfixes are called **affixes.**

Nonconcatenative Morphology

Interdigitation   Not all morphological processes can be viewed as concatenating morphemes to one another by adding a continuous sequence of phonological seg-

TABLE 4-4
Derivational Morphology in Arabic

kita:ba	'writing'	kataba	'he wrote'
ka:tib	'writer'	ka:taba	'he corresponded with'
maktab	'office'	ʔaktaba	'he dictated'
maktaba	'library'	ʔiktataba	'he was registered'
maktu:b	'letter'	taka:taba	'he exchanged letters with x'
mikta:b	'typewriter'	ʔinkataba	'he subscribed'
kutubi:	'bookseller'	ʔistaktaba	'he had a copy made'

ments to a stem. In other words, not all morphological processes add prefixes, suffixes, or even infixes. One interesting morphological phenomenon can be found in the system of marking grammatical and derivational categories in Semitic languages, such as Arabic and Hebrew. We illustrate with Arabic.

Arabic nouns and verbs generally have a root consisting of three consonants, such as KTB /k-t-b/. For example, the Arabic word for 'book' is *kita:b*. By interdigitating /k-t-b/ and various other morphemes, Arabic creates a great many nouns, verbs, and adjectives with this single root. The nouns and verbs in Table 4-4 all contain the same /k-t-b/ root, with other morphemes interdigitated.

Besides the derivational power of such a system, Arabic is able to signal many grammatical categories such as case, number, and definiteness on nouns and to signal person, number, and tense on verbs. Some of the inflected nouns built from the root KTB are listed in Table 4-5. Notice that each word contains the root /k-t-b/, with various vowel patterns interdigitated. Just as the root KTB has a fixed core meaning (having to do with books and writing), so the various combinations of vowels and other consonants are patterned and have a grammatical or derivational meaning that can be transferred systematically among various roots. (See page 93 on nominative, genitive, and accusative cases.) Incidentally, the English words *Moslem, Islam,* and *salaam,* which have been borrowed from Arabic, all contain the root SLM /s-l-m/, with its core meaning of 'peace, submission.'

Portmanteau Words   Another widespread morphological phenomenon is the joining of two or more morphemes in such a way that the phonological segments

TABLE 4-5
Inflectional Morphology in Arabic

kita:b	'book'
kutub	'books'
kita:bun	'a book (nominative)'
kita:bin	'a book (genitive)'
kita:ban	'a book (accusative)'
ʔalkita:bu	'the book (nominative)'
ʔalkita:bi	'the book (genitive)'
ʔalkita:ba	'the book (accusative)'

cannot be assigned partly to each of its morphemes. The classic example of this is the French word *du* representing the two morphemes DE 'of' and LE 'the.'

Hierarchical Ordering of Morphemes

As with all other aspects of language, morphemes are organized within words in patterned ways, as speakers know implicitly.

Besides being arranged in a linear order, the morphemes in words also have a hierarchical (or layered) structure. *Untrue*, for example, is TRUE with UN- prefixed to it (not UN- with TRUE added). *Truthful* is composed of a stem TRUTH with -FUL suffixed to it (and *truth* is itself TRUE with -TH added). Examining more complex words, it is easy to see that *untruthful* would be incorrectly analyzed if we claimed that it was composed of *untrue* with -*thful* suffixed.

How is the word *uncontrollably* organized? Is it *controllably* with UN- prefixed? Or *uncontrol* with -*ably* suffixed? It may be helpful to picture the sequence of morpheme structuring as follows:

control (Verb)
controllable (Adjective)   Verb + -ABLE ⟶ Adjective
uncontrollable (Adjective)   UN- + Adjective ⟶ Adjective
uncontrollably (Adverb)   Adjective + -LY ⟶ Adverb

In looking at a sequence like this, it is clear that the root of *uncontrollably* is CONTROL. We say that CONTROL functions as the stem for -ABLE, that *controllable* functions as the stem for *uncontrollable,* and that *uncontrollable* functions as the stem for *uncontrollably*. A representation using labeled brackets would be as follows:

$$[\ [un \ [\ [control_{Verb}] \ + \ able_{Adj}]_{Adj}] \ ly_{Adv}]$$

It could also be represented using a tree diagram like the one in Figure 4-1.

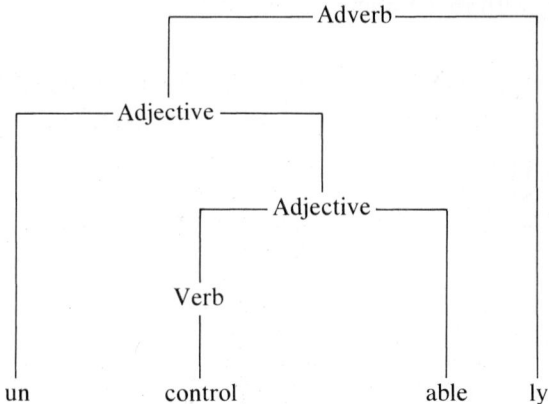

FIGURE 4-1
Hierarchical Structure of *uncontrollably*

THE ROLE OF MORPHOLOGY IN LANGUAGE

Grammatical Functions of Inflectional Morphology

Recall that the principal task of language is to express and communicate thoughts (not ideas only, but wishes, greetings, warnings, requests, and other "thoughts"). To accomplish this work, languages have evolved a wealth of lexical, morphological, and grammatical structures. Different languages reveal different preferences for expressing equivalent "thoughts." Consider the following English sentences:

1. The two doctors expressed their views about Dan's health yesterday.

2. Did the doctor talk to you yesterday about her fear concerning Dan's health?

With respect to the inflectional morphology in these sentences, *doctors, views,* and *Dan's* are inflected nouns, each with two morphemes, while *expressed* is an inflected verb. Note that in the phrase *the two doctors,* the plural suffix *-s* is redundant, given the unambiguously plural word *two.* In the same vein, one could say that the past tense markings of *expressed* and *did* are redundant, given the adverb *yesterday.*

Though the conventional rules of English sentence formation would not allow it, if the sentences were expressed as follows no information would be lost.

3. *The two doctor express their views about Dan's health yesterday.

4. *Do the doctor talk to you yesterday about her fear concerning Dan's health?

As you can see, certain words in these sentences exhibit idiosyncratic characteristics that are required neither for clear communication nor by any general principles of language.

A meaning much the same as that conveyed by sentence 5 below is conveyed by the slightly altered version 6:

5. Did the doctor tell you yesterday about her fear concerning Dan's health?

6. *Did the doctor tell to you yesterday about her fear concerning Dan's health?

This last sentence, of course, is ill formed; it sounds odd.

This comparison shows that the verb *talk* requires the preposition *to* for the indirect object (the person told), while the semantically equivalent verb *tell* does not require a preposition except when a direct object intervenes (as in *She told the story* to *John*). These, then, are facts about the verbs *tell* and *talk,* and such idiosyncratic facts must be part of a word's representation in the lexicon.

A comparison of sentences 2 and 5 indicates that there are alternative ways of saying basically the same thing. Sentences 3 and 4 illustrate that there is considerable redundancy in English, that some of what English requires to be expressed is not necessary for full communication.

The conventional rules of a given language may or may not require such redundant expression. Consider this Indonesian sentence:

harimau	makan	kambing
tiger	eat	goat

$\begin{cases} \text{A tiger ate the goat.} \\ \text{The tigers ate the goats.} \\ \text{Tigers eat goats.} \\ \text{The tigers ate a goat.} \\ \text{The tigers will eat the goat.} \\ \text{A tiger has eaten the goat.} \\ \text{A tiger is eating a goat.} \\ \text{The tigers were eating the goats.} \end{cases}$

Unlike English, Indonesian does not require marking definiteness or plurality on noun phrases, so the word *harimau* can be interpreted as 'tigers,' 'the tiger,' 'the tigers,' or 'a tiger'; the word *kambing* can mean 'a goat,' 'the goat,' 'the goats,' or 'goats.' Indonesian does not require the marking of verbs for tense; hence the verb *makan* can be glossed as 'eats,' 'is eating,' 'ate,' 'was eating,' 'will eat,' and so on. Thus there are a great many possible interpretations for this three-word sentence, and a good many ways to translate it into English. Needless to say, not all the interpretations would be appropriate in all circumstances, and Indonesian does have ways of expressing these differences when it is important to do so. The point is that such categories need not be expressed in Indonesian, though they must be expressed in English.

Now consider the following English sentences. It is obvious that despite the fact that they contain exactly the same words, they do not express the same content.

1. The farmer saw the wolf.

2. The wolf saw the farmer.

These two sentences illustrate how English exploits word order as a device to express meaning; different word orders can communicate different stories about *who* did *what* to *whom*. When semantic relations like *who* did *what* to *whom* are expressed not by inflections but by word order, it is a syntactic, not a morphological, matter and is the subject of the next chapter.

A comparison with Latin may be enlightening. Compared to English, Latin had relatively free word order. If we let X represent "the farmer" and Y "the wolf," speakers of Latin could have arranged sentence 1 in either of these ways (among others):

3. X vīdit Y.

4. Y vīdit X.

Interestingly, sentence 2 (which has a very different meaning) could be expressed in Latin using the same two word orders as in 3 and 4. This is possible because

Latin distinguished who did what to whom not by word order but by inflections on nouns, a device not available in English. The following permissible Latin word orders all mean the same thing.

Agricola vīdit lupum.
Lupum vīdit agricola. } 'The farmer saw the wolf.'
Agricola lupum vīdit.

To express the quite different meaning 'The wolf saw the farmer,' the same word orders could occur, but the nouns would carry different inflections.

Agricolam vīdit lupus.
Lupus vīdit agricolam. } 'The wolf saw the farmer.'
Agricolam lupus vīdit.

From the inflectional suffixes -*a* on *agricola* and -*us* on *lupus*, speakers of Latin would understand these words to be the subjects of their sentences; *agricolam* and *lupum*, with their -*am* and -*um* inflections, would be identified as direct objects.

A parallel to Latin noun inflections can be seen in English in certain pronominal uses in which the form of the pronouns and the word order reinforce one another.

1. She praised him. (*She* is the subject, *him* the object.)

2. He praised her. (*He* is the subject, *her* the object).

Nouns in both English and Latin have inflections for number and case. English nouns exhibit only two cases, referred to as possessive and common. The *common* case is used for all grammatical functions except possession; it can serve as subject of a sentence, direct and indirect object, and object of a preposition. The *possessive* case is also called the *genitive* case, a word traditionally associated with the grammatical descriptions of languages like Latin, Old English, German, and Russian. In English it occurs in phrases like *the teacher's desk* and *a woman's purse*.

Besides a genitive case, Latin exhibited inflections for several other cases, notably *nominative* (used principally to mark subjects), *dative* (for indirect objects and the objects of certain prepositions), *accusative* (for direct objects and the objects of other prepositions), and *ablative/instrumental* (for the objects of still other prepositions and for instrumental functions).

Latin generally had five (or six) case inflections in the singular and a similar number in the plural, although in practice some inflectional forms came to be pronounced alike, as can be seen in Table 4-6. The set of forms constituting the inflectional variants of a particular noun, pronoun, or adjective is known as its inflectional **paradigm.** Latin had several patterns of noun paradigm, each called a *declension*, such as the two given for *agricola* and *hortus*.

Table 4-7 displays the paradigms for the equivalent English words *farmer* and *garden*. Notice that the four orthographic forms in the English paradigms represent only two distinct forms of speech: [farmər] versus [farmərz] and [gardən] versus

TABLE 4-6
Paradigms for Two Latin Nouns

	'farmer'	'garden'
Singular		
Nominative	agricola	hortus
Accusative	agricolam	hortum
Genitive	agricolae	hortī
Dative	agricolae	hortō
Ablative/Instrumental	agricolā	hortō
Plural		
Nominative	agricolae	hortī
Accusative	agricolās	hortōs
Genitive	agricolārum	hortōrum
Dative	agricolīs	hortīs
Ablative/Instrumental	agricolīs	hortīs

[gɑrdənz]. The orthographically distinct forms for possessive singular and for common and possessive plurals do not represent distinct spoken forms. In spoken English, there are generally only two forms of a noun, except that when a plural noun is irregular there are four spoken forms as well as four orthographic forms (as in *man, man's, men, men's; child, child's, children, children's*).

For some English pronouns a third case form exists. Known as the objective case, it is roughly comparable to the dative, accusative, and ablative/instrumental cases of Latin. In Table 4-8, compare the paradigms for first and third person pronouns in English. First person pronouns exhibit distinct forms for three cases in the singular and three cases in the plural. Third person pronouns have distinct masculine, feminine, and neuter forms in the singular, although no distinction for gender is made in the plural. The neuter singular *it* does not have distinct common and objective case forms.

TABLE 4-7
Paradigms for Two English Nouns

Singular		
Common	farmer	garden
Possessive	farmer's	garden's
Plural		
Common	farmers	gardens
Possessive	farmers'	gardens'

TABLE 4-8
Paradigms for First and Third Person Pronouns in English

| | First Person | Third Person | | |
		Masculine	*Feminine*	*Neuter*
Singular				
Common	I	he	she	it
Possessive	my, mine	his	her, hers	its
Objective	me	him	her	it
Plural				
Common	we		they	
Possessive	our, ours		their, theirs	
Objective	us		them	

Second person pronouns and third person singular neuter pronouns do not have distinct objective forms, as can be seen in Table 4-9; like regular nouns, they have only two case forms.

In English, gender distinctions in pronouns are based on natural sex. Males are referred to by the masculine pronoun, females by the feminine pronoun. Things that are neither male nor female are referred to by the neuter pronoun *it*. As we saw above, however, nouns have grammatical gender in some languages, including Latin, German, and Old English, and certain categories of words such as articles and adjectives are inflected to agree with them in gender, number, and case.

In contrast to the English definite article *the* (with a single orthographic form representing the two phonological variants /ðə/ and /ði/), the German definite article has forms for three genders and four cases in the singular, though there are no distinctions of gender in the plural, as Table 4-10 illustrates.

TABLE 4-9
Second and Third Person Pronouns Compared to Nouns in English

| | Pronouns | | Nouns |
	Second	*Third*	
Singular			
Common	you	it	farmer
Possessive	your, yours	its	farmer's
Plural			
Common	you		farmers
Possessive	your, yours		farmers'

TABLE 4-10
Paradigm for Definite Article in German

	Singular			Plural
	Masculine	*Feminine*	*Neuter*	*All Genders*
Nominative	der	die	das	die
Accusative	den	die	das	die
Genitive	des	der	des	der
Dative	dem	der	dem	den

French and Spanish also exhibit variant forms of the definite article, though neither is as varied as German. French distinguishes only two genders in nouns; it marks masculine nouns with the definite article *le* (indefinite *un*), feminine ones with *la* (indefinite *une*); *les* is the plural form for *both* genders. Spanish is similar in having two genders, but it marks them in the plural as well as the singular. Table 4-11 gives examples in French and Spanish.

Some languages have far more complex systems of word classes; Swahili is a frequently cited example of a language with a large number of noun classes.

You have now seen a number of ways in which languages exploit inflectional morphology to mark functions like subject and direct object and certain categorical information like number, gender, and case on nouns and pronouns and to signal tense and person on verbs.

Lexical Functions of Derivational Morphology

Open and Closed Classes of Morphemes and Words   The need for new nouns, adjectives, and verbs arises frequently in some cultures, and additions to these lexical categories occur freely. For this reason, noun, adjective, and verb are called *open classes*. Other lexical categories are relatively closed, and additions are made rarely. Adpositions and pronouns are *closed classes,* and new words are very seldom added to a language in either of these categories.

TABLE 4-11
French and Spanish Definite Articles with Nouns

French	Spanish	
Masculine		
le chat	el gato	'the cat'
les chats	los gatos	'the cats'
Feminine		
la maison	la casa	'the house'
les maisons	las casas	'the houses'

Century after century, English has added thousands (sometimes tens of thousands) of new words, many borrowed from other languages, many more constructed from elements already existing in the English word stock. Nearly all the additions have been nouns, verbs, or adjectives.

A language has basically three ways of extending its word stock. First, entirely new words can be created, although this is not very common. Alternatively, words that already exist in another language can be borrowed, and this often happens. Most commonly, however, a language forms new words from existing words and morphemes in its own word stock.

In order to create new words from existing morphemes and words, several morphological processes can be exploited, and we examine some of them in detail. After looking at the processes of deriving new words from existing elements, we will conclude with a discussion of word borrowing and word invention.

Kinds of Derivational Morphology

Affixation   Adding affixes to an existing word is a very common way of creating new words. English exploits this possibility by adding the agentive suffix *-er* to the prepositions *up* and *down* to create the nouns *upper* and *downer,* which were invented in connection with drugs but have extended their meaning to anything that lifts or dampens one's spirits. More commonly, *-er* is suffixed to verbs (V) and means 'one who Vs' as in *runner* 'one who runs,' *campaigner,* and *designer.*

English takes advantage of two kinds of affixation: prefixing and suffixing. Prefixes like *un-*, *pre-*, and *dis-* serve to change the meaning of words, though not usually their lexical category. Thus the prefix *un-* added to an adjective creates a new adjective with the opposite meaning, as in *untrue, unpopular, unsuccessful,* and *unfavorable.* The prefix *dis-* added to a verb derives a verb with the opposite meaning, as in *disobey, disappear, dishonor,* and *displace. Pre-* serves as a prefix to several categories of words. It can be prefixed to verbs (*preaffirm, preallot, preplan, prewash,* and *premix*), adjectives (*pre-Copernican, precollegiate, precultural, presurgical*), or nouns (*preantiquity, preaffirmation, preplacement*). The prefix *pre-* has roughly the same sense in each of these words, and in each of them it creates from an existing word a new word in the same lexical category.

Suffixes in English usually operate differently from prefixes. More often than not, they change a word's lexical category. The suffix *-ment,* for example, when added to a verb, makes a noun of it, as in *displacement, arrangement, agreement,* and *consignment.* The suffix *-ation* does the same thing: *resignation, organization, implementation, observation,* and *reformation. Discrimination* and *alienation,* which may look like the result of the same affix, are more accurately analyzed as coming from the verbs *discriminate* and *alienate,* the latter itself derived by suffixing *-ate* to the noun *alien.*

Suffixes are widely exploited in other languages as well. The Indonesian suffix *-kan* changes a noun to a verb, and among the various meanings it can produce are these: 'to cause to become X' (as in *budakkan* 'to enslave,' from *budak* 'slave' + *-kan,* and *rajakan* 'to crown,' from *raja* 'king' + *-kan*) and 'to put in X' (as in *penjarakan* 'imprison,' from *penjara* 'prison' + *-kan*).

Reduplication   Reduplication is the morphological process by which a morpheme or part of a morpheme is repeated, thereby creating a word with a different meaning or a different lexical category. For example, the Mandarin Chinese word *sànsanbù* 'to take a leisurely walk' is formed by reduplicating the first syllable of *sànbù* 'to walk' (itself a compound of *sàn* 'to tread' and *bù* 'a step'), and *hónghóng* 'bright red' is formed by reduplicating *hóng* 'red.' Reduplication can be *partial,* repeating only part of the morpheme, or *full,* in which the entire morpheme is reduplicated. In Motu, a language of Papua New Guinea, *mahuta* 'to sleep' reduplicates fully as *mahutamahuta* 'to sleep constantly' and partially as *mamahuta* 'to sleep' (when agreeing with a plural subject). In Turkish, adjectives like *açik* 'open,' *uzun* 'long,' and *ayrı* 'separate' are reduplicated (by prefixing the initial vowel followed by a consonant) as *apaçik* 'wide open,' *apayrı* 'entirely separate' and *upuzun* 'very long.' Reduplication is not to be confused with repetition, which does not create new words but simply reiterates the same word, as in English *very, very (tired)* and *night-night.* English does not have a productive process similar to Chinese, Motu, or Turkish reduplication.

Reduplication can have a variety of functions in the languages in which it is found. It can have a moderating or intensifying effect on the meaning of the word, as illustrated by the Chinese, Motu, and Turkish examples just given. It can be used to mark grammatical categories, as it does in Indonesian, where certain kinds of noun plurals are formed by reduplication: *babibabi* 'an assortment of pigs' is a reduplicated form of *babi* 'pig.'

OTHER WAYS OF EXTENDING THE VOCABULARY

Besides affixation and reduplication, languages have other ways of adding words to their word stock. These other ways do not involve derivational morphology directly, but it may be helpful to discuss them here.

Compounds

English speakers have long shown a strong preference for putting existing words together to create new words. This process is called *compounding.* Recent compounds include *moonshot, waterbed, upfront, color-code, computerlike,* and *radiopharmaceutical.* Notice that the popular compounds *convenience food* and *natural food* are not structured alike. *Convenience food* 'food that is convenient to buy, cook, or eat' is a noun-noun compound. *Natural food* 'food made with natural ingredients, free of chemical preservatives and pesticides' is an adjective-noun compound. Both compounds function as nouns.

To gauge the popularity of compounding in English, consider that one relatively short piece in a recent issue of the *Los Angeles Times* provided the following examples.

Nouns			Adjectives
petroleum engineer	whistle-blower	pay phone	whistle-blowing
government documents	troublemaker	phone call	baby-faced
government witness	debt ceiling	storerooms	highranking

Nouns			Adjectives
subcommittee hearing	brain cancer	cover-up	overzealous
aircraft carrier	reserve account	kickbacks	born-again
training course	sea power	breakup	

The same piece also contained several unusually complex compounds, such as *school records supply schemes, beneficial suggestion program,* and *House government operations subcommittee,* all of which function as nouns.

Compounding occurs in many languages. Chinese, for example, has numerous compounds in its lexicon. Compounds such as *fàn-wǎn* 'rice bowl,' *diàn-nǎo* ('electric' + 'brain') 'computer,' *tái-bù* 'tablecloth,' *fēi-jī* ('fly' + 'machine') 'airplane,' and *hēi-bǎn* ('black' + 'board') 'blackboard' can be found in the Beijing dialect. Another language famous for its compounding tendencies is German: the word *Fernsprecher* (literally 'far speaker') was for a long time the preferred word for what is today usually called *Telefon.* A ballpoint pen is called *Kugelschreiber* ('ball' + 'writer'); a glove is *Handschuh* ('hand' + 'shoe'); a mayor is *Burgermeister* ('citizen' + 'master'). Indonesian has exploited compounding in a word made familiar to westerners from its use as the assumed name of a well-known World War I socialite and spy: *matahari,* meaning 'sun,' comes from *mata* 'eye' and *hari* 'day.' The word for 'eyeglasses' is *kacamata,* a compound of *kaca* 'glass' and *mata* 'eye' (similar to the English compound *eyeglasses* but with a different order of the elements).

Functional Shift, or Conversion

Certain languages permit a word from one lexical category to be converted to another lexical category without any overt marking on the word itself. *Functional shift* is the transfer of a word existing in one lexical class for use in another without altering its form by derivation. In English we request someone to *update* (verb) a report and then refer to the revised report as an *update* (noun). Conversion of this type commonly leads to noun/verb and noun/adjective pairs; as Table 4-12 illustrates, sometimes the same form can be used for all three categories—as noun, verb, and adjective. Once a form has been shifted to a new lexical category, it conforms to the inflectional morphology of that category: *an update, two recent updates, she is updating the report now,* and *he updated it last month.*

Semantic Shift

Existing words can take on new meanings, shrinking or (more commonly) extending the domain of their reference. During the Vietnam War, the word *hawk* came to be used in reference to supporters of the war while *dove* referred to supporters of peace, extending the meaning of these words from the combative nature of hawks and the symbolically peaceful role assigned to doves. The new meanings did not replace the earlier ones but gave us, in effect, new words by extending the domain of reference for old words. This phenomenon, called *semantic shift* or *metaphorical extension,* creates *metaphors.* The metaphorical use of words often leads to new meanings that come to seem perfectly natural and whose

TABLE 4-12
Some English Words Belonging to More Than One Lexical Category

Noun	Verb	Adjective
update	update	
bust	bust	
outrage	outrage	
homer	homer	
delay	delay	
plot	plot	
play	play	
inaugural		inaugural
average	average	average
model	model	model
prime	prime	prime

metaphorical origins are all but lost. Consider the meanings of the underscored parts of the following phrases: *to derail congressional legislation, a buoyant spokesman, an abrasive chief of staff, to sweeten the farm bill with several billion dollars to skirt a veto fight.* Such originally metaphorical uses have become an integral part of the language.

Blends

English speakers are fond of *blending,* creating new words by combining parts of existing words. Among the better-known blends are *smog* (from *smoke* and *fog*) and *motel* (*motor* and *hotel*); others like *glasphalt (glass* and *asphalt)* and *modem (modulator* and *demodulator)* crop up from time to time. There are even blends that capture the degree to which some modern languages have borrowed from each other: *Spanglish, Franglais, Yinglish.*

Shortenings

Shortenings of various sorts are a popular means of increasing the word stock of a language. Regular shortenings like *radial* (from *radial tire*), *jet* (from *jet airplane*), *narc* (from *narcotics agent*), and *obits* (from *obituaries*) are common enough. There are also *acronyms,* in which the initials of a phrase are joined together and pronounced as a word as in *AIDS, UNESCO, NATO, WASP, radar* (from *radio detecting and ranging*), *yuppy* (*young urban professional* + *-y*) and *dink* (from *double income no kids*).

Back Formation

A special type of shortening is suggested by forms derived from *computer.* From the word *computer* (originally formed by affixing the agentive suffix *-er* to the verb *compute* in its mathematical sense), a new verb *compute* has been "back formed" with the meaning 'to use a computer' (for computation or other tasks). Other back formations are the verbs *typewrite* and *baby-sit,* which were invented historically subsequent to their noun forms *typewriter* and *baby-sitter.* The verb *lase* has been back formed from the noun *laser,* possibly on the mistaken notion that *laser* contained the agentive suffix *-er.*

Borrowings

"Neither a borrower nor a lender be," Shakespeare advised, but languages pay no heed. Over the course of its history, English has proved to be an extraordinary host to tens of thousands of borrowed words. Nearly a hundred languages have contributed words to the English word stock during this century alone. As has been true for most of its history, English has borrowed more from French during this century than from any other language, followed at some distance by Japanese and Spanish, Italian and Latin and Greek, German, and Yiddish. In smaller numbers, English has borrowed words from Russian, Chinese, Arabic, Portuguese, and Hindi, as well as from numerous African languages.

In turn, many languages have welcomed English words, although others have been guarded. The Japanese have drafted the words *beesubooru* 'baseball,' *futtobooru* 'football' and *booringu* 'bowling' along with the sports they name, trading them (in sports terminology) for *judo, jujitsu,* and *karate,* which have joined the English-speaking team. Officially at least, the French are not open to borrowings, especially those from English, and have banned the use of *weekend, drugstore, brain-storming,* and *countdown,* as well as the popular term *jumbo jet* (for the use of which Air France was fined by the French government, which had insisted that *gros porteur* be used instead). The Americanism *OK* is now in use virtually everywhere, as are such terms as *jeans* and *discos,* which accompanied the items that they name as they spread around the globe.[2]

The overwhelming majority of borrowings into English have been nouns (and this is true of borrowings into languages in general), but some adjectives have been borrowed, as have a few verbs and interjections. Among the borrowed nouns having to do with food and drink are *hummus* (from Arabic), *aioli* (from Provençal), *mai tai* (from Tahitian), and *frijoles refritos* (from Spanish for 'refried beans'). Yiddish has given us the more general term *nosh.* Other popular recent borrowings include Italian *ciao,* Spanish *macho,* Chinese (Cantonese) *wok,* German *glitch,* and Yiddish *chutzpah, klutz,* and *nebbish.*

---

[2] *Jean* is a Middle English form of the word *Genoa; jeans* is the plural of a shortening of *jean fustian* 'Genoa fustian.' (Denim, also named after a city, is a shortening of *serge de Nîmes,* French for 'serge of Nîmes.') *Disco* also has a fascinating history: it is an abbreviation of the French compound *discothèque* 'record library,' which is made up of two French morphemes, *disque* meaning 'disk' or 'record' and the suffix *-thèque* as in *bibliothèque* 'library.' *Discotheque* is first recorded in English in the year 1954; it was then abbreviated to *disco,* and recorded in print ten years later. First recorded in 1979 is the use of *disco* as a verb meaning 'dance to disco music.' Thus the English verb *disco* has undergone functional shift from the English noun *disco,* a shortening of *discotheque,* which was borrowed from French, where it was formed by affixing *thèque* to *disc* + *o.* It has now spread around the world and can be found in many cities whose inhabitants speak neither English nor French.

Despite their somewhat unusual spellings, these words, like borrowed words in general, come sooner or later to conform to the phonological, morphological, and syntactic rules of the borrowing language. Thus the English word *baseball* /besbɔl/, with its two CVC syllables, was borrowed into Japanese as *beesubooru* to conform to the phonotactic constraints of that language (with its preference for CV syllables—see p. 67). In time, borrowed words undergo the same morphological processes that affect other words. *Nosh,* for example, was borrowed as an intransitive verb *(I feel like noshing)* but has since taken on new use as a transitive verb *(Let's nosh some hot dogs).* It has also added the agentive suffix *-er,* as in *nosher* 'one who noshes.' By a functional shift, the verb *nosh* has come to be used as a noun meaning 'a snack.' In British usage *nosh* has been compounded into the noun *nosh-up* 'a large or elaborate meal.'

Invention

Finally, we can mention invention, a relatively rare kind of word formation. Because of the advantages of using familiar elements in the formation of new words, languages do not often create new words from scratch. In recent years, invention has contributed such words as *granola, zap, quark,* and *lollapalooza* to the English word stock, and they all conform to English phonotactic constraints.

TYPES OF MORPHOLOGICAL SYSTEMS

We have now seen examples of both inflectional and derivational morphology in several languages. Not all languages have inflectional morphology, and some have little or no morphology at all. Still other languages have relatively complex words with quite distinct parts each representing a morpheme. Traditionally, these three types of languages have been said to have inflectional morphology, isolating morphology, or agglutinating morphology. We have already examined inflectional morphology.

Isolating Morphology

Chinese is an oft-cited example of a language with *isolating* morphology—a language in which each word tends to be a single isolated morpheme. In other words, an isolating language lacks both derivational and inflectional morphology. By the use of separate words, Chinese expresses certain content that an inflecting language can express by using inflectional affixes. For example, whereas English permits both an inflectional possessive *(the boy's hat)* and a so-called analytical possessive *(hat of the boy),* Chinese permits only the equivalent of *hat of the boy.* Chinese also lacks tense markers and does not mark gender, number, or case distinctions on pronouns. Where English has six different words—*he, she, him, her, they,* and *them*—Chinese uses the same word (though of course it can indicate plurality with a separate word). The sentence below illustrates the one-morpheme-per-word pattern typical of Chinese.

Wǒ gāng yào gě nǐ   ná   yì bēi chá.

I   just want for you bring one cup tea

'I am about to bring you a cup of tea.'

Vietnamese, even more than Chinese, approximates the one-morpheme-per-word model that characterizes isolating languages. Each word in the sentence below has only one form, and you can see that the word *tôi* is translated as *I, my,* and *we,* the last based upon a coupling of the words for 'I' and 'PLURAL.' Like Chinese, Vietnamese lacks tense markers on verbs and case markers on pronouns, as well as number distinctions (though it can indicate plurality with a separate word).

Khi tôi đến nhà bạn tôi, chúng tôi bắt đầu làm bài.

when I come house friend I Plural I begin do lesson

'When I came to my friend's house, we began to do lessons.'

Some languages that tend to minimize inflectional morphology nevertheless exploit derivational morphology to extend their word stocks in economical ways. Indonesian, for example, has only two inflectional affixes but it utilizes about two dozen derivational morphemes.

Agglutinating Morphology

A third type of morphology besides inflectional and isolating is called *agglutinating*. In agglutinating languages, words can have several prefixes and suffixes, but characteristically they are distinct and readily segmented into their parts—unlike English *sang* (SING + 'PAST') or *us* ('FIRST PERSON' + 'PLURAL' + 'OBJECTIVE CASE'). Greenlandic Eskimo is an example of such a language, as illustrated by the following sentence, in which dashes represent morpheme boundaries within a word:

Qajar-taa-va   asirur-sima-vuq.

kayak-new-his break-done-it

'His new kayak has been destroyed.'

Although there is not always a strict demarcation between agglutinating and inflectional languages, and some languages are difficult to classify, the distinction among the three types of morphology—inflectional, isolating, and agglutinating—is nevertheless useful in characterizing languages with respect to their morphological systems.

ENGLISH MORPHOPHONOLOGY

Before leaving the subject of morphology, let's examine the phonological processes affecting some of the most productive inflectional suffixes of English, namely, the plural and possessive morphemes on nouns and the third person singular and past tense morphemes on verbs. Then we will analyze variation in the surface forms of free morphemes in different lexical environments.

English Plural, Possessive, and Third Person Singular Morphemes

For regular nouns, there are several pronunciations of the plural morpheme, as in lips (lɪp + s], *seeds* [sid + z], and *fuses* [fyuz + əz]. The various surface forms underlying different pronunciations of a morpheme are called **allomorphs** of that morpheme. As the words in the following lists demonstrate, the allomorphs of the plural morpheme are determined by the last sound of the singular noun to which the morpheme is attached.

Allomorphs of the Plural Morpheme for English Nouns

[əz]   bushes, judges, peaches, buses, fuses

[s]   cats, tips, books, whiffs, paths

[z]   pens, seeds, dogs, cars, rays

These lists indicate the pattern of distribution for the plural allomorphs of English:

1. [əz] occurs with nouns ending in /s, z, š, ž, č, ǰ/ (the natural class called *sibilants*[3])

2. [s] occurs following all other voiceless sounds

3. [z] occurs elsewhere (that is, following all other voiced sounds)

You may want to think of arguments for positing one of the three allomorphs as the abstract underlying form of the plural morpheme. We will assume that it is /z/. From this underlying form, all three allomorphs must be derivable by general rules that apply to all regular nouns.

From an underlying /z/, a rule of the following sort would be needed in order to derive the [əz] allomorph following sibilants; note that + marks a morpheme boundary and # marks a word boundary

Schwa Insertion Rule

/z/ ⟶ [əz] / sibilant + _____ #

(schwa is inserted before a word-final /z/ that follows a morpheme ending in a sibilant)

In order to derive the allomorph [s] from the underlying morpheme /z/ following voiceless sounds, a rule that devoices /z/, making it more similar to the unvoiced sound of the stem morpheme would be needed. Phonological rules that make adjacent sounds more similar are called **assimilation** rules.

Assimilation Rule

/z/ ⟶ voiceless / voiceless + _____ #

(word-final /z/ is devoiced following a morpheme ending in a voiceless segment)

---

[3] Sibilants are a class of sounds that function similarly in some languages, including English. They constitute a natural class, but, unlike the natural classes examined in Chapter 2, sibilants do not share an articulatory feature; instead, they share certain acoustic features, including "hissing."

TABLE 4-13
Derivation of English Plural Nouns

	coops	judges	weeds
Underlying Form	/kup + z/	/ǰʌǰ + z/	/wid + z/
Schwa Insertion	DNA		DNA
Derived Form	[kup + z]	[ǰʌǰ + əz]	[wid + z]
Assimilation		DNA	DNA
Surface Form	[kup + s]	[ǰʌǰ + əz]	[wid + z]

These two rules must have considerable generality because they must derive the correct forms of all regular plural nouns. Table 4-13 illustrates this for the nouns *coops, judges,* and *weeds.* (Recall that DNA means that a rule does not apply because the conditions necessary for its application are not present. Slanted lines / / represent underlying forms, and square brackets [ ] represent forms derived by application of a phonological rule.)

If you examine two other inflectional morphemes of English—namely, the possessive of nouns *(judge's, cat's,* and *dog's)* and the third person singular marker on verbs *(teaches, laughs,* and *swims)*—you'll discover that the distribution of the allomorphs of these morphemes is parallel to the distribution of the plural morpheme.

Allomorphs of the Possessive Morpheme for English Nouns

[əz]   church's, judge's, fish's

[s]   ship's, cat's, Pat's

[z]   John's, arm's, dog's

Allomorphs of the Third Person Singular Morpheme for English Verbs

[əz]   preaches, teases, judges, buzzes, rushes

[s]   leaps, eats, kicks, laughs

[z]   seems, leans, craves, sees

If we posit /z/ as the underlying phonological form of these morphemes, then the very same rules that derive the correct allomorphs of the plural morpheme will also derive the correct allomorphs of the possessive morpheme on nouns and the third person singular morpheme on verbs. (Unlike plurals, many of which are irregular, all nouns are regular with respect to the possessive morpheme, and all verbs are regular with respect to the third person singular morpheme except for *is, has, says,* and *does.)*

English Past Tense Morpheme

The inflectional morpheme that marks the past tense of regular verbs in English has three allomorphs.

Allomorphs of the Past Tense Morpheme for English Verbs

[əd]   wanted, waded, waited, hooted, planted, seeded

[t]   wished, kissed, talked, stripped, preached, laughed

[d]   waved, bathed, played, stirred, teased, roamed, ruined, breezed

If we posit /d/ as the underlying phonological form of the past tense morpheme, then we need just two rules to derive the past-tense forms of all regular verbs.

Schwa Insertion Rule

$$/d/ \longrightarrow [əd] \text{ / alveolar stop } + \underline{\quad} \#$$

(schwa is inserted preceding a word-final /d/ that
follows a morpheme ending in an alveolar stop)

Assimilation Rule

$$/d/ \longrightarrow \text{ voiceless / voiceless } + \underline{\quad} \#$$

(word-final /d/ is realized as [t] following a morpheme that ends in a voiceless segment)

Derivations of the past tense forms of the verbs *wish, want,* and *wave* are provided in Table 4-14 as examples.

Inspection of the last two sets of rules reveals striking similarities in both the schwa insertion processes and the assimilation processes required to generate the correct forms of four inflectional morphemes: the plural and possessive forms of nouns, the third person singular forms of verbs, and the past tense forms of verbs.

TABLE 4-14
Derivation of English Past Tense Verbs

	wished	wanted	waved
Underlying Form	/wɪš + d/	/want + d/	/wev + d/
Schwa Insertion	DNA		DNA
Derived Form	[wɪš + d]	[want + əd]	[wev + d]
Assimilation		DNA	DNA
Surface Form	[wɪš + t]	[want + əd]	[wev + d]

Underlying Phonological Form of Morphemes in the Lexicon

Consonants   The same kinds of phonological processes that operate between a stem and an inflectional suffix also operate between a stem and a derivational morpheme. Imagine, for example, that you are a child who knows the words *metal* and *medal*. For many speakers of North American English, the sound that occurs in the middle of both words is an alveolar flap, neither [t] nor [d] but [D].[4]

As a child hearing *metal* and *medal,* you would have entered exactly what you heard into your lexicon—/mɛDəl/ in both cases. But consider what must happen after you have internalized /mɛDəl/ and then hear someone say that her new car is painted *metallic* [mətʰæl + ək] red. If you failed to recognize that *metallic* and *metal* share an element of meaning, you would simply enter a new morpheme into your lexicon. That new morpheme would have the meaning 'metal-like' but would not be related to the morpheme METAL; the two entries would be completely independent of one another. However, once you recognized that *metallic* is made up of METAL plus the derivational suffix -IC, then the two pronunciations [mɛDəl] and [mətʰæl + ək] must be reconciled. (This recognition will accompany the knowledge that -IC is a morpheme that also appears in such words as *atomic, Germanic, alcoholic,* and *demonic.*) The task of a language learner is to posit an underlying form from which all surface forms for pronunciation can be correctly derived given the phonological rules of English.

Now consider the task you faced when you subsequently heard someone report that the car's *medallion* is missing from the hood. For *medal* and *medallion,* you hear [mɛDəl] and [mədælyən]. What underlying form must be posited in the lexicon once the morpheme MEDAL is recognized as occurring in both words?

Assume you recognized that METAL was a common element in both *metal* and *metallic* and that MEDAL was a common element in *medal* and *medallion.* The following pronunciations can be observed:

	metal		**medal**
[mɛDəl]	[mətʰæl + ək]	[mɛDəl]	[mədæl + yən]
metal	metallic	medal	medallion

You can account for the different pronunciations of the morpheme METAL by positing the form /mɛtæl/ in the lexicon and postulating phonological rules that change this abstract underlying form into the various surface forms that do occur. Ignoring the vowels for a moment, the underlying form /mɛtæl/ will require a process that changes /t/ into [D] in the word *metal* [mɛDəl].

---

[4] An alveolar flap, as you recall from Chapters 2 and 3, is the sound created when the tip of the tongue flaps quickly against the alveolar ridge (as in *metal* and *medal*). [D], which is phonetically different from both [t] and [d], is the way most Americans usually say the middle consonant of *metal* and *medal,* so that if the words are differentiated in pronunciation it is usually not by virtue of there being a [t] in one, a [d] in the other.

This same process will be needed to change /d/ into [D] in the word *medal* [mɛDəl]. The flapping rule changes underlying /t/ and /d/ into [D] when they occur between two vowels, the second of which is unstressed (see page 64).

Flapping Rule

$$\begin{array}{c}\text{alveolar}\\\text{stop}\end{array} \longrightarrow \text{flap } / \quad \begin{array}{c}V\end{array} \underline{\quad\quad} \begin{array}{c}V\\\text{unstressed}\end{array}$$

You can see that phonological rules that must be postulated to account for one set of facts sometimes account for other facts. Phonological rules, after all, apply to all morphemes and words unless there is a specific marking in the lexical entry of a particular morpheme to block the application of some process, as irregular plurals like *tooth/teeth* are marked as not taking the regular plural morpheme.

Thus the relationship between the phonological representation of morphemes in the lexicon and their actual pronunciation is mediated by a set of phonological processes that can be represented in rules of significant generality. It is not only *metal* and *medal* that will be affected by the flapping rule but every word that meets the conditions specified in the rule. This includes single-morpheme words like *butter, bitter,* and *meter,* two-morpheme words like *writer, rider, raider, rooter,* and all others.

Vowels   Consider a youngster who knows the words *photograph* [foDəgræf] and *photographer* [fətʰagrəf + ər]. At some point every speaker of English posits a single entry in the lexicon to represent the core of these two words—that is, PHOTOGRAPH. When you think sufficiently about what the underlying form must be, you will see that /fotagræf/ best represents the knowledge needed to produce the two pronunciations above. Given the underlying representation /fotagræf/ and the surface forms [foDəgræf] and [fətʰagrəf + ər], a rule that changes unstressed vowels into [ə] will produce the correct vowels.

If instead we postulated /ə/ in the underlying form, it would be impossible to formulate a rule that would produce the correct surface forms. In order to produce the [a] in [fətʰagrəf + ər] from an underlying form with schwas /fətəgrəf + ər/, we would need a rule that produced [a] from underlying /ə/. For the word *photograph,* on the other hand, we would need a rule that produced [o] from underlying /ə/ in the first syllable and [æ] from underlying /ə/ in the third syllable. This would amount to knowing which vowels exist in the surface pronunciation and encoding that knowledge in the underlying form in the mental lexicon along with the /ə/, but that is exactly what we assume does *not* happen. Instead, if we postulate different vowels in the underlying forms, we can formulate a single rule that derives [ə] from any underlying vowel when it occurs in unstressed position; we can now derive the customary pronunciations for these words. We formulate the rule as follows:

$$\begin{array}{c}V\\\text{unstressed}\end{array} \longrightarrow [\text{ə}]$$

(unstressed vowels become schwa)

This rule will not affect stressed vowels; underlying vowels that are unstressed become schwa [ə]. Of course, a rule that relies on information about stress requires prior assignment of stress. The rules for assigning stress in English are more complex than we can discuss in this book. (The references at the end of Chapter 3 contain treatments of the stress placement rules of English.)

SUMMARY

A morpheme is a minimal unit of meaning or grammatical function in a language. Although some words (like *house, swim,* and *tall*) contain a single morpheme each, many words comprise several smaller units of meaning. As an entry in the lexicon, each morpheme has abstract phonological, morphological, grammatical, and semantic information as part of its structure.

Morphemes can be realized in various phonological shapes depending on their environment in words. The allomorphs of the morpheme 'PLURAL' occur in three principal shapes in English: [əz] after sibilants, [s] after other voiceless sounds, and [z] elsewhere. The plural morpheme in English is an example of a *bound* morpheme—it cannot occur as an independent word but must be attached to another morpheme. Other morphemes are *free*: CAR, HOUSE, FOR.

Bound morphemes serve two principal functions. First, they can mark nouns for information like number (as with 'PLURAL') and case (as with 'POSSESSIVE'), and they can mark verbs for information like tense (as with 'PAST') and person (as with 'THIRD PERSON SINGULAR'). Second, bound morphemes can serve to derive different words from existing morphemes, as in <u>un</u>*true* (an adjective with the opposite meaning derived from an adjective), <u>dis</u>*please* (a verb with the opposite meaning derived from a verb), and *commit<u>ment</u>* (a noun with a related meaning derived from a verb). Bound morphemes can occur as prefixes, suffixes, infixes, or circumfixes (together called affixes). Morphemes are arranged in words with a significant linear and hierarchical structure.

The phonological information that is entered into the internalized lexicon cannot be directly observed in the pronunciation of a word; instead, morphemes have an abstract underlying form from which all the regular allomorphs can be derived by phonological processes of a language.

Every language has a wide range of morphological devices for extending vocabulary, including compounding, reduplication, affixation, and abbreviation. Languages also borrow words from one another, each language eventually submitting most borrowings to its own phonological constraints and regular morphological processes, both inflectional and derivational.

EXERCISES

1. Identify the lexical class of each of the following English words. Interpreting every word as having more than one morpheme, list the morphemes in each word and indicate whether each is free or bound. For each affix indicate whether it is derivational or inflectional.

heard	toys	tiny	saw
unproductive	bookshops	listened	kitten's
improbability	tidiest	disarms	untidiness
reassessment	fatherly	repayment	realignments
unremarkable	realigned	children's	fresheners
unamusing	calculating	forewarned	unpretentiousness

2. a. From a passage of about 500 consecutive words in a newsweekly like *Time* or *Newsweek* make a list of all compound nouns, marking the lexical class of each constituent word of the compound.

   b. Choose five of the compounds and explain the relationship between the lexical class of the elements and the meaning of the compound.

3. a. Analyze the Turkish nouns below and provide a list of their constituent morphemes, along with a gloss for each. (*Note:* In representing Turkish, ɨ is a high back unrounded vowel.)

kitap	'book'	elmalar	'apples'	saplar	'stalks'
at	'horse'	masa	'table'	kɨz	'girl'
oda	'room'	odalar	'rooms'	masalar	'tables'
sap	'stalk'	atlar	'horses'	sonlar	'ends'
elma	'apple'	adamlar	'men'	meyvar	'fruit (sg.)'

   b. On the basis of your analysis, provide the Turkish words for the following English glosses: books, man, girls, end, fruit (pl.).

   c. Given Turkish *odalarda* 'in the rooms' and *masalarda* 'on the tables,' provide the Turkish words meaning 'in the books' and 'on the horse.'

   d. Examine the words below and decide on what basis their plurals are systematically different from those in (a) above. (*Note:* ü represents a high front rounded vowel, ö a mid front rounded vowel.) (*Hint:* The basis is a phonological one.)

gül	'rose'	güller	'roses'	et	'meat'	etler	'meats'
ip	'rope'	ipler	'ropes'	zil	'bell'	ziller	'bells'
el	'hand'	eller	'hands'	köpek	'dog'	köpekler	'dogs'

   e. Provide the plural form of these singular nouns: lokanta 'restaurant'; kalem 'pen'; karar 'decision'; gram 'eye'; ev 'home'; yemek 'meal'.

4. a. Consider the following pairs of singular and plural nouns for human beings in Persian. How does Persian form these noun plurals? Give the underlying form of each noun.

zæn	'woman'	zænan	'women'
mærd	'man'	mærdan	'men'
bæradær	'brother'	bæradæran	'brothers'
pesær	'boy'	pesæran	'boys'
xahær	'sister'	xahæran	'sisters'
doxtær	'daughter'	doxtæran	'daughters'

b. Now consider the following pairs. How does the formation of the plural of these nouns differ from those in (a) above? Give the underlying form of each noun and a rule that will produce the correct plurals.

danešju	'student'	danešǰuyan	'students'
gæda	'beggar'	gædayan	'beggars'
irani	'Iranian'	iraniyan	'Iranians'
dana	'sage'	danayan	'sages'

c. Now consider the following pairs. How does the formation of these plurals differ from those in (a) and (b) above? Give the underlying form of each noun and provide a rule by which the correct plurals will be produced.

bænde	'slave'	bændegan	'slaves'
ferešte	'angel'	freštegan	'angels'
næmayænde	'representative'	næmayændegan	'representatives'

d. Finally, determine whether there is a single derivational process underlying all three sets of singular/plural nouns, and justify your position.

5. Consider the following Persian word pairs with their English glosses. Note the lexical category of the words in column I, and give the complete rule for forming the words of column II from those in column I. Give the underlying form for each word in column I.

	I		II
dana	'wise'	danai	'wisdom'
xub	'good'	xubi	'goodness'
darošt	'thick'	darošti	'thickness'
bozorg	'big'	bozorgi	'size'
zende	'alive'	zendegi	'life'
šayeste	'worthy'	šayestegi	'worthiness'
xæste	'tired'	xæstegi	'fatigue'
širin	'sweet'	širini	'sweetness'

6. Draw trees similar to that on page 90 for these English words.

revaccinations   recapitalization   unlikelihood

disenchantment   unreasonableness   unshockability

7. Consider the two analyses of *untruthful* given below. What arguments could be given for preferring one analysis over the other?

$[[[\text{un} + [\text{true}_{Adj}]_{Adj}] + \text{th}_N] + \text{ful}_{Adj}]$ $[\text{un} [[[\text{true}_{Adj}] + \text{th}_N] + \text{ful}_{Adj}]_{Adj}]$

8. For each of these English words, provide an additional word that will aid a speaker to internalize the correct adult underlying form as compared to the form that would

be posited on the basis of the pronunciation of the given word alone. *Example:* Given *photograph* [foDəgræf] (with stress on the first and third syllables), the word *photographer* [fətʰɑgrəfər] (with stress on the second syllable) will help determine the correct adult form by providing the pronunciation for the second underlying vowel, which cannot be schwa if *photographer* is to be pronounced.

solemn	compute	bomb
history	prosper	record (noun)
professor	sulphur	music

9. In the Niutao dialect of Tuvaluan, a Polynesian language, some verbs and adjectives have different forms with singular and plural subjects, as in these examples:

Singular	**Plural**	
kai	kakai	'eat'
mafuli	mafufuli	'turned around'
fepaki	fepapaki	'collide'
apulu	apupulu	'capsize'
nofo	nonofo	'stay'
maasei	maasesei	'bad'
takato	takakato	'lie down'
valea	valelea	'stupid'

a. Describe the rule of morphology that derives the plural forms of these verbs and adjectives from the singular forms.

b. In the Funaafuti dialect of the same language the process is slightly different, as the following plural forms of the same verbs and adjectives show. (Double consonants indicate that the phoneme is held for a longer period of time.) How are plurals formed from singular forms in this dialect? How does that process differ from the process of plural formation in the Niutao dialect described in (a)?

kkai	nnofo
maffuli	maassei
feppaki	takkato
appulu	vallea

10. Consider the following verb forms in the Tailevu dialect of Fijian.

rai	'see'	kindo	'startle'
raiði au	'see me'	kindori au	'startle me'
raiði iko	'see you'	kindori iko	'startle you'
raiðia	'see him'	kindoria	'startle him'
mbiu	'abandon'	mbese	'be tired of'
mbiuti au	'abandon me'	mbeseki au	'be tired of me'

ᵐbiuti iko	'abandon you'	ᵐbeseki iko	'be tired of you'
ᵐbiutia	'abandon him'	ᵐbesekia	'be tired of him'

a. What underlying form do we need to posit for the root of each of these four verbs? Remember that the underlying form of the root must contain enough phonological information for all forms of the verb to be derived, and bear in mind that morpheme boundaries are not necessarily the same thing as word boundaries.

b. Consider the following short sentences, in which the verbs are the same as in (a). List all the different morphemes that you can identify in these six sentences, and provide an accurate gloss for each.

au a ᵐbiuti iko	'I abandoned you'
e a raiðia	'he saw him'
e a ᵐbiuti au	'he abandoned me'
o a kiⁿdoɾi au	'you startled me'
au a raiðia	'I saw him'
o a ᵐbesekia	'you were tired of him'

c. If *levaðia* means 'be angry at him,' how are the following said in this Fijian dialect?

You were angry at him.	He was angry at me.
I was angry at you.	be angry at

11. The vitality of English suffixation is illustrated by the following sentence from a book review. *The author acknowledges his debt to Marxists, Freudians, structuralists, and McLuhanites.* Do the suffixes *-ist*, *-ian*, and *-ite* have different meanings? If not, what accounts for their differential use in this sentence? Check a good desk dictionary to see what differences in the use of these suffixes are recorded.

12. The following are different forms of the same Russian words. The left-hand column contains simple roots; the right-hand column contains forms that are derived from the corresponding form in the left-hand column by processes of inflectional or derivational morphology.

pərʌxot	'steamboat'	pərʌxody	'steamboats'
zapət	'west'	zapədə	'of the west'
rat	'glad'	radəs't'	'gladness'
most	'bridge'	mastom	'to the bridges'
pot	'perspiration'	paty	'perspirations'
štat	'state'	štatu	'to the state'
pot	'under'	padə	'under'

On the basis of this list, how would you describe the distribution of [t] and [d] in Russian? (*Hint:* You want to be able to derive the word in the left-hand column from the same underlying form as the corresponding morpheme in the right-hand column.)

13. On the basis of the examples given below, determine whether the following languages have an isolating, inflectional, or agglutinative morphology, and justify your answer.

Samoan

ʔua   maalamalama aʔu i   le   mataaʔupu.

Present understand   I   Object the lesson

'I understand the lesson.'

Turkish

Herkes   ben üniversite-ye bašla-yacağ-im san-iyor.

everyone I   university-to start-Future-I believe-Present

'Everyone believes that I will start university.'

Finnish

Tyttö   silitti   paidat.

girl-Subject-Sing. iron-Past-Sing. shirt-Object-Plural

'The girl ironed the shirts.'

Japanese

Akiko ga   Haruko ni mainiti   tegami o   kaku.

Akiko Subject Haruko to everyday letter   Object write

'Akiko writes a letter to Haruko every day.'

Mohawk

t-en-s-hon-te-rist-a-wenrat-eʔ.
Dual-Future-Repetitive-Plural-Reflexive-metal-cross-Punctual

'They will cross over the railroad track.'

Thai

Kʰruu hây sàmùt   nákrian sǎam lêm.

teacher give notebook student three Article

'The teacher gave the students three notebooks.'

14. The following are sentences from Tok Pisin (New Guinea Pidgin English):

Manmeri ol   wokabaut long rot.

people   they stroll   on   road

'People are strolling on the road.'

Mi harim toktok bilong yupela.

I listen speech of you-Plural

'I listen to your (plural) speech.'

Mi harim toktok bilong yu.

I listen speech of you-Sing.

'I listen to your (sing.) speech.'

Em no brata bilong em ol harim toktok bilong mi.

he and brother of he they listen speech of me

'He and his brother listen to my speech.'

Mi laikim dispela manmeri long rot.

I like these people on road

'I like these people (who are) on the road.'

Dispela man no prend bilong mi ol laikim dispela toktok.

this man and friend of me they like this speech

'This man and my friend like this speech.'

Relying on the meaning of the morphemes that you can identify in the sentences above, put the following sentences into Tok Pisin:

(1) These people like my speech.

(2) I am strolling on the road.

(3) I like my friend's speech.

(4) I like my brother and these people.

(5) These people on the road and my friend like his speech.

(6) You and my brother like the speech of these people.

(7) These people listen to my friend's and my brother's speech.

15. The morphophonemic rules of English examined in this chapter (noun plurals and possessives, third-person singular present tense verbs, past tense verbs) are curious in that the schwa insertion rule has the effect of making adjacent sounds dissimilar, whereas the assimilation rule makes adjacent sounds similar. It's interesting to reconsider these processes in light of phonotactic constraints such as those discussed at the end of Chapter 3.

a. Make a list of syllable-final consonant pairs permitted in English (considering any suitable list of words such as those in this question, for example, plus any others needed to complete your survey) and describe the phonotactic constraints of such consonant clusters.

b. In light of your answer to (a), re-examine the assimilation rule of English morphophonology. Provide an explanation for this assimilation rule.

c. Now re-examine the schwa insertion rule in the same light. What explanation can you offer for such a rule?

SUGGESTIONS FOR FURTHER READING

Two good introductions to English word formation are Adams (1973) and Bauer (1983). Aitchison (1987) is an accessible treatment of the mental lexicon. General treatments of morphological processes can be found in Matthews (1991) and Lyons (1968), the latter with separate chapters on morphology and grammatical categories. Matthews (1972) treats inflectional morphology, principally in Latin. Chapter 2 of Langacker (1972) is a good general discussion of morphology with illustrations from many languages, including several American Indian languages. The structural grammarians of the early part of this century gave considerable attention to morphology; useful discussions and interesting examples can be found in Sapir (1921) and Bloomfield (1933). Nida (1949) is a traditional descriptive text with more than two hundred problems from a variety of languages. Our examples of reduplication in Turkish come from Underhill (1976). Recent treatments of morphology can be found in Shopen (1985), especially the chapters by Stephen R. Anderson on "Typological Distinctions in Word Formation" and "Inflectional Morphology," by Bernard Comrie on "Causative Verb Formation and Other Verb-Deriving Morphology," and by Comrie and Sandra A. Thompson on "Lexical Nominalization." Comrie (1987), from which a few of the examples in this chapter are taken, provides valuable descriptions of more than forty major languages, usually including discussion of morphology. The Vietnamese example is taken from Comrie (1989). The newest English words are listed in *12,000 Words* (1987).

REFERENCES

Aitchison, Jean. 1987. *Words in the Mind: An Introduction to the Mental Lexicon* (New York: Blackwell).

Adams, Valerie. 1973. *An Introduction to Modern English Word-Formation* (London: Longman).

Bauer, Laurie. 1983. *English Word-Formation* (Cambridge: Cambridge University Press).

Bloomfield, Leonard. 1933. *Language* (New York: Holt Rinehart and Winston).

Comrie, Bernard. 1989. *Language Universals and Linguistic Typology,* 2nd ed. (Chicago: University of Chicago Press).

———, ed. 1987. *The World's Major Languages* (New York: Oxford University Press).

Langacker, Ronald W. 1972. *Fundamentals of Linguistic Analysis* (New York: Harcourt Brace Jovanovich).

Lyons, John. 1968. *Theoretical Linguistics* (Cambridge: Cambridge University Press).

Matthews, Peter H. 1972. *Inflectional Morphology* (Cambridge: Cambridge University Press).

———. 1991. *Morphology,* 2nd ed. (Cambridge: Cambridge University Press).

Nida, Eugene A. 1949. *Morphology: The Descriptive Analysis of Words,* 2nd ed. (Ann Arbor: University of Michigan Press).

Sapir, Edward. 1921. *Language* (New York: Harcourt Brace Jovanovich).

Shopen, Timothy, ed. 1985. *Grammatical Categories and the Lexicon,* vol. 3 of *Language Typology and Syntactic Description* (Cambridge: Cambridge University Press).

12,000 Words: A Supplement to Webster's Third New International Dictionary. 1987. (Springfield, MA: Merriam).

Underhill, Robert. 1976. *Turkish Grammar* (Cambridge, MA: MIT Press).

5

Syntax: Sentences and Their Structure

INTRODUCTION

This chapter explores how morphemes and words are organized within sentences. It examines the parts of a sentence, the relationships among them, and the relationships among various kinds of sentences, such as statements and questions. It explains how, with a finite system, an infinite number of sentences can be generated by a grammar and how the "creative" aspects of language and the occurrence of novel sentences are part of every person's competence. The structure of sentences, as well as the study of such structures, is called **syntax.**

All languages have ways of referring to entities—to people, places, things, ideas, events, and so on. **Referring expressions** are noun phrases. There are simple ones like the proper nouns *Lauren* and *Paris,* the common nouns *books* and *justice,* and the personal pronouns *you* and *it.* There are also more complex noun phrases like these: *a magical book, his mother, the star of the film, a judge he had known forty years earlier,* and *the strict-constructionist way that Wapner settled another dispute over the ownership of a dog.*

All languages also have ways of saying something about the entities they make reference to. In other words, all languages can make **predications** about the things referred to by the referring expressions. All languages have ways of making statements, both affirmative and negative. They can also ask questions, issue directives, and so on.

Let's illustrate with affirmative statements. In the following sentences, reference is made to an entity and then a predication is made about it.

Referring Expression	Predication
Judge Wapner	has a daughter.
She	uses an answering machine.
The ghost	reappeared last night.

In the first example, reference is made to "Judge Wapner," and something is then predicated of him—namely, that he "has a daughter." Likewise for the second and third examples.

Sentences often consist of more elaborate referring expressions and more elaborate predications than these. The two sentences below illustrate more elaborate predications. In the first example, reference is made to "the dog" and then a predication about the dog is made. In the second example, reference is made to "the lawyer" and then a predication is made about her. In these examples, the predication is underlined.

The dog <u>bit the man who had agreed to care for it.</u>

The lawyer <u>swore that her father had promised to foot the bill.</u>

What constitutes the well-formed strings of words and morphemes that a language uses to refer to things and make predications about them are part of its syntax. Syntax governs the form of the strings by which a language makes statements, asks questions, gives directives, and so on. In other words, the study of syntax treats the structure of sentences and their structural relationships to one another. To repeat: a typical sentence consists of two parts, one a referring expression and the other a predication about the entity referred to. In syntactic terms, referring expressions are noun phrases, and predicates are verb phrases. All languages, however much they differ from one another in the other categories or parts of speech, have nouns (and noun phrases) and verbs (and verb phrases).

SENTENCE TYPES

In many traditional grammars three major sentence types are distinguished. A **simple sentence** consists of a single clause that stands alone as its own sentence. In a **coordinate sentence** (called "compound" in traditional grammars), two or more clauses are joined by a conjunction in a coordinate relationship. A **complex sentence** combines two (or more) clauses in such a way that one clause functions as a grammatical part of the other one.

Simple Sentences = Clauses

Simple sentences are those that contain one clause; a **clause** contains a single verb (or predicate). The following are examples of simple sentences.

1. Dan <u>washed</u> the dishes.
2. Karen <u>assembled</u> the new grill.
3. Joe <u>cooked</u> the hot dogs.
4. A runner from Ohio <u>won</u> the marathon last year.
5. Denise <u>will buy</u> a new raincoat this fall.
6. Her uncle <u>had put</u> the gifts in the car.
7. The psychiatrist <u>should have believed</u> in banshees.

Each of these sentences contains only one verb, but a verb itself can consist of a single word (as in *washed, assembled, cooked,* and *won*) or of more than one word (as in *will buy, had put,* and *should have believed*). In English and in many other languages, the central element in a clause is the verb; each clause—and therefore each simple sentence—contains just one verb.

Coordinate Sentences

Two clauses can be joined to make a coordinate sentence, as in the examples here.

1. Karen assembled the new grill, <u>and</u> Joe cooked the hot dogs.
2. Denise bought a new coat, <u>but</u> she didn't wear it often.

A coordinate sentence consists of two clauses joined by a word such as *and, but,* or *or,* which are called *coordinating conjunctions,* or simply *conjunctions.* Conjunctions can be used to join clauses (as we have just seen), but they can also join other constructions; for example, nouns in *trick OR treat* and *Dungeons AND Dragons;* verbs in *trip AND fall* or *break AND enter;* adjectives in *slow AND painful* or *tried AND true.* When clauses are combined to form a single sentence, we reserve the word *sentence* for the larger structure and refer to the "sentences" that make it up as *clauses.*

The clauses in a coordinate sentence hold equal status: Neither clause is part of the other clause, and each could stand by itself as an independent sentence. Figure 5-1 represents the structure of a coordinate sentence and illustrates the equivalent status of the clauses (called *coordinate clauses*). We use the label S for both the whole sentence and for each coordinate clause in it; CONJ stands for conjunction, a lexical category that links like structures: clauses with clauses, noun phrases with noun phrases, and so on.

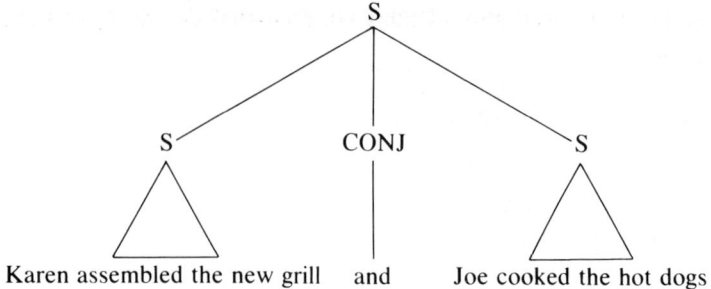

FIGURE 5-1

Complex Sentences

Embedded Clauses   Besides being conjoined to another clause, one clause can be incorporated into another clause. The clause *Dan washed the dishes* can be incorporated into another clause to produce the sentence *Sue said <u>Dan washed the dishes</u>*. In each of the following examples, the underlined portion is a clause that is incorporated (or embedded) into another clause.

1. Sue said <u>Dan washed the dishes</u>.

2. <u>That the runner from Ohio won the marathon</u> surprised us.

3. She is wondering <u>whether Denise will buy a new raincoat</u>.

4. She didn't suspect a party <u>until her uncle put the gifts in the car</u>.

5. It was clear <u>that the patient should have received a refund</u>.

In sentence 1, the clause *Dan washed the dishes* is embedded into the clausal structure *Sue said* ——. The clause *Dan washed the dishes* functions as the direct object of the verb *said*. It is thus functionally equivalent (though not semantically equivalent) to the word *something* in the sentence *Sue said something;* both function as direct objects. In 2, the clause *That the runner from Ohio won the marathon* is embedded into the clausal structure —— *surprised us*. In this case, the embedded clause functions as the subject of the verb *surprised*. The embedded clause in 2 (*That the runner from Ohio won the marathon*) is grammatically equivalent to *It* in *It surprised us* or to *The news* in *The news surprised us*. In 3, the clause *whether Denise will buy a new raincoat* is embedded into the clause *She is wondering* ——; it serves as a complement to the verb *is wondering*.

Subordinators   In most of the examples just given, the embedded clause is introduced by a word that would not occur there if the clause were standing as an independent sentence: words like *that* in 2 and 5, *whether* in 3, and *until* in 4. When a clause is embedded into another clause, it is often introduced by such a **subordinator.** Subordinators serve to mark the beginning of an embedded clause and to help identify its function in the sentence. Not all embedded clauses must be introduced by a subordinator, although in English they usually can be. Compare these sentence pairs:

1. Sue said that Dan washed the dishes.
2. Sue said Dan washed the dishes.

3. That she won surprised us.
4. *She won surprised us.

Notice that 1 and 2 are well formed with or without the subordinator. But of the pair 3 and 4, only 3 is well formed. (The asterisk preceding 4 indicates a structure that is not well formed.)

The Form of Embedded Clauses   When a clause is embedded within certain other clauses, its form may differ from the form it would have if it stood independently as a simple sentence. In these pairs, compare sentence 1 with 2, and compare 3 with 4:

1. Sue said <u>Dan washed the dishes</u>.
2. Sue wanted <u>Dan to wash the dishes</u>.

3. <u>That the runner from Ohio won the marathon</u> surprised us.
4. <u>For the runner from Ohio to win the marathon</u> surprised us.

The clause *Dan to wash the dishes* is not a well-formed English sentence; yet when it is embedded into the clausal structure *Sue wanted* ——, the whole sentence is perfectly well formed. As a matter of fact, any other form would be unacceptable, as illustrated here.

1. *Sue wanted <u>Dan washed the dishes</u>.

2. *Sue wanted that <u>Dan will wash the dishes</u>.

3. *Sue wanted <u>Dan washes the dishes</u>.

The form of an embedded clause can depend on the particular verb of the clause in which it is embedded. Compare the sentences in each of the following pairs.

1. Sue wanted <u>Dan to wash the dishes</u>.
2. *Sue wanted <u>Dan washed the dishes</u>.

3. Sue said <u>Dan washed the dishes</u>.
4. *Sue said <u>Dan to wash the dishes</u>.

These sentences suggest that the verb *want* requires a clause with a tenseless (in this case infinitival) verb form, as in *wanted Dan to wash the dishes,* whereas the verb *say* does not permit an embedded clause to be tenseless (*Dan to wash the dishes)* but does permit the independent sentence form *Dan washed the dishes,* which contains a tensed verb.

Unlike coordinate sentences, which contain clauses of equal status, *complex* sentences contain clauses of unequal status. In the complex sentences we have been examining, one clause is subordinate to another clause and functions as a grammatical part of that clause. We call the subordinate clause an *embedded clause* and the clause into which it is embedded a *matrix clause.* Every subordinate clause is by definition embedded in a matrix clause, in which it serves in a grammatical function such as subject, direct object, or adverbial. For example, in the next sentences, in which brackets set off the embedded clauses, each embedded clause functions as a grammatical unit in its matrix clause. Each embedded clause has the same grammatical function in its matrix clause as the underlined word has in the sentence directly below it.

1.   Sally said [she saw a ghost].
2.   Sally said <u>it</u>. (<u>it</u> is the direct object of the verb <u>said</u>)

3.   [That Jack feared witches] upset his wife.
4.   <u>It</u> upset his wife. (<u>it</u> is the subject of the sentence)

5.   Joe cooked the hot dogs [after Karen assembled the grill].
6.   Joe cooked the hot dogs <u>then</u>. (<u>then</u> is an adverbial)

In 1, the embedded clause *she saw a ghost* functions as the direct object of the verb *said,* just as the word *it* does in 2. In 3, the embedded clause *That Jack feared witches* functions as the subject of the verb *upset,* just as *it* does in sentence 4. In 5, *after Karen assembled the grill* functions as an adverbial modifying the verb phrase *cooked the hot dogs,* just as *then* does in 6.

CONSTITUENCY AND TREE DIAGRAMS

Tree Diagrams

We can represent syntactic relationships in tree diagrams like those on the following pages. The tree in Figure 5-2 represents the fact that the sentence *Sue liked Casper* consists of two parts: the referring expression *Sue* and the predicate

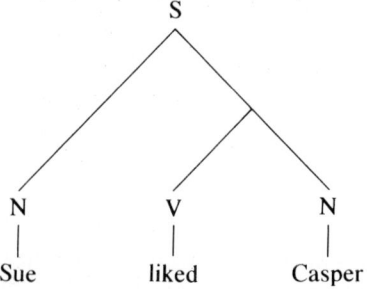

FIGURE 5-2

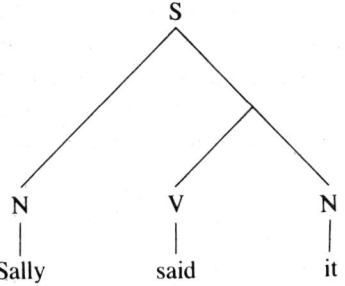

FIGURE 5-3

expression *liked Casper*. In each diagram, *S* stands for sentence (or clause), *N* stands for noun or pronoun, and *V* stands for verb.

This tree diagram can also represent other clauses such as *Sally said it,* as illustrated in Figure 5-3. These trees somewhat oversimplify the structures represented, as you'll see.

Tree diagrams can also illustrate the relationship among the clauses of a sentence like *Sally said she saw a ghost.* In representing a complex sentence, we can substitute the clause *she saw a ghost* for the word *it,* as in Figure 5-4. This diagram captures the fact that the embedded clause S_2 *(she saw a ghost)* functions structurally as part of the matrix clause S *(Sally said ——).* The embedded clause fills the same slot in the matrix clause as the word *it* fills in the clause *Sally said it.*

We saw earlier that coordinate sentences are made up of coordinate clauses. The next examples illustrate that a subordinate clause can be embedded within a coordinate clause of a coordinate sentence.

The tree diagram in Figure 5-5 represents the fact that S_2 and S_3 are coordinate clauses of S_1, and that S_4 is embedded in the matrix clause S_2.

The diagram in Figure 5-6 captures the fact that S_2 and S_3 are coordinate clauses and that S_4 is embedded in the matrix clause S_3.

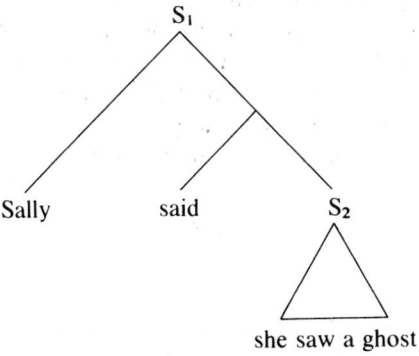

FIGURE 5-4

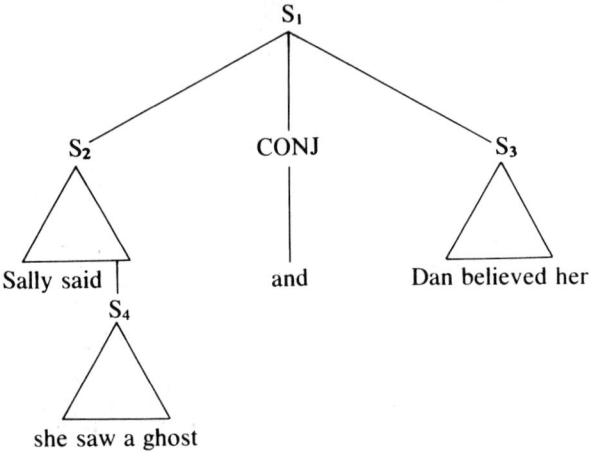

FIGURE 5-5

In the remainder of this chapter, we focus principally on clauses that are embedded in other clauses, and we make only incidental reference to sentences containing coordinate clauses.

Constituency

In analyzing the structure of sentences, one pivotal tool is the simple notion that sentences consist *not of words* but of structural units called **constituents.** For example, the sentence *Sally said she saw a ghost* can be viewed in several ways. Obviously, it is made up of words, each of which contains at least one morpheme. Since these morphemes have sounds associated with them, we could say that the

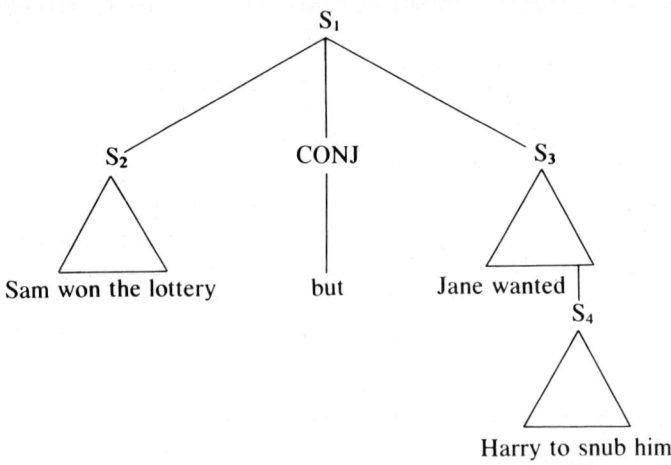

FIGURE 5-6

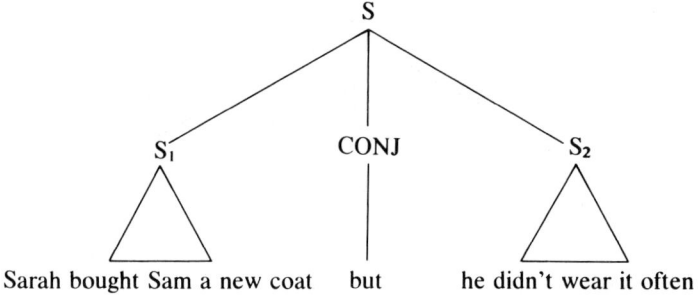

FIGURE 5-7

sentence is made up of sounds (such as /g/, /o/, /s/, /t/ in *ghost* and /s/, /ɛ/, /d/ in *said*), or of morphemes (SAY and 'PAST TENSE'), or of words *(Sally* and *said)*. Such an approach would be like describing a shopping mall as made up of cement and electrical wires—accurate, but beside the point. We want to say that a shopping center has shops, restaurants, parking areas, recreational facilities, and so on. We could then go further and describe the composition and relationship of these units; the point is to identify *structural units* that are relevant to some purpose or some level of organization.

Linguists treat sentences as consisting, first, of the largest grammatical units. These largest units in turn can be analyzed as consisting of smaller units, which in turn can be analyzed. From this point of view, the immediate constituents of a coordinate sentence are the clauses constituting it and the conjunction joining them, as in this example.

<u>Sarah bought Sam a new coat</u> but <u>he didn't wear it often</u>.
clause 1 (S_1)   clause 2 (S_2)

This structure can be represented schematically as in Figure 5-7.

The immediate constituents of a complex sentence are its clauses, as in the next example.

<u>That Jack feared witches</u>   <u>upset his wife</u>.
clause 2 (S_2)   clause 1 (S_1)

This structure can be represented as in Figure 5-8.

Linear Ordering of Constituents It is obvious that the words of a sentence must occur in some order. It follows that constituents, too, have their elements in some order. In speaking, the order is chronological. In writing, the order can be from left to right (as in English), right to left (as in Arabic and Persian), top to bottom (as in Japanese), and so on. Sentences are thus expressed with an ordered sequence of morphemes and words. Sentences such as

The little old plumber from Pasadena sits in the park.

Jill touched the harpie.

Helen claims to be from Xanadu.

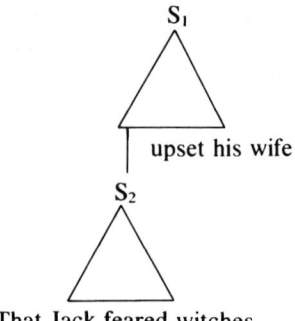

S_1

upset his wife

S_2

That Jack feared witches

FIGURE 5-8

and all other clauses and sentences in every language necessarily express words in a sequential, or linear, order.

Now we ask, is the order in which words are arranged fixed or not? If it is fixed, is it equally fixed across different languages? We begin by examining the following sentences:

> The farmer saw the ghost.
>
> The ghost saw the farmer.

Both are well-formed sentences of English, and both contain exactly the same words. Clearly, however, they do not mean the same thing. Since the words themselves are the same, the only thing that could signal the difference in meaning is the word order. It is the word order in the sentence that signals who is doing what to whom. Now consider the following:

> The farmer saw the ghost.
>
> *Farmer the ghost the saw.

The first is well formed; the second is not. Word order is clearly an essential part of English sentence structure. If we rearrange the words in an English sentence, we sometimes get other well-formed sentences that have a different meaning, but we can also produce sentences that are not well formed. Sometimes, too, a change of word order can produce a different well-formed sentence with the same meaning, as shown.

> Yesterday I heard a poltergeist in the attic.
>
> I heard a poltergeist in the attic yesterday.

Thus word order is not absolutely fixed. However, since rearranging the order of words can sometimes change meaning and sometimes produce an ill-formed sentence, the order of words in an English sentence is significant.

Not all languages exploit word order to the same extent that English does. As we saw in Chapter 4, Latin could express 'The farmer saw the ghost' by using any of the following word orders:

Agricola vīdit umbram.
farmer   saw   ghost

Agricola umbram vīdit.   'The farmer saw the ghost.'

Umbram agricola vīdit.

Grammatical relations like subject and direct object are indicated in Latin not by word order, as they are in English, but by inflectional suffixes; the same is true of Russian, German, and many other languages. Thus, with constant inflections on the nouns, each of the following Latin sentences has the same meaning.

Umbra vīdit agricolam.
ghost   saw   farmer

Umbra agricolam vīdit.   'The ghost saw the farmer.'

Agricolam umbra vīdit.

There are three other possible orders for arranging these three words in sequence, and all would indicate the same content. (Though all are well formed, not all are equally likely to occur in Latin speech; some would seem more natural than others.) Word order is a potential marker of meaning in all the world's languages, but not all languages exploit this potentiality, and very many languages do not exploit it to the same extent that English does.

Hierarchical Ordering of Constituents   Is there any other structure to a sentence besides linear order? To answer this question, consider the phrase *gullible boys and girls*. It can mean either 'gullible boys and gullible girls' or 'gullible boys and (all) girls.' This ambiguity of interpretation reflects the fact that the phrase *gullible boys and girls* has two possible internal organizations for the same linear sequence of words. These internal organizations differ as to whether the adjective *gullible* modifies *boys and girls* or just *boys*. We call the internal organization of a linear string of words its **constituent structure.** Constituent structure refers to the grouping of words (and morphemes) into grammatical units; we represent constituent structure using brackets or tree diagrams. The following illustrates both ways of representing the phrase *gullible boys and girls*. In the tree diagrams of Figure 5-9, notice that at the highest level there are two constituents in the left-hand tree but three in the tree on the right; at the lowest level, there are the same number of constituents in each. Below each tree is an equivalent representation using brackets.

Notice, then, that a string of words with a specified linear order can have more than one constituent structure. Both of these tree diagrams represent the same four words in the same linear order. But the constituent structures are different.

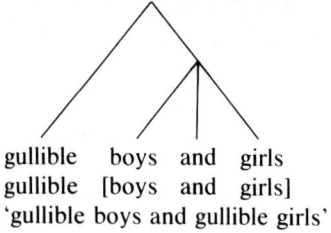
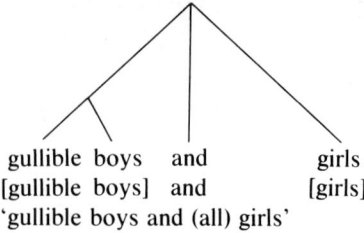

gullible boys and girls   gullible boys and   girls
gullible [boys and girls]   [gullible boys] and   [girls]
'gullible boys and gullible girls' 'gullible boys and (all) girls'

FIGURE 5-9

In the first tree diagram, the phrase *gullible boys and girls* consists of two constituents: (1) *gullible,* (2) *boys and girls.* In the second tree, there are three constituents: (1) *gullible boys,* (2) *and,* (3) *girls.* The difference in meaning between these two identical sequences of words is the result of their having different constituent structures at the highest level of analysis.[1]

Structural Ambiguity   Structural ambiguity of the sort we have just examined is not limited to phrases. It can occur in larger units as well. Consider sentence 1:

   1. He sold the car to his brother in New York.

This string of words is ambiguous: It has more than one possible interpretation. Sometimes ambiguity results from the fact that a word has two meanings, as in *He ate near the bank* (in which *bank* can be a financial institution or the bank of a river) or *He gave her his chair* (in which *chair* can be a physical object or a place to sit). In sentence 1 the ambiguity arises not from the individual words (which are all unambiguous) but from the fact that the string of words has more than one possible constituent structure. We can bracket 1 in different ways to indicate the different constituent structures, as shown here:

   2. He sold the car [to [his brother in New York]].

   3. He sold the car [to his brother] [in New York].

Sentence 2 can be paraphrased as 4 below but not as 5 or 6. Sentence 3 can be paraphrased as 5 or 6 but not as 4.

   4. It was to his brother in New York that he sold the car.

   5. It was in New York that he sold the car to his brother.

   6. In New York he sold the car to his brother.

These examples illustrate that the words of a sentence are organized into units called constituents and that such constituents are not available to inspection—they

---

[1] To refer without ambiguity to the meaning shown in the second tree, you could alter the word order and say *girls and gullible boys.*

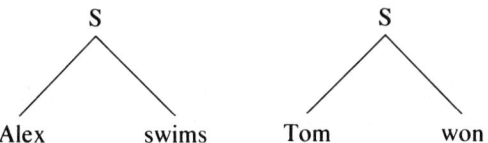

FIGURE 5-10

cannot be identified from the string of words itself. The linear order of words in a written English sentence—which word is first, which second, and so on—is available to inspection (it is obvious), but it takes a speaker of English to recognize constituent structure and to recognize that a given string of words may have two or more possible constituent structures.

MAJOR CONSTITUENTS OF SENTENCES: NOUN PHRASES AND VERB PHRASES

Sentences have a linear order that is obvious and a constituent structure that is not obvious but is nevertheless understood by native speakers. The linear order of speech is automatically represented when we write down a sentence, with each word located sequentially with respect to other words in the sentence. Consider the sentences in Figure 5-10, which have two simple constituents each.

More elaborate sentences can be analyzed similarly, as in Figure 5-11.

An alternative tool in representing constituent structure is bracketing, as illustrated here:

1. [Alex] [swims].

2. [The dog] [is barking].

3. [Bob] [spilled the potion].

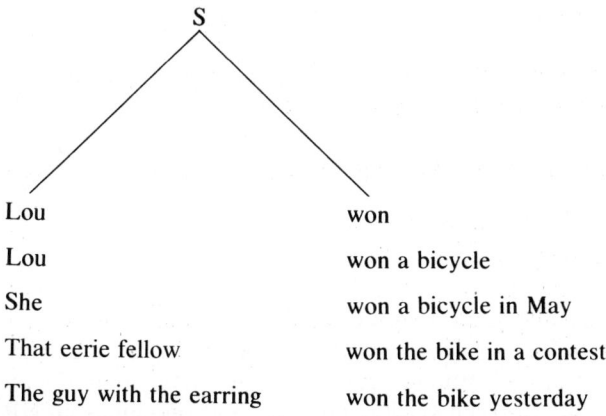

FIGURE 5-11

4.   [The guy with the earring] [won the bike in a contest].

5.   [The witch] [said Bob spilled the potion].

In general, simple sentences (and therefore clauses) consists of two principal constituents. In each of the preceding examples, the constituent on the left is called an NP (for Noun Phrase), and the one on the right is called a VP (for Verb Phrase). Each NP contains a noun (or pronoun). Each VP contains a verb. Functionally, each NP is a referring expression; each VP makes a predication. We identify NPs and VPs sometimes by the slots they fill in a sentence and sometimes from their functions in the sentence. Thus *Alex* in sentence 1 and *The guy with the earring* in 4 function in the same way: they are referring expressions about which the predication in the sentence is made. Similarly, *swims* in 1 and *said Bob spilled the potion* in 5 function alike in their sentences; they are predications made about an NP.

NPs can also be identified by substitution procedures such as those implied in the list of alternatives to the basic two-part structure in Figure 5-11. Thus, for *Lou* we could substitute forms varying from *She* to *The guy with the earring*. Both the short *She* and the longer phrase are NPs because they can occur in the slot —— *won a bicycle*.

Other slots in a sentence can also be filled by an NP. In sentence 3, the VP is *spilled the potion*. Unlike the VP of example 1, which consists of the single word *swims*, the VP of 3 contains two parts: the verb *spilled* and the NP *the potion*. Thus a VP can contain an NP. In fact, several of our sentences have an NP within the VP, as the underlining shows:

	NP	**VP**
1.	[Alex]	[swims].
2.	[The dog]	[is barking].
3.	[Bob]	[spilled the potion].
4.	[The guy with the earring]	[won the bike in a contest].
5.	[The witch]	[said Bob spilled the potion].

The potion, the bike, a contest, and *Bob* are NPs. To repeat two points made earlier, an NP contains a noun (or a pronoun) and in some respects functions like a noun within a sentence. Thus any constituent that you could insert in the slots here would be an NP:

She enjoyed talking about —— incessantly.

Invariably, —— upset her.

The following words and phrases could be inserted in either slot and are therefore NPs; we have italicized the *head noun* in each. (Sometimes an NP contains more than one noun, a topic to which we return below.)

animals
the *weather*
her aged *instructor*
the *thief* who stole her purse
the little old *plumber* from Pasadena

his *return* to his first wife
the *fact* that her family is so poor
Peter's *winning* the race
the *guy* with the earring

Notice that instead of containing a head noun, an NP can be a pronoun, such as *it*. Pronouns are a variety of NP in that they have the same distribution in clauses; they occur where NPs can occur.

Verb Phrases, or VPs, can be identified using similar substitution procedures. Consider the frame *Lou* ———. The following strings fit this frame and are thus VPs (the head verb in each VP is underlined):

<u>won</u>

<u>won</u> the race

<u>claimed</u> she won a prize

<u>claimed</u> she won a prize for her efforts in the tournament

<u>admitted</u> that she would not enter the contest in any case

To this point, we have seen two major constituents in a sentence: NP and VP. The NP often refers to a person or a thing; the VP makes a predication about the NP. What is true of simple sentences applies equally to clauses embedded within other clauses: clauses have two principal constituents—NP and VP.

Active/Passive Sentences   An NP functions as a single unified constituent in a sentence, regardless of how big or small the NP is and regardless of how simple or complex. Even elaborate NPs like *the guy with the earring* and *what she wanted to receive for her twenty-fifth birthday* function structurally as single units in a sentence, exactly like simple NPs such as *lions, she,* and *Bob.* In this section we investigate passive sentences in English to illustrate the unity of NPs.

Consider these active/passive sentence pairs:

1. Zelda auctioned the famous wooden spoon. (Active)
2. The famous wooden spoon was auctioned by Zelda. (Passive)

3. The judge fined an old plumber from Pasadena. (Active)
4. An old plumber from Pasadena was fined by the judge. (Passive)

5. The mail truck crushed the bike I gave Karen. (Active)
6. The bike I gave Karen was crushed by the mail truck. (Passive)

Even schoolchildren who have never heard of active and passive sentences can usually provide the passive version of an active sentence when given a few model pairs. They implicitly know how a passive sentence is related to an active one. Let's attempt to make explicit what that knowledge must be.

On the basis of sentences 1 and 2 above, one might hypothesize this rule: "To make an active sentence passive, interchange the first word with the last four." (For our present purposes, we can ignore the verb *be* and the preposition *by*, but in a complete statement of the rule those aspects of passivization would also have to be addressed.) Our tentative hypothesis produces a well-formed string when applied to sentence 1, but if it is applied to 3 or 5, it produces the ill-formed structures of 7 and 8:

3. The judge fined an old plumber from Pasadena.
7. *Old plumber from Pasadena judge was fined an by the.

5. The mail truck crushed the bike I gave Karen.
8. *Bike I gave Karen mail truck was crushed the by the.

Check for yourself to see that 7 and 8 are indeed the structures that would result from interchanging the first word and the last four words of the active sentences 3 and 5 (and introducing *by* and an appropriate form of *be*). Clearly, what speakers of English know about the relationship between active and passive sentences depends not on counting words, but on knowledge about constituent structure.

Refer again to the constituents that are interchanged in the active/passive pairs of sentences 1 through 6. The strings of words in each of the following sets share a structural property in that they function similarly.

1. <u>Zelda</u>/The <u>judge</u>/The <u>mail truck</u>

2. the famous wooden <u>spoon</u>/an old <u>plumber</u> from Pasadena/the <u>bike</u> I gave Karen

Each NP in sets 1 and 2 contains at least a head noun, which is underlined. The NPs share an ability to function alike in sentences, that is, to fill certain frames and to be movable *as units* in syntactic processes, such as passivization. In relating active and passive sentences, NPs thus function as syntactic units no matter how long they are. We will return to the correct formulation of passives below.

PHRASE-STRUCTURE RULES

Rules for Rewriting Noun Phrases

We can now characterize and exemplify certain types of NP:

Noun (N): *Karen, oracles, justice, swimming*

Determiner (DET) + Noun: *that amulet, a potion, some gnomes, a saucer*

Determiner + Adjective (ADJ) + Noun: *an ancient oracle, these hellish precincts, the first omen, a flying saucer*

Determiner + Adjective + Noun + Prepositional Phrase (PP): *the coldest weather of the year, the first woman on the moon, that loud clap of thunder*

One way of representing these various NP patterns is by the use of **phrase-structure rules** (also called *rewrite rules*) like the following:

1. NP $\longrightarrow$ **N**   (NP consists of N)
2. NP $\longrightarrow$ DET **N**   (NP consists of DET + N)
3. NP $\longrightarrow$ DET ADJ **N**   (NP consists of DET + ADJ + N)
4. NP $\longrightarrow$ DET ADJ **N** PP   (NP consists of DET + ADJ + N + PP)

These four rules can be collapsed into a single rule if we place parentheses around optional elements (that is, around elements that need not be present). Notice that the only constituent required in each NP rewrite rule is N; the other constituents—DET, ADJ, and PP—are optional and must be placed in parentheses. The abbreviated rule looks like this:

5. NP $\longrightarrow$ (DET) (ADJ) **N** (PP)

Rule 5 can be expanded into the four separate rules that we intended to capture in the collapsed version, but 5 has several expansions that we did not anticipate. Because DET, ADJ, and PP are each optional, we can rewrite NP not only as in 1, 2, 3, and 4 above, but also in other ways, including 6 and 7.

6. NP $\longrightarrow$ ADJ **N**
7. NP $\longrightarrow$ DET **N** PP

The collapsed rule thus suggests expansions that we did not set out to capture. If it happens that there are well-formed NP structures consisting of an adjective and a noun (ADJ N) and of a determiner, a noun, and a prepositional phrase (DET N PP), as well as any other expansions 5 would permit, then rule 5 is valid; otherwise, we would have to revise it to exclude structures that are not well formed.

Of course, English does indeed permit NPs that consist of ADJ and N, as in *extraterrestrial life* and *great imagination,* as well as NPs consisting of DET and N and PP, as in *those dishes on the table, the whale on the beach,* and *a cloud in the sky.* (One advantage of formalisms such as the collapsed rewrite rule in 5 is that they sometimes entail unanticipated claims that can be checked against other data—and they thus provide a test of their own validity.)

Prepositional Phrase   The notation PP stands for prepositional phrase, of which previous examples include *in the car, from Xanadu, in New York, to his brother, with the earring,* and *by the judge.* Because every PP consists of a preposition (PREP) and may (but need not) contain a noun phrase (NP), the rewrite rule for PP is this:

PP $\longrightarrow$ **PREP** (NP)

Rules for Rewriting Sentences and Verb Phrases

To capture the fact that sentences and clauses have two basic constituent parts, we formulate the following phrase-structure rule:

$$S \longrightarrow NP\ VP$$

Every rewrite rule can generate a tree diagram, and this phrase-structure rule (rewrite S as NP and VP) would generate the following tree:

Having seen various expansions of NP, we turn now to the internal structure of VP to explore its expansions and the rewrite rules necessary to accommodate them. The following expansions of our frame for identifying VPs reveal that the structures on the right are VPs; the labels under parts of the VPs indicate the categories of constituents of those structures.

```
        _VP_
1.  Lou  won
          V

         _____VP_____
2.  Lou  won  a bicycle
          V      NP

         _____VP_____
3.  Lou  won  the bike in May
          V     NP     PP
```

Sentences 1, 2, and 3 indicate three ways to expand VP:

$$
VP \longrightarrow
\begin{array}{l}
\textbf{V} \\
\textbf{V NP} \\
\textbf{V NP PP}
\end{array}
$$

Using parentheses to enclose optional elements, these three rewrite rules can be collapsed into a single rule, which says that a VP must have a V and may have an NP or a PP or both an NP and a PP:

$$VP \longrightarrow \textbf{V (NP) (PP)}$$

Just as we discovered options that we had not considered when we collapsed four rules for rewriting NP into one rule, so the collapsed rule for VP will generate the structure V PP, which is not represented among sentences 1, 2, and 3, which formed the basis of the rewrite rule for VP. Again we have a way of checking the validity of the rewrite rule: the expansion V PP is needed for VP in order to generate sentences such as *(Jane) swims at noon, (Alex) raced around the track,* and *(Pat) flew to Balnibarbi.*

```
_____VP_____
```
Pat flew <u>to Balnibarbi</u>
V   PP

Phrase-Structure Rules and Tree Diagrams

We have now formulated four phrase-structure rules:

$$S \longrightarrow NP\ VP$$
$$NP \longrightarrow (DET)\ (ADJ)\ N\ (PP)$$
$$VP \longrightarrow V\ (NP)\ (PP)$$
$$PP \longrightarrow PREP\ (NP)$$

These rules represent the fact that every sentence has an NP and a VP; that every NP has an N; that every VP has a V; and that every PP has a PREP. According to these rules, other possibilities are optional.

The following tree diagram can be generated by our rules:

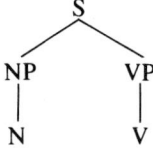

It would represent sentences like *Tom jogged, He fell, Jane swims*. Now consider another structure generated by our rewrite rules; in the example shown in Figure 5-12, we have supplied one sample sentence for the structure.

Refining the Phrase-Structure Rules

Now we examine certain other sentences to see whether they can be generated by the four rewrite rules above. Consider the following on page 136:

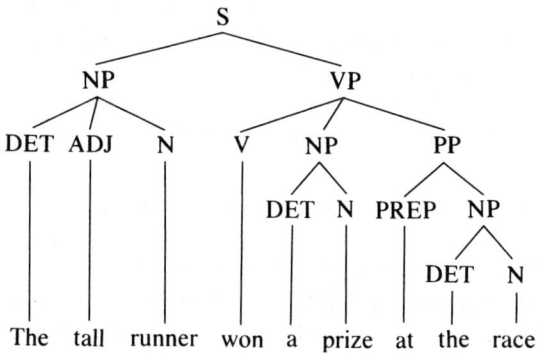

FIGURE 5-12

_____NP_____ _____VP_____
The indictment   charged [that Lou embezzled funds]
               V   S

This sentence cannot be generated by our four phrase-structure rules and thus suggests the following as a rewrite for VP.

$$VP \longrightarrow V\ S$$

Other well-formed English sentences indicate that a VP can also consist of V NP PP S, as here:

_NP_ _____VP_____
Julia   warned [the cook] [on Monday] [that he must wash the celery]
         V   NP   PP   S

From these examples, it appears that a more adequate rewrite rule for VP would be the following:

$$VP \longrightarrow V\ (NP)\ (PP)\ (S)$$

This rule can be expanded into all the following, with an example of each given in parenthesis.

	V	(won)
	V NP	(won the race)
	V NP S	(warned the cook [that he must wash the celery])
VP ⟶	V NP PP S	(told the cook on Monday [that he must wash the celery])
	V S	(charged [that Lou embezzled funds])
	V PP	(flew to Balnibarbi)
	V NP PP	(won the bike in a contest)
	V PP S	(denied in court [that Pat flew to Balnibarbi])

(In addition, PP can be repeated, a fact that we do not account for here.)

We have now arrived at the following phrase-structure rules for English:

$$S \longrightarrow NP\ VP$$
$$NP \longrightarrow (DET)\ (ADJ)\ N\ (PP)$$
$$VP \longrightarrow V\ (NP)\ (PP)\ (S)$$
$$PP \longrightarrow PREP\ (NP)$$

In these rules, we begin with an initial symbol S. S is expanded by a rewrite rule into NP and VP. In turn, both NP and VP can be rewritten. NP can be rewritten as DET and N, for example. Some symbols (NP, VP, and PP) can be rewritten as a sequence of symbols. Other symbols (N or PREP, for example) cannot be expanded further. Finally one arrives at a string in which no symbol can be rewritten or expanded further except by attaching individual morphemes or words. This is called a **terminal string.**

GRAMMATICAL RELATIONS: SUBJECT, DIRECT OBJECT, AND OTHERS

We have had occasion in the course of discussing English clauses and sentences to use the terms subject and direct object. Until now we have used these notions only incidentally, relying on your past acquaintance with them. Using phrase-structure rules, it is possible to define subject and direct object precisely for English. In defining them, two rules are important:

$$S \longrightarrow NP\ VP$$
$$VP \longrightarrow V\ (NP)\ (PP)\ (S)$$

The first rule says that S consists of NP and VP. The second rule says that VP must contain V and may contain NP (it also says that VP may contain other constituents, which are not relevant to the present discussion). We can represent the relevant parts of these phrase-structure rules in a tree diagram that they would generate. Looking at the diagram in Figure 5-13, we see that the circled NP is directly under the S node, that the boxed NP is directly under the VP node, and that the VP node is directly under the S node. When one node is directly under another node, we say that it is *immediately dominated* by that node. Thus V is immediately dominated by VP; the circled NP is immediately dominated by S; the boxed NP is immediately dominated by VP; and both VP and the circled NP are immediately dominated by S.

We can now define subject and direct object in terms of phrase-structure rules and the tree diagrams they generate. In English and many other languages (but not all languages), **subject** is defined as the NP that is immediately dominated by S. In our diagram, the circled NP is the subject of sentence S. Subject NPs appear in tree diagrams as follows:

$$S$$
$$|$$
$$NP$$

Direct object (again, in English and many other languages) is defined as an NP

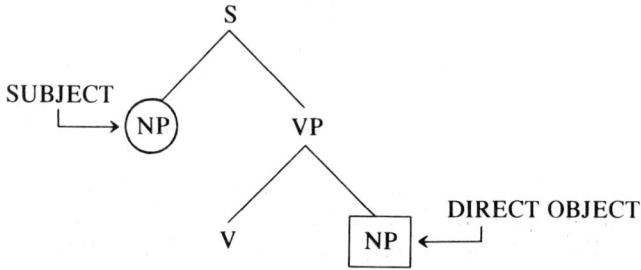

FIGURE 5-13

that is immediately dominated by VP. In Figure 5-13 it is the boxed NP. Direct object NPs appear in tree diagrams as follows:

VP

|

NP

Since NP is an optional element in the expansion of VP, it follows that not every sentence will have an NP immediately dominated by VP; that is, not every sentence will have a direct object. A sentence that does not contain a direct object has what traditional grammars call an *intransitive* verb (see Chapter 4). Intransitive verbs such as *die, hurry,* and *laugh* do not take direct objects. A verb that takes a direct object is called a *transitive* verb. Typical examples are *make, buy,* and *find,* as in *make a potion, buy a pestle,* and *find a penny.* Verbs are specified in the lexicon as being transitive or intransitive. Besides the subject of the sentence, a verb phrase containing a transitive verb requires at least one NP, which is called an **argument** of the verb.

The ghost frightened *the child.*

The king summoned *Beowulf.*

A VP with an intransitive verb contains no argument, although the sentence contains a subject, as illustrated here:

The child screamed.

Grendel perished.

Some verbs can be used both transitively and intransitively, as shown in these sentences:

Intransitive	**Transitive**
Casper won.	Casper won a prize.
Ed sings.	Ed sings lullabies.
Sue studied at Oxford.	Sue studied physics at Oxford.

Grammatical Relations   Subject and direct object are functions known as grammatical relations. **Grammatical relation** is a term used to capture the syntactic relationship that exists in a clause between NPs or between an NP and its predicate—to indicate, in other words, the syntactic role that an NP plays in its clause. Certain structural properties of subjects and direct objects cannot be altogether equated with anything else, including meaning. Besides subject and direct object, sentences can have other grammatical relations, such as **indirect object, oblique** (in English, object of a preposition), and **possessor.** English has the grammatical relations oblique (*The ghost spoke about <u>a toothache</u>*) and possessor (<u>*Joan's*</u> *car*).

There is disagreement about the status of indirect object as a grammatical relation in English.[2]

Passive Construction   Having defined subject and direct object in structural terms, we can now return to a syntactic relationship examined above. The constructs of subject and direct object allow us to reformulate the relationship between active and passive sentences as follows: "To convert an active sentence to a passive one, interchange the subject NP and the direct object NP." (As before, provision must be made for the preposition *by* and a form of the verb *be*.) The following sentences will serve as an example:

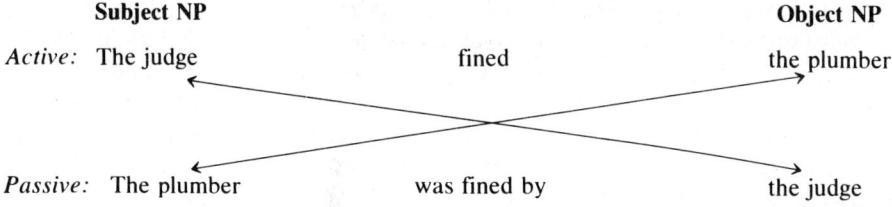

	Subject NP		**Object NP**
Active:	The judge	fined	the plumber
Passive:	The plumber	was fined by	the judge

From these sentences, it is clear that in a passive sentence the direct object NP of the active sentence appears in the position of subject NP (that is, in the NP position dominated by S), and the subject NP of the active sentence appears in the object NP position (the NP position dominated by VP), preceded by the preposition *by* (thus giving it an oblique grammatical relation).

SURFACE STRUCTURES AND DEEP STRUCTURES

We have seen that speakers understand more about the structure of a sentence than is apparent in the linear sequence of its words; for one thing, they have implicit knowledge of constituent structure. In addition, speakers sometimes understand more elements in a sentence than are actually expressed. For example, knowledge of English syntactic rules is essential to understand the meaning of sentences such as the following:

	1. didn't.
	2. didn't care.
	3. didn't tell Sarah.
Mary won a prize but Alex . . .	4. didn't celebrate with her.
	5. didn't visit Paris to buy a tie.
	6. didn't train tigers.
	7. didn't win a prize.

---

[2] It is debatable whether English has indirect object as a distinct grammatical relation and, if so, whether it occurs in sentences like *The witch offered <u>the child</u> a potion* or *The witch offered a potion to <u>the child</u>*. The syntactic properties of *the child* differ in the two sentences (for example, it can be passivized in the first but not in the second), thus demonstrating that they have different grammatical relations. Of course, *the child* has the same *semantic role* in both sentences—namely, recipient, which has traditionally been associated with indirect objects (see Chapter 6 for semantic roles). The point is that semantic and syntactic roles should be distinguished.

Although the list of possible sentences following this pattern is endless, the only legitimate interpretation of 1 is the one represented by 7. Sentences 2 through 6, though well formed, do not represent possible interpretations of 1. Sentence 1 is understood as having the implicit completion "win a prize." How can this fact about our understanding of unexpressed constituents of a sentence be explained?

Earlier we postulated abstract underlying forms of sounds in our discussion of phonology and abstract underlying forms of morphemes in our discussion of words. It will therefore not be surprising to learn that we can accommodate implicit knowledge of sentence structure by positing underlying forms of syntactic structures. For instance, we can represent the meaning of sentence 1 by positing an underlying form something like *Mary won a prize but Alex didn't win a prize.* If we were to assume such an abstract underlying form, certain syntactic processes (or operations) of English would have to be postulated in order to delete the second occurrence of *win a prize* and generate the sentence *Mary won a prize but Alex didn't.* (We call such syntactic processes *transformations,* and we will discuss them shortly.)

Consider the following sentences with an eye to spotting an element in 2 that is not expressed but is nevertheless understood as part of its meaning.

1. Fred wanted Sarah to win.

2. Fred wanted to win.

Given the ordinary interpretation of sentence 2, it would be reasonable to suppose that it has an underlying structure parallel to that of 1, something like the following:

3. Fred wanted Fred to win.

We could represent this sentence by Figure 5-14, in which the subscript $_j$ is an index indicating that *Fred* refers to the same person in both instances. If this structure is taken as a rough approximation of the underlying structure of *Fred wanted to win,* then a syntactic process must be postulated that deletes *Fred* from the embedded clause S_2. Known as equi-NP deletion, this syntactic operation

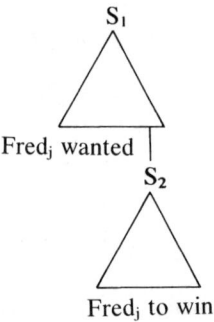

FIGURE 5-14

deletes the subject NP of an embedded clause when that NP is the same as the subject NP of the matrix clause and has the same index. If such a process were not postulated, then *Fred* would not be deleted from the underlying structure and this ill-formed string would result:

Fred_j wanted Fred_j to win.

From these and other examples, we can conclude that the underlying structures of sentences can differ from their surface structures in systematic ways. From the underlying structure of a sentence, the syntactic rules of a language generate surface structures. To capture the facts just examined in sentences like *Fred wanted to win,* we postulate two levels of sentence structure. The level that is represented by the linear string of morphemes and words as uttered or written is called a **surface structure.** Surface structure encompasses both the linear order (which is obvious from inspection) and the hierarchical order of the constituents (which is not expressed explicitly but is understood). The other level of structure is an abstract level underlying the surface structure. Structures at this level are called **deep structures** or **underlying structures.**

From an underlying structure, a surface structure is generated by application of a series of syntactic processes called *transformational rules,* or **transformations,** that change an underlying constituent structure into a surface constituent structure. We can represent the situation schematically as follows:

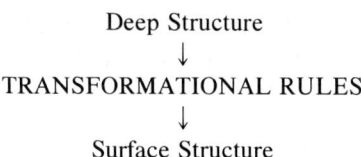

Deep Structure
↓
TRANSFORMATIONAL RULES
↓
Surface Structure

In a widely adopted model of this type, the phrase-structure rules we proposed earlier would actually generate deep structures. Then the syntactic processes—the transformations—would operate on the deep structure generated by the phrase-structure rules to produce a surface structure. It is this surface structure, in turn, that the phonological rules of the language operate upon to produce a pronounceable sentence. The expanded schema would look like this:

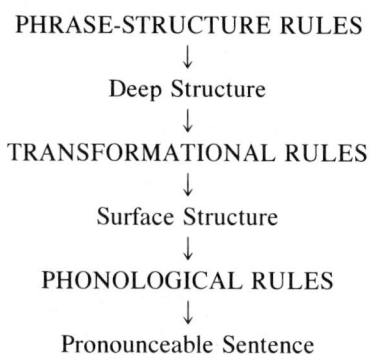

PHRASE-STRUCTURE RULES
↓
Deep Structure
↓
TRANSFORMATIONAL RULES
↓
Surface Structure
↓
PHONOLOGICAL RULES
↓
Pronounceable Sentence

TRANSFORMATIONS

We have already seen several transformational rules of English including passivization and equi-NP deletion. Now we will analyze several other transformational rules that have been proposed by researchers.

Subject-Auxiliary Inversion and WH-Movement Transformations

In this section we explore two movement transformations, both of which are involved in forming questions; we will then note the implications of these transformations for the underlying structure of every English sentence.

Yes/No Questions   Two principal kinds of questions exist in English: yes/no questions and information questions. In the pairs of statements and questions below, the questions are yes/no questions because they can be answered with a simple *yes* or *no* reply.

1. Sue will earn a fair wage.
    Will Sue earn a fair wage?

2. John was winning the race when he stumbled.
    Was John winning the race when he stumbled?

If you compare the form of the statement with the form of the question above, you will see that the formation of a yes/no question requires inverting the subject NP with the auxiliary verb. (Verbs such as *will* in 1 above and *was* in 2—as well as *did* and *does* in 3 and 4 below—are called auxiliary verbs, as distinguished from main verbs like *earn* and *winning;* besides being those that can be inverted with the subject NP in questions, **auxiliary verbs** are those that carry the negative element in contractions such as *can't, shouldn't,* and *wasn't.*) In fact, a yes/no question *must* express an auxiliary verb, even when the corresponding statement form does not, as 3 and 4 show.

3. Alvin studied alchemy in college.
    Did Alvin study alchemy in college?

4. Inflation always hurts the poor.
    Does inflation always hurt the poor?

Sentence pairs like these provide an argument for positing an auxiliary verb in the underlying structure of a sentence, even though not every sentence expresses an auxiliary in the surface form. Notice, however, that in English an auxiliary verb must appear in the surface structure of a negative sentence *(Alvin didn't study alchemy)* and typically appears in the surface structure to express emphasis *(But she does exercise everyday!)* and certain other semantic information such as time reference *(She will win)* and aspect *(They are walking home),* as well as for questions. (Aspect and temporal reference are discussed in Chapter 6).

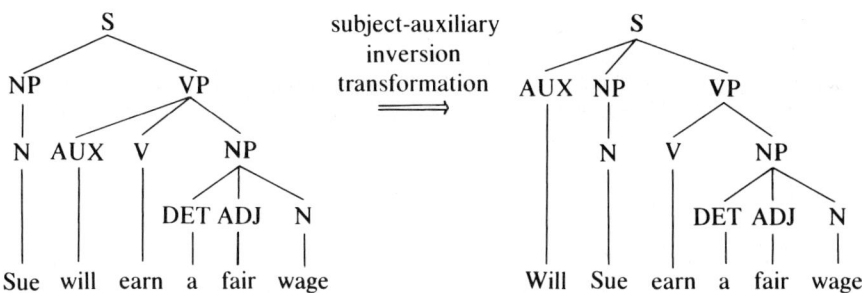

FIGURE 5-15

Given that an auxiliary verb often appears in the surface structure (and for additional reasons that we cannot discuss here), an auxiliary constituent is postulated in the underlying structure of sentences. Abbreviated AUX, the auxiliary is generated by a phrase-structure rule. Instead of the earlier rule that expanded S as NP VP, the following rule is used:

$$S \longrightarrow NP \quad AUX \quad VP$$

We can represent the structure generated by this rule in a tree diagram.

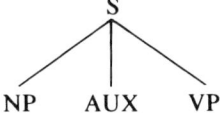

We thus represent the underlying form of the sentences of 1 on page 142 as in the tree on the left in Figure 5-15. The tree on the right is the constituent structure that results from application of the subject-auxiliary inversion transformation, which inverts the subject NP and the AUX.

Information Questions Information questions require more than a simple yes-or-no reply. Because information questions contain a WH-word *(who, why, when, where, which, what, or how)*, they are sometimes called WH-questions. In an information question, the information that is sought—the questioned constituent— is represented by a WH-word.

Information questions occur in two forms. One is called an echo question because it "echoes" the form of a statement, as in the following examples:

1. (He is boiling horsefeathers.)
    He is boiling *what?*

2. (She was looking for Sigmund Freud today.)
    She was looking for *who* today?[3]

---

[3] In the example sentences in the remainder of this chapter, we use what seem to be the most common forms of *who* and *whom* in the context of a particular sentence; in so doing, we sometimes ignore the distinction drawn between these forms in traditional grammar and in much careful writing and speaking.

Echo questions are used when you have failed to hear something completely or cannot believe what you have heard, and their form is identical to that of the statement, except that a WH-word occurs in place of the questioned constituent.

More commonly, information questions take the form illustrated below:

1. What is he boiling ——?

2. Who was she looking for ——today?

If you compare these ordinary information questions with echo questions, you can see that two movements have occurred.

1. The WH-word (the questioned constituent) is moved to the front of its clause.

2. The auxiliary constituent is moved to the position preceding the subject NP constituent.

Notice that ordinary information questions leave a "gap" in the structure at the place vacated by the fronted WH-word (as indicated by the dash ——). This isn't true of echo questions, of course, because the WH-word remains fixed in its underlying position.

Relative Clause Transformation

A **relative clause** is formed when one clause is embedded into an NP of another clause to produce structures like the following (relative clauses are underlined):

1. The board dismissed [the teacher <u>who flunked me</u>].

2. [The jewels <u>that he bought</u>] were fakes.

3. This is [the officer <u>that I talked to last night</u>].

4. Sally saw a new film by [the French director <u>that Tom raves about</u>].

5. Sally saw a new film by [the French director <u>Tom raves about</u>].

When two clauses share a pair of coreferential NPs, a relative clause is formed by embedding one clause into the other, as in this illustration, in which identical indexes indicate coreferential NPs:

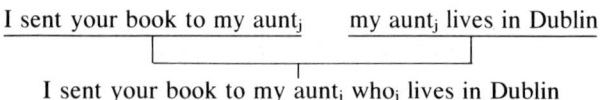

I sent your book to my aunt$_j$ my aunt$_j$ lives in Dublin

I sent your book to my aunt$_j$ who$_j$ lives in Dublin

English relative clauses contain (and are usually introduced by) a relative pronoun, such as *who* (or *whom* or *whose*), *which,* or *that.* As in 5 above, the pronoun can

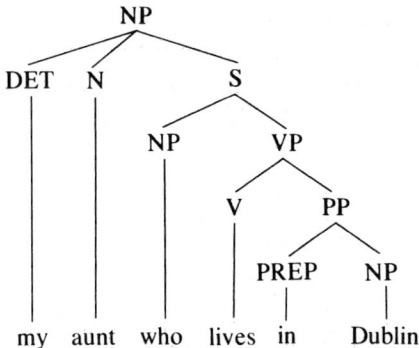

FIGURE 5-16

be omitted in certain structures. Relative clauses modify nouns, and the noun that the relative clause modifies is called the *head noun*. In English, the head noun is repeated in the embedded clause, where it is "relativized." A relative clause is part of the same noun phrase as its head noun. The structure of the resulting noun phrase can be represented as in Figure 5-16, in which the head noun *aunt* is labeled N. Notice that in this instance the relativized NP functions as the subject of its clause (NP immediately dominated by S). In other clauses, the relativized NP may be another grammatical relation like direct object, as in this illustration:

The jewels that he bought were fakes.

Here the relative clause *that he bought* derives from the underlying clause *he bought the jewels*.

A relativized NP can also be an oblique as in 1 or a possessor as in 2:

1. This is the officer whom I told you about.
2. This is the officer whose car was vandalized.

Thus in English a relativized NP can have the following grammatical relations within its clause: subject, direct object, oblique, or possessor.

COMP Node Now let's analyze the syntactic processes associated with relative clause formation in English. Examine the following sentences, noting the "gap" in the structure (indicated by the dash ——):

1. There's the teacher that I warned you about ——.
2. David Lodge wrote the books which I read ——.
3. The fans who —— braved the weather paid a price.

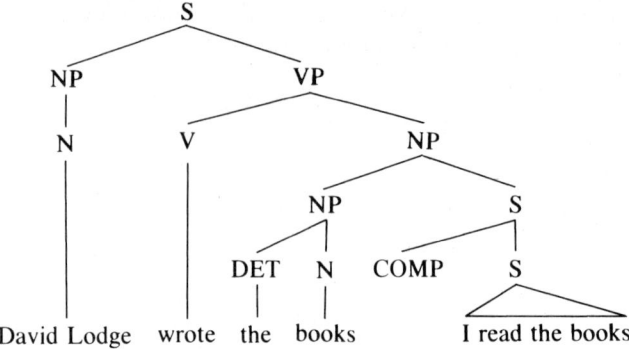

FIGURE 5-17

We can represent the underlying constituent structure of these sentences in a tree diagram, as Figure 5-17 illustrates for sentence 2.

In order to produce the relative clause structure given in 2, the relativized NP *the books* is pronominalized and moved to the front of its clause by the WH-movement transformation that we described for information questions. In Figure 5-17 there is a node labeled COMP (for 'complementizer'), which we have not previously identified. It is possible to discuss the WH-movement transformation for relative clauses without utilizing the COMP node (as we did for information questions), but there is evidence that such a node exists and serves as magnet or landing site for the movement of WH-constituents. Thus the COMP node attracts WH-constituents, such as *that, which, who* (illustrated above), and other relative pronouns, as well as the WH-constituents of information questions.

Since transformations change one constituent structure into another, we can represent the output of the WH-movement transformation applied to Figure 5-17 by the tree given in Figure 5-18. Thus, by the WH-movement transformation, a WH-constituent is extracted from S and attached to the COMP node. We have examined this transformation with respect to relative clauses, but the same trans-

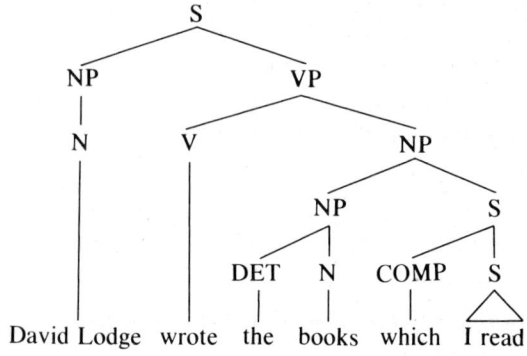

FIGURE 5-18

formation could move any WH-constituent to the COMP node, including question words in the formation of information questions.

TYPES OF TRANSFORMATIONS

While it is not known for certain how many types of syntactic processes exist in human languages, new models of grammar reflect evidence that there may be fewer types of transformation than previously thought. In fact, transformations are probably of a considerably more general nature than our somewhat detailed descriptions of specific transformations might suggest. Movement rules are extremely common in the languages of the world, and in one theoretical model of syntax, all transformations are forms of movement rules.

Constraints on Transformations

One question that continues to challenge grammarians is whether and to what extent limitations exist on the kinds of transformational rules that operate in human language. We can illustrate the kinds of constraints that may exist by analyzing constraints on movement transformations.

Coordinate NP Constraint In each of the two sets of sentences below, the first example is an echo question, the second the corresponding information question, the third an echo question in which the WH-word is contained within a coordinate noun phrase of the type "NP and NP," and the fourth the ill-formed structure that would result if the WH-word were moved to the front of its clause. It is clear from examples 1-d and 2-d that WH-movement cannot occur when the WH-word is part of a coordinate NP structure.

1. a. John invited *who?* (echo)
   b. Who did John invite ——? (WH)

   c. John invited Grendel and *who?* (echo)
   d. *Who did John invite Grendel and ——? (WH)

2. a. The wizard is mixing *what?* (echo)
   b. What is the wizard mixing ——? (WH)

   c. The wizard is mixing *what* and fingernails? (echo)
   d. *What is the wizard mixing —— and fingernails? (WH)

These sentences illustrate that the WH-movement transformation is blocked from moving a WH-constituent out of a coordinate noun phrase. This constraint on movement is called the *coordinate NP constraint*.

Relative Clause Constraint Extraction of WH-words from relative clauses is also blocked in English, as the sentences below indicate. As above, the first sentence in each set is an echo question, in which the WH-word is grammatical. But a

WH-word extracted from its relative clause produces an ungrammatical sentence. The relative clauses are bracketed.

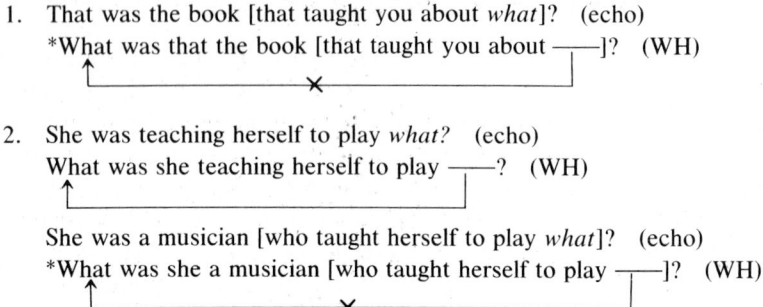

1. That was the book [that taught you about *what*]?   (echo)
    *What was that the book [that taught you about ——]?   (WH)

2. She was teaching herself to play *what?*   (echo)
    What was she teaching herself to play ——?   (WH)

    She was a musician [who taught herself to play *what*]?   (echo)
    *What was she a musician [who taught herself to play ——]?   (WH)

Notice in these sentences that the echo questions, besides being grammatical, make sense in every case; so the difficulty with the ill-formed sentences is not a semantic difficulty but a purely syntactic one: Such movements are blocked from occurring. The ill-formed sentences are prohibited by syntactic rules.

Besides the constraints on WH-movement out of coordinate NPs and relative clauses, there are other constraints on transformations, such as movement out of adverbial clauses *(Pat would buy one whenever who visited?)* and movement out of indirect questions *(Pat would ask why you bought what?)*.

Two important observations may be made about such constraints. The first is that the structures that are blocked by the constraints are not semantically aberrant, as is demonstrated by the straightforward interpretation of the echo questions. Second, the ungrammatical sentences are not found among the utterances of children or second-language learners. This suggests, then, that there is no tendency among first- or second-language learners to overgeneralize movement rules in a way that would violate the constraints. Whereas children do overgeneralize morphological rules *(tooth/tooths; go/goed)*, the constraints that we have noted in the application of movement rules do not get violated by what might seem a natural overgeneralization.

Naturally, to the extent that such general constraints are automatically built into the language faculty, perhaps from birth, the detailed figuring out of how particular transformations operate and what constraints exist becomes unnecessary for a child. Clearly, the more such constraints are built into the operation of transformations, the easier it would be for a child to acquire its language, because it would have less to figure out about the operation of syntactic rules. It would be a formidable task to learn when extraction is possible and when not; but if certain types of extraction are impossible (because the language faculty simply can't handle them, let's say), the conditions blocking those extractions would not have to be learned by a child. That, of course, would simplify the child's task enormously and begin to explain why children are so extraordinarily adept at language acquisition. The exact nature of such constraints and the circumstances in which some languages allow extraction from certain structures remains to be further explored.

SUMMARY

Languages have referring expressions and predication expressions. In syntactic terms, a referring expression is called NP (for noun phrase) and a predication expression VP (for verb phrase). Sentences consist of one or more clauses. An English clause consists of a verb with the necessary set of NP arguments. Simple sentences have a single clause. A clause can be coordinated with another clause to form a coordinate sentence or can be embedded within another clause to form a complex sentence. The rules that govern the formation of clauses and the joining of clauses into coordinate and complex sentences constitute the syntax of a language (and the study of well-formed strings of a language is called syntax as well). Speakers of a language can generate an unlimited number of sentences from relatively few rules for combining words and morphemes. The syntactic rules of a language are of two types. Phrase-structure rules generate underlying constituent structures, which are then altered by transformations that change one constituent structure into another constituent structure until a surface structure is generated.

Underlying constituent structures are posited to capture the striking regularity of certain relationships between sentences. Underlying structures are constructs that help explain certain elements of meaning and certain syntactic and semantic relationships that we understand between sentences. In order to explain how speakers relate two structures to one another (such as *Martha doesn't believe in poltergeists* and *Doesn't Martha believe in poltergeists?*), linguists posit a rule of English that transforms the structure underlying the first sentence into the structure underlying the second sentence. A rule that changes a constituent structure into another constituent structure is called a transformation.

Increasingly, it appears that the most important and most general transformations are movement transformations such as WH-movement and subject-auxiliary inversion. The former applies in the formation of relative clauses, and both apply in the formation of information questions. Certain constraints on transformations limit the ways in which they can operate. In limiting the range of possible grammars of human languages, such constraints may facilitate the process of language acquisition in children.

EXERCISES

1. a. List as many examples of these constituents as you can identify in sentences (1) and (2) below: NP, PP, VP.
   b. List as many examples of these lexical categories as you can identify in sentences (1) and (2) below: N, ADJ, PREP, V.

   (1) A Guns N' Roses concert at an arena near St. Louis ended in disaster after some 2500 fans staged a full-fledged riot.

   (2) The trouble started when Axl Rose asked venue security to confiscate a camera he saw near the front of the stage.

2. For each of the expansions of VP given on page 136, provide an illustrative English example; thus, for V PP, you might give (Sarah) *swims in the pond.*

3. Draw a labeled tree diagram for each of the English phrases given below.

    (1) ancient inscriptions

    (2) in the dark night

    (3) concocted a potion

    (4) bought the book that the teacher recommended

    (5) monstrous members of the reptile kingdom

4. a. Provide a tree diagram for each of the English sentences given below.
    b. For each of the underlined groups of words, determine whether it is a constituent, and, if it is, give its name.

    (1) Witches <u>frighten him</u>.

    (2) The skies deluged the earth <u>with water</u>.

    (3) <u>A ghost has the spirit</u> of a dead person.

    (4) <u>Do ghosts exist in the</u> physical world?

    (5) <u>Does she</u> believe that ghosts exist?

    (6) The teacher <u>that I described to you</u> won the race.

5. Consider the following sentences. What is the difference in the relationship between Harry and the verb *see* in (1) and (2)? Draw tree diagrams of the underlying structure of the two sentences that will reveal the difference in the structures.

    (1) John advised Harry to see the doctor.

    (2) John promised Harry to see the doctor.

6. Examine the tree diagram for this Fijian sentence:

    ea-biuta   na ŋone vakaloloma na tamata ðaa e   na basi
    Past-abandon the child poor   the man   bad on the bus
    'The bad man abandoned the poor child on the bus.'

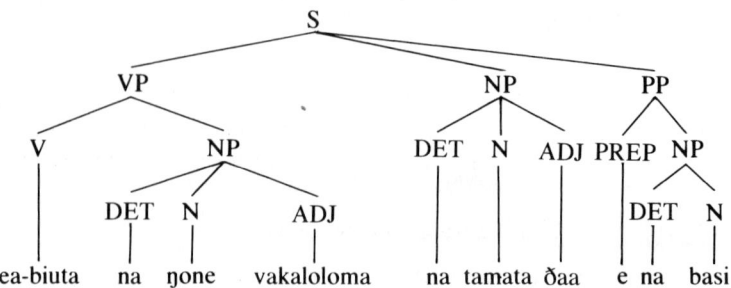

a. Give the phrase-structure rules that will generate this constituent-structure tree.
b. Notice that the order of certain constituents in the Fijian sentence differs from that of English. What are the major differences between Fijian and English with respect to constituent order?
c. On the basis of the tree structure, determine which of the following sequences of words are constituents and which are not; give the name of each constituent.

biuta na	na basi
vakaloloma na tamata	e na basi
na tamata ðaa	na tamata ðaa e na basi
ea-biuta	ea-biuta na ŋone vakaloloma
e	ŋone
	na ŋone vakaloloma na tamata ðaa

7. English has a movement transformation called *dative movement* that derives sentence (2) from the structure underlying sentence (1):

(1) I sent a letter to Hilda.

(2) I sent <u>Hilda</u> a letter.

The following also exemplify sentences with dative movement:

He told <u>his brother</u> a tall tale.

Harold won't give <u>me</u> Hilda's new phone number.

I'm taking <u>my cousin</u> a new pair of pajamas.

a. Give the three basic sentences that correspond to the three derived sentences.
b. Dative movement applies to prepositional phrases that begin with the preposition to and cannot apply to prepositional phrases that begin with most other prepositions.

*I will finish you the homework. (*from* I will finish the homework with you.)

*My neighbor heard the radio the news. (*from* My neighbor heard the news on the radio.)

But dative movement does not apply to *all* phrases that begin with the preposition *to*. The sentences in (1) below cannot undergo dative movement, as witnessed by the ungrammaticality of the corresponding sentences in (2).

(1) He's driving a truck to New Orleans.

He'll take his complaint to the main office.

(2)   *He's driving New Orleans a truck.

    *He'll take the main office his complaint.

Describe in detail the dative movement transformation.

c.   Now observe the ungrammatical sentences in (1) below, which are derived through dative movement from the sentences underlying the corresponding basic sentences in (2). How must your description of the transformation be modified so that it does not generate the ungrammatical sentences of (1)?

(1)   *I gave my new neighbor it.

    *I'm taking my little sister them.

    *They will probably send him me.

(2)   I gave it to my new neighbor.

    I'm taking them to my little sister.

    They will probably send me to him.

8.   Although we have ignored the difference between *who* and *whom* in the examples in this chapter, speakers of English who regularly distinguish these two words in relative clauses do so as follows:

(1)   That's the goblin who visits me each year.

(2)   Where is the author whom you were talking about?

(3)   That's the wizard from whom I bought the potion.

(4)   That's the witch whom I stole the bread crumbs from.

(5)   That's the witch who married the wizard.

(6)   Which is the demon to whom he lost his soul?

(7)   That's the ghost of the man whom Grendel slew.

After examining these sentences, formulate a statement that will capture the facts about when speakers of this variety of English use *who* and *whom* in relative clauses. (*Hint:* Examine the grammatical relation of the relative pronoun in its clause.)

9.   English has two types of relative clauses. Type 1, which was described in this chapter, leaves prepositions where they are in the original clause.

This is the man [who I talked *to* —— last night]. (*original clause:* I talked to the man last night)

In Type 2, the preposition moves to the beginning of the clause with the WH-word.

This is the man [*to* whom I talked last night].

Describe the relative-clause transformation that forms Type 2 relative clauses, focusing on how it differs from the transformation that forms Type I relative clauses. Identify which relative pronouns can occur in which type of relative clause, and in which cases the two types differ. Base your discussion on the following data:

This is the man [that left]. (Types 1 and 2).

*This is the man [left]. (Types 1 and 2).

This is the man [that I saw]. (Types 1 and 2)

This is the man [who I saw]. (Types 1 and 2)

This is the man [whom I saw]. (Types 1 and 2)

This is the man [I saw]. (Types 1 and 2)

This is the man [who I gave the book to]. (Type 1)

This is the man [whom I gave the book to]. (Type 1)

This is the man [that I gave the book to]. (Type 1)

This is the man [I gave the book to]. (Type 1)

*This is the man [to who I gave the book]. (Type 2)

This is the man [to whom I gave the book]. (Type 2)

*This is the man [to that I gave the book]. (Type 2)

*This is the man [to I gave the book]. (Type 2)

This is the woman [who Harry left his wife for]. (Type 1)

This is the woman [whom Harry left his wife for]. (Type 1)

This is the woman [that Harry left his wife for]. (Type 1)

This is the woman [Harry left his wife for]. (Type 1)

*This is the woman [for who Harry left his wife]. (Type 2)

This is the woman [for whom Harry left his wife]. (Type 2)

*This is the woman [for that Harry left his wife]. (Type 2)

*This is the woman [for Harry left his wife]. (Type 2)

10. There are two types of relative clauses in English: *restrictive* relative clauses provide essential information about the head noun as in (1); *nonrestrictive* relative clauses provide incidental information about the head noun as in (2). In (1), the hearer must have the information provided in the relative clause in order to understand which potion the speaker is referring to; in (2), this is not the case.

(1) The potion *that I mixed yesterday* is in the pestle.

(2) The potion, *which I mixed yesterday*, is in the pestle.

Compare the following sets of restrictive and nonrestrictive relative clauses, and describe in detail the structural differences between the two types of relative clauses.

The man *who had been standing outside* suddenly dashed away.

The man, *who had been standing outside,* suddenly dashed away.

The detective movie *that I saw yesterday* was terrible.

The detective movie, *which I saw yesterday,* was terrible.

*The detective movie, *that I saw yesterday,* was terrible.

Those books *which I hadn't opened in years* were all dusty.

Those books, *which I hadn't opened in years,* were all dusty.

The jacket *I wore at the reception* cost me $250.

*The jacket, *I wore at the reception,* cost me $250.

SUGGESTIONS FOR FURTHER READING

There have been exciting developments in the study of syntax in the last three decades. The major works in this line of development are Chomsky (1957, 1965, 1981); except for the first, these works require considerable background, though Chomsky (1965) can be grasped with this chapter as background. Chomsky (1981) should probably not be attempted before Radford (1981, 1988), and van Riemsdijk and Williams (1986), but even these may be too advanced for those whose only knowledge of syntax is what is contained in this chapter. These works focus on syntactic theory and syntactic argumentation, neither of which has been stressed here. Lightfoot (1982) is a useful introduction to Chomsky's work.

A more basic and more accessible presentation of syntax than those above can be found in Smith and Wilson (1979) (which covers more than syntax). Newmeyer (1980) provides an account of the development of syntactic theory during the preceding decades. Given the enormous impact of Chomsky on linguistics and other fields, Newmeyer's book is interesting for what it reveals about how Chomsky's ideas were spread. Comrie (1989), a clear and accessible discussion of syntactic universals across a wide range of languages, expresses reservations about the generative-transformational approach to syntax; as a follow-up to the present chapter, Comrie's chapters on "Word Order," "Subject," "Case Marking," and "Relative Clauses" are recommended.

The volumes edited by Shopen (1985) contain a wealth of useful material; volume I, *Clause Structure,* and volume II, *Complex Constructions,* are relevant to this chapter. Probably accessible to most interested readers who have mastered the present chapter are two excellent chapters of volume I: "Parts of Speech Systems" and "Passive in the World's Languages." Volume II contains valuable discussions of "Complex Phrases and Complex Sentences," "Complementation," and "Relative Clauses."

REFERENCES

Chomsky, Noam. 1957. *Syntactic Structures* (The Hague: Mouton).
———. 1965. *Aspects of the Theory of Syntax* (Cambridge, MA: MIT Press).
———. 1981. *Lectures on Government and Binding* (Dordrecht: Foris).

Comrie, Bernard. 1989. *Language Universals and Linguistic Typology: Syntax and Morphology,* 2nd ed. (Chicago: University of Chicago Press).

Lightfoot, David. 1982. *The Language Lottery* (Cambridge, MA: MIT Press).

Newmeyer, Frederick J. 1980. *Linguistic Theory in America: The First Quarter-Century of Transformational Generative Grammar* (New York: Academic).

Radford, Andrew. 1981. *Transformational Syntax: A Student's Guide to Chomsky's Extended Standard Theory* (Cambridge: Cambridge University Press).

———. 1988. *Transformational Grammar: A First Course* (Cambridge: Cambridge University Press).

Shopen, Timothy, ed. 1985. *Language Typology and Syntactic Description* (Cambridge: Cambridge University Press).

Smith, Neil, and Deirdre Wilson. 1979. *Modern Linguistics: The Results of Chomsky's Revolution* (New York: Penguin).

van Riemsdijk, Henk, and Edwin Williams. 1986. *Introduction to the Theory of Grammar* (Cambridge, MA: MIT Press).

6

Semantics: The Study of Meaning in Words and Sentences

INTRODUCTION

Of the various parts of grammar that people may refer to, "semantics" is a more familiar term than phonology, morphology, or syntax. "That's just semantics" is a frequent claim in arguments and debates. Even the proverbial man (and woman) in the street knows that semantics has something to do with meaning. Linguistic **semantics** is the study of the systematic ways in which languages structure meaning, especially in words and sentences.

In defining linguistic semantics (which we refer to as *semantics* from now on), we must invoke the word *meaning*. Just as we have many everyday notions of what semantics is, we use the words *meaning* and *to mean* in different contexts and for different purposes. For example:

1. The word *perplexity means* 'the state of being puzzled.'

2. The word *rash* has two *meanings:* 'impetuous' and 'skin irritation.'

3. In Spanish, *espejo means* 'mirror.'

4. I did not *mean* that he is incompetent, just inefficient.

5. The *meaning* of the cross as a symbol is complex.

6. I *meant* to bring you my paper, but left it at home.

What Is Meaning?

Linguists also attach different interpretations to the word *meaning*. Because the goal of linguistics is to explain precisely how languages are structured and used, it is important to distinguish among the different ways of interpreting the word *meaning*.

A few examples will illustrate why we need to develop a precise way of talking about meaning. Consider these sentences:

1. I went to the store this morning.

2. All dogs are animals.

The sentences make sense—that is, have meaning—for quite different reasons. Whether sentence 1 is true depends on whether or not the speaker is in fact telling the truth; nothing about the words of the sentence makes the sentence inherently true. Sentence 2, in contrast, is true because we know the word *dogs* describes entities that are also described by the word *animals*. The truth of 2 does not depend on whether or not the speaker is telling the truth; it has solely to do with the meanings of the words *dogs* and *animals*.

Now compare the following pairs of sentences:

3. You are too young to drink.
   You are not old enough to drink.

4. Harold spent several years in northern Tibet.
   Harold was once in northern Tibet.

The sentences of 3 basically "say the same thing" in that the first describes exactly what the second describes—no more, no less. We say that they are *synonymous* sentences, or that they paraphrase each other. In 4, the first sentence *implies* the second but not vice versa. If indeed Harold spent several years in northern Tibet, then he must have set foot in that area of the world at some stage in his life; but if he was once in northern Tibet, it is not necessarily the case that he spent several years there.

Next, consider the following sentences:

5. The unmarried woman is married to a bachelor.

6. My toothbrush is pregnant.

Sentences 5 and 6 are well formed syntactically, but there is something amiss with their semantics. The meanings of the words that make up sentence 5 contradict each other: an unmarried woman cannot be married, and certainly not to a bachelor. Sentence 5 thus presents a *contradiction*. Sentence 6 is different: given that toothbrushes are not capable of being pregnant, its meaning is *anomalous*. To diagnose precisely what is wrong with these sentences, we need to distinguish between contradictory and anomalous sentences.

Finally, examine sentences 7 and 8:

7. I saw her duck.

8. She ate the pie.

Sentence 7 may be interpreted in two ways: *duck* may be a verb referring to the act of bending over quickly (while walking through a low doorway, for example), or it may be a noun referring to a domesticated bird. These two word meanings give the sentence distinct meanings. Because there are two possible readings for 7, it is said to be **ambiguous.** While sentence 8 is not ambiguous, taken out of context there is an imprecise quality to it. While we know that the subject is a female, we cannot know who *she* refers to, or what particular pie was eaten, although the structure of the phrase *the pie* indicates that the speaker has a particular one in mind. Taken out of context, 8 is thus *vague* in that certain details are left unspecified, but it is not ambiguous.

These observations illustrate that meaning is a multifaceted notion. A sentence may be meaningful and true because it states a fact about the world or because the speaker is telling the truth. Two sentences may be related to each other because they mean exactly the same thing or because one implies the other. Finally, when we feel that there is something wrong with the meaning of a sentence, it may be because the sentence is contradictory, anomalous, ambiguous, or merely vague. One purpose of semantics is to distinguish among these different ways in which language "means."

REFERENTIAL, SOCIAL, AND AFFECTIVE MEANING

For our purposes we can distinguish three types of meaning. **Referential meaning** is the object, notion, or state of affairs described by a word or sentence. **Social meaning** is the level of meaning that we rely on when we identify certain social characteristics of speakers and situations from the character of the language used. **Affective meaning** is the emotional connotation that is attached to words and utterances.

Referential Meaning

One way of defining meaning is to say that the meaning of a word or sentence is the person, object, abstract notion, state, or event to which the word or sentence makes reference. The meaning of *John Smith,* for example, is the person who goes by that name. The phrase *Scott's dog* refers to the particular domesticated canine that belongs to Scott. That particular animal can be said to be the meaning of the linguistic expression *Scott's dog*. This type of meaning is *referential* meaning. The canine described by the expression *Scott's dog* is the **referent** of the referring expression *Scott's dog*. Speakers of English know what the referents of referring expressions like *father, book,* and *truth* are, although they may be hard put to explain exactly what these referents look like and may have slightly different notions of what these referents are, particularly in the case of abstract referring expressions like *truth*.

Words, of course, are not the only linguistic units to carry referential meaning. Sentences also have meaning because, like words and phrases, they *refer* to actions, states, and events in the world around us. *Lou is resting on the sofa* refers to the fact that a person known as Lou is currently lying down (or sitting) on an elongated piece of furniture generally meant to be sat upon. The referent of the sentence *Lou is resting on the sofa* is thus the action (or, in this case, state of being) of Lou on the piece of furniture in question.

Social Meaning

Referential meaning is not the only type of meaning that language users communicate to each other. Consider the following sentences.

1. Then I says to him he can't do nothin' right.

2. Is it a doctor in here?

3. Y'all gonna visit over the holiday?

4. I adore your lavender shawl; it's absolutely gorgeous!

5. Great chow!

In addition to representing actions, states, and mental processes, these sentences convey information about the identity of the person who has uttered them. In 1, the use of the verb *says* with the first person singular pronoun reveals something about the speaker's social class. In 2, the form *it* where some other varieties use *there* indicates a speaker of an ethnically marked variety of English. In 3, the pronoun *y'all* identifies a particular regional dialect of American English. The choice of words in 4 suggests a female speaker; it is thus marked with respect to gender. Finally, the choice of words in 5 indicates that the comment was made in an informal context. Social class, ethnicity, regional origin, gender, and context are all *social* factors. In addition to referential meaning, therefore, every utterance also conveys *social* meaning, not only in the sentence as a whole but in word choice (*y'all* and *chow*) and pronunciation (*gonna* or *nothin'*).

Affective Meaning

Besides referential and social meaning, there is a third kind of meaning. Compare the following examples.

1. Harold, who always boasts about his two doctorates, lectured me the entire evening on Warhol's art.

2. Harold, who has two doctorates, gave me a fascinating overview of Warhol's art last night.

These two sentences can be used to describe exactly the same event: They have similar referential meaning. At another level, however, the information they convey is different. Sentence 1 gives the impression that the speaker considers Harold a pretentious bore. Sentence 2, in contrast, indicates that the speaker finds Harold interesting. The "stance" of the utterances is thus quite different.

Word choice is not the only means of communicating feelings and attitudes toward utterances and contexts. A striking contrast is provided by sentences that differ only in terms of stress or intonation. The following string of words can be interpreted in several ways, depending on intonation.

Harold is really smart.

The sentence can be uttered in a matter-of-fact way, without emphasizing any word in particular, in which case it will be interpreted literally as a remark acknowledging Harold's intelligence. But if the words *really* and *smart* are stressed in an exaggerated manner, the sentence may be interpreted sarcastically to mean exactly the opposite. Intonation (often accompanied by appropriate facial expressions) can be used as a device to communicate attitudes and feelings, and it can override the literal meaning of a sentence.

Consider a final example. Suppose that John Smith, happily married to Mary Smith, addresses his wife as follows:

Mary Smith, how many times have I asked you not to flip through the TV channels?

There would be reason to look beyond the words for the "meaning" of this unusual form of address. Mr. Smith may address his wife as *Mary Smith* to show his exasperation, as in this example. What he conveys by choosing to address her as *Mary Smith* instead of the usual *Mary* is frustration and annoyance. His choice of name thus "means" that he is exasperated. Contrast the tone of that sentence with a similar one in which John Smith addresses Mary Smith as *dear*.

The level of meaning that conveys the language user's feelings, attitudes, and opinions about a particular piece of information or about the ongoing context is called *affective* meaning. Affective meaning is not an exclusive property of sentences: Words like *Alas!* and *Hurray!* obviously have affective meaning, and so can words like *funny, sweet,* and *obnoxious*. Even the most common words—like *father, democracy,* and *old*—can evoke particular emotions and feelings in us. The difference between synonymous or near-synonymous pairs of words like *vagrant* and *homeless* is essentially a difference at the affective level; in this particular pair, the first word carries a rather negative affective meaning, while the second is neutral or positive. Little is known yet about how affective meaning works, but it is of great importance to all verbal communication.

From our discussion so far, you can see that meaning is not a simple notion, but a complex combination of several aspects: referential meaning (the real-world object or concept described by language); social meaning (the information about the social nature of the language user or of the context of utterance); and affective meaning (what the language user feels about the content or about the ongoing context). The referential meaning of a word or sentence is frequently called its *denotation*, in contrast to the *connotation*, which includes both its social and affective meaning.

This chapter focuses primarily on referential meaning, the traditional domain of semantics, but we occasionally refer to the three-way distinction. Social meaning will be investigated in detail in Chapters 12 and 13.

WORD MEANING, SENTENCE MEANING, AND UTTERANCE MEANING

Meaning of Words and Sentences

We have talked about words and sentences as the two units of language that carry meaning. **Content words**—principally nouns, verbs, adjectives, and adverbs—have meaning in that they refer to objects, events, and abstract concepts; are marked as being characteristic of particular social, ethnic, and regional dialects and of particular contexts; and convey information about the feelings and attitudes of language users. **Function words,** such as prepositions and determiners, also carry meaning, though in a different way from content words, as you will see later in this chapter. Like individual words, sentences also have social and affective connotations. The study of word meaning, however, differs from the study of sentence meaning because the units are different in kind.

In order to understand the meaning of a sentence, we must rely on the meaning of individual words that make it up. How we accomplish the task of retrieving sentence meaning from word meaning is a complex question. One obvious hypothesis is that the meaning of a sentence is simply the sum of the meanings of its words. To see that this is *not* the case, consider the following sentences, in which the individual words (and therefore their *sum* meanings) are the same.

The hunter bit the lion.

The lion bit the hunter.

Obviously, the sentences refer to different events and hence have distinct referential meanings. This is conveyed by the fact that the words of the sentences are ordered differently. In English, the order in which words are arranged in a sentence can be crucial to meaning (see Chapter 5). Thus we cannot simply say that in order to retrieve the meaning of a sentence, all we need to do is add up the meanings of its components. What we must take into consideration, in addition to the meaning of individual words, is the *semantic role* assigned to each word. By semantic role we mean such things as *who* did *what* to *whom*, with *whom*, and for *whom*. In other words, the semantic role of a word is the role that its referent plays in the action or state of being described by the sentence. Sentence semantics is concerned with semantic roles and with the relationship between words within a sentence.

Scope of Word Meaning   While it is important to distinguish between word meaning and sentence meaning, the two interact on many levels, as the following sentence indicates.

He may leave tomorrow if he finishes his term paper.

In this sentence, the words *may, tomorrow,* and *if* have meanings as individual function words: *may* denotes permission or possibility; *tomorrow* indicates a future time unit that begins the following midnight; and *if* indicates a condition. But the impact of these words goes beyond the phrases in which they occur and affects the meaning of the entire sentence. Indeed, if we replace *may* with *will,* the sentence takes on a completely different meaning.

He will leave tomorrow if he finishes his term paper.

The sentence with *may* denotes permission or possibility, while the sentence with *will* is simply the description of a future event. Thus *may* affects the meaning of the entire sentence.

The *scope* of the meaning of the function word *may* is the entire sentence. This is also true of *tomorrow* and of *if.* Many function words (and grammatical morphemes, for that matter) have sentence scope. What this example illustrates is that word meaning and sentence meaning are intimately related.

Meaning of Utterances

In addition to words and sentences, there is a third unit that also carries meaning, though we may not notice it as clearly because we take it for granted in day-to-day interactions. Consider this utterance:

I now pronounce you husband and wife.

This sentence may be uttered in at least two different sets of circumstances: (1) by a pastor presiding at a ceremony to a young couple getting married in the presence of their assembled families; or (2) by an actor dressed as a pastor to two actors before a congregation of Hollywood extras assembled in the same church by a director giving instructions for the filming of a soap opera. In the first instance, *I now pronounce you husband and wife* will effect a marriage between the couple intending to get married. But that same utterance will have no effect on the marital status of any party on the movie location. Thus the circumstances of utterance create different meanings, although the referential meaning of the sentence remains unchanged. It is therefore necessary to know the circumstances of utterance in order to understand the effect or force of the utterance. We say that the sentence uttered in the wedding context and the sentence uttered in the film context have the same referential meaning but are different **utterances,** each with its own *utterance meaning.*

The difference between sentence meaning and utterance meaning can be further illustrated by the question *Can you shut the window?* There are at least two ways in which the addressee might react to this question. One possible response would be to say *Yes* (meaning 'Yes, I am physically capable of shutting the window') and to do nothing about it. This is the "smart-aleck" interpretation; it is of course not the way such a question is intended in most cases. Another way in which the addressee might react would be to get up and shut the window. Obviously, these interpretations of the same question are different: The smart-aleck interpretation treats the question as a request for information; the second interpretation treats it as a request for action. To describe the difference between these interpretations, we say that they are distinct utterances.

Sentence semantics is not concerned with utterance meaning. (Utterances are the subject of investigation of another branch of linguistics called *pragmatics,* which is the topic of Chapters 7 and 11.) One of the premises of sentence semantics is that sentences must be divorced from the context in which they are uttered. In other words, sentences and utterances must be distinguished. To experienced language users, this stance may appear strange and counterintuitive, since so much *meaning* depends on context. The point is not to discard context as unimportant. Rather, it is to recognize that, in a fundamental sense, sentence meaning is independent of context, while utterance meaning depends crucially on the circumstances of the utterance. **Semantics** is the branch of linguistics that examines word meaning and sentence meaning while generally ignoring context; pragmatics, in contrast, pays less attention to the relationship of word meaning to sentence meaning and more attention to the relationship of an utterance to its context.

LEXICAL SEMANTICS

The *lexicon* can be viewed as a compendium of all the words of a language. Words are sometimes called **lexical items,** or *lexemes* (the *-eme* ending as in *phoneme* and *morpheme*). The branch of semantics that deals with word meaning is called **lexical semantics.**

Lexical semantics is concerned with relationships among word meanings. What, for example, is the relationship between the words *man* and *woman* on the one hand and *human being* on the other hand? How are the adjectives *large* and *small* in the same relationship to each other as the pair *dark* and *light?* What is the difference between the meaning of words like *always* and *never* and the meaning of words like *often* and *seldom?* What do language users actually mean when they say that a dog is "a type of" mammal? Lexical semantics is concerned with such questions: It is the study of how the lexicon is organized and of how the meanings of lexical items are interrelated. The principal goal of lexical semantics is to build a model for the structure of the lexicon by categorizing the types of relationships between words.

Lexical Fields

Consider the following sets of words:

1. cup, mug, wineglass, tumbler, plastic cup, goblet

2. hammer, cloud, tractor, eyeglasses, leaf, justice

The words of set 1 all refer to concepts that can be described as 'vessels from which one drinks,' while the words of set 2 denote concepts that have nothing in common with each other. The words of set 1 constitute a **lexical field**—a set of words with identifiable semantic affinities. The following set of words is also a lexical field, all of whose words refer to emotional states.

angry, sad, happy, exuberant, depressed, afraid

Thus we see that words can be classified into sets according to their meaning.

In a lexical field, not all lexical items necessarily have the same status. Consider the following sets, which together form the lexical field of color terms (of course there are other terms in the same field).

1. blue, red, yellow, green, black, purple

2. indigo, saffron, royal blue, aquamarine, bisque

The colors referred to by the words of set 1 are more "usual" than those described in set 2. They are said to be less **marked** than those of set 2; therefore the words in set 1 are less marked members of the lexical field than the words in set 2. The less marked members of a lexical field will usually be easier to learn and remember than more marked members; children learn the term *blue* before they learn the terms *indigo, royal blue,* or *aquamarine.* Typically, a less marked word consists of only one morpheme, in contrast to more marked words (contrast *blue* and *royal blue*). The less marked member of a lexical field cannot be described by using the name of another member of the same field, while more marked members can be thus described (indigo is a kind of blue). Less marked terms also tend to be used more frequently than more marked terms; *blue,* for example, occurs considerably more frequently in conversation and writing than either *indigo* or *aquamarine.* (One survey of a million words of written English found 126 examples of *blue,* one of *indigo,* and none of *aquamarine.*) Less marked terms also are often broader in meaning than more marked terms; *blue* describes a broader range of colors than *indigo* or *aquamarine.* Finally, less marked words are not the result of the metaphorical usage of the name of another object or concept, whereas more marked words often are (for example, saffron is the color of a spice that lent its name to the color).

Using our definitions of lexical field and markedness, we now turn to the identification of types of relationships between words. We will see how the words of a lexical field can have different types of relationships to each other and to other words in the lexicon, and we will classify these relationships.

Hyponymy

Consider again this set of unmarked color terms: *blue, red, yellow, green, black, purple.* Any speaker of English can identify these words as referring to different colors. The description that these terms have in common is that they refer to colors. The terms *blue, red, yellow, green, black,* and *purple* are called hyponyms of the term *color.* A **hyponym** is a term whose referent is totally included in the referent of another term (the prefix *hypo-* in *hyponym* means 'below'). Blue is a color; red is a color; and so forth. The relationship may be illustrated by the following diagram, in which the lower terms are the hyponyms. (The higher term—in this case, *color*—is sometimes called the *hypernym.*)

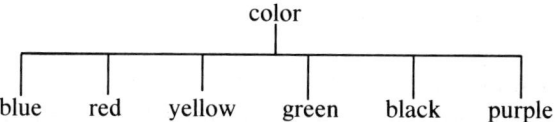

Another example is the term *mammal,* whose referent includes the referents of many other terms.

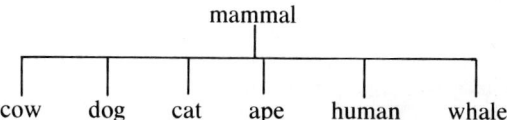

The relationship between each of the "lower" terms and the "higher" term is called *hyponymy.*

Hyponymy is not restricted to objects like mammals and abstract concepts like color—or even to nouns, for that matter. Hyponymy can be identified in many other areas of the lexicon. The verb *cook,* for example, has many hyponyms.

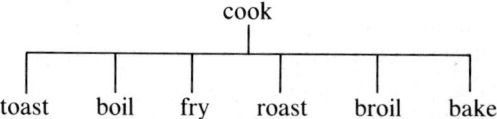

Not every set of hyponyms has a hypernym, that is, a term that includes them all. Consider the terms *uncle* and *aunt;* they obviously form a lexical field because we can easily identify a property that their referents share. Yet in English we do not have a term that refers specifically to both uncles and aunts (that is, to 'siblings of parents and their spouses').

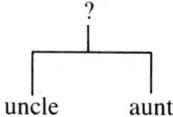

Other languages, in contrast, have a hypernym for the equivalent field. In Spanish, the plural term *tios* can include both aunts and uncles, and the Spanish equivalent of the terms *uncle* and *aunt* are its hyponyms.

While hyponymy is found in all languages, which concepts will have words in hyponymic relationships varies from one language to the next. In Tuvaluan (a

Polynesian language), the higher term *ika* (roughly translated as 'fish') has as hyponyms not only all terms that refer to the animals that English speakers would recognize as fish but also terms for whales and dolphins (which speakers of English recognize as mammals) and for sea turtles (which are reptiles). Of course, we are dealing with folk classifications here, not scientific classifications.

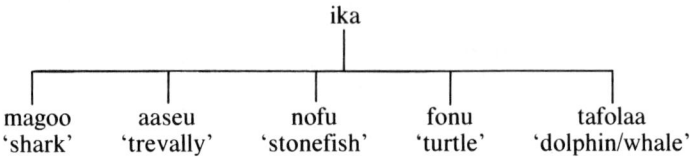

Thus there is variability across languages as to the exact nature of particular hyponymic relationships.

In a lexical field, hyponymy often exists at more than one level. A term may at the same time have a hyponym and a hypernym, as *blue* does in Figure 6-1. Because they refer to different "types" or "shades" of blue, the terms *turquoise, aquamarine,* and *royal blue* are hyponyms of *blue*. The term *blue* in turn is, along with many other color terms, a hyponym of the term *color*. We thus obtain a hierarchy of terms related to each other through hyponymic relationships. Similar hierarchies can be established for many lexical fields almost without limit. In the "cooking" field, *fry* has hyponyms in the terms *stir-fry, saute,* and *deep-fry* and is itself a hyponym of *cook*. The "lower" we get in a hierarchy of hyponyms, the more marked the terms: *cook* is relatively unmarked; *stir-fry* is considerably more marked. The intermediate term *fry* is less marked than its hyponym *stir-fry* but more marked than *cook*.

Examples of multiple layers of hyponymic relationships abound in the area of folk biological classification, as illustrated by Figure 6-2. Note that the term *animal* appears on two different levels. English speakers indeed use the word to refer to at least two different referents: animals as distinct from plants and rocks, and animals (generally mammals other than humans) as distinct from humans, birds, and bugs. Cases in which a word has different meanings at different levels of a hyponymic hierarchy are not uncommon.

Hyponymy is one of several relationship types with which language users organize the lexicon. It is based on the notion of reference *inclusion:* If the referent

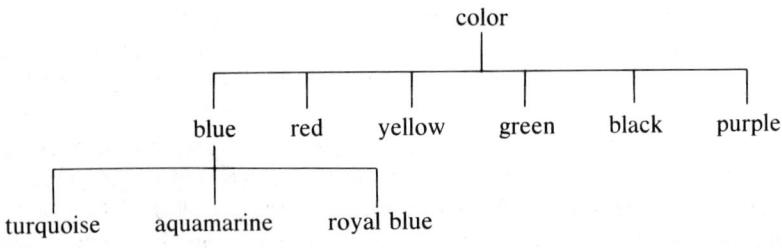

FIGURE 6-1

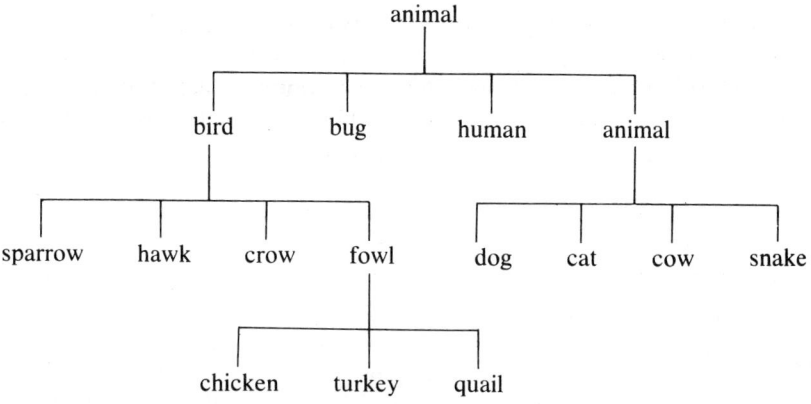

FIGURE 6-2

of term A (for example, *color*) includes a referent of term B (for example, *red*), then term B *(red)* is a hyponym of term A *(color)*. Note that hyponymy is important to everyday conversation—we use it whenever we say "B is a kind of A" (red is a kind of color)—and to such tasks as using a thesaurus, which is organized according to hyponymic relationships.

Part/Whole Relationships

A second important hierarchical relationship between words is the one found in pairs of words like *hand* and *arm* or *room* and *house*. In each pair, the referent of the first term is included in the referent of the second term. A hand, however, is not 'a kind of' arm, and thus the relationship between *hand* and *arm* is not hyponymic. A distinct relationship type is needed to capture the relationship of the term *hand* to the term *arm*, and we call this a *part/whole relationship*. Part/whole relationships are not a property of pairs of words only: *hand, elbow, forearm, wrist,* and several other words are in a part/whole relationship with *arm*. Other important examples of part/whole relationships include words like *second* and *minute, minute* and *hour, hour* and *day,* none of which could be described without reference to the fact that it is a subdivision of another.

Synonymy

Two words are said to be **synonymous** if they "mean the same thing." The terms *movie, film, flick,* and *motion picture* all refer to the same set of referents in the real world and are usually taken to be synonymous terms. To address the notion of synonymy more formally, we can say that term *A* is synonymous with term *B* if every referent of term *A* is a referent of term *B* and vice versa. The "vice versa" is important: without it, we would be defining hyponymy.

You may have wondered why speakers of a language would bother to keep synonyms, since they only add redundancy to the lexicon. In English, we have many pairs of synonymous words like *cloudy* and *nebulous, help* and *assist, skewed* and *oblique* that result from English having borrowed the second term of each pair from French or Latin. When we assert that two terms are synonymous, we usually base our conclusion on referential meaning only. For example, even though *movie, film, flick,* and *motion picture* have the same referential meaning, the terms differ in social and affective meaning. *Film* may strike you as British or as appropriate for movie classics or art movies. You recognize that *flick* is used chiefly in very informal contexts, while *motion picture* is quaintly outdated and has connotations as a term from the thirties or forties. Thus we can consider the terms to be synonymous if we specify that we are taking only referential meaning into account. At the social and affective levels, however, the terms are not synonymous.

In fact, there are very few true synonyms in the lexicon. More often than not, terms that appear to be synonymous have different social and affective connotations. Even if we restrict the definition of meaning to referential meaning, we often find that words that appear synonymous at first glance actually refer to slightly different sets of concepts or are used in different situations. The adjectives *fast, quick,* and *rapid* may be used interchangeably in reference to someone's running speed, but a *fast talker* is different from a "quick talker," some people lead their lives in the *fast lane,* not the "rapid lane," while *quick* is the most appropriate term to describe a mind or a glance, and *rapid* is the usual term when reference is made to a person's strides, especially metaphorical strides, as in learning to type or do mathematics. Under the circumstances, is it accurate to say that the three adjectives are synonymous?

The fact that there are few true synonyms in the lexicon of a language reflects the general tendency of language users to make the most of what is available to them. If two terms have the same referent, the meaning of one of them is usually modified to express differences in referential, social, or affective meaning. Although true synonymy is rare, the notion is useful because it helps describe similarities between the meanings of different terms in the lexicon.

Antonymy

The word **antonymy** derives from the Greek root *anti-* (meaning 'opposite') and denotes opposition in meaning. In contrast to synonymy and hyponymy, antonymy is a *binary* relationship in that it can characterize the relationship between only two words at a time.

The prototypical antonyms are pairs of adjectives that describe opposite notions: *large* and *small, wide* and *narrow, hot* and *cold, open* and *closed, married* and *single, alive* and *dead*. Antonymy is not restricted to adjectives. The nouns *male* and *female* are also antonyms because an individual cannot be described by both terms at once. *Always* and *never* form an antonymous pair of adverbs because they have mutually exclusive referents. The verbs *love* and *hate* can also be viewed as antonyms because they refer to mutually exclusive emotions. Antonymy is thus a binary relationship between terms with *complementary* meanings.

Intuitively, we see a difference between the antonymous pair *large* and *small* and the antonymous pair *single* and *married*. The adjectives of the first pair denote notions that are relatively subjective. Most of you would agree that humpback whales are large mammals and that mice are small mammals, but whether German shepherds are small or large dogs depends on your perspective. The owner of a Chihuahua will say that German shepherds are large, but the owner of a Great Dane may find them on the small side. Furthermore, adjectives like *large* and *small* have superlative and comparative forms: humpback whales are the *largest* of all mammals; German shepherds are *larger* than Chihuahuas but *smaller* than Great Danes. Antonymous pairs that have these characteristics are called *gradable* pairs.

In contrast to *large* and *small*, *single* and *married* are mutually exclusive and complementary. A person cannot be single and married at the same time. With respect to marital status, a person cannot be described with a term that does not have either *single* or *married* as a hyponym; thus *single* and *married* are complementary. Furthermore, *single* and *married* generally cannot be used in a comparative or superlative sense (someone being legally "more single" than another single person is impossible). The pair constitute an example of *nongradable* antonymy (also sometimes called *complementarity*).

There are thus two types of antonymy: gradable and nongradable. If terms *A* and *B* are *gradable* antonyms and if *A* can be used to describe a particular referent, then *B* cannot be used to describe the same referent, and vice versa. If *A* and *B* are *nongradable* antonyms, the same condition applies along with an additional condition: If *A* cannot describe a referent, then that referent must be describable by *B*, and vice versa. So *male* and *female, married* and *single, alive* and *dead* can be viewed as nongradable antonyms, while *hot* and *cold, love* and *hate, always* and *never* are gradable. Typically, for gradable antonyms, there will be words to describe intermediate stages: *sometimes, seldom, occasionally, often* are gradations between *always* and *never*.

As you recognize, the distinction between gradable and nongradable antonymy is sometimes blurred by language users. In English, for example, it is reasonable to assume that whatever is alive is not dead and that whatever is dead is not alive, and thus that the adjectives *dead* and *alive* form a nongradable pair. However, we do have expressions like *half-dead, barely alive,* and *more dead than alive,* which suggest that, in some contexts, we see *alive* and *dead* as gradable antonyms. The distinction between the two types of antonymy is nevertheless useful in that it describes an important distinction between two types of word relationships.

Finally, words that are in an antonymous relationship often do not have equal status with respect to markedness. For example, when you inquire about the weight of an object, you say *How heavy is it?* and not *How light is it?* unless you already know that the object is light. Notice also that the noun *weight,* which describes both relative heaviness and relative lightness, is associated with *heavy* rather than with *light* (as in the expressions *carry a lot of weight* and *throw one's weight around*). Of the antonymous pair *heavy* and *light, heavy* is more neutral than *light* and is thus less *marked*. In the same fashion, *tall* is less marked than *short,* and *married* less marked than *single* (we say *marital status,* not *singleness status*). Although there is some variation across languages as to which word of a pair is considered less marked, there is a surprising agreement in this respect from language to language.

Converseness

Another important relationship type invokes the notion of oppositeness, although it does so in a different way from antonymy. Consider the relationship between *wife* and *husband*. If A is the husband of B, then B is the wife of A. Thus *wife* is the *converse* of *husband,* and vice versa. **Converseness** characterizes a reciprocal semantic relationship between pairs of words. Other examples of converse pairs include terms denoting many other kinship relations like *grandchild* and *grandparent* or *child* and *parent,* terms describing professional relationships like *employer* and *employee* or *doctor* and *patient,* and terms denoting relative positions in space or time such as *above* and *below, north of* and *south of,* or *before* and *after.*

Converse pairs can combine with other types of opposition to form complex relationships. The antonymous pair *father : mother* is in a converse relationship with the antonymous pair *son : daughter.* Generally, converse pairs denote relationships between objects or between people.

Some converse relationships are a little more complex. The verb *give,* for example, is usually ditransitive, which means that it requires a subject and two objects *(She gave him the book).* The converse of *give* is *receive,* except that the relationship is not a "reversal" of the subject and the direct object as it would be with *kiss* and *be kissed (Smith kissed Jones* v. *Jones was kissed by Smith)* or a mutual subject/possessor relation like *husband* and *wife;* rather, it is a relationship between the subject and the indirect object.

John gave a present to Harold.

Harold received a present from John.

Other pairs of words with a similar relationship include *lend* and *borrow,* and *buy* and *sell.* Note that *rent* is its own converse in American English.

John rents an apartment to Harold.

Harold rents an apartment from John.

When there is a possibility of confusion, the preposition *out* can be attached to *rent* in the meaning of 'lending out for money.' In British English, this sense of *rent* is described by the verb *let (flat to let).* In some languages, a single word is used for 'buy' and 'sell.' In Samoan, for example, the word *faʔatau* carries both meanings, while the Mandarin Chinese words *mǎi* 'buy' and *mài* 'sell' are etymologically related. These facts suggest that converseness is an intuitively recognizable relationship.

Polysemy and Homonymy

Two additional notions that are closely related to the basic relationship types are **polysemy** and **homonymy.** In contrast to the notions discussed above, polysemy and homonymy refer to similarities rather than differences between meanings. A word is *polysemic* when it has more than one meaning. The word *plain,* for example, can have several meanings, among which figure (1) 'easy, clear'; (2) 'undecorated'; (3) 'not good-looking'; and (4) 'a level area of land.' *Plain* is thus polysemic. Two or more words are *homonymic* when they sound the same but have different meanings. *I, eye,* and *aye* are homonymic: they have different meanings but are pronounced alike. Languages exhibit polysemy and homonymy in their lexicons to varying degrees. A language like Hawaiian, for example, which has a restricted set of possible words because of its phonological structure, has a good deal more homonymy than English (see Chapter 3).

A difficulty arises in distinguishing between polysemy and homonymy: How do you know when you have separate lexical items rather than a single word with different meanings? Because *plain* 'a level area of land' is a noun, it is a distinct word from *plain* in the first three meanings, all of which are adjectives. How would you know whether or not the three adjectival meanings of *plain* constitute different words that happen to sound the same? Using spelling as a criterion is misleading: many sets of words are obviously distinct but have the same spelling—as, for example, the noun *sound* 'noise' and the adjective *sound* 'healthy,' or *bank* 'financial institution' and *bank* 'shore of a river.' Yet the problem is an important one, especially for anyone who wants to arrange or use the entries of a dictionary (in which different meanings of the same word are grouped under a single entry but each homonymous form has its own distinct entry).

There is no simple solution to the problem. If there is a clear distinction between polysemy and homonymy, it must involve several criteria, no one of which is sufficient by itself and several of which may yield different results. We have already excluded spelling as an unreliable criterion. One modestly reliable criterion is the word's *etymology,* or historical origin. We can consider that there are two words of the form *sound* corresponding to the two meanings given earlier because they derive from different Anglo-Saxon roots. On the other hand, the word *bank* meaning 'financial institution' is an early borrowing from French, while *bank* meaning 'shore of a river' has a Scandinavian origin. The various antonyms and synonyms of a word provide a different kind of criterion that can be useful in distinguishing between polysemy and homonymy. *Plain* in the sense of 'easy, clear' and in the sense of 'undecorated' share a synonym in *simple* and an antonym in *complex.* This fact suggests that they are indeed two meanings of the same polysemic word. No such shared synonym or antonym can be identified for the two meanings of *sound.* Finally, we can ask whether there is any commonality between the different meanings of what appears to be the same word. The first two meanings of *plain* can be characterized as 'devoid of complexity,' which suggests that they are related, but no such hypernymic description exists for *bank* and *bank.* Thus *plain* in these two senses is polysemic, while the two senses of *bank* reflect homonymous lexical items. (Of course, other meanings of *plain* may or may not belong to separate words.)

While the criteria just outlined help distinguish between polysemy and homonymy, they are not foolproof. It is often difficult to decide whether a particular pair of look-alike and sound-alike word forms are separate homonymous words or simply the same polysemic word with different meanings. Though homonymy and polysemy can be distinguished as different notions, the boundary between them is not clear-cut.

Metaphorical Extension

The difficulties in defining the distinction between polysemy and homonymy partly arise from the fact that language users often extend the primary meaning of words to form metaphors. A **metaphor** is an extension in the use of a word beyond its primary meaning to describe referents that bear similarities to the word's primary referent. The word *eye,* for example, can be used to describe the hole at the dull end of a needle, the bud on a potato, or the center of a storm. The similarities between these referents and the primary referent of the word *eye* are their roundish shape and their more or less central role or position in a larger form. People constantly create new metaphors. Once a metaphor becomes accepted, speakers tend to view the metaphorical meaning as separate from its primary meaning—as in *booking* a flight, *tabling* a motion, *seeing* the *point, stealing* the *head*lines, *buying* time, studying a foreign *tongue.* Hence difficulty exists in determining whether one word exists with two meanings or two words exist with different but metaphorically related meanings.

All languages appear to have metaphors, and metaphors are so fundamental to human communication that small children can be observed creating them in the process of acquiring language. Very early, children extend the meaning of the words that they know to cover objects and concepts for which they do not yet know the adult word. Linguist Eve Clark reports the example of a child who first said the word *mooi (moon)* while looking at the moon; before long, the child was using the word *mooi* to describe cakes, circles drawn on foggy windows, postmarks, and the letter ⟨o⟩. Obviously, the child noticed that all these objects shared a round shape and used the word *mooi* to refer to round objects. This early process of applying a particular word to meanings that resemble the primary meaning of the word is called *overgeneralization* and can be thought of as a primitive kind of metaphor. As adults, we use metaphors not because we are unaware of the names of objects and concepts, but because we find in metaphors a tool to be creative and to describe things vividly.

Metaphors occur constantly in day-to-day speaking and writing. The following examples were gleaned from the front page of a typical newspaper.

> Tennis star Martina Navratilova *breezed* through the championship match.
>
> The dollar is *falling sharply.*
>
> His speech was the *catalyst* that gave the *signal* for a new popular upheaval.

In the first example, the verb *breeze* is of course not meant literally; it is used to give the impression that Navratilova won the championship effortlessly, as a breeze would blow over a tennis court. Similarly, the italicized words in the other two sentences are meant to be interpreted as metaphors, whose effectiveness relies on our ability to see that in some contexts words are not to be interpreted

literally. (The mechanisms that we use in figuring out when a word must be interpreted metaphorically will be discussed in Chapter 11.)

Metaphors aren't formed haphazardly. Observe, for example, the following
metaphors that refer to the notion of time.

I look *forward* to seeing you again this weekend.

Experts do not *foresee* an increase in inflation in the near future.

He *drags up* old grudges from his youth.

Once in a while, we need to *look back over our shoulders* at the lessons that history
has taught us.

A pattern is apparent in these examples: in English, we construct time metaphors
as if we physically moved through time in the direction of the future. Thus the
future is forward in the first two examples. Metaphors that refer to the past use
words that refer to what is left behind, as in the latter two examples. Metaphors
that violated this pattern would sound very strange.

*I look *back* to seeing you again this weekend.

*He *drags down* old grudges from his youth.

Another principle that governs the creation of metaphors is the following:
"Ideas are objects that can be sensed." Thus ideas can be smelled, felt, and heard.

Your proposal *smells* fishy.

I failed to *grasp* what they were trying to prove.

I'd like your opinion as to whether my plan *sounds* reasonable.

Writers and critics often talk about the writing process as "cooking."

I let my manuscript *simmer* for six months.

Who knows what kind of a story he is *brewing!*

Their last book was little more than a *half-baked concoction* of earlier work.

"The heart is where emotions are experienced" is a common principle on which
our metaphors for emotions are based.

It is with a *heavy heart* that I tell you of her death.

You shouldn't speak *lightheartedly* about this tragedy.

The rescuers received the survivors' *heartfelt* thanks.

The construction of metaphors thus follows preset patterns.

Most of the metaphors discussed so far are relatively conventionalized—that is, they are found in the speech and writing of many language users because they are preset. But language lends itself to creative activities, and language users do not hesitate to create new metaphors of their own. Even when speakers and writers create their own metaphors, however, they must follow the principles that regulate conventionalized metaphors. In English, metaphors that refer to time must obey the convention of "moving through time in the direction of the future."

There is strong evidence that some metaphorical patterns are frequent across the world's language. For example, in many languages the word for "eye" is used metaphorically to refer to roundish objects like protuberances on a potato and the pivotally located portion of an object like the center of a storm.

But other principles of metaphorical extension vary from language to language. Mandarin Chinese metaphors for time move in the direction of the *past*. Similarly, "the heart is the seat of emotions" does not apply to metaphors in many languages. Polynesian languages like Samoan and Tahitian treat the *stomach* as the metaphorical seat of emotions. It is likely that some of these principles reflect different cultures' views of the world. The exact workings of the link between culture and language are still poorly understood. Increased knowledge about metaphors in different languages should help us determine which principles are shared by most or all languages, which are specific to some languages, and to what extent metaphors reflect cultural perspectives.

Lexical Semantics: Discovering Relationships in the Lexicon

Hyponymy, part/whole relationships, synonymy, gradable and nongradable antonymy, converseness, polysemy, homonymy, and metaphorical extension—lexical semantics is primarily concerned with discovering relationships in the lexicon of languages. The semantic relationships of a word are, in a sense, part of its meaning: The word *cold* can be defined as a gradable antonym of *hot*, as having the expression *sensation of heat* as hypernym, and as being more marked than *hot* but less marked than *chilly* and *freezing*. By knowing how the meaning of a word interacts with the meaning of other words, we can begin to understand the meaning of that word.

Lexical semantics, of course, does not explain the difference in meaning between words like *gorilla* and *doubtful*. For lexical semantics to be useful, it must be applied to particular areas of the lexicon where words' senses have shared characteristics. Thus the notion of lexical field becomes useful. If the word *gorilla* is placed in its appropriate lexical field, its relationship to *chimpanzee* and *great ape* can be investigated. Similarly, the word *doubtful* can be contrasted with *certain, probable,* and other words that express likelihood or certainty.

The different types of relationships described above are the most basic tools of lexical semantics. They are basic because one type cannot be characterized in terms of another type. For example, an antonymous relationship between two words cannot be explained in terms of hyponymy, part/whole relationships, synonymy, converseness, or metaphorical extension.

FUNCTION WORDS AND CATEGORIES OF MEANING

The lexicon is not made up exclusively of content words like *father, pigeon, stir-fry,* and *democracy,* which refer to objects, actions, or abstract concepts. It also contains function words like the prepositions *to, from,* and *about;* the conjunctions *if, however,* and *or;* the determiners *a, the,* and *some;* and the auxiliaries *may, should,* and *will.* The role of these lexical items is to signal grammatical relationships.

Tense and Modality

Many categories of meaning are associated with function words and function morphemes. Bound morphemes can denote several categories of meaning in English, including number *(toys),* tense *(walked),* and person *(walks).* In other languages, the same categories are expressed not by means of bound morphemes but by separate words. In Tongan, the function word *ʔoku,* which precedes the verb, denotes present tense, while *naʔe* denotes past tense.

ʔoku ʔalu e fineʔeiki ki kolo.
Present go the lady to town

'The lady is going to town.'

Naʔe ʔalu e fineʔeiki ki kolo.
Past go the lady to town

'The lady was going to town.'

Whether tense is expressed through bound morphemes or separate lexical items is not important for semantics. What is important is that there is a semantic category *tense* that affects the meaning of sentences in both Tongan and English.

Semantic categories like tense are conveyed by function words and function morphemes, but their scope goes beyond the noun phrase or verb phrase in which they occur. The meaning of tense morphemes affects the whole sentence, since the **tense** of the verb determines the time reference of the entire clause. The category *tense* (and other semantic categories like it) thus refers to both word meaning and sentence meaning.

Modality, or *mood,* is the category through which speakers convey their attitude toward the truth of their assertions (called *epistemic modality*) or express obligation, permission, or suggestion (called *deontic modality*). The sentences in the following pairs differ as to their *epistemic* modality.

1. She has *probably* left town by now. (probability)
   She has left town by now. (assertion)

2. Harry *must*'ve been very tall when he was young. (conjecture)
   Harry was very tall when he was young. (assertion)

3. They *may* come to the party. (possibility)
   They are coming to the party. (assertion)

And those in the following pairs differ as to their *deontic* modality.

4. He *must* come tomorrow. (command)
   He is coming tomorrow. (statement)

5. They *may* take the dishes away. (permission)
   They are taking the dishes away. (statement)

The two types of modality are interrelated, as witnessed by the fact that the same words (*must* and *may,* among others) can denote either type, depending on the context. Modality may be expressed through auxiliary verbs, such as *may, should,* or *must,* which are called *modal* auxiliaries; through *modal* verbs like *order, assume,* and *allow;* through *modal* adverbs like *possibly* or *certainly;* and in some languages through affixes attached to verbs or nouns. The latter type is common in American Indian languages, some of which have extremely complex systems of modal affixes and particles.

Reference

Another important semantic category is **reference,** through which we provide information about the relationship between noun phrases and their referents. For example, there is a semantic difference between the following sentences:

1. *The* woman came to see you.

2. *A* woman came to see you.

In 1, the speaker assumes that the hearer is able to identify which woman is in question, while no such assumption is made in 2. (Reference is investigated in depth in Chapter 7.)

Deixis

The word *deixis* comes from the Greek adjective *deiktikos* meaning 'pointing, indicative.' **Deixis** is the marking of the orientation or position of objects and events with respect to certain *points of reference.* Take, for example, the following sentence addressed by a restaurant customer to a waiter and uttered while the speaker points to items on a menu.

I want this dish, this dish, and this dish.

In order to interpret this utterance, the waiter needs to have information about who *I* refers to, about the time at which the utterance is produced, and about what the three noun phrases *this dish* refer to. We say that *I,* the present tense form of the verb, and the three noun phrases *this dish* are *deictic expressions.* Our ability to interpret them enables us to decipher the meaning of the sentence.

Deixis consists of three semantic notions, all related to the orientation or position of events or objects in the real world. *Personal deixis* is commonly conveyed through personal pronouns: *I* versus *you* versus *he* or *she. Spatial deixis* refers to orientation in space: *here* versus *there* and *this* versus *that. Temporal deixis* refers to orientation in time: present versus past, for example.

Personal Deixis   Many of the utterances that you produce daily are comments or questions about yourself or your interlocutors.

> *I* really should be going now.
>
> Did *you* pick up the carton of milk *I* asked *you* to?
>
> In this family, *we* rarely smoke or drink.

The pronouns *I, you,* and *we*—along with *she, he, it,* and *they* (and alternative forms)—are markers of personal deixis. When we use these pronouns, we orient or place our utterances with respect to ourselves, our interlocutors, and third parties.

Personal pronouns are of course not the only tool used to mark personal deixis. The phrase *this person* in the sentence *You may enjoy scary roller-coaster rides, but this person doesn't care for them at all* may be used to refer to the speaker if the speaker wishes to express annoyance or disdain. Similarly if you happen to be entertaining royalty, etiquette requires you to use the noun phrase *Her Majesty* to refer to the addressee: *Would Her Majesty like some more fried oysters?*

Personal deixis is thus not associated exclusively with pronouns, although pronouns are the most common way to express personal deixis. In this discussion, we will concentrate primarily on pronouns as markers of personal deixis.

The most basic opposition of personal deictic systems is that between speaker (*I* or *me*) and addressee (*you*). This opposition in *person* is so basic that it is reflected in the pronominal systems of *all* languages. Pronouns that refer to the speaker (or to a group that includes the speaker) are called *first person* pronouns, and pronouns that refer to the addressee (or to a group including the addressee) are called *second person* pronouns.

Besides the contrast between first person and second person, pronoun systems often have separate forms for the *third person*—that is, any entity other than the speaker and the person spoken to. In English, *he, she,* and *it,* and *they* denote third person entities. But third person pronouns are not found in all languages. Some languages simply do not have special forms to refer to third person entities; in these languages, third person entities are referred to with a demonstrative like *this* or *that,* or they remain unexpressed. In Tongan, a verb without an expressed subject is understood as having a third person subject.

> Naʔe aʔu.
>
> Past   arrive
>
> '(He/She/It) arrived.'

Tongan does have a third person pronoun form, but it is used only for emphasis.

Naʔe   aʔu   ia.

Past   arrive   he/she

'He/She is the one that arrived.'

The fact that some languages lack separate third person pronouns reflects the fact that the third person is less important than the first and second persons in personal deixis. In fact, the third person can be defined as an entity other than the first person and other than the second person. Because it can be described in terms of the other two persons, it is a less basic distinction in language in general. The singular pronoun system of English can thus be described as follows:

speaker only	I
hearer only	you
neither speaker nor hearer	he/she/it

Some languages make finer distinctions in their pronominal systems, while others make fewer distinctions (see Chapter 8). In all languages, though, there are separate first person and second person pronouns.

Besides person, personal-deixis systems may mark distinctions in gender and number. The gender distinction is made in English in the third person only: *he* for masculine referents and *she* for feminine referents. In other languages, gender may be marked in the other persons as well. In Hebrew, the second person singular pronoun is *ata* for masculine referents but *at* for feminine referents. Number is marked on English pronouns in the first person (*I* versus *we*) and the third person (*he/she/it* versus *they*); the second person pronoun *you* is used for reference to both singular and plural entities. In many languages, including French, there are separate second person singular and plural pronouns. Singular and plural are not the only number categories that can be distinguished: some languages have distinct *dual* forms to refer to exactly two people, and a few languages even mark a distinction between "a few" and "many" referents (see Chapter 8).

Finally, personal deixis frequently reflects the social status of referents. In French and in many other languages, the choice of a pronoun in the second person depends on the nature of the speaker's relationship to the addressee. If speaker and addressee are of roughly equal social status, the pronoun *tu* is used; but to mark or create social distance or social inequality, a speaker uses the plural pronoun *vous* instead of *tu,* even when addressing one person. Considerably more complex systems are found in languages like Japanese, Thai, and Korean. Strictly speaking, the use of deictic devices to reflect facts about the social relationship of the participants is a distinct type of deixis, commonly referred to as *social deixis*.

Thus personal deixis can mark a number of overlapping distinctions: person, gender, number, and social relations. Languages express these distinctions in different combinations, marking some and not others. The basic distinction between first person and second person, however, is found in all languages and appears to be a basic semantic category in all deictic systems.

Spatial Deixis   Spatial deixis is the marking in language of the orientation or position in space of the referent of a linguistic expression. The categories of words that are most commonly used to express spatial deixis are demonstratives (*this* versus *that*) and adverbs like *here* and *there*. Demonstratives and adverbs of place are by no means the only categories that have spatial deictic meaning; the directional verbs *go* and *come* also carry deictic information, as do *bring* and *take*.

Languages differ in terms of the number and meaning of demonstratives and adverbs of place. The demonstrative system of English distinguishes only between *this* (proximate—close to the speaker) and *that* (remote—relatively distant from the speaker). It is one of the simplest systems found. At the other extreme are languages like Eskimo, which has thirty demonstrative forms. In all languages, however, the demonstrative system treats the speaker as a point of reference. Thus the speaker is a basic point of reference for spatial deixis.

Many spatial deixis systems have three terms. Three-term systems fall into two categories. In one type, the meanings of the terms are 'near the speaker,' 'a little distant from the speaker,' and 'far from the speaker.' The Spanish demonstratives *este, ese, aquel* have these three respective meanings. In another type of three-term demonstrative system, the terms have the meanings 'near the speaker,' 'near the hearer,' and 'away from both speaker and hearer.' Fijian exemplifies such a system.

na   ŋone   oŋgo

the   child   this (near me)

'this child (near me)'

na   ŋone   oŋgori

the   child   this (near you)

'that child (near you)'

na   ŋone   oya

the   child   that (away from you and me)

'that child (away from you and me)'

In both systems, however, the speaker is taken as either the sole point of reference or as one of two points of reference.

Spatial deixis thus represents the orientation of actions and states in space, and it is most commonly conveyed by demonstratives and by adverbs of place. Languages may have anywhere from two to thirty distinct demonstrative forms, but all demonstrative systems take the speaker as a basic point of reference.

Temporal Deixis   A third type of deixis is *temporal deixis*—the orientation or position of the referent of actions and events *in time*. All languages have words and phrases that are inherently marked for temporal deixis, like the English terms *before, last year, tomorrow, now,* and *this evening*. In many languages (but not all), temporal deixis can be marked through tense, encoded on the verb with affixes, or expressed in an independent morpheme. In English, we must make an obligatory choice between the past tense and the nonpast-tense form of verbs.

> I walk to school every day. (nonpast tense)

> I walked to school every day. (past tense)

To express a future *time,* English has no distinct verbal inflection (it lacks a future *tense*) but uses a phrasal verb in the nonpast tense.

> I will walk to school next week. (nonpast tense for future time)

Tuvaluan is like English: *e* denotes nonpast, while *ne* is a past tense marker.

> Au   e   fano ki te   fakaala.
>
> I   Nonpast   go   to the   feast
>
> 'I am going/will go to the feast.'

> Au   ne   fano ki   te   fakaala.
>
> I   Past go   to   the   feast
>
> 'I went to the feast.'

In some languages, the choice is between future and nonfuture (with undifferentiated present and past).

In a number of languages, temporal deixis can be marked only with optional adverbs. This Chinese sentence can be interpreted as past, present, or future, depending on the context.

> Xià   yǔ.
>
> down   rain
>
> 'It was/is/will be raining.'

When there is the possibility of ambiguity, an adverb of time ('last night,' 'right now,' 'next week') is added to the sentence.

In languages that do not mark tense on verbs, another semantic category called **aspect** is frequently obligatory. Aspect is not directly related to temporal deixis but refers to the ways in which actions and states are viewed: as continuous *(I was talking)*, repetitive *(I talked (every day))*, instantaneous *(I talked)*, and so on.

Tense is thus not the only marker of temporal deixis, although it is very frequently exploited by languages as the primary means of marking temporal deixis.

The most basic point of reference for tense is the moment at which the sentence is uttered. Any event that occurs before that moment may be marked as past, and any event that occurs after that moment may be marked as future.

The train arrived. (any time before the utterance moment)

The train is arriving. (at the moment of utterance)

The train will arrive. (any time after the utterance moment)

When the point of reference is some point in time other than the moment of utterance, we say that tense is *relative*. Relative tense is used in many languages when speakers wish to compare the time of occurrence of two different events.

After I had bought two, they gave me another one.

Before I saw you yesterday, I had been sick for a week.

Languages sometimes have complex rules of *tense concord* that dictate the form of verbs in relative contexts.

Deixis as a Semantic Notion   The three types of deixis illustrate how semantic categories permeate language beyond the simple meaning of words. The deictic orientation of a sentence or part of a sentence can be conveyed through bound morphemes such as tense endings, through free morphemes and function words such as pronouns and demonstratives, or through content words such as *here* and *bring*. Deictic meaning is independent of the means used to convey it.

One of the purposes of semantics is to describe which parameters are important or essential to characterize deixis (as well as other semantic categories) in language in general. We noted, for example, that distinguishing between the speaker and the addressee is an essential function of the personal deixis system of all languages. Similarly, we found that every spatial deixis system has at least one point of reference, a location near the speaker. A spatial deixis system may also have a secondary point of reference near the hearer.

There is considerable overlap between the different types of deixis. For example, personal, spatial, and temporal deixis all share a basic point of reference: the speaker's identity and location in space and time. Many linguistic devices can also be used to mark more than one kind of deixis. The English demonstrative *this* can be used for personal deixis *(this person)*, spatial deixis *(this object)*, and temporal deixis *(this morning)*. Clearly, personal, spatial, and temporal deixis are closely related notions.

There is one type of deixis that we have not yet discussed. *Textual deixis* is the orientation of utterances with respect to other utterances in the string of utterances in which it occurs. Consider for example the following pair of sentences:

He started to swear at me and curse. *This* made me very angry.

The demonstrative *this* at the beginning of the second sentence refers not to a direction in space or time but rather to something previously mentioned. It marks textual deixis. Textual deixis is thus a tool that enables language users to "package" utterances together and indicate relationships across utterances. Because textual deixis is primarily concerned with utterances and their context, it goes beyond the scope of semantics as traditionally defined, and its importance is not to be underestimated.

SEMANTIC ROLES AND SENTENCE SEMANTICS

We have noted that, like words, sentences must "carry" meaning for language speakers to understand each other at all, but that the meaning of sentences cannot be determined merely by adding up the meaning of each content word of the sentence. This fact was illustrated in the last section, where you saw that bound morphemes and function words may also carry meaning that has implication for the meaning of the entire sentence. We also noted that sentences like *The hunter bit the lion* and *The lion bit the hunter* have very different meanings, even though they contain exactly the same words. Clearly, adding together the meaning of each word will not produce the full meaning of a sentence. Such a process will not even distinguish between the two simple illustrative sentences in this paragraph. In defining what the meaning of a sentence consists of, more than just the meaning of the individual content words must be taken into consideration.

Consider the following active/passive counterparts, which, at the level of referential meaning at least, describe the same situation.

1. The hunter bit the lion.
2. The lion was bitten by the hunter.

These sentences differ in that the derivation of 2 involves passivization, whereas 1 does not. Since our concern here is with meaning, we must ask how to account for the synonymy between 1 and 2.

Furthermore, consider the following sentences:

3. Seymour sliced the salami with a knife.
4. Seymour used a knife to slice the salami.

Here is a situation not unlike the active/passive counterparts of 1 and 2, in that the sentences have the same referential meaning. But 3 and 4 have different deep structures. Nevertheless, we need to describe how sentences 3 and 4 mean "the same thing."

A different situation is presented by the contrast between these examples.

5. Harold was injured by a stone.
6. Harold was injured with a stone.

Sentences 5 and 6 share some properties (for example, both describe someone being injured and a stone being involved), but they are not completely synonymous: if the stone was part of a natural rockfall, only sentence 5 applies, because 6 implies that someone threw a stone at Harold with intent to do harm. How can we describe such meaning differences?

The three situations just presented all suggest that the crucial factor in the way sentence meaning is constructed is the *role* played by each noun phrase in relation to the verb. We thus need to introduce the notion **semantic role** of a noun phrase—semantic role refers to the way in which the referent of the noun phrase contributes to the state, action, or situation described by the sentence. The semantic role of a noun phrase differs from its syntactic role (as subject, object, and so on), as illustrated by the contrast between sentences 1 and 2. In both 1 and 2, the way in which the lion is involved in the action is the same; and the way in which the hunter is involved is the same. By contrast, despite its having the same semantic role in both, *the lion* is the direct object of the verb in sentence 1 and the grammatical subject of sentence 2.

Semantic role, furthermore, is not an inherent property of a noun phrase, since a given noun phrase can have different semantic roles in different sentences, as in the following contrast.

Harold was injured by *a friend*.

Harold was injured with *a friend*.

Rather, semantic role is a way of characterizing the meaning relationship between a noun phrase and the verb of a sentence.

The first semantic roles we need to identify are *agent* (the responsible initiator of an action) and *patient* (the entity that undergoes a certain change of state). In both 1 and 2 above, the agent is *the hunter,* and the patient is *the lion.* That the sentences describe the same situation (and hence have the same referential meaning) can thus be explained by the fact that in both sentences a given noun phrase has the same semantic role.

The role of the subject noun phrases in the following sentences is not that of agent, because Lou is not really the responsible initiator of the actions denoted by the verbs.

Lou likes blueberry pancakes.

Lou felt threatened by the lion.

In both sentences, Lou is experiencing a physical or mental sensation. The semantic role of *Lou* is *experiencer*, defined as that which receives a sensory input. In

English, experiencers can be either subjects or direct objects, depending on the verb. Compare these sentences, in which the experiencer is the subject, with the following sentence, in which the experiencer is the direct object.

Harold sometimes astounds *me* with his stupidity.

So far, we have identified the semantic roles of agent, patient, and experiencer. Now consider again the semantic roles of the noun phrases in the following sentences.

5. Harold was injured by a stone.

6. Harold was injured with a stone.

Recall that the difference between the sentences is that 6 implies that someone used a stone to attack Harold, while 5 does not require this implication. In sentence 6, we say that *a stone* is the *instrument*—the intermediary through which the agent performs the action; note that the definition requires that there be an agent, which is consistent with our interpretation of sentence 6. In sentence 5, *a stone* could be assigned the role of an instrument only if there was an agent doing the injuring; if the stone that injured Harold were part of a rockfall, *a stone* would be assigned the semantic role of *cause*—defined as any natural force that brings about a change of state. Instruments and causes can be expressed as prepositional phrases (as in the previous examples) or as subjects.

The silver key opens the door to the wine cellar. (instrument)

The snow caved in the roof. (cause)

That the noun phrase *the silver key* is indeed an instrument and not an agent is supported by the fact that it cannot be conjoined (linked by *and*) with an agent, as the following anomalous example shows.

*The silver key and John open the door to the cellar.

However, an instrument *can* be conjoined with another instrument, and an agent can be conjoined with another agent.

A push and a shove opened the door to the cellar.

Harold and Hilda opened the door to the cellar.

In addition to agent, patient, experiencer, instrument, and cause, a noun phrase can be a *recipient* (that which receives a physical object), a *benefactive* (that for which an action is performed), a *locative* (the location of an action or state), or a *temporal* (the time at which the action or state occurred).

I gave *Hilda* a puppy. (recipient)

Harold passed the message to me for *Hilda*. (benefactive)

The Midwest is cold in winter. (locative)

She left home *the day before yesterday*. (temporal)

The point of this enterprise is to characterize all possible semantic roles that noun phrases can fill in a sentence. Every noun phrase in a clause is assigned a semantic role, and, aside from coordinate NPs, the same semantic role cannot be assigned to two different noun phrases within the same clause. So, for example, a sentence like the following is ruled out as being semantically anomalous because it contains two different instrumental noun phrases, namely the two italicized noun phrases.

*This ball broke the window with *a hammer*.

In addition, in most cases a single noun phrase can be assigned only one semantic role. In rare instances, a noun phrase can be assigned two different roles; in the sentence *Harold rolled down the hill,* if Harold rolled down the hill deliberately, he is both agent and patient, because he is at once the responsible initiator of the action and the entity that undergoes the change of state.

Semantic Roles and Grammatical Relations

It is important to understand the relationship between semantic roles and grammatical relations (or syntactic roles). We noted earlier that the two notions are different. In English, for example, the subject of a sentence can be an agent (as in the italicized noun phrase in sentence 1); a patient (2); an instrument (3); a cause (4); an experiencer (5); a benefactive (6); a locative (7); or a temporal (8), depending on the verb.

1. *The janitor* opened the door.

2. *The door* opened easily.

3. *His first record* greatly expanded his audience.

4. *Bad weather* ruined the corn crop.

5. *Serge* heard his father whispering.

6. *The young artist* won the prize.

7. *Arizona* attracts asthmatics.

8. *The next day* found us on the road to Alice Springs.

Furthermore, in certain English constructions the subject does not have any semantic role; such is the case of the so-called "dummy *it*" construction, in which the pronoun *it* fills a semantically empty subject slot.

It became clear that the government had jailed him there.

So the notion of subject is independent of the notion of semantic role, and we could show the same thing for direct objects and other grammatical relations. Conversely, semantic roles do not appear to be constrained by grammatical relations. A locative, for example, may be expressed as a subject (as in sentence 1); a direct object (2); an indirect object (3); or the object of a preposition (4).

1. *The garden* will look great in the spring.
2. Harold planted *the garden* with cucumbers and tomatoes.
3. The begonias give *the garden* a cheerful look.
4. The gate opens on *the garden*.

Nevertheless, there is a relationship between grammatical relations and semantic roles. Consider the following sentences, all of which have *open* as a verb:

Harold opened the door with this key.

The door opens easily.

This key will open the door.

The wind opened the door.

The grammatical subjects of the sentences above are an agent *(Harold)*, a patient *(the door)*, an instrument *(this key)*, and a cause *(the wind)*. Such extreme variety is not found with all verbs. The verb *soothe* can take an instrument or a cause as subject.

This ointment will soothe your sunburn.

The cold stream soothed my sore feet.

To have an experiencer as the grammatical subject of the verb *soothe*, we must use a passive construction.

I was soothed by the herbal tea.

Clearly, the verb controls the range of variation allowed in each case. Language users know the semantic roles that each verb allows as subject, direct object, and so on. Attached to the verb *soothe* is a "tag" indicating that only instruments and causes are allowed in subject position, whereas the tag attached to the verb *open* permits the subject to be agent, patient, instrument, or cause.

Semantic roles are universal features of the semantic structure of all languages, but how they interact with grammatical relations like subject and direct object differs from language to language. Equivalent verbs in different languages do not carry similar tags. The tag attached to the English verb *like,* for example, permits only experiencers as subjects.

I like French fries.

But only patients can be the subjects of the equivalent Spanish verb *gustar.*

Las papas fritas me   gustan.

the French-fries to-me like

'I like French fries.' (literally: 'French fries to me are pleasing.')

A similar situation is found for verbs of "liking" and "pleasing" in many other languages including Russian. In some languages, the verb 'to understand' carries a tag that allows its subjects to be either experiencers or patients, as in Samoan. The choice depends on emphasis and the focus of discussion.

ʔua   maalamalama aʔu i   le   mataaʔupu.

Present-tense understand   I   Object-marker the lesson

'I understand the lesson.'

ʔua   maalamalama le   mataaʔupu iate a ʔu.

Present-tense understand   the lesson   to   me

'I understand the lesson.' (literally: 'The lesson understands to me.')

Some languages distinguish between agent and experiencer much more carefully than English does. For example, the verb might take a subject when the action described is intentional but take a direct object when the action is unintentional.

In addition to cross-linguistic variation with respect to specific verbs, languages vary in the degree to which different semantic roles can fit into different grammatical slots in a sentence. In English, the subject slot can be occupied by noun phrases of any semantic role—depending, of course, on the verb. Many English verbs allow different semantic roles for subject, direct object, and so on. But the situation is different in many other languages. In languages such as Russian and German, verbs do not allow nearly as much variation in semantic roles as English verbs do, and there is a much tighter bond between semantic roles and grammatical relations.

SUMMARY

Semantics is the study of meaning in language. While semantics has traditionally focused on referential meaning, language also conveys social meaning (information about the social characteristics of the context of production) and affective meaning (information about the emotional characteristics of the context of production). Referential meaning is often called *denotation,* while social and affective meanings are covered by the term *connotation.* Words, sentences, and utterances can all carry meaning, and sentence meaning and utterance meaning must be distinguished. While the study of sentence meaning is primarily the responsibility of semantics, the branch of linguistics that concerns itself with utterance meaning is called pragmatics.

Lexical semantics is the study of meaning relationships in the lexicon. The types of relationships must be universal, though the word sets to which they apply vary from language to language. Lexical fields are sets of words whose referents belong together on the basis of one or more fundamental characteristics. The words in a lexical field are often arranged in terms of the following relationships: hyponymy (a kind of), part/whole (subdivision), synonymy (similar meaning), gradable and nongradable antonymy (opposite meaning), converseness (reciprocal meaning), polysemy (many meanings), homonymy (same phonological shape), and metaphorical extension (derived meaning).

Content words are not the only units of language that carry meaning. Semantic notions like deixis, for example, can be conveyed through bound morphemes and function words as well as content words. Several types of deixis are recognized: personal deixis, spatial deixis, and temporal deixis. All necessitate that a point of reference be identified. The here-and-now (in relation to the speaker and the moment of utterance) is highly privileged as a point of reference for all three types of deixis, although it is not the only possible reference point.

The meaning of a sentence is not simply the sum meaning of its words. Rather, sentence semantics aims to uncover the basic relationships that exist between noun phrases and the verb of the sentence. These semantic roles are relational notions and not inherent properties of noun phrases. They are also independent of the grammatical function of the noun phrase in the sentence; the verb determines which semantic role may be used in particular grammatical slots of the sentence. We have described these semantic roles: agent, patient, experiencer, instrument, cause, benefactive, locative, and temporal. While these categories must be universal, different languages may have different rules as to how semantic role is encoded in syntax.

EXERCISES

1. In the first section of the chapter we introduced the terms *synonymy, implication, contradiction, anomaly, ambiguity,* and *vagueness* to describe various sentences and sentence pairs. Determine which of these notions applies to each of the following sentences and sentence pairs.

   Harry's cat called me on the phone.

   Visiting relatives can be boring.

   His daughter is her brother's grandmother.

   My husband just returned from the store. I am a married woman.

I don't like locking my car. My car's doors can be locked.

The basil I will plant next weekend is growing well.

She swims.

I was fatally ill last year.

It is still too warm to start a fire. It is not cold enough to start a fire.

The wine I didn't drink tasted sour to me.

My dog wants out. The canine creature that belongs to me is experiencing the desire to proceed outdoors.

Hilda kissed Harold, and Jerry too.

2. The following sentences are ambiguous. Based on the discussion in this chapter and Chapter 5, describe the ambiguity in detail.

They found the peasants revolting.

The car I'm getting ready to drive is a Lamborghini.

There is nothing more alarming than developing nuclear power plants.

Hilda does not like her dentist, and neither does Gertrude.

They said that they told her to come to them.

Challenging wrestlers will be avoided at all costs.

He met his challenger at his house.

3. Identify the differences in referential, social, and affective meaning among the words and phrases in each of the following sets.

   (1) hoax, trickery, swindle, rip-off, ruse, stratagem

   (2) delightful, pleasant, great, far-out, nice, pleasurable, bad, cool

   (3) man, guy, dude, jock, imp, lad, gentleman, hunk, boy

   (4) eat, wolf down, nourish oneself, devour, peck, ingest, chow down, graze, fill one's tummy

   (5) tired, fatigued, pooped, weary, languorous, zonked out, exhausted, fordone, spent

   (6) stupid person, idiot, nerd, ass, jerk, turkey, wimp, punk, airhead, bastard

4. Some of the sets of terms below form lexical fields. For each set:

   a. Identify the words that do not belong to the same lexical field as the others in the set.
   b. Identify the hypernym of the remaining lexical field, if there is one (it may be a word in the set).
   c. Determine whether some terms are less marked than others, and justify your claim.

(1)   acquire, buy, collect, hoard, win, inherit, steal

(2)   whisper, talk, narrate, report, tell, harangue, scribble, instruct, brief

(3)   road, path, barn, way, street, freeway, avenue, thoroughfare, interstate, method

(4)   stench, smell, reek, aroma, bouquet, odoriferous, perfume, fragrance, scent, olfactory

5.   Traditionally, a thesaurus is used to find the synonyms of a word. The following is a typical entry from *Roget's Thesaurus* (Harmondsworth, England: Penguin Books, 1962):

> **710.** Concord—N. *concord,* harmony, unison, unity, duet   24 n. *agreement;* unanimity, bi-partisanship   488 n. *consensus;* understanding, rapport; solidarity, team-spirit   706 n. *cooperation;* reciprocity, sympathy, fellow-feeling, compatibility, coexistence, league, amity   880 n. *friendship;* rapprochement, reunion, reconciliation   719 n. *pacification;* entente cordiale, happy family   717 n. *peace;* goodwill, honeymoon.
>
>   Adj. *concordant,* harmonious; en rapport, eye to eye, unanimous, of one mind, bi-partisan   24 adj. *agreeing;* co-existent, compatible, united; amicable, on good terms   880 adj. *friendly;* frictionless, happy   717 adj. *peaceful;* agreeable, congenial   826 adj. *pleasurable.*
>
>   Vb. *concord,* harmonize; agree   24 vb. *accord;* see eye to eye   706 vb. *cooperate;* reciprocate, respond, run parallel; fraternize 880 vb. *be friendly;* keep the peace, work for peace.

a.   Using the terms introduced in our discussion of lexical semantics, describe how this entry is organized. Include information on how punctuation is used in the entry.

b.   To what extent are the words in the entry synonymous? Provide specific examples to support your point.

c.   What are the advantages and limitations of using a thesaurus? In particular, what kinds of information does an entry offer and not offer?

d.   On the basis of your answer to (c), describe in detail some of the difficulties that (i) children and (ii) nonnative speakers of English might encounter in using a thesaurus.

6.   Consider the following two sequences of dictionary entries, taken (slightly abbreviated) from the *American Heritage Dictionary of the English Language* (Boston: American Heritage and Houghton Mifflin, 1975):

Sequence 1

husk·y[1] *adj.* **-ier, -iest. 1.** Hoarse, as from overuse or emotion. **2.** Like or resembling a husk. **3.** Full of or containing husks. [Originally, "dry as a husk."]—**husk′i·ly** *adv.*—**husk′i·ness** n.
husk·y[2] *adj.* **-ier, -iest.** *Informal.* Rugged and strong; burly. —*n.,pl.* **huskies.** A husky person. [From HUSKY (hoarse).]—**husk′i·ness** n.

husk·y³ *n., pl.* **-kies. 1.** *Sometimes capital H.* A dog of a breed developed in Siberia for pulling sleds, having a dense, furry, variously colored coat. Also called "Siberian husky." **2.** A dog of any of several breeds of Arctic origin. [Probably a shortened variant of ESKIMO.]

Sequence 2

junior *adj.* **1.** *Abbr.* **Jr., Jun.** Younger. Used to distinguish the son from the father of the same name, and written after the full name: *William Jones, Jr.* **2.** Designated for or including youthful persons: *a junior tennis match; junior dress sizes.* **3.** Lower in rank or shorter in length of tenure: *the junior senator.* **4.** Designating the third or penultimate year of a U.S. high school or college. **5.** Lesser in scale than the usual.—*n. Abbr.* **Jr., jr., Jun., jun. 1.** A younger person or individual. **2.** A person lesser in rank or time of participation or service; subordinate. **3.** An undergraduate in his third or penultimate year of a U.S. high school or college.

Using the terms introduced in our discussion of lexical semantics, describe in detail how these dictionary entries are organized. Include a discussion of the criteria that are used to create different entries or subentries for homonymous words.

7. In the following sets of sentences one or more words are used metaphorically. Provide a general statement describing the principle that underlies these sets of metaphors; then add to the set one metaphor that follows the principle.

Example

I let my manuscript *simmer* for six months.

She *concocted* a retort that readers will appreciate.

There is no easy *recipe* for writing effective business letters.

General statement: "The writing process is viewed as cooking." Additional example: He is the kind of writer that *whips up* another trashy novel every six months.

(1) Members of the audience *besieged* him with counterarguments.

   His opponents *tore* his arguments to *pieces.*

   My reasoning left them *with no ammunition.*

   The others will never be able to *destroy* this argument.

   His question betrayed a *defensive* stance.

(2) This heat is *crushing.*

   The sun is *beating down* on these poor laborers.

   The clouds seem to be *lifting.*

   The northern part of the state is *under* a heavy snowstorm.

   The fresh breeze *cleared up* the *oppressive* heat.

   (3)   She has *an eye* for handsome men.

         He has *a palate* for good Indian curry.

         My neighbor has *an ear* for gossip.

         I used to have *an eye* for good etchings.

         The french have *a nose* for cheese.

8.   Determine whether the words in each of the following sets are polysemic, homonymous, or metaphorically related. In each case, state the criteria used to arrive at your conclusion. You may use a dictionary.

   (1)   to run down (the stairs); to run down (an enemy); to run down (a list of names)

   (2)   the seat (of one's pants); the seat (of the government); the (driver's) seat (of a car)

   (3)   an ear (for music); an ear (of corn); an ear (as auditory organ)

   (4)   to pitch (a baseball); pitch (black); the pitch (of one's voice)

   (5)   to spell (a word); (under) a spell; a (dry) spell

   (6)   vision (the ability to see); (a man of) vision; vision (during a hallucination)

   (7)   the butt (of a rifle); the butt (of a joke); to butt (as a ram)

9.   Identify the semantic role of each noun phrase in the sentences below.

   (1)   In October, I gazed from the wooden bridge into the small river behind our college.

   (2)   I have forgotten everything that I learned in grade school.

   (3)   The Grand Tetons tower majestically over the valley.

   (4)   The snow completely buried my car during the last storm.

   (5)   Fifty kilos of cocaine were seized by the DEA.

   (6)   Lou was awarded one thousand dollars' worth of travel.

   (7)   The hurricane destroyed the island.

   (8)   Their ingenuity never ceases to amaze me.

10.   In this chapter we said that a "tag" is attached to every verb in the lexicon indicating which semantic role can be assigned to each noun argument. The verb *bake,* for example, can have as its subject an agent (as in sentence (1)); a patient, (2); a cause, (3); or an instrument, (4). But it does not allow locatives (5) or temporals (6) in subject position.

   (1)   Harold baked scones.

   (2)   The cake is baking.

   (3)   The sun baked my lilies to a crisp.

(4)   This oven bakes wonderful cakes.

(5)   *The kitchen bakes nicely.

(6)   *Tomorrow will bake nicely.

a.   Determine which semantic roles these verbs allow in subject position on the basis of the sentences provided: *feel, provide, absorb, thaw, taste*.

His hands felt limp and moist.

I could feel the presence of an intruder in the apartment.

This room feels damp.

They all felt under the blanket to see what was there.

This semester feels very different from last year to me.

Gas lamps provided light for the outdoor picnic.

These fields provide enough wheat to feed a city.

Who provided these scones?

The Middle Ages provided few famous mathematicians.

The accident provided me plenty to worry about.

Your textbooks provide many illustrations of this phenomenon.

The bylaws provide for dissolution of the board in these cases.

The students have absorbed so much material that they can't make sense of it.

This kind of sponge does not absorb water well.

The United States absorbed the Texas Republic in 1845.

My work hours are absorbing all my free time.

The soil is absorbing the rain.

If Antarctica suddenly thawed, the sea level would rise dramatically.

Chicken does not thaw well in just two hours.

The crowd thawed after Kent arrived.

Kent's arrival thawed the party.

The heat of the sun will thaw the ice in the ice chest.

Ice thaws at 0 degrees Celsius.

The peace treaty will thaw relations between the United States and China.

This wine tastes like vinegar.

He's tasted every single hors d'oeuvre at the party.

I can taste the capers in the sauce.

b. Languages may differ with respect to the semantic roles that particular verbs may take. The following are semantically well-formed French sentences with the verb *goûter* 'taste':

Il   n'a   jamais goûté   au caviare.

he   not-have ever   tasted   the caviar

'He's never tasted caviar.'

Je   goûte   un   goût   amer   dans   ce   café.

I   taste   a   taste   bitter   in   this   coffee

'I taste a bitter taste in this coffee.'

The following sentence, in contrast, is not well constructed:

*Les   cuisses   de   grenouille   goûtent   bon.

  the   thighs   of   frog   taste   good

'Frog's legs taste good.'

What is the difference between *taste* and *goûter* in terms of the range of semantic roles that they permit?

SUGGESTIONS FOR FURTHER READING

The major reference work for semantics is Lyons (1977), which is thorough and provides a wealth of information and critical discussion. Palmer (1981) and Leech (1974) provide concise overviews of the field. Bierwisch (1970) is a clear and concise summary of lexical semantics, though it is a little outdated. More detailed and up-to-date discussions of lexical semantics are provided in Lehrer (1974), which focuses on semantic universals (discussed in Chapter 8 of this text), and in Wierzbicka (1985), in which the main concern is the meaning of the notion 'kind of.' Cruse (1986) is a good overview of lexical semantics. Several of the papers in Holland and Quinn (1987) investigate connotation and the cultural elements in the organization of semantic fields. A basic work on metaphors is Lakoff and Johnson (1980); some of the ideas presented in that earlier work are developed further in Lakoff (1987). Deixis is discussed in detail in Anderson and Keenan (1985) and in Chapter 2 of Levinson (1983). For a concise discussion of tense and related notions, consult Chung and Timberlake (1985); further details on aspect can be found in Comrie (1985); further details on mood and modality are in Palmer (1986). Sentence semantics and semantic roles were originally discussed in Fillmore (1968) and refined in Fillmore (1977); good critical overviews of the brand of sentence semantics presented in this chapter can be found in the general works on semantics mentioned above. For a textbook on the areas of semantics not covered in this chapter, see Kempson (1977). The example of semantic overgeneralization in child language quoted here is from Clark (1975).

REFERENCES

Anderson, Stephen R., and Edward L. Keenan. 1985. "Deixis," in Timothy Shopen, ed., *Language Typology and Syntactic Description* (Cambridge: Cambridge University Press), 3, pp. 259–308.

Bierwisch, Manfred. 1970. "Semantics," in John Lyons, ed., *New Horizons in Linguistics* (New York: Penguin), pp. 166–184.

Chung, Sandra, and Alan Timberlake. 1985. "Tense, Aspect, and Mood," in Timothy Shopen, ed., *Language Typology and Syntactic Description* (Cambridge: Cambridge University Press), 3, pp. 202–258.

Clark, Eve V. 1975. "Knowledge, Context, and Strategy in the Acquisition of Meaning," in D. P. Dato, ed., *Georgetown University Roundtable in Language and Linguistics 1975* (Washington, DC: Georgetown University Press), pp. 77–98.

Comrie, Bernard. 1985. *Tense* (Cambridge: Cambridge University Press).

Cruse, D. A. 1986. *Lexical Semantics* (Cambridge: Cambridge University Press).

Fillmore, Charles J. 1968. "The Case for Case," in Emmon Bach and Robert T. Harms, eds., *Universals in Linguistic Theory* (New York: Holt), pp. 1–88.

———. 1977. "The Case for Case Reopened," in Peter Cole and Jerold M. Saddock, eds., *Syntax and Semantics 8: Grammatical Relations* (New York: Academic), pp. 59–82.

Holland, Dorothy, and Naomi Quinn, eds., 1987. *Cultural Models in Language and Thought* (Cambridge: Cambridge University Press).

Kempson, Ruth M. 1977. *Semantic Theory* (Cambridge: Cambridge University Press).

Lakoff, George. 1987. *Women, Fire, and Dangerous Things: What Categories Reveal about the Mind* (Chicago: University of Chicago Press).

Lakoff, George, and Mark Johnson. 1980. *Metaphors We Live By* (Chicago: University of Chicago Press).

Leech, Geoffrey. 1974. *Semantics* (New York: Penguin).

Lehrer, Adrienne. 1974. *Semantic Fields and Lexical Structure* (Amsterdam: North-Holland).

Levinson, Stephen C. 1983. *Pragmatics* (Cambridge: Cambridge University Press).

Lyons, John. 1977. *Semantics,* 2 vols. (Cambridge: Cambridge University Press).

Palmer, F. R. 1981. *Semantics,* 2nd ed. (Cambridge: Cambridge University Press).

———. 1986. *Mood and Modality* (Cambridge: Cambridge University Press).

Wierzbicka, Anna. 1985. *Lexicography and Conceptual Analysis* (Ann Arbor, MI: Karoma).

7

Pragmatics:
Information Structure

THE ENCODING OF INFORMATION STRUCTURE

Syntax and semantics are not the only regulators of sentence structure. A sentence may be grammatically and semantically well formed but still exhibit problems when used in a particular context. Examine the sentences that make up the following two versions of a typical local news report.

Version 1

At 3 A.M. last Sunday, the Santa Clara Fire Department evacuated two apartment buildings at the corner of Country Club Drive and 5th Avenue. Oil had been discovered leaking from a furnace in the basement of one of the buildings. Firemen sprayed chemical foam over the oil for several hours. By 8 A.M., the situation was under control. Any danger of explosion or fire had been averted, and the leaky furnace was sealed. Residents of the two apartment buildings were given temporary shelter in the Country Club High School gymnasium. They regained possession of their apartments at 5 P.M.

Version 2

As for the Santa Clara Fire Department, it evacuated two apartment buildings at the corner of Country Club Drive and 5th Avenue at 3 A.M. last Sunday. There was someone who had discovered a furnace in the basement of one of the buildings from which oil was leaking. What was sprayed by firemen over the oil for several hours was chemical foam. It was by 8 A.M. that the situation was under control. What someone had averted was any danger of explosion or fire, and as for the leaky furnace, it was sealed. What the residents of the two apartment buildings were given in the Country Club High School gymnasium was temporary shelter. Possession of their apartments was regained by them at 5 P.M.

Virtually the same words are used in the two versions, and every sentence in both versions is grammatically and semantically well formed. Still, there is something fundamentally odd about Version 2: it runs counter to expectations of how information should be presented in a text. Somehow, the second version emphasizes the wrong elements at the wrong time. The structures are grammatical, but they seem inappropriate.

The problem with Version 2 is the way in which different pieces of information are marked for relative significance. In any sequence of sentences, it is essential to mark elements as being more or less important or essential. Speakers and writers are responsible for highlighting certain elements and backgrounding other elements, exactly as a painter highlights particular details and deemphasizes others with a judicious use of color, shape, and position.

In language texts, this highlighting and deemphasizing are called **information structure.** Unlike syntax and semantics, which are sentence-based aspects of language, information structure requires consideration of whole texts—of sequences of sentences rather than isolated ones. Out of context, there is nothing wrong with the first sentence of Version 2.

As for the Santa Clara Fire Department, it evacuated two apartment buildings at the corner of Country Club Drive and 5th Avenue at 3 A.M. last Sunday.

It is only when this sentence serves to open a news report that it is inappropriate. Thus, when we talk about information structure we must take into account the *discourse context* of a sentence—that is, the environment in which it is produced, especially what comes before it. We can describe a **discourse** as a sequence of sentences that "go together": a conversation over the family dinner table, a newspaper column, a personal letter, a radio interview, or a subpoena to appear in court. We may also say that *Oh, look!* (uttered, for example, to draw attention to a beautiful sunset) is discourse, even though it is not a sequence of utterances, because the utterance is produced within an extralinguistic environment that helps determine an appropriate information structure.

In marking (or encoding) information structure in a sentence, speakers rely on the fact that the rules of syntax permit alternative ways of shaping sentences. The following is an incomplete list of alternative sentences that "say the same thing." It illustrates how broad a choice we have in expressing even simple predications.

The fireman discovered a leak in the basement.

A leak was discovered by the fireman in the basement.

A leak in the basement was discovered by the fireman.

It was the fireman who discovered a leak in the basement.

What the fireman discovered in the basement was a leak.

What the fireman discovered was a leak in the basement.

It was a leak that the fireman discovered in the basement.

What was discovered by the fireman was a leak in the basement.

As for the fireman, he discovered a leak in the basement.

In the basement, the fireman discovered a leak.

It is such a choice of alternatives that we exploit to mark information structure. You might ask yourself what question each of the sentences above is an appropriate answer to. This chapter will describe how that is done.

The term **pragmatics** is often used as an alternative to the term *information structure*. Pragmatics is the branch of linguistics that studies information structure. (Chapter 11 will discuss another aspect of language that is also sometimes referred to as "pragmatics.")

One of the first tasks that pragmatics must tackle is identifying the categories needed to talk about information structure. The fact that there are so many different ways to express the same thought demonstrates the need to make more subtle distinctions to describe the differences between these alternatives. A set of basic constructs must be developed to describe pragmatic differences in English and other languages.

CATEGORIES OF INFORMATION STRUCTURE

In order to describe the differences between alternative ways of "saying the same thing," we must identify the basic categories of information structure. These categories must be applicable to all languages (though the ways they are used may differ). With these categories, we want to explain how discourse is constructed in any language. Ultimately, these explanations may suggest hypotheses about how the different components of the human mind (such as memory, attention, and logic) work and interact with each other. Thus categories of information structure, like other aspects of linguistics, should be as independent of particular languages as possible.

There is an important difference between the types of syntactic constructions found in particular languages and the categories of information structure. The range of syntactic constructions available in different languages differs considerably; for example, some languages have a passive construction, while others do not. Since the categories of information structure are not language dependent, they cannot be defined in terms of particular structures.

Nevertheless, there is a close kinship between pragmatics and syntax. In all languages, one principal function of syntax is to encode pragmatic information. What differs from language to language is the way in which pragmatic structure maps onto syntax.

Given and New Information

One major category of information structure is the distinction between given and new information. **Given information** is information currently in the forefront of the hearer's mind; **new information** is information being introduced into the discourse. Consider the following two-turn interaction:

Alice: Who ate the custard?

Tom: Mary ate the custard.

The noun phrase *Mary* represents new information in Tom's answer because it is just being introduced into the discourse there; *the custard,* in contrast, is given information in the reply because it can be presumed to be in the mind of Alice, who has just introduced it into the discourse in the previous turn. (Because it is given information in Tom's reply, *the custard* would normally be expressed simply by the pronoun *it: Mary ate it.*)

Given information need not be introduced into a discourse by a second speaker. In the following sequence of sentences, uttered by a single speaker, the underlined element represents given information because it has just been introduced in the previous sentence and can thus be assumed to be in the hearer's mind.

A man called while you were on your break. He said he'd call back later.

A piece of information is sometimes taken as given because of its close association with something that has been introduced into the discourse. For example, when a noun phrase is introduced into a discourse, all the subparts of the referent can be treated as given information.

Kent returned my car last night after borrowing it for the day. One of the wheels was about to fall off and the dashboard was missing.

My mother went on a Caribbean cruise last year. She loved the food.

Because face-to-face conversation and most other kinds of discourse have at least implicit speakers and addressees, interactors always take first person (speaker) and second person (addressee) pronouns to be given information. These noun phrases thus do not need to be introduced into the discourse as new information.

Noun phrases carrying new information usually receive more stress than those carrying given information, and they are commonly expressed in a more elaborate fashion—for example, with a full noun phrase instead of a pronoun, and sometimes with a relative clause or adjectival modifiers. The following is typical of how new information is introduced into a discourse.

> When I entered the room, there was <u>a tall man with an old-fashioned hat on, quite elegantly dressed</u>.

In contrast, given information is commonly expressed in more attenuated ways—ways that are abbreviated or reduced. Typical attenuating devices used to encode given information include pronouns and unstressed noun phrases. Sometimes given information is simply left out of a sentence altogether. In the following interaction, the given information *is at the door* is omitted entirely from B's answer, which expresses only new information.

> A: Who's at the door?
>
> B: The mailman.

The contrast between given and new information is important in characterizing the function of several constructions in English and other languages, as we will show in the next section.

Topic

The **topic** of a sentence is its center of attention—what the sentence is about, its point of departure. The notion of topic is opposed to the notion of *comment*, the element of the sentence that says something about the topic. Often, given information is the sentence element about which we say something; in other words, given information is the topic. New information, on the other hand, represents what we want to say about the topic; it is the comment. Thus, if *Mary ate the custard* is offered in answer to the question *What did Mary do?*, the topic would be *Mary* (the given information) and the comment would be *ate the custard* (the new information). The topic of a sentence can sometimes be phrased as in this example:

> <u>Speaking of Mary</u>, she ate the custard.

Given information is not always the topic. In the second sentence of the following sequence, the noun phrase *her little sister* is both new information and the topic.

> Mary ate the custard. As for <u>her little sister</u>, she drank the cod-liver oil

Similarly, given information can serve as comment, as the underlined element in the following sequence illustrates.

> Harold didn't believe anything the charlatan said. As for Hilda, she <u>believed everything he said</u>.

So the given/new contrast differs from the topic/comment contrast.

It is difficult to define precisely what a topic is. While the topic is the element of a sentence that functions as the center of attention, a sentence like *Oh, look!*, uttered to draw attention to a beautiful sunset, has an unexpressed topic ("the setting sun" or "the sky"). Thus topic is not necessarily a property of the sentence; it may be a property of the discourse context.

Topics are less central to the grammar of English than to the grammar of certain other languages. Indeed, the one construction of English that unequivocally marks topics is the relatively rare *as for* construction. In English, marking the topic of a sentence is far less important than marking the subject.

Marking topic is considerably more important in certain other languages. Languages such as Japanese and Korean have function words whose sole purpose is to mark a noun phrase as topic (Japanese is discussed in the section on "Information-Structure Morphemes," page 213). In Chinese and other languages, no special function words attach to topic noun phrases, but they are marked by word order. In these three languages, noun phrases marked in one way or another as the topic occur very frequently. Thus, despite the difficulty in defining it, the notion of topic is important and needs to be distinguished from other categories of information structure.

Contrast

A noun phrase is said to be **contrastive** when it occurs in opposition to another noun phrase in the discourse. Here, for example, the noun phrase *Hilda* in B's answer is contrasted with the noun phrase *Matt*.

A: Did Matt see the ghost?

B: No, Hilda saw the ghost.

Contrast that answer by B with the following one, in which *Matt* is not contrastive.

B: Yes, Matt saw the ghost.

Contrast is also marked in sentences that express the narrowing down of a choice from several candidates to one. In such sentences, the noun phrase that refers to the candidate thus chosen is marked contrastively.

Of everyone present, only Hilda knew what was going on.

Compare that sentence with the following one, in which *Hilda* is not contrastive.

Gerard knew what was going on, and Hilda knew what was going on.

A simple test exists for contrast: if a noun phrase can be followed by *rather than,* it is contrastive.

A: Did Matt see the ghost?

B: No, <u>Hilda</u>, rather than Matt, saw the ghost.

A single sentence can have several contrastive noun phrases; in B's answer in the following exchange, *Hilda* contrasts with *Matt,* and *an entire cast of spirits* contrasts with *a ghost.*

A: Did Matt see a ghost?

B: Yes, Matt saw a ghost, but <u>Hilda</u> saw <u>an entire cast of spirits</u>.

The entity with which a noun phrase is contrasted is understood sometimes from the discourse context and sometimes from the nonlinguistic context. In the following example, *Hilda* could be marked contrastively if the sentence were part of a conversation about how the interlocutors dislike going to Maine during the winter.

<u>Hilda</u> likes going to Maine during the winter.

In the next exchange, between an employee and one of several managers, the noun phrase *I* in the manager's reply can be made to contrast with "other managers," which is understood from the context.

Employee: Can I leave early today?

Manager: <u>I</u> don't mind.

The implication of the manager's answer is 'It's fine with me, but I don't know about the other managers.' The employee can readily understand the implication from knowledge of the context.

In English, contrastive noun phrases can be marked in a variety of ways, the most common of which is by pronouncing the contrastive noun phrase with strong stress.

You may be smart, but <u>he</u> is good-looking.

Other ways of marking contrastiveness will be investigated in the next section.

Definiteness

Speakers mark a noun phrase as **definite** when they assume that the listener can identify the referent of the noun phrase; otherwise, the noun phrase is marked as **indefinite.** In this example, the definite noun phrase *the neighbor* in B's answer presupposes that A can determine which neighbor B is talking about.

A: Who's at the door?

B: It's <u>the neighbor</u>.

B's answer is appropriate if A and B have only one neighbor or have reason to expect a particular neighbor. If they have several neighbors, none of whom they know particularly well, B cannot assume that A will be able to identify which neighbor is at the door, and the answer to A's question must be indefinite.

> B: It's a neighbor.

Pronouns and proper nouns are generally definite. Pronouns like *you* and *we* usually refer to particular individuals, who are identifiable in the context of the discourse. And a speaker who refers to someone by the name *Hilda* or *Harry* assumes that a listener will be able to determine the referents of these names. Still, there are exceptions. Clerks in a government office may say to each other:

> I have a Susie Schmidt here who hasn't paid her taxes since 1947.

And they can do this irrespective of whether the speaker or hearer knows which particular individual goes by the name of Susie Schmidt.

Definiteness in English and many other languages is marked by the choice of articles (definite *the* versus indefinite *a*) or demonstratives (*this* and *that,* both definite). But article choice is not always a way to mark definiteness. Some languages have only one article. In Fijian, *na,* the only article, is definite, while indefiniteness is marked with the help of the expression *e dua* 'there is one.'

> na   tuuraŋa   (definite)
>
> Article gentleman
>
> 'the gentleman'

> e dua   na   tuuraŋa   (indefinite)
>
> there is one Article gentleman
>
> 'a gentleman'

Hindi, in contrast, has only an indefinite article *ek;* a noun phrase with no article is interpreted as definite.

> Maĩ kɪtaab ḍʰũũṛʰ rahii tʰii.   (definite)
>
> I   book   search -ing   Past-tense
>
> 'I was looking for the book.'

> Maĩ ek kɪtaab ḍʰũũṛʰ rahii tʰii.   (indefinite)
>
> I   a   book   search -ing   Past-tense
>
> 'I was looking for a book.'

Many languages do not have articles and must rely on other means to mark definiteness, if they mark it at all. In Mandarin Chinese, word order is used to mark definiteness. When the subject comes before the verb, as in 1, it must be interpreted as definite; if it follows the verb, as in 2, it is indefinite.

1. Huǒchē lái   le.

   train   arrive New-situation   (definite)

   'The train has arrived.'

2. Lái   huǒchē le.   (indefinite)

   arrive train   New-situation

   'A train has arrived.'

More exotic systems also exist; in Rotuman, spoken in the South Pacific, most words have two forms, one definite and one indefinite.

Definite		**Indefinite**	
futi	'the banana'	füt	'a banana'
vaka	'the canoe'	vak	'a canoe'
rito	'the young shoot'	ryot	'a young shoot'

The indefinite form can be derived from the definite form through a series of phonological rules.

Definiteness must be distinguished from givenness because a noun phrase can be definite and given, indefinite and given, definite and new, or indefinite and new. The first and the last combinations are the most common: here, the underlined noun phrase in the first sentence is indefinite and new, and the one in the second sentence is definite and given.

> Once upon a time, there was a young woman who lived on a remote farm in the country. The young woman was named Mary.

But a noun phrase that refers to new information can also be definite. The following sentence, in which *the plumber* is definite, is acceptable whether or not the speaker has introduced a particular identifiable plumber into the previous discourse.

> The kitchen faucet is leaking; we have to call the plumber.

In certain circumstances, a noun phrase can be both indefinite and given, as with the underlined noun phrase in this example:

> I ate a hamburger for breakfast—a hamburger, I might add, that was one of the worst I've ever eaten.

Clearly, definiteness and givenness are distinct categories of information structure.

Referentiality

A noun phrase is **referential** when it refers to a particular entity. In the first example, the noun phrase *an Italian with dark eyes* does not refer to anyone in particular and is therefore nonreferential. In the second example, in contrast, the same noun phrase does have a referent and is referential.

Katie wants to marry an Italian with dark eyes, but she hasn't found one yet.

Katie wants to marry an Italian with dark eyes; his name is Mario.

Out of context, *Katie wants to marry an Italian with dark eyes* is ambiguous because nothing in the sentence indicates whether or not a particular man is intended. In real-life natural discourse, sentences of this type are rarely ambiguous because of the power of context to clarify.

Referentiality and definiteness must be distinguished because a noun phrase can be:

Referential and definite

I'm looking for the dog. (that is, the family dog)

Referential and indefinite

I'm looking for a dog. It's a fawn-colored boxer with a white chest and floppy ears.

Nonreferential and definite

I'm looking for the most intelligent dog. But I haven't found it yet.

Nonreferential and indefinite

I'm looking for a dog. Do you have any for sale?

While pronouns and proper nouns are usually referential, certain pronouns, such as *you, it, they,* and *one,* are often nonreferential.

If *you* can't stand the heat, get out of the kitchen.

It is widely suspected that linguistics is fun to study.

They have just changed the tax laws.

One just doesn't know what to do in these circumstances.

None of these pronouns refers to a particular person or entity: they are nonreferential.

Generic and Specific

A noun phrase may be *generic* or *specific* depending on whether it refers to a category or to a particular member of a category. In the first of the following sentences, *the giraffe* is generic because it refers to the set of all giraffes; but *the giraffe* in the second sentence, which could have been uttered during a visit to the zoo, must refer to a particular animal, and is thus specific.

> The giraffe has a long neck.

> The giraffe has a sore foot.

The generic/specific contrast thus differs from definiteness and referentiality, and must be considered a separate category.

Relational and Inherent Categories

Of the categories discussed in this section, givenness, topic, and contrast are not inherent properties of particular noun phrases. Like semantic roles, these categories can be defined only in relation to the context in which the noun phrase occurs. For example, we can identify whether a noun phrase is contrastive or not only if we know the sentence or even the discourse in which it occurs. Givenness, topic, and contrast are thus *relational* categories of information structure.

Definiteness, referentiality, and the generic/specific contrast are *inherent* properties of a noun phrase. Given a particular noun phrase (and some information about what it refers to), we can usually decide whether it is definite or indefinite, referential or nonreferential, and generic or specific without knowing the sentence in which it occurs.

Information Structure and Lexical Categories

Information structure is not marked solely on noun phrases. Other lexical categories, verbs in particular, can be given or new information and can also be contrastive. In the following exchange, the underlined verb represents contrastively marked new information.

> Jerry comes to visit occasionally, but Lou <u>moves in</u> every holiday.

Similarly, function words like prepositions can sometimes be marked for information structure. It is not difficult to come up with examples of contrastively marked prepositions.

> I said the phone book was <u>on</u> the table, not under it!

In this chapter, we concentrate almost exclusively on the marking of information structure on noun phrases, in part because the role of other constituents in the structure of discourse is still poorly understood.

PRAGMATIC CATEGORIES AND SYNTAX

The categories of information structure can now be used to describe the functions of transformations and other phenomena found in different languages. As noted earlier, every language can express the same content in a variety of ways. The difference between these various ways of expressing the same thing is most frequently a pragmatic one. In this section we will analyze a number of constructions, many of which are found in English, and illustrate how information structure is an important determiner of the choices that we make in expressing ourselves verbally.

Languages differ in the extent to which and the way in which pragmatic information is encoded in morphology and syntax. Some languages, like Japanese, have function words whose sole purpose is to indicate pragmatic categories. Other languages, like English, depend on syntactic structures like passives to convey pragmatic information. Intonation is also used in many languages to mark contrast. In English, intonation is an important tool in marking information structure; it is less important in languages like French and unimportant in Chinese. Thus different languages use different strategies to encode pragmatic information. What follows is a sampling of some of these strategies.

Fronting

The first strategy that may be used to mark information structure is fronting. *Fronting* is a movement transformation that operates in many languages, although its exact function varies from language to language. In English, it creates sentence 1 from the structure underlying sentence 2, which has the same meaning.

1. Lou I cannot stand.

2. I cannot stand Lou.

In English, the main function of fronting is to mark givenness. The fronted noun phrase must represent given information.

A: I heard that you really like mushrooms.

B: <u>Mushrooms</u> I'd kill for.

A noun phrase can be fronted if its referent is part of a set that has been mentioned previously in the discourse, even though it may not represent given information itself. In the following, *mushrooms* is a hyponym of *vegetable,* which is mentioned in the question that immediately precedes the fronted noun phrase; the result is pragmatically acceptable.

A: What's your favorite vegetable?

B: Mushrooms I find delicious.

Fronted noun phrases are often contrastive in English.

A: Do you eat cauliflower?

B: I hate cauliflower, but <u>mushrooms</u> I find delicious.

The fronted noun phrase must be the more salient element of the sentence. If this requirement is violated, the result is pragmatically ill formed. In B's answer in the following interaction, *mushrooms* is not the most salient element in the sentence, because the hearer's attention is distracted by the phrase *with butter and parsley*.

A: What's your favorite vegetable?

B: *Mushrooms I love to eat with butter and parsley.[1]

In other languages, fronted noun phrases do not necessarily have the same function as in English. In Mandarin Chinese, fronted noun phrases are commonly used to represent the topic of the sentence.

Zhèi	běn	shū	pízi	hěn	hǎokàn.
this	Classifier	book	cover	very	good-looking

'This book, the cover is nice looking.'

Zhèi	ge	zhǎnlǎnhuì,	wǒ	kàndào	hěn	duō	yóuhuàr.
this	Classifier	exhibition	I	see	very	many	painting

'(At) this exhibition, I saw many paintings.'

What is interesting about Chinese fronted noun phrases is that they do not necessarily have a semantic role in the rest of the sentence. In the following sentence, for example, *mógū* 'mushrooms' cannot be a patient because the sentence already has a patient: *zhèi ge dōngxi* 'that sort of thing.' Yet the sentence is both grammatical and pragmatically acceptable.

Mógū	wǒ	hěn	xǐhuan	chī	zhèi	ge	dōngxi.
mushroom	I	very	like	eat	this	Classifier	thing

'Mushrooms, I like to eat that sort of thing.'

Furthermore, fronted noun phrases do not need to be contrastive in Chinese, though they frequently are in English. The comparison of English and Chinese fronting illustrates an important point: A grammatical process such as a movement

---

[1] In this chapter, asterisks * are used to mark not ungrammatical sentences but sentences that are pragmatically ill formed—that is, sentences that do not fit well into the discourse context in which they occur.

transformation may have comparable syntactic properties in two languages, but its pragmatic functions may differ considerably.

Left-Dislocation

Left-dislocation is a transformation that derives sentences like 1 from the same underlying structures as basic sentences like 2.

1. Margaret, I can't stand her.
2. I can't stand Margaret.

Though left-dislocation is syntactically similar to fronting, there are several differences between the two. In particular, a fronted noun phrase does not leave a pronoun in the sentence, whereas a left-dislocated noun phrase does.

Margaret, I can't stand. (fronting)

Margaret, I can't stand her. (left-dislocation)

Unlike fronted noun phrases, a left-dislocated noun phrase is also set off from the rest of the sentence by a very short pause, represented in writing by a comma. Left-dislocation is similar in nature and function to *right-dislocation,* which moves the noun phrases to the right of a sentence.

I can't stand her, Margaret. (right-dislocation)

In this discussion, we will concentrate on left-dislocation.

Left-dislocation is primarily used to reintroduce given information that has not been talked about for a while. In the following long example, the speaker lists a number of people and comments on them. Harold, one of the people mentioned earlier in the discourse, is reintroduced in the last sentence. Because nothing has been said about Harold in the previous two sentences, the speaker reintroduces *Harold* as a left-dislocated noun phrase.

I've kept in touch with many people from my school days. I still see Harold, who was my best friend in high school. And then there's Jim, who was my college roommate, and Stan and Hilda, who I met in my sophomore year at State. I really like Jim and Stan and Hilda. But *Harold,* I can't stand him now.

In addition to reintroducing given information, left-dislocation is contrastive. In this example, *Harold* clearly contrasts with *Jim, Stan,* and *Hilda.* As a result of its double function, left-dislocation is typically used when speakers go through lists and make comments about each individual element in the list. Some languages exploit left-dislocation considerably more frequently than English does. In spoken colloquial French, left-dislocated noun phrases are frequent, considerably more so than the equivalent basic sentences.

<u>Mon frère</u>,   il   s'en va   en   Mongolie.

my   brother   he   is-going   to   Mongolia

'My brother, he is leaving for Mongolia.'

Right-dislocation, illustrated by the following sentence, is equally common.

J'sais   pas,   <u>moi</u>,   c'qu'il   veux.

I know   not   me   what-he   wants

'Me, I don't know what he wants.'

Left-dislocation in colloquial French has a different function from the equivalent transformation in English. In French, a left-dislocated noun phrase represents a topic. Left-dislocated noun phrases are particularly frequent when a new topic is introduced into the discourse (as in the first of the following examples) or when the speaker wishes to shift the topic of the discourse (as in the second example).

[Asking directions of a stranger in the street]

Pardon,   <u>la</u>   <u>gare</u>,   où   elle   est?

excuse-me   the   station   where   it   is

'Excuse me, where is the station?'

Pierre: <u>Moi</u>,   j'aime   bien   les   croissants.

me   I like   the   croissants

'Me, I like croissants.'

Marie: Oui,   mais   <u>le</u>   <u>pain</u>   <u>frais</u>,   c'est   bon   aussi.

yes   but   the   bread   fresh   it-is   good   too

'Yes, but fresh bread is also good.'

The pragmatic function of left-dislocation in French is thus considerably broader than its function in English.

Clefting and Pseudoclefting

Clefting and *pseudoclefting* are transformations that are commonly used in English and many other languages to mark information structure in the sentence. In the next examples, sentence 1 is a cleft sentence, sentence 2 is a pseudocleft sentence, and sentence 3 is the basic sentence that corresponds to 1 and 2—that is, the sentence that is derived from the same underlying structure but to which no transformation has applied.

1. It was Harold that Stan saw at the party. (cleft)

2. What Stan saw at the party was Harold. (pseudocleft)

3. Stan saw Harold at the party.

Cleft sentences are of the form *It* BE . . . *that,* in which BE stands for some form of the verb *to be* (such as *is, was,* or *will be*) and what comes between the first part and the second part of the construction is the clefted noun phrase or prepositional phrase. Pseudocleft constructions can be of the form WH-word . . . BE, in which the WH-word is usually *what.* In pseudocleft constructions, the pseudoclefted noun phrase or prepositional phrase is placed after the verb *to be,* and the rest of the clause is placed between the two parts of the construction. Other variants of pseudocleft sentences also exist.

the one that/who . . . BE

The one who saw Harold at the party was Stan.

. . . BE *what/who* . . .

Harold is who John saw at the party.

Both cleft and pseudocleft constructions are used to mark givenness. In a cleft construction, the clefted noun phrase presents new information, and the rest of the sentence is given information. Thus the information question in 1 can be answered with 2, in which the answer to the question is clefted, but not with 3 because the clefted element is not the requested new information.

1. Who did Stan see at the party?

2. It was Harold that Stan saw at the party.

3. *It was Stan who saw Harold at the party.

That the part of the sentence following *that* in a cleft sentence presents given information is illustrated by the fact that it can refer to something just mentioned in the previous sentence. In the following example, the second sentence is a cleft construction in which the elements following *that* are simply repeated from the previous sentence in the discourse.

Alice told me that Stan saw someone at the party that he knew from his high school days. It turns out that it was Harold that Stan saw at the party.

Clearly, the element following *that* in a cleft sentence represents given information.

Pseudocleft constructions are similar to cleft constructions. In pseudocleft sentences, the new information comes after the verb *to be,* and the rest of the clause is placed between the WH-word and the *be* verb.

1.   What did Stan see at the party?

2.   What Stan saw at the party was Harold dancing the rumba.

Question 1 could not be answered with either of the following pseudoclefted sentences because in neither 3 nor 4 is the pseudoclefted noun phrase the new information.

3.   *The one who saw Harold dancing the rumba was Stan.

4.   *Where Stan saw Harold was at the party.

The rest of a pseudoclefted sentence marks given information, as in clefted sentences. The following sentence pair, in which given information is underlined, illustrates this fact.

I liked her latest novel very much. In particular, what <u>I liked about it</u> was the way the characters' personalities are developed.

The effect of both clefting and pseudoclefting is to highlight which element is new information and which element is given information.

In addition, both constructions can mark contrast. Consider the following two sequences. In the first sequence (in which the second sentence is a cleft construction) and the second (whose second sentence is a pseudocleft), the new information can easily be understood as being contrastive. Possible implied information is provided in square brackets after each example.

Alice said that Stan saw someone at the party that he knew from his high school days. It turns out it was Harold <u>that Stan saw at</u> the party. [. . . not Larry, as you might have thought.]

I liked her latest novel very much. In particular, what <u>I liked about it</u> was the way the characters' personalities are developed. [. . . I liked the character development more than the style of writing.]

You might wonder why English should have two constructions with the same function. Languages usually exploit different structures for different purposes—and, indeed, there is a subtle difference in the uses for these two constructions. A cleft construction can be used to mark given information that the listener or reader is not necessarily thinking about; in a pseudocleft construction, though, the listener or reader must be thinking about the given information. Thus it is possible to begin a narrative with a cleft construction but not with a pseudocleft construction. This first sentence, a cleft construction, would be an acceptable opening sentence for a written historical narrative; but the second sentence, a pseudocleft construction, would not normally make a good beginning.

It was to gain their independence from Britain that the colonists started the Revolution.

*What the colonists started the Revolution to gain was their independence from Britain.

The first sentence is an acceptable opening because it does not necessarily assume that the reader has in mind the given information ("the colonists started the Revolution") when the narrative begins. The second sentence does assume that the given information is in the reader's mind and thus does not make a good opening sentence.

The difference between cleft and pseudocleft constructions shows that given information is not an absolute notion. There may be different types of givenness: information that the listener knows but is not necessarily thinking about at the moment versus information that the listener both knows and is thinking about.

Sentence Stress

In English and some other languages, intonation is an important information-marking device. Generally, noun phrases representing new information receive stronger stress than noun phrases representing given information, and they are uttered on a slightly higher pitch than the rest of the sentence. This is called *new-information stress*.

A: Whose foot marks are these on the sofa?

B: They're <u>Lou's</u> foot marks.

English speakers also exploit stress to mark contrast.

A: Are these your foot marks on the sofa?

B: No, they're not mine, they're <u>Lou's</u>.

They told Harold he had to put in two more years to graduate, but they gave <u>Hilda</u> an <u>honorary doctorate</u>.

Phonetically new-information stress and contrastive stress are very similar but functionally they are different. English uses stress in very complex ways, much more so than such languages as French and Chinese.

Information-Structure Morphemes

Some languages have grammatical morphemes whose sole function is to mark categories of information structure. In Japanese, the function word *wa,* which is placed after noun phrases, marks either givenness or contrastiveness. When a noun phrase is neither given nor contrastive, it is marked with a different function word (usually *ga* for subjects and *o* for direct objects). That *wa* is a marker of given information is illustrated by the following exchange.

A: Basu   ga   kimasuka?

bus   Subject   come-Question

'Is the bus coming?'

B: <u>Basu</u>   <u>wa</u>   kimasu.

    bus   Given   coming-is

    'The bus is coming.'

In A's question, *basu* could not be marked with *wa* unless A and B had been talking about it in the previous discourse. But in B's answer, *basu* is given information and must be marked with *wa*. Here is another example.

Basu   ga   kimasu.   <u>Basu</u>   <u>wa</u>   konde-imasu.

bus   Subject   coming-is   bus   Given   crowded-is

'The bus is coming. The bus is crowded.'

Japanese *wa* also marks contrastive information, as in the following sentence:

<u>Basu</u>   <u>wa</u>   kimasu.   Demo   <u>takushii</u>   <u>wa</u>   kimasen.

bus   Contrast   coming-is.   But   taxi   Contrast   coming-isn't

'The bus is coming. But the taxi isn't (coming).'

Here, *basu wa* need not represent given information, for *wa* can simply mark the fact that the noun phrase to which it is attached is in contrast with another noun phrase also marked with *wa* (*takushii* 'taxi').

Like Japanese, many languages use function words to mark different categories of information structure. This device is the most transparent way of marking information structure. Unlike movement transformations, such grammatical morphemes as Japanese *wa* do not affect the overall shape of a sentence; rather, in a straightforward fashion, they point out which element of a sentence is given, which is contrastive, and so on.

Passives

As with other languages that have a passive construction, the choice between an active sentence and its passive equivalent can be exploited in English to mark information structure. Compare the following sentences:

1. The old man was scolding the mermaid.

2. The mermaid was being scolded by the old man.

3. The mermaid was being scolded.

Of these three sentences, all of which can describe the same situation, 1 is active, while the other two are passive structures. In 2, the agent is expressed *(by the old man),* whereas there is no expressed agent in 3. We call a passive construction like 2 an *agent passive* construction; 3 is an example of an *agentless passive.*

In general, speakers and writers of English prefer active to passive sentences. What makes a sentence like *A good time was had by all* humorous is the fact that it is passive without a reason. Such unmotivated passives occur frequently among beginning writers, who appear to labor under the misapprehension that passive structures are more literary than active ones. (On the distribution of active and passive structures, see Chapter 12.)

Agentless and agent passives are used in English for specific purposes. First of all, a sentence is expressed as an agentless passive if the agent is particularly unimportant in the action or state that the sentence describes. Such a situation may arise, for example, when the agent is a generic entity whose identity is irrelevant to the point of the sentence.

A new shopping mall is being built near the Interstate.

New Christmas stamps are issued every year.

In the first sentence, the agent is likely to be some real-estate developer; in the second sentence, the postal authorities. In each case, the exact identity of the agent is either known or irrelevant to the situation described by the sentence. In spoken language, agentless passives are often equivalent to active sentences with an indefinite and nonreferential pronoun *they*.

They're building a new shopping mall near the Interstate.

They issue new Christmas stamps every year.

An agent passive construction is used if a noun phrase other than the agent is given information. Suppose that a news report begins as follows:

The World Health Organization held its annual meeting last week in Geneva.

This sentence establishes the *meeting* as given information for the rest of the report. If the next sentence uses the noun phrase *the meeting,* it is likely that the phrase will occur in subject position because it is given information. If the noun phrase *the meeting* does not have the semantic role of agent in the next sentence, the sentence is likely to be expressed as a passive construction in order to allow *the meeting* to be the grammatical subject.

The meeting was organized by health administrators from fifty countries.

This rule is of course not absolute, and indeed there is nothing fundamentally wrong with the following sequence, in which the second sentence is active rather than the passive predicted by the rule.

The World Health Organization held its annual meeting last week in Geneva. Health administrators from fifty countries organized the meeting.

But the equivalent sequence with a passive second sentence seems to flow better and may be easier to understand.

> The World Health Organization held its annual meeting last week in Geneva. The meeting was organized by health administrators from fifty countries.

Clearly, in English the choice of a passive sentence over its active counterpart is regulated by information structure. Specifically, agentless passives are used when the agent is either known or is not significant; agent passives are used when a noun phrase other than the agent of the sentence is more prominent as given information than the agent itself.

Not all languages have a passive construction. Samoan, for example, does not, but it has other ways of saying what English speakers express with the passive. In Samoan, when the agent of a sentence is not important, it is simply not expressed; the sentence remains an active structure.

> ʔua   ʔoteŋia le   teiŋe.
>
> Present-tense scold   the   young-woman
>
> 'The young woman is being scolded.' (Literally: 'Is scolding the young woman.')

Word Order

Many languages use the sequential order of noun phrases to mark differences in information structure. English cannot use the full resources of word order for this purpose because it uses word order to mark subjects and direct objects (see Chapter 5). In the following sentence, the word order indicates who is doing the chasing and who is being chased.

> The cat is chasing the dog.

If we invert the two noun phrases, the semantics of the sentence (who is agent and who is patient) changes.

> The dog is chasing the cat.

In a language like Russian, however, we can scramble the noun phrases without changing the semantics. All the following sentences mean the same thing.

> Koška presleduet sobaku.
> cat   is chasing dog
>
> Sobaku presleduet koška.
> Presleduet koška sobaku.   'The cat is chasing the dog.'
> Presleduet sobaku koška.
> Koška sobaku presleduet.
> Sobaku koška presleduet.

In each of these sentences we know who is doing what to whom because the inflections on the noun vary with the noun's grammatical function. The *-u* ending of *sobaku* 'dog' marks it as the direct object (if it were the subject, it would be *sobaka*), and the *-a* ending of *koška* 'cat' marks it as the subject (as direct object, it would be *košku*).

The differences among these versions of the same sentence reside in their information structure. More precisely, word order marks givenness in Russian. The information question *Što koška presleduet?* 'What is the cat chasing?' can only be answered as followed:

Koška   presleduet   sobaku.

cat   is chasing   dog

'The cat is chasing the dog.'

On the other hand, the question *Što presleduet sobaku?* 'What is chasing the dog?' must be answered as follows:

Sobaku   presleduet   koška.

dog   is chasing   cat

'The cat is chasing the dog.'

Thus what comes first in the Russian sentence is not the subject but the given information, and what comes last is the new information. In answer to the question *What is the cat chasing?, the dog* is new information and comes at the end of the Russian sentence. In contrast, *the cat* is new information in answer to the question *What is chasing the dog?,* and, therefore, it comes last in the sentence. Word order in Russian, as in many other languages, is thus used to mark givenness. Similar explanations could be offered for the other four variants of the Russian sentence we have cited, but we will not develop them here.

Typically, in languages that exploit word order to encode pragmatic information, syntactic constructions like passives, clefts, and pseudoclefts do not exist (or are rare). Russian has a grammatical construction that resembles the English passive, but it is rarely used. The reason is simple: Given the rich inflectional system that marks grammatical relations, word order can be used to mark information structure, and there is really no need to use complex structures like passives to mark givenness. Passives are useful only in languages in which word order is exploited for other purposes and thus cannot be manipulated to indicate pragmatic structure.

PRAGMATICS: THE RELATIONSHIP OF SENTENCES TO DISCOURSE

We have outlined some of the basic notions needed to describe how information is structured in discourse and have analyzed a number of constructions in terms of information structure. From the discussion in this and the previous chapter, it should be clear that the syntactic structure of any language is driven by two factors. On the one hand, syntax must encode semantic structure. The syntactic structure of a sentence must enable language users to identify who does what to whom—the agent of a sentence, the patient, and other semantic roles. On the other hand, syntax must encode information structure: which element of a noun phrase is given information, which is new information, which can be easily identified by the hearer, which cannot, and so on. Schematically, the relationship is as follows:

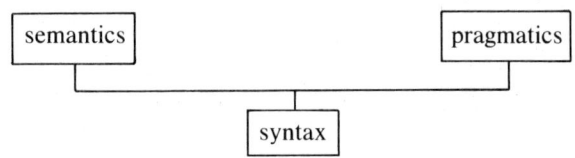

Syntax thus is used to convey two types of information: semantic information and pragmatic information.

SUMMARY

Pragmatics is concerned with the encoding of information structure—the relative significance of different elements in a clause, principally noun phrases. Pragmatics treats the relationship of sentences to their discourse environment.

Several categories of information structure must be distinguished. Relational categories include *givenness* (whether a piece of information is new or already exists in the discourse context), *topic* (the center of attention), and *contrast* (whether or not a piece of information is contrasted with another piece). Nonrelational notions include *definiteness* (whether or not the referent of a noun phrase is identifiable) and *referentiality* (whether or not a noun phrase has a referent).

The function of many syntactic transformations is to mark certain elements of sentences for these different pragmatic categories. In English, structures like left-dislocation, cleft, pseudocleft, and passive have the effect of singling out particular noun phrases as sentence topics or as given or new information. The marking of contrast is achieved through sentence stress and is a secondary function of certain transformations like fronting. Many languages exploit word order and grammatical morphemes to mark information structure. The functions of a particular transformation or information-structure device may differ from one language to another: Each language favors particular strategies over others.

Syntax is thus used to encode two types of information: *semantic* information (the semantic role of a noun phrase) and *pragmatic* information (the relative significance of noun phrases in a discourse).

EXERCISES

1.   Describe in detail why the following text is poorly constructed. Analyze each of the seven sentences in its context and state what is wrong with it in terms of information structure.

(1) As for the Fire Department, it evacuated two apartment buildings at the corner of Country Club Drive and 5th Avenue at 3 A.M. last Sunday. (2) There was some-one who had discovered a furnace in the basement of one of the buildings from which oil was leaking. (3) What was sprayed by firemen over the oil for several hours was chemical foam. (4) It was by 8 A.M. that the situation was under control. (5) What someone had averted was any danger of explosion or fire, and as for the leaky furnace, it was sealed. (6) What the residents of the two apartment buildings were given in the Country Club High School gymnasium was temporary shelter. (7) Possession of their apartments was regained by them at 5 P.M.

2. Choose a short article (approximately one newspaper column) or an excerpt of an article from the front page of a newspaper. Identify all the sentences in the article that have undergone a transformation of some kind (such as passivization or clefting). In each case, provide a likely reason for using a transformed sentence instead of the equivalent basic sentence.

3. In certain dialects of English there is a rule that moves a noun phrase to the beginning of its clause. This transformation derives sentence (1) from the same underlying struc-ture as the basic sentence (2):

    (1)   A bottle of champagne and caviar he wants.

    (2)   He wants a bottle of champagne and caviar.

The transformation is called *Yiddish movement* because it is characteristic of the English dialect spoken by some native speakers of Yiddish. Yiddish movement is syntactically similar to fronting but differs in terms of its pragmatic function. Here are three pragmatic contexts in which Yiddish movement is appropriate. On the basis of these data, describe succinctly the pragmatic function of Yiddish movement.

    A: What does he want?

    B: A bottle of champagne and caviar he wants!

    A: How's your daughter?

    B: The troubles in school she's having!

    A: Are you willing to help me?

    B: A finger I would not lift for you!

Compare in particular the following interactions; in the first, the answer can undergo Yiddish movement; in the second, it cannot.

    A: Who is Lou going to marry?

    B: A scoundrel Lou is going to marry!

    A: Who is going to marry Lou?

    B: *Lou a scoundrel is going to marry!

4.   In English, *presentational constructions* are sentences in which a noun phrase is preceded by *there is/was* (or any other tense variant) and followed by a relative clause. Here are two typical examples.

> Once upon a time there was a poor peasant who had three sons.

> There's a man who wants to talk to you; he's been waiting for more than an hour.

Presentational constructions must be distinguished from constructions with *there* that indicate location, as in: *There's my lavender shawl*. Describe succinctly the pragmatic function of presentational constructions. In your discussion, you may refer to the following additional examples:

(1)   There is a dog I've been looking for. It's a fawn boxer with a white chest and cropped ears.

(2)   *There's a dog I've been looking for. Any dog will do.

(3)   There's the new Fellini movie that's playing at the Arts Theater.

(4)   There's that weird guy who called yesterday who's waiting for you in your office.

5.   As in Russian, word order in Spanish is used to encode information structure. The constituents of a sentence may be ordered in a variety of ways, as shown by the following examples from Castilian Spanish, all of which can describe the same event. (S = subject; V = verb; O = direct object)

Consuelo envió el   paquete. (SVO)
Consuelo sent   the package

Envió Consuelo el   paquete. (VSO)
sent   Consuelo the package

Envió el   paquete Consuelo. (VOS)
sent   the package Consuelo

El   paquete lo envió Consuelo. (OVS)
the package it sent   Consuelo

'Consuelo sent the package.'

Consider the following conversational exchanges, focusing on the order of constituents in the answers.

(1)   Q: ¿Qué   hizo Consuelo?

        what did   Consuelo

        'What did Consuelo do?'

        A: Consuelo preparó   la   sangria.

        Consuelo prepared   the sangria

        'Consuelo made the sangria.'

(2) Q: ¿Quién comió mi bocadillo?

      who   ate   my sandwich

      'Who ate my sandwich?'

    A: Tu   bocadillo lo comió Consuelo.

      your sandwich it ate   Consuelo

      'Consuelo ate your sandwich.'

(3) Q: ¿A quién dió   Consuelo este regalo?

      to whom gave Consuelo this present

      'Who did Consuelo give this present to?'

    A: Este regalo lo dió   Consuelo a su madre.

      this present it gave Consuelo to her mother

      'Consuelo gave this present to her mother.

(4) Q: ¿Que pasó?

      what occurred

      'What happened?'

    A: Se murió Consuelo

      died   Consuelo

      'Consuelo died.'

(5) Q: ¿Recibió Consuelo el premio?

      received Consuelo the prize

      'Did Consuelo get the prize?'

    A: No, el premio lo recibió Paquita.

      no the prize it received Paquita

      'No, *Paquita* got the prize.'

(6) Q: ¿Recibió Consuelo esta carta?

      received Consuelo this letter

      'Did Consuelo get this letter?'

    A: No, Consuelo recibió este paquete.

      no Consuelo received this package

      'No, Consuelo got this *package*.'

(7)   Q: ¿Recibió   Consuelo   el   premio?

received   Consuelo   the   prize

'Did Consuelo get the prize?'

A: Si, el   premio lo recibió   Consuelo.

yes the prize   it received Consuelo

'Yes, Consuelo got the prize.'

a.   On the basis of these data, describe how word order is used to mark information structure in statements (but not in questions). In particular, state which categories of information structure are marked through which word order possibility. Make the statement of your rules as general as possible.

b.   Notice that in certain sentences the pronoun *lo* 'it' appears before the verb. What is the syntactic rule that dictates when it should and should not appear? Which rule of English does the presence of the pronoun in these sentences remind you of?

SUGGESTIONS FOR FURTHER READING

Overviews of the issues addressed in this chapter can be found in Leech (1983), Brown and Yule (1983), Foley and Van Valin (1985), Givón (1979a), and Chafe (1976). The papers in Givón (1979b) and Li (1976) investigate the interaction of syntax and pragmatics in various languages. Chafe (1970) is an important study of this interaction in English. Givenness and related topics are discussed in Gundel (1977) and Prince (1979), definiteness in Hawkins (1979). Japanese *wa* and other particles are discussed in Kuno (1973). Our discussion of English cleft and pseudocleft constructions is based on Prince (1978) and that of fronting and Yiddish movement on Prince (1981). Lambrecht (1981) is an analysis of left- and right-dislocation in spoken French; left-dislocation in Italian is discussed in Duranti and Ochs (1979).

English passive constructions are investigated in Thompson (1987) and in Weiner and Labov (1983). There is a concise discussion of the function of Russian word order in Comrie (1979), with which Thompson's (1978) study of English word order can be usefully contrasted. For an overview of research on intonation and sentence stress and their pragmatic functions, see Bolinger (1986). Other means of marking pragmatic structure in English are discussed in Halliday and Hasan (1976). Quirk et al. (1985), an extensive description of English grammar, discusses the pragmatic functions of particular constructions.

REFERENCES

Bolinger, Dwight L. 1986. *Intonation and Its Parts: Melody in Spoken English* (Stanford: Stanford University Press).

Brown, Gillian, and George Yule. 1983. *Discourse Analysis* (Cambridge: Cambridge University Press).

Chafe, Wallace L. 1970. *Meaning and the Structure of Language* (Chicago: University of Chicago Press).

———. 1976. "Givenness, Contrastiveness, Definiteness, Subjects, Topics, and Point of View," in Charles N. Li, ed. *Subject and Topic* (New York: Academic), pp. 25–55.

Comrie, Bernard. 1979. "Russian," in Timothy Shopen, ed., *Languages and Their Status* (Cambridge, MA: Winthrop), pp. 91–151.

Duranti, Alessandro, and Elinor Ochs. 1979. "Left-dislocation in Italian Conversation," in Talmy Givón, ed. *Syntax and Semantics 12: Discourse and Syntax* (New York: Academic), pp. 377–416.

Foley, William, and Robert Van Valin, Jr. 1985. "Information Packaging in the Clause," in Timothy Shopen, ed., *Language Typology and Syntactic Description* (Cambridge: Cambridge University Press), 3, pp. 282–384.

Givón, Talmy. 1979a. *On Understanding Grammar* (New York: Academic).

———, ed. 1979b. *Syntax and Semantics 12: Discourse and Syntax* (New York: Academic).

Gundel, Jeannette K. 1977. *Role of Topic and Comment in Linguistic Theory* (Bloomington: Indiana University Linguistics Club).

Halliday, M. A. K., and Ruqaiya Hasan. 1976. *Cohesion in English* (London: Longman).

Hawkins, John A. 1979. *Definiteness and Indefiniteness* (London: Croom Helm).

Kuno, Susumu. 1973. *The Structure of the Japanese Language* (Cambridge, MA: MIT Press).

Lambrecht, Knud. 1981. *Topic, Antitopic, and Verb Agreement in Non-standard French* (Amsterdam: Benjamins).

Leech, Geoffrey N. 1983. *Principles of Pragmatics* (London: Longman).

Li, Charles N., ed. 1976. *Subject and Topic* (New York: Academic).

Prince, Ellen F. 1978. "A Comparison of WH-clefts and *It*-clefts in Discourse," *Language* 54:883–906.

———. 1979. "On the Given/New Distinction," *Papers from the Fifteenth Regional Meeting of the Chicago Linguistics Society* (Chicago: Chicago Linguistics Society), pp. 267–278.

———. 1981. "Topicalization, Focus Movement, and Yiddish Movement: A Pragmatic Differentiation," *Proceedings of the Seventh Annual Meeting of the Berkeley Linguistics Society* (Berkeley: Berkeley Linguistics Society), pp. 249–264.

Quirk, Randolph, Sidney Greenbaum, Geoffrey Leech, and Jan Svartvik. 1985. *A Comprehensive Grammar of the English Language* (London: Longman).

Thompson, Sandra A. 1978. "Modern English from a Typological Point of View: Some Implications of the Function of Word Order," *Linguistische Berichte* 54:19–35.

——— 1987. "The Passive in English: A Discourse Perspective," in Robert Channon and Linda Shockey, eds., *In Honor of Ilse Lehiste* (Dordrecht: Foris), pp. 497–511.

Weiner, Judith E., and William Labov. 1983. "Constraints on the Agentless Passive," *Journal of Linguistics* 19:29–58.

8

Language Universals and Language Typology

SIMILARITY AND DIVERSITY ACROSS THE LANGUAGES OF THE WORLD

The various languages of the world are structured according to many different patterns at the level of phonology, morphology, syntax, and semantics. For example, some languages have very large inventories of phonemes, while others have very few phonemes. In some languages, such as English, French, and Italian, the basic structure of the clause is SVO: subject first, then verb, then direct object; other languages, like Japanese, place both the subject and the direct object before the verb in a pattern of SOV. One might legitimately wonder whether the world's languages have any characteristics in common.

As it happens, there are basic principles that govern the structure of *all* languages. These language **universals** regulate what is possible and what is impossible in the structure of a language. For example, some languages have both voiceless stops and voiced stops in their phonemic inventory. Other languages have only voiceless stops among their phonemes. No language has yet been encountered, however, that has voiced stops but lacks voiceless stops. This observation can be translated into a rule expressing what is possible in the structure of a language (that is, a language can have both voiced and unvoiced stops or only voiceless stops in its phonemic inventory) and into a law that excludes a combination of phonemes that is not known to occur in any of the world's languages (that is, voiced stops without voiceless stops).

The Value of Uncovering Universals

The study of language universals is valuable for several reasons. First of all, language universals are statements of what is possible and impossible in language. Viewed from a purely practical perspective, such principles are useful in that, if we can assume them to apply to all languages, they need not be repeated in the description of each language. Thus the study of language universals underscores the unity underlying the enormous variety of languages found in the world.

Language universals are also important to our understanding of the brain and of the principles that govern interpersonal communication in all cultures. In the course of evolution, the ability to speak is something that the human species alone has developed, thus distinguishing itself from other higher mammals. However, the human species has developed not a single language spoken and understood by every human being but, rather, nearly five thousand different languages, many of which are completely unrelated and each of which is as complex and sophisticated as the next. If basic principles exist that govern all languages, they are likely to be the direct result of whatever cognitive and social skills enabled human beings to develop the ability to speak in the first place. By studying language universals and by trying to explain why they exist, we begin to understand what in the human brain and the social organization of everyday life enables people to communicate through language. The study of language universals offers a glimpse of the cognitive and social foundations of human language, about which so little is known.

When postulating language universals, researchers must exercise caution. First of all, universals are statements to the effect that some characteristics are found in all the world's languages while others are not found in any. When we make such statements, it is sobering to bear in mind that, of the thousands of languages spoken in the world, only a relatively few have been adequately described. Furthermore, a great deal more is known about European languages and the major non-Western languages (such as Chinese, Japanese, Hindi, and Arabic) than about the far more numerous other languages of Africa, Asia, the Americas, and Oceania. In Papua New Guinea alone, more than seven hundred languages are spoken, although grammatical descriptions of only a few dozen are available; very little—and sometimes nothing at all—is known about the rest. Linguists proposing language universals must be very cautious that the proposed principles are not applicable only to European languages. Language universals must be valid for all (or nearly all) languages of the world, whether those languages are spoken by only a few dozen people in a small highlands village of Papua New Guinea or by millions of people in Europe, Africa, or Asia. Since little or nothing is known about the structure of hundreds of languages, universal principles can be proposed only as tentative hypotheses based on the languages for which descriptions are available.

Fortunately, many linguists are studying lesser-known languages and those about which nothing is yet known; more often than not, as first-time grammars become available they confirm rather than disprove the language universals that have been proposed.

Caution must also be exercised in drawing inferences from language universals. As mentioned earlier, these universal principles help explain why language is species specific; but there is a big step between uncovering a language universal and explaining it as a symptom of the cognitive or social abilities that humans have developed in the course of evolution. More often than not, explanations for language universals as symptoms of cognitive or social factors rely on logical arguments rather than solid empirical proof. Of course, the fact that explanations can be only tentative does not mean they should not be proposed. Rather, it means that linguists must be cautious and keep in mind that languages fulfill many roles at once.

Language Types

A prerequisite to the study of universals is a thorough understanding of the variety found among the world's languages. Language **typology** is a field of inquiry that focuses on classifying languages according to their structural characteristics. (*Typology* means the study of types or the classification of objects into types.) An example of a typological classification would be languages that have both voiced and voiceless stops in their phonemic inventories (like English, French, and Japanese) and languages that have only voiceless stops (like Mandarin Chinese, Korean, and Tahitian). Remember, there is no language in the world that has voiced stops but no voiceless stops, so that type does not exist. Of course, if we look at other criteria of classification, the composition of each category will be different. For instance, if we establish a typology of languages according to whether or not they have nasal vowels in their phonemic inventory, English, Japanese, Mandarin Chinese, Korean, and Tahitian will fall into the category of languages that lack nasal vowels. In contrast, Standard French has four nasal vowels (some French dialects have only three): /ɛ̃/ as in *faim* /fɛ̃/ 'hunger'; /œ̃/ as in *brun* /bʀœ̃/ 'brown'; /ɑ̃/ as in *manger* /mɑ̃že/ 'to eat'; and /ɔ̃/ as in *maison* /mɛzɔ̃/ 'house.' Standard French thus falls into the category of languages that have nasal vowels, along with Hindi, Tibetan, and Yoruba (widely spoken in Nigeria). Of course, linguists can establish categories only according to specific criteria; the world's languages are so diverse in so many different ways that no overall typological classification of languages exists, even within a single level of linguistic structure such as phonology.

Typological categories have no necessary correspondence with groups of genetically related languages. Typological categories cut across language families. In the example just given, English, Japanese, and Tahitian are not related languages; yet they fall into the same language type with respect to the presence or absence of nasal vowels. On the other hand, French and English *are* related, but they fall into two different types. Though language types are in principle independent of language families, it is not uncommon for members of the same family to share certain typological characteristics as a result of a common heritage. Therefore linguists are always careful to include as many unrelated languages as possible in their proposed language types, so as to make certain that the similarities between languages of any category are not the result of genetic relationships.

This chapter explores both the variety found among the world's languages and the unity that underlies this variety. Uncovering language universals and classifying languages into different types are related but complementary tasks. In order to uncover universal principles, we first need to know the extent to which languages differ from one another in terms of their structure. We would not want to posit a language universal on the basis of a limited sample of languages, only to discover that our putative universal did not work for a type of language that we had failed to consider. A universal must work for all language types and all languages.

Similarly, the way in which we go about classifying languages and describing the different types of structures is determined in large part by the search for universals. It would be possible, for example, to set up a typological category grouping all languages that have the sound /o/ in their phonemic inventory. But such a typology would tell us nothing about any universal principle underlying the structure of these languages; indeed, their structures might have little else in common. In contrast, a typology of languages based on the presence or absence of nasal vowels reveals interesting patterns. It turns out that no language has *only* nasal vowels. All languages must have oral vowels, whether they have nasal vowels or not. This suggests that oral vowels are in some sense more "basic" or more indispensable than nasal vowels, a fact that could be of great interest to our understanding of language structure. So this typology is a useful one in that it has helped uncover a language universal.

EXAMPLES OF LANGUAGE UNIVERSALS AND LANGUAGE TYPES

This section presents examples of language universals and of language types from semantics, phonology, syntax, and morphology. For each example, observe carefully the interaction of language typologies with linguistic universals, and note how different types of language universals are stated. A number of the examples will be taken up again in the last section of this chapter, which will examine some cognitive and social explanations for language universals and language types.

Semantic Universals

Semantic universals are rules that govern the composition of the vocabulary of all the world's languages. That semantic universals should exist at all may seem surprising at first. Anyone who has studied a foreign language knows how greatly the vocabularies of two languages can differ. Some ideas that are conveniently expressed with a single word in one language may require an entire sentence in another language. The English word *privacy*, for example, does not have a simple equivalent in French (which does not mean that the French do not have the notion that the word denotes!). Similarly, English lacks an equivalent for the Hawaiian word *aloha*, which can be roughly translated as 'love,' 'compassion,' 'pity,' 'hospitality,' or 'friendliness' and is also used as a general greeting and farewell.

Despite these cross-linguistic differences, however, there are some fundamental areas of the vocabulary of every language that are subject to universal rules. These areas include body part terms, animal names, and verbs of sensory perception.

Semantic universals typically deal with the less marked members of lexical fields (see Chapter 6), which are called *basic terms* in this context. Consider, for example, the following terms, all of which refer to shades of blue: *turquoise, royal blue,* and *blue.* Intuitively, *blue* is a more basic term than the others. *Turquoise* derives from the name of a precious stone of the same color, while *royal blue* refers to a shade of blue. The word *blue* is thus more basic than each of the other words, though for different reasons: unlike *turquoise, blue* refers primarily to a color, not an object; unlike *royal blue,* it is a simple, unmodified term. The combination of these characteristics makes *blue* a less marked (more basic) color term than the others. Basic terms are morphologically simple, are less specialized in meaning, and have not been recently borrowed from another language. Semantic universals deal with basic terms.

Pronouns   Pronoun systems can differ greatly from language to language; yet the pronoun system of every language follows the same set of universal principles.

First, all known languages, without any exception, have pronouns for at least the speaker and the addressee: the first person *(I, me)* and the second person *(you).* But there is great variability among the world's languages in the number of distinctions that are made by pronouns. The following chart presents the English pronominal system (we limit ourselves to subject pronouns).

	Singular	Plural
First person	I	we
Second person	you	you
Third person	he, she, it	they

In this chart, the first column represents "singular," the second column "plural"; the first row lists first person pronouns, the second row second person pronouns, and the third row third person pronouns. In standard American English the same form is used for second person singular and plural.

Turning to the pronoun systems of other languages, we encounter different patterns. Spoken Castilian Spanish has separate forms for the singular and plural in each person; in this example, the two forms of the plural are the masculine and feminine forms (the "polite" pronoun forms have been ignored).

	Singular	Plural
First person	yo	nosotros, nosotras
Second person	tú	vosotros, vosotras
Third person	él, ella	ellos, ellas

Some languages make finer distinctions in number. For example, speakers of Sanskrit made a distinction between two and more than two. The form for two is called the *dual,* and the form for more than two is referred to as the *plural* (the three forms of the third person are the masculine, feminine, and neuter forms).

	Singular	Dual	Plural
First person	aham	āvām	vayam
Second person	tvam	yūvām	yūyam
Third person	sas, tat, sā	tau, te, te	te, tāni, tās

Other languages have a single pronoun to refer to the speaker and the addressee together (and perhaps other people) and a separate pronoun to refer to the speaker along with other people but not the addressee; the first of these is called a first-person *inclusive* pronoun, and the second a first-person *exclusive* pronoun. In English, both notions are encoded with the pronoun *we.* In contrast, Tok Pisin (or New Guinea Pidgin) has separate inclusive and exclusive pronouns.

	Singular	Plural
First person	mi	mipela
First person inclusive		yumi
Second person	yu	yupela
Third person	em	ol

Tok Pisin is an English-based creole (see Chapter 9), and thus most of its vocabulary comes from English. The English pronouns and other words that were taken by Tok Pisin speakers to form the Tok Pisin pronoun system are easily recognizable: *mi* is from *me, yu* from *you, em* probably from *him, yumi* from *you-me, ol* from *all,* and the plural suffix *-pela* probably from the English *fellow.*

Fijian has one of the largest pronoun systems of any language. It has a singular form for each pronoun, a dual form for two people, a trial form that refers to about three people, and a plural form that refers only to more than three people (in actual usage, trial pronouns refer to a few people and the plural refers to a multitude). In addition, in the first person dual, trial, and plural, Fijian has separate inclusive and exclusive forms, like Tok Pisin. Here is the Fijian pronoun system.

	Singular	Dual	Trial	Plural
First person exclusive	au	keirau	keitou	keimami
First person inclusive		kedaru	kedatou	keda
Second person	iko	kemudrau	kemudou	kemunii
Third person	koya	irau	iratou	ira

Between the extremes represented by English and Fijian are many variations. Some languages have separate dual pronouns, others do not; some pronoun systems make a distinction between inclusive and exclusive reference, others do not.

All of the world's languages, however, have distinct first and second person pronouns; and most languages have third person pronouns, inclusive first person pronouns, and exclusive first person pronouns. A four-person system (inclusive first and exclusive first, second, and third person) is by far the most common. The four-person type of pronoun system is thus somehow more basic than a two- or three-person type. English, in this respect, is atypical.

Furthermore, variations in pronoun systems are governed by a set of universal rules. To discover these universals, we need to establish a typology of pronoun systems. Here are some of the types.

1. systems with singular and plural forms (like English and Spanish)

2. systems with singular, dual, and plural forms (like Sanskrit)

3. systems with singular, dual, trial, and plural forms (like Fijian)

4. systems that do not make an inclusive/exclusive distinction in the first person plural (like English, Spanish, and Sanskrit)

5. systems that make an inclusive/exclusive distinction in the first person plural (like Tok Pisin and Fijian)

Types that we will *not* find include:

6. systems with no pronouns for the first and second persons

7. systems with singular and dual forms but no plural forms

8. systems with singular, dual, and trial forms but no plural forms

9. systems that make an inclusive/exclusive distinction, but not in the first person (a logical impossibility)

Based on what we do and do not find in our typology, we can derive the following universal rules:

1. All languages have pronouns for at least two persons: first and second persons.

2. If a language has separate singular and dual forms, then it will have separate plural forms.

3. If a language has separate singular, dual, and trial forms, then it will have separate plural forms.

4. If a language makes an inclusive/exclusive distinction in its pronoun system, it will make it in the first person.

Note that the converse of these rules is not true. The converse of universal rule 2, for instance, would state that if a language had separate plural forms then it would have separate dual forms. But even English proves this generalization wrong: It has separate plural forms but no dual. The implications thus go in only one direction.

It is important to note that semantic typologies and universals do not represent a measure of complexity in language or culture. The most we can infer from these differences is that some categories are more salient in some cultures than in others. The pronoun system of English is one of the most restricted in the world, despite the fact that English has very rich scientific and color lexicons, to mention only two arenas. Thus different arenas of the lexicon exhibit different degrees of elaboration in different languages. This fact does not mean that some languages are "richer" or "better" or "more developed" than others.

Phonological Universals

Vowel Systems   Another level of linguistic structure in which we can identify universal rules and classify languages into useful typological categories is phonology. In Chapter 2 we discussed the fact that languages could have very different inventories of sounds. Figure 8-1 represents the vowel system of Standard American English, arranged according to place of articulation. Compare this with Figure 8-2, which represents the vowel system of Standard Parisian French (a conservative dialect retaining certain oppositions that have been lost in many other French dialects). The symbol /ü/ represents a high front rounded vowel as in the word /ʁü/ *rue* 'street'; /ø/ is an upper-mid front rounded vowel as in /fø/ *feu* 'fire'; /œ/ is a lower-mid front rounded vowel as in /bœʁ/ *beurre* 'butter'; and /ɛ̃/, /œ̃/, /ɔ̃/, and /ɑ̃/ are nasal vowels.

Finally, in Figure 8-3, compare the vowel systems of two other languages: Quechua (spoken in Peru and Ecuador) and Hawaiian. The first thing these four examples demonstrate is that different languages may have very different sets of vowels: English has several vowels in its inventory that French does not have, and vice versa. Second, the number of vowels in a language can also vary considerably. Quechua has only three distinct vowels; along with the vowel systems of Greenlandic Eskimo and Moroccan Arabic, the Quechua vowel system is one of the smallest in the world. (Kabardian, a language spoken in the Caucasus, may have only a two-vowel system that consists of /a/ and /ə/, with many allophones, but the facts are still unclear.) Hawaiian has five vowels, a very common number

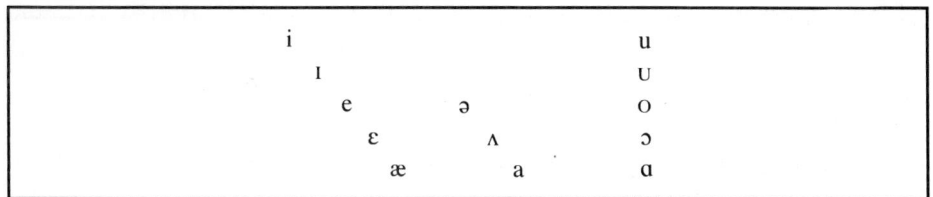

FIGURE 8-1
Vowels of American English

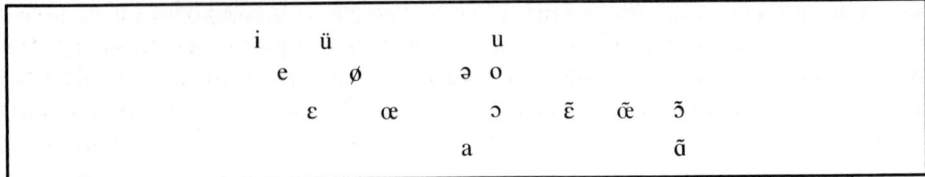

FIGURE 8-2
Oral and Nasal Vowels of Parisian French

among the world's languages. At the other end of the spectrum, English has thirteen vowels and French has fifteen.

Underlying such diversity, however, we find universal patterns. If we charted the vowel inventories of all known languages, we would confirm that all languages have vowel systems that fall between the two extremes represented by Quechua and French. Thus every language has at least three vowel phonemes. Some have four vowels, like Malagasy, the language of Madagascar (whose vowels are /i ɛ a ʊ/), and the American Indian language Kwakiutl (which has /i a ə u/). Some, like Hawaiian and Mandarin Chinese, have five vowels; others, such as Persian and Malay, have six; and so on up to fifteen.

Comparing all the charts, we find that all languages include in their vowel inventory a high front unrounded vowel (/i/ or /ɪ/), a low vowel (/a/), and a high back rounded (/u/ or /ʊ/) or unrounded (/ɯ/) vowel. These vowels may have allophones in some languages, particularly in languages with few vowels. In Greenlandic Eskimo, for example, /i/ has the allophones [i], [e], [ɛ], and [ə], depending on the consonants that surround it; but there are no minimal pairs that depend on these variants. Small variations exist, but these variations do not really contradict the universal rule, which can be stated as follows: **All languages have a high front unrounded vowel, a low vowel, and a high back vowel in their phoneme inventory.** Note that this first universal rule describes what constitutes the minimal type and what is included in all other types.

The second universal rule states this: **Of the languages that have four or more vowels, all have vowels similar to /i a u/** (as indicated by the first universal rule) **plus either a high central vowel /ɨ/** (as in Russian vɨ 'you') **or a mid front unrounded vowel /e/ or /ɛ/.** The third universal rule we can uncover from our vowel charts is this: **Languages with a five-vowel system include a mid front unrounded vowel.** In the five-vowel system of Hawaiian, for example, /e/ has allophones [ɛ] and [e]. Other languages with five-vowel inventories include Japanese (whose inventory

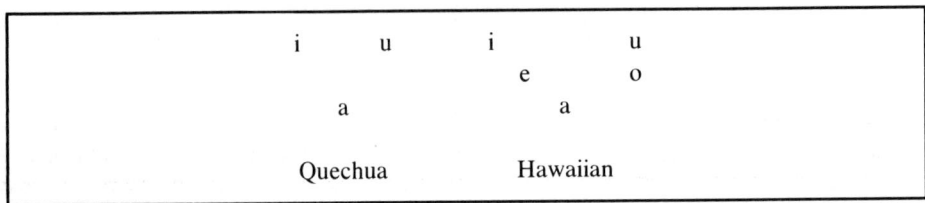

FIGURE 8-3
Vowels of Quechua and Hawaiian

is /i ɛ a ɔ ɯ/) and Zulu (/i ɛ a ɔ u/). Most languages with five vowels also have a mid back rounded vowel (either /ɔ/ or /o/) in their inventory, like Japanese, Hawaiian, and Zulu. A few languages with a five-vowel system lack a mid back rounded vowel, although a very similar sound is often included, as with Mandarin Chinese, whose inventory (/i ü a ë u/) includes the lower-mid back unrounded vowel /ë/.

We can thus state that languages with five-vowel inventories *generally* (but not always) have a mid back rounded vowel. This observation is applicable to languages with more than five vowels as well. The fourth universal rule thus reads: **Languages with five or more vowels in their inventories generally have a mid back rounded vowel phoneme.** This rule is stated in a different way from the first three rules in that it is not absolute. But it is a useful observation because it describes a significant tendency across languages.

Languages with six-vowel inventories like Malayalam (spoken in southwestern India) include /ɔ/ in their inventory and either /ɨ/ or /e/. Malayalam has in its inventory the three "obligatory" vowels /i a u/; the vowels /e/ and /ɔ/, as predicted by the second and third universal rules; and /ɨ/. These universal rules can be summarized as in Figure 8-4.

Nasal and Oral Vowels   Many more universal rules that regulate the vowel inventories of the world's languages can be uncovered, but we mention only two more. The first states: **When a language has nasal vowels, the number of nasal vowels never exceeds the number of oral vowels.** Thus we can find examples of languages with fewer nasal vowels than oral vowels: Standard French, for example, has four nasal vowels and eleven oral vowels. We can also find examples of languages with an equal number of oral and nasal vowels: Punjabi (a language of northern India) has ten of each. But there are no languages with a greater number of nasal vowels than oral vowels.

The second universal rule is not a rule in the usual sense but a description of *the most common vowel system:* a five-vowel system consisting of a high front unrounded vowel (/i/ or /ɪ/), a mid front unrounded vowel (/e/ or /ɛ/), a low vowel (/a/), a mid back rounded vowel (/o/ or /ɔ/), and a high back rounded vowel (/u/ or /ʊ/). Hawaiian is an example of such a system, as you can see by looking at

	Language Type			
	1	*2*	*3*	*4*
	i		ɛ	ɔ
	a ⟨	ɨ ⟨		e
	u	ɛ	ɔ ⟨	
Number of vowels	3	4	5	6
Example	Quechua	Malagasy	Hawaiian	Malayalam

FIGURE 8-4
Summary of Universal Vowel Rules

the symmetry in the chart for Hawaiian vowels (page 232). Each vowel is maximally distant from the others, thus minimizing the possibility of two vowels being confused. There is thus an ideal quality to such a five-vowel system, to which we will return later in this chapter.

Consonants   Vowel systems are not the only area of phonology in which universal rules operate. The consonant inventories of the languages of the world also exhibit many universal properties. A few examples are presented here, though not in great detail because they do not differ in nature from universals of vowel systems.

Recall (from Chapter 2) that the sounds /p t k/ are voiceless stops. Every language has at least one of these voiceless stops as a phoneme. Some languages lack affricates or trills, but voiceless stops are found in all languages. In fact, most languages have all three of these sounds, even languages with small consonant inventories. For example, Niuean (a Polynesian language) has only three stops, three nasals, three fricatives, and an approximant, totaling ten consonants (in contrast to the twenty-four of American English). Yet the three stops are /p t k/. Put in the form of a universal, this generalization reads: **Most languages have the three stops /p t k/ in their consonant inventory.** This universal suggests that these three consonants are in some sense more basic than others.

It is clear, given our discussion, that this universal is not an absolute rule. Hawaiian (a language related to Niuean) has only /p/ and /k/. (That is why English words with the sound /t/ are borrowed into Hawaiian with a /k/, like *kikiki* 'ticket'). This universal is thus a *tendency,* rather than a statement of what is and is not found among the world's languages.

Another important universal referring to stops has already been mentioned. Recall that the difference between the two sets of stops /p t k/ and /b d g/ is that the first set is voiceless, the second voiced. All six sounds have phonemic status in English, as in French, Spanish, Quechua, and many other languages. In some languages, however, we find only voiceless stops; such is the case of Hawaiian (and all other Polynesian languages), Korean, and Mandarin Chinese. Thus far, we have identified two types of languages: languages with both voiced and voiceless stops and languages with only voiceless stops. As noted, every language has at least one voiceless stop in its inventory; consequently, there are no languages that have voiced stops but no voiceless stops and no languages that have neither voiced nor voiceless stops. This typology allows us to derive the following universal rule: **No language has voiced stops without voiceless stops.**

Note that of the universals of stop inventories explored thus far, only one rule (and it is only a tendency) says anything about *which* stops are included in the inventories of languages. But there are other universals that deal with this question. We give only one example here: **If a language lacks a stop, there is a strong tendency for that language to include in its inventory a fricative sound with the same place of articulation as the missing stop.** For instance, Standard Fijian, Amharic (the principal language of Ethiopia), and Standard Arabic all lack the phoneme /p/, which is a labial stop. As predicted by the universal rule, all these languages have a fricative whose place of articulation is similar to that of /p/—namely, /f/

or /v/. The fricative thus "fills in" for the missing stop. This rule, too, is only a tendency, as there are languages that violate it. Hawaiian, which lacks a /t/, has none of the corresponding fricatives /ð/, /θ/, /z/, or /s/. But most languages do follow the rule.

Syntactic and Morphological Universals

Word Order   Speakers of English and other European languages commonly assume that the normal way of constructing a sentence is to place the subject of the sentence first, then the verb, and then the direct object (if there is one). Indeed, in English, the sentence *Mary hit John,* which follows this order, is well formed, while variations like *John Mary hit* and *hit Mary John* are not well formed.

However, the normal order of words in a sentence differs considerably from language to language. Consider the following Japanese sentence, in which the subject is a girl called *Akiko,* the verb is *butta* 'hit (past tense),' and the direct object is a boy named *Taro.*

Akiko	ga	Taroo	o	butta.
Akiko	Subject	Taro	Object	hit

'Akiko hit Taro.'

In Japanese, the normal word order is thus subject first, direct object second, and verb last—SOV. If we changed this order (in an effort to make Japanese syntax conform to English syntax, for example), the result would be ungrammatical.

Now consider Tongan, in which the verb must come first, the subject second, and the direct object last—VSO. In the following sentence, the verb is *taaʔi* 'to hit,' the subject is a person named *Hina,* and the direct object is a person called *Vaka.*

Naʔe	taaʔi	ʔe	Hina	ʔa	Vaka.
Past	hit	Subject	Hina	Object	Vaka

'Hina hit Vaka.'

Of course, not all English sentences follow the order subject-verb-direct object—SVO. To emphasize particular noun phrases, English speakers sometimes place direct objects in clause-initial position *(It was John that Mary hit);* such constructions are called cleft sentences. In questions like *Who did John hit?,* the direct object is placed in first position. Similar word order variants are found in most languages of the world. But cleft sentences and questions are derived from more basic sentences. Cleft sentences and questions are also less common than sentences that follow the SVO order subject-verb-direct object. Thus, even though some English constructions do not follow this order, we say that the order SVO is "basic" in English, and that English is an SVO language. Examples of SVO languages include Romance languages (such as French, Spanish, and Italian),

Thai, Vietnamese, and Indonesian. Japanese is an SOV language, as are Turkish, Burmese, Hindi, and the American Indian languages Navajo, Hopi, and Luiseño. Tongan is a VSO language, as are most other Polynesian languages, some dialects of Arabic, Welsh, and a number of American Indian languages like Mam, Chinook, and some Salishan languages.

There are, of course, three other logical possibilities for combining verbs, subjects, and direct objects besides the orders VSO, SVO, and SOV. Remarkably, however, very few languages in the world have VOS, OVS, or OSV as basic word order. There are only a handful of VOS languages, the best known being Malagasy and Fijian. Following is a basic sentence in Fijian showing that the direct object precedes the subject.

Ea   taya   na   ŋone   na   yalewa.

Past   hit   the   child   the   girl

'The girl hit the child.'

OVS and OSV are confirmed as the basic word order of only a handful of languages of the Amazon Basin, including Hixkaryana (OVS) and Nadëb (OSV). By far the most common word orders found among the world's languages are SVO, SOV, and, to a lesser extent, VSO.

What is the difference between VSO, SVO, and SOV, on the one hand, and VOS, OVS, and OSV, on the other hand? In the first three configurations, the subject *precedes* the direct object, while it *follows* the direct object in the last three configurations. We can thus make the following generalized statement: **In the basic word orders of the languages of the world there is an overwhelming tendency for the subject of a sentence to precede the direct object.**

There is a great deal more to universals of syntax. Let us focus on the two extreme cases: languages in which the verb comes first in the clause (called verb-initial languages and illustrated by Tongan) and languages in which the verb comes last (called verb-final languages and illustrated by Japanese). For the sake of simplicity, we will exclude VOS and OSV languages from our discussion, though they follow basically the same rules as VSO and SOV languages respectively.

Possessor and Possessed Noun Phrases   If we look at the order of other syntactic constituents in these two types of languages, we find extremely regular and interesting patterns. First of all, in most verb-final languages, possessor noun phrases precede possessed noun phrases, as in Japanese.

Taroo   no   imooto

Taro   of   sister

'Taro's sister'

In verb-initial languages the opposite order is most commonly found; in the following example from Tongan, the possessed entity is expressed first, the possessor last.

ko e   tuongaʔane ʔo Vaka

the   sister   of Vaka

'Vaka's sister'

We have thus established the following rule: **There is a strong tendency for possessor noun phrases to** *precede* **possessed noun phrases in verb-final languages and to** *follow* **possessed noun phrases in verb-initial languages.**

Adpositions   To express position or direction, many languages use prepositions. As the word indicates, prepositions come *before* modified nouns. In Tongan, for example, the prepositions *ki,* which indicates direction, and *ʔi,* which denotes location, both precede the NP they modify.

ki	Tonga	ʔi	Tonga
to	Tonga	in	Tonga
'to	Tonga'	'in	Tonga'

Other languages have postpositions instead of prepositions. Postpositions fulfill exactly the same functions as prepositions, but they follow NPs, as in this Japanese example.

Tookyoo   ni

Tokyo   to

'to Tokyo'

Overwhelmingly, verb-initial languages have prepositions and verb-final languages have postpositions. The third rule can be stated as follows: **There is a strong tendency for verb-initial languages to have prepositions and for verb-final languages to have postpostions.**

Relative Clauses   In different languages, relative clauses either precede or follow head nouns. In English relative clause constructions *(the book that Mary wrote),* the relative clause *(that Mary wrote)* follows its head *(the book)*. The same is true in Tongan.

ko e tohi   [naʔe faʔu ʔe   Hina]

the   book   Past   write Subject Hina

'the book that Hina wrote'

In Japanese, however, the relative clause precedes its head.

[Hiroo ga   kaita] hon

 Hiro   Subject wrote   book

'the book that Hiro wrote'

The great majority of verb-initial languages place relative clauses after the head noun, and the great majority of verb-final languages place relative clauses before the head noun. We can therefore note the following universal: **There is a strong tendency for verb-initial languages to place relative clauses after the head noun and for verb-final languages to place relative clauses before the head noun.**

Overall Patterns of Ordering   We have established that verb-initial languages (VSO) place possessors after possessed nouns, place relative clauses after head nouns, and have prepositions. Verb-final languages (SOV), on the other hand, place possessors before possessed nouns, place relative clauses before head nouns, and have postpositions.

In all these correlations a pattern emerges. Notice that possessors and relative clauses modify nouns; the noun is a more essential element to a noun phrase than any of the modifiers. In a similar sense, noun phrases modify prepositions or postpositions; likewise, though it is not intuitively obvious, the most important element of a prepositional phrase is the preposition itself, not the noun phrase—it is the preposition that makes it a prepositional phrase. Finally, in a verb phrase, the direct object modifies the verb. In light of these remarks, we can draw a generalization about the order of constituents in different language types: **In verb-initial languages the modifying element** *follows* **the modified element, while in verb-final languages the modifying element** *precedes* **the modified element.** This pattern is illustrated in Table 8-1.

This generalization is of course based on tendencies rather than absolute rules. At each level of the table, some languages violate the correlations. Persian, for example, is an SOV language like Japanese and thus should have the properties listed in the righthand column of the chart. But in Persian, possessors follow possessed nouns, prepositions are used, and relative clauses follow head nouns—all of which are properties of verb-initial languages. Such counterexamples to the correlations are rare, however.

Notice that our discussion has mentioned nothing about verb-medial (SVO) languages like English. SVO languages appear to follow no consistent pattern. English, for example, places relative clauses after head nouns and has prepositions (both properties of verb-initial languages). With respect to the order of possessors and possessed nouns, English has both patterns *(the man's arm* and *the arm*

TABLE 8-1
Summary of Constituent Orders

Verb-Initial Languages	Verb-Final Languages
(Example: Tongan)	(Example: Japanese)
Modified—Modifier	*Modifier—Modified*
verb—direct object	direct object—verb
possessed—possessor	possessor—possessed
preposition—noun phrase	noun phrase—postposition
head noun—relative clause	relative clause—head noun

of the man). In contrast, Mandarin Chinese, another verb-medial language, has characteristics of verb-final languages.

Word order universals are an excellent illustration of the level that linguists attempt to reach in their description of the universal properties of language. Table 8-1 implies that in the structure of virtually all verb-initial and verb-final languages the same ordering principle is at play at the level of the noun phrase, the prepositional phrase, and the whole sentence. This fact is remarkable in that it applies to a great many languages whose speakers have never come in contact with each other. It is thus likely that underlying this ordering principle there may be some cognitive process shared by all human beings.

Relativization Hierarchy   Another area of syntactic structure in which striking universal principles are found is the structure of relative clauses. English can relativize the subject of a relative clause, the direct object, the indirect object, obliques, and possessor noun phrases, as the examples below illustrate.

the teacher [who talked at the meeting] (subject)

the teacher [whom I mentioned—to you] (direct object)

the teacher [that I told the story to—] (indirect object)

the teacher [that I heard the story from—] (oblique)

the teacher [whose book I read] (possessor)

Other languages might not allow all these possibilities. Some languages allow relativization on only some of these categories but not others. For example, a relative clause in Malagasy is grammatical only if the relativized noun phrase is the subject of the relative clause.

ny   mpianatra   [izay   nahita   ny   vehivavy]

the   student   who   saw   the   woman

'the student who saw the woman'

In Malagasy there is no way of directly translating a relative clause whose direct object has been relativized ('the student whom the woman saw—'), or the indirect object ('the student whom the woman gave a book to—'), or an oblique ('the student that the woman heard the news from—'), or a possessor ('the student whose book the woman read'). If speakers of Malagasy need to convey what is represented by these English relative constructions, they must use a passive sentence before constructing the relative clause. Thus the head noun phrase becomes the grammatical subject ('the student who was seen by the woman'). Alternatively, they can express their idea in two clauses—that is, instead of 'the teacher saw the student whom she failed,' they might say, 'the teacher saw the student, and that same teacher failed that student.'

Some languages permit relative clauses in which either the subject or the direct object can be relativized, but not the indirect object, an oblique, or a possessor.

TABLE 8-2
Relativization Hierarchy: Types of Relative Clause Systems

Language Type	Subject	Direct Object	Indirect Object	Oblique	Possessor	Example
1	+	–	–	–	–	Malagasy
2	+	+	–	–	–	Kinyarwanda
3	+	+	+	–	–	Basque
4	+	+	+	+	–	Catalan
5	+	+	+	+	+	English

An example of such a language is Kinyarwanda, spoken in East Africa. Other languages, like Basque, have relative clauses in which the subject, the direct object, and the indirect object can be relativized, but not an oblique or a possessor. Yet another type of language adds obliques to the list of categories that can be relativized; such is the case in Catalan, spoken in northeastern Spain. Finally, languages like English and French allow all possibilities.

In Table 8-2, which recapitulates the types of relative clause systems found among the world's languages, the plus sign indicates a grammatical category that can be relativized, while a minus sign indicates one that cannot be relativized.

Remarkably, there are no languages in which, for example, an oblique can be relativized ('the man [that I heard the story from]') but not subjects, direct objects, and indirect objects as well. Indeed, relative clause formation in all languages is sensitive to the following *hierarchy* of grammatical relations.

subject < direct object < indirect object < oblique < possessor

The hierarchy predicts that if a language allows a particular category on the hierarchy to be relativized, then the grammar of that language will also allow all positions to the left to be relativized. For example, in English possessors can be relativized ('the woman [whose book I read]'); the hierarchy predicts that English would allow all positions to the left of possessor (namely, oblique, indirect object, direct object, and subject) to be relativized. The hierarchy also predicts that Basque, which permits indirect objects to be relativized, will also allow direct objects and subjects to be relativized; it does *not* allow categories to the right of indirect object on the hierarchy (obliques or possessors) to be relativized. The hierarchy is thus a succinct description of the types of relative clause formation patterns found in the languages of the world.

TYPES OF LANGUAGE UNIVERSALS

In this section we will draw on the universals treated in the last section in order to classify the different types of universals. It should be clear by now that language universals are not all alike. Some do not have any exceptions; others hold for most languages but are violated by a handful of languages. It is important to distinguish between these two types of universals because the first type appears to be the result of an absolute constraint on language in general, while the other is the result of a tendency.

Absolute Universals and Universal Tendencies

The first two types of universals are distinguished by whether or not they may be stated as absolute rules. The typology of vowel systems established earlier indicates that the minimum number of vowels a language can have is three: /i a u/. The two universal rules that are suggested by the typology read as follows: (1) all languages have at least three vowels; and (2) if a language has only three vowels, these vowels will be /i a u/. From the descriptions of all languages studied to date, it appears that these two rules have no exceptions. The two rules are thus examples of **absolute universals**—universal rules that have no exceptions. Other examples of absolute universals include these: If a language has a set of dual pronouns, it must have a set of plural pronouns; if a language has voiced stops, it must have voiceless stops.

In contrast to absolute universals, we have seen a number of universal rules that had some exceptions. A good example is the rule stating that if a language has a gap in its inventory of stops, it is likely to have a fricative with the same place of articulation as the missing stop. This rule holds for most languages that have gaps in their inventory, but not all. Such rules are called **universal tendencies** (or *relative universals*). The fact that they describe strong tendencies across languages is significant, but they are different in nature from absolute universals.

Naturally, we must be careful when deciding that a particular rule is absolute. Until a few years ago, it would have been easy to assume that no language existed with OVS or OSV as basic word order (since none had been described) and that there was an absolute universal stating that "no language has OVS or OSV for basic word order." However, we now know of a few OVS and OSV languages, all spoken in the Amazon Basin. Thus the rule that had been stated as an absolute universal seemed absolute only because no one had come across a language that violated it.

Implicational and Nonimplicational Universals

Independently of the contrast between absolute universals and tendencies, we can draw another important distinction: one between implicational universals and nonimplicational universals. Some universal rules are in the form of a conditional implication, as in the following examples: If a language has five vowels, it generally has the vowel /o/ or /ɔ/; if a language is verb-final, then in that language possessors are likely to precede possessed noun phrases. All these rules are of the form "if condition P is satisfied, then conclusion Q holds"; they are called **implicational universals.** Other universals can be stated without the help of a condition: All languages have at least three vowels. Such universals are called *nonimplicational* universals.

There are thus four types of universals: implicational absolute universals; implicational tendencies; nonimplicational absolute universals; and nonimplicational tendencies. Examples of each type can be identified in the discussion of the previous section.

EXPLANATIONS FOR LANGUAGE UNIVERSALS

By any standard, it is remarkable that all languages of the world should fall into clearly defined types and be subject to universal rules, given the extreme structural diversity they otherwise exhibit. It is thus reasonable to ask why universal rules exist at all. The question is extremely complex, and no one can claim to have come up with a definitive explanation for any universal. However, for many universals, we can make empirically based hypotheses at best, and educated guesses at worst, about the reasons for their existence.

Original Language Hypothesis

The first explanation for language universals that may come to mind is that all languages of the world derive historically from the same original language. This hypothesis is difficult to support, however. First of all, archaeological evidence strongly suggests that the ability to speak developed in our ancestors in several parts of the globe at about the same time; it is difficult to imagine that different groups of speakers not in contact with one another would have developed exactly the same language. Secondly, even if we ignore the archaeological evidence, the existence of an original language is impossible to prove or disprove because we have no evidence for or against the hypothesis at our disposal. Finally, if the "original" language had been a verb-final language with all the characteristics of SOV languages, for example, how would VSO languages have acquired the regularities they exhibit today? Conversely, if it had been a verb-initial language with typical characteristics, how did verb-final languages develop? Thus the original language hypothesis is not a very good explanation; at best, it is so hypothetical that it does not adequately fulfill the function of an explanation.

Universals and Perception

A more likely explanation for language universals is the hypothesis that they are symptoms of how all humans perceive the world and conduct verbal interactions. In the discussion of vowel systems, you may have noticed that the three vowels found in all languages—/i a u/—are mutually very distant in a vowel chart. The two vowels /i/ and /u/ differ in terms of both frontness and usually rounding, and /a/ differs from the other two in terms of frontness, height, and usually rounding. There is no other set of three vowels that differ from each other more dramatically. From these observations, it is not difficult to hypothesize why these three vowels would be the most fundamental vowels across languages.

Acquisition and Processing Explanations

Some language universals have psychological explanations that have no physiological basis. The explanations for word order universals that have been proposed, for example, are based on the notion that the more regular the structure of a language, the easier it is for children to acquire it. Thus the fact that verb-initial languages have prepositions and place adjectives after nouns, possessors after possessed nouns, and relative clauses after head nouns can be summarized by the following rule: In verb-initial languages, the modifier follows the modified element. Languages that strictly follow this rule exhibit a great deal of regularity from one construction to the other; a single ordering principle regulates the order of verbs and direct objects, adpositions and noun phrases, nouns and adjectives, possessors and possessed nouns, and relative clauses and head nouns. Such a language would be easier to acquire as a native tongue than a language with two or more ordering principles underlying different areas of the syntax. The fact that so many languages in the world follow one overall ordering pattern (modified-modifier) or the other (modifier-modified) with such regularity reflects the general tendency for the structure of language to be as regular as possible to make it as easy as possible to acquire.

Psychological explanations have also been proposed to explain the relative clause formation hierarchy. Relative clauses in which the head functions as the subject of the relative clause ('the woman [that left]') are easier to learn and to understand than relative clauses in which the head functions as the direct object of the relative clause ('the man [that I saw]'). Small children generally acquire the ability to use the first type before they begin using the second type. Finally, people take less time to understand the meaning of relative clauses on subjects than on direct objects. Relative clauses on direct objects, in turn, are easier to understand than those on indirect objects, and so on down the hierarchy.

subject < direct object < indirect object < oblique < possessor

There is thus a psychological explanation for the cross-linguistic patterns in the typology of relative clause formation: A language allows a ''difficult'' relative clause type only if all the ''easier'' types are also allowed in the language.

Social Explanations

Finally, recall that language is both a cognitive and a social phenomenon (see Chapter 1). While some language universals have a basis in cognition, others reflect the fact that language is a social tool.

Universals of pronoun systems must be explained in terms of the uses of language. Why, for example, do all languages have first and second person singular pronouns? The most basic type of verbal interaction that humans engage in is face-to-face conversation. Other contexts in which language is used to communicate (through writing, over the telephone, on the radio, and so on) are relatively recent inventions compared to the development of the ability to carry on a conversation; they occur less frequently and perhaps less naturally than face-to-face interactions. In a face-to-face interaction, it is essential to be able to refer to the speaker and the addressee, the two most important entities involved in the interaction, in an efficient and concise manner. Imagine an argument between two individuals who were unable to refer to *I* and *you,* or who had to refer to themselves and each other by name! Obviously, first and second person singular pronouns are essential for ordinary efficiency of social interaction. It is thus not surprising that every language has first and second person singular pronoun forms, even though it may have a gap elsewhere in its pronoun system. The universal that all languages have first and second person pronoun forms thus has a social motivation.

Furthermore, as noted earlier, the most frequent pronoun system has separate first, second, and third person forms, and separate first person inclusive ('you and me and perhaps other people') and exclusive ('other people and me, but not you') forms. Why would this system be so frequent and in some way more basic than other systems? Pronoun systems can be viewed as a matrix, each slot of the matrix being characterized by whether or not the speaker and the addressee are included in the reference of the pronoun.

	Speaker Included	Speaker Excluded
Addressee included	——— first person inclusive plural	second person singular second person plural
Addressee excluded	first person singular first person exclusive plural	third person singular third person plural

It should come as no surprise that speaker and addressee inclusion or exclusion are the crucial factor in defining each slot of the matrix in light of the fact that speaker and addressee are the more important elements of face-to-face interactions. The more basic (and most common) type of pronoun system is thus the most balanced matrix, one in which each slot is filled with a separate form.

Language universals may thus stem from the way in which humans perceive the world around them, learn and process language, and organize their social interactions. Underlying the search for universals is the desire to learn more about each of these areas of cognition and social life.

SUMMARY

The languages of the world offer a diverse panorama of structures. Some languages have many vowels in their phonemic inventory, others have few; some are verb-final, others verb-initial; some languages have extensive pronoun systems, others have only a restricted number of pronoun forms. Underlying this diversity, however, universal principles are at play in many areas of language structure. The study of language typology aims to catalog languages according to types, while the study of language universals aims to formulate the universal principles themselves.

Universals are found at all levels of language. In lexical semantics, the composition of pronoun systems, in which cross-linguistic variation is found, is dictated by several universal rules that regulate distinctions in number and person. Vowel systems and inventories of stops are two examples of universals at play in phonology. In syntax and morphology, universals are found regulating the basic order of constituents in sentences and phrases. The relativization hierarchy is another striking example of a universal principle at the level of syntax. The salient characteristic of all universals is that the most common patterns at all levels of linguistic structure are also the most regular and harmonious.

Four types of universal rules can be distinguished, according to whether or not they have exceptions (absolute universals versus universal tendencies) and according to their logical form (implicational versus nonimplicational universals).

The ultimate goal of the study of language universals is to provide explanations for such universal principles. Language universals are often indicative of how we perceive the world around us. For example, languages tend to highlight categories that are physiologically and perceptually salient, as with vowels. Secondly, structural simplicity and consistency make language easier to acquire and process; thus many universals predict that the simplest and most consistent systems will be preferred. Finally, distinctions drawn in the expression side of language reflect important social distinctions on the content side. Universals thus may have physiological, psychological, or social explanations.

EXERCISES

1. Determine whether each of the following is an absolute implicational universal, an absolute nonimplicational universal, an implicational universal tendency, or a nonimplicational universal tendency.

   (1) The consonant inventories of all languages include at least two different stops that differ in place of articulation.

   (2) Languages always have fewer nasal consonants than oral stops.

   (3) In all languages, the number of front vowels of different height is greater than or equal to the number of back vowels of different height.

   (4) Most VSO languages have prepositions, not postpositions.

   (5) Diminutive particles and affixes tend to exhibit high vowels.

   (6) If a language has separate terms for 'foot' and 'leg,' then it must also have different terms for 'hand' and 'arm.'

   (7) The future tense is used to express hypothetical events in many languages, and the past tense is often used to express nonhypothetical events.

   (8) Languages that have a relatively free word order tend to have inflections for case.

   (9) Many verb-initial languages place relative clauses after the head of the relative clause.

2. In English, conditions can be expressed in two ways: by placing the conditioning clause first and the conditioned clause second, as in (1), or by placing the conditioning clause second and the conditioned clause first, as in (2). In numerous languages, however, only the first pattern is grammatical. In Mandarin Chinese, the conditioning clause must come first, as in (3); if it is placed second, as in (4), the resulting sentence

is ungrammatical. No language allows only pattern (2)—conditioning clause second, conditioned clause first.

(1) If you cry, I'll turn off the TV.

(2) I'll turn off the TV if you cry.

(3) Rúguǒ wǒ dìdi   hē   jiǔ, wǒ jiù hěn shēngqì.

     if   my younger-brother drink wine I   then very angry

     'If my younger brother drinks wine, I'll be very angry.'

(4) *Wǒ hěn shēngqì rúguǒ wǒ dìdi   hē   jiǔ.

     I   very angry if   my younger-brother drink wine

a. From this information, formulate descriptions of an absolute implicational universal, an absolute nonimplicational universal, and a universal tendency, all of which refer to conditional clauses.

b. Propose an explanation for the universal ordering patterns that you formulated in (a). (*Hint:* Think of the order in which the actions denoted by the conditioning and the conditioned clauses must take place.)

3. The composition of vowel inventories of the world's languages is predicted by the hierarchy given in Figure 8-4 (p. 233). The hierarchy predicts the composition of a vowel inventory that consists of six phonemes. Complete the next step in the hierarchy by determining the composition of seven-vowel inventories; use the following information on the composition of the seven-vowel inventories of four languages, which you should assume are representative of possible seven-vowel inventories.

Burmese	i	e	ɛ	a	ɔ	o	u
Sundanese	i	ɨ	ɛ	a	o	u	ə
Washkuk	i	ɨ	e	ɛ	a	ɔ	u
Tunica	i	e	ɛ	a	ɔ	o	u

4. Consider the following typology of pronoun systems found among the world's languages. The first column of each set represents singular pronouns, the second column dual pronouns, and the third column plural pronouns; and an example of a language also is given for each type (incl. = inclusive, excl. = exclusive).

Eight-pronoun Systems

(1) I   we-2   we   Greenlandic Eskimo

    thou   you-2   you   (Greenland)

    s/he   they

(2) I   we   Arabic

    thou   you-2   you

    s/he   they-2   they

(3)	I	we-2-incl	we-incl.	Southern Paiute
			we-excl.	(North America)
	thou		you	
	s/he		they	

Nine-pronoun Systems

(1)	I	we-2	we	Lapp
	thou	you-2	you	(Arctic Scandinavia)
	s/he	they-2	they	
(2)	I	we-2-incl.	we-incl.	Maya
		we-2-excl.	we-excl.	(Central America)
	thou		you	
	s/he		they	
(3)	I	we-2-incl.	we	Lower Kanauri
		we-2-excl.		(India)
	thou	you-2	you	
	s/he		they	

Ten-pronoun Systems

(1)	I	we-2-incl	we	Coos
		we-2-excl.		(North America)
	thou	you-2	you	
	s/he	they-2	they	
(2)	I	we-2-incl	we-incl.	Kanauri
		we-2-excl.	we-excl.	(India)
	thou	you-2	you	
	s/he		they	

Eleven-pronoun Systems

(1)	I	we-2-incl.	we-incl.	Hawaiian
		we-2-excl.	we-excl.	
	thou	you-2	you	
	s/he	they-2	they	
(2)	I	we-2-incl.	we-incl.	Ewe
		we-2-excl.	we-excl.	(West Africa)
	thou	you-2	you	
	s/he		they	
			he and they	

a.   On the basis of these data, which you may assume to be representative, formulate a set of absolute universal principles that describe the composition of eight-, nine-, ten-, and eleven-pronoun systems. State your principles as generally as possible.

b.   Of these systems, the most commonly found is the eleven-pronoun system of type 1, exemplified by Hawaiian, followed by the nine-pronoun system of type 1, exemplified by Lapp. Formulate a set of universal tendencies that describe the preponderance of examples of these two systems.

5.   From a logical standpoint, the possible basic ordering combinations of subject, verb, and direct object are SOV, SVO, VSO, VOS, OVS, and OSV. We have seen that there is great variation in the number of languages exhibiting each combination as a basic word order. Linguists have recognized this fact for several decades, but there has been little agreement on the exact distribution of these basic word order variations across the world's languages. Here are results from five researchers who conducted cross-linguistic analyses of the distribution of basic word order possibilities. (The figures are cited from Tomlin 1986.)

Researcher	Languages Sampled	Percentage of Sampled Languages That Are						
		SOV	SVO	VSO	VOS	OVS	OSV	Unclassified
Greenberg	30	37	43	20	0	0	0	0
Ultan	75	44	34.6	18.6	2.6	0	0	0
Ruhlen	427	51.5	35.6	10.5	2.1	0	0.2	0
Mallinson, Blake	100	41	35	9	2	1	1	11
Tomlin	402	44.8	41.8	9.2	3.0	1.2	0	0

a.   In what ways do these researchers agree, and where do they disagree? Describe in detail.

b.   What are the possible causes of the discrepancies in the results?

c.   What lesson can typologists learn from this comparison?

6.   Relative clauses in the world's languages can be formed in a variety of ways. In English, we "replace" the relativized element by a relative pronoun that links the relative clause to its head (type 3). Other languages do not have relative pronouns but replace the relativized element with a personal pronoun (type 2). For example, in Gilbertese (spoken in the central Pacific), the position of the relativized element in the relative clause is marked with a personal pronoun.

te ben   [e bwaka iaon te   auti]   te anene   [i nori-a]

the coconut it fall   on the house   the coconut I saw-it

'the coconut [that fell on   the house]'   'the coconut [that I saw]'

In other languages like Finnish, relative clauses are formed simply by deleting the relativized element from the relative clause; no relative pronoun or personal pronoun is added to the relative construction (type 1).

[tanssinut] poika   [nakemani] poika

had-danced boy   I-had-seen boy

'the boy [that had danced]'   'the boy [that I had seen]'

Some languages have several types of relative clauses. Mandarin Chinese has types 1 and 2. (In Chinese, the relative clause is ordered before its head and is separated from the head by the particle *de*.)

Type 1	**Type 2**
[mǎi píngguǒ de] rén	[tā jiějie zài Měiguó de] rén
buy apples Particle man	he sister is-in America Particle man
'the man [who bought apples]'	'the man [whose sister is in America]'

Type 1 is used only when relativizing a subject or direct object, while type 2 can be used when relativizing a direct object, an indirect object, an oblique, or a possessor, as indicated in the table below. Whenever two types of relative clauses are found in a language, the pattern is the same: As we go down the relativization hierarchy (from subject to direct object to indirect object to oblique to possessor), one type can end but the other type takes over. Here are the patterns for some languages:

		Grammatical Relation Relativized				
		Subject	*Direct Object*	*Indirect Object*	*Oblique*	*Possessor*
Aoban (South Pacific)	*Type 1*	+	−	−	−	−
	Type 2	−	+	+	+	+
Dutch	*Type 1*	+	+	−	−	−
	Type 2	−	−	+	+	+
Japanese	*Type 1*	+	+	+	+	+
	Type 2	−	−	−	−	+
Kera (Central Africa)	*Type 1*	+	−	−	−	−
	Type 2	−	+	+	+	+
Mandarin Chinese	*Type 1*	+	+	−	−	−
	Type 2	−	+	+	+	+
Roviana (South Pacific)	*Type 1*	+	+	+	−	−
	Type 2	−	−	−	+	+
Tagalog (Philippines)	*Type 1*	+	−	−	−	−
	Type 2	+	−	−	−	−
Catalan (Spain)	*Type 1*	+	+	+	−	−
	Type 2	−	−	−	+	−

What cross-linguistic generalizations can you draw from these data on the distribution of relative clause types in each language? How can we expand the universal rules associated with the hierarchy to describe these patterns?

SUGGESTIONS FOR FURTHER READING

The most readable basic book on the study of language universals and linguistic typology is Comrie (1989), which focuses principally on syntax and morphology. Mallinson and Blake (1981) is another good introduction to typology. Shopen (1985) is a collection of excellent essays by different authors on selected areas of syntactic typology; it is also useful on the range of variation found among the world's languages in morphology and syntax. Volume I treats *Clause Structure*, volume 2 *Complex Constructions*, and volume 3 *Grammatical Categories and the Lexicon*. Some of the most influential work on language universals was conducted by Greenberg, who has edited a four-volume compendium of detailed studies of universals on specific areas of linguistic structure (1978); several papers from these volumes provided data for the exercises of this chapter. Volume 1 treats *Method and Theory*, volume 2 *Phonology*, volume 3 *Word Structure*, and volume 4 *Syntax*. Brown (1984) is an interesting investigation of universals of words for plants and animals. Lehrer (1974) is a good summary of research on semantic universals. Tomlin (1986) surveys the basic word orders of the world's languages. The relativization hierarchy was uncovered by Edward L. Keenan and Bernard Comrie, and Chapter 7 of Comrie (1989), from which we have taken some examples, offers an accessible discussion of the topic. Butterworth et al. (1984) is a collection of papers on theoretical explanations for language universals.

REFERENCES

Brown, Cecil H. 1984. *Language and Living Things: Uniformities in Folk Classification and Naming* (New Brunswick, NJ: Rutgers University Press).

Butterworth, Brian, Bernard Comrie, and Osten Dahl, eds. 1984. *Explanations for Language Universals* (Berlin: Mouton).

Comrie, Bernard. 1989. *Language Universals and Linguistic Typology: Syntax and Morphology*, 2nd ed. (Chicago: University of Chicago Press).

Greenberg, Joseph H., ed. 1978. *Universals of Human Language*, 4 vols. (Stanford: Stanford University Press).

Lehrer, Adrienne. 1974. *Semantic Fields and Lexical Structure* (Amsterdam: North-Holland).

Mallinson, George, and Barry J. Blake. 1981. *Language Typology* (Amsterdam: North-Holland).

Shopen, Timothy, ed. 1985. *Language Typology and Syntactic Description*, 3 vols. (Cambridge: Cambridge University Press).

Tomlin, Russell S. 1986. *Basic Word Order: Functional Principles* (London: Croom Helm).

9

The Historical Development of Languages

LANGUAGES: ALWAYS CHANGING

It's no secret that languages change over the years. Sometimes, especially in times of social and political upheaval, they may change dramatically. Usually, though, the changes are more subtle. Still, all of us can recognize different speech patterns between one generation and the next. There are probably notable differences between the speech patterns of your parents and your friends and even greater ones between your grandparents and your friends. The most noticeable differences between one generation and another are in vocabulary. What one generation calls *ice box, record player* or *hi-fi, car phone,* and *studious young man* a younger generation calls *fridge, stereo, cellular phone,* and (in some instances) *nerd.* Our grandparents certainly didn't hear of *double speak, tank tops, six packs,* or *sitcoms* in their youth, nor did they refer to certain verbal actions as *bad-mouthing* or *dumping on* someone.

Pronunciations change too. A change is currently underway for the word *nuclear,* which a couple of decades ago was more commonly pronounced /nukliər/ but today is increasingly pronounced /nukyələr/. In the same vein, the word *realtor,* formerly pronounced /riəltər/, is increasingly pronounced /rilətər/. Regional accents and dialects change. The /r/ in words like *car* and *beard,* which is pronounced in most of the United States, is coming to be pronounced more and more in New York City, where it has been missing for a couple of centuries. Southerners and Yankees raised in an age of national television programming sound more alike than their parents do. And throughout the United States, there is an increasing tendency not to differentiate the vowel sounds in word pairs like *knot* and *nought* or *cot* and *caught.*

The meaning of a term can also change. About a thousand years ago, the English verb *starve* (Old English *steorfan*) meant simply 'die (by any cause)'; today, *starve* refers principally to deprivation and death by hunger (or, by metaphorical extension, 'deprive of affection'). Similarly, the Old English verb *berēafian* meant 'to deprive of, take away, rob'; today, the much narrower principal meaning of *bereave* is 'to deprive of life or hope.' Until recently, the 700-year-old adjective *natural* did not have the meaning 'without chemical preservatives' that it now commonly has, as in *all natural ice cream.* And the meanings of *joint, bust, fix,* and many other words have been extended by their use in the world of drugs.

There can also be morphological and syntactic differences in the speech of different generations. *Goes the king hence today?* is what Shakespeare wrote in Macbeth. Today, the same inquiry would have a form more like *Is the king going out today?* because certain syntactic and lexical features of seventeenth-century English are no longer available.

Linguistic alterations very often prompt comment, especially from people who feel that language change reflects corruption; for many, the best language forms are those that have stood the test of time. Though generalizing from one's own linguistic experience can be risky, it is safe to say that the common experience of noticing linguistic differences between one generation and another reflects the simple fact that languages do not stand still: They are always in the process of changing.

In this chapter, we explore language change: What kinds of change occur, how languages are related to one another historically, and how language families are established. We also describe the linguistic and cultural prehistory of the Polynesians as a way of illustrating how some challenges of historical linguistics are met.

LANGUAGE FAMILIES

One result of the ongoing changes that affect a language is that a single language can develop into several languages. The early stages of such development are apparent in the differences among Australian, American, Canadian, Indian, and Irish English dialects, all of which have sprung from the English spoken in the United Kingdom. In order for different dialects to develop into separate languages, groups of speakers must remain relatively isolated from one another, separated either by physical barriers, such as impassable mountains and bodies of water, or by social and political barriers, such as those drawn along tribal, religious, racial, and national boundaries.

You have probably heard it said that French, Spanish, and Italian come from Latin. This statement is true, provided that by "Latin" one understands the different dialects spoken throughout the Roman Empire, not the written variety of classical Latin still studied in school. The "Vulgar Latin" spoken throughout the Roman Empire lives on in today's French, Italian, Spanish, and Portuguese as well as in Rumanian, Catalan, and Provençal, all of which are its direct descendants. On the other hand, the classical Latin of Cicero, Virgil, Caesar, and other Roman writers is "dead": The written varieties of French, Spanish, and Italian are based on the modern spoken languages, not the classical written language.

You may also have heard it claimed that English comes from Latin. That claim is false. English and Latin are indeed related, but Latin is not an ancestor of English. Both English and Latin come from a common ancestor, but they traveled along different genealogical paths. Then, during the Renaissance, English borrowed thousands of words from Latin and thereby created striking lexical parallels, especially in the sciences and humanities. But by no stretch of the imagination is English a daughter of Latin in the sense that Spanish, French, Italian, and Portuguese are. English is descended from Proto-Germanic, a language that was spoken about the time of classical Latin and a few centuries earlier and that ultimately gave rise not only to English but to German, Dutch, Norwegian, Danish, and Swedish (among others). Thus, as Latin is the parent language of French and Spanish, so Proto-Germanic is the parent language of English and German.

Except for a few carved runic inscriptions from the third century A.D., Proto-Germanic (unlike Latin) has left no written records. Modern knowledge of Proto-Germanic—and it is considerable—has been inferred from its daughter languages through *comparative reconstruction,* a technique explained in this chapter. Proto-Germanic and Latin are themselves daughters of Proto–Indo-European, another *unattested* (unrecorded) language. In a simplified manner, we can represent the situation by the family tree in Figure 9-1, which has two *branches*.

While the notion that languages change and give rise to new languages is not strange to modern readers, it is a notion that was postulated clearly only two centuries ago. In 1786, while serving as a judge in Calcutta, Sir William Jones addressed the Royal Asiatic Society of Bengal about his experience.

> The Sanskrit language, whatever be its antiquity, is of a wonderful structure; more perfect than the Greek, more copious than the Latin, and more exquisitely refined than either, yet bearing to both of them a stronger affinity, both in the roots of verbs and in the forms of grammar, than could possibly have been produced by accident; so strong indeed, that no philologer could examine them all three, without believing them to have sprung from some common source, which, perhaps, no longer exists: there is a similar reason, though not quite so forcible, for supposing that both the Gothic and the Celtic, though blended with a very different idiom, had the same origin with the Sanskrit; and the old Persian might be added to the same family. . . .

Today linguists would shy away from such judgmental comparative statements as Sanskrit having a "more perfect" structure than Greek and being "more exquisitely refined" than Latin, but we must credit Jones for his clear recognition that languages give rise to other languages. Indeed, we now know that Sanskrit, Latin, Greek, Celtic, Gothic, and Persian *did* spring from a "common source" that "no

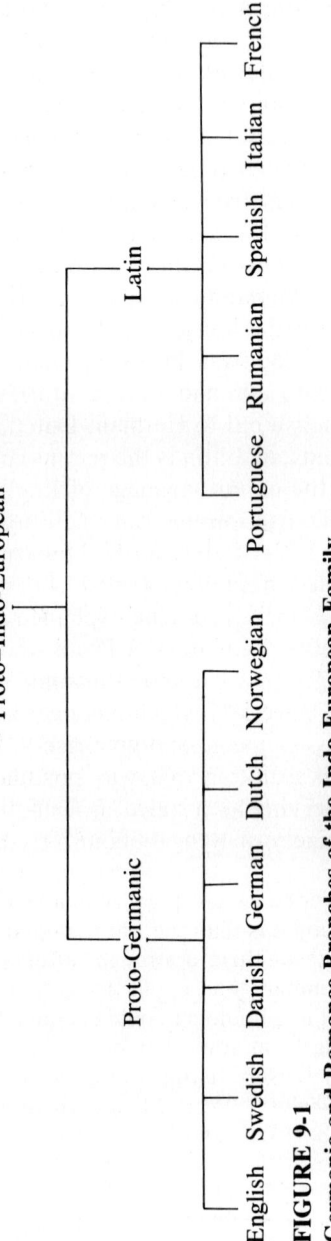

FIGURE 9-1
Germanic and Romance Branches of the Indo-European Family

longer exists." Jones had made an important discovery, and his formulation has proved to be a most influential hypothesis. The common source of Latin, Greek, Sanskrit, Celtic, Gothic, Persian, and many other languages (including English and its Germanic relatives, and French and Spanish and their Romance relatives) is Proto–Indo-European. A parent language and the daughter languages that have developed from it are collectively referred to as a **language family,** and the family that Jones discovered is called the **Indo-European** family. While there are no written records of Proto–Indo-European itself, a rich vein of inference about its words and structures can be mined from the linguistic characteristics of its daughter languages. Exercising certain well-defined precautions, scholars can confidently reconstruct a parent language from the shared characteristics of its daughters.

The working assumption of historical linguists is this: A feature that occurs widely in daughter languages and whose presence cannot be explained by reference to language typology, language universals, or borrowing from another tongue is likely to have been inherited from the parent language.

RECONSTRUCTING THE LINGUISTIC PAST

People have always been on the move. The past century has witnessed great migrations from one end of the globe to another—from Europe to the Americas and Australia, from the Far East to North America and Southeast Asia. There is evidence of massive migrations from Central Asia to Europe in about 4000 B.C. by a people who probably spoke Proto–Indo-European. There are no written records to document these migrations, but archaeologists have found buried remains from the daily life of people who inhabited particular parts of the globe. Combined with what we can reconstruct of ancestral languages, archaeological records enable researchers to make educated guesses about where our ancestors came from and where they migrated to, as well as how they lived and died.

When scholars reconstruct an ancestral language, they also implicitly reconstruct an ancestral society and culture. Every language lives on the lips of its speakers; words that are ascribed to a prehistoric group represent artifacts in their culture and facets of the social and physical activities of their daily life. In this chapter, we concentrate not on Indo-European culture and the Indo-European homeland (which are discussed in other accessible sources) but on the Polynesians, whose linguistic development presents another interesting case of reconstruction of a protolanguage and the culture of its speakers.

Polynesian and Pacific Background

On land, the only physical obstacles to sustained contacts between people are insurmountable mountains and wide rivers, which are in fact not very common. As a result, boundaries between different languages and cultures are often blurred. In contrast, once people settle on an isolated island, contact with inhabitants of other islands is difficult, and languages and cultures develop in relative isolation. Islands thus offer an opportunity to study what happens when a protolanguage evolves into distinct daughter languages. Because the South Pacific region consists of small islands and island groups quite isolated from one another, it provides an almost ideal "laboratory" for researchers interested in the past.

The South Pacific is home to three different cultural areas—Polynesia ('many islands'), Melanesia ('black islands'), and Micronesia ('small islands')—whose approximate boundaries are shown in Figure 9-2. Among other things, each area is distinguished by the physical appearance of its inhabitants: Polynesians are generally large, with olive complexions and straight or wavy hair; Melanesians typically are dark skinned, with smaller frames and curlier hair; and Micronesians are slight of frame, with light brown complexions and straight hair. We will concentrate on Polynesians and ask what we can learn about their origins and their early life in Polynesia from the languages they speak today.

The islands of Polynesia vary greatly in size and structure. The main island of Hawaii and the islands of Samoa and Tahiti are comparatively large land masses formed through volcanic eruptions. Other islands are tiny atolls, little more than sand banks and coral reefs that barely reach the surface of the ocean; typically, one can walk (or wade) around an atoll in a few hours. Atolls are found in Tuvalu, the Tuamotu Archipelago, and the northern Cook Islands. Some coral islands in Tonga and elsewhere have been raised by underground volcanic activities and are medium-sized and often hilly—in contrast to atolls, which are utterly flat.

There are no written records to aid in tracing the Polynesians' cultural and linguistic development because they had no system of writing before literacy was introduced by Westerners. But the modern languages and the archaeological record provide useful tools for reconstruction.

There is every indication that all the islands of Polynesia were settled by a people who shared a common language, a common culture, and a common way of dealing with the environment. That they traveled by sea from west to east, settling islands on their way, we know because the languages of Polynesia are clearly related to languages spoken to the west in Melanesia but have no connection with languages spoken to the east in South America. In addition, Polynesian cultures have many affinities with Melanesian cultures but virtually none with those of South America. Finally, the human bones, artifacts, and other archaeological remains found on the western islands of Polynesia are older than those found on the eastern islands. The obvious conclusion that western Polynesia was settled prior to eastern Polynesia contradicts the theory, popularized by Norwegian explorer Thor Heyerdahl, that the Polynesians originated in South America.

The oldest archaeological records in Polynesia were found in western Polynesia: in Tonga, Samoa, Uvea, and Futuna. Consisting mostly of pottery fragments similar to those found in Melanesia, these records date to between 1500 and 1200 B.C. This implies that people moved from somewhere outside Polynesia and settled on these western islands about thirty-five hundred years ago. No pottery has been found in eastern Polynesia (the Cook Islands, Tahiti and the Society Islands, the Marquesas Islands, and the Tuamotu Archipelago), but other remains indicate that these eastern islands were settled around the first century A.D. The most recent archaeological remains are found in Hawaii and New Zealand. That these two island groups were settled last is not surprising, given that they are the most remote from other islands of the region. The earliest artifacts found on these

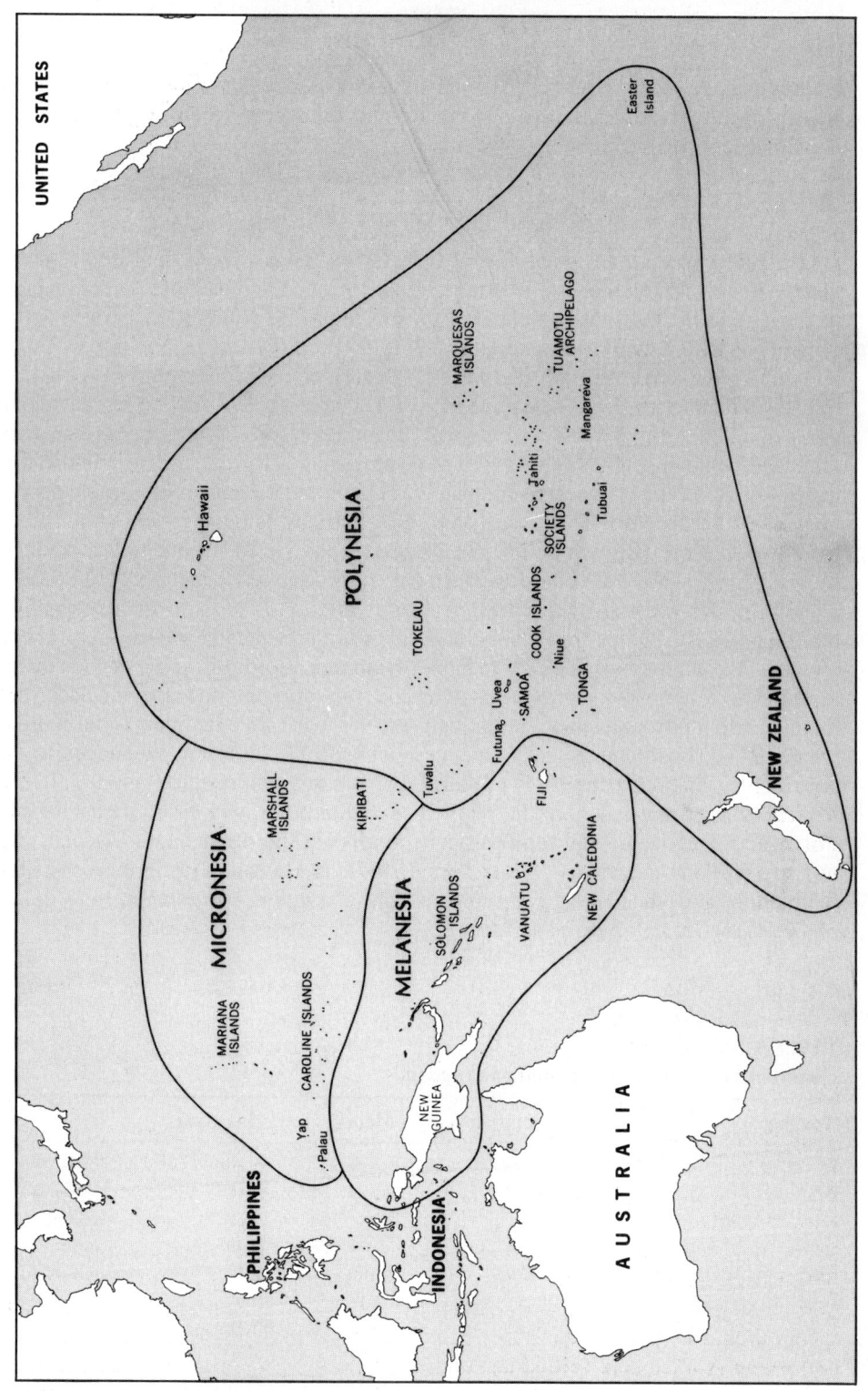

FIGURE 9-2
Cultural Areas in the Pacific

islands suggest that the ancient Hawaiians and the ancestors of the New Zealand Maoris first arrived on their respective island homes between the seventh and eleventh centuries A.D.

Polynesian Languages and Their History

We said earlier than all of Polynesia was settled by the same people or by groups of closely related people from a single region. Linguistic evidence can help us determine the original homeland of the Polynesians. Table 9-1 illustrates some typically striking similarities among words in five Polynesian languages. These and other widespread similarities of expression for equivalent content demonstrate that the languages of Polynesia are manifestly related. Not finding similar close correspondences in vocabulary between the languages of Polynesia and any other language, we can safely say that Polynesian languages form a language family. In other words, all the Polynesian languages are daughter languages of a single parent language, the ancestor of the thirty or so Polynesian languages and of no other existing language. Known as Proto-Polynesian, the parent language was spoken by the people who first settled western Polynesia between 1500 and 1200 B.C.

In Table 9-1, the word *manu* 'bird' is exactly the same—in form and content—in all five languages. The other words have the same vowel correspondences (where one has /a/, all have /a/) and differ slightly from one another in some of the consonants. The Polynesian words in each line of the table are **cognates**—words that have developed from a single, historically earlier word. In examining other words, we find the consonant correspondences between the different languages to be strikingly regular. On the basis of many words such as those in Table 9-1, it can be seen that in words where the phonemes /m/ and /n/ (as in *manu*) occur in one Polynesian language, they tend to occur in all. On the other hand, Tongan, Samoan, Tahitian, and Maori /t/ corresponds to /k/ in Hawaiian (as in the words for 'forbidden' and 'face'). We can represent these *sound correspondences* as in the chart below Table 9-2 on page 259.

TABLE 9-1
Common Words in Five Polynesian Languages

Tongan	Samoan	Tahitian	Maori	Hawaiian	
manu	manu	manu	manu	manu	'bird'
ika	iʔa	iʔa	ika	iʔa	'fish'
kai	ʔai	ʔai	kai	ʔai	'to eat'
tapu	tapu	tapu	tapu	kapu	'forbidden'
vaka	vaʔa	vaʔa	waka	waʔa	'canoe'
fohe	foe	hoe	hoe	hoe	'oar'
mata	mata	mata	mata	maka	'face'
ʔuta	uta	uta	uta	uka	'bush'
toto	toto	toto	toto	koko	'blood'

TABLE 9-2

Cognates in Five Polynesian Languages I

Tongan	Samoan	Tahitian	Maori	Hawaiian	
toki	toʔi	toʔi	toki	koʔi	'axe'
taŋi	taŋi	taʔi	taŋi	kani	'to cry'
taŋata	taŋata	taʔata	taŋata	kanaka	'man'
kafa	ʔafa	ʔaha	kaha	ʔaha	'rope'
kutu	ʔutu	ʔutu	kutu	ʔuku	'louse'
kata	ʔata	ʔata	kata	ʔaka	'to laugh'
moko	moʔo	moʔo	moko	moʔo	'lizard'

Tongan	Samoan	Tahitian	Maori	Hawaiian
m	m	m	m	m
n	n	n	n	n
t	t	t	t	k

If we examine still other words, these sound correspondences are maintained, and additional **correspondence sets** can be established. As the words in Table 9-2 reveal, Tongan and Maori /k/ corresponds to a glottal stop /ʔ/ in Samoan, Tahitian, and Hawaiian, while Tongan, Samoan, and Maori /ŋ/ corresponds to Tahitian /ʔ/ and Hawaiian /n/. We can thus establish regular sound correspondences among modern-day Polynesian languages. Table 9-3 presents the consonant correspondences exhibited in the words presented so far.

In comparative reconstruction, it is important to exclude all borrowed words because the only words that can profitably provide sounds for use in a correspondence set are those that have descended directly from the ancestor language. For example, because Proto-Polynesian *s became /h/ in Tongan (but remained /s/ in other daughter languages), Tongan has very few words with /s/—among them *sikaleti,* meaning 'cigarette.' While *sikaleti* was obviously borrowed from a language outside the Polynesian family, words borrowed from other languages within the same family may not be so easy to spot.

TABLE 9-3

Sound Correspondences in Five Polynesian Languages

Tongan	Samoan	Tahitian	Maori	Hawaiian
m	m	m	m	m
n	n	n	n	n
ŋ	ŋ	ʔ	ŋ	n
p	p	p	p	p
t	t	t	t	k
k	ʔ	ʔ	k	ʔ

Comparative Reconstruction   The method just illustrated is known as **comparative reconstruction.** It aims to reconstruct an ancestor language from the evidence that remains in daughter languages. Its premise is that, borrowing aside, similar forms with similar meanings across related languages are *reflexes* of a single form with a related meaning in the parent language. This commonsense approach is at the foundation of the comparative method and, indeed, of historical linguistics.

When we examine *correspondence sets* such as m-m-m-m-m and t-t-t-t-k in Table 9-3, it seems reasonable to assume that *m and *t existed in the parent language and that /m/ was retained in each of the daughter languages, while /t/ was retained except in Hawaiian, where it became /k/. Such assumptions are the everyday fare of historical linguistics. When we assume the existence of a sound (or other structure) in a language for which we have no evidence except what can be inferred from daughter languages, that sound (or structure) is said to be *reconstructed*. Reconstructed forms are "starred" to indicate that they are unattested. We can represent the reconstructions from correspondence sets this way:

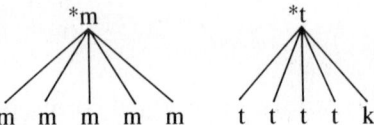

In describing the development of Hawaiian from Proto-Polynesian, we would postulate a historical rule of the form: *t > k. (Note that a shaftless arrow is used to indicate that one form developed into another form over time.)

Instead of *t, we could have reconstructed a *k in Proto-Polynesian that was retained in Hawaiian and became /t/ in all the other languages, but cautious reconstruction and experience with many languages have led historical linguists to prefer reconstructions that assume the *least* change consistent with the facts, unless there is good reason to do otherwise.

Let's inspect the reconstruction of *m more closely. That *m existed in the protolanguage and was retained in all the daughter languages is the simplest but not the only logical hypothesis. We could hypothesize some other sound in the protolanguage that independently became /m/ in each daughter language. Both the *bilabial* *b and the *nasal* *n would be likely candidates for this reconstruction in that they share phonetic features with /m/, a *bilabial nasal*. However, since Polynesian languages generally lack the phoneme /b/, it seems more reasonable to assume that the parent language also lacked *b. Alternatively, we could reconstruct an *n that changed to /m/ in all the daughter languages independently of one another. This hypothesis must be rejected for two reasons: First, it is not a minimal assumption; second, the daughter languages have an /n/ that also must have a source in the parent language. We thus postulate reconstructed Proto-Polynesian *m and *n, which were retained unchanged in all the daughter languages.

Let's examine one other correspondence set: ŋ-ŋ-ʔ-ŋ-n. We have just postulated Proto-Polynesian *n as the reconstructed **etymon,** or earlier form, of the correspondence set n-n-n-n-n. It is interesting to compare this reconstruction with one for the correspondence set ŋ-ŋ-ʔ-ŋ-n, for which the most likely reconstruction is *ŋ.

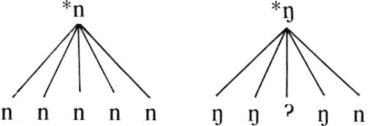

Thus *ŋ was retained in Tongan, Samoan, and Maori but became /ʔ/ in Tahitian and /n/ in Hawaiian. As a result, the distinction between *n and *ŋ that existed in Proto-Polynesian and is maintained in Tongan, Samoan, and Maori does not exist in Hawaiian, in which *n and *ŋ have merged in /n/. Hawaiian /n/ therefore has two historical sources. We can represent the historical merger in rules (*n > n; *ŋ > n) or schematically.

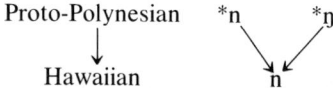

Subgroups   On the basis of lexical and structural characteristics, it is apparent that some Polynesian languages are more closely linked than others. As shown in Table 9-4, Tongan differs from other Polynesian languages in at least two respects: It has initial /h/ where other languages do not have anything; and it has nothing where other languages have either /l/ or /r/. Niuean, another Polynesian language, shares these and certain other characteristics with Tongan. On the basis of such evidence, Tongan and Niuean can be seen to form a **subgroup,** or *branch,* of Polynesian. This implies that Tongan and Niuean were at one time a single language distinct from Proto-Polynesian and that Proto-Tongic, as it is called, developed certain features before splitting into Tongan and Niuean. The retention in both languages of these features (those that developed after Proto-Tongic split from Proto-Polynesian but before Tongan and Niuean split into separate

TABLE 9-4
Cognates in Five Polynesian Languages II

Tongan	Samoan	Tahitian	Maori	Hawaiian	
hama	ama	ama	ama	ama	'outrigger'
hiŋoa	iŋoa	iʔoa	iŋoa	inoa	'name'
mohe	moe	moe	moe	moe	'to sleep'
hake	aʔe	aʔe	ake	aʔe	'up'
ua	lua	rua	rua	lua	'two'
ama	lama	rama	rama	lama	'torch'
tui	tuli	turi	turi	kuli	'knee'

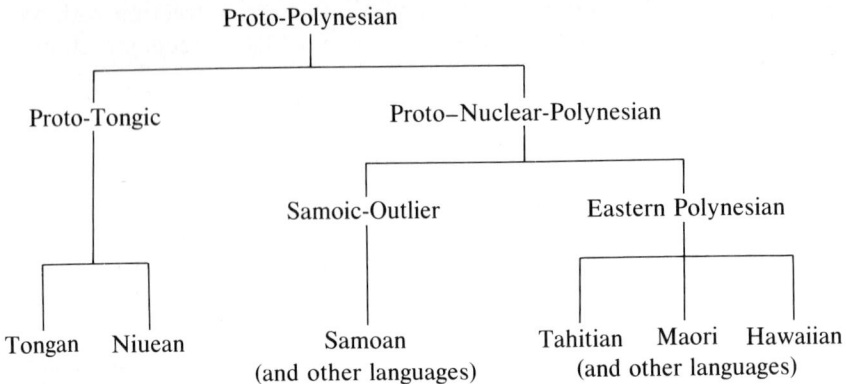

FIGURE 9-3
Polynesian Languages

languages) constitutes the characteristic shared features of the Proto-Tongic branch of the Polynesian family.

In the meantime, the other branch of Proto-Polynesian also evolved independently after its speakers lost contact with speakers of Proto-Tongic. As this second branch, called Proto–Nuclear-Polynesian, developed its distinctive characteristics, it emerged as a separate language that gave rise to still other languages. Except for Tongan and Niuean, all modern Polynesian languages share certain features inherited from Proto–Nuclear-Polynesian. In turn, Proto–Nuclear-Polynesian has two main subgroups: Samoic-Outlier and Eastern Polynesian. The evolution of Polynesian languages can be represented in the *family tree* shown in Figure 9-3. Family trees such as these are useful in representing the general genetic relationships in a family of languages, but they inevitably oversimplify the complex facts of history, especially by excluding borrowing and other influences that languages can exert on one another.

Reconstructing the Proto-Polynesian Vocabulary

On the basis of the evidence provided by modern-day Polynesian languages, we can reconstruct the phonology and lexicon of Proto-Polynesian (and make educated guesses about its grammatical structure). In turn, reconstructed linguistic information can tell us a good deal about the people who first settled Polynesia more than three thousand years ago.

A word can be reconstructed for Proto-Polynesian if we find **reflexes** of it—that is, cognates—in at least one language of each major subgroup (Tongic, Samoic-Outlier, and Eastern Polynesian) and are confident that the cognates are not borrowed words.[1]

---

[1] If we reconstructed a lexical item for Proto-Polynesian based simply on evidence from Tongan and, say, Samoan, we would run the risk of having found a word that existed originally only in Tongan (after Tongan became a separate language) and was borrowed by the early Samoans. (You can see from Figure 9-2 that Tonga and Samoa are close enough to have had contacts in prehistoric times.)

TABLE 9-5
Reconstructed Terms in Proto-Polynesian I

*awa	'channel'	*hafu	'waterfall'
*hakau	'coral reef'	*lanu	'fresh water'
*kilikili	'gravel'	*lolo	'flood'
*peau	'wave'	*mato	'precipice'
*sou	'rough ocean'	*maʔuŋa	'mountain'
*tahi	'sea'	*rano	'lake'
*ʔone	'sand'	*waitafe	'stream'

For example, since cognate words for 'bird,' 'fish,' and 'man' are found in all major subgroups of the Polynesian family (as shown in Tables 9-1 and 9-2), we can reconstruct a Proto-Polynesian form for each. According to regular sound correspondences and the most plausible reconstructed sounds, these words are: *manu, *taŋata,* and *ika.* In contrast, the word for a 'night of full moon,' which in Maori and Tahitian is *hotu* and in Hawaiian *hoku,* cannot be reconstructed for Proto-Polynesian because there is no cognate in any Tongic or Samoic-Outlier language. Similarly, an etymon for the Tongan and Niuean word *kookoo* 'windpipe' cannot be reconstructed for Proto-Polynesian because there is no reflex in any Samoic-Outlier or Eastern Polynesian language.

Using the comparative method of historical reconstruction just outlined, the lexical items in Table 9-5, all referring to the physical environment, can be reconstructed for Proto-Polynesian.

From Table 9-5, you can see that the Proto-Polynesian people had words for ocean-related notions (the left-hand column) and for topographic features typically found on large volcanic islands (the right-hand column). As it happens, there are no waterfalls, mountains, precipices, or lakes on coral atolls, and only rarely are they found on raised coral islands.

In interpreting such results, linguists make the commonsense assumption that the presence of a word for a particular object in a language usually indicates the presence of that object in the speakers' environment. (There are exceptions to this rule, as we will see, but they are few and far between.) In particular, complete landlubbers will not normally have an elaborate native vocabulary for the sea and for seafaring activities (barring the possibility of a recent move inland from a coastal area). We thus surmise that the early Polynesians inhabited a high island or a chain of high islands but lived close enough to the ocean to be familiar with the landscape and phenomena of the sea.

In Table 9-6, we reconstruct still other Proto-Polynesian names for animals and make the assumption that the ancient Polynesians were familiar with them. Names of many other reef and deepwater fish and other sea creatures can be reconstructed besides those listed in the second and fourth columns. In contrast, we can reconstruct only a handful of names for land animals: a few domesticated animals (dog, pig, chicken) and a few birds and reptiles. We surmise that the Polynesians' original habitat was rich in sea life but probably relatively poor in land fauna—that the Polynesians originally inhabited coastal regions and not island interiors.

TABLE 9-6
Reconstructed Terms in Proto-Polynesian II

*maŋoo	'shark'	*kulii	'dog'
*kanahe	'mullet'	*puaka	'pig'
*sakulaa	'swordfish'	*moko	'lizard'
*ʔatu	'bonito'	*kumaa	'rat'
*ʔono	'barracuda'	*ŋata	'snake'
*ʔume	'leatherjacket'	*fonu	'turtle'
*manini	'sturgeon'	*peka	'bat'
*nofu	'stonefish'	*namu	'mosquito'
*fai	'stingray'	*lulu	'owl'
*kaloama	'goatfish'	*matuku	'reef heron'
*palani	'surgeonfish'	*akiaki	'tern'
*toke	'eel'	*moa	'chicken'

The character of the land fauna offers pointed information about the Proto-Polynesian homeland. Since the Proto-Polynesian terms *peka 'bat' and *lulu 'owl' can be reconstructed, we can exclude as possible homelands Tahiti, Easter Island, and the Marquesas, where bats and owls are not found.

Furthermore, snakes are found only east of Samoa. Though we find reflexes of Proto-Polynesian *ŋata 'snake' in many languages, we find no snakes west of Samoa. Had the Proto-Polynesians inhabited an island west of Samoa, they would very likely have lost the term *ŋata over the centuries. Similarly, we know that pigs (for which the word *puaka can be reconstructed) are not native to Polynesia, but Europeans first arriving between the sixteenth and nineteenth centuries found them everywhere except in Niue, Easter Island, and New Zealand. These three regions are thus unlikely homelands.

Words for some animals have undergone interesting changes in certain Polynesian languages. For example, New Zealand is much colder than the rest of Polynesia, and its native animals are very different from those found on the tropical islands to the north. On arrival in New Zealand, the ancient Maoris encountered many new species to which they gave the names of animals they had left behind in tropical Polynesia; thus the following correspondences exist.

Proto-Polynesian		Maori	
*pule	'cowrie shell'	pure	'bivalve mollusk'
*ŋata	'snake'	ŋata	'snail'
*ali	'flounder'	ari	'small shark'

Other animals names were dropped from the Maori vocabulary or applied to things commonly associated with the animal.

Proto-Polynesian		Maori	
*ane	'termite'	ane	'rotten'
*lupe	'pigeon'	rupe	'mythical bird'

Other changes are more complex. The word *lulu* (or *ruru*) refers to owls in languages (such as Tongan, Samoan, and Maori) that are spoken in areas where owls are found. On some islands like the Marquesas and Tahiti, owls do not exist, and the reflex of Proto-Polynesian **lulu* 'owl' has either disappeared from the language, as in Marquesan, or been applied to another species, as in Tahitian. Owls inhabit Hawaii, but the Proto-Polynesian term **lulu* has been replaced by the word *pueo* there.

Why would the early Hawaiians replace one word with the other? In the Marquesas, as we have said, there are no owls, and the language spoken there has no reflex of **lulu*. Apparently the ancient Polynesians settled the Marquesas and stayed there for several centuries, during which they lost the word **lulu* for lack of anything to apply it to. When they subsequently traveled north and settled Hawaii, they encountered owls, but by that time the word *lulu* had long been forgotten, and a new word had to be found.

The linguistic evidence argues that the ancestors of the Polynesians were fishermen and cultivators. Here are a few of the many terms that refer to fishing and horticulture.

*mataʔu	'fishhook'	*too	'to plant'
*rama	'to torch-fish'	*faki	'to pick'
*paa	'fish lure'	*lohu	'picking pole'
*kupeŋa	'fishnet'	*hua	'spade'
*afo	'fishing line'	*maʔala	'garden'
*faaŋota	'to fish'	*pulapula	'seedling'

In contrast to this rich vocabulary, hunting terms are limited, with three words apparently exhausting all possible reconstructions for verbs related to hunting: **fana* 'to shoot with a bow,' **welo* 'to spear,' and **seu* 'to snare with a net.' It is probably safe to infer that the major source of food for the ancient Polynesians was not the bush but sea and garden.

One field with a notable array of vocabulary is canoe navigation, with the following reconstructions: **folau* 'to travel by sea,' **ʔuli* 'to steer,' **fohe* 'paddle,' **fana* 'mast,' **laa* 'sail,' **kiato* 'outrigger boom,' **hama* 'outrigger.' That the speakers of Proto-Polynesian were expert seafarers comes as no surprise, given that they traveled enormous distances between islands (two thousand miles stretch between Hawaii and the closest inhabited island).

Historical Linguistics and Prehistory

The linguistic evidence combined with evidence from archaeology leads to the following hypotheses:

1. The speakers of Proto-Polynesian inhabited the coastal region of a high island or group of high islands.

2. This homeland is likely to have been in the region between Samoa and Fiji, including the islands of Tonga, Uvea, and Futuna.

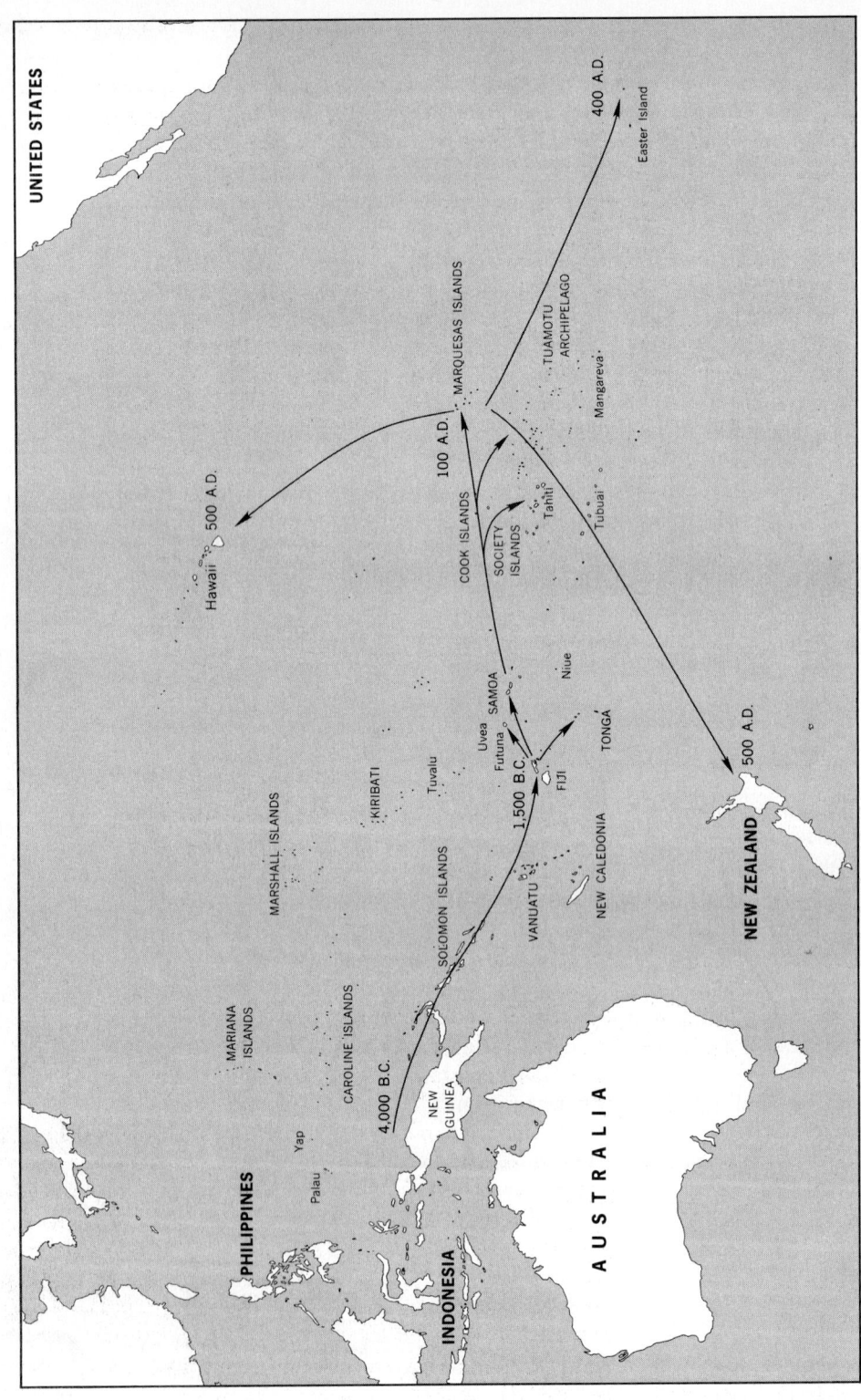

FIGURE 9-4
The Settlement of Polynesia

3. The ancient Polynesians were fishermen, cultivators, and seafarers.

4. Around the first century A.D., the ancient Polynesians traveled eastward from their homeland, settling eastern Polynesia: Tahiti, the Cook Islands, the Marquesas, the Tuamotu, and the neighboring island groups.

5. Then, between the fourth and sixth centuries, Easter Island, Hawaii, and New Zealand were settled from eastern Polynesia.

The history of Polynesian settlement and migrations is summarized in Figure 9-4.

Our discussion has focused on Polynesian origins and migrations. By judiciously combining linguistic evidence with evidence from other disciplines, we constructed a probable picture of an ancient people, the environment they lived in, and the skills they developed for survival. Linguists have applied the same methods to other peoples, including the Indo-Europeans and the Algonquian Indians.

THE LANGUAGE FAMILIES OF THE WORLD

The same comparative method used to trace the historical development of languages can be applied to determine which languages are related within families. In this section we survey the major language families of the world, paying particular attention to those families with the greatest number of speakers and those that include most languages.

Counting Speakers and Languages

It is not easy to determine with certainty how many people speak languages like English, Chinese, and Arabic. Nevertheless, these and a few others stand out for the sheer number of people that claim them as a native language. Of the world's several thousand languages, about a dozen are spoken natively by 100 million individuals or more. In the following table, numbers have been rounded off to the nearest 50 million.

Chinese	1 billion
English	350 million
Spanish	300 million
Hindi-Urdu	150 million
Portuguese	150 million
Indonesian-Malay	150 million
Russian	150 million
Arabic	150 million
Bengali	150 million
French	100 million
German	100 million
Japanese	100 million

Six of these languages—Chinese, English, Spanish, Russian, Arabic, and French—are the working languages of the United Nations.

Equally difficult to estimate is the number of languages currently spoken in the world. The figure commonly cited is 4,000 to 5,000, while a more conservative estimate would be about 2,000. It is difficult to determine, in many cases, whether particular communities speak different dialects of the same language or different languages. Furthermore, little is known about many of the world's languages. In Papua New Guinea, a nation of only 3 million people, as many as 800 languages (about one fifth of the world's total) are spoken, although we have descriptions of a mere handful. Many Papuan languages are spoken in remote communities by only a few hundred speakers, or even a few dozen.

The discussion below is arranged by language family, beginning with Indo-European, Sino-Tibetan, Austronesian, and Afroasiatic, which together are the four most important families in terms of both numbers of speakers and numbers of languages. The three major language families of sub–Saharan Africa are then discussed together, followed by other language families of Europe and Asia, including important isolated languages like Japanese. Finally, we discuss the native languages of the Americas, Australia, and central Papua New Guinea. Following a brief discussion of the proposed Nostratic macrofamily, we conclude with a discussion of pidgins and creoles.

The Indo-European Family

To the Indo-European language family belong most languages of Europe (which are now spoken natively in the Americas and Oceania and play prominent roles in Africa and Asia), as well as most languages of Iran, Afghanistan, Pakistan, Bangladesh, and most of India. Of the 12 languages with more than 100 million native speakers, 8 belong to the Indo-European family. Yet Indo-European languages number only about 150, a small fraction of the world's languages. The extensive spread of Indo-European languages is shown in Figure 9-5. The Indo-European family is divided into several groups, which we discuss briefly. Figure 9-6 is a family tree showing a few languages for each group.

Germanic Group   Modern-day Germanic languages include English, German, Yiddish, Norwegian, Swedish, Danish, Dutch (and its derivative Afrikaans), and a few other languages like Icelandic, Faroese, and Frisian. Frisian, spoken in the northern Netherlands, is the closest relative to English. As Table 9-7 illustrates, Germanic languages bear striking similarities to one another in vocabulary, and similarities in phonology and syntax are also numerous. Some Germanic languages are mutually intelligible, and all bear the imprint of their common ancestor, Proto-Germanic.

Swedish, Danish, Norwegian, Icelandic, and Faroese—the North Germanic group—are more closely related to each other than to the other languages of the Germanic group. They descended from Proto–North-Germanic, which evolved as a single language for a longer period of time than the West Germanic subgroup that includes English, Frisian, Dutch, and German. We also have written records of Gothic, which was spoken in central Europe but which disappeared around the eighth century. Gothic alone forms the East Germanic subgroup. Figure 9-7 is the family tree for the Germanic group. (Gothic is in parentheses because it is extinct.)

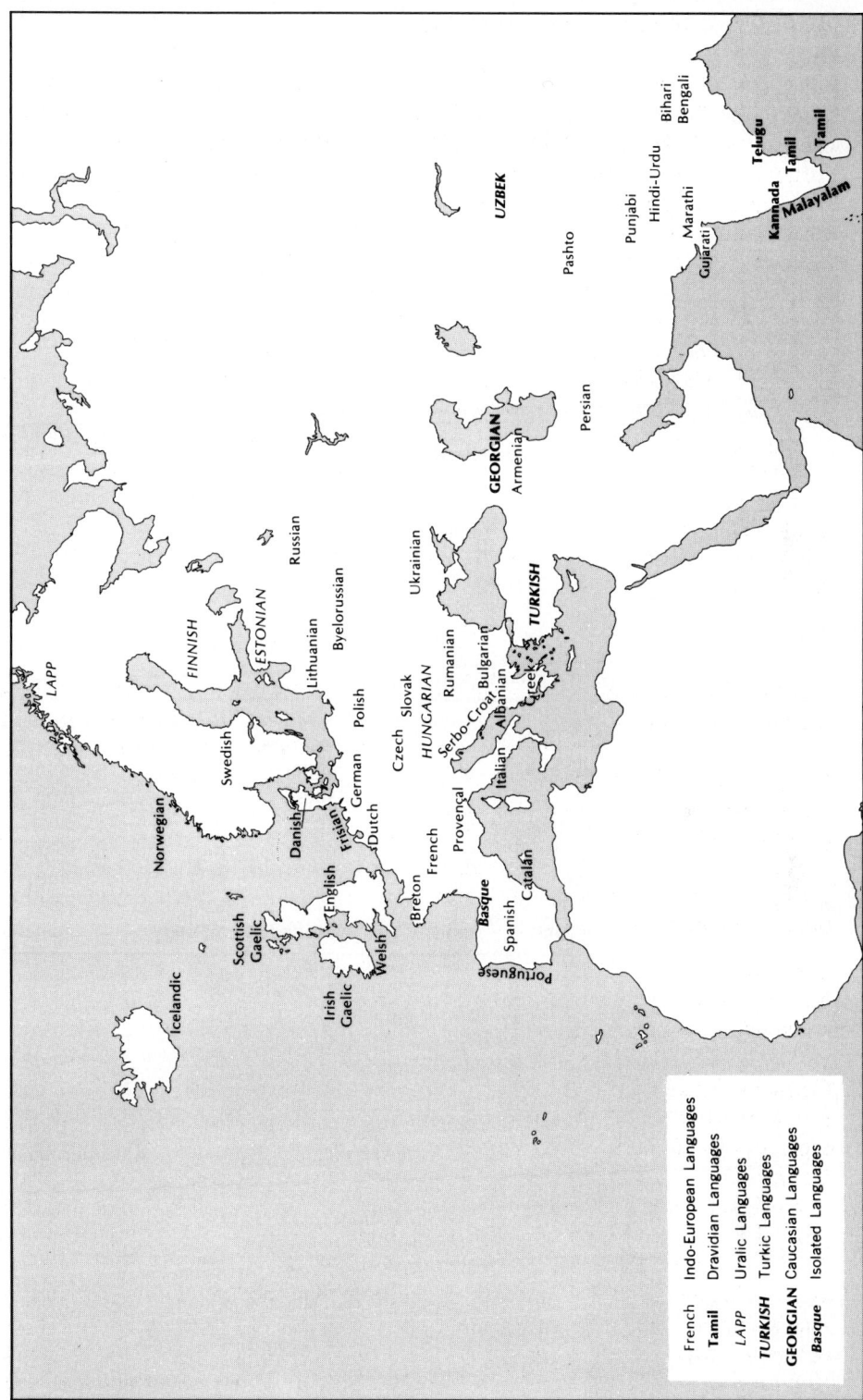

FIGURE 9-5
Location of the Major Indo-European, Dravidian, Caucasian, Uralic, and Turkic Languages

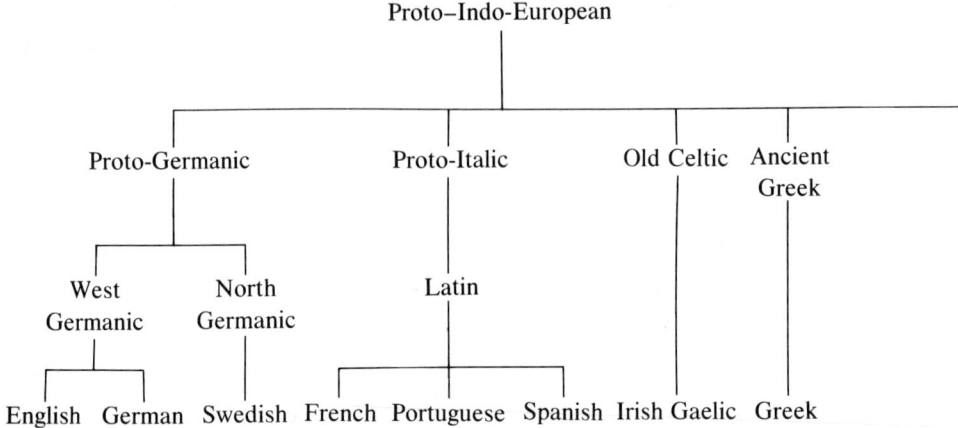

FIGURE 9-6
Partial Tree of the Indo-European Language Family

TABLE 9-7
Common Words in Seven Germanic Languages

English	German	Dutch	Swedish	Danish	Norwegian	Icelandic
mother	Mutter	moeder	moder	moder	moder	móðir
father	Vater	vader	fader	fader	fader	faðir
eye	Auge	oog	óga	øje	øye	auga
foot	Fuss	voet	fot	fod	fot	fótur
one	ein	een	en	en	en	einn
three	drei	drie	tre	tre	tre	þrír
month	Monat	maand	månad	maaned	måned	mánaður

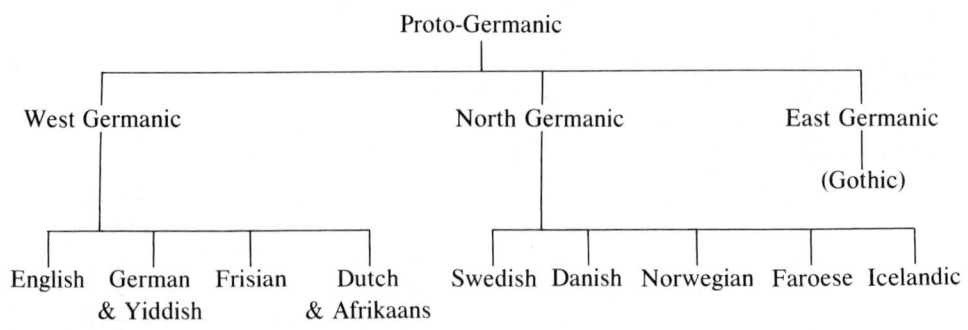

FIGURE 9-7
Germanic Languages

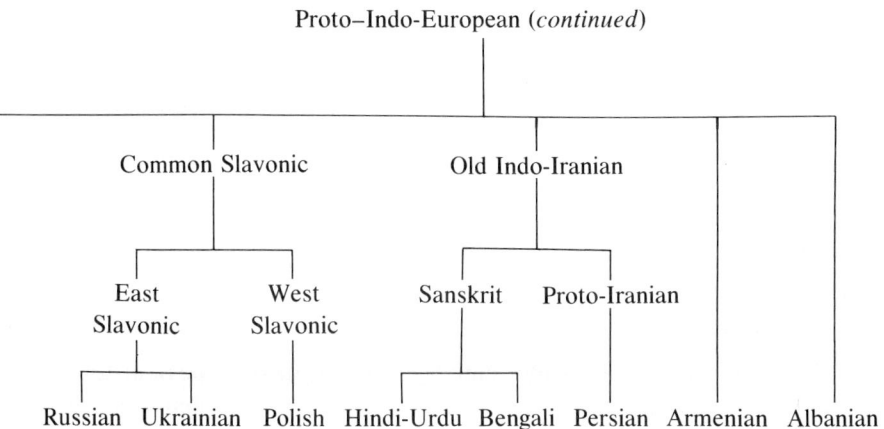

Proto–Indo-European (*continued*)

Common Slavonic

Old Indo-Iranian

East Slavonic

West Slavonic

Sanskrit

Proto-Iranian

Russian   Ukrainian   Polish   Hindi-Urdu   Bengali   Persian   Armenian   Albanian

FIGURE 9-6   (*continued*)

With about 350 million speakers, English is native to many inhabitants of the British Isles, the United States, most of Canada, the Caribbean, Australia, New Zealand, and South Africa. In addition, there are numerous bilinguals in English and another language on the Indian subcontinent, in eastern and southern Africa, and in Oceania. To these we must add the countless speakers of English as a second language scattered around the globe. English is the second most populous spoken language in the world after Chinese, but it is unrivaled in terms of its geographical spread and popularity as a second language. German, which has not spread as much as English, is still one of the world's most widely spoken languages. It claims about 100 million native speakers, mostly in central Europe.

Italic Group and Romance Subgroup   The Romance languages include French, Spanish, Italian, Portuguese, and Rumanian, as well as Provençal (spoken in the south of France), Catalan (spoken in northern Spain), and Romansch (spoken in Switzerland). The Romance languages are closely related to each other, as witnessed by the sample of vocabulary correspondences in Table 9-8. The Rumanian words for 'mother,' 'father,' 'foot,' and 'month,' which are not derived from the

TABLE 9-8
Common Words in Six Romance Languages

French	Italian	Spanish	Rumanian	Catalan	Portuguese	
mère	madre	madre	mamă	mare	mãe	'mother'
père	padre	padre	tată	pare	pai	'father'
œil	occhio	ojo	ochiu	ull	ôlho	'eye'
pied	piede	pie	picior	peu	pé	'foot'
un	uno	uno	un	un	um	'one'
trois	tre	tres	trei	tres	três	'three'
mois	mese	mes	lŭna	mes	mês	'month'

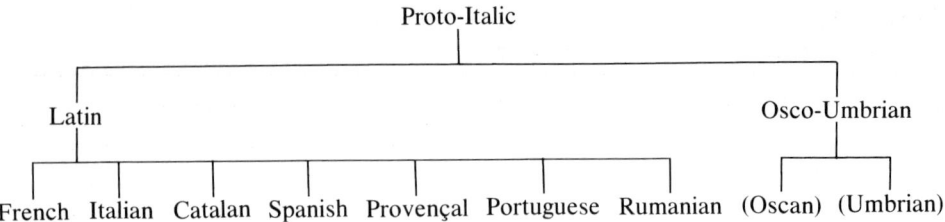

FIGURE 9-8
Italic Languages

same roots as those in the other Romance languages, illustrate the type of historical change that hinders communication between speakers of closely related languages. Such examples are particularly common in Rumanian, which is geographically isolated from other Romance languages.

The languages of the Romance family are descendants of Vulgar Latin. Because the Romance languages have remained in close contact over the centuries, subgroups are more difficult to identify than for Germanic languages. Latin is one descendant of Proto-Italic. Oscan and Umbrian, the other principal descendants, were once spoken in southern Italy but are now extinct. While written records abound for Latin, little is known about Oscan and Umbrian. The tree for Italic and Romance languages is shown in Figure 9-8.

Spanish, with approximately 300 million native speakers in Spain and the Americas, is the third most populous language. Portuguese is spoken by nearly 150 million people, principally in Portugal and Brazil. French has almost 100 million native speakers in France, Canada, and the United States, as well as many second-language speakers, particularly in North Africa and West Africa.

Slavonic Group   Slavonic languages are spoken in eastern Europe and the former Soviet Union. The Slavonic group can be divided into three subgroups: East Slavonic, which includes Russian, Ukrainian, and Byelorussian (spoken in the westernmost part of the former USSR); South Slavonic, which includes Bulgarian and Serbo-Croat; and West Slavonic, which groups together Polish, Czech, Slovak, and a few minor languages. All are derived from Common Slavonic (see Figure 9-9).

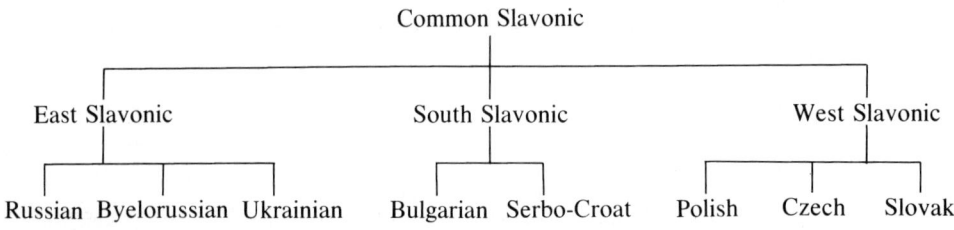

FIGURE 9-9
Slavonic Languages

TABLE 9-9
Common Words in Six Slavonic Languages

Russian	Ukrainian	Polish	Czech	Serbo-Croat	Bulgarian	
mat'	mati	matka	matka	mati	mayka	'mother'
otec	otec'	ojciec	otec	otac	bašča	'father'
oko*	oko	oko	oko	oko	oko	'eye'
noga	noga	noga	noha	noga	krak	'foot'
odin	odin	jeden	jeden	jedan	edin	'one'
tri	tri	trzy	tři	tri	tri	'three'
mesyac	misyac'	miesiac	mešíc	mjesec	mesec	'month'

Russian *oko* 'eye' is archaic; the more modern word is *glaz*.

Even more so than the Germanic and Romance languages, Slavonic languages are remarkably similar to each other, especially in their vocabulary (see Table 9-9).

By far the most widely spoken Slavonic language is Russian, which is spoken natively by 150 million people and as a foreign language by an additional 65 million. Ukrainian has 50 million speakers, Polish 35 million, Serbo-Croat 17 million, Czech 10 million, and Byelorussian 10 million.

Indo-Iranian Group   At the other geographical extreme of the Indo-European family we find the Indo-Iranian group, which is subdivided into Iranian and Indic (see Figure 9-10). The two most important Iranian languages are Persian (also called Farsi), with 35 million speakers in Iran, and Pashto, with 15 million speakers in Afghanistan and northern Pakistan. Indic languages include Hindi-Urdu, spoken by about 150 million people in India (where it is called Hindi and is written in Davanāgari script) and Pakistan (where it is called Urdu and uses the Arabic script); Bengali, spoken in India and Bangladesh by 150 million people; Bihari, spoken in northeastern India by 40 million; Punjabi, with 40 million speakers in northern India and Pakistan; Marathi, spoken in central India by 30 million people; and Gujarati, spoken in western India by 25 million. Many of these languages are also spoken by ethnic Indian populations in Southeast Asia, Africa, the Americas, Great Britain, and Oceania. The parent language of the modern Indic languages

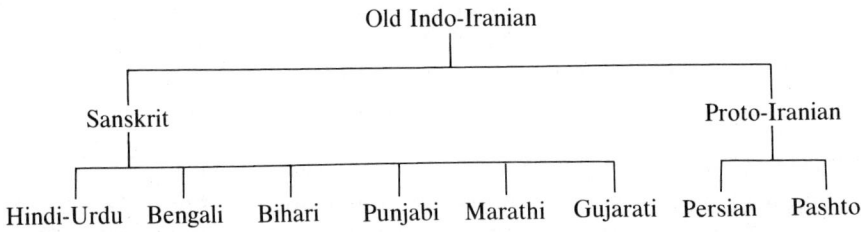

FIGURE 9-10
Indo-Iranian Languages

TABLE 9-10
Common Words in Six Indic Languages

Hindi	Bengali	Marathi	Gujarati	Persian	Pashto	
mã:	ma	ma:	ma:	madær	mo:r	'mother'
ba:p	ba:p	baba:	ba:p	pedær	pla:r	'father'
ã:kʰ	cókʰ	dola	a:nkʰ	čæšm	starga	'eye'
pã:w	pa:	pa:	pa:g	pa	xpa	'foot'
ek	ak	ek	e:k	yek	yau	'one'
ti:n	ti:n	ti:n	tra:n	se	dre:	'three'
mahi:na:	mas	mahi:na:	mahi:no	mah	mia:sht	'month'

is Sanskrit, the ancient language of India immortalized in the Vedas and other classical texts.

Table 9-10 presents sample vocabulary correspondences among a few Indo-Iranian languages. Not all the words with one meaning are cognates because some have sources other than a common parent language.

Hellenic Group   The sole member of the Hellenic group is Greek. Certain languages, while belonging to a major language family, were isolated early enough that they do not bear any particularly close affiliations to other languages of the family. Such is the case with Greek, which evolved through the centuries in relative isolation. Greek stands out from other isolated Indo-European languages because of its relatively large number of speakers (10 million) and its historical importance in Indo-European linguistics, owing to the fact that early written records of Ancient Greek have survived.

Other Indo-European Language Groups   Of the other Indo-European groups, Celtic includes Irish Gaelic, Scottish Gaelic, Breton, and Welsh, which together are spoken by no more than 1 million people today; Baltic includes Lithuanian, with 3 million speakers, and Latvian. Tocharian and Anatolian (including Hittite) are now extinct. Armenian and Albanian, each with 4 million speakers, form two additional language groups.

The Sino-Tibetan Family

Included in the Sino-Tibetan family are about 300 East Asian languages, many of which remain relatively unexplored. This family is divided into a Sinitic group and a Tibeto-Burman group.

The Sinitic group includes a dozen languages, most of which are structurally similar and are regarded as dialects of a single language. With more than 1 billion speakers, this language is the world's most populous language; it is of course Chinese. At least five dialect groups can be identified. The Mandarin group includes the Běijīng (Peking) dialect, which serves as the official language of the People's Republic of China; the Yuè dialects include the dialect of Guǎngzhōu (Canton), which is spoken by the greatest number of overseas Chinese, now scat-

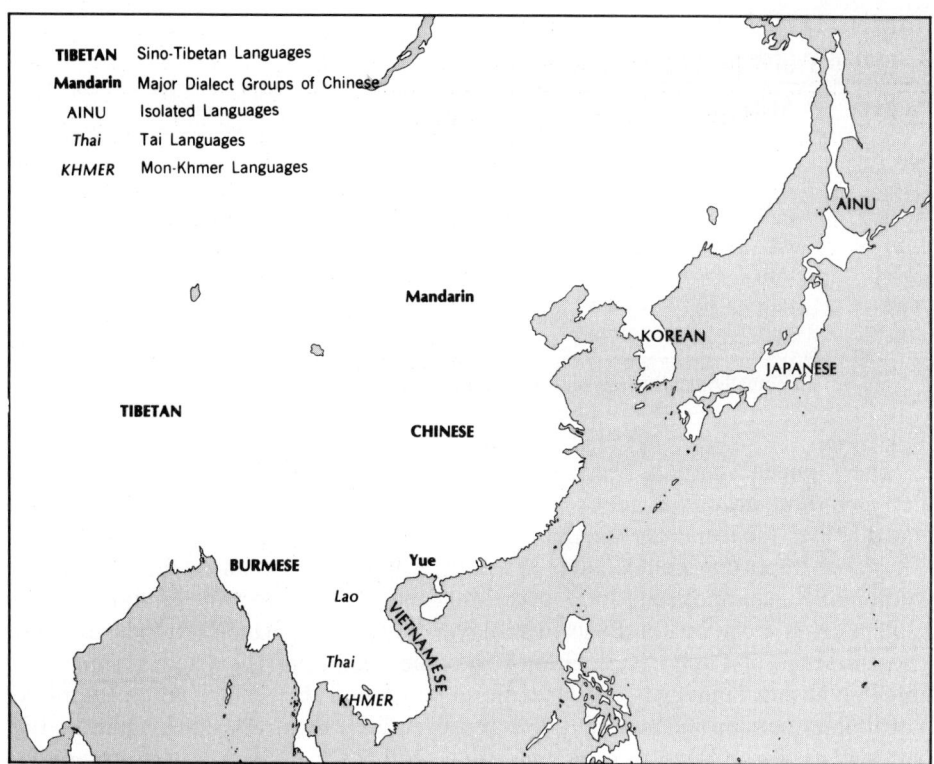

FIGURE 9-11
Location of the Major Sino-Tibetan, Mon-Khmer, and Tai Languages, and of the Major Isolated Languages of Asia

tered throughout the world. In addition, there are the Wú dialects, the Mǐn dialects, and the Hakka dialects.

By comparison, the Tibeto-Burman group includes many different languages, each with relatively few speakers. The only members of this group that have more than a million speakers are Burmese (20 million) and Tibetan (3 million). Figure 9-11 maps the major Sino-Tibetan languages.

The Austronesian Family

The Austronesian family has up to 1,000 different languages scattered over one-third of the Southern Hemisphere. It includes Indonesian-Malay, spoken by about 150 million people in Indonesia and Malaysia; Javanese, with 60 million speakers on the island of Java in Indonesia; Tagalog or Pilipino, the official language of the Philippines, with 12 million speakers; Cebuano, another language of the Philippines (10 million speakers); and Malagasy, the principal language of Madagascar (9 million speakers). Most other Austronesian languages have fewer than 1 million speakers each, and many of them are spoken by only a few hundred people.

TABLE 9-11
Common Words in Six Austronesian Languages

Malay	Malagasy	Tagalog	Motu	Fijian	Samoan	
ibu	ineny	inâ	sina	tina	tinaa	'mother'
bapa	ikaky	amá	tama	tama	tamaa	'father'
mata	maso	mata	mata	mata	mata	'eye'
satu	isa	isa	ta	dua	tasi	'one'
tiga	telo	tatló	toi	tolu	tolu	'three'
batu	vato	bato	nadi	vatu	fatu*	'stone'
kutu	hao	kuto	utu	kutu	ʔutu	'louse'

* Samoan *fatu* actually means 'fruit pit,' a meaning closely related to 'stone.'

The Austronesian family contains several groups. The most ancient division is between three groups of minor Formosan languages spoken in the hills of Taiwan and all other Austronesian languages; the latter group is called Malayo-Polynesian. The most important split divides Western Malayo-Polynesian, which groups together languages spoken in Indonesia, Malaysia, Madagascar, the Philippines, and Guam, from Oceanic (or Eastern Malayo-Polynesian), which extends from the coastal areas of Papua New Guinea into the islands of the Pacific. Fijian and the Polynesian languages are Oceanic languages. Table 9-11 gives a sample of vocabulary correspondences between representative Austronesian languages. Figure 9-12 is a simplified tree of the family, and the distribution of Austronesian languages is illustrated in Figure 9-13.

The Afroasiatic Family

The Afroasiatic family comprises about 250 languages scattered across the northern part of Africa and western Asia. It includes Arabic, dialects of which

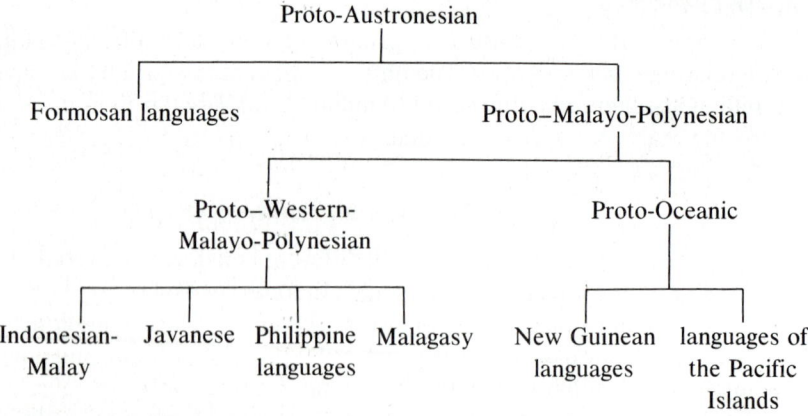

FIGURE 9-12
Tree of Austronesian Languages

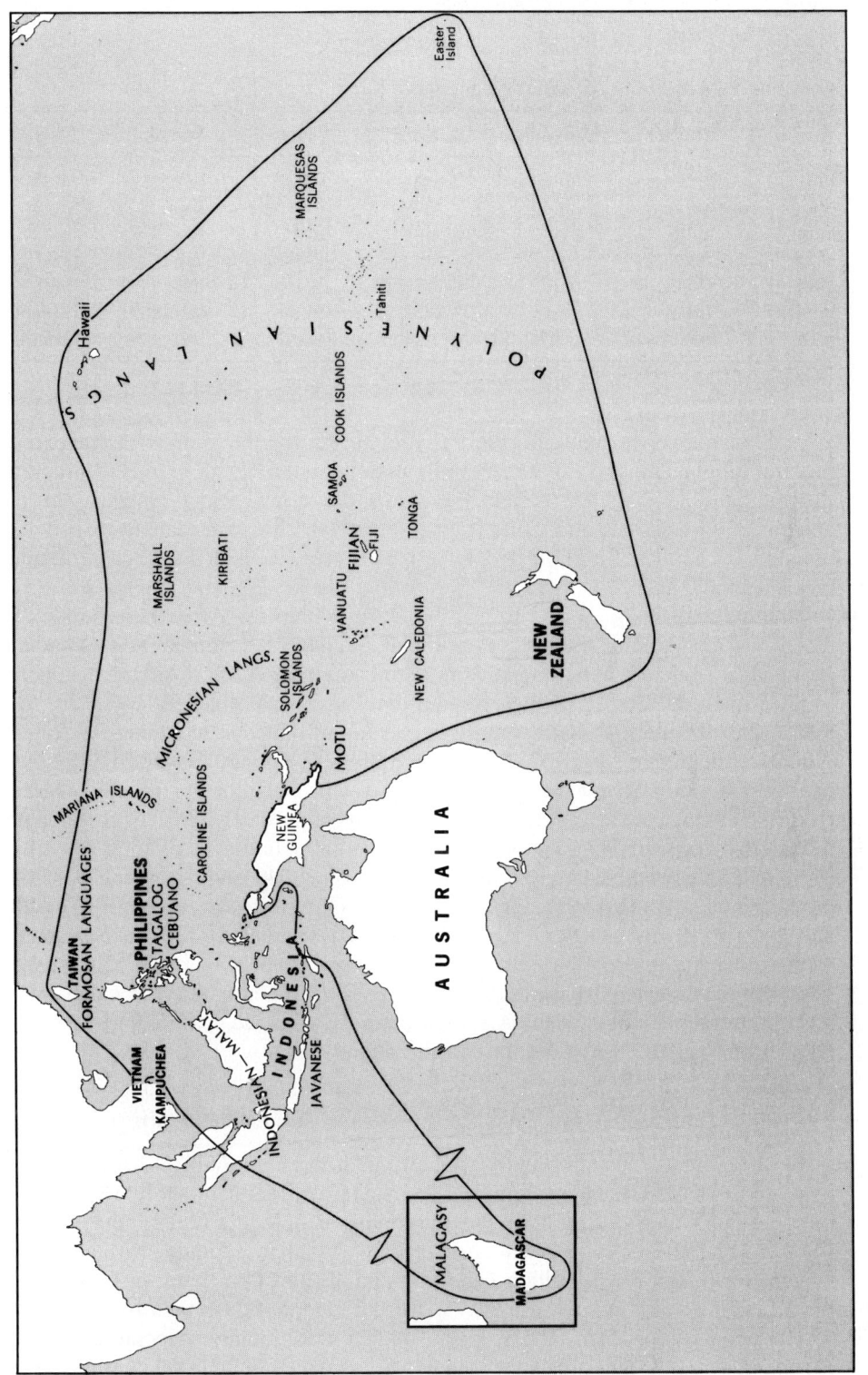

FIGURE 9-13
Map of Austronesian Languages

TABLE 9-12
Common Words in Six Afroasiatic Languages

Arabic	Hebrew	Amharic	Kabyl	Hausa	Somali	
um	ɛm	annat	yemma	inna	hooyyo	'mother'
ab	av	abbat	baba	baba	aabe	'father'
ʕain	ayin	ayn	allen	ido	il	'eye'
ʔežer	rɛgɛl	agar	aḍaṛ	k'afa	ʕag	'foot'
waḥad	ɛxad	and	waḥed	'daya	hal	'one'
ṭalaṭa	šloša	sost	tlata	uku	saddeħ	'three'
šaher	xodɛš	wár	eccher	wata	bil	'month'

are spoken across the entire northern part of Africa and the Middle East; Hebrew, the traditional language of the Jewish nation and revived in this century as the national language of Israel; Egyptian, the now extinct language of the ancient Egyptian civilization; and Hausa, one of Africa's major languages, spoken natively by about 20 million people in Chad, Nigeria, and neighboring nations (see Figure 9-14).

Hebrew and Arabic form the Semitic group within the Afroasiatic family. To this group also belong Amharic, the official language of Ethiopia, and Akkadian, a language of ancient Mesopotamia (modern Iraq), now extinct. Akkadian appears to have been the first language ever written, but it was replaced largely by Aramaic, also Semitic. Aramaic comprises a group of dialects, including Palestinian Aramaic, the native language of Jesus, and Modern Syriac, spoken by Christians in Iran, Iraq, and Soviet Georgia. A distinctive property of Semitic languages is their morphological system; noun and verb roots consist of a series of consonants, in which vowels are interdigitated to represent inflection (see Chapter 4).

Somali, the principal language of Somalia, is one of 40 languages of the Cushitic group. Kabyl and other languages that belong to the Berber group (with 10 million speakers) are scattered across North Africa. Hausa and about 130 other languages form the Chadic group, all of which have developed tone systems. Ancient Egyptian forms a separate Afroasiatic group. Table 9-12 is a comparative vocabulary for representative members of the Afroasiatic family. (ħ is the symbol for a voiceless pharyngeal fricative and ʕ for its voiced counterpart.)

The Three Major Language Families of Sub–Saharan Africa

Besides the Afroasiatic family spoken north of the Sahara Desert, Africa is home to three other language families: the Niger-Kordofanian family, with several hundred languages spoken by about 150 million people in a region that stretches from Senegal to Kenya to South Africa; the Nilo-Saharan family, with about 100 languages spoken by 10 million people in and around Chad and the Sudan; and the Khoisan family in southern Africa, with 50 languages spoken by fewer than 75,000 people altogether. The Khoisan family, traditionally associated with the Bushmen of the Kalahari Desert, is the only language family in the world that has

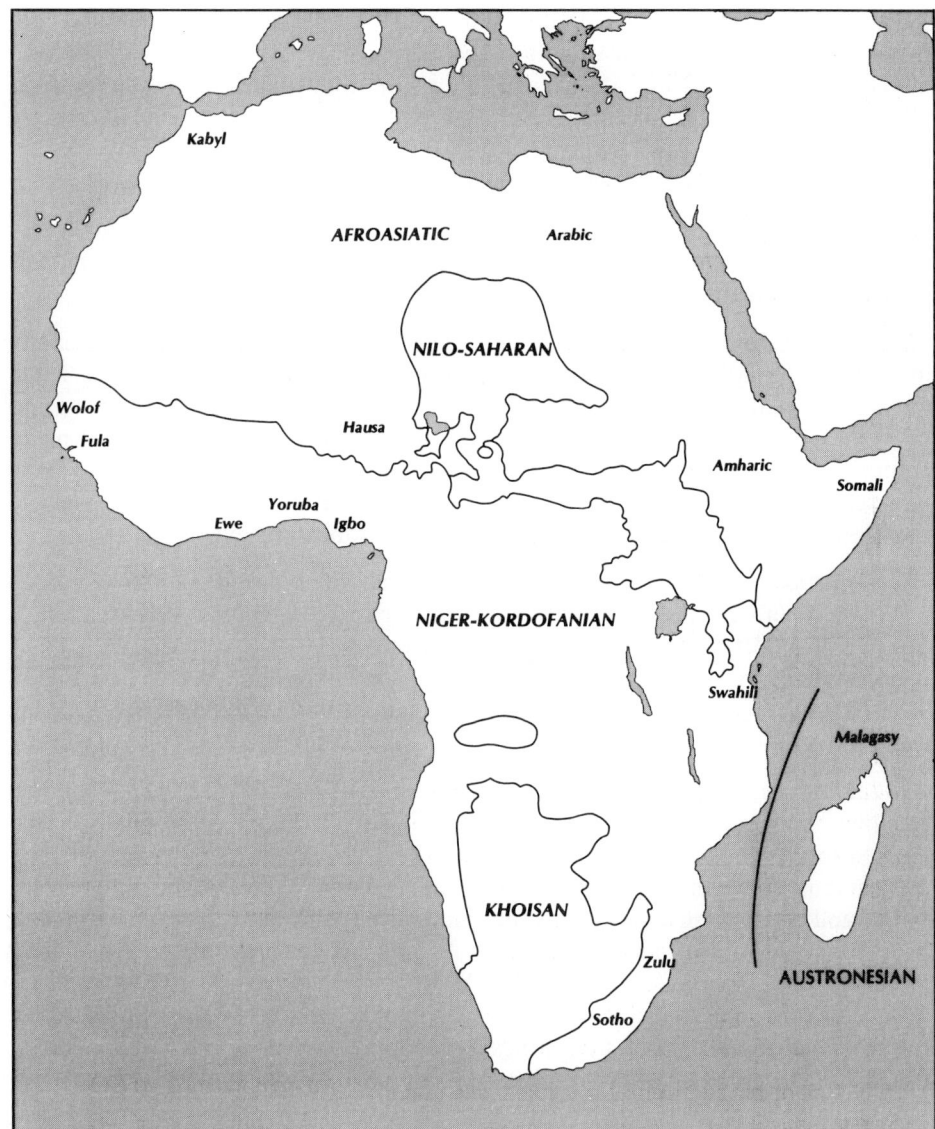

FIGURE 9-14
The Language Families of Africa

Source: Adapted from Gregersen 1977

click sounds (discussed in Chapter 2). The boundaries between these language families are shown in Figure 9-14.

Most of the better known languages of sub–Saharan Africa belong to the Niger-Kordofanian family. These include Fula, spoken by 6 million speakers in Senegal; Wolof, with 2 million speakers in Senegal, Gambia, Mali, and Guinea; Yoruba, spoken in Nigeria by more than 150 million; Ewe, spoken by 1 million in Togo, Benin, and Ghana; Igbo, with 5 million speakers in Nigeria; Swahili, with approximately 20 million in East Africa; and other Bantu languages of southern Africa like Zulu (5 million speakers) and Sotho (4 million).

Other Language Families of Asia and Europe

Scattered throughout Asia and Europe are a few smaller language families and a few languages that seem not to be genetically related to any other language family, so far as linguists can determine, and are therefore called *isolates*.

The Dravidian Family   Languages of the Dravidian family are spoken principally in southern India (see Figure 9-5). The four major Dravidian languages are Tamil (30 million speakers), Malayalam (20 million speakers), Kannada (20 million speakers), and Telugu (40 million speakers), all of which have been written for many centuries. All Dravidian languages have been somewhat influenced by the Indic languages spoken to their north. In Table 9-13, the Indic influence is evident in the Tamil word for 'month,' which is of Indo-European origin.

The Mon-Khmer Family   The Mon-Khmer family includes about 100 languages spoken in Southeast Asia (Vietnam, Laos, Kampuchea, Thailand, and Myanmar). The most important of these is Cambodian or Khmer, the official language of Kampuchea (formerly Cambodia), spoken by nearly 8 million people (see Figure 9-11). The Mon-Khmer languages may be related to other minor families of the same region.

The Tai Family   The best known languages of the Tai family are Thai (40 million speakers) and Lao (10 million speakers), the official languages of Thailand and Laos respectively (shown in Figure 9-11). There are about 50 other members of the Tai family scattered throughout Thailand, Laos, Vietnam, Myanmar, eastern India, and southern China, where they intertwine with Sino-Tibetan languages, Mon-Khmer languages, and Vietnamese. Tai languages may be related to a number of languages spoken in Vietnam, with which they may form a Kam-Tai family. It has also been suggested that Tai languages may be related to Austronesian, but the evidence supporting that hypothesis is scanty.

TABLE 9-13
Common Words in Four Dravidian Languages

Tamil	Malayalam	Kannada	Telugu	
amma:	amma	awwa	amma	'mother'
appa:	a:chchan	tande	na:nna	'father'
kaṇṇu	kaṇṇu	kaṇṇu	kannu	'eye'
ka:lu	ka:l	ka:lu	ka:lu	'foot'
onru	oru	ondu	okaṭi	'one'
mu:nru	mu:nnu	mu:ru	mu:ḍu	'three'
ma:sam	nela	tingaḷu	tingḷu	'month'

The Caucasian Family   With about 30 languages, the Caucasian family is confined to the mountainous region between the Black Sea and the Caspian Sea, which is part of the former Soviet Union, Turkey, and Iran. Spoken by about 5 million people altogether, Caucasian languages typically have complex phonological and morphological systems. The best known Caucasian language is Georgian (see Figure 9-5).

The Turkic Family   This family comprises 60 languages, all of which are quite similar. The better-known members are Turkish, spoken by 25 million people, and Uzbek, with 10 million speakers in the southern Soviet Union. Most Turkic languages are spoken in Turkey and central Asia (see Figure 9-5). Some scholars include Turkic in a larger Altaic family.

The Uralic Family   With about 30 members, the Uralic family is thought by some to be related to the Turkic family, though this link is tenuous. The better-known Uralic languages are Finnish (5 million speakers) and Hungarian (15 million speakers); also included are Estonian and Lapp (see Figure 9-5).

Japanese   Japanese, with more than 115 million speakers, does not have any universally agreed upon relatives, although many scholars regard it and Korean as belonging to an Altaic family, along with Turkic. Ryūkyūan, spoken in Okinawa, is a dialect of Japanese, and Ainu, spoken by about 15,000 people in the north of Japan, may also be related. Japanese has absorbed considerable influence from Chinese, to which it is *not* related (see Figure 9-11).

Korean   Korean is spoken by about 50 million people. Many scholars regard Korean and Japanese as related members of the Altaic family, but this hypothesis remains unproven. Like Japanese, Korean has been greatly influenced by Chinese over the centuries (see Figure 9-11).

Vietnamese   Vietnamese, the language of the 55 million inhabitants of Vietnam and neighboring areas, does not have any clear genetic relationships, although it may be a distant relative of Mon-Khmer languages (see Figure 9-11).

Other Isolated Languages of Asia and Europe   Of the remaining isolated languages of Eurasia, Basque is the best known. It is spoken by almost 1 million inhabitants in an area that straddles the Spanish-French border on the Atlantic coast (see Figure 9-5).

Native American Languages

Compared to the Old World, the linguistic situation in the New World is bewildering, with numerous American Indian language families in North and South America. While proposals for the genetic integration of these languages have been made, solid evidence for a pan-American link is lacking. Below are listed a few of those families and some of their members. The approximate locations of selected languages are shown in Figure 9-15.

Eskimo-Aleut   A distinction is generally drawn between the Eskimo-Aleut family (whose speakers are not genetically related to Amerindians) and all other

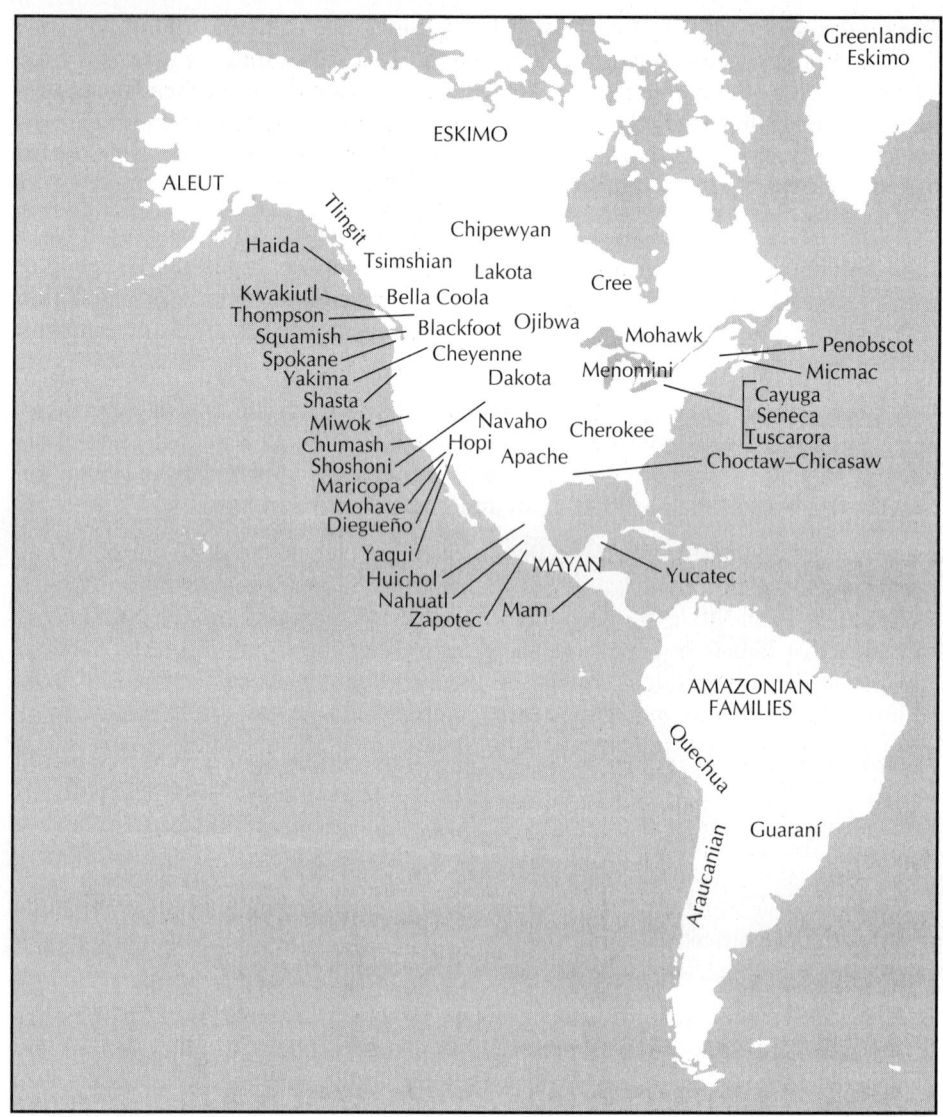

FIGURE 9-15
Native American Languages

language families. Inuit has 21,500 speakers across northern Canada and Alaska, and Yupik has about 16,000 speakers in Alaska and several hundred in Siberia.

Algonquian   Among the Algonquian languages are Cree (with 67,000 speakers in Canada and Montana) and Ojibwa (with more than 50,000 speakers living in Ontario, Manitoba, Michigan, Minnesota, and North Dakota). Represented by fewer speakers are Arapaho (1,500 in Wyoming and Oklahoma), Blackfoot (9,000 in Montana and Canada), Cheyenne (2,000 in Montana and Oklahoma), Kikapoo (1,200 in Kansas, Oklahoma, and Coahuila, Mexico), Malecite-Passamaquoddy (1,500 in Maine and New Brunswick), Micmac (with 8,100 in Maritime Canada and 2,000 in Boston), Potawatomi (500 spread across Wisconsin, Michigan, Kansas, Oklahoma, and Ontario), and Shawnee (with 200 in Oklahoma). Related to the Algonquian languages are the Muskogean languages, discussed next.

Muskogean   The largest Muskogean language is Choctaw-Chickasaw, with 12,000 speakers in Oklahoma, Mississippi, and Louisiana. Also Muskogean are Koasati (270 speakers in Louisiana and Texas) and Alabama (200–300 in Texas).

Athabaskan   In the Athabaskan family, some varieties of Apache are becoming extinct, but Western Apache has 11,000 speakers in Arizona, and Mescalero-Chiricahua Apache has 1,800 speakers chiefly in New Mexico. Navaho has 130,000 speakers in Arizona, Utah, and New Mexico. Chipewyan has 4,000 speakers in Alberta, Saskatchewan, Manitoba, and the Northwest Territories. Often included with the Athabaskan languages in a group called Na-Dene are Tlingit and possibly Haida, both spoken in Alaska and British Columbia.

Iroquoian   Excepting principally Cherokee (with 22,500 speakers in Oklahoma and North Carolina), the Iroquoian languages are spoken mainly in Ontario and Quebec, Canada, and in upstate New York. Cayuga has 380 speakers, Mohawk 3,000, Oneida 250, and Seneca 200.

Siouan   The Siouan family, located mainly in the upper midwest and Canada, includes Dakota, with 19,000 speakers in Manitoba and Saskatchewan, as well as Minnesota, Montana, Nebraska, and the Dakotas. Crow has 5,500 speakers in Montana, and Lakota has 6,000 in Manitoba and Saskatchewan, as well as Nebraska, Minnesota, Montana, and the Dakotas. Omaha has 1,500 speakers in Nebraska, while Winnebago has 1,500 in Nebraska and Wisconsin.

Penutian   The Penutian family includes Tsimshian (with 1,435 speakers in Canada), Yakima (with 3,000 in Washington), and Walla Walla (with 100 speakers in Oregon).

Salishan   Among the languages of the Salishan family are Shuswap (with 500 speakers in British Columbia), Spokane (with 50 in Washington), and Thompson (with 500 in British Columbia).

Uto-Aztecan   The Uto-Aztecan language family remains robust. Varieties of Nahuatl are spoken by about 1 million people in central and southern Mexico. On a much smaller scale, Huichol has 12,500 speakers in Nayarit and Jalisco, and Papago-Pima has 15,000 in Arizona and Mexico. Hopi is spoken by 5,000 speakers in Arizona and Yaqui by 17,000 near Phoenix and Tucson and in Mexico. Shoshoni has 3,000 speakers in California, Nevada, Idaho, Wyoming, and Utah, while Ute–Southern Paiute is spoken by 2,500 speakers in Colorado, Utah, Arizona, and Nevada. Comanche has 500 speakers in Oklahoma. Also Uto-Aztecan are Cahuilla (50) and Luiseño (100), spoken in Southern California.

Hokan   Hokan includes Diegueño (with 350–400 speakers in Baja California and Southern California), Havasupai-Walapai-Yavapai (with 1,200 in Arizona),

Karok (with 100 in northwestern California), Maricopa (with 150 near Phoenix), Mohave (with 700 on the California–Arizona border), and Washo (with 100 on the California–Nevada border).

Mayan   The largest Mayan language is Yucatec, whose 940,000 speakers live mostly in the Yucatán Peninsula. Mam has about 16,000 speakers in Chiapas, Mexico. The Mayan family also embraces Kekchi, Quiché, and Cakchiquel, each with more than 100,000 speakers, and possibly Araucanian, spoken by 200,000 people in Chile.

Quechua   The language of the ancient Inca Empire, Quechua has 6 million speakers in the Andes and is the most popular indigenous South American language; its genetic affiliation is unclear.

Tupi   The Tupi family includes Guaraní, with about 4 million speakers in Paraguay (where it is an official language) and in southwestern Brazil.

Oto-Manguean   Members of the Oto-Manguean family include Zapotec (with almost half a million speakers), Mixtec (with about 250,000), and Otomi (with 100,000), all spoken in central and southern Mexico.

Totonacan   Totonacan includes Totonaco, with about 250,000 speakers in Mexico.

Extinct and Dying Amerindian Languages   Scores of indigenous languages of the Americas have fallen silent over the past few decades. The last speaker of Tilla-mook, a Salishan language, died in 1970, eight years after the last speaker of Wiyot, related to the Algonquian languages. Algonquian has also lost Miami, spoken in Indiana and Oklahoma, and Massachusett (also called Natick and Wampanoag). Also now extinct are Huron (or Wyandot) of the Iroquoian family, and the Hokan languages Chumash, spoken around Santa Barbara but extinct since 1965, and Salinan, spoken on the central California coast. Other extinct Amerindian languages include Chinook, of Washington and Oregon; Natchez and Tonkawa, both of Oklahoma; and Mohegan-Montauk-Narragansett, heard earlier in Wisconsin and from Long Island to Connecticut and Rhode Island.

Amerindian languages are disappearing in the face of mounting pressure for younger speakers to adopt English, Spanish, or Portuguese, and many native languages are known only to a few older speakers. Among languages with fewer than fifty speakers are Abnaki-Penobscot, spoken in Maine and Canada; several varieties of Apache; the Salishan languages Coeur d'Alene (in Idaho) and Squamish (near Vancouver); Cupeño (of the Uto-Aztecan family in Southern California), Delaware and Menomini (Algonquian languages, the latter spoken in Wisconsin), Iowa and Osage (Siouan), Miwok and Yokuts (Penutian languages, spoken in California), Pomo and Shasta (both Hokan), and Tuscarora (an Iroquoian language formerly of North Carolina and now spoken in upstate New York).

Languages of Aboriginal Australia

Before settlement by Europeans in the eighteenth century, Australia had been inhabited by Aborigines for up to fifty millennia. It is estimated that at the time of first contact with Europeans about two hundred to three hundred Aboriginal languages were spoken. Today many of these languages have disappeared, along with their speakers, decimated by imported diseases and sometimes (as on the island of Tasmania) by genocide. Today, only about a hundred Aboriginal languages survive, most spoken by tiny populations of older survivors.

Virtually all Australian languages fall into a single family with two groups: the large Pama-Nyungan group, which covers most of the continent and includes most Aboriginal languages, and the Non–Pama-Nyungan group, which includes about fifty languages in northern Australia.

Papuan Languages

Papuan languages are spoken on the large island of New Guinea, which is divided politically between the nation of Papua New Guinea and the Indonesian-controlled section called Irian Jaya. While the inhabitants of coastal areas of the island speak Austronesian languages, about eight hundred of the languages are not Austronesian languages. Referred to as Papuan languages, most are not in any danger of extinction, though many are spoken by small populations. They fall into more than sixty different families, with no established genetic link among them. Little is known about most of these languages.

Nostratic Macrofamily

Recent years have seen renewed focus on linking certain language families within larger "macrofamilies." One proposed macrofamily that has received attention even in the popular press is the Nostratic macrofamily. Some scholars, especially in the former Soviet Union and the United States, have proposed that several of the language families that are generally regarded as distinct should be viewed as having a common source further back in time. Among the families in the proposed Nostratic macrofamily is Indo-European. The languages hypothesized to belong to Nostratic differ slightly from scholar to scholar, but most scholars espousing this theory include Indo-European, Afroasiatic, Uralic, Altaic, Dravidian, and Eskimo-Aleut. Assuming for the moment that detailed comparative reconstruction confirms this hypothesis, the Nostratic macrofamily would then make cousins (albeit quite distant cousins) of English (Indo-European), Hebrew, Arabic, Somali, and Hausa (Afroasiatic), Finnish and Hungarian (Uralic), perhaps Korean and Turkish (Altaic), Tamil (Dravidian), and Eskimo.

Although the links among these far-flung languages are not widely accepted among scholars, the hypothesis is provocative in an important way. As we demonstrated in this chapter, the principal method for establishing genetic relations among languages is by comparative reconstruction, whereby the forms of a parent language are hypothesized and the forms of the various daughter languages are derived by regular rules. As a moment's thought will convince you, before any comparative reconstruction can be attempted, there must be hypotheses about which languages are and are not related. Without such hypotheses, just which languages would constitute the bases for establishing the sound correspondences (and other correspondences not emphasized in this chapter) that make the stuff of comparative reconstruction? With the Nostratic hypothesis in mind, you may find it thought provoking to reexamine the tables of common words for those Nostratic languages illustrated in this chapter: Tables 9-7 through 9-10 for four Indo-European groups, 9-12 for Afroasiatic, and 9-13 for Dravidian. Bear in mind that the sound correspondences among these languages would not be between the sounds of the daughter languages directly but between the sounds of the reconstructed parent languages, so any immediate correspondences that you might spy may be deceptive.

LANGUAGES IN CONTACT

At no other time in history have there been such intensive contacts between language communities as in the last few centuries. As a result of the exploratory and colonizing enterprises of the English, French, Dutch, Spanish, and Portuguese, European languages have come into contact with languages of Africa, Native America, Asia, and the Pacific. These colonizing efforts put members of different speech communities in contact with each other. For example, the importing of slaves from Africa to the Americas forced speakers of different African languages to live side by side. Several language contact phenomena can take place when speakers of different languages interact.

Multilingualism

Bilingualism   The first of these phenomena is **bilingualism** or multilingualism, in which members of a community acquire more than one language natively. In a multilingual community, children grow up speaking several languages. In many multilingual communities, use of each language is compartmentalized, as when one language is used at home and another at school or at work. Multilingualism is such a natural solution to the problem of language contact that it is extremely widespread throughout the world. In this respect, industrialized societies like the United States and Japan, in which bilingualism is not widespread, are exceptional. In the United States, bilingualism is mostly relegated to immigrant communities, whose members are expected to learn English upon arrival. The adaptation is one-sided in contrast to what is found in many other areas of the globe, where neighboring communities learn each other's languages with little ado. In central Africa, India, and Papua New Guinea, it is commonplace for small children to grow up speaking four or five languages. In Papua New Guinea, multilingualism is a highly valued attribute that enhances a person's status in the community.

Nativization   A possible side effect of multilingualism is **nativization,** which takes place when a community adopts a new language (in addition to its native language) and modifies the structure of that new language, thus developing a dialect that becomes characteristic of the community. That is precisely what has happened with English in India, where Indian English is recognized as a separate dialect of English with its own structural characteristics. Indeed, it has become one of the two national languages (along with Hindi, the most widely spoken indigenous language) and is used in education, government, and communications within India and with the rest of the world. Nativization is a widespread phenomenon, and one could even argue that the emergence of American English as a socially recognized variety of English was a nativization process.

Pidgins   Another process that may take place in language contact situations is pidginization. Though probably derived from the word *business,* the origin of the word **pidgin** is uncertain, but it is used to refer to a contact language that develops where groups are in a dominant/subordinate situation, often in the context of colonization. Pidgins arise when members of a politically or economically dominant group do not learn the native language of the people they interact with as political or economic subordinates. To communicate, members of the subordinate community create a simplified variety of the language of the dominant group as their own second language. Pidgins then become the language of interaction between the colonizer and the colonized. Pidgins are thus defined in terms of sociological and linguistic characteristics: They are based on the language of the dominant group but are structurally simpler. They have no native speakers and are typically used for a restricted range of purposes.

Pidgins have arisen in many areas of the world, including West Africa, the Caribbean, the Far East, and the Pacific. Many pidgins have been based on English and French, the languages of the two most active colonial powers in the eighteenth and nineteenth centuries. Other languages that have served as a base for the development of pidgins include Portuguese, Spanish, Dutch, Swedish, German, Arabic, and Russian.

From Pidgin to Creole   Today, most pidgins have given way to creole languages. At some point, a pidgin may begin to fulfill a greater number of roles in social life; instead of using the pidgin language only in the workplace to communicate with traders or colonizers, speakers of a pidgin may begin to use the language at home or among themselves. Such situations frequently arise when the colonized population is linguistically diversified. Members of that community may find it convenient to adopt the new language as a **lingua franca**—a means to communicate across language boundaries. As a result, small children begin to grow up speaking the new language, and as greater demands are put onto that language its structure becomes more complex in a process called *creolization*. A **creole** language is thus a former pidgin that has "acquired" native speakers. Creoles are structurally complex, eventually as complex as any other language, and they differ from pidgins in that they exhibit less variability from speaker to speaker than pidgins do.

The boundary between pidgin and creole is often difficult to establish. Creolization is a gradual process, and in many situations pidgins are undergoing creolization. In such situations, there will be much variability from speaker to speaker and from situation to situation. For some speakers and in some contexts, the language will clearly be at the pidgin stage; for speakers whose language is more advanced in the creolization process, or in contexts that call for a more elaborated variety, the language will be structurally more complex. Furthermore, as a creole gains wider usage and becomes structurally more complex, it often comes to resemble the language on which it is based. For example, in the Caribbean and in Hawaii, English-based creoles are very similar to standard English for many speakers. Typically in such situations we find a continuum from speaker to speaker and from situation to situation—from a nonstandard dialect of the parent language to a very basic pidgin.

Figure 9-16 shows the location of the more important creoles in the world. Note that in common parlance many creoles are called pidgins, as with Hawaiian "Pidgin" and Papua New Guinea "Tok Pisin" (from *talk Pidgin*), both of which are actually creoles.

Some creoles have low status where they are spoken. Such is the case with Hawaiian "Pidgin," or Da Kine Talk, which is often referred to as a "bastardized" version of English or as "broken English." The fact is that Hawaiian creole has its own structure, different from that of English, and one cannot pretend to speak Da Kine Talk by speaking "broken" English.

In contrast, in many areas of the world creoles have become national languages used in government proceedings, education, and the media. In Papua New Guinea, Tok Pisin is one of the three national languages (along with English and Kiri Motu, also a creole) and has become a symbol of national identity. Some creoles have become the language of important bodies of literature, particularly in West Africa. Elsewhere, creoles are used in newspapers and on the radio for various purposes, including cartoons and commercials. Figure 9-17 is a publicity cartoon in Papua New Guinea Tok Pisin; the English translation of the captions is given underneath. Tok Pisin is even used to write about linguistics, as illustrated by the discussion of relative clause formation in Tok Pisin given next; it begins with three example sentences.

1. Ol ikilim pik bipo.

2. Na pik bai ikamap olosem draipela ston.

3. Na pik *ia* [ol ikilim bipo *ia*] bai ikamap olosem draipela ston.

Sapos yumi tingting gut long dispela tripela tok, yumi ken klia long tupela samting. Nambawan samting, sapos pik istap long (1) em inarapela pik, na pik istap long (2) em inarapela, orait, yumi no ken wokim (3). Tasol sapos wanpela pik tasol istap long (1) na (2), em orait long wokim (3). Na tu, tingting istap long (1) ia, mi bin banisim insait long tupela banis long (3), long wonem, em bilong kliaim yumi long wonem pik Elena itok long en.

[Translation]

1. They killed the pig.

2. The pig looks like a big rock.

3. The pig [that they killed] looks like a big rock.

If we think carefully about these three sentences, we can obtain two interpretations. First, if the pig of sentence (1) is one pig, and the pig of sentence (2) is another pig, then we cannot construct (3). However, if the pig in (1) and (2) is the same, then we can construct (3). Thus, I have bracketed in (3) the meaning corresponding to (1) with two brackets, because it has the purpose of identifying for us which pig Elena [the speaker who produced these sentences] is talking about.

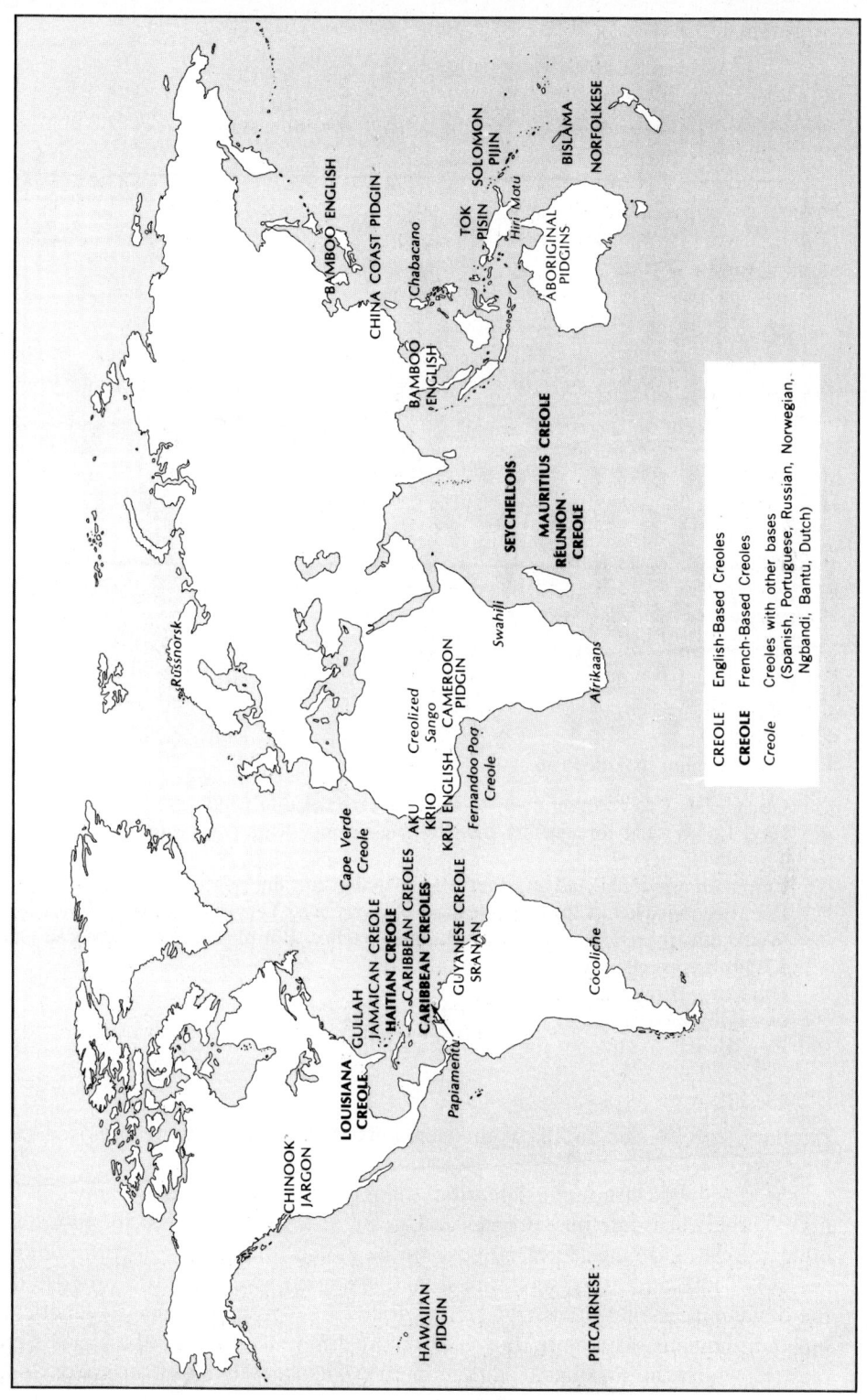

FIGURE 9-16
Location of Major Pidgin and Creole Languages

FIGURE 9-17
Publicity Cartoon in Tok Pisin

① Oh, please. I'm running away to Port Moresby. I don't like this kind of party.
② Hey, Lu! It's not for nothing that this big fat one beats your wife (in size).
③ The bloody nerve!
④ I am so happy. They all say that we are going to a big party. Oh, boy.
⑤ Hee, hee, hee, hee. I know what kind of party too. Very sorry, Piggy. Bye bye.
⑥ We frequently sell pigs for eating at dance parties. But pigs are very heavy so Isuzu KB20s are excellent to carry them all away.
⑦ One, two, three, up . . .
⑧ (speaking in Hiri Motu) Friend, I don't speak Tok Pisin.
⑨ Hey, Henry! Watch out for your things.

In short, creoles can fulfill all the demands that are commonly imposed on a language.

The worldwide structural similarities among creoles are striking. Many creoles, for example, lack indefinite articles and lack a distinction between the future and other tenses, and many have preposition stranding (like the English *the house I live in*). These and other similarities have led some researchers to propose that the development of pidgins and creoles follows a ''program'' that is genetically innate in humans. There are, however, many differences among the world's creoles, in which the imprint of various native languages is clear. In many South Pacific creoles, for example, a distinction is made in the pronoun system between dual and plural and between inclusive first person dual and plural and exclusive first person dual and plural (see Chapter 8, page 229, where the Tok Pisin pronoun system is given). These distinctions are not found in West African creoles, and their presence in South Pacific creoles reflects the fact that many languages spoken in the South Pacific make these distinctions. In Nigerian creole, on the other hand, we find honorific terms of address *(Mom* and *Dad)* that are used when addressing high-status individuals. These honorifics are not found in any other creole; again, they are transferred from local languages. Thus there is both homogeneity and heterogeneity among the creoles of the world.

SUMMARY

Languages are ever changing. All levels of the grammar change: phonology, morphology, lexicon, syntax, and semantics. From one language many other languages can develop in the course of time if groups of speakers remain physically or socially separated from one another. The method of comparative reconstruction enables linguists to make educated guesses about the structure and vocabulary of prehistoric peoples and to infer a good deal about their cultures from the nature of the reconstructed lexicon. The thousands of languages in the world can be grouped for the most part into language families, whose branches represent languages that are genealogically closer to one another than other languages of the family. When speakers of different languages come into contact, bilingualism may develop, with speakers commanding two or more languages. In some circumstances—usually when a dominant and a subordinate group are in contact—a pidgin may spring up for very limited use, usually in trade. If in time the pidgin comes to be used for other purposes and children learn it at home as a first language, the process of creolization starts. Creolization is a process of expansion in terms of both uses and structures.

EXERCISES[2]

1. The following is a comparative word list from seven languages spoken in the South Pacific. (β represents a voiced bilabial fricative and ɣ a voiced velar fricative.)

Hiw	*Waskia*	*Motu*	*Amara*	*Sowa*	*Mota*	*Raɣa*	
yoŋ	utuwura	lai	akauliŋ	laiŋ	laŋ	laŋi	'wind'
en	laŋ	miri	olov	on	one	one	'sand'
βət	maŋa	nadi	epeiouŋo	βət	βət	fatu	'stone'
yə	didu	matabudi	opon	tariβanaβi	uwə	afua	'turtle'
eyə	wal	gwarume	ouŋa	ek	iɣa	iɣe	'fish'
noɣa	kasim	namo	ovinkin	tapken	nam	namu	'mosquito'

[2] The Amara data used here are taken from an unpublished Amara lexicon by Bil Thurston; the Hiw, Sowa, Mota, and Raɣa data, from Darrell Tryon, *New Hebrides Languages* (Pacific Linguistics, series C, vol. 50, 1976); the Waskia data, from Malcolm Ross and John Natu Paol, *A Waskia Grammar Sketch and Vocabulary* (Pacific Linguistics, series B, vol. 56, 1978); the Lusi and Bariai data, from Rick Goulden, "A Comparative Study of Lusi and Bariai" (McMaster University M.A. thesis, 1982).

Hiw	Waskia	Motu	Amara	Sowa	Mota	Raɣa	
yo	nup	lada	serio	se	sasa	iha	'name'
moɣoye	kulak	natu	emim	dozo	natu	nitu	'child'
suɣe	buruk	boroma	esnei	bo	kpwoe	poe	'pig'
tø	kemak	tohu	elgo	ze	tou	toi	'sugarcane'

a.   Identify which languages are likely to be related and which are not, and justify your claims.

b.   Of the languages that appear to be part of the same family, which are more closely related? Justify your answer.

2.   The following is a comparative word list from Lusi and Bariai, closely related languages spoken on the island of New Britain in Papua New Guinea.

Lusi	Bariai		Lusi	Bariai	
βaza	bada	'to fetch'	βua	bua	'Areca nut'
kalo	kalo	'frog'	niu	niu	'coconut'
ɣali	gal	'to spear'	uβu	ubu	'hip'
ahe	ae	'foot'	rai	rai	'trade wind'
zaŋa	daŋa	'thing'	oaɣa	oaga	'canoe'
tazi	tad	'sea'	mata	mata	'eye'
tupi	tup	'to peck'	zoɣi	dog	'type of plant'
tori	tol	'to dance'	hani	an	'food'
ŋiŋi	ŋiŋ	'to laugh'	aŋari	aŋal	'type of bird'

a.   List the consonant correspondences between Lusi and Bariai.

b.   Identify which vowel is lost in Bariai and give a rule that states where it is lost.

3.   Table 9-3 (p. 259) provides some correspondence sets among five Polynesian languages. We noted that Tongan had lost a phoneme /r/ from its inventory, which was kept as /r/ or became /l/ in the other four languages. Furthermore, Tongan has kept a phoneme /h/ in certain words, which has been lost in all other Polynesian languages. The following cognates illustrate these two changes.

Tongan	Samoan	Tahitian	Maori	Hawaiian	
hama	ama	ama	ama	ama	'outrigger'
ama	lama	rama	rama	lama	'torch'

a.   On the basis of this information and the following words, complete the table of consonant correspondences for Tongan, Samoan, Tahitian, Maori, and Hawaiian.

Tongan	Samoan	Tahitian	Maori	Hawaiian	
leʔo	leo	reo	reo	leo	'voice'
ʔuha	ua	ua	ua	ua	'rain'
lili	lili	riri	riri	lili	'angry'

Tongan	Samoan	Tahitian	Maori	Hawaiian	
hae	sae	hae	hae	hae	'to tear'
hihi	isi	ihi	ihi	ihi	'strip'
huu	ulu	uru	uru	ulu	'to enter'
fue	fue	hue	hue	hue	'type of vine'
afo	afo	aho	aho	aho	'fishing line'
vela	vela	vera	wera	wela	'hot'
hiva	iva	iva	iwa	iwa	'nine'

b. Using your table of consonant correspondences and assuming that vowels have not undergone any change in any Polynesian language, complete the following comparative table by filling in the missing words.

Tongan	Samoan	Tahitian	Maori	Hawaiian	
kaukau					'to bathe'
	mata				'eye'
	tafe		kahe		'to flow'
laʔe					'forehead
			waʔa		'canoe'
laŋo					'fly'

c. Reconstruct the Proto-Polynesian consonant system, on the basis of the information you now have, and taking into account the genetic classification of Polynesian languages discussed in this chapter. (*Hint:* The protosystem has to be full enough to account for all the possible correspondences found in the daughter languages. No daughter language has innovated new phonemes, but all have lost one or more from the protosystem.)

d. Reconstruct the Proto-Polynesian words for 'outrigger,' 'rain,' 'to enter,' 'strip,' and 'nine.'

4. Following is a list of Modern French words in phonetic transcription with the Vulgar Latin words from which they derive. (Notice that word-initial /k/ in Latin becomes /k/, /š/, or /s/ in Modern French, depending on where it occurs.)

Modern French	Vulgar Latin	
koʁd	korda	'rope'
šɑ̃	kampus	'field'
sɛdʁ	kɛdrus	'cedar'
kʁaše	krakkāre	'to spit'
šamo	kamēlus	'camel'
sɛʁkl	kirkulus	'circle'
kuʁiʁ	kurrere	'to run'
šaʁ	karrus	'carriage'
kle	klavis	'key'
sitɛʁn	kistɛrna	'tank'
kɔlɔ̃b	kolomba	'dove'
ša	kattus	'cat'
ku	kollum	'neck'

a. Describe a rule that predicts which of the three French phonemes will appear where Latin had /k/. (Consider only the first phoneme of words.)

b. Consider the additional data below.

Modern French	Vulgar Latin	
šov	kalvus	'bald'
šɛn	katena	'chain'
šo	kalidum	'hot'
šɛʁ	karo	'flesh'

At first glance, these forms are problematic for the rule that you stated in (a). Note, however, that these four words are spelled in Modern French *chauve, chaine, chaud,* and *chair,* respectively. Given the fact that French orthography often reflects an earlier pronunciation of the language, explain in detail what has happened to the four words in the history of the language.

5. Consider the following Proto–Indo-European reconstructions. Conspicuously, no word for 'sea' can be reconstructed for Proto–Indo-European.

*rtko	'bear'	*peisk	'fish'
*laks	'salmon'	*sper	'sparrow'
*er	'eagle'	*trozdo	'thrush'
*gwou	'cow/bull'	*su:	'pig'
*kwon	'dog'	*agw^{h}no	'lamb'
*mori	'lake'	*sneigw^h	'snow'
*b^{h}erəg	'birch'	*grəno	'corn'
*yewo	'wheat'	*med^{h}u	'honey'
*weik	'village'	*sel	'fortification'
*se:	'to sow'	*kerp	'to collect (food)'
*yeug	'to yoke'	*web^h	'to weave'
*sne:	'to spin'	*arə	'to plow'
*ayes	'metal'	*agro	'field'

a. Describe in detail what these reconstructions (or lack of reconstruction) tell us about the Proto–Indo-Europeans, the environment in which they lived, and their activities.

b. Based on these reconstructions and on what you know about the current distribution of Indo-European languages, which area or areas of the world would be the best candidates as the homeland of the Proto–Indo-Europeans? Defend your claim.

6. The following is a list of Proto–Indo-European reconstructions. Cite a Modern English word that contains a reflex for each one of them; ignore the question as to whether the Modern English word is itself a borrowing or not.

*akwa:	'water'	*b^{h}ugo	'ram, goat'
*agro	'field'	*b^{h}reu	'to boil'
*kwetwer	'four'	*carcer	'prison'

*pel	'skin'	*genə	'to give birth'
*reg	'to rule'	*gel	'to freeze'
*wen	'to strive for'	*gʰans	'goose'
*yeug	'to join together'	*macula	'blemish'
*ped	'foot'	*med	'to measure'

SUGGESTIONS FOR FURTHER READING

There are several good textbooks on historical linguistics, including Hock (1986), Lehmann (1993), Anttila (1989), and Jeffers and Lehiste (1979); Bynon (1977) and Aitchison (1991) combine traditional historical analysis with sociolinguistic insights. Arlotto (1972) is a good next step after the present chapter, although his treatment is largely Indo-European. Lehmann (1967) provides many of the original documents of historical work from the nineteenth century, including the speech of Sir William Jones quoted on page 253. Bellwood (1979; 1987) and Jennings (1979) are surveys of research on Polynesian and Austronesian migrations; all include extensive discussions of language history. Pawley and Green (1971) discuss the linguistic evidence for the location of the Proto-Polynesian homeland. Bomhard (1992) and Kaiser and Shevoroshkin (1988) discuss the Nostratic macrofamily.

A convenient reference work treating about a dozen language families and forty of the world's major languages is Comrie (1987), with a list of references for each family and language. For more detailed information, the encyclopedic fourteen-volume survey edited by Sebeok (1963–1976), several volumes of which are dedicated to particular linguistic areas, can be consulted. In addition, there are two series of books on language areas and language families: the older Faber and Faber Language Series, which includes volumes on language families and groups like Romance and Germanic and on particular languages like Chinese, and the more up-to-date Cambridge Language Survey Series. The latter includes volumes on lesser-known areas and language families by Comrie (1981), Dixon (1980), Foley (1986), and Suárez (1983), and on Japanese by Shibatani (1990). Outside these series, African languages are succinctly surveyed in Gregersen (1977), the languages of China in Ramsey (1987), North American Indian languages in Campbell and Mithun (1979), Amazonian languages in Derbyshire and Pullum (1986), and South American languages in Manelis Klein and Stark (1985). A proposal that all Amerindian languages can be classified into three families appears in Greenberg (1987). Using a method like that used to determine the Proto-Polynesian homeland, Siebert (1967) discusses the original home of the Proto-Algonquian people.

Conveniently appended to the third edition (1992) of *The American Heritage Dictionary of the English Language*—and also published separately as Watkins (1985)—is a list of Indo-European roots with cognates in several languages, as well as a valuable article describing Indo-European and the cultural inferences that can be drawn from the reconstructed lexicon. Buck (1949) is a compilation of Indo-European roots with the reflexes in various languages. Lockwood (1969; 1972) and Baldi (1983) are useful overviews of the Indo-European language family.

Nativization is discussed in Kachru (1982). Good recent surveys of the structure and use of pidgins and creoles include Mühlhäusler (1986) and Romaine (1988). The papers in Hymes (1971) and Valdman (1977) also touch on aspects of pidgins and creoles worldwide. An interesting hypothesis about pidginization as an innate program is advanced by Bickerton (1981). On Hawaiian Da Kine Talk, see Carr (1972). The Tok Pisin excerpt on linguistics is taken from Gillian Sankoff's paper entitled ''Sampela Nupela lo Ikamap Long Tok Pisin'' ('Some New Rules of Tok Pisin') published in McElhanon (1975).

Two reference volumes list the languages of the world and their genetic affiliation: Voegelin and Voegelin (1977) and Ruhlen (1986). Our data on Amerindian languages are taken from Grimes (1992). Additional problems of comparative reconstruction are provided in Cowan (1971) and, with some solutions, in Chapter 5 of Langacker (1972).

REFERENCES

Aitchison, Jean. 1991. *Language Change: Progress or Decay?*, 2nd ed. (Cambridge: Cambridge University Press).

Anttila, Raimo. 1989. *Historical and Comparative Linguistics* (Amsterdam: Benjamins).

Arlotto, Anthony. 1972. *Introduction to Historical Linguistics* (Lanham, MD: University Press of America).

Baldi, Philip. 1983. *An Introduction to the Indo-European Languages* (Carbondale: Southern Illinois University Press).

Bellwood, Peter. 1979. *Man's Conquest of the Pacific: The Prehistory of Southeast Asia and Oceania* (New York: Oxford University Press).

——— 1987. *The Polynesians. Prehistory of an Island People*, rev. ed. (London: Thames and Hudson).

Bickerton, Derek. 1981. *Roots of Language* (Ann Arbor, MI: Karoma).

Bomhard, Allan R. 1992. "The Nostratic Macrofamily (with Special Reference to Indo-European)" *Word* 43:61–83.

Buck, Carl D. 1949. *A Dictionary of Selected Synonyms in the Principal Indo-European Languages* (Chicago: University of Chicago Press).

Bynon, Theodora. 1977. *Historical Linguistics* (Cambridge: Cambridge University Press).

Campbell, Lyle, and Marianne Mithun, eds. 1979. *The Languages of Native America: Historical and Comparative Assessment* (Austin: University of Texas Press).

Carr, Elizabeth Ball. 1972. *Da Kine Talk. From Pidgin to Standard English in Hawaii* (Honolulu: University Press of Hawaii).

Comrie, Bernard. 1981. *The Languages of the Soviet Union* (Cambridge: Cambridge University Press).

———, ed. 1987. *The World's Major Languages* (New York: Oxford University Press).

Cowan, William. 1971. *Workbook in Comparative Reconstruction* (New York: Holt, Rinehart and Winston).

Derbyshire, Desmond C., and Geoffrey K. Pullum, eds. 1986. *Handbook of Amazonian Languages,* 3 vols. (New York: Mouton).

Dixon, R. M. W. 1980. *The Languages of Australia* (Cambridge: Cambridge University Press).

Foley, William A. 1986. *The Papuan Languages of New Guinea* (Cambridge: Cambridge University Press).

Greenberg, Joseph H. 1987. *Language in the Americas* (Stanford: Stanford University Press).

Gregersen, Edgar A. 1977. *Language in Africa: An Introductory Survey* (New York: Gordon & Breach).

Grimes, Barbara F., ed. 1992. *Ethnologue: Languages of the World,* 12th ed. Dallas, TX: Summer Institute of Linguistics.

Hock, Hans Henrich. 1986. *Principles of Historical Linguistics* (New York: Mouton).

Hymes, Dell, ed. 1971. *Pidginization and Creolization of Languages* (Cambridge: Cambridge University Press).

Jeffers, Robert J., and Ilse Lehiste. 1979. *Principles and Methods for Historical Linguistics* (Cambridge, MA: MIT Press).

Jennings, Jesse D., ed. 1979. *The Prehistory of Polynesia* (Cambridge, MA: Harvard University Press).

Kachru, Braj, ed. 1982. *The Other Tongue: English Across Cultures* (Urbana: University of Illinois Press).

Kaiser, M., and V. Shevoroshkin. 1988. "Nostratic," *Annual Review of Anthropology* 17: 309–329.

Langacker, Ronald W. 1972. *Fundamentals of Linguistic Analysis* (New York: Harcourt Brace Jovanovich).

Lehmann, Winfred P. 1993. *Historical Linguistics*, 3rd ed. (London: Routledge).

———, ed. 1967. *A Reader in Nineteenth-Century Historical Linguistics* (Bloomington: Indiana University Press).

Lockwood, W. B. 1969. *Indo-European Philology* (London: Hutchinson).

———. 1972. A *Panorama of Indo-European Languages* (London: Hutchinson).

Manelis Klein, Harriet E., and Louisa R. Stark, eds. 1985. *South American Indian Languages: Retrospect and Prospect* (Austin: University of Texas Press).

McElhanon, K. A., ed. 1975. *Tok Pisin i Go We?* (Ukarumpa: Linguistic Society of New Guinea).

Mülhäusler, Peter. 1986. *Pidgin and Creole Linguistics* (Oxford: Blackwell).

Pawley, Andrew, and Kaye Green. 1971. "Lexical Evidence for the Proto-Polynesian Homeland," *Te Reo* 14:1–35.

Romaine, Suzanne. 1988. *Pidgin and Creole Languages* (London: Longman).

Ramsey, S. Robert. 1987. *The Languages of China* (Princeton, NJ: Princeton University Press).

Ruhlen, Merritt. 1986. *A Guide to the World's Languages* (Stanford: Stanford University Press).

Sebeok, Thomas A., ed. 1963–1976. *Current Trends in Linguistics* (The Hague: Mouton).

Shibatani, Masayoshi. 1990. *The Languages of Japan* (Cambridge: Cambridge University Press).

Siebert, Frank T. 1967. "The Original Home of the Proto-Algonquian People," *Bulletin No. 214* (Ottawa: National Museum of Canada), pp. 13–47.

Suárez, Jorge A. 1983. *The Mesoamerican Indian Languages* (Cambridge: Cambridge University Press).

Valdman, Albert. 1977. *Pidgin and Creole Linguistics* (Bloomington: Indiana University Press).

Voegelin, Charles F., and Florence M. Voegelin. 1977. *Classification and Index of the World's Languages* (Amsterdam: Elsevier).

Watkins, Calvert, ed. 1985. *The American Heritage Dictionary of Indo-European Roots* (Boston: Houghton Mifflin).

10

The Historical Development of English

A THOUSAND YEARS OF CHANGE

Nearly every secondary school student in the English-speaking world has studied the writings of William Shakespeare and Geoffrey Chaucer, two of the greatest writers ever to use English (or any language) as a poetic vehicle. You may recall that when you read Shakespeare's plays, some of his lines were opaque, as with the opening lines of *I Henry IV:*

So shaken as we are, so wan with care
Find we a time for frighted peace to pant
And breathe short-winded accents of new broils
To be commenced in stronds afar remote.

That some of Shakespeare's lines are opaque has a straightforward explanation (besides the fact that they are verse): The English spoken in and around London four centuries ago is often subtly and sometimes strikingly different from the English spoken today. Still, much of it is altogether accessible, and very little of it is so foreign that it eludes us completely. Many of the words in the brief passage just cited are familiar enough, though some are used in ways that strike the modern reader as peculiar. While the words of the opening line are mostly familiar and can be sorted out syntactically, line two is tougher, even though all the words (except *frighted*) exist in Modern English in exactly the same forms. (The line means 'Let us find a time for frightened peace to catch its breath.')

As the many Shakespearean productions around the world testify, reciting Shakespeare with his sixteenth-century lexicon and syntax but with a modern pronunciation enables twentieth-century audiences to follow his plays with little difficulty. With the support of costumed actors interacting with props on a rich visual set, there is not much in *Romeo and Juliet, Henry IV,* or *King Lear* that modern audiences fail to grasp.

Far more difficult to understand than Shakespeare's English is the English of Chaucer, who lived in London two centuries earlier. Chaucer's *Canterbury Tales,* whose opening lines follow, was the first major book to be printed in England. William Caxton published it in 1476, almost a century after it was written and long after Chaucer's death in 1400.

> Whan that Aprill with his shoures soote
> The droghte of March hath perced to the roote,
> And bathed every veyne in swich licour,
> Of which vertu engendred is the flour; . . .
> Thanne longen folk to goon on pilgrimages.

Though their pronunciation may differ from ours, quite a few of Chaucer's four-teenth-century words have the same written form now as they did then: *that, with, his, the, of, bathed, every, folk, pilgrimages,* along with seven or eight others. Still others can be recognized though their Modern English counterparts differ: *droghte* 'drought,' *perced* 'pierced,' *veyne* 'vein,' *vertu* 'virtue, strength,' and *flour* 'flower.' Of course, some are more opaque: *soote* 'sweet,' *swich* 'such,' *thanne* 'then,' and the verbs *longen* 'to long' and *goon* 'to go.' As a whole, the Chaucer passage is harder to grasp than the Shakespeare. Thus, in the two centu-ries between Chaucer (1340–1400) and Shakespeare (1564–1616), English changed—as languages always do. Chaucer understood language change and the arbitrariness of linguistic form for accomplishing its ends, as we learn in these lines from his *Troilus and Criseyde* (II, 22–26).

> Ye knowe ek, that in forme of speche is chaunge
> Withinne a thousand yeer, and wordes tho
> That hadden pris, now wonder nyce and straunge
> Us thinketh hem, and yet thei spake hem so,
> And spedde as wel in love as men now do.[1]

[1] You know also that in speech's form (there) is change
Within a thousand years, and words then
That had value, now wondrously foolish and strange
To us seem them, and yet they spoke them so,
And fared as well in love as men now do.

The English spoken in Chaucer's time is far enough removed from today's English that students often study the *Canterbury Tales* in "translation"—from fourteenth-century English into twentieth-century English. Though we are not yet so estranged from Shakespeare's English to require a translation, editions of his plays have glosses and footnotes aplenty.

If we now examine the language of the epic poem, *Beowulf*, written down almost four centuries before Chaucer lived, we are struck by the utterly foreign appearance of these forms of Old English. Indeed, speakers of Modern English cannot recognize *Beowulf* as English; it is as far removed as Dutch or German (if such impressionistic comparisons have any meaning). The *Beowulf* poet, whose identity is lost to history, composed his grim epic in the first half of the eighth century, about six hundred years before Chaucer, who surely would have found its language about as unintelligible as modern readers do. Here are the first three lines from a *Beowulf* manuscript transcribed around the year 1000:

> Hwæt wē Gār-Dena   in gēardagum
> þēodcyninga   þrym gefrūnon,
> hū ðā æþelingas   ellen fremedon.[2]

No one needs to be persuaded that Old English is a "foreign" language. Scarcely a word in the passage seems familiar (though when you have finished reading this chapter, a few may not seem so formidably strange). Even some of the letters are different: Modern English no longer uses ⟨æ⟩, ⟨þ⟩, or ⟨ð⟩. Still, an imaginative inspection may reveal that some function words remain in present-day English (*wē* = *we, in* = *in*, and *hū* = *how*). Perhaps you also recognized *ðā* as Modern English *the* and *hwæt* as *what*, but it is not easy to recognize *gēardagum* as *year + days* or *cyninga* as *kings*. Even knowing these words, however, you would find the passage far from transparent. You would need to know the meaning of the nouns *þēod, þrym*, and *æþelingas* (none of which survives in Modern English), the verbs *gefrūnon* and *fremedon*, and the adjective *ellen* (here used as a noun). And given all that lexical information, the syntax of Old English would still be elusive. About a thousand years old, Old English is indeed a long way from Modern English.

THE BACKGROUND OF ENGLISH

Historical Background

Where did English come from, and how long has it been spoken in England? What are its principal ancestors and its closest relatives?

---

[2] A rough word-for-word translation:

What! We of Spear-Danes in yore-days
Nation-kings' glory have heard,
How the nobles heroic-deeds did.

A more idiomatic rendering: 'Yes, we have heard of the might of the kings of the Spear-Danes in days of yore, how the chieftains carried out deeds of valor.'

Before the beginning of the modern era, Britain was inhabited by Celtic-speaking peoples, ancestors of today's Irish, Scots, and Welsh. In 55 B.C., Britain was invaded by Julius Caesar, but that attempt to colonize it failed, and the Romans conquered Britain only in A.D. 43. When the Roman legions withdrew in A.D. 410, the Celts, who by then had become accustomed to their protection, were at the mercy of the Picts and the Scots from the north of Britain. In a profoundly important development for the English language, Vortigern, king of the Romanized Celts in Britain, sought help from three Germanic tribes, who in A.D. 449 set sail from what is today northern Germany and southern Denmark to aid the Celts. But when they landed in Britain, they decided to settle, leaving the Celts only the remote corners—today's Scotland, Wales, and Cornwall.

The invaders spoke closely related varieties of West Germanic—the dialects that were to become English. The word *England* derives from the name of one of the tribes, the Angles. Thus England, originally *Englaland,* is the 'land of the Angles.' The Old English language used by the early Germanic inhabitants of England and their offspring up to about A.D. 1100 is often called Anglo-Saxon, after two of the tribes (the Jutes were the third tribe). Early Anglo-Saxon has left no written records. The oldest surviving English-language materials come from the end of the seventh century, and there is an increasing quantity after that, giving rise to an abundant and impressive literature including *Beowulf.*

Once the Anglo-Saxon peoples had settled in Britain, there were additional onslaughts from other Germanic groups starting in A.D. 787. In the year 850, a fleet of three hundred fifty Danish ships arrived. In 867, Vikings captured York. Danes and Norwegians settled in much of eastern and northern England and from there launched attacks into the kingdom of Wessex in the southwest. In 878, after losing a major battle to King Alfred the Great of Wessex, the Danes agreed by the Treaty of Wedmore to become Christian and to remain outside Wessex in a very large section of eastern and northern England that became known as the Danelaw because it was subject to Danish law. After the treaty, Danes and Norwegians were assimilated to Anglo-Saxon life, so much so that fourteen hundred English place names are Scandinavian including all those ending in *-by* 'farm, town' *(Derby, Rugby), -thorp* 'village' *(Althorp), -thwaite* 'isolated piece of land *(Applethwaite),* and *-toft* 'piece of ground' *(Brimtoft, Eastoft).*

Attacks from the Scandinavians continued throughout the Viking Age (roughly 750–1050), until finally King Svein of Denmark was crowned King of England and was succeeded almost immediately by his son Cnut in 1016. England was then ruled by Danish kings until 1042 when Edward the Confessor regained the throne his father, Aethelred, had lost to the Danes. The intermingling between the Anglo-Saxon invaders and the subsequent Scandinavian settlers created a mix of Germanic dialects in England that molded the particular character of the English language and distinguishes it markedly from its cousins.

English as a Germanic Language

As you saw in Chapter 9, West Germanic is distinguished from two other branches of the Germanic group of languages: from North Germanic (which includes Swedish, Danish, and Norwegian) and from East Germanic (including only Gothic, which has since died out).

During the first millennium B.C., before Germanic had split into three branches but after it had split from the other branches of Indo-European, Common (or Proto) Germanic developed certain characteristic features that continue in its daughter languages, setting them apart from all other Indo-European varieties. Among these characteristics are features belonging to every level of grammar: phonology, lexicon, morphology, and syntax.

Phonology   The most striking phonological characteristic of the Germanic languages is a set of consonant correspondences found in none of the other Indo-European languages. It was Jacob Grimm, one of the brothers of fairy-tale fame, who in 1822 formulated these correspondences in what is now called "Grimm's Law." Grimm described the regular sound shifts that had occurred within three natural classes of sounds in developing from Indo-European into Germanic.

Grimm's Law

1. voiceless stops became voiceless fricatives: p > f; t > θ; k > h
2. voiced stops became voiceless stops: b > p; d > t; g > k
3. voiced aspirated stops became unaspirated: b^h > b; d^h > d; g^h > g

The impact of these changes can be seen in Figure 10-1 by examining the shift of voiceless stops in Indo-European to voiceless fricatives in Germanic. We illustrate this shift by citing English words that have inherited the sounds /f θ h/ from Germanic and contrasting them with corresponding words in Romance languages, which (like all the other branches of Indo-European) did not undergo these sound shifts.

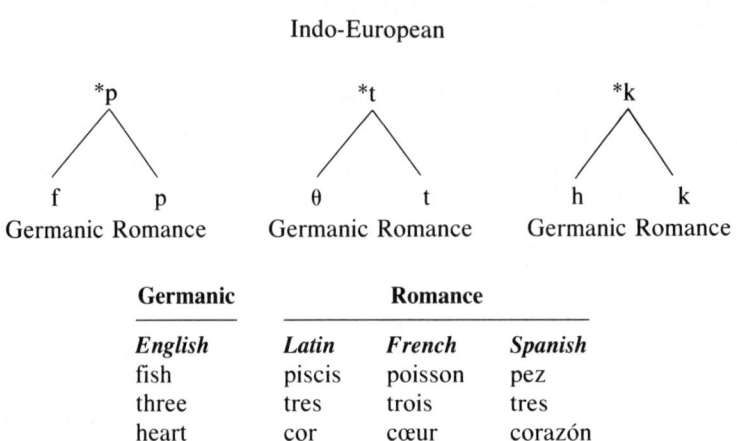

Germanic	Romance		
English	*Latin*	*French*	*Spanish*
fish	piscis	poisson	pez
three	tres	trois	tres
heart	cor	cœur	corazón

FIGURE 10-1
Reflexes of Indo-European Voiceless Stops in Germanic and Romance

Another important phonological development of Common Germanic was a shifting of stress patterns. Indo-European had variable stress on its words: A morpheme could be stressed on one syllable in the context of a given word and elsewhere in a different word. But in Common Germanic, stress shifted systematically to a word's first or root syllable. Compare Modern English *fáther, fátherly, unfátherly,* and *fátherless,* all having stress on the root syllable in the Germanic fashion, with the Greek borrowings *phótograph, photógrapher,* and *photográphic,* which have variable stress in the Indo-European fashion.

Lexicon   The regular pattern of sound shifting described by Grimm's Law set the phonological shape of the Germanic vocabulary apart from that of other Indo-European languages (as seen in the Romance examples in Figure 10-1). In addition, the Germanic languages have a set of words found nowhere else in Indo-European. Once the Germanic tribes separated from the rest of the Indo-European peoples, any words innovated or borrowed from speakers of a non–Indo-European tongue would be distinctively Germanic within Indo-European. Among the English words found in other Germanic languages but not in any other Indo-European languages are the nouns *arm, blood, earth, finger, hand, sea,* and *wife;* the verbs *bring, drink, drive, leap,* and *run;* and the adjectives *evil, little,* and *sick.* Here are the strictly Germanic nouns from English and German (to illustrate the similarity among Germanic tongues) and from French (to illustrate the striking contrast between Germanic and Romance languages).

English	German	French
arm	Arm	bras
blood	Blut	sang
earth	Erd	terre
finger	Finger	doigt
hand	Hand	main
sea	See	mer
wife	Weib	femme

It is conceivable that these Germanic words could have existed in Indo-European and been lost in all daughter languages except Germanic, but it is hardly likely. Hence we can assume they were not inherited from Indo-European but were innovated or borrowed during the Common Germanic period.

Grammar: Morphology and Syntax

Indo-European—at least at some stages—was certainly a highly inflected language. Because Sanskrit, one of the oldest attested Indo-European languages, had eight case inflections on nouns, it is possible that Indo-European itself had eight cases (though, alternatively, case distinctions not in Proto–Indo-European could have arisen in the Indic branch to which Sanskrit belongs). If we assume that the rich inflectional morphology of Sanskrit reflects the complexity of Indo-European, then Indo-European nouns would have had eight *cases,* three *numbers* (singular, dual, and plural), and three *genders* (masculine, feminine, and neuter). Verbs were also highly inflected, probably for two *voices* (active and a kind of passive), four *moods* (indicative, imperative, subjunctive, and optative), and three *tenses* (present, past, and future). In addition, verbs carried markers for *person* and *number*.

The Indo-European system of indicating verb tenses was principally word internal (as in English *sing/sang/sung*). While this internal sound *gradation* (sometimes called *ablaut*) is typical of Indo-European languages, the typical English inflection [t] *(kissed)* or [d] *(judged)* for the past tenses is characteristically Germanic. Thus the two-tense system, with past tense marked by a dental or alveolar suffix, sets the Germanic group apart from all its Indo-European cousins.

Periods in the History of English

Because languages change continuously, any division into historical stages or periods is necessarily somewhat arbitrary. Nevertheless, scholars have divided the history of English into three main periods representing very different stages of the language. We now refer to the language spoken in England from the end of the seventh century to the end of the eleventh century (700–1100) as Old English (or Anglo-Saxon). The English spoken since 1450 or 1500 is called Modern English. The language spoken in between—from 1100 to 1450 or 1500—is known as Middle English. Thus *Beowulf* is written in Old English, the *Canterbury Tales* in Middle English, and *Henry IV* in (early) Modern English.

OLD ENGLISH: 700–1100

When the Angles, Saxons, and Jutes began to invade England in 449, they settled in different parts of the island. Thus four principal dialects of Old English sprang up: Northumbrian in the north (above the Humber River); Mercian in the Midlands; Kentish in the southeast; and West Saxon in the southwest (see Figure 10-2). Because Wessex was the seat of the powerful King Alfred, its dialect, West Saxon, achieved a certain status; it forms the basis of most surviving Old English literature and of the study of Old English today.

Like the classical Latin of Roman times and the German and Russian of today, Old English was a highly inflected language. It had an elaborate system of inflectional suffixes on nouns, pronouns, verbs, adjectives, and even determiners. Only traces of these inflectional forms of Old English survive in Modern English.

Orthography

Only a few Old English letters differ from those of Modern English, but they occurred in some of the most frequently used words, giving Old English an exaggerated air of strangeness. Among the graphs no longer used in English are ⟨þ⟩ (called thorn), ð (eth), ⟨ƿ⟩ (wynn), and ⟨æ⟩ (ash). Modern-day editors usually let the graphs ⟨þ⟩, ⟨ð⟩, and ⟨æ⟩ stand in texts, but they almost invariably substitute ⟨w⟩ for wynn.

Both ⟨þ⟩ and ⟨ð⟩ (and their capitals ⟨Þ⟩ and ⟨Ð⟩) were alternative spellings for two sounds; each graph, much like Modern English ⟨th⟩, represented the sounds

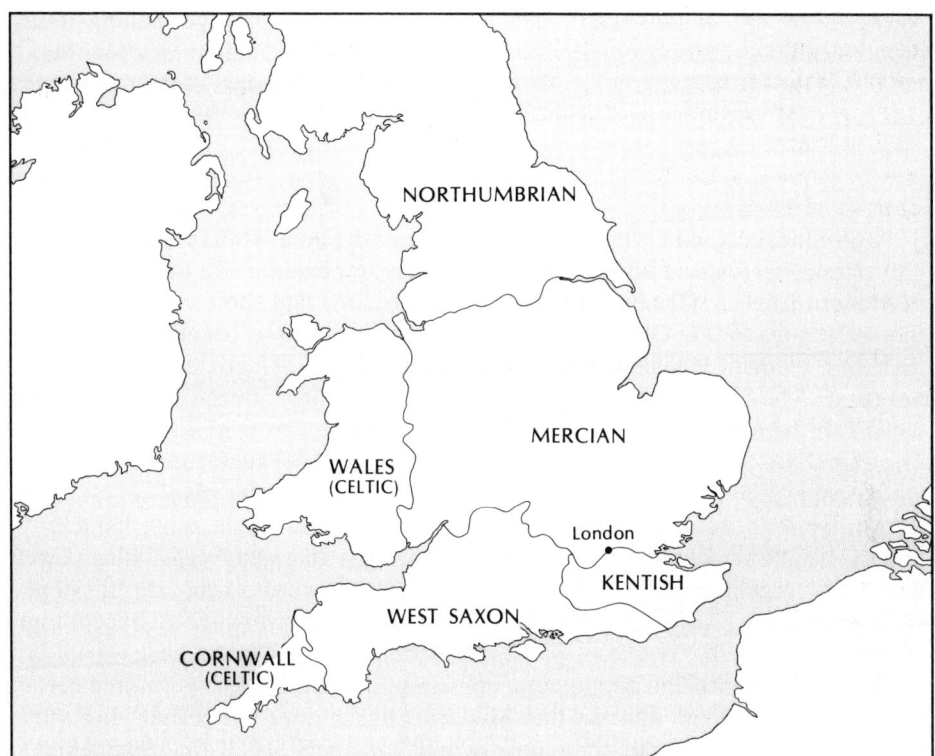

FIGURE 10-2
The Old English Dialects

[θ] or [ð], which were allophones of a single phoneme in Old English. Old English scribes did not assign one graph to the sound [θ] and the other to [ð] because the two sounds were not perceived as different: They were allophones of a single phoneme. Old English speakers were no more aware of the difference between [θ] and [ð] than Modern English speakers are aware that they are pronouncing different /p/ sounds in *pot* and *spot*. Besides, alphabetic systems ideally assign different symbols not to different sounds (allophones) but to different *distinctive* sounds (phonemes).

The graph ⟨æ⟩, rarely used in Modern English, represented the same pronunciation in Old English that it has in the phonetic alphabet used today (the vowel of *hat*). The Old English vowel combinations ⟨ēo⟩ and ⟨ēa⟩ represented the diphthongs [e:ɔ] and [ɛ:ə] respectively. The letter sequence ⟨sc⟩ (as in *Englisce*) is equivalent to Modern English ⟨sh⟩ [š]. The letter ⟨c⟩ represented two sounds: [k] as in *cȳpmenn* or [č] as in *æðellīce*. The letter ⟨g⟩ represented three sounds: [y] initially when it preceded front vowels and finally when it followed them (as in *gelamp*, *gȳt*, and *Rōmānabyrig*) and [g] or [ɣ] elsewhere. The letter ⟨y⟩ was always the vowel [ü]. The letters ⟨j⟩ and ⟨q⟩ were not used in Old English and ⟨k⟩ was rare (hence *folc* 'folk'), though the sounds they represent today did exist (compare *cwēn* 'queen' and *cēpan* 'keep'). The letter ⟨x⟩ was an alternative spelling of ⟨cs⟩, pronounced [ks], as in *axode* [ɑksɔdɛ] 'asked.' Finally, we might mention that ⟨⅂⟩ 'and' was the customary representation in original manuscripts of the Old English equivalent of an ampersand sign ⟨&⟩.

Phonology

A good deal could be said about the Old English sound system. We shall make only a few observations about patterns that have implications for the development of Modern English. Old English had a system of long and short vowels and diphthongs, though in late Old English the diphthongs tended to become simplified to their first element. (A similar process occurs today in American dialects of the South, in which words like *time* /taym/ tend to be pronounced [tʰam], like the word *I* throughout the United States in a phrase like *I'm gonna* . . . [amgʊnə].) The short vowels have remained relatively constant over the centuries, so many words are pronounced today as they were in Old English: *fisc* 'fish', *æt* 'at,' *þorn* 'thorn,' *benc* 'bench,' and *him* 'him.' The long vowels, on the other hand, have undergone marked changes. Suffice it to say for now that Old English long vowels had their "continental" values, as in the following words: *stān* [stɑːn] 'stone,' *sēon* [seːɔn] 'see,' *sōðlīce* [soːðliːčɛ] 'truly'; *būton* [buːtɔn] 'without, except'; and *swīðe* [swiːðɛ] 'very.'

As to consonants, the phonotactic constraints of Old English permitted certain word-initial consonant clusters that Modern English does not permit: /hl-/, /hn-/, /hr-/, and /kn-/. Three pairs of sounds whose members are distinct phonemes in Modern English were allophones of single phonemes in Old English: [f] and [v]; [θ] and [ð]; and [s] and [z]. The voiceless allophones [f θ s] occurred at the beginning and end of words and when adjacent to voiceless sounds within words; between voiced sounds, however, the voiced allophones occurred. Thus in the nominative case of the word *wīf* [wiːf], ⟨f⟩ represented the allophone [f], but in the genitive case it represented the allophone [v]: *wifes* [wiːvɛs] (note the final [s] too). The phonemes /s/ and /θ/ figure prominently in the history of English because so many inflections and so many function words contain them.

Morphology

Compounds Old English writers (and presumably speakers) were fond of compounding. The three lines of *Beowulf* cited earlier contain three compounds: *Gār-Dena* meaning 'spear Danes,' *gēardagum* meaning 'yore days' (that is, 'days of yore'), and *þēodcyninga* meaning 'nation-kings.'

Noun Inflections Old English had several inflections for noun phrases, depending on their grammatical and semantic role in a sentence. Four principal cases could be distinguished: *nominative* (usually for subjects), *genitive* (for possessive and certain other functions), *dative* (for indirect objects and certain other functions), and *accusative* (for direct objects and objects of certain prepositions). Each noun carried a grammatical gender, which occasionally coincided with natural

TABLE 10-1
Four Old English Noun Declensions

	Masculine 'fox'	Feminine 'learning'	Neuter 'animal'	Masculine 'foot'
Singular				
Nominative	fox	lār	dēor	fōt
Accusative	fox	lār-e	dēor	fōt
Genitive	fox-es	lār-e	dēor-es	fōt-es
Dative	fox-e	lār-e	dēor-e	fēt
Plural				
Nom./Acc.	fox-as	lār-a	dēor	fēt
Genitive	fox-a	lār-a	dēor-a	fōt-a
Dative	fox-um	lār-um	dēor-um	fōt-um

gender: *guma* 'man' and *broðor* 'brother' were masculine, while *brȳd* 'bride' and *sweostor* 'sister' were feminine. But usually gender had little to do with the natural sex of a noun's referent. For example, the nouns *mīl* 'mile,' *wist* 'feast,' and *lēaf* 'permission' were feminine; *hund* 'dog,' *hungor* 'hunger,' *wīfmann* 'woman,' and *wīngeard* 'vineyard' were masculine; and *wīf* 'woman, wife,' *manncynn* 'mankind,' and *scip* 'ship' were neuter. Thus gender is simply a grammatical category that determined the way each noun was inflected (and also the inflections on adjectives and other agreeing constituents of the noun phrase).

Table 10-1 shows the paradigms for the nouns *fox* 'fox,' *lār* 'learning, lore,' *dēor* 'animal,' and *fōt* 'foot.' From the Old English *fox* declension (*declension* is the name for a noun paradigm) come the only productive Modern English noun inflections: the genitive singular in *-s* and all plurals in *-s*. The *dēor* paradigm survives in uninflected modern plurals like *deer* (whose meaning has been narrowed from 'animal') and *sheep*, but new words never follow this pattern. The *fōt* declension has yielded a few nouns (like *foot, goose, tooth, louse, mouse*, and *man*) whose plurals are signaled by an internal vowel change rather than by the common *-s* suffix. Modern English phrases like *a ten-foot pole* are relics of the Old English genitive plural ('a pole of ten feet'), whose form *fōta* has given rise to *foot*. Over the centuries, most nouns that had earlier been inflected according to other paradigms have come to conform to the *fox* paradigm, and new nouns (with the exception of a few borrowings) are also inflected like it.

Articles   The Modern English definite article is simple in form. It has a single orthographic shape *the* with two standard pronunciations, [ði] before vowels and [ðə] elsewhere. In sharp contrast, the Old English demonstratives—forerunners of today's definite article—were inflected for five cases and three genders in the singular and for three cases without gender distinction in the plural (see Table 10-2). The fifth case, the instrumental, was used either with or without a preposition to indicate such semantic roles as accompaniment or instrument ('with the

TABLE 10-2
Old English Declension of Demonstrative 'that'

	Singular			Plural
	Masculine	*Feminine*	*Neuter*	*All genders*
Nominative	sē	sēo	þæt	þā
Accusative	þone	þā	þæt	þā
Genitive	þæs	þǣre	þæs	þāra
Dative	þǣm	þǣre	þǣm	þǣm
Instrumental	þȳ	þǣre	þȳ	þǣm

chieftains,' 'by an arrow'). It may be instructive to compare the Old English demonstrative as represented in Table 10-2 with the Modern German definite article represented in Table 4-10 (page 96). The similarities are striking indeed.

As in Modern English, Old English indefinite noun phrases were frequently unmarked *(She writes books),* except that *sum* 'a certain' and *ān* 'one' occurred sometimes in the singular for emphasis and were inflected like adjectives.

Adjective Inflections   The Old English adjective system owes its complexity to innovations that had arisen in Common Germanic and consequently do not appear in other Indo-European languages; they also have not survived into Modern English.

Old English adjectives were inflected for gender, number, and case to agree with their head noun. There were two distinct kinds of adjective declensions. When a noun phrase had as one of its constituents a highly inflected possessive pronoun or demonstrative, adjectives were declined with one set of inflections—the so-called ''weak'' (or *definite*) declension. In other instances, such as predicative usage *(It is tall),* when indicators of grammatical relations were few or nonexistent, the more varied forms of the strong (or *indefinite*) declension were required. Table 10-3 gives the indefinite and definite adjective paradigms for *gōd* 'good.' Notice that Old English has ten different forms as compared to a single one for Modern English.

Nothing remains of the Old English inflectional system for adjectives. Today all adjectives occur in a single shape such as *tall, old,* and *beautiful* (except for the comparative and superlative inflections, as in *taller* and *tallest*). For any gender, number, or case of the modified noun, and for both attributive functions *(the tall ships)* and predicative functions *(the ship is tall),* the form of a Modern English adjective remains invariant.

Personal Pronouns   The Modern English personal pronouns preserve more of their earlier complexity than any other lexical category. The Old English paradigms for personal pronouns are given in Table 10-4, alongside their modern counterparts. As can be seen, besides singulars and plurals Old English had a dual number in the first and second persons ('we two' and 'you two'). The dual was

TABLE 10-3
Old English Declensions of the Adjective 'good'

| | **Singular** | | | **Plural** | | |
	Masc.	Fem.	Neut.	Masc.	Fem.	Neut.
Indefinite						
Nom.	gōd	gōd	gōd	gōd-e	gōd	gōd
Acc.	gōd-ne	gōd-e	gōd	gōd-e	gōd	gōd
Gen.	gōd-es	gōd-re	gōd-es	gōd-ra	gōd-ra	gōd-ra
Dat.	gōd-um	gōd-re	gōd-um	gōd-um	gōd-um	gōd-um
Ins.	gōd-e	gōd-re	gōd-e	gōd-um	gōd-um	gōd-um
Definite				*All genders*		
Nom.	gōd-a	gōd-e	gōd-e	gōd-an		
Acc.	gōd-an	gōd-an	gōd-e	gōd-an		
Gen.	gōd-an	gōd-an	gōd-an	gōd-ra (gōd-ena)		
Dat.	gōd-an	gōd-an	gōd-an	gōd-um		

already weakening in late Old English and eventually disappeared from English, as did the distinct number and case forms of the second person pronoun (*þū* 'thou'/*þē* 'thee' and *gē* 'ye'/*ēow* 'you' are all now *you*); the distinct dative case form for the third person singular neuter pronoun has also disappeared.

TABLE 10-4
Old English and Modern English Pronouns

| | **Old English** | | | | | **Modern English** | | | | |
| | First | Second | *Third person* | | | First | Second | *Third person* | | |
			Masc.	Fem.	Neut.			Masc.	Fem.	Neut.
Singular										
Nom.	ic	þū	hē	hēo	hit	I	you	he	she	it
Acc.	mē	þē	hine	hie	hit	me	you	him	her	it
Gen.	mīn	þīn	his	hiere	his	mine	yours	his	hers	its
Dat.	mē	þē	him	hiere	him	me	you	him	her	it
Dual										
Nom.	wit	git								
Acc.	unc	inc								
Gen.	uncer	incer								
Dat.	unc	inc								
Plural			*All Genders*					*All Genders*		
Nom.	wē	gē	hīe			we	you	they		
Acc.	ūs	ēow	hīe			us	you	them		
Gen.	ūre	ēower	hiera			ours	yours	theirs		
Dat.	ūs	ēow	him			us	you	them		

Relative Pronouns   In Old English, an invariant particle *þe* or *ðe* marked the introduction of relative clauses, though *þe* was often compounded with the demonstrative *sē, sēo, þæt,* as in *sē þe* (for masculine reference) and *sēo þe* (for feminine reference) 'who, that.' The forms of the demonstrative *sē, sēo, þæt* also occurred alone as relatives.

ānne	æðeling	sē	wæs	Cyneheard	hāten
a	prince	Rel	was	Cyneheard	called

'a prince who was called Cyneheard'

Old English relative clauses were also sometimes introduced by *þe*, while a form of the personal pronoun was retained, as in this example with *þe* and *him*.

Nis	nū	cwicra	nān	þe	ic	him	mōdsefan	mīnne	durre	āsecgan.
(there) isn't	now	alive	no one	Rel	I	him	mind	my	dare	speak

'There is no one alive now to whom I dare speak my mind.'

As this example shows, Old English relativized indirect objects. Therefore, according to the universal hierarchy examined in Chapter 8, we would assume that it also relativized direct objects and subjects—which in fact it did.

Verbs and Verb Inflections   Like other Germanic languages, Old English and its descendants exhibit two types of verbs. The characteristically Germanic regular verbs have a [d] or [t] suffix in the past tense (and are called "weak"). The so-called irregular verbs (the traditional Indo-European "strong" type) show a vowel alternation (as in *sing/sang/sung*). Old English had seven patterns of irregular verbs. Table 10-5 lists the principal parts (the forms from which all other inflected forms can be derived) of the seven Old English verb classes. These illustrative words survive as irregular verbs in Modern English, but quite a few Old English irregular verbs have developed into *regular* verbs in the course of time. (*Shove, melt, wash,* and *step,* for instance, were irregular in Old English.)

Two tenses—present and past (the latter sometimes called the *preterit*)—and two moods (indicative and subjunctive) could be formed from a verb's principal

TABLE 10-5
Seven Classes of Old English Strong Verbs

Infinitive	Past Singular	Past Plural	Past Participle	
1. rīdan	rād	ridon	geriden	'ride'
2. frēosan	frēas	fruron	gefroren	'freeze'
3. drincan	dranc	druncon	gedruncen	'drink'
4. beran	bær	bǣron	geboren	'bear'
5. licgan	læg	lǣgon	gelegen	'lie'
6. standan	stōd	stōdon	gestanden	'stand'
7. feallan	fēoll	fēollon	gefeallen	'fall'

TABLE 10-6
Conjugation of 'judge, deem' in Old English

	Indicative Mood	Subjunctive Mood
Present Tense		
Singular		
first person	dēm-e	dēm-e
second person	dēm-st (or dēm-est)	
third person	dēm-þ (or dēm-eþ)	
Plural		
first, second, and third	dēm-aþ	dēm-en
Past Tense		
Singular		
first person	dēm-d-e	dēm-d-e
second person	dēm-d-est	
third person	dēm-d-e	
Plural		
first, second, and third	dēm-d-on	dēm-d-en
Gerund	tō dēm-enne (or dēm-anne)	
Present Participle	dēm-ende	
Past Participle	dēm-ed	

parts. Table 10-6 gives a typical Old English regular verb conjugation for *dēman* 'judge, deem.' (*Conjugation* is the name for a verb paradigm.) Note that the present tense indicative had three singular forms and one plural, but the present tense subjunctive had only one singular and one plural form. Compared to the twelve distinct forms of an Old English regular verb paradigm, the Modern English paradigm has only four separate forms (*judge, judges, judged,* and *judging*) and does not include any distinctly subjunctive forms.

Compared to its elaborate Indo-European ancestors and some of its even more elaborate cousins, Old English had a simple verbal system. Old English verbs were inflected for person, number, and tense in the indicative mood and for number and tense in the subjunctive mood; the subjunctive mood was used far more frequently in Old English than it is in Modern English. Latin, by way of contrast, was inflected for active and passive *voice,* for perfective and imperfective *aspect,* and for present, past, and future *tenses,* as well as for three *moods.* Scholars are uncertain whether Latin inherited all those distinctions from Indo-European or innovated some on its own.

Inflections and Word Order

Having a rich inflectional system, Old English could rely on its morphological distinctions to indicate the grammatical relations of nouns (and, to a lesser extent, their semantic roles). Noun phrases had agreement in gender, number, and case among the demonstrative/definite article, the adjective, and the head noun; adjectives were declined, either definite or indefinite, as already described. Using some of the declensions provided in Tables 10-1, 10-2, and 10-3, and two other adjectives, we can form the following Old English noun phrases. Note that in each instance the adjective and demonstrative article must *agree* with the noun (that is, they must be inflected for the same gender, case, and number).

sē gōda fox	'the good fox' (masc. nom. sg.)
gōd dēor	'good animals' (neuter nom./acc. pl.)
þā gōdan fēt	'the good feet' (masc. nom./acc. pl.)
langra fōta	'of long feet' (masc. genitive pl.)
þǣre micelan lāre	'of/for the great learning' (fem. genitive/dative sg.)

The rich inflectional system operating within Old English noun phrases could indicate grammatical relations and certain semantic roles without having to rely on word order as Modern English must. Word order was therefore more flexible in Old English than in Modern English. Still, by late Old English, word order patterns were already similar in many respects to those of Modern English. Both Old English and Modern English show a preference for SVO order (subject preceding verb preceding object) in main clauses. Modern English prefers SVO in subordinate clauses as well; Old English (like Modern German) preferred verb-final order (SOV) in subordinate clauses.

As in Modern English, the order of elements in Old English noun phrases was usually determiner-adjective-noun: *sē gōda mann* 'the good man.' Far more frequently than in Modern English, genitives preceded nouns, as in the following:

folces weard   'people's protector'

mǣres līfes mann   'a man of splendid life'
(literally '(a) splendid life's man')

fōtes trym   'the space of a foot'
(literally '(a) foot's space')

We saw in Chapter 4 that adpositions can either follow or precede their nouns. Old English generally had prepositions, though with pronouns the same adposition often served in postposition (that is, after the pronoun), as shown in this example.

sē   hālga   Andreas   him tō cwæþ . . .

the   holy   Andrew   him to said . . .

'St. Andrew said to him . . .'

Like Modern English adjectives, Old English adjectives almost uniformly preceded their head nouns (*sē foresprecena here* 'the aforesaid army'), though they could sometimes follow them.

wadu   weallendu

waters   surging

'surging waters'

As they do in Modern English, relative clauses generally followed their head nouns in Old English.

ðā   cyningas   ðe   ðone onwald hæfdon

the   kings   who the   power   had

'the kings who had the power'

AN OLD ENGLISH NARRATIVE TEXT

The Old English passage in Figure 10-3 originates in Bede's *Ecclesiastical History of the English People,* completed in A.D. 731 and subsequently translated from Latin into English perhaps by Alfred the Great during his reign as king of Wessex (871–899). The version here is slightly edited from a later translation by the English abbot Ælfric (about 955–1020). Written in the plain style that Ælfric sometimes used, the story tells of how Gregory the Great, who reigned as pope between 590 and 604, first learned of the English people as he walked through a marketplace in Rome and saw boys being sold as slaves. The passage seems as foreign as any language written in the Roman alphabet and more so than some, given its unusual letters.

Lexicon of the Text

Function Words   Focusing on such function words as prepositions, demonstratives, and pronouns, we see some notable similarities between the Old English passage and Modern English: in the prepositions *æt* 'at,' *tō* 'to'; *betwux* 'between, among,' *of* 'of, from'; in the conjunction ⟨⟩ 'and,' which occurs more than half a dozen times in the passage; in the conjunction *þā* 'then,' used frequently to introduce sentences (usually with the verb following, as in lines 1, 4, and 8). The subordinator *þæt* (lines 8 and 17) was used exactly as it is in Modern English. Some of the personal pronouns functioned exactly as they do in Modern English (but their pronunciations have in most instances changed): *hit* 'it,' *hē* 'he,' *hī* 'they,' *him* 'him.' We can see in the verb *be* the singular past tense inflection *-e* (*wǣre*) and the plural past tense inflection *-on* (*wǣron*).

Content Words   There is greater difference between Old English and Modern English in nouns, verbs, and adjectives than in function words, but some of this unfamiliarity is due to inflections (*mannum,* the dative plural of 'man') and much of it to spelling differences or pronunciation. Thus we can see in the words *Englisce, strǣt, ðing, menn,* and *nama* the earlier forms of the nouns *English, street, thing, men,* and *name.* In *brōhton, behēold, sǣde,* and *wǣre* are the etymons of the modern verbs *brought, beheld, said,* and *were.* Among other words that still

1 Ðā gelamp hit æt sumum sǣle, swā swā gȳt for oft dēð,
Then happened it at a certain time as yet very oft does,

2 þæt Englisce cȳpmenn brōhton heora ware tō Rōmānabyrig,
that English traders brought their wares to Rome

3] Grēgōrius ēode be þǣre strǣt tō ðām Engliscum mannum,
and Gregory went through the street to the English men,
heora ðing scēawigende.
their things looking at.

4 Þā geseah hē betwux ðām warum cȳpecnihtas gesette,
Then saw he among the wares slaves seated

5 þā wǣron hwītes līchaman] fægeres andwlitan menn,] æðellīce gefexode.
who were of white body and of fair countenance men, and nobly haired.

6 Grēgōrius ðā behēold þǣra cnapena wlite,
Gregory then saw the boys' countenances.

7] befrān of hwilcere þēode hī gebrōhte wǣron.
and asked from which people they brought were.

8 Þā sǣde him man þæt hī of Englalande wǣron,
Then said to him someone that they from England were,

9] þæt ðǣre ðēode mennisc swā wlitig wǣre.
and that that nation's people so handsome were.

10 Eft ðā Grēgōrius befrān, hwæðer þæs
Again then Gregory asked, whether that

11 landes folc crīsten wǣre ðe hǣðen.
land's people Christian were or heathen.

12 Him man sǣde þæt hī hǣðene wǣron. . . .
Him someone told that they heathen were. . . .

13 Eft hē āxode, hū ðǣre ðēode nama wǣre þe hī of cōmon.
Later he asked, how the people's name was that they from came.

14 Him wæs geandswarod, þæt hī Angle genemnode wǣron.
To him was answered that they Angles named were.

15 Hwæt, ðā Grēgōrius gamenode mid his wordum tō ðām naman] cwæð,
Well, then Gregory played with his words on the name and said,

16 "Rihtlīce hī sind Angle gehātene, for ðan ðe hī engla wlite habbað,
"Rightly they are Angles called, because they angels' countenances have,

17] swilcum gedafenað þæt hī on heofonum engla gefēran bēon.
and for such it is right that they in heaven angels' companions be.

FIGURE 10-3
A Narrative Written in Old English around the Year 1000

exist today are *hwæðer* 'whether,' *hū* 'how,' *crīsten* 'Christian,' and *hǣðen* 'heathen.' A few others are not quite so transparent, but they can trigger a flash of recognition once the connection is pointed out: *rihtlīce* 'rightly,' *cwæð* 'quoted,' *heofonum* 'heaven,' *engla* 'angel.'

Grammar: Syntax and Morphology in the Text

Given its highly inflected nature, Old English had considerable freedom of word order. Note, however, that the verb occurred in second position following the introductory adverb *þā* (*þā geseah hē,* line 4, and also lines 1 and 8); otherwise, it tended to occur in final position in subordinate clauses (*þæt hī hǽðene wǽron,* line 12, and 1, 7, 9, 13, 14, and 17). As in Modern English, noun phrases had the order (article)-(adjective)-noun (*sumum sǽle* 'a certain time,' *þǽre strǽt* 'the street') and prepositional phrases had the order preposition-adjective-noun *(æt sumum sǽle, be þǽre strǽt)*.

Text Structure

One striking characteristic of Old English writing was the strong preference for linking clauses together with ⟨⟩ 'and' and *þā* 'then,' much as is done in Modern English oral narratives. Frequent use of subordinators making explicit the relation between one clause and another *(because, since, until)* was a later development. Clauses are introduced with 'and' or 'then' often in the passage, including lines 1, 3, 4, 8, and 17. There are a few example of subordination, as in *hwæðer* 'whether' in line 10 and *for ðan ðe* 'because' in line 16.

MIDDLE ENGLISH: 1100–1500

The Norman Invasion

In the year 1066, William, Duke of Normandy, sailed across the Channel to claim the English throne. After winning the Battle of Hastings, William was crowned king of England in Westminster Abbey on Christmas Day, and Anglo-Saxon England passed into history. Thus was established a Norman kingdom in England: For generations the king of England and the duke of Normandy would be one person. The Norman invasion would not only reshape England's institutions but exercise a profound effect on its language.

The Norman French spoken by the invaders quickly became the language of England's ruling class, while the lower classes remained English-speaking. Following the invasion, the English language had a recess from many of its previous duties. In particular, it was relieved of service in the affairs of government, the court, the church, and education, for these important activities were now conducted in French. Indeed, for two centuries after the Conquest, the kings of England did not know the language of many of their subjects, and English-speaking subjects could not understand the French of their king. The most famous king of this period, Richard the Lion-Hearted, was in every way French, and during his reign (1189–1199) he visited England only twice and stayed a total of less than ten months. Eventually the middle classes became bilingual, speaking to peasants in English and to the ruling classes in French.

After 1200 the situation began to change, when King John lost Normandy to King Philip of France. On both sides of the Channel, decrees were issued commanding that no one could own land in both England and France. Cut off from its Norman origins, the force that had sustained the use of French in Britain began to collapse.

Lexicon

A hundred years later, around 1300, English came to be known again by all inhabitants of England. Not surprisingly, however, the language that emerged was strikingly different from the Old English used prior to the Norman invasion, at least as that Old English is reflected in the surviving written documents. The vocabulary of Middle English was heavily spiced by Norman French. The English word stock was swollen by the addition of thousands of French words because speakers learning English used French words to refer to things whose English labels they no longer knew. Based on calculations by the Danish scholar Otto Jespersen, it has been estimated that approximately ten thousand French words came into English during the Middle English period—and most of them remain in use today! Especially plentiful were words pertaining to religion, government, the courts, and the army and navy, though many borrowings relate to food, fashion, and education—those arenas in which the invaders and their successors wielded great influence in England.

Once English had been reestablished as the language of the law, the residents of England found themselves without sufficient English terminology to carry on the activities that had been conducted for centuries in French. Hence a good many French legal terms were borrowed, including even the words *justice* and *court* (the word *law* itself, however, derives from Old English *lagu*). To discuss events in a courtroom today, the following words—all borrowed from French during the Middle English period—are used: *judgment, plea, verdict, evidence, proof, prison,* and *jail.* The actors in a courtroom now have French names: *bailiff, plaintiff, defendant, attorney, jury, juror,* and *judge.* The names of certain crimes are French, including *felony, assault, arson, larceny, fraud, libel, slander,* and *perjury,* as is the word *crime* itself. We have cited examples only from the law, and by no means all of them; extensive lists of French borrowings could also be provided for the other arenas in which the French were socially and culturally influential.

Phonology

Vowels   Most Old English long vowels were maintained in Middle English unchanged. But the Old English long vowel /ɑ:/ in words like *bān, stān,* and *bāt* became in Middle English long /ɔ:/ (and in Modern English /o/) as in *boon* 'bone,' *stoon* 'stone,' and *boot* 'boat.' Many diphthongs were simplified in late Old English and early Middle English. Thus the vowels of the words *sēon* 'see' and *bēon* 'be' were leveled to long /e:/, a sound that went on to become [i] in Modern English.

Short vowels in unstressed syllables, which had been kept distinct at least in early West Saxon, tended to merge in schwa [ə], usually written ⟨e⟩.

Consonants and Consonant Clusters   The Old English initial consonant clusters /hl-/, /hn-/, /hr-/, and /kn-/ were simplified to /l/, /n/, and /r/, all losing their initial /h/ or /k/: *hlāf* 'loaf,' *hlot* 'lot,' *hnecca* 'neck,' *hnacod* 'naked,' *hrōf* 'roof,' *hræfn* 'raven,' *hring* 'ring,' *cnīf* 'knife,' *cnoll* 'knoll,' *cniht* 'boy, knight.' A phonological change of considerable consequence was the merging of word-final /-m/ and /-n/ in a single sound (/-n/) when they occurred in unstressed syllables (*foxum* > *foxun*). Significantly, unstressed syllables included all the inflections on nouns, adjectives, and verbs. By the end of the Middle English period even this /-n/ was dropped

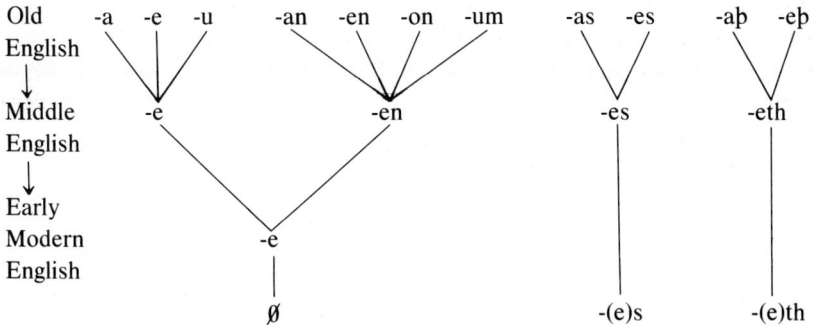

FIGURE 10-4
The Historical Reduction of English Inflections

altogether *(foxun > foxen > foxe),* and the final *-e* was also dropped, as you can infer.

Morphology

Three of the phonological changes just mentioned had profound effects on the morphology of Middle English.

1. -m > -n   (in unstressed syllables)

2. -n > ø

3. a, o, u, e > e [ə] (when not stressed)

Figure 10-4 shows how, as a consequence of these sound changes, certain sets of Old English inflections merged, becoming indistinguishable in Middle English and being further reduced or dropping altogether in early Modern English. As a result of these mergers, the Old English noun paradigms became greatly simplified in Middle English, and grammatical gender disappeared (see Table 10-7).

TABLE 10-7
Four Middle English Noun Declensions

	'fox'	'lore'	'animal'	'foot'
Singular				
Nom./Acc.	fox	loor	deer	foot
Genitive	foxes	loor(e)	deeres	footes
Dative	fox(e)	loor(e)	deer(e)	foot
Plural				
Nom./Acc.	foxes	loor(e)	deer	feet
Genitive/Dative	foxes	loor(e)	deer(e)	foot(e)

The frequently used subject and object noun phrase forms (nominative and accusative cases) established the nominative and accusative plural form *foxes* (and the *-es* inflection for other nouns in general) throughout the plural; it also established the nominative and accusative singular throughout the singular except that the genitive in *-s* was maintained. Thus the Middle English paradigm for a noun like *fox* came to be what it is in Modern English: *fox* and *foxes* (now spelled *fox's*) in the singular and *foxes* throughout the plural (now spelled *foxes'* in the genitive).

In some of the other noun paradigms, the damage to the morphological distinctions brought on by the merging of unstressed vowels was even greater. Old English *dēor* was reduced to three forms *(deer/deeres/deere),* while *lār* was reduced to two *(loor* and *loore),* a distinction that was itself lost when final inflected *-e* vanished about 1500.

We have the Modern English forms of the word *deer (deer* and *deer's)* from the nominative and accusative singular inflection, which was extended throughout the singular (except that the ending in *-s* has been kept in the genitive). The parallel nominative and accusative plural form extended throughout the plural (except that by analogy with all other English nouns the genitive plural is formed by adding *-s* to the form of the nominative plural).

From the *foot* declension, the origins of the Modern English forms are clear: Middle English nominative and accusative *foot* was extended throughout the singular, with the *-s* of the genitive form *footes* maintained; the nominative and accusative plural *feet* was extended throughout the plural (and, as usual, the inflected genitive is formed by adding *-s* to the nominative). Modern English expressions like *a ten-foot pole* 'a pole of ten feet' and *a three-day weekend* 'a weekend of three days' are simply relics of the Old English constructions with genitive plurals (for example, *fōta*), whose final *-a* became *-e* in Middle English and then was dropped.

Adjectives   The same merging of distinct inflections that collapsed the noun paradigms also had a devastating effect on adjectives. The only indefinite forms surviving the phonological change from Old English were *goodne* (masculine accusative singular), *goodes* (masculine and neuter genitive singular), and *goodre* (feminine genitive, dative, and instrumental singular, and genitive plural). Then *good* became the universal form for the singular. In the plural, the nominative, accusative, and dative forms for all genders became *good,* and the genitive plural also became *good* by analogy. That left only a single form in the singular and plural, namely *good,* which yielded Modern English *good* as the invariable form of the adjective (comparative and superlative forms aside).

In the definite declension, the only two forms surviving were *good* and *goodre.* Then *goodre* was re-formed by analogy (whereby one form takes on the shape of other forms in the same or another paradigm) to *good,* thus leaving only a single definite adjective form, which was the same as the indefinite. Thus a few simple phonological changes (and some analogical adaptations) reduced the complex forms of Old English adjectives to the striking simplicity of today's single forms.

Syntax

Much could be said about Middle English syntax, but the language changed so thoroughly during the four centuries of this period that a good deal of provision would have to be made for intermediate stages. Since we have described Old English and Modern English syntax at some length, suffice it to say that Middle English was a transitional period. This is especially true with respect to the change from a reliance on inflection to a reliance on word order for a considerable amount of information about grammatical relations. As the inflections of Old English disappeared, the word order of Middle English became increasingly fixed. The communicative work that had previously been done for nouns by inflectional morphology still needed doing, and it fell principally to prepositions and word order to perform these tasks. We have already said that Old English preferred SVO order in main clauses but often had SOV order in subordinate clauses. The nearly exclusive use of the SVO pattern emerged in the twelfth century and has remained part of English ever since.

A MIDDLE ENGLISH TRAVEL FABLE

We can now see how some of these features of morphology and syntax came together in Middle English prose. Figure 10-5 is a brief passage from *The Travels of John Mandeville,* a translation made from Mandeville's French work by an unknown but gifted English writer in the early fifteenth century (about the time of Chaucer's death). These travel stories, in large part fables, were extremely popular and survive in more than three hundred manuscripts. In the passage quoted here, Mandeville is describing a fabulous place called Lamary.

We analyze this passage with a view to how English of the early fifteenth century differs from today's. First of all, it should be noted that the passage is quite intelligible, though a few marked differences (and some subtle ones) can be noted between it and today's English.

Lexicon in the Fable

As to vocabulary, not a single word in the passage will be unknown to readers today, though a few (such as *lond* 'land,' *hete* 'heat,' *ʒeer* 'year,' *byʒen* 'buy,' and *hem* 'them') might not be instantly recognizable. (The graph ⟨ʒ⟩, called *yogh,* was pronounced like [y].) Not all the words borrowed from French during the Middle English period immediately took their current form, but most are nevertheless transparent: *custom, strange, clothed, nature, comoun, clos, contradiccioun, contree, habundant, marchauntes.*

Morphology in the Fable

Only a few inflections remain from Old English that have not survived in Modern English. For example, third person singular present tense verbs end in *-(e)th: holdeth, hath, lyketh, taketh* (but compare past tense *made*); and plural present tense verbs end in *-n* or *-en: gon, scornen, seyn, ben, eten, bryngen, byʒen,* and others. This *-n* or *-en* is not the direct reflex of the Old English plural form *-aþ* but was apparently introduced from the subjunctive plural so as to maintain a distinction between the singular and the plural. This distinction otherwise would have been lost when the unstressed vowels of the singular *-eþ* and the plural *-aþ* merged to give Middle English *-eth* for both forms. While Mandeville's translator

1 In þat lond is full gret hete,
   In that land is very great heat.

2 and the custom þere is such þat men and wommen gon all naked.
   and the custom   there is such that men and women   go all naked.

3 And þei scornen, whan thei seen ony strange folk goynge clothed.
   And they scorn,   when they see any strange folk going   clothed.

4 And þei seyn, þat god made Adam and Eue all naked
   And they say,   that God made Adam and Eve all naked

5 and þat no man scholde schame him to schewen him such as god made him;
   and that no man should   shame himself to show   himself such as God made him;

6 for no thing is foul þat is of kyndely nature . . . .
   for no thing is foul that is of natural   nature. . . .

7 And also all the lond is comoun; for all þat a man
   And also all the land is common; for all that a man

8 holdeth o ȝeer, another man hath it anoþer ȝeer,
   keeps   one year, another man has it another year,

9 and euery man taketh what part þat him lyketh.
   and every man takes   what part that him pleases.

10 And also all the godes of the lond ben comoun, cornes and all oþer þinges;
   And also all the goods of the land are common, grains and all other things;

11 for no þing þere is kept in clos, ne no þing þere is vndur lok,
   for no thing there is kept in a closet nor no thing there is under   lock,

12 and euery man þere taketh what he wole, withouten ony contradiccioun.
   and every man there takes   what he wants, without   any contradiction.

13 And als riche is o man þere as is another.
   And as rich is one man there as is another.

14 But in þat contree þere is a cursed custom:
   But in that country there is a cursed   custom:

15 for þei eten more gladly mannes flesch þan ony oþer flesch.
   for they eat more gladly man's   flesh   than any other flesh.

16 And ȝit is þat contree habundant of flesch, of fissch,
   And yet is that country   abundant with flesh, with fish,

17 of cornes, of gold and syluer, and of all oþer godes.
   with grains, with gold and silver, and with all other goods.

18 Þider gon marchauntes and bryngen with hem children,
   Thither go   merchants   and bring   with them children,

19 to selle to hem of the contree; and þei byȝen hem.
   to sell to them of the country; and they buy   them.

20 And ȝif þei ben fatte, þei eten hem anon; and ȝif þei ben lene,
   And if they are fat,   they eat them at once; and if they are lean,

21 þei feden hem till þei ben fatte, and þanne þei eten hem.
   they feed   them until they are fat,   and then   they eat them.

22 And þei seyn, þat it is the best flesch and the swettest of all the world.
   And they say,   that it is the best flesh   and the sweetest of all the world.

FIGURE 10-5
A Travel Fable Written in Middle English around the Year 1400

alternates between the two spellings *þei* and *thei* for the third person plural subject pronoun, the *þ/th* forms of the objective case do not yet appear in this passage, which instead shows the objective form *hem* (lines 19, 20, and 21). Otherwise, several of the Modern English inflections have their current form (after some slight spelling adjustments): *goynge* 'going,' *clothed, godes* 'goods,' *þinges* 'things,' *marchauntes* 'merchants,' and *swettest* 'sweetest.' Even certain words that had kept their exceptional forms from Old English are basically the same in 1400 and today: *men, wommen, folk, children,* and *best.* Being among the more common words of the language they were more likely to maintain their unusual forms than were words used less frequently.

Syntax in the Fable

The first notable difference in syntax occurs in line 1. Where Modern English requires a "dummy subject" (without a referent), Middle English did not: *In þat lond is.* . . . But note the dummy *þere* in line 14: *But in þat contree þere is.* . . . Another striking difference is the double negative *ne no þing* 'nor nothing' in line 11.

There are marked word order differences. Compare in line 13 this word-for-word equivalent with its current English version (which follows the slash): *And as rich is one man there as is another/And one man there is as rich as another.* Note, too, that the adverbial phrase *more gladly* (line 15) follows its verb instead of preceding it as it would in Modern English. Finally, note the relic of Old English verb-second word order in line 18 *(Thither go merchants)* and the prepositional phrase *with hem* in the same line, which in current English would follow the direct object *children.*

Among some of the subtler syntactic differences are the intransitive use of *scorn* (that is, without a direct object) in line 3, which is no longer possible, and the use of the nonreflexive pronoun *him* where current English would reflexivize (line 5). One final interesting difference occurs in line 9, where *him* is an object form that complements the verb *lyketh* (in a benefactive semantic role); *him lyketh* literally translates *to him (it) likes* 'it pleases him.' Since Old English times, this "impersonal" construction had required not a nominative but a dative (or, later, objective) case form of the pronoun; it resembles the French *s'il vous plait* 'if it you pleases,' which may have influenced the now archaic formulation *if it please you* or *if it please my lord.*

We may tend to overlook some of the syntactic differences that do exist in this passage as compared to current English because we are accustomed to finding relatively conservative syntax in such places as the King James Bible and certain formal prose styles such as legalese. Still, this Middle English passage, now six centuries old, is obviously English and almost completely transparent to modern readers.

MODERN ENGLISH: 1500–PRESENT

Chapters 2 through 6 of this book examined the structure of twentieth-century English in detail, and there is no need to rehearse that material here. This section focuses instead on what changes occurred in the earliest stages of Modern English to move the language from its Middle English forms to those we know today.

Early and Late Modern English

As our analysis of Mandeville's travel fable shows, Middle English had developed many of the principal syntactic patterns we know today by the beginning of the fifteenth century. The complex inflectional system of Old English had been drastically simplified; and today's system, with fewer than ten inflections, had emerged. Most nouns that had been inflected in Old English according to various patterns now conformed to the *fox* pattern. By the time of Shakespeare, the third person plural pronouns with *th-* instead of *h-* (*they, their,* and *them*) had been in general use for a century: Chaucer and the Mandeville translator had used *they,* but both still used the older possessive *her* 'their' and objective *hem* 'them.' In addition, word order had become more fixed, essentially as it is in Modern English.

The language of the late fifteenth century is in most ways Modern English—though in so saying, one should be mindful that the principal phonological development of English vowels took place sometime between 1450 and 1650, when all the long vowels changed their quality very markedly, as we shall see. If that phonological change is not apparent, it is simply because the modern spellings of English vowels had essentially been established by the time of William Caxton, who founded his printing press in the vicinity of Westminster Abbey in 1476—before the phonlogical change had progressed very far at all. Caxton's spellings thus disguise the fundamental alteration that has transformed the system of English vowels, throwing it out of harmony with the representations that these same written vowels have in the continental languages.

Phonology: The English Vowel Shift

In the Mandeville travel passage, certain words are easily recognized by their similar spellings to Modern English. In particular, the words, *gret, hete, schame,* and *foul* resemble their modern counterparts. The written similarity, however, disguises the fact that the words as *pronounced* in Chaucer's time are not likely to be recognizable by a modern listener. Sometime in the two centuries between 1450 and 1650, all the long vowels of Middle English underwent a systematic shift. Each long front vowel was raised and became pronounced like another vowel higher in the system. The same thing occurred with back vowels: Each long vowel was systematically raised to be pronounced like the vowel next higher in the vowel chart. Thus, /ɔ:/ came to be pronounced /o:/, /e:/ came to be pronounced /i:/, and so on. The two highest long vowels, high front /i:/ and high back /u:/, could not be raised any farther and instead were diphthongized to /ay/ and /aw/ respectively. Thus Middle English *I* /i:/ became /ay/, *hous* /hu:s/ became /haws/ 'house,' and so on. We can represent the situation as in Figure 10-6.

Morphology

Verbs   Of the hundreds of irregular (strong) verbs in Old English, fewer than half survive in Modern English. Of those that do, many came to be inflected like

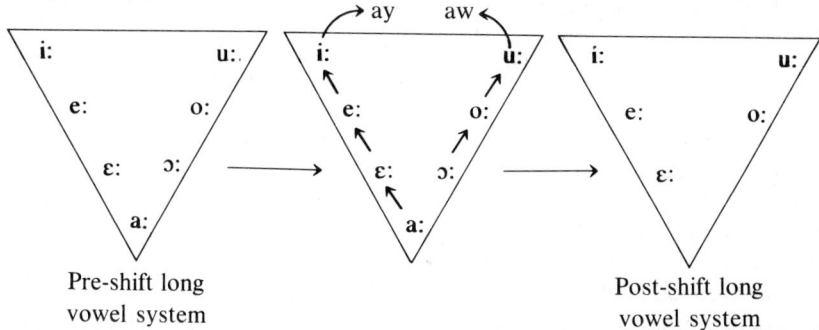

Pre-shift long
vowel system

Post-shift long
vowel system

FIGURE 10-6
The English Vowel Shift

Source: Adapted from Theodora Bynon, *Historical Linguistics* (Cambridge: Cambridge University Press, 1977), p. 82.

the regular verbs, with an alveolar stop suffix rather than the vowel gradation characteristic of irregular verbs. One tally suggests that of the 333 irregular verbs of Old English, only 68 continue as irregular verbs in Modern English. Among those that have become regular over the centuries are *burn, brew, climb, flow, help,* and *walk.* Slightly more than a dozen verbs have become irregular in the history of English, including *dive,* which has recently developed a past tense form *dove* alongside the historical form *dived.* You may also have heard *drug* for *dragged,* as its use seems to be on the rise as well. Among other verbs that are now irregular but were formerly regular are *wear, spit,* and *dig.*

Definite Article   The initial consonant of *sē* and *sēo,* the Old English masculine and feminine nominative singular demonstratives, differed from all other forms, which began with [θ] (orthographic ⟨þ⟩). *Sē* was apparently reshaped by analogy with forms having initial [θ]. By Middle English, *þe* had become the invariant definite article in the north, and its use spread to all dialects. Chaucer uses only *the,* pronounced [θə]. The voicing of the initial consonant as we have it today occurred because the customary lack of stress on *the* encouraged assimilation to the vowel nucleus, which of course is voiced. Such a history is somewhat surprising for what is by far the most commonly used word in Modern English.

Indefinite Article   The history of the indefinite article *a/an* is also remarkable, for while Old English did not use an indefinite article, *a/an* has today become the fifth most common word in English.

Personal Pronouns   Though the personal pronouns retain more of their Old English diversity than any other lexical category, our earlier comparison of Old and Modern English pronouns (Table 10-4) indicates that the dual was lost entirely (starting at the beginning of the Middle English period). During the early Modern English period, the distinction between the second person singular and plural forms—between *thou* and *thee* singular and *ye* and *you* plural—disintegrated.

Under the apparent influence of French, speakers of English began using the plural forms *ye, your,* and *you* as a sign of respect or formality, much as happens with the French pronoun *vous,* which is grammatically plural but is used to show respect and deference even when addressing a single stranger, elder, or "social superior." Among the higher social classes in England, the historical plural form *you* came to be used as a mutual sign of respect even in informal conversation between equals. In time, the singular forms all but disappeared as did the distinction in the plural between the subject and object forms *ye* and *you.* Thus, from the six-fold distinction found in Old English and much of Middle English, Modern English has only a two-fold distinction—between *you* and *yours.*

The loss of a singular/plural distinction for *you* is a kind of accident of history, and Modern English speakers seem to find it difficult to get along without a distinctive second person plural pronoun. In fact, certain varieties of Modern English have created distinct plural forms, although these are regionally marked (*y'all* in the American South) or socially stigmatized (*yous* [yuz] or [yɪz] in New York City and parts of Ireland, and *y'uns* in western Pennsylvania and the Ohio valley). Standard English has no way to mark the second person pronoun for plurality, though of course one can say such things as *you two* or *you all.*

Syntax

Deprived of the richness of its earlier inflectional signposts to meaning, Modern English has become a more analytical language—more like Chinese than like Latin and the other early daughters of Proto–Indo-European. With nouns inflected only for the possessive case (and for number, of course), word order is now the chief signal of grammatical relations, displacing the earlier inflectional morphology. Even the fuller pronominal inflections are subordinate to the grammatical relations signaled by word order, so that *Him and me saw Scott at the party,* though not standard, is nevertheless not confusing in any way as to subject and object.

Why English should have advanced further than its Germanic cousins along the path to becoming an analytical language (rather than remaining an inflected language) is not clear. Possible explanations may be found in the thoroughgoing contact between the Danes and the English after the ninth century, in the French ascendance over English for numerous secular and religious purposes in the early Middle English period, and in the preservation of the vernacular chiefly in folk speech and therefore without the conservationist brake of writing for several generations in the eleventh and twelfth centuries. The influence of the Danes is particularly important: When they invaded England in the eighth and ninth centuries, the Danes spoke varieties of Germanic that must have been quite similar to the dialects spoken in England but with different inflections. It is easy to imagine that children exposed to parents using different inflectional suffixes and to friends whose inflectional suffixes were not uniform might readily look for other means to signal the differences formerly indicated by inflections.

In any case, decades before the Norman Conquest, those inflectional reductions started that became apparent when English reemerged; doubtless they had advanced further in speech than the written texts of the day indicate. Thus phonological reductions undermined the inflectional morphology, and, as inflection grew less able to signal grammatical relations and semantic roles, word order and the deployment of prepositions came to bear those communicative tasks less redundantly. Gradually, the freer word order of Old English yielded to the relatively fixed order of Modern English, whose linear arrangements are the chief carrier of grammatical functions.

Spurred by an almost total absence of inflections on nouns, Modern English syntax has evolved to permit unusually free interplay among grammatical relations and semantic roles. With nouns marked only for possessive case, and pronouns additionally for objective case, Modern English exercises minimal inflectional constraint on subject noun phrases, which are consequently free to represent an exceptionally wide range of semantic roles (as illustrated in Chapter 6, page 185).

Lexicon

As in the course of the Middle English period, when English supplanted French and borrowed thousands of French words, so in the course of early Modern English, as English came to be used where Latin had previously been used, a great many words were borrowed from Latin (and through Latin from Greek). The words borrowed from Latin are not common words like the courtroom terminology from French but are instead learned words, reflecting the arenas in which Latin had been used. Even with these borrowings, English found itself in need of a great many more words as it spread from principally literary and personal uses into every sphere of activity. The *Oxford English Dictionary* records words from about fifty different languages borrowed into English during the first century-and-a-half of Modern English (1500–1650), the period during which the vernacular came to replace Latin in nearly every learned arena.

Among the words that can be cited as Latin borrowings of this early Modern English period are the following: *allusion, anachronism, antipathy, antithesis, appendix, atmosphere, autograph,* and *axis* among the nouns (to stick to those beginning with *a*); *abject, agile,* and *appropriate* among the adjectives; and *adapt, alienate,* and *assassinate* among the verbs. Some of these words, though introduced to English from Latin, came originally from Greek. During the Renaissance, words were borrowed directly from Greek as well; these include *acme, anonymous, catastrophe, criterion* (and its plural, *criteria*), *idiosyncrasy, lexicon, ostracize, polemic, tantalize,* and *tonic.* Not everyone appreciated borrowed words, and many writers who used these then-strange terms were criticized for their "inkhorn" words. Not every borrowed term was successful; many failed to survive.

SUMMARY

English belongs to the West Germanic group of the Germanic branch of the Indo-European family. Among the major languages, its closest relatives are German and Dutch. In the course of its history, English has been greatly enriched by thousands of words borrowed from more than one hundred languages—most notably from French, as the descendants of the Norman invaders started using English in the thirteenth century, and from Latin, during the Renaissance, as the vernacular came to be used in arenas previously reserved for the classical language.

Beowulf is an epic poem of the Old English period (700–1100). Chaucer wrote during the Middle English period (1100–1500), and Shakespeare's works are from early in the Modern English period (1500–present). While Old English was a highly inflected language, a few critical sound changes left little inflectional morphology in Middle English. Modern English is thus an analytical language, relying principally on word order to express grammatical relations that were formerly marked inflectionally.

EXERCISES

1. Modern English words that were borrowed from Latin or Greek do not show the influence of Grimm's Law (which affected only the Germanic branch of Indo-European). For many such borrowed words, English also has a related word that has been directly inherited from Indo-European through Germanic. Any such inherited word that contained an affected consonant did undergo the consonant shifts described by Grimm. For each borrowed word given below, cite an English word that is related in meaning and whose pronunciation shows the result of the consonant shift. For this exercise, focus only on the initial consonant of each word. For example, given *pedal,* you would seek a word like *foot* that has a related meaning and begins with [f] (because Indo-European [p] became [f] in Germanic).

cardiac	dual	capital	cordial
paternal	pentagon	piscatorial	canine
plenitude	dentist	triangle	decade

2. This exercise is like the preceding one, except that here we provide English words that have undergone the Germanic consonant shift and ask you to provide another English word that is likely to have been borrowed because it has a closely related meaning and does not show the results of Grimm's Law. Bear in mind that most Latin and Greek borrowings tend to be more learned and technical than the related ones inherited directly from Indo-European. Focus only on the underlined consonant. For example, given *foot,* you would cite a word that begins with *p* such as *podiatrist* 'foot doctor.'

tooth	ten	lip
hound	fire	eat

3. You know that, by the effects of Grimm's Law, Indo-European *[bʰ] became [b], and Indo-European *[gʰ] became [g] in Germanic. Latin, not being a Germanic language, did not undergo these consonant shifts. Instead, Indo-European *[bʰ] became [f] in Latin, and Indo-European *[gʰ] became [h] in Latin. We can represent these facts in the following correspondences:

Indo-European

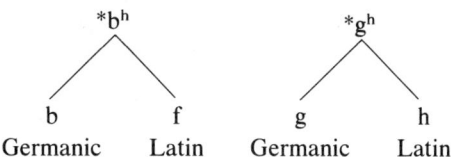

b   f   g   h
Germanic   Latin   Germanic   Latin

With this information, you may be able to provide an English word inherited directly from Indo-European for each of the following words, which are all borrowed from Latin. Focus on the initial consonant, and bear in mind that other changes may have affected the remainder of the word so that the resemblance is distant.

fraternity   fundamental
fragile   flare
hospitable   fracture

4. Indicate which allophone of /f/, /θ/, or /s/ was pronounced in each of the following Old English words (use the description of the allophonic distribution given on p. 306 to help you determine the correct answer): *þæt, sēo, his, ūs, wæs, æðeling* 'prince,' *frēosan* 'freeze,' *dēmst* 'judge,' *līfes* 'of life,' *þā* 'then,' *drīfan* 'drive,' *wulfas* 'wolves,' *hræfn* 'raven,' *bosm* 'bosom,' *seofon* 'seven,' *bæþ* 'bath,' *sceaft* 'shaft.'

5. a. Identify the grammatical gender of the following Old English nouns, and then write out the full declension (all cases, singular and plural) for each of the noun phrases in which they appear; use the paradigms given in this chapter as models.

    sē stān 'the stone'

    ðæt word 'the word'

    sēo wund 'the wound'

    b. For each of these Old English noun phrases, provide the Old English pronoun that would be used in the space given.

    Sē stān, _____ is gōd.   'The stone, it is good.'

    Ðæt word, _____ is gōd.   'The word, it is good.'

    Sēo wund, _____ nis gōd.   'The wound, it isn't good.'

6. Compare the Old English passage on p. 314 with the Middle English passage on p. 320 and identify ways in which Middle English differs from Old English in orthography, lexicon, morphology, and word order. Provide an example from the passages to illustrate each point.

7. You have seen several words in this chapter whose meaning has changed from Old English to Modern English. One example is the word *dēor,* which meant 'animal' in Old English but has narrowed its meaning to 'deer' in Modern English. Among several other ways, words can change their meaning by becoming more specialized, as with

deer, or becoming more generalized. Examine the Old English words and meanings that follow and note what each word has become in Modern English. State whether the word's meaning has become more specialized or more generalized in the course of its development from Old English into Modern English.

Old English	Modern English
steorfan 'die'	starve
berēafian 'deprive of'	bereave
hlāf 'bread'	loaf
spēdan 'prosper'	speed
spellian 'speak'	spell
hund 'dog'	hound
mete 'food'	meat
wīf 'woman'	wife
dōm 'judgment'	doom
sellan 'give'	sell
tīd 'time'	tide

8. Nearly all of the words listed below were borrowed into English from other languages. Keeping in mind the character of the words and what they signify, make an educated guess as to the likely source language for each word and the approximate date of borrowing. Then, for each word, look up its origin in a good dictionary, noting for borrowed words the actual source language and the date of borrowing. For which words has no source been identified? (While the source language will be identified in most good dictionaries, the date of borrowing may not be. *Webster's Ninth New Collegiate Dictionary* does supply dates. It may be useful for different students or student groups to tackle different columns of words and then to compare their findings.)

barf	kerchief	denim	mutton
zilch	teriyaki	algebra	klutz
duffel	catsup	alarm	glitch
mai tai	hunk	a la mode	schlock
hummus	honcho	nosh	kvetch
tortilla	macho	ginger	glasnost
tandoori	moped	giraffe	kayak
ginseng	jeans	ciao	shtick
kibble	disco	karate	moussaka
bummer	dude	kimono	whiskey
dinosaur	sphere	kung fu	karma
leviathan	taffy	paparazzi	caucus
tae kwon do	dim sum	taffeta	caddy
piña colada	cadaver	falafel	goober

SUGGESTIONS FOR FURTHER READING

Baugh and Cable (1993)—from which our examples of French borrowings in Middle English, Latin and Greek borrowings of early Modern English, and regular and irregular verbs are taken—is excellent on the external history of English. Pyles and Algeo (1993), from which we have borrowed a few examples, is balanced between linguistic history and social history, and it complements Baugh and Cable by being stronger on the linguistic history; Algeo (1993) is a workbook in the history of English. Bolton (1982) and Millward (1990), the latter with a workbook, are also good general histories of English, as is Strang (1970). All include references to more specialized works for each period. A useful and easy-to-use reference grammar of Old English is Quirk and Wrenn (1957), from which several of our examples are taken. Especially valuable for Old English syntax is Mitchell and Robinson (1986). For Middle English, Mossé (1952), with grammar and texts, is useful. Good selections of texts, some with detailed apparatus, can be found in Fisher and Bornstein (1974) and Rigg (1968). Kaiser (1961) prints a large, carefully edited collection with minimal apparatus. For the early Modern English period, Görlach (1991) concentrates on linguistic aspects and has a chapter on writing and spelling, while Barber (1976) is also good on attitudes toward borrowing and correctness, and on semantic change in the lexicon. Traugott (1972) has a helpful discussion of historical English syntax. Machan and Scott (1992) contains accessible essays aiming to contextualize change in English within the social contexts of the historical periods; it also has chapters on current British, American, and Australian English, and on the spread of English around the globe. Dillard (1992) is a history of American English.

Background information is conveniently found in the chapters on "Indo-European Languages" and "Germanic Languages" in Comrie (1987). Two excellent books about life in Anglo-Saxon Britain are Campbell et al. (1982) and Wood (1986), which contain photographs of artifacts, ruins, and manuscripts; Wood's book is designed to accompany a BBC television series. Evans (1986), also lavishly illustrated, describes the treasures evacuated at the site of a burial ship for a seventh-century king of an Anglo-Saxon kingdom. Also useful and readable is Laing (1982), with a bias toward the archaeological.

There are excellent recordings of English representing all periods. EAV Lexington offers *A Thousand Years of English Pronunciation,* a selection of readings by Helge Kökeritz from Old, Middle, and early Modern English texts, and *Beowulf/Chaucer,* with *Beowulf* read by John C. Pope and Chaucer by Kökeritz. On the Spoken Arts label is *Beowulf,* read in Old English by Norman Davis and Nevill Coghill. Yale University Press offers a recording (manufactured by Columbia Records) with Kökeritz reciting selections from Shakespeare. The National Council of Teachers of English has issued audiocassettes called *The Sounds of Chaucer's English* with a study pamphlet and script. Linn and Zuber (1984) offer a handy bibliography of language recordings. Finally, a series of videos called "The Story of English," hosted by Robert MacNeil, treats the history of English in two segments, "The Mother Tongue" and "A Muse of Fire"; they are readily available in libraries and video rental outlets and are highly recommended.

REFERENCES

Algeo, John. 1993. *Problems in the Origins and Development of the English Language,* 4th ed. (Fort Worth: Harcourt Brace Jovanovich).

Barber, Charles. 1976. *Early Modern English* (London: Andre Deutsch).

Baugh, Albert C., and Thomas Cable. 1993. *A History of the English Language,* 4th ed. (Englewood Cliffs, N.J.: Prentice-Hall).

Bolton, W. F. 1982. *A Living Language: The History and Structure of English* (New York: Random House).

Campbell, James, Eric John, and Patrick Wormald. 1982. *The Anglo-Saxons* (Oxford: Phaidon).

Comrie, Bernard, ed. 1987. *The World's Major Languages* (New York: Oxford University Press).

Dillard, J. L. 1992. *A History of American English* (London: Longman).

Evans, Angela Care. 1986. *The Sutton Hoo Ship Burial* (London: British Museum Publications).

Fisher, John H., and Diane Bornstein. 1974. *In Forme of Speche Is Chaunge* (Englewood Cliffs, NJ: Prentice-Hall).

Görlach, Manfred. 1991. *Introduction to Early Modern English* (Cambridge: Cambridge University Press).

Kaiser, Rolf. 1961. *Medieval English: An Old English and Middle English Anthology* (West Berlin: Rolf Kaiser).

Laing, Lloyd, and Jennifer Laing. 1982. *Anglo-Saxon England* (London: Paladin).

Linn, Michael D., and Maarit-Hannele Zuber. 1984. *The Sound of English* (Urbana, IL: National Council of Teachers of English).

Machan, Tim William, and Charles T. Scott, eds. 1992. *English and Its Social Contexts: Essays in Historical Sociolinguistics* (New York: Oxford University Press).

Millward, C. M. 1990. *A Biography of the English Language* (Fort Worth: Holt, Rinehart and Winston).

Mitchell, Bruce, and Fred C. Robinson. 1986. *A Guide to Old English: Revised with Prose and Verse Texts and Glossary* (New York: Blackwell).

Mossé, Fernand. 1952. *A Handbook of Middle English,* trans. J. A. Walker (Baltimore: Johns Hopkins Press).

Pyles, Thomas, and John Algeo. 1993. *The Origins and Development of the English Language,* 4th ed. (Fort Worth: Harcourt Brace Jovanovich).

Quirk, Randolph, and C. L. Wrenn. 1957. *An Old English Grammar* (New York: Holt, Rinehart and Winston).

Rigg, A. G. (1968). *The English Language: A Historical Reader* (New York: Appleton-Century-Crofts).

Strang, Barbara M. H. 1970. *A History of English* (London: Methuen).

Traugott, Elizabeth Closs. 1972. *A History of English Syntax* (New York: Holt, Rinehart and Winston).

Wood, Michael. 1986. *Domesday: A Search for the Roots of England* (London: BBC Books).

LANGUAGE USE

11

Speech Acts and Conversation

LANGUAGE IN USE

People use language principally as a tool for *doing* things: to ask questions, request favors, make comments, report news, give directions, offer greetings, and perform hundreds of other ordinary verbal actions in daily life. Through language, people actually *do* things: propose marriage, declare a mistrial, swear to tell the truth, fire an employee, insult a relative, invite friends to dinner, and so on. These speech *acts* are part of speech *events,* such as telephone and face-to-face conversations, student-teacher conferences, news broadcasts, office meetings, marriage ceremonies, and courtroom trials. Much of what is reported in the pages of newspapers are speech acts: claims, denials, threats, promises, and so forth (in addition to births, deaths, hurricanes, fires, robberies, and the like, which are not speech acts).

The early chapters of this book examined the structure of sentences. We now turn to the question of what people do with sentences and describe some of the ways in which sentences are used in verbal interactions. This chapter examines the nature of speech acts and how sentences are used in speech events to accomplish all that is achieved through language.

Knowing a language is not simply a matter of knowing how to encode messages and transmit them to a second party, who by decoding them understands what we intended to say. If language use were simply a matter of encoding and decoding messages—in other words, of *grammatical* competence—every sentence would have a fixed interpretation irrespective of its context of use. That is not the case, of course, as the following scenarios illustrate.

1. You are stopped by a police officer, who surprises you by informing you that you have just driven through a stop sign. "I didn't see the stop sign," you say.

2. A friend has given you directions to her new house, including the instruction to turn left at the first stop sign after the intersection of Sixth and Main. You arrive about thirty minutes late and say, "I didn't see the stop sign."

3. You are driving with an aunt, who is in a hurry to get to church. You slow down and glide through a stop sign, knowing that there is seldom traffic at that intersection on Sunday mornings. As you enter the intersection, you see a car approaching and you jam on the brakes, unsettling your aunt. "I didn't see the stop sign," you say.

To the police officer, your comment ("I didn't see the stop sign") is an *explanation* for failing to stop and a *plea* not to be cited for the violation. To the friend, your utterance is an *excuse* for your tardiness and an *explanation* that it was neither intended nor entirely your fault. To your aunt, the same sentence—an untruthful one in this case—is uttered as an *apology* for having frightened her. She recognizes your intention to apologize and says, "It's all right. But *please* be careful." The linguistic meaning of the sentence *I didn't see the stop sign* is the same in all three cases, but its utterance meaning in different contexts serves various purposes, conveys distinct messages, and is interpreted in quite different ways.

SENTENCE STRUCTURE AND THE FUNCTION OF UTTERANCES

Traditional grammar books would lead you to assume that declarative sentences make statements *(It's raining.)*, imperative sentences issue directives *(Close the door!)*, and interrogative sentences seek information *(What time is it?)*. These assumptions, however, are oversimplified and misleading. Consider the sentence *Can you shut the window?* Taken literally, its interrogative structure (marked, among other ways, by the inversion of the subject and auxiliary) asks about the addressee's *ability* to shut some particular window. If asked this question by a roommate trying to study while a marching band practiced nearby, you would likely interpret it not as a yes/no question about your abilities and therefore requiring a verbal response but as a request for a physical action—a request to shut the window.[1] Conversely, the imperative structure *Tell me your name again* would

---

[1] A request in question form is marked in speech by the absence of voice raising and sometimes in writing by the absence of a question mark *(Would you please respond promptly.)*.

normally be taken not as a directive to do something but as a request for information.

Take another case: Suppose that a knock is heard at the door, and Mary says to Alice *I wonder who's at the door.* If Mary believed that Alice knew the answer, this declarative sentence might be uttered as a request for information. More often, though, it would actually be a polite request for Alice to open the door. Finally, interrogative sentences can sometimes be used to make statements, as in Sarah's reply to Fred's question.

Fred: Is Amy pretty easy to get along with?

Sarah: Do hens have teeth?

Sarah's yes/no *question* communicates an emphatically negative *reply* to Fred's inquiry.

Two things are clear, then: First, people often employ declarative, interrogative, and imperative sentences for purposes other than making statements, asking questions, and giving commands, respectively. Second, an essential element in the interpretation of an utterance is the *context* in which it is uttered.

Recall that a sentence is a structured string of words that carries a certain meaning. An *utterance,* in contrast, is a sentence that is said, written, or signed *in a particular context* by someone *with a particular intention,* by means of which the "speaker" intends *to create an effect* on the addressee. Thus, as an interrogative sentence, *Can you shut the window?* has the meaning of a request for *information* ('Are you able to shut the window?'), but as a contextualized utterance it would more often than not be a request for *action* ('Please shut the window.'). Drawing the requisite inferences from conversation is an essential ingredient for interpreting utterances appropriately. To understand utterances, one must be skilled at "reading between the lines," and the skills one employs in using the sentences that are shaped by *grammatical competence* are part of one's *communicative competence.*

SPEECH ACTS

Besides what we accomplish through physical acts, such as cooking, bicycling, gardening, or getting on the bus, we accomplish a great deal each day by verbal acts. In face-to-face conversation, telephone calls, job application letters, notes scribbled to a roommate, and a multitude of other speech events, we perform verbal actions of different types. In fact, language is the principal means we have to greet, compliment, and insult one another, to plead or flirt, to seek and supply information, and to accomplish hundreds of other tasks in a typical day. Actions that are carried out through language are called **speech acts.**

Types of Speech Acts

Various kinds of speech acts have been identified, chiefly by philosophers taking a functional approach to sentences in use. Among the various kinds of speech acts, six have received particular attention:

Representatives   Speech acts that represent a state of affairs: assertions, statements, claims, hypotheses, descriptions, and suggestions. Representatives can generally be characterized as true or false.

Commissives   Speech acts that commit a speaker to a course of action: promises, pledges, threats, and vows.

Directives   Speech acts intended to get the addressee to carry out an action: commands, requests, challenges, invitations, entreaties, and dares.

Declarations   Speech acts that bring about the state of affairs they name: blessings, firings, baptisms, arrests, marrying, declaring a mistrial.

Expressives   Speech acts that indicate the speaker's psychological state or attitude: greetings, apologies, congratulations, condolences, and thanksgivings.

Verdictives   Speech acts that make assessments or judgments: ranking, assessing, appraising, condoning. Because some verdictives (such as calling a baseball player "out") combine the characteristics of declarations and representatives, these are sometimes called *representational declarations*.

Locutions and Illocutions

Every speech act has several principal components, two of which directly concern us here: the utterance itself and the intention of the speaker in making it. First, every utterance is represented by a sentence with a grammatical structure and a linguistic meaning; this is called the **locution** or the utterance act. Second, speakers have some intention in making an utterance, something they intend to accomplish; that intention is called an **illocution,** and every utterance consists of performing one or more illocutionary acts. (A third component of a speech act—one we will address only incidentally—is the effect of the act on the hearer; this is called the *perlocution* of the utterance, or its "uptake.")

The utterance *Can you shut the window?,* for example, can be viewed as comprising a locution and an illocution. The locution is a yes/no question about the addressee's ability to close a particular window; as such, an answer of *yes* or *no* would be appropriate. The illocution, let us assume, is a request for the addressee to shut the window; as such, convention would enable the addressee to recognize the structural question as a request for action and to comply or not. In discussions of speech acts, it is common for the illocutionary act itself to be called the speech act; thus promises, assertions, questions, directives, and so on would be speech acts.

Distinguishing among Speech Acts

How do language users distinguish among different types of speech acts? How do we know whether a locution such as *Do you have the time?* is a yes/no question (*Do you have the time* [to help me]*?*) or a request for information about the time of day? To put the matter in more technical terms, given that a locution can serve many functions, how do addressees determine the illocutionary force of a speaker's utterance? The answer of course is "context." But how do people interpret context accurately?

We begin our analysis by distinguishing between two broad types of speech acts. Compare the following two utterances.

1. I now pronounce you husband and wife.

2. It's going to be very windy today.

In an appropriate context, the first utterance creates a new relationship between two individuals; it is a declaration that effectuates a marriage. The second utterance is a simple statement or representation of a state of affairs. As any weather predictor will attest, it certainly will have no effect on the weather. As you saw earlier, utterances such as 2 that make assertions or state opinions are called *representatives*. Utterances like 1 that change the state of things are called *declarations;* they provide a striking illustration of how language in use is a form of action. Children exposed to fantastical declarations like "Abracadabra, I change you into a frog!" eventually learn that real-life objects are more recalcitrant than fairy-tale objects, but all speakers come to recognize a verbal power over certain aspects of life, especially with respect to social relationships.

With the utterance *I now pronounce you husband and wife,* the nature of the social relationship between two people can be profoundly altered. Similarly, the utterance *You're under arrest!* can have consequences for one's social freedom, as can *Case dismissed.* An umpire can change a baseball game with so simple a declaration as *Foul ball!* or *Safe!* Typically, to be effective, declarations of this type must be uttered by a specially designated person. If called by a nondesignated individual—a fan in the stands, for example—*Out!* would be a verdictive, not a declaration. Indeed, a declaration by a single designated umpire will override a contrary call by a whole team of players and an entire stadium of fans.

Appropriateness Conditions and Successful Declarations

The efficacy of any declaration depends on well-established conventions. *I now pronounce you husband and wife* can bind two individuals in marriage only if a number of conditions are satisfied: The setting must be a wedding ceremony and the utterance made at the appropriate moment; the speaker must be designated to marry others (a pastor, rabbi, justice of the peace) and must intend to marry the two individuals; the two individuals must be legally eligible to marry each other; and they must intend to become spouses. Finally, of course, the words themselves must be uttered. If any condition is not satisfied, the utterance of the words will be ineffectual as a performative. Made on a Hollywood movie set by an actor in the role of a pastor and addressed to two actors playing characters about to marry, the utterance will be vacuous (see Chapter 6).

The conventions that regulate the conditions under which an utterance serves as a particular speech act—as a question, marriage, promise, arrest, invitation—are called **appropriateness conditions,** and they can be classified into four categories. The first condition, the *propositional content condition,* requires merely that the words of the sentence be conventionally associated with the intended speech act and convey the content of the act. The locution must exhibit conventionally acceptable words for effecting the particular speech act: *Is it raining out?*, *I now pronounce you husband and wife, You are under arrest, I promise to . . . , I swear . . . .*

The second condition requires a conventionally recognized context in which the speech act is embedded. In a marriage, the situation must be a genuine wedding ceremony (however informal) at which two people intend to exchange vows in the presence of a witness. This condition is called the *preparatory condition.*

The third condition requires the speaker to be sincere in uttering the declaration. At a wedding, the speaker must intend that the marriage words should effectuate a marriage; otherwise, the *sincerity condition* will be violated and the speech act will not be successful.

Finally, the fourth condition requires that the involved parties all intend by this ceremony and the utterance of the words *I now pronounce you husband and wife* to create a marriage bond; this is the *essential condition.*

Successful Promises   Now consider the commissive *I promise to help you with your math tonight.* In order for such an utterance to be successful, it must be recognizable as a promise; in addition, the preparatory, sincerity, and essential conditions must be met. In the propositional content condition, the speaker must state the intention of helping the addressee. The preparatory condition requires that speaker and hearer are sane and responsible, that the speaker believes she is able to help with the math, and that the addressee wishes to have help. The preparatory condition would be violated if, for example, the speaker knew that she could not be there or that she was incapable of doing the math herself, or if the participants were reading the script of a movie in which the utterance appears. If the speaker knew that the hearer did not *want* help, the promise would not succeed. For the sincerity condition to hold, the speaker must sincerely intend to help the addressee. This condition would be violated (and the promise formula abused) if the speaker had no such intention. Finally, the essential condition of a promise is that the speaker must intend by the utterance to place herself under an obligation to provide some help to the hearer. These four appropriateness conditions define a successful promise.

Successful Requests and Other Speech Acts   Appropriateness conditions are useful in describing not only declarations and commissives but all other types of speech act. In a typical request *(Please pass me the salt),* the content of the utterance must identify the act requested of the hearer (passing the salt), and its form must be a conventionally recognized one for making requests. The preparatory condition includes the speaker's belief that the addressee is capable of passing the salt and that, had he not asked her to pass the salt, she would not have ventured to do so. The sincerity condition requires that the speaker genuinely desire the hearer to pass the salt. Finally, the essential condition is that the speaker intends by the utterance to get the hearer to pass the salt to him.

THE COOPERATIVE PRINCIPLE

The principles that govern the interpretation of utterances are diverse and complex, and they differ somewhat from culture to culture. Even within a single culture, they are so complex that we may wonder how language succeeds at communication as well as it does. The principles that we examine in this section, however commonsensical they may seem to western readers, are by no means universal; as you will see later, what seems commonsense to one group is not necessarily commonsense to all groups.

Despite occasional misinterpretations, people in most situations manage to understand utterances essentially as they were intended. The reason is that, without cause to expect otherwise, interlocutors normally trust that they and their conversational partners are honoring the same interpretive conventions. *Hearers* assume simply that speakers have honored the conventions of interpretation in constructing their utterances. *Speakers*, on the other hand, must make a two-fold assumption: not only that hearers will themselves be guided by the conventions, but also that hearers will trust speakers to have honored those conventions in constructing utterances. There is an unspoken pact that people will *cooperate* in communicating with each other, and speakers rely on this cooperation to make conversation efficient.

The **cooperative principle,** as enunciated by philosopher H. Paul Grice, is as follows:

Make your conversational contribution such as is required, at the stage at which it occurs, by the accepted purpose or direction of the talk exchange in which you are engaged.

This pact of cooperation touches on four areas of communication, each of which can be described in a *maxim,* or general principle.

Maxim of Quantity

First, speakers are expected to give as much information as is necessary for their interlocutors to understand their utterances, but to give no more information than is necessary. If you ask an acquaintance whether she has any pets and she answers, "I have two cats," it is the *maxim of quantity* that permits you to assume that she has no other pets. The conversational implication of such a reply is 'I have two (and only two) cats (and no other pets).' Notice that *I have two cats* would be true even if the speaker had six cats, two dogs, and a llama, so truth value is not at issue here. But if she had such other pets, you would have reason to feel deceived. While her reply was not false as far as it went, your culturally defined expectation that relevant information will not be concealed would have been violated. Listeners, in most Western cultures (but not in all cultures), expect speakers to abide by this maxim, and—equally important—speakers know that hearers believe them to be abiding by it. It is this unspoken cooperation that creates conversational implicatures.

To take another example, suppose you asked a man painting his house what color he had chosen for the living room, and he replied:

> The walls are going to be off-white to contrast with the black sofa and the Regency armchairs that I inherited from my great-aunt. (Bless her soul, she passed away last year after a long but distressing marriage to a man who really wasn't able to appreciate her extraordinary love of the visual and performing arts.) Then the trimmings will be peach except for the ones near the door, which Alice said should be salmon because otherwise they will clash with the yellow, black, and red Picasso print that I brought back from Spain—I was on vacation in Spain in August of, let's see, 1982, and I bought it then. Or was it July? I forget, actually. Gosh! time goes fast, don't you think? Oh, never mind. And the stairway leading to the bedrooms will be a pale yellow.

In providing too much information, far more than was sought or expected, the man would be as uncooperative as the woman who withheld information about her pets. The maxim of quantity provides that, in normal circumstances, speakers say just enough, that they supply no less information—and no more information—than is necessary for the purpose of the communication. Stated succinctly, the maxim of quantity requires one to *Be appropriately informative*.

Society stigmatizes individuals who habitually violate the maxim of quantity; those who give too much information are described as "never shutting up" or "always telling everyone their life story," while those who habitually fail to provide enough information are branded as sullen, secretive, or untrustworthy.

Maxim of Relevance

The second maxim directs speakers to organize their utterances in such a way that they are relevant to the ongoing context: *Be relevant at the time of the utterance*. The following interaction illustrates a violation of this maxim.

> Speaker A: How's the weather outside?
>
> Speaker B: There's a great movie on TV Thursday night.

Taken literally, B's utterance seems unrelated to what A has said immediately before; if so, it would violate the *maxim of relevance*. Because of the maxim of relevance, when someone produces an apparently irrelevant utterance, hearers typically strive to understand how it might be relevant (as a joke, perhaps, or an indication of displeasure with the direction of the conversation). Chronic violations of this maxim are characteristic of schizophrenics, whose sense of "context" differs radically from that of healthier people.

Maxim of Manner

Third, people follow a set of miscellaneous rules that are grouped under the *maxim of manner*. Summarized by the directive *Be orderly and clear,* this maxim dictates that speakers and writers avoid ambiguity and obscurity and be orderly in their utterances. In the following example, the maxim of manner is violated with respect to orderliness.

> A birthday cake should have icing; use unbleached flour and sugar in the cake; bake it for one hour; preheat the oven to 325 degrees, and beat in three fresh eggs.

This recipe is odd for the simple reason that English speakers normally follow a chronological order of events in describing a process such as baking.

Orderliness is dictated not only by the order of events: In any language there are conventions that dictate a "natural" order of details in a description. Because, in American English, more general details usually precede more specific details, when a speaker violates this rule the result appears odd.

> My hometown has five shopping malls. It is the county seat. My father and my mother were both born there. My hometown is a midwestern town of 105,000 inhabitants situated at the center of the Corn Belt. I was brought up there until I was thirteen years old.

As a third example, consider the utterance, "Ted died and was hit by lightning." If it was the lightning that killed Ted, the maxim of manner has been violated here. Although in logic *and* joins clauses whose time reference is not relevant (thus, *She studied chemistry, and she studied biology* is logically equivalent to *She studied biology, and she studied chemistry*), the maxim of manner dictates that an utterance like *They had a baby and got married* has different conversational implications from those like *They got married and had a baby*. The maxim of manner in this instance would suggest that the sequence of expressions reflects the sequence of events or is irrelevant to an appropriate interpretation. Of course English and other languages provide ways around misinterpretation: *They had a baby before they got married; First they had a baby, and then they got married; They got married after they had a baby,* and so on.

Maxim of Quality

The fourth principle governing norms of language interpretation is the maxim of quality: *Be truthful.* Speakers and writers are expected to say only what they believe to be true and to have evidence for what they say. Again, the other side of the coin is that speakers are aware of this expectation; they know that hearers expect them to honor the *maxim of quality*. Without the maxim of quality, the other maxims are of little value or interest. Whether brief or lengthy, relevant or irrelevant, orderly or disorderly, all lies are false. Still, it should be noted that the maxim of quality applies principally to assertions, and certain other "representative" speech acts. Expressives and directives can hardly be judged true or false in the same sense.

It is useful to reflect further on the maxim of quality. On the one hand, it is this maxim that constrains interlocutors to tell the truth and to have evidence for their statements. Ironically, however, it is this maxim that also makes lying possible. Without the maxim of quality, speakers would have no reason to expect hearers to take their utterances as true, and without the assumption that one's interlocutors assume one to be telling the truth, it would be impossible to tell a lie. Lying requires that speakers are expected to be telling the truth.

VIOLATIONS OF THE COOPERATIVE PRINCIPLE

It is no secret that people sometimes violate the maxims of the cooperative principle. Certainly not all speakers are completely truthful on all occasions; others, though truthful, have not observed that efficiency is the desired Western norm in conversational interaction. More interestingly, speakers are sometimes forced by competing cultural norms or other external factors to violate a maxim. For example, irrespective of your aesthetic judgment, you may feel constrained to say *What a lovely painting!* to a host who is manifestly proud of some newly finished art work. The need to adhere to social conventions of politeness sometimes invites people to violate maxims of the cooperative principle.

Indirect Speech Acts

As mentioned earlier, interrogative structures can be used to make polite requests for action, imperative structures can be used to ask for information, and so on. Such uses of an utterance with one meaning for a different purpose play a frequent role in ordinary interaction, as in this exchange between colleagues who have stayed at the office after dark.

> Sue: Is the boss in?
>
> Alan: The light's on in her office.
>
> Sue: Oh, thanks.

Alan's answer makes no apparent reference to the information Sue is seeking. Thus in theory it would appear to violate the maxim of relevance. Yet Sue is satisfied with the answer. Recognizing that the *literal* interpretation of Alan's reply violates the maxim of relevance but assuming that as a cooperative interlocutor Alan is being relevant, Sue seeks an *indirect* interpretation. To help her, she knows certain facts about their boss's habits: that she works in her own office, that she does not work in the dark, and that she is not in the habit of leaving the light on when out of her office. Relying on this information, Sue infers an interpretation from Alan's utterance: Alan believes the boss is in.

Alan's reply is an example of an indirect speech act. **Indirect speech acts** involve an apparent violation of the cooperative principle but are in fact indirectly cooperative. For example, an indirect speech act can be based on an apparent violation of the maxim of quality. When we describe a friend as *someone who never parts with a dime,* we don't mean it literally; we are exaggerating. By exaggerating the information, we may seem to be flouting the maxim of quality. But listeners will usually appreciate that the statement should not be interpreted literally and will make an appropriate adjustment in their interpretation. Similarly, we may exclaim in front of the World Trade Center *That's an awfully small building!* This utterance too appears to violate the maxim of quality in that we are expressing an evaluation that is manifestly false. But speakers readily spot the irony of such utterances and take them to be indirect speech acts intended to convey an opposite meaning to what the sentence means literally.

Characteristics of Indirect Speech Acts   From the prior examples, we can identify four characteristics of indirect speech acts.

1. Indirect speech acts violate at least one maxim of the cooperative principle.
2. The literal meaning of the locution of an indirect speech act differs from its intended meaning.
3. Hearers and readers identify indirect speech acts by noticing that an utterance has characteristic 1 and by assuming that the interlocutor is following the cooperative principle.
4. As soon as they have identified an indirect speech act, hearers and readers identify its intended meaning with the help of knowledge of the context and of the world around them.

Thus, to interpret indirect speech acts, hearers use the maxims to sort out the discrepancy between the literal meaning of the utterance and an appropriate interpretation for the context in which it is uttered.

Indirect Speech Acts and Shared Knowledge   One prerequisite for a successful indirect speech act is that interactors share sufficient background about the context of the interaction, about each other and their society, and about the world in general. If Fred asks Ellen *Are you done with your sociology paper?* and she replies *Is Rome in Spain?*, he will certainly recognize the answer as an indirect speech act. But whether or not he can interpret it will depend on his knowledge of geography.

Using and understanding indirect speech acts requires familiarity with both language and society. To cite an example from a distant culture, when speakers of the Polynesian language Tuvaluan want to comment on the fact that a particular person is in the habit of talking about himself, they may say *Koo tagi te tuli ki tena igoa* 'The plover bird is singing its own name.' The expression derives from the fact that the plover bird's cry sounds like a very sharp "tuuuuuliiiii," from which speakers of Tuvaluan have created the word *tuli* to refer to the bird itself. Thus the expression has become an indirect way of criticizing the trait of singing one's own praises. In order to interpret the utterance as an indirect speech act, one must be familiar not only with the plover bird's cry and the fact that it resembles the bird's name but also with the fact that Tuvaluans view people who talk about themselves as being similar to a bird "singing its own name." The amount of background information about language, culture, and environment needed to interpret indirect speech acts is thus considerable.

POLITENESS

Indirect speech acts appear to be a complicated way of communicating. Not only must you spot them, but you must then go through a complex reasoning process to interpret them. It would be more efficient to communicate directly, one might think. The fact is, though, that indirect speech acts have uses besides asking and answering questions, criticizing others, and so on. They sometimes add humor and sometimes show politeness. Ellen's indirect reply of ''Is Rome in Spain?'' in answer to Fred's question suggests 'Don't be ridiculous; of course I'm not done.' Questions such as *Can you shut the window?* are perceived as more polite and less intrusive and abrasive than a command such as *Shut the window!* One message that indirect speech acts can convey is 'I am being polite toward you.' Indirect speech acts are thus an efficient tool of communication: they can convey two or more messages simultaneously.

Positive and Negative Politeness

There are two basic aspects to being polite. The first rests on the fact that human beings respect one another's presence, privacy, and physical space. We *avoid* intruding on other people's lives, try *not* to be overly inquisitive about their activities, and take care *not* to impose our presence on them. This is called *negative politeness* and involves avoidance. On the other hand, when we let people know that we enjoy their company, feel comfortable with them, like something in their personality, or are interested in their well-being, we show *positive politeness*. While everyone expects both negative and positive politeness, the first requires us to leave people alone, while the second requires us to do the opposite. Fortunately, the needs for negative and positive politeness usually arise in different contexts. When we shut ourselves in a room or take a solitary walk on the beach, we affirm our right to negative politeness. When we attend a party, invite someone to dinner, or call friends on the telephone to check up on them, we extend positive politeness.

In conversation, interlocutors give one another messages about their needs for negative and positive politeness and acknowledge the other's needs for both types as well. The expectation that others will not ask embarrassing questions about our personal lives stems from the need for negative politeness. When you tell a friend about personal problems and expect sympathy, you are seeking positive politeness. Excusing yourself before asking a stranger for the time acknowledges the stranger's right to negative politeness (that is, privacy). When we express the hope of meeting an interlocutor at a later date *(Let's get together sometime soon!),* we acknowledge that person's need for positive politeness (that is, sociability).

SPEECH EVENTS

A political rally or debate, a public speech, a classroom lecture, a religious sermon, and a disk jockey's ''Top 40 countdown'' are all speech events—social activities in which language plays a particularly important role. ''Speech'' events need not involve speaking: personal letters, short stories, shopping lists, office memos, and birthday cards are also speech events.

Conversation provides the matrix in which native languages are acquired, and it stands out as the most frequent, most natural, and most representative of verbal interactions. A person can spend a lifetime without writing a letter, composing a poem, or debating public policy, but only in rare circumstances does anyone *not* have frequent conversation with companions. Conversation is an everyday speech event. We engage in it for entertainment (gossiping, passing the time, affirming social bonds) and for accomplishing work (getting help with studies, renting an apartment, ordering a meal at a restaurant). Whatever its purpose, conversation is a most basic verbal interaction.

Though movie-screen lovers can conduct heart-to-heart conversations with their backs to each other, conversation usually involves individuals facing each other and taking turns at speaking, neither talking simultaneously nor letting the conversation lag. In some societies, even with several conversationalists in a single conversation, there are only tenths of a second between turns and extremely little overlap in speaking. At the beginning of a conversation, people go through certain rituals, greeting one another or commenting about the weather. Likewise, at the end of a conversation people don't simply turn their backs and walk away; they take care that all participants have finished what they wanted to say and only then utter something like *I have to run* or *Take care*. Throughout the entire interaction, conversationalists maintain a certain level of orderliness—taking turns, not interrupting one another too often, and following certain other highly structured but implicit guidelines for conversation.

These guidelines can be considered norms of conduct that govern how conversationalists comport themselves. Though it is tempting to think of relaxed conversation as essentially free of rules or constraints, the fact is that many rules are operating, and the unconscious recognition of these rules helps identify particular interactions as conversations.

THE ORGANIZATION OF CONVERSATION

If it seems surprising that casual conversation should be organized by rules, the reason is that, as in most speech events, more attention is paid to content than to organization; we take for granted the organization of conversations. A conversation can be viewed as a series of speech acts—greetings, inquiries, congratulations, comments, invitations, requests, refusals, accusations, denials, promises, farewells. To accomplish the work of these speech acts, some organization is essential: We take turns at speaking, answer questions, mark the beginning and end of a conversation, and make corrections when they are needed. To accomplish such work expeditiously, interlocutors could give one another traffic directions.

Okay, now it's your turn to speak.

I just asked you a question; now you should answer it, and you should do so right away.

If you have anything else to add before we close this conversation, do it now because I am leaving in a minute.

Such instructions would be inefficient, however, and would deflect attention from the content. In unusual circumstances, conversationalists do invoke the rules

(*Would you please stop interrupting?* or *Well, say something!*), but such cases are avoided whenever possible because they underscore the fact that rules have been violated and thus can seem impolite. Conversations are usually organized covertly, and the organizational principles provide a discreet interactional framework.

The covert architecture of conversation must achieve the following: Organize turns so that more than one person has a chance to speak and the turn taking is orderly; allow for interlocutors to anticipate what will happen next and, where there is a choice, how the selection is to be decided; provide a way to repair glitches and errors when they occur.

Turn Taking and Pausing

Participants must tacitly agree on who should speak when. Normally we take turns at holding the floor and do so without overt negotiation. A useful way to uncover the conventions of turn taking is to observe what happens when they break down. When a participant fails to take the floor despite indications that it is his turn, other speakers usually pause, and then someone else begins speaking. In this example, Alice repeats her question, assuming that Bill either did not hear or did not understand it the first time.

Alice: Is there something you're worried about?

[pause]

Alice: Is there something you're worried about?

Bill: No, but I was wondering if you could help me with a problem I'm having with my brother.

Turn-taking conventions are also violated when two people attempt to speak simultaneously. In the next example, the beginning and end of the overlap are marked with brackets.

Speaker 1. After John's party we went to Fred's house.

Speaker 2: So you— so you— you—

            [   ]

Speaker 3:   What— what— time did you get there?

When such competition arises in casual conversation, a speaker may either quickly relinquish the floor or turn up the volume and continue speaking. Both silence and simultaneous speaking are serious problems in conversation, which the turn-taking norms are designed to minimize.

Different cultures have different degrees of tolerance for silence between turns, overlaps in speaking, and competition among speakers. In some cultures, including certain Native American nations and the Eskimos, people sit comfortably together in silence. At the other extreme, in French and Argentinian cultures several conversationalists often talk simultaneously and interrupt each other more frequently than Americans typically feel comfortable doing.

However much tolerance they may have for silences and overlaps, people from all cultures appear to regulate turn taking in conversation in basically similar ways. To do this, there are two basic rules: (1) speakers signal when they wish to end their turn, either selecting the next speaker or leaving the choice open; (2) the next speaker takes the floor by beginning to talk. This simple principle, which seems second nature to us, regulates conversational turn taking very efficiently.

Turn-Taking Signals   Speakers signal that their turn is about to end with verbal and nonverbal cues. As most turns end in a complete sentence, the completion of a sentence may signal the end of a turn. A sentence ending in a tag question *(isn't it?, are you?)* explicitly invites an interlocutor to take the floor.

> Speaker A: Pretty windy out today, isn't it?
>
> Speaker B: Sure is!

The end of a turn may also be signaled by sharply raising or lowering the pitch of your voice, or by drawling the last syllable of the final word of the turn. In very informal conversations, one common cue is the phrase *or something.*

> Speaker 1: So he was behaving as if he had been hit full speed by a truck, or something.
>
> Speaker 2: Really?

Other expressions that can signal the completion of a turn are *y'know, kinda, I don't know* (or *I dunno*), and a trailing *uhm.* As with *y'know,* some of these can also function within a turn for the speaker to keep the floor while thinking about what to say next. Another way to signal the completion of a turn is to pause and make no attempt to speak again.

> Speaker A: I really don't think he should've said that at the meeting, particularly in front of the whole committee. It really was pretty insensitive.
>
> [pause]
>
> Speaker B: Yeah, I agree.

Of course, speakers often have to pause in the middle of a turn to think about what to say next, or to emphasize a point, or to catch a breath. To signal that a speaker has finished a turn, the pause must be long enough, although what can constitute "long enough" differs from culture to culture.

Nonverbal as well as verbal signals can indicate the end of a turn. Although in speaking the principal role of gestures is to support and stress what we say, continuing our hand gestures lets our interlocutors know that we have more to say. Once we put our hands to rest, our fellow conversationalists may infer that we are yielding the floor.

In a more subtle vein, eye gaze can help control floor holding and turn taking. In mainstream American society, speakers do not ordinarily stare at their interlocutors; instead, their gaze goes back and forth between their listener and another point in space, alternating quickly and almost imperceptibly. But because listeners usually fix their gaze on the speaker, a speaker reaching the end of a turn can simply return her gaze to an interlocutor and thereby signal her own turn to listen and the interlocutor's to speak. In cultures in which listeners look away while speakers stare, a speaker who wishes to stop talking simply looks away. While eye gaze plays a supportive role in allocating turns, the success of telephone conversations makes it clear that eye gaze is not essential in the allocation of turns.

Getting the Floor   In multiparty conversations, the speaker holding the floor can select who will speak next, or the next speaker can select himself. In the first instance, the floorholder may signal the choice by addressing the next speaker by name *(What have you been up to these days, Helen?)* or by turning toward the selected next speaker. If the floorholder does not select the next speaker, anyone may take the floor, often by beginning the turn at an accelerated pace so as to block other potential claims for the floor.

When the floorholder does not select who will talk next, competition can arise, as in the following example, in which overlaps are indicated with square brackets.

Speaker 1: Who's gonna be at Jake's party Saturday night?

          [pause]

Speaker 2: Todd to—

                [   ]

Speaker 3: I don't kn—

          [pause]

Speaker 2: Todd told me—

             [   ]

Speaker 3:   I don't know who's—

          [short pause]

Speaker 2: [to speaker 3] Go ahead!

Speaker 3: Todd told me a lotta people would be there.

Speaker 2: Yeah, that's what I was gonna say. I don't know who's gonna be there, but I know it'll be pretty crowded.

Friendly participants strive to resolve such competition quickly and smoothly.

Social or situational inequality between conversationalists (boss and employee, parent and child, doctor and patient) is often reflected in how often and when participants claim the floor. In American work settings, superiors commonly initiate conversations by asking a question and letting subordinates report. Thus subordinates hold the floor for longer periods of time than superiors; subordinates perform while superiors act as spectators. In some cultures, superiors talk while subordinates listen.

Adjacency Pairs

One useful mechanism in the covert organization of conversation is that certain turns have specific follow-up turns associated with them. Questions take answers. Greetings are returned by greetings, invitations by acceptances or refusals, and so on. Certain sequences of turns go together, as in these exchanges.

Question and Answer

Speaker 1: Where's the milk I bought this morning?

Speaker 2: On the counter.

Invitation and Acceptance

Speaker 1: I'm having some people to dinner Saturday, and I'd really like you to come.

Speaker 2: Sure!

Assessment and Disagreement

Speaker 1: I don't think Harold would play such a dirty trick on you.

Speaker 2: Well, you obviously don't know Harold very well.

Such **adjacency pairs** comprise two turns, one of which directly follows the other. In a question/answer adjacency pair, the question is the first part, the answer the second part. Here are other examples of adjacency pairs.

Request for a Favor and Granting

Speaker 1: Can I use your phone?

Speaker 2: Sure.

Apology and Acceptance

Speaker 1: Sorry to bother you this late at night.

Speaker 2: No, that's all right. What can I do for you?

Summons and Acknowledgment

Mark: Bill!

Bill: Yeah?

The Structure of Adjacency Pairs   Three characteristics of adjacency pairs can be noted. First, the two parts are contiguous and are uttered by different speakers.

An interaction in which a speaker makes a statement before answering a question that has been posed sounds strange (and can provoke anger) because the parts of the adjacency pair are not consecutive:

Speaker 1: Where's the milk I bought this morning?

Speaker 2: They said on the radio that the weather would clear up by noon. It's on the counter.

Second, the two parts are ordered. Except on certain TV game shows, the answer to a question cannot precede the question; in ordinary conversation, one cannot accept an invitation before it has been offered; and an apology cannot be accepted before uttered (except sarcastically).

Third, the first and second parts must be appropriately matched to avoid such odd exchanges as the following.

Speaker 1: Do you want more coffee?

Speaker 2: That's all right, you're not bothering me in the least!

Insertion Sequences   Occasionally, the requirement that both parts be adjacent is violated in a systematic and socially recognized way.

Speaker 1: Where's the milk I bought this morning?

Speaker 2: The skim milk?

Speaker 1: Yeah.

Speaker 2: On the counter.

In order to provide an accurate answer to Speaker 1's question, Speaker 2 must first know the answer to another question and thus initiates an *insertion sequence*—another adjacency pair that interrupts and puts the original adjacency pair "on hold." The interaction thus consists of one adjacency pair embedded in another one, as in the following telephone conversation.

main adjacency pair
⎡ Speaker 1:   Can I speak to Mr. Higgins?
⎢   Speaker 2: May I ask who's calling? ⎤   secondary
⎢   Speaker 1: Arthur Wilcox.   ⎥   adjacency pair
⎣ Speaker 2:   Please hold.   (insertion sequence)

Preferred and Dispreferred Responses   Certain kinds of adjacency pairs are marked by a preference for a particular type of second part. For example, requests, questions, and invitations have preferred and dispreferred answers. Compare the following interactions, in which (1) has a preferred (positive) second part and (2) has a dispreferred (negative) second part.

(1) Speaker 1: I really enjoyed the movie last night. Did you?

Speaker 2: Yeah, I thought it was pretty good.

(2) Speaker A: I really enjoyed the movie last night. Did you?

Speaker B: No, I thought it was pretty crummy, though I can see how you could've liked certain parts of it.

To an assessment also, the preferred second part is agreement.

Speaker 1: I think Ralph's a pretty good writer.

Speaker 2: I think so too.

Speaker A: I think Ralph's a pretty good writer.

Speaker B: Well, I can see how you'd find his imagery interesting, but apart from that I don't really think he writes well at all.

Dispreferred second parts tend to be preceded by a pause and to begin with a hesitation particle such as *well* or *uh*. Preferred second parts tend to follow the first part without a pause and to consist of structurally simple utterances.

Speaker 1: Would you like to meet for lunch tomorrow?

Speaker 2: Sure!

Speaker A: Would you like to meet for lunch tomorrow?

Speaker B: Well, hmm, let's see. . . .
Tommorrow's Tuesday, right?
I told Harry I'd have lunch with him.
And I told him so long ago that I'd feel bad canceling. Maybe another time, okay?

In addition, dispreferred second parts often begin with a token agreement or acceptance, or with an expression of appreciation or apology, and usually include an explanation.

Speaker 1: Can I use your phone?

Speaker 2: Oh, I'm sorry, but I'm expecting an important long-distance call. Could you wait ten minutes?

Opening Sequences

Conversations are opened in socially recognized ways. Before beginning their first conversation of the day, conversationalists normally greet each other, as when two office workers meet in the morning.

Jeff: Mornin', Stan!

Stan: Hi. How's it goin'?

Jeff: Oh, can't complain, I guess.
　　　　Ready for the meeting this afternoon?

Stan: Well, I don't have much choice!

Greetings exemplify opening sequences, utterances that ease people into a conversation. They convey the message 'I want to talk to you.'

Greetings are usually reserved for acquaintances who have not seen each other for a while, or as opening sequences for longer conversations between strangers. Some situations do not require a greeting, as with a stranger approaching in the street to ask for the time: *Excuse me, sir, do you know what time it is?* The expression *Excuse me, sir* serves as an opening sequence appropriate to the context. Thus greetings are not the only type of opening sequences.

Very few conversations do not begin with some type of opening sequence, even as commonplace as the following.

Speaker A: Guess what.

Speaker B: What?

Speaker A: I broke a tooth.

Conversationalists also use opening sequences to announce that they are about to invade the personal space of their interlocutors. Here, two friends are talking on a park bench next to a stranger; at a pause in their conversation, the stranger interjects:

Stranger: Excuse me, I didn't mean to eavesdrop, but I couldn't help hearing that you
　　　　　　were talking about Dayton, Ohio. I'm from Dayton.

[Conversation then goes on among the three people.]

It is not surprising that opening sequences should take the form of an apology in such situations

Finally, opening sequences may serve as a display of one's voice to enable the interlocutor to recognize who is speaking, especially at the beginning of telephone conversations. Here, the phone has just rung in Alfred's apartment.

Alfred: Hello?

Helen: Hi!

Alfred: Oh, hi, Helen! How you doin'?

In the second turn, Helen displays her voice to enable Alfred to recognize her. In the third turn, Alfred indicates his recognition and simultaneously provides the second part of the greeting adjacency pair initiated in the previous turn.

Opening Sequences in Other Cultures   In many cultures, the opening sequence appropriate to a situation in which two people meet after not having met for a while is an inquiry about the person's health, as in the American greeting *How are you?* Such inquiries are essentially formulaic and not meant literally. Indeed, most speakers respond with a conventional upbeat formula (*I'm fine* or *Fine, thanks*) even when feeling terrible. In other cultures, the conventional greeting may take a different form. Traditionally, Mandarin Chinese conversationalists ask *Nǐ chī guo fàn le ma?* 'Have you eaten rice yet?' When two people meet on a road in Tonga, they ask *Ko hoʔo ʔalu ki fe?* 'Where is your going directed to?' These greetings are as formulaic as the American *How are you?*

In formal contexts, or when differences of social status exist between participants, many cultures require a lengthy and formulaic opening sequence. In Fiji, when an individual visits a village, a highly ceremonial introduction is conducted before any other interaction takes place. This event involves speeches that are regulated by a complex set of rules governing what must be said, and when, and by whom. This ceremony serves the same purpose as opening sequences in other cultures.

Functions of Opening Sequences   One last aspect of opening sequences in which cultural differences are found is the relative importance of their various functions. In American telephone conversations, opening sequences serve primarily to identify speakers and solicit the interlocutor's attention. In France, opening sequences normally apologize for invading someone's privacy.

Person called: Allo?

Caller: Allo? Je suis désolé de vous déranger.
Est-ce que j'peux parler à Marie-France?
('Hello? I'm terribly sorry for disturbing you. Can I speak to Marie-France?')

In an American telephone conversation, such an opening sequence is not customary. Thus, in two relatively similar cultures, the role played by the opening sequence in a telephone call is different. As a result, the French can find Americans intrusive and impolite on the telephone, while Americans are puzzled by French apologetic formulas, which they find pointless and exceedingly ceremonious.

Closing Sequences

Conversations must also be closed appropriately. A conversation can be closed only when the participants have said everything they wanted to say. Furthermore, a conversation must be closed before participants begin to feel uncomfortable about having nothing more to say. As a result, conversationalists carefully negotiate the timing of closings, seeking to give the impression of wanting neither to rush away nor to linger on.

These objectives are reflected in the characteristics of the closing sequence. First of all, a closing sequence includes a conclusion to the last topic covered in the conversation. In conclusions, conversationalists often make arrangements to meet at a later time or express the hope of so meeting. These arrangements may be genuine, as in the first example here, or formulaic, as in the second.

Speaker 1: Okay, it's nice to see you again.
            I guess you'll be at Kathy's party tonight.

Speaker 2: Yeah, I'll see you there.

Speaker A: See you later!

Speaker B: See ya!

The first step of a closing sequence helps ensure that no one has anything further to say. This is accomplished by a simple exchange of short turns such as *okay* or *well*. Typically, such preclosing sequences are accompanied by a series of pauses between and within turns that decelerate the exchange and prepare for closing down the interaction. In the following example, Speaker 2 takes the opportunity to bring up one last topic, after which Speaker 1 initiates another closing sequence.

Speaker 1: Okay, it's nice to see you again.
            I guess you'll be at Kathy's party tonight.

Speaker 2: Yeah, I'll see you there.

Speaker 1: Okay.

Speaker 2: I hear there's gonna be lots of people there.

Speaker 1: Apparently she invited half the town.

Speaker 2: Should be fun.

Speaker 1: Yeah.

Speaker 2: Okay.

Speaker 1: Okay. See you there.

Speaker 2: Later!

Sometimes, after a preclosing exchange, speakers refer to the original motivation for the conversation. In a courtesy call to inquire about someone's health, the caller sometimes refers to this fact after the preclosing exchange.

Caller: Well, I just wanted to see how you were doing after your surgery.

Person called: Well that was really nice of you.

If the purpose of a conversation was to seek a favor, this short exchange might take place:

Speaker 1: Well, listen, I really appreciate your doing this for me.

Speaker 2: Forget it. I'm glad to be of help.

Finally, conversations close with a parting expression: *bye, goodbye, see you, catch you later.*

The striking thing about closings is their deceptive simplicity. In fact, however, they are complex. Participants exercise great care not to give the impression that they are rushing away or that they want to linger on, and they try to ensure that everything on the unwritten agenda of any participant has been touched on. However informal and abbreviated, closing sequences are characterized by a great deal of negotiated activity.

Conversational Routines

Both openings and closings are more routinized than the core parts of conversations. Core parts are relatively less predictable, and whereas children are trained not to ask certain kinds of questions, they are drilled on the proper way to open and close conversations. Because of the routinized nature of openings and closings, conversations can be begun and, equally important, ended expeditiously.

Repairs

A **repair** takes place in conversation when a participant feels the need to correct herself or another speaker, to edit a previous utterance, or simply to restate something, as in these examples, in which a dash indicates an abrupt cutoff.

1. Speaker: I was going to Mary's— uh, Sue's house.

2. Speaker: And I went to the doctor's to get a new— uh— a new whatchamacallit, a new prescription, because my old one had expired.

3. Speaker 1: Look at these daffodils, aren't they pretty?

    Speaker 2: They're pretty, but they're narcissus.

4. Speaker 1: Todd came to visit us over the spring break.

    Speaker 2: What?

    Speaker 1: I said Todd was here over the spring break.

In 2, the trouble source is the fact that the speaker cannot find a word. In 4, Speaker 2 indicates a repair because he has not heard or has not understood Speaker 1's utterance. Conversationalists thus make repairs for a variety of reasons.

To initiate a repair is to signal that one has not understood or has misheard an utterance, that a piece of information is incorrect, or that one is having trouble finding a word. To resolve a repair, someone must repeat the misunderstood or misheard utterance, correct the inaccurate information, or supply the word. To initiate a repair, we may ask a question, as in 4; repeat part of the utterance to be repaired, as in example 5 below; abruptly stop speaking, as in example 6, or use particles and expressions like *uh, I mean,* or *that is,* as in example 1.

5. Speaker: I am sure—I am *absolutely* sure it was him that I saw last night prowling around.

6. Speaker 1: And here you have what's called the—

     [pause]

     Speaker 2: The carburetor?

     Speaker 1: Yeah, that's right, the carburetor.

Repairs can be initiated and resolved by the person who uttered the words that need to be repaired or by another conversationalist. There are thus four possibilities: repairs that are self-initiated and self-repaired; repairs that are other-initiated and self-repaired; repairs that are self-initiated and other-repaired; and repairs that are other-initiated and other-repaired. Of these possibilities, conversationalists show a strong preference for self-initiated self-repairs, which are least disruptive to the conversation and to the social relationship between the conversationalists. In general, conversationalists wait for clear signals of communicative distress before repairing an utterance made by someone else. The least preferred pattern is for repairs that are other-initiated and other-repaired. Individuals in the habit of both initiating and repairing utterances for others get branded as poor conversationalists or know-it-alls.

Found in many cultures, these preference patterns reflect a widespread but unspoken rule that all participants in a conversation among equals be given a chance to say what they want to say by themselves. Conversationalists provide assistance to others in initiating and resolving repairs only if no other option is available.

Politeness: An Organizational Force in Conversation

Violations of the turn-taking principles by interrupting or by failing to take turns are considered impolite. Turning one's back on interlocutors at the end of a conversation without going through a closing sequence is also stigmatized by the conventions of politeness. Other aspects of politeness are more subtle but nevertheless play an important role in structuring conversation.

There are also covert ways in which we communicate negative and positive politeness. When we expect interlocutors to allow us to both initiate and resolve a repair ourselves, we are expecting them to respect our right to make a contribution to the conversation without intrusion from others; that is, we are asking them to show negative politeness. Similarly, we recognize another person's need for negative politeness when, instead of ending a conversation, we initiate a preclosing exchange, affording the interlocutor a chance to say something further before closing. In contrast, when we initiate a conversation with a greeting, we convey concern about the addressee's health and well-being, thereby acknowledging the other's need for positive politeness. Many of the principles of conversational architecture can be explained in terms of politeness and the recognition of the politeness needs of others.

CROSS-CULTURAL COMMUNICATION

When people of different cultures have different norms about what type of politeness is required in a particular context, trouble can easily arise. We have described how callers in France begin telephone conversations with an apology; such apologies seldom form part of the opening sequence of an American telephone conversation. Obviously, members of the two cultures view telephone conversations differently: Americans generally see the act of calling as a sign of positive politeness, while the French tend to view it as a potential intrusion.

When two cultures are in close contact with each other, such differences can have unfavorable consequences. In the United States, social conflicts sometimes arise between African Americans and whites as a result of differences in the norms of communication in particular contexts. Take flirting, for example. White working-class men and women tend to be more attentive to each other's needs for negative politeness and, generally speaking, make relatively few overt references to sexual matters; they allude to, rather than state, their interest in each other. In contrast, African-American working-class men and women may make sexual overtures more bluntly and do not shy away from making explicit complimentary remarks about physique; their patterns of flirting thus place greater emphasis on positive politeness needs than on negative politeness needs. As long as both parties share the same norms of flirting, no problems arise. But when two people holding different views of the social and cultural norms appropriate to a particular situation flirt with one another, it is not difficult for misunderstanding to occur.

As a consequence of such variability, people from different cultures often misinterpret each other's signals. In the conversations of Athabaskan Indians, a pause of up to about one and a half seconds does not necessarily indicate the end of a turn, and Athabaskans often pause that long within a turn. In contrast, most European-Americans consider a pause of more than one second sufficient to signal the end of a turn (though there may be social variation). When Athabaskan Indians and European-Americans interact with each other, the latter often misinterpret the Athabaskans' mid-turn pauses as end-of-turn signals and feel free to claim the floor. From the Athabaskans' perspective, the European-Americans' claim of the floor at this point constitutes an interruption, and with the same situation occurring time and again in interactions between the two groups, negative stereotypes arise. Athabaskans find European-Americans rude, pushy, and uncontrollably talkative, while the European-Americans find Athabaskans conversationally uncooperative, sullen, and incapable of carrying on a coherent conversation. Carrying those stereotypes unwittingly into a classroom, white teachers may judge Indian students unresponsive or unintelligent, for their unspoken cultural expectations would have students speaking up, interacting, and being quick in their responses. While these tend to be the reactions of children in mainstream European-American culture, Athabaskan children, honoring the norms of their own culture, do not have these characteristics, at least not to the same degree. Though most people are totally unaware of such subtle cross-cultural differences, they can have profound social consequences.

SUMMARY

Utterances are used to accomplish things like asserting, promising, pleading, and greeting. Actions accomplished through language are called *speech acts*. That language is commonly used to perform actions is most clearly illustrated by declarations. All speech acts, whether declarations or not, can be described with a set of four appropriateness conditions, each of which describes one aspect of, or prerequisite for, a successful speech act: the content of the speech act, the preparatory condition, the sincerity condition, and the essential condition.

Language users are bound by an unspoken pact, which they adhere to in most normal circumstances and expect others to adhere to. This *cooperative principle* consists of four maxims—of quantity, quality, relevance, and manner. On occasion, a speaker or writer may flout a maxim to signal that the literal interpretation of the utterance is not the intended one. To encode and decode the intended meaning of such indirect speech acts, people use patterns of conversational implicature based on knowledge of their language, their society, and the world around them. Indirect speech acts convey more than one message; they are commonly used for politeness and humor. Respecting other people's needs for privacy expresses negative politeness, while showing interest and displaying sympathy shows positive politeness.

A *speech event* is a social activity in which spoken or written language plays an important role. Speech events are structured; appropriate verbal and nonverbal behavior characteristic of particular speech events can be described systematically. Conversations are organized according to a number of principles that regulate various aspects of conversational behavior. Turn taking is regulated by one set of norms. Adjacency pairs are structured by a local set of organizational principles; many have preferred and dispreferred second parts. Still other organizational principles shape conversational openings and closings. The organization of repairs can be described with a set of rules that rank different repair patterns in terms of preference; self-initiated self-repairs are favored. At the root of many organizational principles in conversation is the need for human beings to display both positive and negative politeness to one another. When and where negative and positive politeness behaviors are appropriate is determined by culture-specific norms. Because cross-cultural variation is considerable in the organization of polite behavior in conversation, miscommunication of intent is common.

EXERCISES

1. Make a list of the headlines on the first two pages of a daily newspaper. Indicate which of the headlines report physical actions and which report speech acts.

2. Observe a typical lecture meeting of one of your courses and identify the characteristics that define it as a lecture (as distinct from an informal conversation, workshop, seminar, or lab meeting). Identify characterizing features in the areas listed. To what

extend is there room for variability in how a lecture is conducted (depending, for example, on the personality of the participants)? List several signals that a lecture has stopped being a lecture.

(1) setting (physical setting, clothing, social identity of the participants, and so on)

(2) nonverbal behavior of the participants (body movement, stance and position with respect to each other, and so on)

(3) verbal behavior of the participants (turn taking, openings, closings, assignment of pair parts among participants, and so on)

(4) topic (what is appropriate to talk about? to what extent can this be deviated from? and so on)

3. Make a tape recording of the first minute of a radio interview. Transcribe what is said during that first minute in as much detail as possible (indicating, for example, who talks, when pauses occur, and what hesitations occur). Label each turn as to its illocutionary force (greeting, inquiry, compliment, and so on). Then describe in detail the strategies used in opening the radio interview. Illustrate your description with specific examples taken from your transcript.

4. Make a tape recording of the first forty-five seconds of a broadcast of the evening news on radio or television. Transcribe what is said during that period in as much detail as possible. Then answer the following questions, citing specific illustrations from your transcript.

a. What effect do radio or television newscasters try to achieve initially?

b. How is this accomplished? Describe two strategies, using specific illustrations.

c. Suppose you played your tape recording to friends without identifying what was taped. Exactly what features would help them recognize it as a recording of the evening news? Cite three specific telltale characteristics other than content.

d. Is your first news item a report of a physical action or a speech act?

5. Observe the following interaction between two people who are working at nearby desks.

Anne: Ed?

Ed: Yeah?

Anne: Do you have a ruler?

Anne's first turn is an opening sequence. What does it signal, and what does Ed's response indicate? Why did Anne not merely open with *Do you have a ruler?*

6. The next time you talk on the telephone to a friend, observe the distinctive characteristics of talk over the telephone, and take notes immediately after you hang up. Identify several ways in which a telephone conversation differs from a face-to-face conversation. Recreate specific linguistic examples from your telephone conversation to illustrate your points.

7. Consider the following excerpts, each of which contains a repair. For each excerpt, determine whether the repair is (a) self-initiated and self-repaired, (b) self-initiated and other-repaired, (c) other-initiated and self-repaired, or (d) other-initiated and other-repaired.

   a. Pierre: What's sales tax in this state?

      James: Five cents on the dollar.

      Patricia: *Five* cents on the dollar? You mean *six* cents on the dollar.

      James: Oh, yeah, six cents on the dollar.

   b. Anne: There's a party at Rod's tonight. Wanna go?

      Sam: At Rod's? Rod's outta town!

      Anne: I mean Rick's.

   c. Peter: And then he comes along an' tells me that he's dropping his accounting— uh, his economics class.

      Frank: Yeah, he told me the same thing the next mornin'.

   d. Rick: His dog's been sick since last month an' he can't go to the wedding because he's gotta take care of him.

      Alice: Well, actually, his dog's been sick for at least two months now. So it's nothin' new.

   e. Samantha: Do you remember the names of all their kids? The oldest one is Daniel, the girl's Priscilla, then there's another girl— what's her name again?

      Reginald: Susie, I think.

      Samantha: Yeah, Susie, that's it.

   f. Ellie: What do they charge you for car insurance?

      Ted: Two thousand bucks a year, but then there's a three-hundred-dollar deductible. Three hundred or one hundred— I can't remember.

      Ellie: Probably's one hundred, right?

      Ted: Yeah, I think you're right. One hundred sounds right.

   g. Sarah: He's been cookin' all day for that dinner party.

      Anne: Actually he's been cooking for three days now.

   h. Will: There wasn't much I could do for her. She needed five thousand bucks to pay for tuition and I just didn't have it.

      David: I thought it was four thousand.

      Will: Yeah, four thousand, but still I didn't have that much.

8. Consider the following excerpts, all of which are prestructures initiating conversation. Describe in detail the structure and the function of each prestructure using the terms

turn (or *turn-taking*) *signal, adjacency pair, first part, second part,* and *claiming the floor.*

Larry: Guess what.

Lauren: What?

Larry: Pat's coming tomorrow.

Tom: [reading the newspaper] I can't believe this!

Fred: What?

Tom: Congress passed that new immigration law.

Ruth: [chuckles while reading a book]

Anne: What're you chuckling about?

Ruth: This story, it's so off the wall!

9.   Consider the following excerpt from a conversation among three friends.

Cindy: Heard from Jill recently? She hasn't written or called in ages.

Larry: Yeah, she sent me a postcard from England.

Barb: From England?

Larry: Oh, maybe it was from France, I can't remember.

Cindy: What's she doin—

Barb: No, I know it must've been from France 'cause she was gonna stay there all year.

Cindy: What's she doin' in France?

Larry: Why are you asking about her?

Cindy: I don't know, I've just been thinkin' about her.

Larry: She's on some sort of exchange program. Studyin' French or somethin'.

Cindy: Sounds pretty nice to me.

Larry: Yeah. Well, I don't know. She said she was tired of Europe and wants to come home.

a.   In the conversation here, how many turns does each interlocutor have?

b.   Identify an example of each of the following in the conversation: *turn-taking signal, claiming the floor, preferred response, dispreferred response, repair, trouble source, initiation,* and *resolution.*

c.   Identify an *adjacency pair* in the conversation, giving the name of the *first part* and *second part.*

10.   Conversations in fiction and drama and re-created in movies or on the stage differ from the ordinary conversations of daily living. The following is an excerpt of a

conversation from Part III of Isak Dinesen's autobiographical novel *Out of Africa* (New York: Random House, 1937).

> "Do you know anything of book-keeping?" I asked him.
>
> "No. Nothing at all," he said, "I have always found it very difficult to add two figures together."
>
> "Do you know about cattle at all?" I went on. "Cows?" he asked. "No, no. I am afraid of cows."
>
> "Can you drive a tractor, then?" I asked. Here a faint ray of hope appeared on his face. "No," he said, "but I think I could learn that."
>
> "Not on my tractor though," I said, "but then tell me, Emmanuelson, what have you even been doing? What are you in life?"
>
> Emmanuelson drew himself up straight. "What am I?" he exclaimed. "Why, I am an actor."
>
> I thought: Thank God, it is altogether outside my capacity to assist this lost man in any practical way; the time has come for a general human conversation. "You are an actor?" I said, "that is a fine thing to be. And which were your favourite parts when you were on the stage?"
>
> "Oh I am a tragic actor," said Emmanuelson, "My favourite parts were that of Armand in 'La Dame aux Camelias' and of Oswald in 'Ghosts'."

On the basis of this example, analyze the differences between the organization of conversations quoted in writing and the organization of actual conversations. Why do these differences exist?

SUGGESTIONS FOR FURTHER READING

The analysis of speech acts has been an enterprise chiefly of philosophers. Austin (1962) is a set of twelve readable lectures laying out the nature of locutionary acts, illocutionary acts, and perlocutionary acts. Grice (1975) formulates the cooperative principle and enumerates the conversational maxims discussed in this chapter. Searle (1976) discusses the classification of speech acts and their syntax, while Searle (1975) lays out the structure of indirect speech acts. Besides these primary sources, there are several good discussions of the work of Austin, Grice, and Searle in various chapters of Cole and Morgan (1975), Levinson (1983), and Wardhaugh (1991).

Profoundly differing from the philosophical traditions in their methodological approach, the inductive studies of the conversation analysts are technical and challenging to read: Turn taking was first analyzed systematically by Sacks et al. (1974), closings by Schegloff and Sacks (1973), and repairs by Schegloff et al. (1977). Atkinson and Heritage (1984) and Schenkein (1978) are good collections of papers on various aspects of the organization of conversation. More accessible are these textbooks on conversation analysis and language use in various informal contexts: Levinson (1983), McLaughlin (1984), Chapters 8 and 10 of Ellis and Beattie (1986), and Chapters 10 and 12 of Wardhaugh (1991); Wardhaugh (1985) is very accessible.

The theoretical background to the study of speech events is presented in Goffman (1974) and Hymes (1974). Goffman (1981) presents interesting and entertaining analyses of various speech events including lectures and radio talk. Kendon et al. (1975) and Goodwin (1981) describe how talk and gestures are integrated in conversation. The organization of conversation in the workplace is investigated by Boden (1988), and verbal communication (and miscommunication) between doctors and patients is analyzed in West (1984). The characterization of communication between subordinates and superordinates as spectator/performer or performer/spectator was proposed in Bateson (1972), which lays out the philosophical foundation for the study of human communication. Cross-social and cross-cultural differences in the organization of conversation are analyzed in Gumperz (1982), Gumperz (ed., 1982), Kochman (1981), and Scollon and Scollon (1981). A few examples from the latter two books were used in this chapter. Gumperz et al. (1979), a one-hour video on miscommunication between East Indian immigrants and the British in institutional settings in England, is a moving demonstration of the painful difficulties that can arise from differing conversational norms across cultural boundaries. Godard (1977) is an interesting study of Franco-American differences in behavior on the telephone. Tannen (1990) discusses misunderstanding between the sexes. Brown and Levinson (1987) and various chapters of Levinson (1983) and Wardhaugh (1991) discuss politeness. Drew and Heritage (1993) is a collection of essays discussing interaction in institutional settings.

REFERENCES

Atkinson, J. Maxwell, and John Heritage, eds. 1984. *Structures of Social Action: Studies in Conversation Analysis* (Cambridge: Cambridge University Press).

Austin, John. 1962. *How to Do Things with Words* (New York: Oxford University Press).

Bateson, Gregory. 1972. *Steps to an Ecology of Mind* (New York: Bantam).

Boden, Deirdre. 1988. *The Business of Talk: Organizations in Action* (Cambridge: Polity).

Brown, Penelope, and Stephen C. Levinson. 1987. *Politeness: Some Universals in Language Usage* (Cambridge: Cambridge University Press); repr. from Esther Goody, ed., *Questions and Politeness: Strategies in Social Interaction* (Cambridge: Cambridge University Press), pp. 56–311.

Cole, Peter, and Jerry L. Morgan, eds. 1975. *Syntax and Semantics 3: Speech Acts* (New York: Academic).

Drew, Paul, and John Heritage, eds. 1993. *Talk at Work* (Cambridge: Cambridge University Press).

Ellis, Andrew, and Geoffrey Beattie. 1986. *The Psychology of Language and Communication* (New York: Guilford).

Godard, Daniele. 1977. "Same Setting, Different Norms: Phone Call Beginnings in France and the United States," *Language in Society* 6:209–219.

Goffman, Erving. 1974. *Frame Analysis: An Essay on the Organization of Experience* (New York: Harper & Row).

———. 1981. *Forms of Talk* (Philadelphia: University of Pennsylvania Press).

Goodwin, Charles. 1981. *Conversational Organization: Interaction between Speakers and Hearers* (New York: Academic).

Grice, H. Paul. 1975. "Logic and Conversation," in Peter Cole and Jerry L. Morgan, eds. *Syntax and Semantics 3: Speech Acts* (New York: Academic), pp. 41–58.

Gumperz, John J. 1982. *Discourse Strategies* (Cambridge: Cambridge University Press).

———, ed. 1982. *Language and Social Identity* (Cambridge: Cambridge University Press).

Gumperz, John J., T. C. Jupp, and C. Roberts. 1979. *Crosstalk: A Study of Cross-cultural Communication* (London: National Centre for Industrial Language Training and BBC).

Hymes, Dell. 1974. *Foundations in Sociolinguistics* (Philadelphia: University of Pennsylvania Press).

Kendon, Adam, Richard M. Harris, and Mary Ritchie Key, eds. 1975. *Organization of Behavior in Face-to-Face Interaction* (The Hague: Mouton).

Kochman, Thomas. 1981. *Black and White Styles in Conflict* (Chicago: University of Chicago Press).

Levinson, Stephen C. 1983. *Pragmatics* (Cambridge: Cambridge University Press).

McLaughlin, Margaret L. 1984. *Conversation: How Talk Is Organized* (Beverly Hills, CA: Sage).

Sacks, Harvey, Emanuel A. Schegloff, and Gail Jefferson. 1974. "A Simplest Systematics for the Organization of Turn-taking in Conversation," *Language* 50:696–735.

Schegloff, Emanual A., Gail Jefferson, and Harvey Sacks. 1977. "The Preference for Self-correction in the Organization of Repair in Conversation," *Language* 53:361–382.

Schegloff, Emanuel A., and Harvey Sacks. 1973. "Opening Up Closings," *Semiotica* 7: 289–327.

Schenkein, Jim, ed. 1978. *Studies in the Organization of Conversational Interaction* (New York: Academic).

Scollon, Ron, and Suzanne B. K. Scollon. 1981. *Narrative, Literacy and Face in Interethnic Communication* (Norwood, NJ: Ablex).

Searle, John R. 1975. "Indirect Speech Acts," in Peter Cole and Jerry L. Morgan, eds. *Syntax and Semantics 3: Speech Acts* (New York: Academic), pp. 59–82.

———. 1976. "A Classification of Illocutionary Acts," *Language in Society* 5:1–23.

Tannen, Deborah. 1990. *You Just Don't Understand: Women and Men in Conversation* (New York: Ballantine).

Wardhaugh, Ronald. 1985. *How Conversation Works* (New York: Blackwell).

———. 1991. *An Introduction to Sociolinguistics,* 2nd ed. (New York: Blackwell).

West, Candace. 1984. *Routine Complications: Troubles in Talk Between Doctors and Patients* (Bloomington: Indiana University Press).

12

Registers: Language Variation across Situations of Use

INTRODUCTION: THE CLOCKS OF BALLYHOUGH

Ballyhough railway station in Ireland has two clocks, which disagree by some six minutes. When a helpful traveler pointed out this fact to a porter, the porter's reply was "Faith, sir, if they was to tell the same time, why would we be having two of them?" Though the porter's logic may be faulty when applied to railway clocks, it may legitimately be applied to the many competing languages that exist throughout the world. If every language variety were to do the same work as the others, there would be no need for more than one. Each language variety serves a distinct purpose. Among the socially significant functions of a language is affirmation of the identity and unity of its speakers; languages can also mark speakers as distinct from members of other groups. It is possible to imagine a fantasy world in which all social groups spoke alike, with no dialect variations of any kind. For better or worse, this imaginary situation is not what we find in the real world. Rather, a multitude of tongues exists, each with several regional and social dialects, all changing continuously so that each generation speaks differently from those preceding it.

In the next chapter, we discuss language variation across different groups of speakers. In this chapter we discuss language variation that is associated not with groups of language *users* but with various *situations of use*. We explore the varieties of language that individuals in communities use in the course of daily living. To cite some simple examples, we don't talk to close friends the way we talk to our teachers, nor do we write to our parents the same way we would write to an attorney or a minister. In different circumstances, we all vary our use of language forms. In some societies, different situations call for different languages altogether; in other societies, different situations call for alternative varieties of a single language. Language varieties that are characteristic of particular situations of use are called **registers.**

LANGUAGE VARIATION WITHIN A COMMUNITY

Language Choice in Multilingual Societies

You might assume that in multilingual countries like Switzerland, Belgium, and India, different languages are spoken by different groups of people. Typically, though, each language is systematically allocated to specific social situations. In speech communities employing several languages, language choice is not arbitrary. Instead, a particular setting, such as school or government, may favor one language, and other languages will be appropriate to other speech situations. Where one language is appropriate, another will be inappropriate. Though there may be roughly equivalent expressions in two languages, the social meaning that attaches to use of one language generally differs from that attached to use of the other. As a result, speakers must attend to the social import of language choice, however unconsciously that choice may be made.

Linguistic Repertoires in Brussels, Teheran, and Los Angeles' Koreatown   The use of selected varieties from two languages among government workers in the capital of Belgium illustrates the nature of language choice among various languages in one European community.

> Government functionaries in Brussels who are of Flemish origin do not always speak Dutch to *each other,* even when they all know Dutch *very* well and *equally* well. Not only are there occasions when they speak French to *each other* instead of Dutch, but there are some occasions when they speak standard Dutch and others when they use one or another regional variety of Dutch with each other. Indeed, some of them also use different varieties of French with each other as well, one variety being particularly loaded with governmental officialese, another corresponding to the non-technical conversational French of highly educated and refined circles in Belgium and still another being not only a 'more colloquial French' but the colloquial French of those who are Flemings. All in all, these several varieties of Dutch and of French constitute the *linguistic repertoire* of certain social networks in Brussels.[1]

[1] Fishman (1972), pp. 47–48.

The language variety that Brussels residents choose for use is occasioned by the setting in which the talk takes place, by the topic, by the social relations among the participants, and by certain other features of the situation. In general, the use of Dutch is associated with interaction that is informal and intimate, whereas French has more official or highbrow connotations. Given these associations, the choice of French or Dutch carries an associated social meaning in addition to its referential meaning.

We use the term **linguistic repertoire** for the set of language varieties exhibited in the speaking and writing patterns of a speech community. As in Brussels, the linguistic repertoire of any speech community may consist of several languages and may include several varieties of each language. Here we describe two.

At least into the mid 1970s, there was considerable multilingualism in the Iranian city of Teheran. Christian families spoke Armenian or Syriac at home and in church, Persian at school, all three in different situations while playing or shopping, and Azerbaijani Turkish at shops in the bazaar. Moslem men from northwest Iran, who were working as laborers in the booming capital, spoke a variety of Persian with their supervisors at construction sites but switched to a variety of Turkish with their fellow workers and to a local Iranian dialect when they visited their home villages on holidays; in addition, they listened daily to radio broadcasts in standard Persian and heard passages from the Koran recited in Arabic. It was not uncommon for individuals of any social standing to command as many as four or five languages and to deploy them in different situations.

To take another example, the Korean-speaking community in Los Angeles supports bilingual institutions of various sorts: banks, churches, shops, and a wide range of services from pool halls and video rentals to hotels and construction companies. At several banks all the tellers are bilingual, and in the course of a day's work they switch often between Korean and English. As the tellers alternate between Korean-speaking and English-speaking patrons, the language in which they conduct business alternates just as naturally.

Switching Varieties within a Language

If we examine the situation in Europe, we see examples of language-internal switching in addition to switching between languages. Brussels residents switch not only between French and Dutch but also among varieties of French and among varieties of Dutch. In Hemnes, a village in northern Norway, residents speak two quite distinct varieties of Norwegian. Ranamål is a local dialect and serves to identify speakers of that region. Bokmål, one of two forms of standard Norwegian (the other being Nynorsk), is in use in Hemnes for education, religion, government transactions, and the mass media. All members of the community control these two varieties and regard themselves at any given time as speaking one *or* the other. There are differences of pronunciation, morphology, lexicon, and syntax, and speakers do not perceive themselves as mixing the two varieties in their speech. We illustrate with a simple sentence meaning 'Where are you from?'

Ranamål: ke du e ifrå

Bokmål: vor ær du fra

While Bokmål is the expected variety in certain well-defined situations, the residents of Hemnes do not accept the use of Bokmål among themselves outside those situations. In situations in which Ranamål is customarily used, the employment of Bokmål would signal social distance and even contempt for community spirit. In Hemnes, to use Bokmål with fellow locals is to *snakkfint* or *snakk jalat* 'put on airs.' As the researchers who reported these findings wrote, "Although locals show an overt preference for the dialect, they tolerate and use the standard in situations where it conveys meanings of officiality, expertise, and politeness toward strangers who are clearly segregated from their personal life."[2] Regard for the social situation is thus important even in choosing varieties of the same language.

SPEECH SITUATIONS

As we have seen in Hemnes, Koreatown, Brussels, and Teheran, language switching can be triggered by a change in any one of several situational factors, including the setting and purpose of the communication, the person being addressed, the social relations between the interlocutors, and the topic.

Elements of the Speech Situation

If we define a speech situation as the coming together of various significant situational factors, such as location, topic, and social relations, then each speech situation in a bilingual community will generally allow for only one of the two languages to be used. Table 12-1 illustrates this concept for a bilingual community in Los Angeles.

As you see from the table, in situation A a variety of Spanish is appropriate; in situation C a variety of English. Only in the relatively rare case of situation E might an individual have a genuine choice between Spanish and English without calling attention to the language chosen. In situation E, a choice is allowed because of the conflict between intimacy (which usually requires Spanish, as in situations A or B) and an academic topic (for which English is usually preferred).

TABLE 12-1
Linguistic Repertoire

Speech Situation	Relation of Speakers	Location	Topic Type	Spanish	English
A	intimate	school	not academic	X	
B	intimate	home	not academic	X	
C	not intimate	school	not academic		X
D	not intimate	home	academic		X
E	intimate	school	academic	X	X

[2] Blom and Gumperz (1972), pp. 433–434.

TABLE 12-2
Elements of a Speech Situation

Purpose	Setting	Participants
Activity	Topic	Speaker
Goal	Location	Addressee
	Mode	Social roles of speaker and addressee
		Character of audience

Table 12-2 charts certain aspects of a speech situation that may require a change in language variety.

Related to *purpose,* the kind of activity that is involved is crucial. Are you making a purchase, giving a sermon, telling a story? The activity may have an influence on the selection of a language. Are you entertaining, reporting information, affirming a social relationship? Greeting a friend or inviting an aunt to dinner?

As to *setting,* you may switch from one language to another as the topic switches, from a topic of local interest, say, to one of national concern; or from a personal topic to one about your studies. Even the location can influence language choice in that you might well use one language in a university setting but a different one in church or at home for otherwise equivalent situations. The mode—that is, whether you are speaking or writing—can certainly influence the forms of language selected.

As to the *participants,* the identity of the speaker will influence the language choice, as will the person being addressed. Speakers of probably all languages adapt their utterances to the age of their addressee. In some societies, the older the person, the higher his or her social standing; younger people must address older people more respectfully than they address peers. In French the second person singular pronoun 'you' has two forms: The grammatically singular form *tu* is used when addressing a social equal or as an expression of intimacy with an addressee, while the plural form *vous* is reserved for a person of higher social status or to mark social distance (as well as for addressing more than one person, irrespective of status). A younger person addressing an older person is expected to use *vous,* not *tu,* unless the older person is a close relative. The French pronoun system illustrates one way in which morphology may vary according to the age of the addressee. Persian also shows many of the same patterns, and so do several European tongues.

Also with respect to participants, it is not just the social identity of speaker and addressee that is relevant but their roles in the particular speech situation. A judge, for example, typically speaks one variety at home and another in the courtroom. A parent who works as a teacher and has his child for a student may speak different varieties at home and at school, even when the topic and the addressee are the same.

The various aspects of the speech situation come together in a particular choice of language variety. In each bilingual situation—whether a general one, such as home or church, or a specific one, such as discussing politics in a cafe with a close friend—only one variety is usually appropriate. In fact, people get so accustomed to speaking a particular language in a given setting that they often have difficulty communicating in another language in that setting, no matter how familiar the other language may be in other settings.[3] As a result, switching between language varieties is very common throughout the world.

REGISTERS IN A MONOLINGUAL SOCIETY

Thus, the recognition that there are settings and speech situations in multilingual societies in which one language or another is appropriate has a direct parallel in monolingual speech communities, in which varieties of a single language constitute the entire linguistic repertoire. Consider the difference between the full forms of careful speech and the abbreviations and reductions characteristic of fast speech that occur in face-to-face relaxed communication: not only workaday contractions like *won't* and *I'll* but reduced sentences like [ǰityɛt] for 'Did you eat yet?'

To take a second example, you know that you do not typically use the same terms in referring to certain body parts when speaking to friends, family, and physician. The term *collarbone* might be used at home, with *clavicle* reserved for use with a physician; either could be used with friends, depending on other aspects of the speech situation. The choices that you make for certain other body parts will be much more striking.

The distribution of alternative terms for the same referent may seem arbitrary and without communicative benefit; indeed, in the case of body parts, all the terms may be known and used by all the parties under equivalent circumstances. A physician speaking with her own physician may use the term *clavicle;* with her family and friends, however, she will be expected to use the same terms the rest of us would use with equivalent addressees in comparable speech situations. When nonmedical people address a physician, they use the terms appropriate to discussion of a medical situation.

Since all the terms would be equally well understood and could communicate referential meaning equally well, the choice of a socially appropriate variant is *cognitively* unhelpful. One may ask, then, why language forms differ in different speech situations. The answer is that different forms for the same content can indicate your affective relationship to salient aspects of the situation (setting, addressee, topic, and so on). Such variation as has lasted for centuries in a language can be assumed to be serving a fundamental need of human communication.

Thus, just as a multilingual linguistic repertoire allocates different language varieties to different speech situations, so does a monolingual repertoire. For all speakers—monolingual and multilingual—there is marked variation in the forms of language used for different activities, addressees, topics, and settings. These marked forms of language constitute the registers of a linguistic repertoire. By choosing among the varieties, situational variation is both created and communicated.

---

[3] Exceptions to this generalization include professional translators, bilingual educators, and certain business people who are regularly engaged in negotiations with members of their own and another culture.

From a relatively young age, everyone learns to control several varieties for use in different speech situations. No one is limited to a single variety of a single language. For some, the language varieties they control belong to one language; for others, they are drawn from more than one language. Just which speech situations—which purposes, settings, participants—prompt a different variety depends on the norms in particular cultures. In one society, the presence of in-laws may call for a different variety (as it does in Dyirbal and several other aboriginal Australian societies); in other societies, the presence of in-laws may have no independent influence on the selection of an appropriate language variety, whereas the presence of children or members of the opposite sex may be crucial. In Western societies, there are many words that adults avoid saying in the presence of children. And of course there are differences associated with mode, whether language is written or spoken, as you will see shortly.

MARKERS OF REGISTER

As languages and dialects differ from one another at every grammatical level, so registers can differ in vocabulary, phonology, morphology, syntax, and semantics. There may also be different interactional patterns in different speech situations—how the allocation of turns is decided, for example. In addition, there are rules governing nonlinguistic behavior, such as physical proximity, face-to-face positioning, standing, and sitting, that also accompany register variation; both the interactional patterns and the body language are beyond the scope this book, and we mention them only incidentally.

When you find characteristic features of a register at one level of the grammar, you can expect to find corresponding features at other grammatical levels as well. For example, to describe the register known as legalese we must describe its characteristic lexicon, sentence structure, and semantics, as well as its characteristic terms of address, rules of interaction, and so forth.

Lexical Markers

Registers vary along certain dimensions. For example, people generally speak (and write) in markedly different ways in formal and informal situations. Formality and informality can be seen as opposite poles of a situational continuum along which the various levels of language may vary.

We begin our analysis of register variation with an examination of word choice. The five words that follow generally mean the same thing and can have the same referent, but it wouldn't be difficult for you to rank them according to degrees of formality. It would be surprising if you did not generally agree that these words should be ranked as follows, with the least formal word first: *pissed, pickled, high, drunk, intoxicated.*

Think of other terms for the state that results from having consumed too much alcohol. In one context, to suggest inebriation may require the word *intoxicated,* while in another a more appropriate expression may be *drunk* or *under the influence.* The words *bombed* and *pissed* are also sometimes used, especially by younger people in situations of considerable informality. One thesaurus lists more than 125 words or phrases for 'intoxicated.' But by no means are they situationally equivalent.

Not every word that can be glossed as 'inebriated' is suitable for use on all occasions when reference to intoxication is intended. Word choice can indicate quite different attitudes toward the state, the addressees, the person being described, and so on. It can also index the speech situation in which the term is being used—as intimate or distant, formal or informal, serious or jocular, and so forth. Different expressions for "intoxication" have different connotations, depending on the situations of use with which they are customarily associated. These affiliated situations of use add a dimension of meaning that is quite distinct from the referential meaning of a word.

Imagine the following dialogue between a judge and a defendant at an arraignment in a courtroom:

> Judge: I see that the cops say you were pickled last night and were driving an old jalopy down the middle of the road. True?
>
> Defendant: Your honor, if I might be permitted to address this allegation, I should like to report that I was neither inebriated nor under the influence of an alcoholic beverage of any kind; I imbibed no booze last evening.

Of the many possible observations about this exchange, we make just a few. In the first place, the judge's language seems out of place: Words like *cops, pickled,* and *jalopy* strike us as inappropriate for a judge in a courtroom, perhaps even bizarre. As for the defendant's response, it too seems out of place, especially following the very informal speechways of the judge. Indeed, the defendant's language might well seem too formal, too elevated, even if the judge had used more formal language. There is an incongruity in the defendant's using more formal terms than the judge. It also seems odd to have the informal word *booze* used in an utterance in which the more formal *imbibed, inebriated, beverage,* and *allegation* also occur.

Compare the judge's language in the first example with the following, which is more appropriate to the speech situation.

> Judge: You are charged with driving a 1982 blue Ford while under the influence of alcohol. How do you plead?

Thus we see that within a single language certain registers are appropriate to specific circumstances. Like all language varieties, registers constrain which words can be used together and which others cannot be, even though their use together would not violate grammatical constraints. These kinds of *co-occurrence restrictions* also apply to phonological and syntactic patterns, as you'll see.

Address Terms   Appropriate forms of address differ in different situations. Judges are addressed in court as *Your Honor,* though they may well be addressed by their friends and neighbors quite differently. Each of us can be addressed in several ways: by first name *(Sally);* family name *(Smith);* family name preceded by a title *(Mister, Doctor, Professor);* the second person pronoun *(you);* terms showing respect *(Sir, Madam).* Cardinals in the Catholic church are addressed as *Your Eminence,* the Queen of England as *Your Majesty* (or *Ma'am).* At the opposite end of the scale of respect are terms of disrespect, such as *you bastard* or *you son of a bitch.* A given individual may be addressed in different ways in the course of several speech situations. A judge's spouse does not employ *Your Honor* as a form of address, nor do parents normally address their children with a title of any sort, nor children (of any age) ordinarily address their parents with a title and name.

Slang   Perhaps the most infamous register, certainly one with a familiar name, is *slang,* the variety used in situations of extreme informality, often with rebellious undertones or an intention of distancing its users from certain mainstream values. Slang is therefore particularly popular among underworld groups and among teenagers. But by no means is its use limited to such groups, for slang has its wellsprings in specialized groups of all sorts, from physicians and computer ''hacks'' to police officers and stock brokers. Slang and argot, however, are not the same. Argot is the specialized vocabulary of a group, often an occupational or recreational group, but argot is not limited to situations of extreme informality and it generally lacks rebellious undertones.

It is risky providing examples of slang in a book such as this, because much slang is as changing as fashions in clothing. Still, there are dictionaries of slang, and that suggests that some slang expressions have more than a very brief existence. It would be safer to ask student readers of this book, whose social circumstances likely put them within earshot of more slang than teachers, to provide your own examples, and in an exercise at the end of this chapter, that is exactly what happens. In the meanwhile, the following, taken from the dust jacket of a 1986 slang dictionary, may be illustrative: *Barbie Doll, bean counter, bells and whistles, cover your ass, designer drug, glitterati, kick ass, mallie, pocket pool, puzzle palace,* and *tits and zits.* If any of these happens to be unfamiliar, some of your classmates may be able to provide a gloss (or you can check the dictionary, which is identified in the ''Suggestions for Further Reading'' at the end of the chapter).

Slang has a legitimate place in the linguistic repertoire of speech communities. Like all registers, however, its effectiveness depends crucially on the circumstances of its use. In appropriate circumstances anyone of any socioeconomic or educational status can use slang, usually without calling attention to its use.

The observation that the effectiveness of a particular register depends not on the socioeconomic status of the user but on the circumstances of use applies equally to all registers: Even the most formal varieties of English are not appropriate to all occasions, any more than a tuxedo is suited to all occasions. A tuxedo at the beach is as out of place as a bathing suit at a church wedding.

Just as informal clothing can extend its welcome from informal circumstances into somewhat more formal circumstances, so slang expressions often climb up the social ladder, becoming acceptable in more formal circumstances. The words *mob* and *pants* are among many that were considered slang at an earlier period of their history but can now be used in any circumstances. As words become used

TABLE 12-3

Percentage of Pronunciation of *-ing* as /ıŋ/ in Three Speech Situations among Four Social Groups in New York City

	Speech Situation		
	Casual	*Careful*	*Reading*
Lower class	20	47	78
Working class	51	69	89
Lower-middle class	68	79	99
Upper-middle class	95	96	100

in more formal circumstances, they lose their status as slang, and other slang terms develop in their stead.[4]

Slang is a variety for which we have a name in English; that is, we recognize it as a register by a combination of the lexical features that it exhibits and the circumstances in which it is used, and we name it. Slang differs from other registers in that it is characterized chiefly by lexical peculiarities.

Phonological Markers

Different registers are marked not only by word choice but by all other levels of the grammar, and for spoken registers this includes phonology. In a study of New York City speechways that we will discuss in detail in the following chapter, considerable variation was uncovered among all groups of speakers in different situations of use.

Table 12-3 presents figures for the pronunciation of *-ing* as /ıŋ/ in three speech situations. (Here we focus on the variation that occurs in the speech of a single social group across different situations. In the next chapter we examine the variation across the social groups themselves.) The speech situations in this case consist of three kinds of interaction in the course of a sociolinguistic interview in the homes of the respondents. The style of the interview, with its interlaced questions and answers, can be regarded as "careful" speech. In addition, respondents were asked to read a set passage aloud; this "reading" style was taken to be representative of more careful speech than that represented by interview style. At the end of the interview, in order to prompt relaxed speech, the interviewer asked respondents whether they had ever had a close call with death. This gambit usually elicited a very relaxed, unguarded variety, here called "casual" speech.

In their casual speech, lower-class respondents pronounced the *-ing* suffix as /ıŋ/ 20 percent of the time (and as /ın/ the other 80 percent). In their careful speech, the occurrence of /ıŋ/ increases to 47 percent (while /ın/ decreases to 53 percent).

---

[4] Though this climb up the social ladder is quite common for slang expressions, some are apparently designed to remain forever suited only to the most informal circumstances. *Bones* meaning 'dice' was used by Chaucer in the fourteenth century, and *beat it* meaning 'scram' by Shakespeare.

TABLE 12-4

Percentage of -ing Pronounced as /ɪŋ/ in Two Speech Situations by Males and Females in Los Angeles

	Speech Situation	
	Joking	*Arguing*
Males	54	76
Females	72	79

When reading a passage aloud, the same lower-class respondents pronounce /ɪŋ/ 78 percent of the time (and /ɪn/ only 22 percent). This represents a dramatic increase of /ɪŋ/ pronunciations as the speech situation becomes more formal. Exactly the same overall pattern holds for the other three groups: Each class increases its pronunciation of /ɪŋ/ as formality increases.

In data gathered by college students in Los Angeles, both males and females increased the percentage of /ɪŋ/ in arguments, as compared with joking. The figures are given in Table 12-4. Though men and women differ in their use of this phonological variable (a topic we return to in Chapter 13), both exploit it in the same way as a marker to signal different situations of use.

A study in Norwich (England) uncovered similar patterns of variation across registers. Among five different socioeconomic status groups, the middle-middle class (the highest ranking group in the study) *always* used /ɪŋ/ in the formal register of reading style, while lower-working-class residents *never* used it in their most casual speech. Thus, at the extremes of socioeconomic status and situational formality, the range of difference was 100 percent, but all classes used both pronunciations in their speech. As the figures in Table 12-5 show, the pattern in Norwich is the same as in New York City: Each socioeconomic status group uses /ɪŋ/ most in reading style and least in its casual speech, with an intermediate percentage for careful speech. It is clear that on this variable, three widely separated English-speaking communities use /ɪŋ/ differentially to mark situations of greater and lesser

TABLE 12-5

Percentage of Pronunciation of -ing as /ɪŋ/ in Three Speech Situations among Five Social Groups in Norwich

	Speech Situation		
	Casual	*Careful*	*Reading*
Lower-working class	0	2	34
Middle-working class	5	12	56
Upper-working class	13	26	85
Lower-middle class	58	85	90
Middle-middle class	72	97	100

TABLE 12-6
Number of Contractions per Thousand Words of British English in Different Situations of Use

Situation of Use	Contractions
Telephone conversation with friends	59.9
Telephone conversation with strangers	48.8
Interviews	25.4
Broadcasts	21.5
Romantic fiction	19.0
Spontaneous speeches	17.8
Prepared speeches	13.3
Science fiction	6.5
Press	1.5
Academic journals	0.1
Official documents	0.0

formality. It should be stressed that it is not the absolute percentage that marks situations but the *relative* percentage with respect to other situations. The data indicate that this linguistic marker of situation is a continuous variable, able to indicate fine distinctions in degrees of formality across a wide range of speech situations.

As another example of phonological variation (or its equivalent spelling variation) across different speech situations, we examine the distribution of ordinary contractions like *can't, won't,* and *I'll* in different situations of use, from telephone conversations between personal friends and between strangers to writing in newspapers and academic journals. Even in so straightforward a linguistic feature as contractions, English speakers exhibit differential use of forms in different speech situations. The figures in Table 12-6 are based on a large sample of written and spoken British English and represent the average number of contractions per one thousand words.

Syntactic Markers

Syntactic variables also mark situations of use. As an example, consider the occurrence of sentence-final prepositions. You may recall from your school days that sentence-final prepositions are disfavored by prescriptive textbooks and some teachers: *That's the teacher I was telling you ABOUT* as compared with *That's the teacher ABOUT whom I was telling you.* Using the same large number and wide range of texts as for contractions, the number of sentence-final prepositions per thousand prepositions for several spoken and written registers is given in Table 12-7. This table does not show the same continuous incline from least formal to most formal that we saw with contractions. Instead, there is a major distinction between spoken varieties and nonfiction writing, with fiction writing (which includes fictional dialogue) having intermediate values between the two. In the spoken texts, somewhere between thirty-three and fifty-six prepositions per thousand

TABLE 12-7
Number of Sentence-Final Prepositions per Thousand Prepositions in Different Situations of Use in British English

Situation of Use	Sentence-Final Prepositions	
Face-to-face conversation	56	
Telephone conversation with friends	50	
Interviews	50	Speech
Spontaneous speeches	48	
Broadcasts	39	
Prepared speeches	33	
Science fiction	21	
Romantic fiction	18	Fiction writing
General fiction	14	
Academic journals	8	
Press	4	Nonfiction writing
Official documents	1	

appear in sentence-final position. In nonfiction writing, however, in all situations of use, the number of final prepositions is less than for all spoken registers; the range is between one and eight per thousand. Thus for this feature there is a marked difference between speech and writing.

As a second example of syntactic variation across different situations of use, examine this brief passage of *legalese*—another register that is identified by name in English.

> Upon request of Borrower, Lender, at Lender's option prior to full reconveyance of the Property by Trustee to Borrower, may make Future Advances to Borrower. Such Future Advances, with interest thereon, shall be secured by this Deed of Trust when evidenced by promissory notes stating that said notes are secured hereby.

This passage illustrates several characteristic syntactic features of legalese.

1. Frequent use of passive structures: *shall be secured, are secured*

2. Preference for repetition of nouns in lieu of pronouns: *Lender/at Lender's option, promissory notes/said notes, Future Advances/Such Future Advances*

3. Avoidance of indefinite and definite articles: *Upon request, of Borrower, to Borrower, Lender, at Lender's, by Trustee*

Semantic Markers

A given word often carries different meanings in different registers. Consider, for example, the word *notes:* As used in the legalese passage, *notes* means promissory notes, or IOUs. In its everyday meaning, however, *notes* refers to brief, informal written messages on any topic. Among other words with one meaning in common everyday use but with a different meaning in legal register are the following:

> hearing, action, to continue, to alienate, to serve, save, party, reasonable man, executed, consideration, suit, sentence, rider, motion

Not only lawyers but also some of their clients may give specialized meanings to words. Criminal argot (now understood by a wider stripe of people than those with connections to the underworld) contains many words and expressions that are in common use but carry a different meaning when used in the context of crime or criminal behavior. The following two lists are illustrative (the first is more general; the second refers specifically to the drug world).

> mob, hot, fence, excess baggage, sting, sing, rat, racket, a mark, confidence game, bug, bird cage, slammer, joint ('prison')

> crack, coke, snow, rock, dime, pot, grass, toot, high, down, downer, speed, pusher, dealer, joint ('marijuana cigarette')

Each of these expressions is used with one meaning in everyday situations but bears a quite different meaning in the underworld.

SPOKEN AND WRITTEN REGISTERS: SIMILARITIES AND DIFFERENCES

Though it is sometimes said that writing is simply speech written down or visual language as distinct from audible language, writing and speaking ordinarily serve different purposes and have somewhat different linguistic characteristics. Conversation is not a written register, although it can be represented in novels, plays, and screenplays. Nor are legal contracts ordinarily spoken (though one made in that mode may be legally binding). Imagine how the words and the syntax of a handwritten will would differ from one made by a testator speaking before a video-tape. Or consider the linguistic differences between a note stuck on a refrigerator door and the same basic message spoken to someone face to face. Speaking and writing are thus not mirror images of one another.

Oral communication can exploit such channels as intonation and voice pitch to convey information; face-to-face oral communication can also utilize gestures, posture, and physical proximity between participants. In writing, the only channels available are words and syntax, along with certain conventions of typography and punctuation. In speaking, communication is possible on different levels simultaneously; we can criticize someone's personality in a seemingly objective manner while expressing with intonation or body language how much we greatly admire the person. In writing, much more must be communicated lexically and syntactically, though there are ways of achieving ironic and sarcastic tones, enabling addressees to read "between the lines."

A second important difference between speech and writing is in the amount of planning that is possible. For most written registers, more time is available for composing and for revising afterward. During a conversation, on the other hand, pausing to find just the right word risks losing the floor. This difference in the time available for planning and editing in written registers produces characteristic syntactic patterns that are very difficult to achieve under the on-line processing constraints imposed in spoken registers. Written registers also typically show a more specific and varied vocabulary because writers have time to choose words carefully and even to consult a thesaurus if they wish.

As you recognize, written registers are not always more planned than spoken registers. For academic lectures or job interviews, language reflecting some of the characteristics of planned writing is expected. On the other hand, some types of writing are produced with relatively little planning; the language of a letter scribbled a few minutes before the mail pickup is likely to be quite speechlike.

A third distinction is that speakers and addressees are often face-to-face, whereas writers and readers are not. In many face-to-face interactions, the immediacy of the interlocutors and the contexts of interaction allow them to refer to themselves and their own opinions (*I think, you see*) and to be more personal in their interaction. The contexts of writing, in contrast, limit the degree to which written expression can be personal. Again, however, we must be careful not to overgeneralize. Consider, for example, a personal letter and a personal conversation. Language users often feel that they have a right to be equally personal in both contexts. An impersonal stance is thus a feature of only some written registers, as a personal stance is a feature of only some spoken registers.

Finally, written registers tend to rely on the context of the interaction less than spoken registers do. In spoken registers, expressions of spatial deixis (like *this* and *that*) and temporal deixis (like *today* and *next Tuesday*) are likely to be understood, whereas the lack of a shared environment might tend to make such expressions opaque or confusing in writing. To what day would *today* refer in an undated written text? And to which pencil would *this pencil* be referring when found in a printed document? Like other distinctions among registers, reliance on deictic expressions does not constitute an absolute difference between speech and writing. In telephone conversations, for example, you cannot say *this thing* (referring to something in the environment of the speaker) without risking opaqueness. In contrast, you can leave a written note on the kitchen table that reads *Please don't eat this!* as long as the referent of *this* is obvious from what is near the note.

There are many ways in which spoken and written registers differ. But when we examine those differences (as we have just done), we find no absolute dichotomy. It is difficult, for example, to think of words that could occur *only* in speech or *only* in writing, even though certain words may occur more frequently in one mode or the other. Instead, written registers *tend* to be more formal, more informational, and less personal. Along a "personal/impersonal" continuum, for example, the type of writing found in legal documents will be at the impersonal end, while informal conversation will tend toward the personal end. But personal letters may be very close to conversation in their linguistic character. Writing and speaking thus do not form a simple dichotomy, and to describe the differences between them, we must ask in each case what register of writing or what register of speaking is being considered. With all language, the situation of use is the most influential factor in determining linguistic form.

A COMPARISON OF TWO REGISTERS

Let's examine two brief passages of text as a way of illustrating the nature of register variation in some detail. You will see how the various levels of grammar come together to form a coherent register. The first passage will be immediately recognizable as legalese. While critics have remarked that legalese should be considered a foreign language because it is so different from ordinary writing and speaking, legalese is simply one of the many registers of English. That it may be more difficult to understand than other registers (for people not accustomed to using it) does not give grounds for considering it a foreign tongue.

This passage comes from a rider to a deed of trust. A deed of trust is a written agreement that places the title to real estate in the hands of a trustee to ensure that money borrowed with the property as collateral will be repaid; a rider is an addition to the basic document.

	Line	Sentence
Notwithstanding anything in the Deed of Trust to the	1	1
contrary, it is agreed that the loan secured by this	2	
Deed of Trust is made pursuant to, and shall be	3	
construed and governed by the laws of the United	4	
States and the rules and regulations promulgated	5	
thereunder, including the federal laws, rules and	6	
regulations for federal savings and loan	7	
associations. If any paragraph, clause or provision	8	2
of this Deed of Trust or the Note or other	9	
obligations secured by this Deed of Trust is	10	
construed or interpreted by a court of competent	11	
jurisdiction to be invalid or unenforceable, such	12	
decision shall affect only those paragraphs, clauses	13	
or provisions so construed or interpreted and shall	14	
not affect the remaining paragraphs, clauses and	15	
provisions of this Deed of Trust or the Note or other	16	
obligations secured by this Deed of Trust.	17	

The second passage is from a 1961 face-to-face interview with former President Harry Truman by biographer Merle Miller.[5]

[5] Merle Miller, *Plain Speaking* (New York: Berkley Books, 1974), p. 242.

	Line	Sentence
Q. What do you consider the biggest mistake you made	1	1
as President?	2	
A. That damn fool from Texas that I first made	3	2
Attorney General and then put on the Supreme Court.	4	
I don't know what got into me.	5	3
He was no damn good as Attorney General, and on the	6	4
Supreme Court . . . it doesn't seem possible, but he's	7	
been even worse.	8	
He hasn't made one right decision that I can think of.	9	5
And so when you ask me what was my biggest mistake,	10	6a
that's it.	11	
Putting Tom Clark on the Supreme Court of the United	12	6b
States.	13	
I thought maybe when he got on the Court he'd improve,	14	7
but of course, that isn't what happened.	15	
I told you when we were discussing that other fellow.	16	8a
After a certain age it's hopeless to think people are	17	8b
going to change much.	18	

It is apparent at a glance how strikingly different these two passages are. Of course, the linguistic differences are not as great as those between different languages. But in some respects these samples from different registers differ substantially from one another.

First consider sentence length. The first passage (the trust deed) is 139 words long and comprises two sentences. By contrast, the 135 words of the second passage occur in eight sentences. (The interviewer, in writing down Truman's words as represented here, made nine sentences of them; in our numbering of the sentences, we have used the letters *a* and *b* to indicate a combining of two of the interviewer's sentences into a single sentence so as not to exaggerate the number of separate sentences.) Thus average sentence length differs significantly in these register samples: 70 words for the trust deed, 17 for the interview.

It is instructive to examine the passages carefully to discover other linguistic features that contribute to the marking of register difference. We recommend that you review the passages and jot down as many characteristics of vocabulary, syntax, and lexical category as you can before reading the analysis that follows; note contrasting features as well as any features the passages may have in common.

Vocabulary

One easily observed difference between the passages is in vocabulary. The deed of trust contains certain words and phrases that might seem odd if they appeared in the interview: *notwithstanding, pursuant to, thereunder, jurisdiction.* Likewise, Truman's earthy language contains certain words that would strike us as highly inappropriate in a legal document: *damn, fool, fellow, hopeless,* and *maybe* would stand out in a deed of trust, though they seem perfectly natural in the interview. Furthermore, while the words *no* and *good* might not individually call attention to themselves in a deed of trust, they would certainly be remarkable in the combination *no good,* all the more so in *no damn good.*

We are not suggesting that the words mentioned from the trust deed could never occur in Truman's interview, or vice versa. Rather we are suggesting that, at least as they are actually used in these passages, they would seem out of place and would call attention to themselves if used in the other register. The few words that actually do occur in both passages are chiefly the simple and most common words of English—the ones that occur in nearly all registers and might be expected to appear in most sample passages: *the, of, and, a, to, it, is,* and *that.* These monosyllabic words are everyday pronouns, prepositions, conjunctions, and articles; they are among the twenty most common words of English, although they do not occur with the same frequency in all registers (consider headlines and classified ads). The few instances of nouns and verbs that occur in both our passages will be discussed later.

You have now seen that in the selection of words and the collocation of these words into phrases, as well as in sentence length, there are striking differences between the passages. It is precisely such features—not in isolation but taken together—that help us identify passages as being particular *kinds* of text, particular language varieties suitable in different situations, particular registers.

Phonology

Besides sentence length, lexical collocations, and vocabulary, there are other distinctive characteristics of these passages, though they may not jump off the page so dramatically.

Since only one of the two passages originated in speech, we cannot make straightforward phonological comparisons between them, except as it is reflected in spelling conventions. We do not have a phonetic transcription, but we can infer from the text that Truman exhibited frequent phonological abbreviation. Instead of full forms like *do not,* you can find eight contractions even in this small sample of text: *don't, doesn't, isn't, hasn't, he's, he'd, that's,* and *it's.* In the one place in the deed of trust where a comparable form might appear, you find *it is,* not *it's.* If we were comparing two forms of spoken English and had suitable transcriptions, we could perhaps say more about phonological similarities and differences. Even comparing these two passages, however, we can observe the equivalent of phonological differences between varieties.

Morphology and Lexicon

We next ask whether there are morphological and lexical differences between the passages. We begin our analysis by examining lexical categories. In looking at nouns, prepositions, and verbs, you'll see that the trust deed is very "nominal," the interview much more "verbal."

Nouns and Pronouns   In comparable amounts of text, the trust deed has forty nouns, the interview only seventeen. On the other hand, the interview has many more pronouns than the trust deed.

Prepositions   The trust deed has nineteen prepositions compared to only ten in the interview. Given the need for a trust deed to be quite specific and the fact that the function of prepositional phrases is to express specific semantic roles—for example, agent *(by a court)*, instrument *(by this Deed)*, location *(of the United States)*—the frequency of prepositions in the deed is not surprising. Informational registers generally show a much higher proportion of prepositions than other kinds of registers precisely because each preposition provides a frame for additional semantic information.

Verbs   The number of verbs in the trust deed is nine, about one-third the number in the Truman interview. Thus the interview is very verbal. As to particular verbs, Truman uses *think* (and *thought*), *know*, and *seem*, and his interviewer uses *consider*. Such "private" verbs have to do with internal states of the speaker or writer and are appropriate in an interview and very frequent in conversation, though they would be out of place in the trust deed. Truman also employs pro-verbs of various sorts (pro-verbs take the place of other verbs, much as pronouns take the place of nouns): *do* and *happen*, which can be substituted for many verbs; *put* and *get*, which are more limited but still have far-ranging uses. In conversation, where there is pressure to find your words speedily, pro-verbs tend to occur frequently. In this short passage *got* appears twice, and Truman uses *put on* and *putting on* (the Supreme Court) instead of, say, *appointed to*. The verb *to be*—the most common one in English—occurs as a main verb seven times, whereas in the trust deed it occurs four times as an auxiliary (*is agreed, is made, be construed,* and *is construed*) but just once as main verb *(to be void)*.

The following verbs of the trust deed are related to the topic of discussion and therefore to the register of the passage: *agree, construe, govern, promulgate, interpret,* and *affect*. Not related to topic but also characteristic of legalese is the use of *shall* as an auxiliary verb. While *shall* can occur in many registers of English, its use is exceptionally common in legalese.

Verb Tenses   The interview concerns the years of Truman's presidency, as the preponderance of verbs in the past tense reflects. Among its twenty-three verbs, fourteen are in the past tense, while its eight present-tense verbs generally make reference to the ongoing interaction or to Truman's own thought processes in the course of the interview: *what do you consider, when you ask, I don't know, I can think*. The one verb that refers to future time uses the construction *are going to* instead of the more formal *shall* or *will*. *Shall*, on the other hand, occurs as an auxiliary in both sentences of the trust deed.

Negation   In the interview, four out of five negative morphemes occur as the separate negative adverb *not* (attached to the verb as a contraction); the fifth negative is the simple adverb *no* modifying *damn good*. In contrast, the trust deed incorporates the elements of negation into adjectives or prepositions by the processes of derivational morphology (*invalid* and *unenforceable*) or compounding (*notwithstanding*); there is one isolated *not* (which occurs with reference to future time *shall not*, in contrast to a future positive *shall*); in addition, there are several words that have negative content built into their definitions, as in *void* and *contrary*. One characteristic difference between speech and writing is the much higher frequency of negation in spoken registers, where the vast majority of negative elements are separate (like *not*, often realized as *-n't*) rather than incorporated into words (like *unpleasant*).

Impersonal Constructions   The deed of trust is also characterized by several impersonal constructions, especially passives: *is agreed, is made, shall be construed*. Passive constructions demote agent subjects to be objects of a preposition and in turn permit omission of the agent *(Lightning struck the house/The house was struck by lightning/The house was struck)*. In legalese, agentless passives and passives with *by* are both common. Also in keeping with the impersonal character of this passage, there are no occurrences of first or second person pronouns (and only a single occurrence of any third person pronoun: the nonreferential *it* in *it is agreed*). In contrast, the interview uses first and second person pronouns frequently: *I, me*, and *we* a total of eleven times; *you* four times; the possessive *my* once.

Latinate Vocabulary   In contrast to the short everyday words of the interview, the deed of trust uses more uncommon words, as is notoriously characteristic of legalese. The vocabulary in the deed of trust is more "Latinate" or learned, the words themselves longer: *promulgated, construed, governed, regulations, obligations, decision, jurisdiction, provisions, invalid, unenforceable, remaining, secured*. There is also the markedly legal collocation *competent jurisdiction*, in which the word *competent* does not carry its ordinary meaning of 'capable' but its legal meaning of 'having proper jurisdiction over the matter to be decided.' Many words that are used in other registers with one meaning carry a different sense in legalese. Besides *competent*, the following words from the passage have a sense quite specific to legalese: *deed, trust, obligation, decision, provisions*, and *note*.

Syntax

The interview and the legal document exhibit striking syntactic differences, of which sentence length is one indication.

Passive Voice   One striking feature of the deed of trust is its frequent use of the passive voice *(is agreed, is made, shall be construed and governed, is construed or interpreted)*. In marked contrast, Truman and his interviewer use *only* active voice verbs.

Questions   In using the form of a direct question *(When you ask me what was my biggest mistake)* instead of an indirect question *(When you ask me what my biggest mistake was)*, Truman contributes to the overwhelming impression of informality that characterizes the passage. And though it may seem too obvious to mention, the interview naturally contains a question, a syntactic structure that not only does not appear in the trust deed but would seem very odd there.

Prepositions   Prepositions were discussed in the lexical section, but two further aspects can be mentioned here. First is the use of series of prepositional phrases in the deed of trust. Whereas in the interview there is only one instance of two prepositional phrases used consecutively *(on the Supreme Court of the United States)*, the trust deed has seven, including a sequence of three consecutive prepositional phrases: *in the deed of Trust to the contrary.* Second, the interview has an example of a sentence-final preposition *(He hasn't made one right decision that I can think of)*, something that does not occur in the passage of legalese and occurs very rarely in formal writing of any kind as you saw in Table 12-7.

Pronominalization   We have already discussed first and second person pronouns. There are other differences in pronominal use as well, reflecting a major difference between the customary usage of legalese and conversation. Truman uses the pronoun *that* as a "sentence" pronoun, referring not to a noun phrase but to an entire clause, as in *that isn't what happened* and *that's it.*

The interview also exhibits frequent third person pronouns: Truman uses *he* five times in reference to Tom Clark. This can be contrasted with the repetition of full noun phrases in the trust deed, in which *Deed of Trust* occurs six times, the compound noun phrase *rules and regulations* occurs twice, and the lengthy compound noun phrase *paragraph, clause or provision* three times (once in the singular and twice in the plural). One exceptionally long noun phrase is repeated, and it contains a repetition of the noun phrase *Deed of Trust* within it: *this Deed of Trust or the Note or other obligations secured by this Deed of Trust.*

Reduced Relative Clauses   Another characteristic feature of legalese is the occurrence of reduced relative clauses, in which the relative pronoun and a form of the verb *be* do not appear where they might (this feature is sometimes referred to as "whiz deletion"). The following examples show the omitted words in parentheses.

loan (that is) secured

rules and regulations (that are) promulgated thereunder

paragraphs, clauses or provisions (that are) so construed or interpreted

Conjunctions   The Truman interview is marked by frequent coordinating conjunctions, such as *and, but, and then, and so,* which serve chiefly to link clauses, as in lines 6, 7, and 15. These conjunctions are lacking in the legalese passage except for *and,* which is used to link verbs, or nouns, or adjectives, but *not* clauses.

Triple Conjoining   Another syntactic feature typical of legalese is triple phrasal conjunction: "X, Y conjunction Z" or "X conjunction Y conjunction Z." In legal registers, X, Y, and Z can be members of almost any lexical category, most commonly nouns (or noun phrases), adjectives, or verbs; X, Y, and Z are ordinarily members of the same lexical or phrasal category. The following exemplify the pattern.

laws, rules and regulations (nouns)

paragraph, clause or provision (nouns)

deed of trust or the note or other obligation (noun phrases)

void, invalid or unenforceable (adjectives)

Sometimes variation within the X, Y, and Z constituents produces very similar but not completely parallel structures, as in these examples.

1. is made pursuant to, and shall be construed and governed by

2. the laws of the United States and the rules and regulations

In 1, there are two verb-phrase structures joined by *and,* but the second itself contains two conjoined verbs *(construed and governed).* In 2, we might more accurately describe the structure not as X, Y, and Z but as X and Y, with Y a compound M and N; thus, the X and the (M and N).

Adverbs and Adjectives   Legalese is famous for its use of words like *thereto, hereinunder,* and *wherefore.* There is only one instance of such a compound adverb in our passage *(thereunder).* A strikingly marked adjective of legalese does, however, occur in *such decision.* The adverbials of the legalese passage are phrasal *(notwithstanding anything . . .),* clausal *(If any paragraph . . . is construed),* or, when simply lexical, peculiarly legal *(thereunder).*

Truman's adverbials are quite different. When clausal, they are often introduced by *when (when you ask me, when he got on the court, when we were discussing).* Truman's simple adverbs commonly make reference to time *(first, then);* others are hedges of various sorts that indicate Truman's stance toward what he is saying: *of course, maybe.*

As for adjectives, Truman's are judgmental and simple: *good, worse, right, biggest, hopeless;* one is a comparative *(worse)* and another a superlative *(biggest).* The legalese adjectives, none of them common in English, are limiting: *federal, competent, void, invalid, unenforceable, remaining.*

Comparing Registers

In comparing and contrasting the two passages, it is not any single feature alone that leads to our judgment about what registers they exemplify. Rather, various features occurring in combination characterize the first passage as legalese and the second as a spoken interview. Truman's style is so informal that it suggests a conversation rather than a formal interview. This may be partly the result of the interviewer's having spent several months with Truman, morning and afternoon. No doubt the interview came increasingly to resemble conversation between friends as the days passed.

You have now seen that language features differ from one speech situation to another. Sometimes there is more of one feature in a given register than in another; occasionally a feature occurs in one register exclusively, or almost exclusively. Sometimes the same form occurs in more than one register but with different meanings or different uses.

THE DIMENSIONS OF REGISTER VARIATION

The linguistic resources from which registers must draw their particular features produce consistent and coherent texts from a single grammatical system. It is by differentially drawing on the same grammatical resources at each level of the grammar that different texts in different registers are created.

Using computers and large data bases, linguists have begun to identify systematically which sets of linguistic features tend to co-occur in texts. Analyzing sets of co-occurring features has contributed to our understanding of the underlying dimensions of register variation and of how sets of features co-occur in the service of common functions.

Sets of Co-Occurring Features

One set of linguistic features that commonly occur together in texts includes the following:

Set A (Involved Features)

first and second person pronouns *(I, me, we, us; you)*

that omission from subordinate clauses *(She said ø he lied)*

private verbs *(think, consider, assume, know)*

demonstrative pronouns *(this, that, these)*

contractions *(he's, isn't)*

emphatics *(really, such a, so, even)*

hedges *(kind of, more or less, maybe, about)*

sentence relatives *(Then he lied, <u>which</u> bothered her a lot.)*

clause-final prepositions *(the teacher I told you <u>about</u>)*

Wh-questions *(What do you consider . . . ?)*

Be as a main verb *(It is hopeless)*

To make some of the features of this set more concrete, it will help to reinspect the Truman interview. First and second person pronouns go together because they commonly occur in face-to-face interaction (and in personal letters), in which there is a personalized speaker/writer addressing a particular known addressee. In such a circumstance, it is also appropriate to express one's inner thoughts and feelings (and inquire about the addressee's), which thus requires the use of private verbs. The use of emphatics (Truman's *damn fool* and *even worse*), and hedges *(maybe)* is also characteristic of such interaction. The occurrence of sentence-final and clause-final prepositions *(that I can think of)* marks relatively informal person-to-person speech and writing (see also Table 12-7). The use of demonstrative pronouns *(that,* as in line 11) is characteristic of a shared context between speaker and addressee, in that in many instances the addressee must be present to understand the reference of words like *that* and *these*. Virtually all the features of Set A do indeed occur in the brief Truman interview, even though the determination of which features occur together was based on a much larger sample of texts, not including the two examined here.

Another set of features that commonly occur together in texts are these:

Set B (Informational Features)

(frequent) nouns

(frequent) prepositions

longer words

lexical variety

attributive adjectives (*federal laws*)

It is not surprising that prepositions and nouns should occur commonly together. After all, prepositional phrases include noun phrases. What is less obvious is why frequent nouns and prepositions would occur with longer words and with lexical variety. A moment's thought will help explain this pattern. Lexical variety results from using a relatively larger number of alternative words. Given that alternative words usually have somewhat different meanings (or different connotations), lexical variety generally indicates an attempt to be exact in expressing meaning or to expand the meaning of a referent already mentioned. Contrast Truman's use of different referring expressions for Tom Clark. Instead of repeating *Tom Clark* or the pronoun *he,* the use of various referring expressions permits Truman to make additional comments that expand on his opinionated description of Justice Clark. (In the deed of trust, the use of attributive adjectives—*federal laws, competent jurisdiction, remaining paragraphs*—has a related function of specifying noun phrases.)

As you may have anticipated already, there is a very strong tendency for the linguistic features of Set A to occur frequently in registers in which the features of Set B are not frequent, and vice versa. That is, in texts and registers where you find first and second person pronouns, *that* omission, questions, and the other features of Set A, you will typically not find many long words, much lexical variety, frequent nouns, prepositions, or attributive adjectives—that is, the features of Set B. If you think about it, this makes sense, for it is precisely in contexts that require lexical specificity that speakers and writers have less occasion to use personal pronouns, private verbs, and the other features of Set A. And vice versa: When you are in a face-to-face interactional situation requiring the features of Set A, you do not have much of an opportunity to choose your words very carefully, and it is just such an opportunity that permits us to produce lexical variety, longer words, and so on.

You can think of these two sets of features as representing opposite poles of a single dimension of linguistic variation. At one pole are registers with a heavy emphasis on interaction and personal involvement; at the other pole are registers with virtually no interaction or personal involvement but a heavy emphasis on sharing information. Each text will fall somewhere along a continuum between extremely informational and extremely involved, and by calculating the average values for an adequate sample of texts in various registers, linguists have determined average values for those registers, as you will see next.

Involved versus Informational Texts

We could count the features just discussed as a way of gauging involved and informational focus in the texts of various registers. A register whose texts had higher-than-average frequencies for the features of Set A and lower-than-average frequencies for the features of Set B would show a high degree of personal involvement (like the interview represented in the Truman passage). A register whose texts had higher-than-average frequencies for the features of Set B (and would in general then have lower-than-average frequencies for the features of Set A) would show a high degree of informational focus (rather than involvement).

Based on the number of features in a wide range of registers and a large number of texts, average values for all the features discussed here have been determined for English speech and writing. In Figure 12-1, the baseline represents the average number of occurrences for the relevant features, and distances above the baseline indicate above-average frequencies for the particular features represented by that end of the dimension. The bar graphs extending well above the baseline represent registers that show high degrees of involvement (that is, high frequencies of the

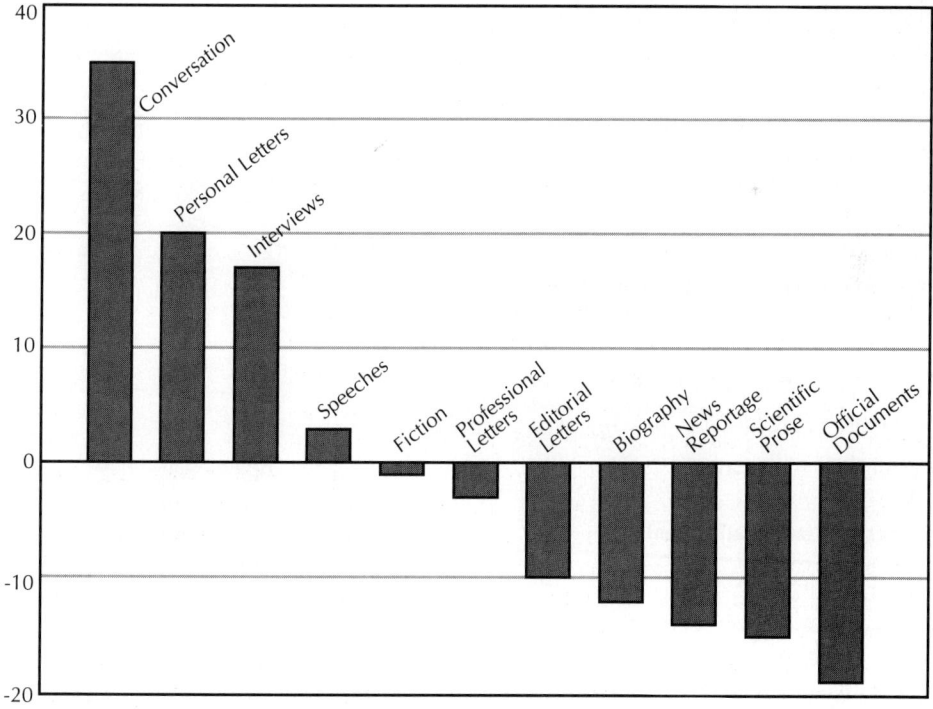

FIGURE 12-1
Register Values on the Involved/Informational Dimension (Defined by Feature Sets A and B)

Source: Data from Douglas Biber, *Variation across Speech and Writing* (Cambridge: Cambridge University Press, 1988).

features in Set A); those extending well below the baseline represent registers showing high degrees of informational focus (that is, frequent occurrence of the features of Set B). A register whose texts had the average number of features of Set A and Set B would have a value of zero in Figure 12-1, and the bar for that register would neither rise above nor fall below the baseline.[6]

As Figure 12-1 strikingly illustrates, conversation is a register that ranks very high in involvement, while scientific prose and official documents (which would be similar to documents like trust deeds) are registers that rank very low on involvement but very high on informational focus. Registers with values below the baseline are characterized by *high* frequencies of the information features (Set B) and *low* frequencies of the involvement features (Set A). Personal letters and interviews rank high on involvement. Recall that the Truman interview had many examples of features that contribute to the "involved" characterization. By contrast, the trust deed had higher frequencies of the features defining Set B (longer words, more lexical variety, and prepositions). In other words, if you calculated the values for the various features of sets A and B needed to place our illustrative texts on this scale, the Truman interview would rank close to conversation and interviews, well above the baseline, while the trust deed would rank with official documents, well below the baseline.

Narrative Texts

Two other sets of linguistic features have been shown to co-occur with great frequency in texts, and they are given below as Set C and Set D. The features of Set C characterize texts that are very narrative (that is, story-like), while those of Set B are characteristic of nonnarrative texts.

Set C (Narrative Features)

past tense verbs

perfect aspect verbs (with *have* as in *have seen*)

public verbs *(discuss, tell, say, write, explain)*

third person pronouns

Set D (Nonnarrative Features)

present tense verbs

attributive adjectives *(high office)*

As with sets A and B, sets C and D also tend to be complementary. Registers marked by frequent occurrence of the features of Set C typically have very few features of Set D, and vice versa.

---

[6] The scale of values in Figures 12-1 and 12-2 represents standard deviations from the average (that is, mean) value for the sets of features; as indicated above, the average value is set at zero; hence, a value of −1 would represent one standard deviation below the average.

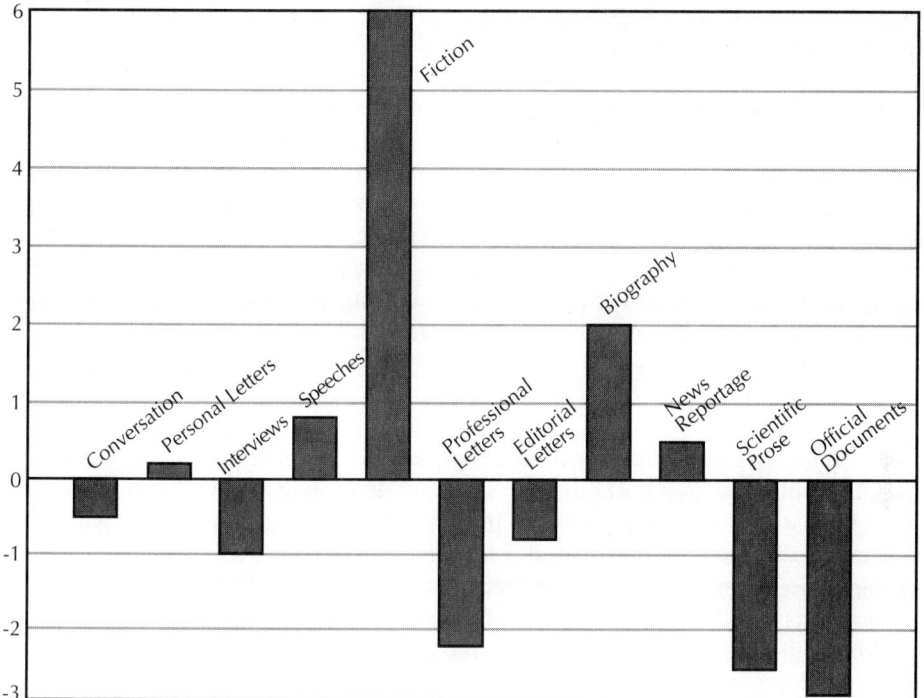

FIGURE 12-2
Register Values on the Narrative Dimension (Defined by Feature Sets C and D)

Source: Data from Douglas Biber, *Variation across Speech and Writing* (Cambridge: Cambridge University Press, 1988).

Now we turn to Figure 12-2. As with Figure 12-1, the baseline of Figure 12-2 is set at zero, which represents the average values for the features in Sets C and D (as determined for the same wide range and large number of texts as for Figure 12-1). A register whose texts had the average number of features of Sets C and D would have a value of zero in Figure 12-2. As you can see in Figure 12-2, the registers that rank above the baseline (those that are highly narrative) are fiction, biography, speeches, and news reportage, while official documents, scientific prose, and professional letters fall well below the baseline on this dimension (with below-average frequencies for the features of Set C but above-average values for the features of Set D). Our trust deed would also stand well below the baseline toward the nonnarrative end of this dimension. You may recall that the trust deed has *no* past tense verbs, *no* perfect aspect verbs, and only a single third person pronoun (the semantically empty *it*). By contrast, the Truman interview has fourteen out of twenty-three verbs in the past tense. The interview also has a relatively high number of perfect aspect verbs, public verbs, and third person pronouns.

If you compare particular registers on the two dimensions, you will note on Figure 12-1 that conversation ranks extremely high on involvement (indicating lots of features of Set A and very few of Set B), while on Figure 12-2 it ranks below the baseline on the narrative/nonnarrative dimension (indicating lower-than-average values for the features of Set C or higher-than-average values for those of Set D). By way of contrast, the register of fiction ranks far above the baseline on the narrative dimension (Figure 12-2) but below the baseline on the involvement dimension (Figure 12-1), which means it has relatively more informational features than involved features. Looking at a third register, you can see that the official documents register ranks far below the baseline on the involved/informational dimension, which indicates that it is a very informational and not very involved register, and it ranks far below the baseline on the narrative/nonnarrative dimension, which indicates that it is very nonnarrative.

English and Other Languages

It would be challenging to uncover other sets of co-occurring features representing different dimensions of textual variation. Each pair of complementary sets would constitute another dimension in a multidimensional "space" in which the range of texts could be represented. More than two or three additional dimensions of linguistic variation would be needed to represent textual variation adequately, but analysis of other dimensions lies beyond our scope.

We should mention, however, that the distribution of features comparable to those we have examined here has been investigated in several languages other than English, with comparable results. Korean, Somali, and Nukulaelae Tuvaluan have all been investigated, and dimensions of variation have been found that in some instances resemble those found in English and in other instances reflect the particular characteristics of the cultures whose languages they represent. As an example of the latter phenomenon, we can mention that Korean, which is a language with a highly evolved set of deferential address terms and other grammatical features showing respect, has a dimension defined solely by features related to markers of deference and respect.

SUMMARY

Three principal elements determine each situation of use: setting, purpose, and participants. As part of the setting, one must consider the topic and the location. As you wear different clothing to different places and for different activities, so you do not generally speak the same in court, at dinner, and on the soccer field. As part of the purpose, one must consider such things as activity type and goals. With respect to participants, it is not only the people themselves who influence language form but the roles they are playing in the speech situation.

In multilingual communities, different situations of use call sometimes for different languages and sometimes for different varieties of the same language. *Registers* are language varieties appropriate for use in particular speech situations (in contrast to dialects, which are language varieties characteristic of social groups). The set of varieties used in a speech community in various speech situations is called its *linguistic* (or verbal) *repertoire*. In the linguistic repertoire of a monolingual

appear in nearly all registers of English. Headlinese is one register in which these words are relatively infrequent; identify three other registers in which you can observe a relatively infrequent use of these words and, after choosing a sample from one of them or from headlines, make a list of the lexical categories that strike you as occurring with higher frequency than in conversation and another for those that occur relatively infrequently. Then offer a hypothesis as to why the distribution is as you found it.

8. Examine the following three letters. The first is a letter of recommendation for a student seeking admission to a master's degree program in linguistics, the second a letter to a magazine, and the third a personal letter from a woman to a female friend in another state. Identify the particular characteristics of each type of letter in terms of the co-occurring features on the two dimensions examined in this chapter. Then, using the features as a guide, indicate approximately where each letter might fall on the two dimensions.

Letter of Recommendation

I have known Mr. John Smith as a student in three of my courses at State, and on the basis of that acquaintance with him, it is my recommendation that he should certainly be admitted to graduate school.

John was a student of mine in Linguistics 100, where he did exceptionally well, writing a very good paper indeed. On the basis of that paper, I encouraged him to become a linguistics major and subsequently had the good fortune to have him in two more of my classes. In one of these (historical linguistics) he led the class, obviously working more insightfully than the other seventeen students enrolled. In the other course (introduction to phonology), he did less well, perhaps because he was under some financial pressure and was forced to work twenty hours a week while carrying a full academic load. In all three courses, John worked very hard, doing much more than was required.

I recommend John Smith to you without reservation of any kind. He knows what he wants to achieve and is clearly motivated to succeed in graduate school.

Editorial Letter

Your story on Afghanistan was in error when it stated that the Russian-backed coup of 1973 was bloodless. As a Peace Corps volunteer in Afghanistan at the time, I saw the bodies and blood and ducked the bullets. It was estimated that between 1,000 and 1,500 died, but it is hard to get an accurate count when a tank pulls up to the house of the shah's supporters and fires repeatedly into it from 30 feet away, or when whole households of people disappear in the middle of the night.

Personal Letter

So, what's up? Not too much going on here. I'm at work now, and it's been so slow this week. We haven't done anything. I hate it when it's so slow. The week seems like it's never going to end.

Well how have you all been? Did you get the pictures and letter I sent you? We haven't heard from you in a while. Mother has your B'day present ready to send to you and Dan's too, but no tellin when she will get around to sending it.

How are the kids? Does Dan like kindergarten? Well, Al has gone off to school. I miss him so much. He left Monday to go to LLTI. It's a trade school upstate. You only have to go for two years, and he's taking air conditioning and refrigeration and then he's going to take heating.

9.   a.   Review what was said about *competent* (jurisdiction) in the discussion of Latinate vocabulary on p. 384, and then specify the specialized legal senses of these words, also used with specialized meanings in the trust deed passage: *deed, trust, obligation, decision, provisions,* and *note*. List any words used with specialized senses in the Truman interview and specify the sense.

   b.   List at least one other example of a reduced relative clause ("whiz deletion") in the trust deed besides the three identified on p. 385.

   c.   List any examples of a reduced relative clause in the Truman passages on p. 381 and in Exercise 4 above.

10.   The following are several personal ads (very slightly adapted) from a weekly newspaper published in Los Angeles. Examine them for their linguistic characteristics.

   (1)   Aquarius SWM, 33, strong build, blue eyes, You: marriage-minded, bilingual Latin Female 23–30, children ok.

   (2)   Busty, brilliant, stunning entrepreneur, 40s (looks 30). Seeks possibly younger, tall, handsome, caring SWM, who respects individuality. Someone who lives the impossible dream, financially secure, good conversation, for relationship, n/s.

   (3)   SWM, 28, attractive college student, works for major U.S. airlines, enjoys traveling. Seeks Female, 23–32, humorous and intelligent for world class romance and possibly marriage.

   (4)   English vegetarian. SWM, 31. Sincere, sensitive, original, thinking, untypical, amusing, shy, playful, affectionate professional. Seeking warm, witty, open-minded WF, under 29, to share my life with.

   (5)   Slim, young, GWM, masculine, athletic, healthy, clean-shaven, discreet. Seeks similar good-looking WM, under 25, for monogamous relationship.

   (6)   Very romantic SBM, 24, college educated. Seeks wealthy, healthy and beautiful Lady for friendship and maybe romance. Phonies and pranksters need not apply.

   (7)   Hispanic DF, petite but full of life, likes sports, dancing, traveling, looking for someone with same interests, 30+, race unimportant.

   (8)   Evolved, positive thinking, spiritual, affectionate, honest, handsome, healthy, secure, 36, 6', 160#, blue-eyed, unpretentious, unencumbered, professional. Seeking counterpart, soulmate, marriage, family.

   a.   What lexical categories (parts of speech), if any, are very frequent in the ads (compared to conversation, let's say)? What lexical categories are particularly rare?

   b.   Identify eight characteristic linguistic features of personal ads; they can be features of syntax, morphology, lexicon, abbreviatory conventions, etc.

    c.   List the verbs in all the ads, and identify their grammatical person (first, second, third) and number (singular, plural) where possible. (*Hint:* Supply the pronoun that would serve as subject of each verb in order to determine person and number.)

    d.   Choose one of the ads and attempt to write it out fully in conversational English *solely* by supplying additional words; keep the same word order and word forms as the original ad.

    e.   On the basis of your attempt, what indication is there that the ads represent a reduced or abbreviated form of conversational English? If you judge the ads not to be reductions of the sentences of conversational English, what explanation can you offer for the form of the sentences?

    f.   Which linguistic features of personal ads strike you as having become conventionalized to the point of requiring previous knowledge of the customs of the register in order to write or understand the register?

11.   Examine a current issue of your school newspaper, and list as many different registers as you can identify in it (such as editorials, letters to the editor, reviews). Choose one register, and list eight linguistic features that contribute by their frequency to the characterization of that register, including an example of each from your passage.

12.   Recipes, obituaries, classified ads, display ads, telegrams, birthday cards, credit applications, course descriptions in college catalogs, directions for using medicines, and essay questions are just a few of the many distinctive registers you have occasion to meet daily. Choose a small textual sample from one of these, and provide a list of characteristic features, with an example of each from your sample.

13.   Identify several instances of linguistic features that vary across registers in a foreign language that you have studied. (Some features may be alluded to in your foreign language textbook; others may have been mentioned by your instructor). Attempt to identify at least one phonological, one syntactic, and several lexical items. Specify for each feature the situation in which you believe it to be appropriate and another situation in which it would not be. (*Hint:* Consider gross differences of situation, such as writing versus speech, formal versus informal, deferential versus equal status, fast speech versus careful speech).

SUGGESTIONS FOR FURTHER READING

We borrowed the story of Ballyhough railway station from Joos (1962), which is an entertaining introduction to the notion of register, which he calls "style." Brown and Fraser (1979) survey the elements of speech situations that influence language. The description of switching in Brussels comes from Fishman (1972), while Blom and Gumperz (1972) describe switching between Bokmål and Ranamål. Biber (1988) is a quantitative study of variation in a computerized corpus of spoken and written registers of English; it is the basis of our discussion of dimensions of register variation. Shopen and Williams (1981), a collection of essays suitable for a general audience, treats discourse, literary style, and other styles; our data on *-ing* in Los Angeles come from a chapter by Benji Wald and Shopen in that collection. O'Donnell and Todd (1991) treat English in the media, advertising, literature, and the classroom. Crystal and Davy (1969) contains chapters on the language of conversation, religion, newspaper reporting, and legal documents. Discussions of still other written registers can be found in Ghadessy (1988). Chapters in the volume edited by Biber and Finegan (1993) describe sports coaching register, personal ads, and dinnertable conversations, as well as register variation in Somali and Korean. Duranti and Goodwin (1992) is a collection of studies about the interaction of language and context. Chapman's (1986) dictionary of slang, from whose dust jacket our examples of slang expressions are taken, also discusses the nature and sources of slang. Andersen (1990) describes register use among children. Lambert and Tucker (1976) report several social-psychological studies of address forms, principally in Canadian French and Puerto Rican and Colombian Spanish.

REFERENCES

Andersen, Elaine S. 1990. *Speaking With Style*. (London: Routledge).

Biber, Douglas. 1988. *Variation Across Speech and Writing* (Cambridge: Cambridge University Press).

Biber, Douglas, and Edward Finegan, eds. 1993. *Sociolinguistic Perspectives on Register* (New York: Oxford University Press).

Blom, Jan-Petter, and John J. Gumperz. 1972. "Social Meaning in Linguistic Structure," in John J. Gumperz and Dell Hymes, eds., *Directions in Sociolinguistics* (New York: Holt), pp. 407–434.

Brown, Penelope, and Colin Fraser. 1979. "Speech as a Marker of Situation," in Klaus Scherer and Howard Giles, eds., *Social Markers in Speech* (Cambridge: Cambridge University Press), pp. 33–62.

Chapman, Robert L., ed. 1986. *New Dictionary of American Slang* (New York: Harper & Row).

Crystal, David, and Derek Davy. 1969. *Investigating English Style* (London: Longman).

Duranti, Alessandro, and Charles Goodwin, eds. 1992. *Rethinking Context: Language as an Interactive Phenomenon* (Cambridge: Cambridge University Press).

Fishman, Joshua A. 1972. "The Sociology of Language," in Pier Paolo Giglioli, ed., *Language and Social Context* (New York: Penguin), pp. 45–58.

Ghadessy, Mohsen, ed. 1988. *Registers of Written English: Situational Factors and Linguistic Features* (London: Pinter).

Joos, Martin. 1962. *The Five Clocks* (New York: Harcourt).

Lambert, Wallace E., and G. Richard Tucker. 1976. *Tu, Vous, Usted: A Social-Psychological Study of Address Patterns* (Rowley, MA: Newbury House).

O'Donnell, W. R., and Loreto Todd. 1991. *Variety in Contemporary English*, 2nd ed. (London: Harper Collins).

Shopen, Timothy, and Joseph M. Williams, eds. 1981. *Style and Variables in English* (Cambridge, MA: Winthrop).

13

Dialects: Linguistic Variation across Regions and Social Groups

LANGUAGES AND DIALECTS

It is an obvious fact that people of different nations tend to use different languages. Along with physical appearance and cultural characteristics, language differences are part of what distinguishes one nation from another. Of course, it is not only across national boundaries that people speak different languages. In Canada, inhabitants of some cities have spoken different languages for centuries. In Quebec province, ethnic French-Canadians maintain a strong allegiance to the French language, while ethnic Anglos maintain a loyalty to English. In India, literally dozens of languages are spoken, some confined to small areas, others spoken regionally or nationally.

Among speakers of a single language there is considerable international variation. Thus we distinguish Australian, American, British, Indian, and Irish English, among others. Striking differences can be noticed between the varieties of French spoken in Montreal and in Paris, and marked distinctions exist among the varieties of Spanish in Spain, Mexico, and the South American countries. In basically monolingual countries like Germany, France, England, and the United States, there is also variation from one group to another: Even casual observers know that residents of different parts of the country speak regional varieties of the national language. When Americans speak of a "Boston accent," a "Southern drawl," or "Brooklynese," they reveal that American English is perceived as varying from place to place and, in general, that languages have regional dialects. These linguistic markers of region serve to identify people as belonging to a particular social group, even though that group may be loosely bound together (as are most regional groups in the United States). In countries where regional affiliation may have other social correlates—of ethnicity or religion or clan—regional varieties are relatively more important markers of social affiliation. The existence of regional varieties of a language, like the existence of different languages themselves, demonstrates that people who speak *with* one another tend to speak *like* one another and that people who view themselves as distinct from one another tend to mark that distinction in their speech, however else it may be marked as well.

A language can be thought of as a collection of dialects that are usually related to one another historically and similar to one another structurally and lexically; the dialects are used by different social groups who *choose* to say that they are speakers of the same language.

Social Boundaries and Dialects

Language varies not only from region to region but also across ethnic, socioeconomic, and gender boundaries. Speakers of American English know that white Americans and black Americans tend to speak differently, even when they live in the same city. Similarly, middle-class speakers can often be distinguished from working-class speakers. You know too that women and men differ in how they use language. These variations across ethnic groups, socioeconomic classes, and gender groups also constitute dialects. African-American and white residents of the United States speak the same language, though somewhat differently. The American middle class and working class share the same language, though each class has distinctive speech characteristics. And though mainstream American women and men speak the same language, their speech differs in patterned ways. Throughout the world, in addition to regional dialects, there are ethnic, social, and gender dialects.

Dialects and Registers

The term **dialect** refers to the language varieties characteristic of different regional or social groups. Partly through a dialect we recognize a person's regional, ethnic, social, and gender affiliation; thus dialect has to do with language *users,* with groups of speakers. In addition, as we saw in the preceding chapter, all dialects vary according to the situation in which they are used. The term *register* refers to language varieties characteristic of different situations of use. Languages, dialects, and registers are all called language **varieties.** In this chapter we deal with dialects—language varieties characteristic of particular social groups.

DIFFERENTIATION AND MERGER OF LANGUAGE VARIETIES

How is it that certain language varieties, once similar to one another, can come to differ so greatly, while other varieties remain very much alike? There is no simple answer to that question, but this much seems clear: The more people interact with one another, the more alike their language remains or becomes. The less contact two social groups have, the more likely it is that their languages will become differentiated.

Geographical separation and social distance can give rise to notable differences in speechways. From the Proto–Indo-European spoken about six millennia ago have come most of today's European languages, as well as many tongues of Central Asia and the Indian subcontinent. Not only the Romance languages but the Celtic, Greek, Baltic, Slavic, and Indo-Iranian tongues have developed from Proto–Indo-European, as have the Germanic languages, including English, Norwegian, Swedish, Danish, Dutch, and German. When we consider that only some two hundred generations have lived and died during that six-thousand-year period, we can appreciate how quickly a multitude of different tongues can develop from a single parent language. Scores of mutually unintelligible languages have developed from Proto–Indo-European, all within about six thousand years.

In the same vein, the Spanish varieties of the New World are developing along lines somewhat different from the Spanish of the Iberian Peninsula. Similar contrasts can be observed between the French spoken in Paris and Montreal and among the British, American, Australian, Canadian, New Zealand, Indian, and Irish varieties of English. So physical distance can be a crucial factor in promoting dialect distinctions.

Similarly, social distance can contribute to creating and maintaining distinct dialects. Middle-class dialects differ from working-class dialects partly because of the relative lack of sustained contacts across class boundaries in American society. African-American Vernacular English remains distinct from other varieties of American English partly because of the social distance between whites and African Americans in the United States. A dialect links its users through recognition of shared linguistic characteristics; speakers' ability to use and understand a dialect marks them as "insiders" and allows them to identify (and exclude) "outsiders."

All languages and language varieties change and develop continuously. When two groups of people speaking a common tongue stop having sufficient social interaction to keep their language developing along the same path, the changes in the speech patterns of each group can eventually produce mutual unintelligibility. That is what happened in the evolution of the many derivatives of Proto–Indo-European and Proto-Polynesian.

Dialects or Languages?

The Romance languages arose from the regional varieties of Latin spoken in different parts of the Roman Empire. Those dialects of Latin eventually gave rise to Italian, French, Spanish, Portuguese, and Rumanian, now the distinct languages of different countries. Though these tongues share many structural features of syntax, phonology, and lexicon, the nationalistic pride taken by the Italians, French, Spaniards, Portuguese, and Rumanians contributes to the varieties' being viewed as different languages rather than as dialects of a single language. The opposite situation characterizes the Chinese language, which comprises several distinct dialects. Though not all Chinese dialects are mutually intelligible, their speakers choose to regard themselves as sharing the same language.

Thus the difference between a language and a dialect is as much a social as a linguistic question; it is strongly influenced by social and psychological factors, such as nationalistic and religious attitudes. The Hindus of northern India speak Hindi, while the Moslems there and in neighboring Pakistan speak Urdu. Opinions differ among them as to the extent to which they can understand one another. The fact that linguists write grammars of "Hindi-Urdu" reflects their professional judgment that these varieties require only a single grammatical description, despite the different language names assigned to them by their speakers. Naturally, with the passing years, these varieties—whose different names proclaim that their speakers belong to different social, political, and religious groups—will become increasingly differentiated, as French and Spanish have done over the centuries.

As physical and social distance enable speakers of particular varieties to distinguish themselves from speakers of other varieties, so close contact and frequent communication foster linguistic uniformity. As dialects spoken by people in close social contact tend to become alike, so different languages spoken in a community can become more similar and even tend to merge in some circumstances. The type and degree of merger are determined by the type and degree of social integration and shared values.

Language Merger in an Indian Village

One fascinating case of merger has occurred in Kupwar, a village in India on the border between two major language families: the Indo-European family (which includes the languages of North India) and the unrelated Dravidian family (comprising the languages of South India). Kupwar's three thousand inhabitants regularly use three languages in their daily activities. There are three principal groups: the Jains, who speak Kannada (a Dravidian language); the Moslems, who speak Urdu (an Indo-European language closely related to Hindi); and the Untouchables, who speak Marathi (the regional Indo-European language surrounding Kupwar and the principal literary language of the area). These groups have lived in the village for centuries, and most villagers are bilingual or multilingual. Over the course of time, with individuals switching back and forth among at least two of these languages, the varieties used in Kupwar have come to be more and more alike. In fact, the grammatical structures of the village varieties are now so similar that a word-for-word translation is possible among the languages. This means that the word order and other structural characteristics of the three languages are now virtually identical. This merging is all the more remarkable because the varieties of these same languages that are used elsewhere are very different from one another. Indeed, they belong to two unrelated language families and cannot be translated word for word into one another.

Even in Kupwar, however, where the grammars of the different languages have been merging, the vocabulary of each variety has remained quite distinct. On the one hand, the need for communication among the different groups has fostered a convergence of grammars; on the other hand, the social separation needed to maintain religious and caste differences has supported the continuation of separate lexicons. The need for intercommunication among the groups has had the effect of making it easy to communicate across the languages; and the fact that the groups remain distinct from one another has kept their languages from becoming so much alike that it would prove difficult to tell linguistically what group an individual belonged to. As things now stand, communication is relatively easy (easier, certainly, than speaking across different languages), while affiliation and group identification remain clear.[1] This is the linguistic equivalent of having your cake and eating it too.

In the following example sentence, the word order and morphology are relatively uniform across the three Kupwar varieties, but the vocabulary leaves no doubt as to which language is being spoken in each case.

Urdu	pala	jəra	kaat	ke	le	ke	a		ya
Marathi	pala	jəra	kap	un	gʰe	un	a	l	o
Kannada	tapla	jəra	kʰod	i	təgond	i	bə		yn
	greens	a little	cut	having	taken	having	come	Past	I

'I cut some greens and brought them.'

Thus, while the three grammars have merged to a remarkable extent, combining grammatical elements from each language, social distinctions remain linguistically marked (and are partly maintained) by clear differences in vocabulary.

Language/Dialect Continua

In contrast to the situation in Kupwar, the Romance languages, including Spanish, French, Italian, and Portuguese, have evolved distinct national varieties from the relatively uniform colloquial Latin that was spoken throughout their regions in Roman times. Whereas language varieties have converged in Kupwar, the language varieties spoken in the area where Latin was used have diverged over the centuries. The reasons in both cases are the same. First, people use language to mark their social identity. Second, people who talk with one another tend to talk *like* one another. A corollary of the second principle is that people not talking with one another tend to become linguistically differentiated.

Today the languages of Europe (in the Romance-speaking area and elsewhere) look separate and tidily compartmentalized on a map. In reality they are not so neatly distinguishable. Instead, there is a continuum of variation, and languages

---

[1] We accomplish a related thing in the United States with nearly identical grammars but distinct regional pronunciations, or accents. As a result, we have no difficulty communicating, but there is little doubt about regional affiliation.

"blend" into one another. Near language-area borders the change is slightly more abrupt. The national border between France and Italy, for example, also serves as a dividing line between the French-speaking and the Italian-speaking area. But in practice the French spoken just over the French border shares features with the Italian spoken by Italians on the Italian side. From Paris to the Italian border, there is a continuum along which the local French varieties become more and more "Italian-like." Likewise, from Rome to the French border, Italian varieties can be viewed as becoming more "French-like."

Similar situations exist all over Europe. As a result, Swedes of the far south using their local dialects can communicate better with Danish speakers in nearby Denmark than with fellow countrymen in distant northern Sweden. The same situation exists with residents along the border between Germany and Holland. Using their own local varieties, speakers of German can communicate better with speakers of Dutch living near them than with speakers of southern German dialects. Examples of geographical dialect continua are found throughout Europe. In fact, while the standard varieties of Italian, French, Spanish, Catalan, and Portuguese are not mutually intelligible, the local varieties form a continuum from Portugal through Spain and halfway through Belgium and then through France and down to the southern tip of Italy. There is also a Scandinavian dialect continuum, a West Germanic dialect continuum, and South Slavonic and North Slavonic dialect continua.

Just as different languages may form a dialect continuum, so different dialects of a single language can constitute a continuum. This is the case in China, where several mutually unintelligible varieties constitute a single language. In the case of Kupwar, if there were no outside reference varieties against which to compare the varieties spoken in the village, we might be inclined to say that the varieties spoken there were dialects of one language; they do, after all, have basically one grammar. The residents of Kupwar, however, have found it socially valuable to continue speaking "different" languages, despite increasing grammatical similarity. Among the factors that count in deciding on designations for varieties and on whether they represent dialects of a single language or separate languages is the view of native speakers.

REGIONAL VARIETIES OF ENGLISH

British and American Varieties

The principal varieties of English throughout the world are customarily divided into British and American types. British English is the basis for the varieties spoken in England, Ireland, Wales, Scotland, Australia, New Zealand, India, Pakistan, Malaysia, Singapore, and South Africa. American (or North American) includes chiefly the English of Canada and the United States.

This division inevitably oversimplifies the facts. For example, despite the groupings just suggested, certain characteristics of Canadian English are closer to British English, while certain characteristics of Irish English are closer to North American English. And there are many differences between, say, Standard British English and Standard Indian English. But we can still make a number of generalizations about British-based varieties and American-based varieties, provided we keep in mind that neither group is completely homogeneous.

There are well-known spelling differences between British and American English. Red, white, and blue are *colours* in Britain and *colors* in America. The British put *tyres* on their cars and drive to the *theatre,* where they park near the *kerb.* Interestingly, Canadians usually follow British spelling rather than American, a reflection of the close historical association between Canada and Britain. But these minor spelling differences do not reflect spoken differences. On the other hand, in the phonology, morphology, syntax, and lexicon of the two sets of varieties you can note some marked differences.

Speakers of most American varieties, for example, consistently pronounce the vowel of words like *can't* as [æ], while speakers of British varieties usually have the sound [ɑ:] in such words. Between two vowels the first of which is stressed, Americans and Canadians usually pronounce the stop /t/ as a flap [D] so that the word *sitter* is pronounced [sɪDər]. Speakers of British varieties, in contrast, do not readily change /t/ to [D] between vowels. Again, most American varieties have a retroflex /r/ in word-final position in words like *car, sir,* and *near,* whereas in many British varieties /r/ is dropped in these words. With respect to the last feature, speakers of Irish and Scottish English follow the American pattern rather than the British pattern, while residents of New York City and Boston, among others, follow the British pattern. This patterning illustrates the fact that British varieties can differ widely from one another, as do American varieties.

There are also a few morphological and syntactic differences between British and American varieties. Many noun phrases that denote locations in time or space take an article in American English but not in British English.

American	British
in the hospital	in hospital
to the university	to university
the next day	next day

Collective nouns (those that refer to groups of people or institutions) are plural in British varieties but usually singular in American varieties. An American watching a college soccer game would say *Cornell is ahead by two,* while a British observer would say *Cornell are ahead by two.* A final illustration of the grammatical differences between the two varieties is the use of the verb *do* with the auxiliaries *do, can,* and *have.* If asked *Did he find the book?*, an American may answer *Yes, he did,* while a speaker of a British variety can also answer *Yes, he did do.* If asked *Have you finished the assignment?*, an American may say *Yes, I have,* while British English also allows *Yes, I have done.* Asked whether flying time to Los Angeles varies, a British flight attendant might reply *It can do* as well as *It can.*

Finally, there are differences between the word stocks of American and British varieties of English, many of which are well known.

American	British
elevator	lift
second floor	first floor
TV	telly
flashlight	torch
hood (of a car)	bonnet
trunk (of a car)	boot
cookies	biscuits
gas/gasoline	petrol
highway	motorway
truck	lorry
bus	coach
can	tin
intermission	interval
line	queue
exit	way out

In general, structural differences between British varieties and American varieties are not great. But combined with social and political factors, the structural differences are sufficient to make speakers of English everywhere intensely aware of the dialect boundary that the Atlantic Ocean constitutes.

Regional Varieties of American English

Although regional differences have always been greater in Great Britain than in the United States, recent presidents have highlighted regional differences in American speech. John F. Kennedy and his successor Lyndon B. Johnson spoke markedly different dialects. George Bush and Bill Clinton, also successive occupants of the White House, articulate strikingly different policies with strikingly different speechways, the latter a reflection of their different regional origins.

Starting in the late 1940s, investigation of vocabulary patterns in the eastern United States suggested distinguishing among Northern, Midland, and Southern dialects, each with subdivisions. Midland was divided into North Midland and South Midland varieties. Boston and metropolitan New York were seen as distinct varieties of the Northern dialect. Midwestern states, such as Illinois, Indiana, and Ohio, formerly thought of as representing General American, were seen as situated principally in the North Midland dialect, with a narrow strip of Northern dialect across their northernmost counties and a small strip across their southern counties belonging to the South Midland variety. The most recent research has suggested a refinement of that scheme, and the results are shown in the geographical patterns of Figure 13-1.

Mapping Dialects   In order to propose a map like Figure 13-1, dialectologists investigate word usage and pronunciation as well as characteristic patterns of morphology and syntax. Typically, a researcher visits a town and, using a lengthy questionnaire, inquires of residents what they call certain things or how they express certain meanings.

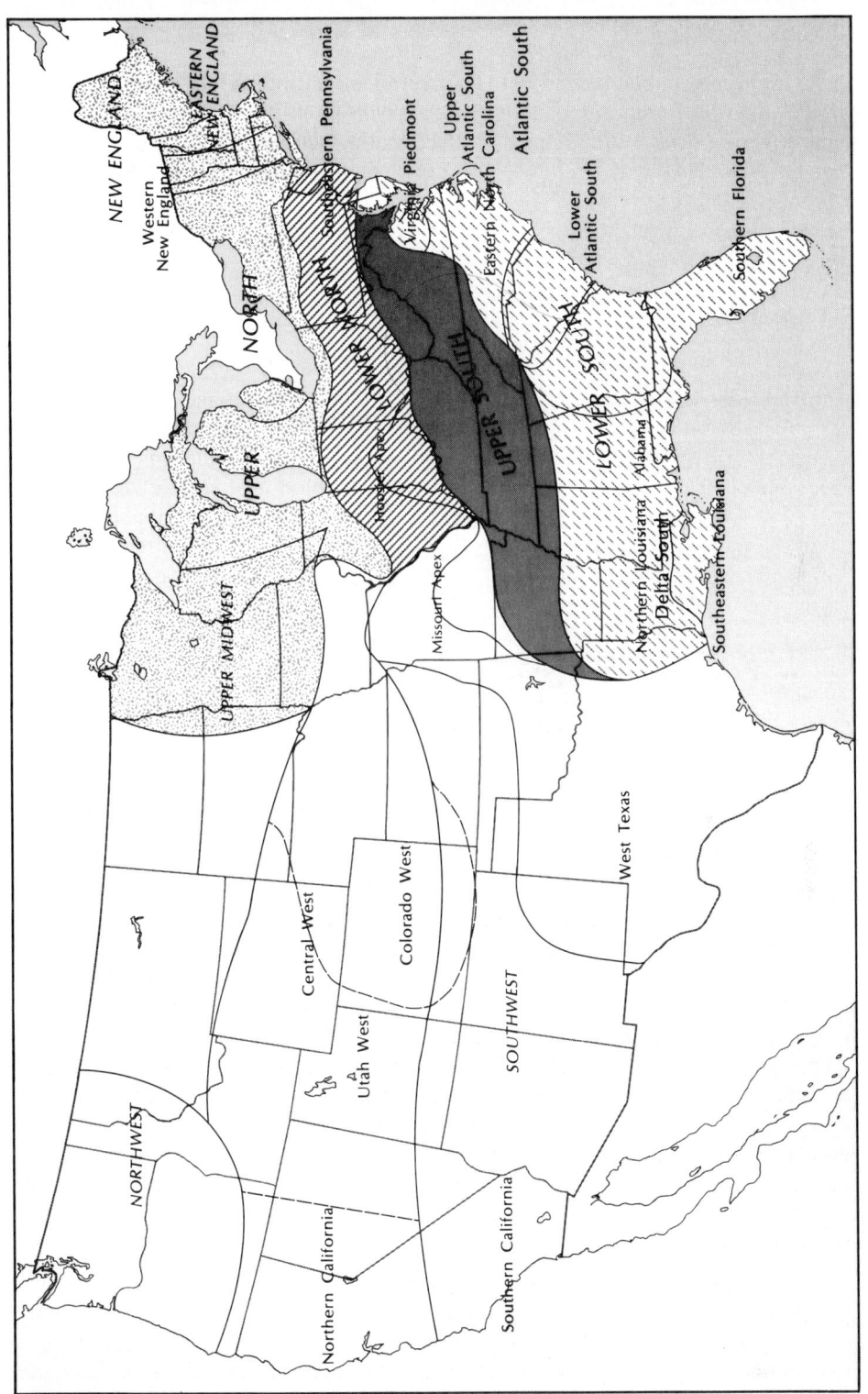

FIGURE 13-1
Major Dialect Regions of the United States

Source: Carver 1987

To take an example, researchers uncovered surprising variety when they asked what word was commonly used for the large insect with transparent wings often seen hovering over water. Figure 13-2 shows that *darning needle* was most common in New England, upstate New York, metropolitan New York (including

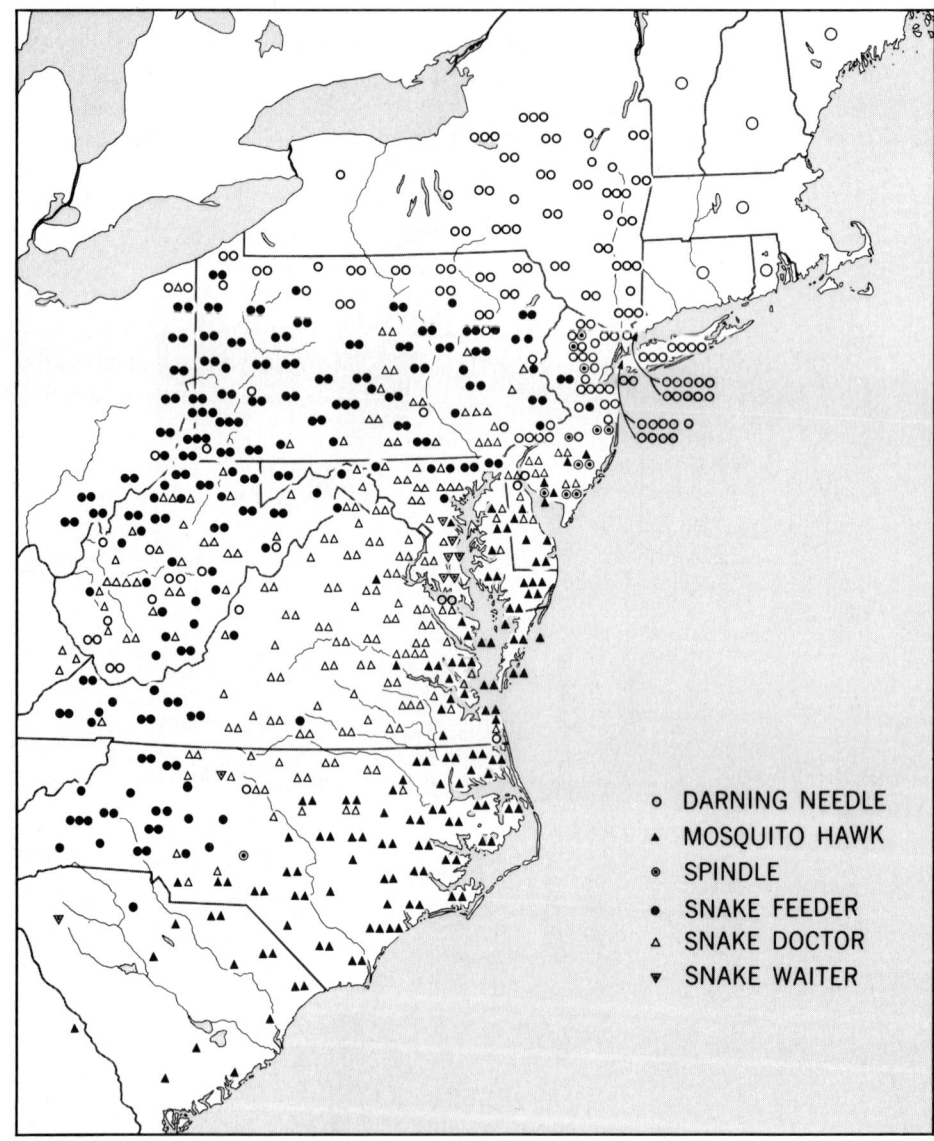

FIGURE 13-2
Words for 'dragonfly' in the Eastern States

Source: Kurath 1949

northern and eastern New Jersey and Long Island), and northern Pennsylvania. *Mosquito hawk* predominated in coastal North Carolina and Virginia, *snake doctor* occurred widely in inland Virginia, and *snake feeder* predominated along the northern Ohio River in West Virginia, Ohio, western Pennsylvania, and the upper Ohio Valley toward Pittsburgh. Notice that not all the words were tidily limited to an area in which no other word was used. In some areas, a mixture of two or more forms occurred. In other areas a single form occurred exclusively. The Os on the map in New England and New York indicate that *darning needle* was the only regional term found among respondents there.

As you can see in Figures 13-3 and 13-4, *mosquito hawk* was virtually the only regional response given in much of southeast Texas and portions of central Texas, as well as all of Louisiana and Florida, and much of southern Alabama, Mississippi, and Georgia. But *snake doctor* was the favored form in west, north, and northwest Texas, the western half of Tennessee, the northern parts of Alabama and Mississippi, and a part of northwestern Georgia. *Snake feeder* occurred occasionally along the Canadian and Arkansas rivers in Oklahoma and throughout eastern Tennessee. Both *mosquito hawk* and *snake doctor* were found in the southern half of Arkansas. *Darning needle,* so popular in New York and New England,

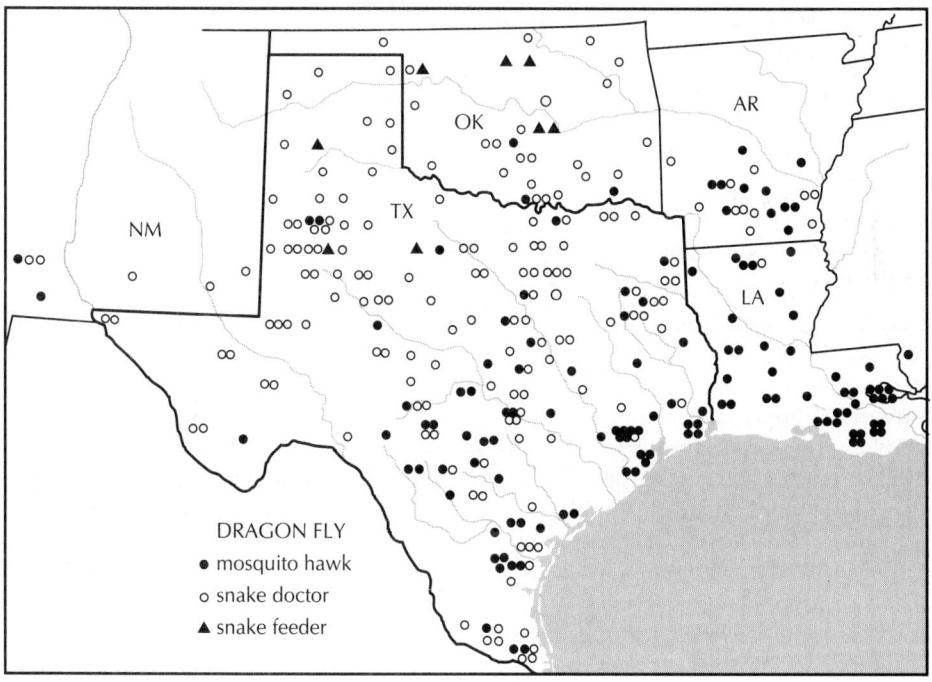

FIGURE 13-3
Words for 'dragonfly' in Texas, Arkansas, Louisiana, Oklahoma

Source: Atwood 1963

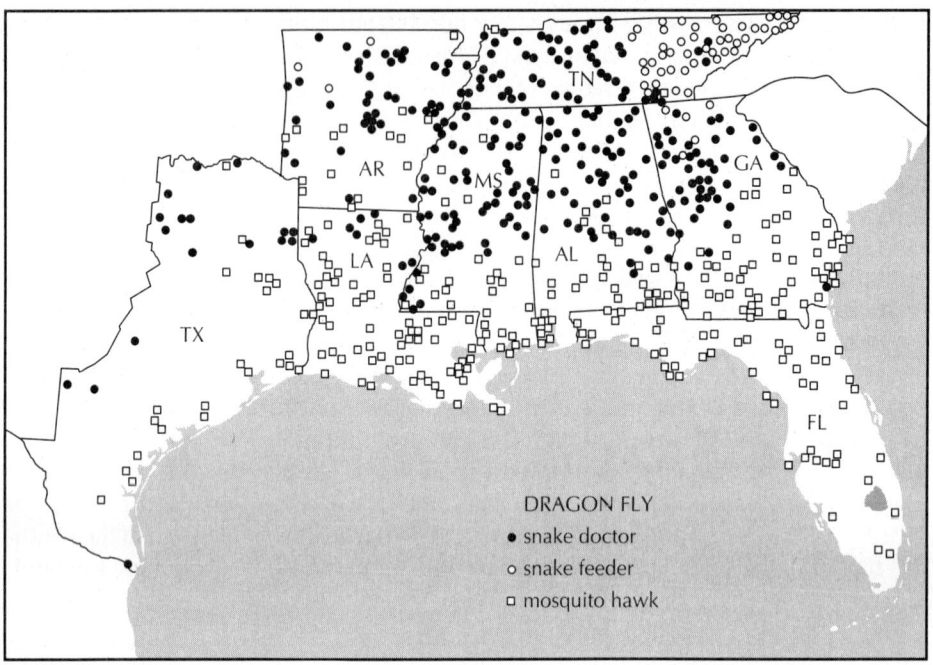

FIGURE 13-4
Words for 'dragonfly' in the Gulf States

Source: Pederson 1986

occurred too infrequently even to be recorded on these maps of the South. Some respondents were unacquainted with local terms and reported using only *dragon fly*.[2]

Determining Isoglosses   Once a map has been marked with symbols for various features, lines called **isoglosses** can be drawn at the boundary between regions that use different forms. From Figure 13-2, showing the distribution of regional words for the dragonfly in the eastern states, and from other maps (not provided here) showing the distribution of *I want off* and *Sook!* (a call to cows), dialect geographers derive Figure 13-5, on which the easternmost boundaries of the three features have been marked.

Figure 13-6 shows four isoglosses traversing the three North-Central states of Ohio, Indiana, and Illinois. These isoglosses represent the northernmost limits of *greasy* pronounced as /grizi/, of *snake feeder* for 'dragonfly,' of *Sook!* as a call to cows, and of *sugar tree* meaning 'maple.'

Figure 13-7 represents seven isoglosses in the Upper Midwest. Three are the southernmost boundaries of northern features: *humor* pronounced [hyumər]; *bou-*

---

[2] If you hail from an area represented on the maps and find the terms indicated there unfamiliar, bear in mind that the data were often gathered in rural areas and represent not only "cultivated" speech but "folk" speech as well. Moreover, some of the data are now more than fifty years old, and a preference was given to older respondents in the survey.

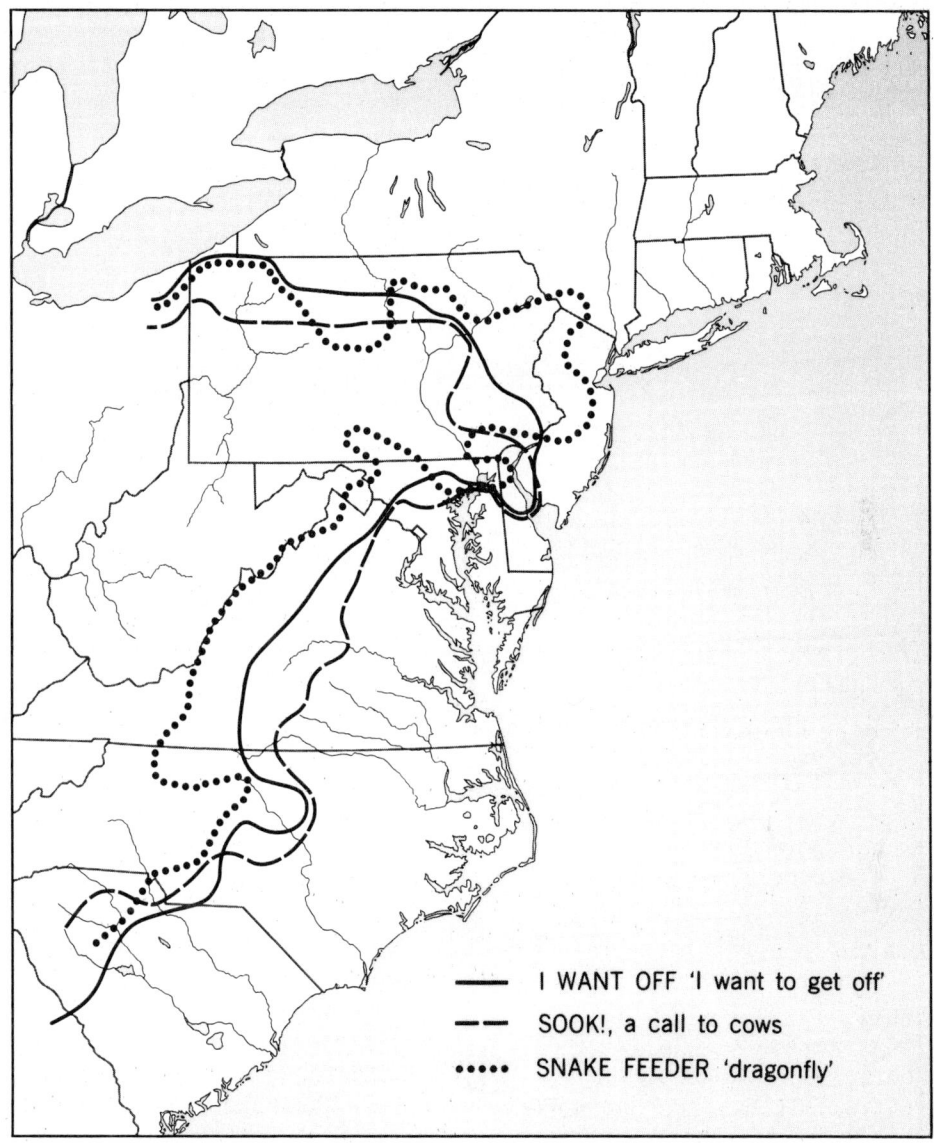

FIGURE 13-5
Three Isoglosses in the Eastern States (Eastern Limits)

Source: Kurath 1949

levard referring to the grass strip between curb and sidewalk; and *come in (fresh)*, meaning 'to give birth, usually said of a cow.' Four are the northernmost boundaries of midland features: *on* pronounced with /ɔ/ or /ɒ/ (the latter a rounded /ɑ/) instead of /ɑ/; *caterwampus* for 'askew, awry'; *roasting ears* for 'corn on the cob';

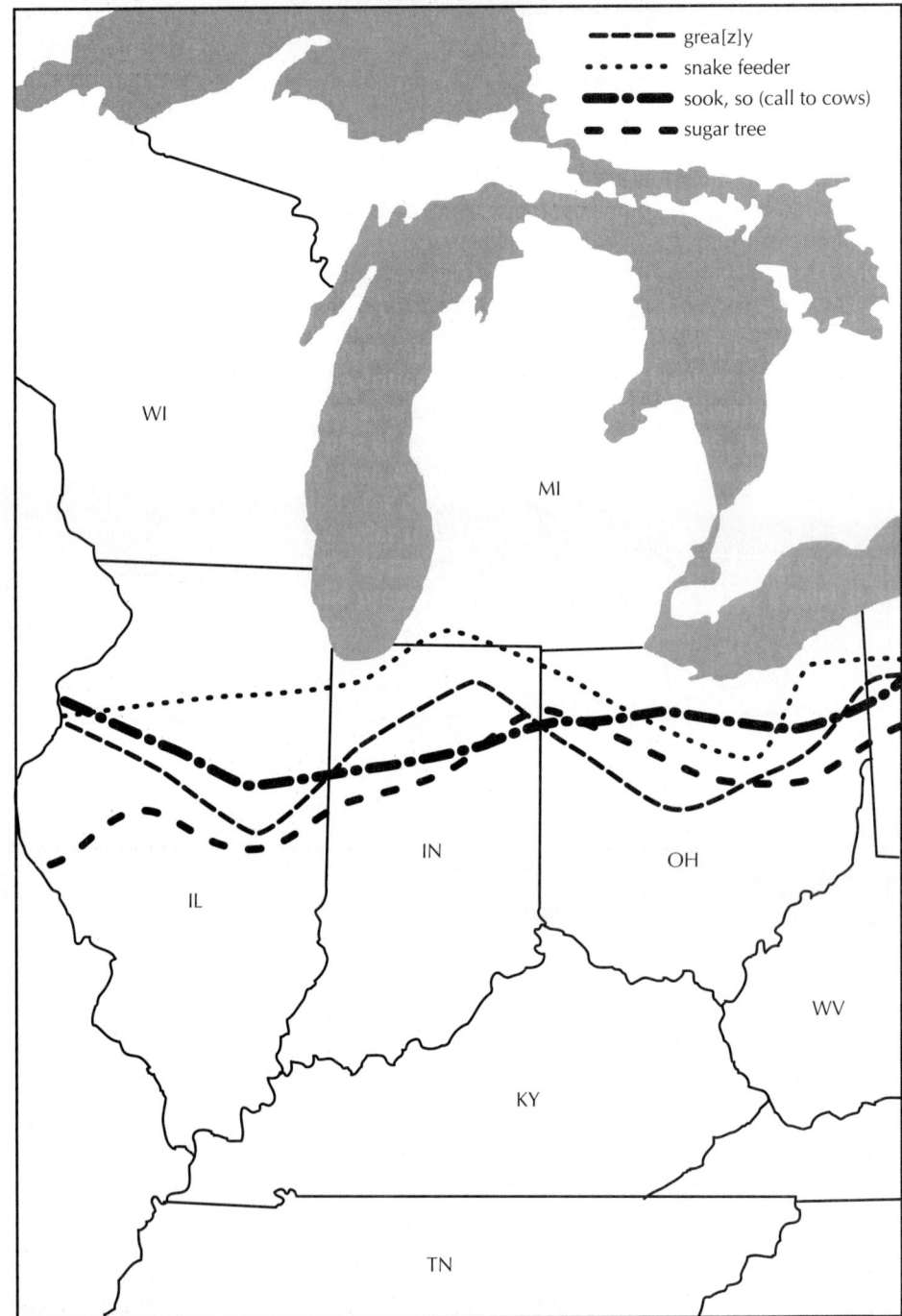

FIGURE 13-6
Four Isoglosses in the North-Central States (Northern Limits)

Source: Marckwardt 1957

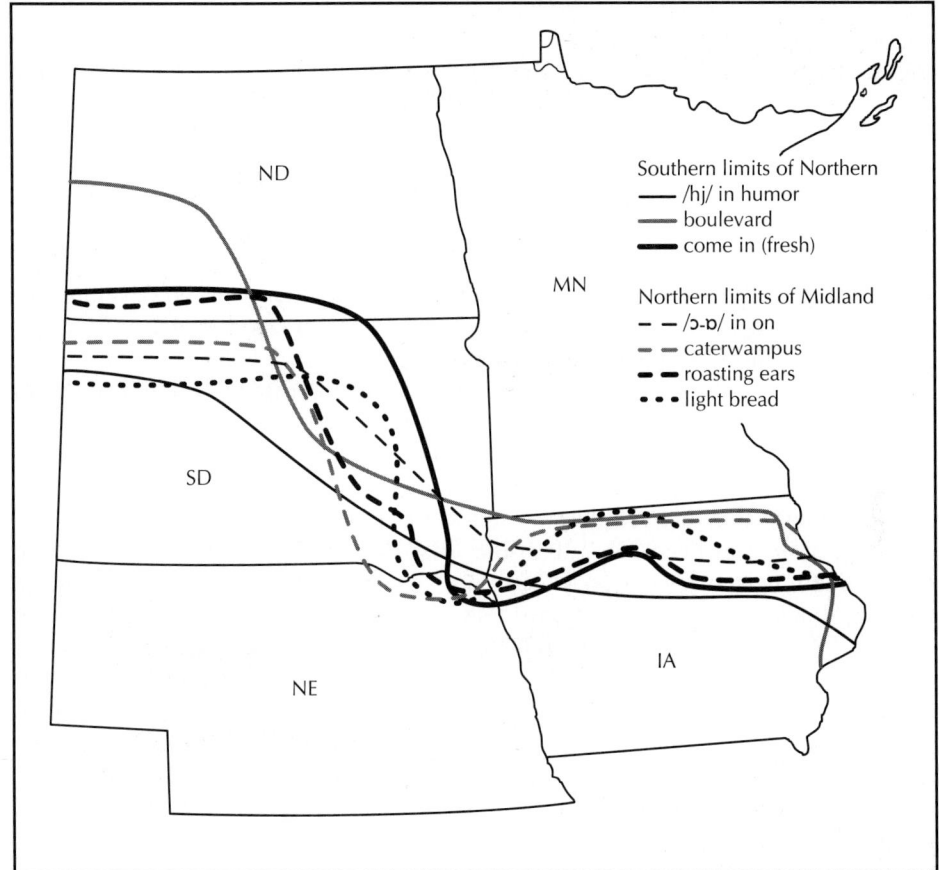

FIGURE 13-7
Seven Isoglosses in the Upper Midwest

Source: Allen 1973

and *lightbread* for 'white bread.' You can see that each feature has a unique distribution.

Dialect Boundaries   Imagine each isogloss map drawn on a transparency and stacked one on top of the other. The result would be a map similar to that shown in Figure 13-7 and would show the extent to which the isoglosses from the different feature maps "bundle" together. The geographical limit for the use of a particular word (say, *caterwampus*) often corresponds roughly to the limit for the use of other pronunciations or words (say, *roasting ears*). Where isoglosses bundle, dialectologists draw dialect boundaries; thus, a *dialect boundary* is simply the location of a bundle of isoglosses. The map in Figure 13-1 is a distillation of dozens of maps similar to those in Figures 13-5, 13-6, and 13-7.

Speech patterns in the United States, as elsewhere in the world, are determined partly by the geographical and physical boundaries that inhibit communication and partly by the migration routes that were followed in settling the country. Among the isoglosses of Figure 13-6, the one for /grisi/ versus /grizi/ essentially follows a line (now approximated by Interstate 70) that was the principal road for the migration of pioneers during the postcolonial settlement period.

In the western United States, the dialect situation is more complex than in the longer established areas of the East, the South, and the Midwest. The West drew settlers speaking a range of dialects from various parts of the country. California especially continues to welcome immigrants from other parts of the country and the world, and it is a melting pot not only of races and cultures but of dialects and languages. Such extreme heterogeneity is not conducive to the development of distinctive regional varieties of English and therefore does not lend itself so readily to the tidiness suggested by isoglosses.

An illustration of California's diversity can be seen in Figure 13-8, which shows the distribution of the words *curtains* 'window shades,' *seed* 'pit,' *green beans* 'string beans,' and *took sick* for 'got sick.' The small numerals on the map represent the number of respondents (if more than one) using that feature in that location. 270 residents were interviewed in California (and 30 in Nevada): 55 in Los Angeles, 25 in San Francisco, 20 in the East Bay and 5 on the Peninsula (both near San Francisco), 8 in San Diego, 5 in Sacramento, 4 in San Bernardino, 3 each in San Jose, Stockton, Fresno, Pomona, Riverside, and Bakersfield, and 2 each in 65 other communities. Looking at Figure 13-8, you can infer that most respondents used expressions other than the ones plotted; they used *shades* or *blinds* instead of *curtains; pit* or *stone* instead of *seed; string beans* instead of *green beans;* and *got sick* instead of *took sick.* You can also see that within the substantial area marked by the dialect boundary along the coast (including San Luis Obispo, Santa Barbara, Oxnard, and Oceanside) not a single respondent used any of the four mapped features. Patterns of usage in California and Nevada are not so tidy as elsewhere.

The special mixed character of California can also be heard in its pronunciations, as you can see in the map of Figure 13-9, showing locations for two pronunciations of *rodeo*—the Spanish pronunciation [rodéo] (with stress on the second syllable) and the anglicized pronunciation [ródio] (with stress on the first syllable). At least in the 1950s, when the dialect survey was made, the anglicized pronunciation predominated in Nevada and was the sole pronunciation in central Nevada, as well as in the California communities along the Oregon border. The Spanish pronunciation predominated in the great bulk of California and was the *only* pronunciation in communities along the coast from Monterey to Santa Barbara and Oxnard. Even in Los Angeles, residents favored the Spanish pronunciation by almost two to one, and pronunciations in San Diego were evenly divided. The influence of Spanish thus remained strong on some pronunciations (as it continues to be in such place names as Los Angeles, San Diego, San Francisco, and Santa Barbara).

Dictionary of American Regional English

When in 1985 the first volume of the *Dictionary of American Regional English* appeared, it made available more information about regional words and expres-

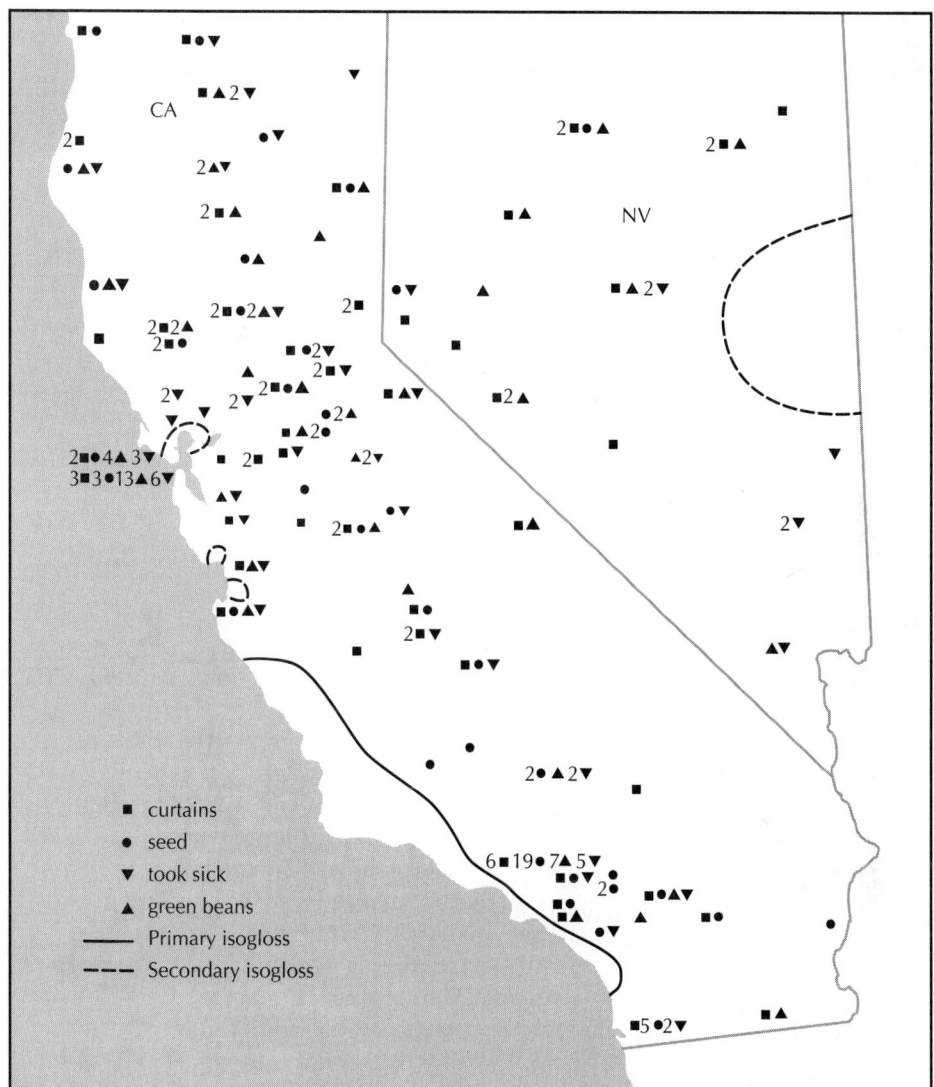

FIGURE 13-8
Distribution of Four Features in California and Nevada

Source: Bright 1971

sions throughout the United States than had ever been known before. *DARE* (as the project and the dictionary are called) represents the most up-to-date knowledge of American regional vocabulary.

Based on answers to 1,847 questions asked by field workers who visited 1,002 communities across the country, the computer-produced maps that *DARE* uses for exhibiting its findings represent not geographical space but population density.

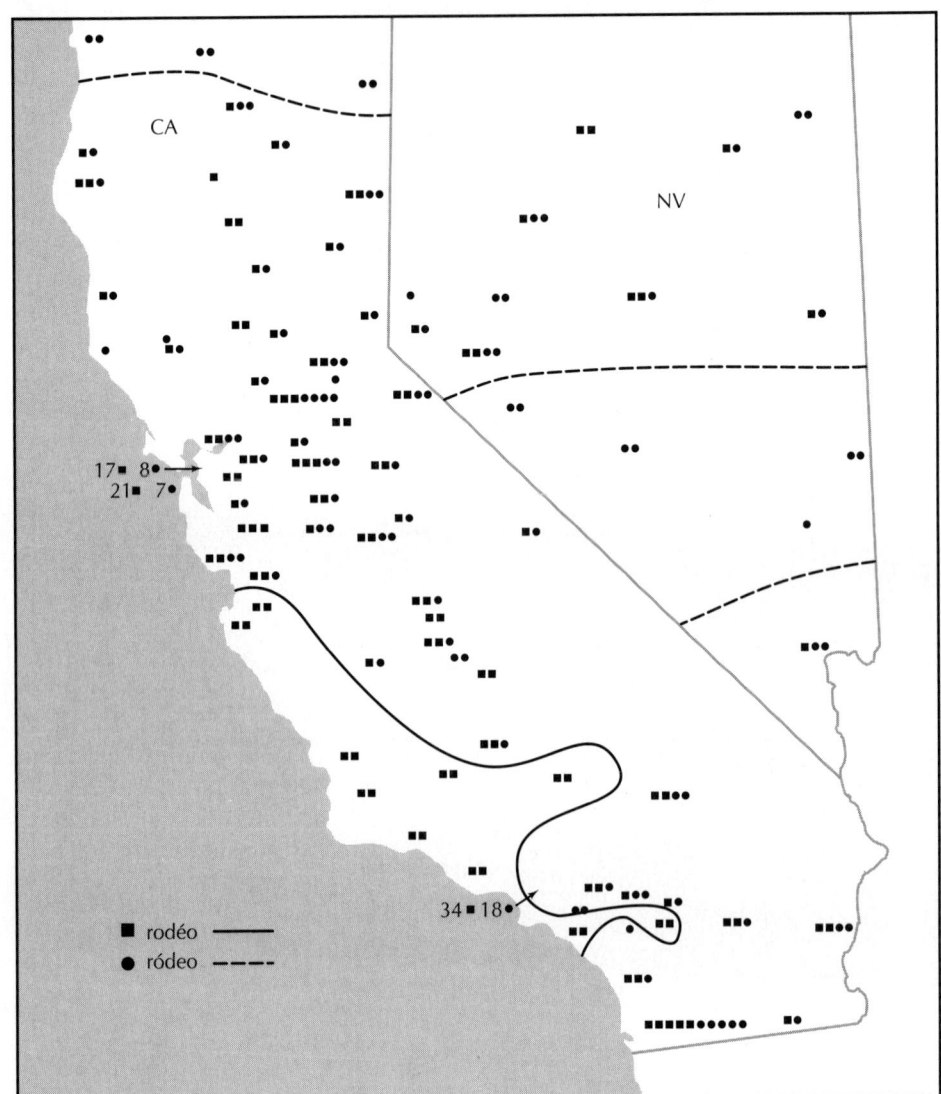

FIGURE 13-9
Two Pronunciations of *rodeo* in California and Nevada

Source: Bright 1971

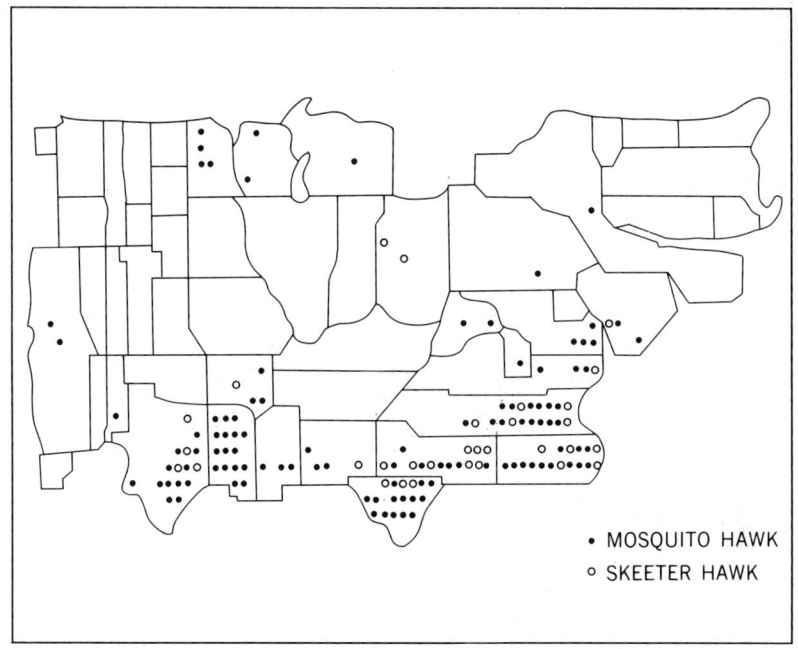

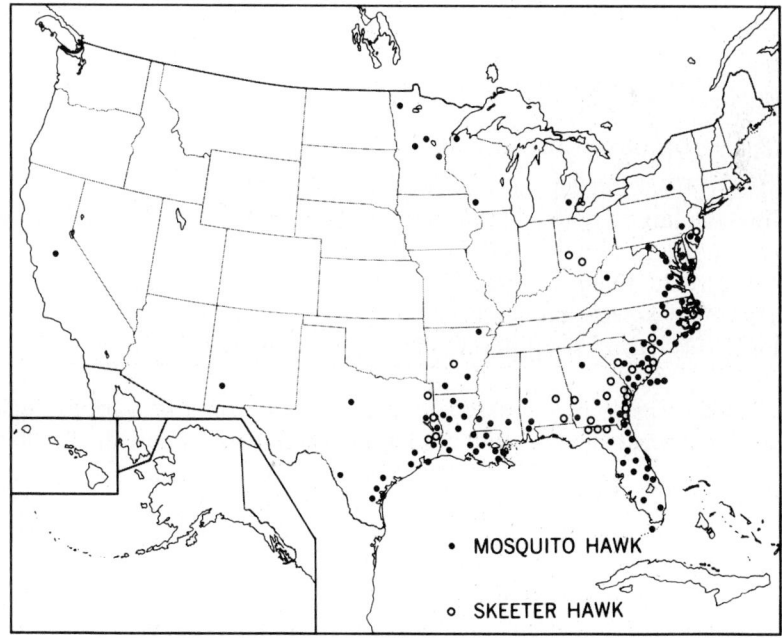

FIGURE 13-10
Distribution of *mosquito hawk* and *skeeter hawk* on *DARE* Map and Conventional Map

Source: Dictionary of American Regional English, I, 1985

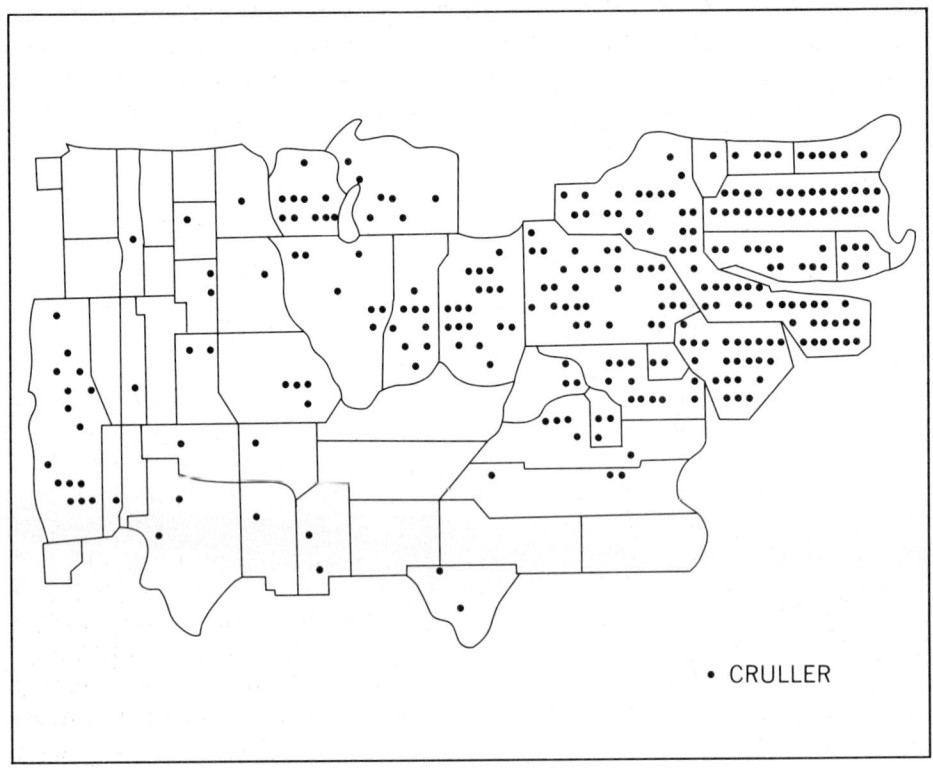

FIGURE 13-11
Distribution of *cruller* **on a** *DARE* **Map**

Source: Dictionary of American Regional English, I, 1985

Thus the largest states are those with the largest populations. As a result, *DARE* maps appear oddly shaped.

Figure 13-10 shows the distribution of the terms *mosquito hawk* and *skeeter hawk* on a *DARE* map and on a conventional map. The word *cruller* 'a twisted doughnut' has a very different distribution, as shown in the *DARE* map of Figure 13-11.

As the result of increased knowledge, the fruits of various regional dialect projects, especially *DARE,* a complex picture of American English dialects is emerging, as Figure 13-1 shows. The darker the shading of a dialect area in that figure, the greater the number of lexical items that distinguish that dialect area from others. As you can see, the farther west you go, the fewer the peculiar linguistic characteristics of an area. The boundaries of American dialects are better established in the eastern states than in the more recently settled western ones.

Current View of Dialect Patterns in the United States

Recent research indicates that there are basically northern and southern dialects, each divided into upper and lower regions (see Figure 13-1). In the Upper

North, there are dialects of New England, the Upper Midwest, and the Northwest, with some lesser-marked dialect boundaries in the Central West and Northern California. The Southwest is also a dialect area, with Southern California having some distinct characteristics. The South is divided into an Upper South and Lower South, each having subdialects as well.

Comparing American and British Regional Distributions

Because not much information is available about the patterns of English in seventeenth- and eighteenth-century America, it is not easy to trace particular patterns of American English to their British sources. But the maps in Figure 13-12 and 13-13, showing distributions for the regional forms of past tense *see* (as in standard *He saw me*) are suggestive. Because the map in Figure 13-12 represents three forms other than *saw,* the blank spaces indicate that *saw* is universal only in central Massachusetts, metropolitan New York City, and southeastern New York state. Throughout the rest of New England, *see (He see me)* predominates (by five to one: hence the large black circles). *Seen (He seen me)* occurs all over the map and is strongly favored in Pennsylvania except along its northern border, in most of New Jersey and West Virginia, and in much of Delaware, Maryland, and the Shenandoah Valley of Virginia. *Seed* has a single occurrence in western Massachusetts but otherwise is limited to the area south of the Pennsylvania/Maryland border, particularly North Carolina and inland South Carolina; in parts of the Carolinas, *seed* is the only regional form used (other than the standard *saw*).

England too has sharply marked regional distribution of these same forms. The blank portions in Figure 13-13 indicate that *saw* is favored in rural speech only in the counties bordering Scotland and in parts of the northeast Midlands. Most of the southwest Midlands and Kent (in the far southeast) favor *seen,* with a narrow band of *seen* linking the two. *Seed* predominates in southwest England, most of the northwest Midlands, and the north.

From Figure 13-13 it is clear that England has its own regional patterns, and dialect geographers hope one day to be able to trace the vocabulary, pronunciations, and other linguistic features from one region to another and from one country to another. With additional information, a good deal may be learned about the diffusion of linguistic and cultural patterns alike.

SOCIAL VARIETIES

Just as oceans and mountains separate people and lead eventually to distinct speech patterns, so social and political boundaries also separate people and can be instrumental in promoting separate speechways. To the extent that such technology as the automobile, jet plane, telephone, radio, and television have reduced the effect of physical boundaries and distances between communities, physical separation has become a less significant barrier to communication. Still, social barriers continue to play an important role in promoting and maintaining characteristic speech patterns among groups of people.

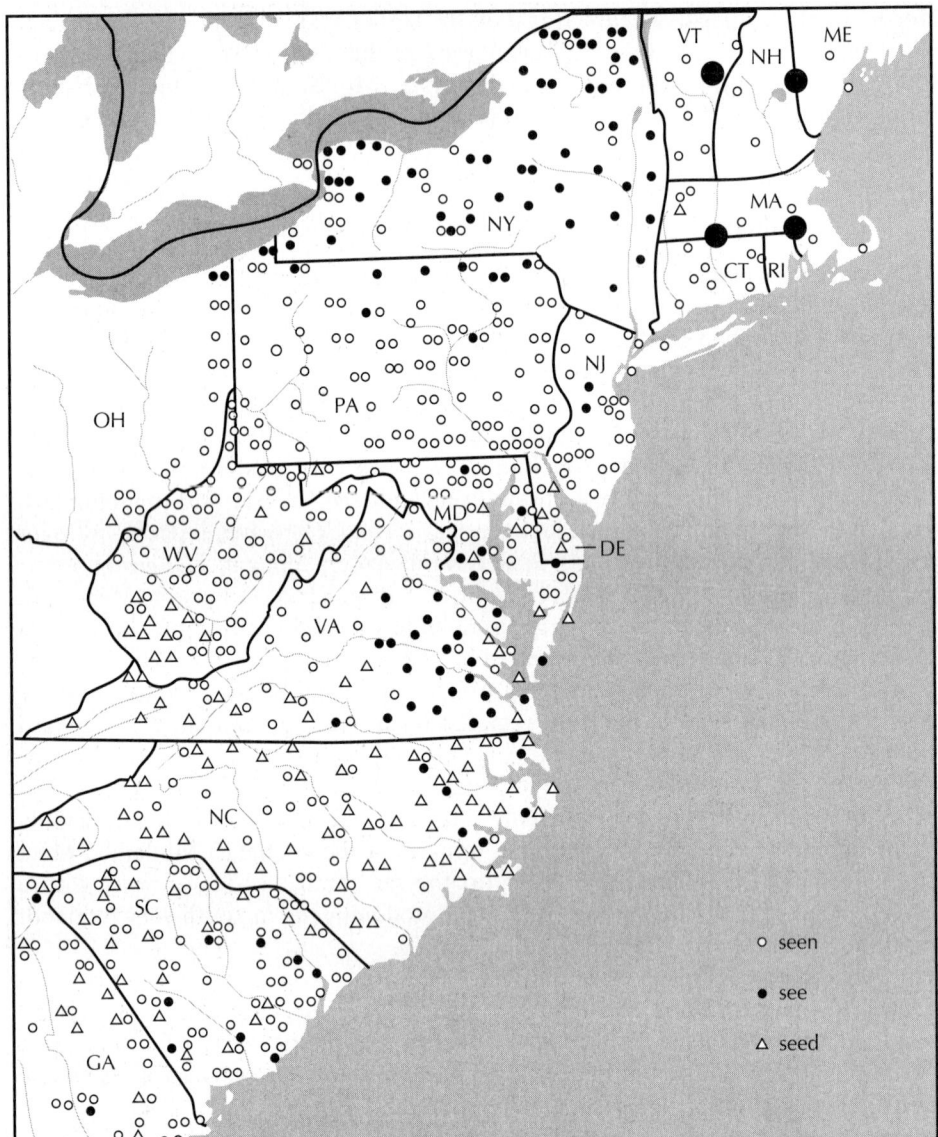

FIGURE 13-12
Distribution of Past Tense of *see* in Eastern States

Source: Atwood 1953

Thus we can speak of **social dialects** as validly as we have spoken of regional ones. The social groups that claim various social dialects as their own may identify themselves as separate classes or separate ethnic groups or separate religions. In addition, cutting across all other social boundaries are differences in the ways women and men speak. In this section we explore several examples of how lan-

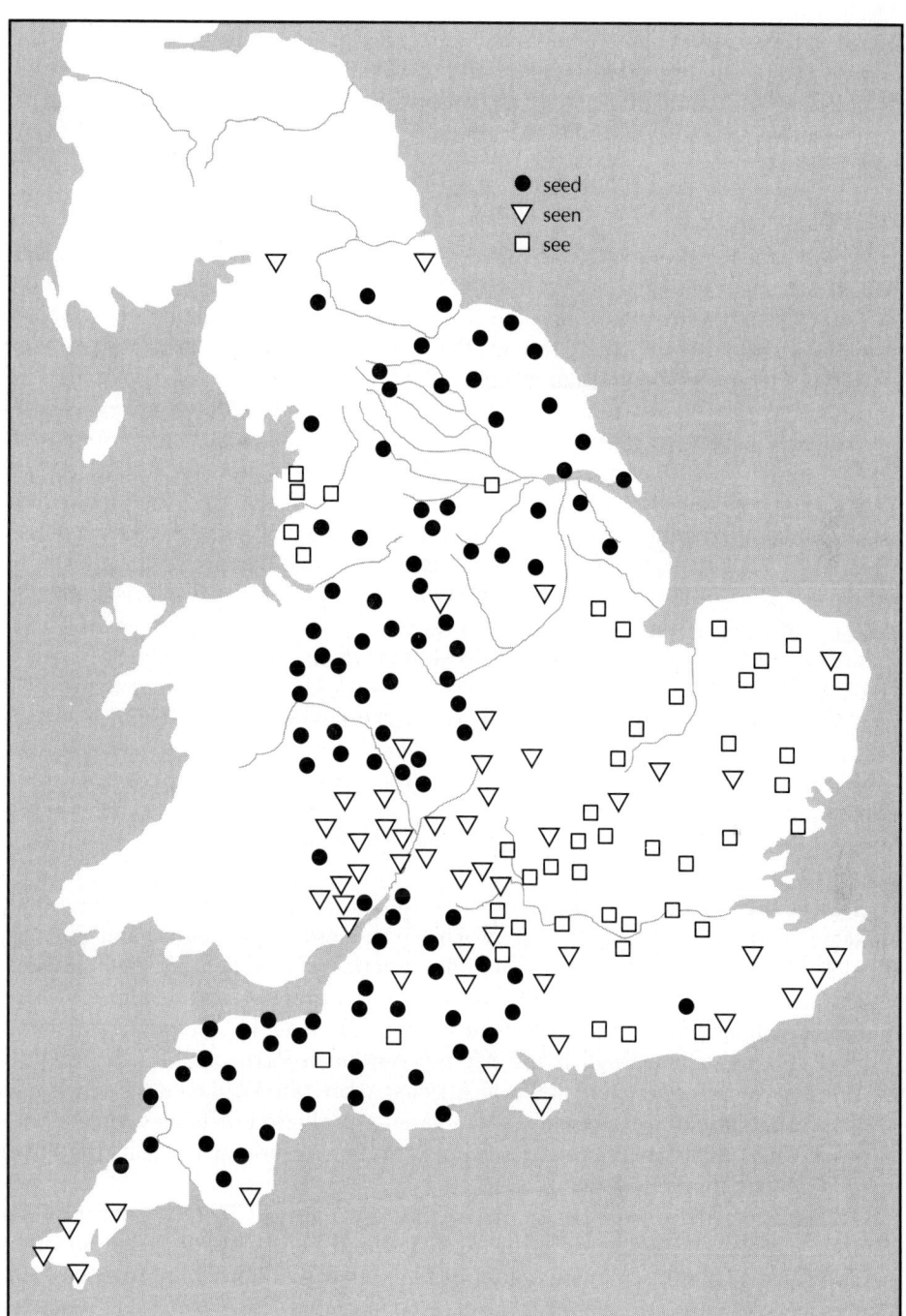

FIGURE 13-13
Distribution of Past Tense of *see* in England

Source: Francis 1961

guage varies across social boundaries, especially in America. As will be evident, society can be subdivided in a multiplicity of ways: by religion, ethnic background, social-class affiliation, and gender, to name a few. As a mirror of society, language varies across all these boundaries.

Ethnic Varieties

Americans commonly believe that American society is essentially homogeneous. If language is any indicator, this belief is a myth. Even though Americans may be less class-conscious than, say, the British, social-group affiliation nevertheless remains extremely important. In fact, the language of each American marks him or her as a member of particular groups, which we unconsciously learn to identify and react to as we grow up.

The most salient socially defined dialects of American English are *ethnic varieties*. Ethnicity is sometimes racial and sometimes not. For example, differences in the speech of Jewish and Italian New Yorkers have been noted, and bookstores carry books describing "Yinglish," the variety of English influenced by Yiddish speakers who have settled in America. But the social separation that leads to ethnic varieties of language is particularly noticeable in the characteristic speech patterns of urban African Americans. In some cities, the speech of African-American residents is becoming increasingly distinct from the speech of white residents. Such a distinction between social groups is also noticeable in the characteristic speech patterns of other ethnic groups. Spanish-speaking immigrants in Los Angeles, New York, Chicago, Miami, and elsewhere have learned English as a second language, and their English is marked by a foreign accent. The children of these immigrants acquire English as a native language (and many are bilingual to some degree), but the variety of English that many Hispanic Americans speak natively identifies them as being of Latin ancestry.

The discussion that follows identifies certain major characteristics of two ethnic dialects of American English: African-American Vernacular English and Chicano English. Both these dialects are bona fide varieties of American English like any other regional or social variety. Both have complete grammatical systems overlapping to a great degree with other varieties of English. And, like Standard American English, both Chicano English and African-American Vernacular English have a wide range of registers. Speakers of African-American Vernacular English and Chicano English do not speak the same variety in all circumstances. While both dialects share many characteristics with Standard American English, they also exhibit certain distinctive features.

To think of African-American Vernacular English or Chicano English as an inferior variety of English or as ill formed would be erroneous. Like all other social dialects, these two ethnic varieties have rules that determine what can and cannot be said. As in Standard English, a construction can be ungrammatical in African-American Vernacular English or in Chicano English. Rules govern the structures and use of all the world's dialects, and no dialect exists without phonological, morphological, and syntactic rules, among others.

African-American Vernacular English   Probably the most widespread and most familiar ethnic variety of American English is African-American Vernacular English (formerly called Black English or Black English Vernacular). Not that all African Americans are fluent speakers of African-American Vernacular English, but neither are all speakers of African-American Vernacular English African Americans. After all, people grow up speaking the language variety spoken around them. As you could have grown up speaking Japanese, Swahili, or Arabic had you been born into Japanese-, Swahili-, or Arabic-speaking families, children growing up among speakers of different regional and social varieties speak the variety that surrounds them. In an ethnically diverse city like Los Angeles, one can meet teenage speakers of African-American Vernacular English whose foreign-born parents speak Chinese or Vietnamese. The variety of English spoken by these Asian Americans reflects the characteristic speechways of their friends and of the neighborhoods in which they acquired English. To underscore an obvious but often misunderstood fact, the acquisition of a particular language or dialect is as independent of one's skin color as it is of one's height or weight.

The history of African-American Vernacular English in the United States is not completely understood, and there are conflicting theories about its origins and subsequent development. But there is no disagreement concerning its structure and functioning. African-American Vernacular English has characteristic phonological, morphological, and syntactic features, as well as vocabulary of its own. Speakers of African-American Vernacular English, like all other social groups, also share characteristic ways of interacting. In this section we examine some of the phonological and syntactic features of African-American Vernacular English; we will not discuss lexical or interactional characteristics.

One of the most prominent phonological features of African-American Vernacular English is the frequent simplification of consonant clusters, as in "des" [dɛs] for *desk,* "pass" [pæs] for *passed,* and "wile" [wayl] for *wild.* This feature also occurs (though to a lesser degree) in several regional varieties of American English. In Standard English the consonant clusters in *desk* and *wild* are also commonly simplified, as in "asthem" [æsðəm] for *ask them* and "tole" [tol] for *told.* But consonant cluster simplification occurs more frequently and to a greater extent in African-American Vernacular English than in other varieties.

Another salient characteristic concerns the final stop consonants in words like *side* and *borrowed.* Speakers of African-American Vernacular English frequently delete some word-final stops, pronouncing *side* like *sigh* and *borrowed* like *borrow.* The deletion rule is governed by the linguistic circumstances of the utterance. When a final stop consonant represents a separate morpheme (as it would in the words *followed* and *tried*), the final [d] is preserved much more frequently than when it is part of the word stem (as in the words *side* and *rapid*). Another factor influencing the deletion of word-final stops is whether they occur in a syllable that is strongly stressed *(tried)* or weakly stressed *(rapid);* strongly stressed syllables tend to preserve final stops more than weakly stressed syllables do. A third factor is whether the stop has a vowel following it (as in *side angle* and *tried it*) or a consonant (as in *tried hard* and *side street*). A following vowel serves to preserve the stop; in fact, it appears to be the most significant factor in determining whether a final stop is deleted in this variety of English.

African-American Vernacular English distinguishes itself not only at the phonological level but also in its syntax. One prominent syntactic feature is a characteristic use of the verb BE. Compare the uses of this verb in African-American Vernacular English and in Standard American English:

African-American Vernacular	Standard American
1. That my bike.	That's my bike.
2. The coffee cold.	The coffee's cold.
3. The coffee be cold there.	The coffee's (always) cold there.

As sentences 1 and 2 illustrate, African-American Vernacular English permits omitting the verb BE in the present tense in just those environments in which standard English permits a contracted form of it. As example 3 shows, speakers of African-American Vernacular English express recurring or repeated action by using the form *be*. It may seem that *be* is equivalent to Standard American English *is,* but in fact *be* in a sentence like 3 is equivalent to a verb expressing a habitual or continuous state of affairs. As Geneva Smitherman, herself an African-American linguist, wrote about sentences like 2 and 3, "If you the cook and *the coffee cold,* you might only just get talked about that day, but if *the coffee bees cold,* pretty soon you ain't gon have no job!"

Thus, in African-American Vernacular English, the verb *be* (or its inflected variant *bees*) is used to indicate continuous, repeated, or habitual action. The following examples illustrate its function further.

African-American Vernacular	Standard American
Do they be playing all day?	Do they play all day?
Yeah, the boys do be messin' around a lot.	Yeah, the boys do mess around a lot.
I see her when I bees on my way to school.	I see her when I'm on my way to school.

Another feature of African-American Vernacular English is the use of the expression *it is* where Standard American English uses *there is*.

African-American Vernacular	Standard American
Is it a Miss Jones in this office?	Is there a Miss Jones in this office?
She's been a wonderful wife and it's nothin' too good for her.	She's been a wonderful wife and there's nothing too good for her.

A final illustration of the distinctiveness of this ethnic variety is provided by these examples of multiple negation:

African-American Vernacular	Standard American
Don't nobody never help me do my work.	*Nobody* ever helps me do my work.
He *don't never* go *nowhere*.	He *never* goes anywhere.

The African-American Vernacular English sentences contain more than one word marked for negation. In African-American Vernacular English, multiple-negative constructions are well formed, as they are in several other varieties of American English. The fact that these constructions are not appropriate in Standard English has no effect on their grammaticality or appropriateness in other varieties.

Chicano English   Another important ethnic dialect of American English is Chicano English, spoken by many people of Mexican descent in the major urban areas of the country and in rural areas of the Southwest. Chicano English has not been studied as much as African-American Vernacular English, and our knowledge of it is therefore somewhat tentative. Certain features of Chicano English also occur in other varieties of Hispanic English, such as those spoken in the Cuban community in Miami and the Puerto Rican community in New York City.

Chicano English—like the language used by any social group—is not a single variety but many varieties, depending on the circumstances of use. While some characteristics of Chicano English may result from the persistence of Spanish as one of the language varieties of the Hispanic-American community, Chicano English has nevertheless become a distinct variety of American English and cannot be regarded as English spoken with a foreign accent. Chicano English is acquired as a first language by many children and is the native language of hundreds of thousands of adults. It is a stable variety of American English, with characteristic patterns of grammar and pronunciation.

Among other well-known phonological characteristics of Chicano English is the substitution of *ch* [č] for *sh* [š], as in saying [či] for *she* [ši], [čuz] (homophonous with *choose*) for *shoes* [šuz], and [ɛspɛčəli] for *especially*. This feature is so distinctive that it has become a stereotype for Mexican-Americans. There is also substitution of *sh* for *ch*, as in "preash" for *preach* and "shek" [šɛk] for *check* [čɛk], though this phenomenon seems not to be stereotyped. Other phonological characteristics of Chicano English are consonant cluster simplification, as in [ɪs] for *it's*, "kine" for *kind*, "ole" for *old*, "bes" for *best*, "un-erstan" [ʌnərstæn] for *understand*. Much of this can be represented in the phrase "It's kind of hard," which is pronounced [ɪs kanə har] in Chicano English. Another major characteristic of the phonological system of Chicano English is the devoicing of /z/, especially in word-final position. Because of the widespread occurrence of /z/ in the inflectional morphology of English (plural and possessive nouns and third person singular present tense verbs), this salient characteristic is also stereotypical. Chicano English pronunciation is also characterized by the substitution of stops for the standard fricatives represented in spelling by *th:* [t] for [θ] and [d] for [ð], as in [tɪk] for *thick* and [dɛn] for *then*. Still another notable characteristic is the pronunciation of the morpheme *-ing* as [in] ("een") rather than as /ɪn/ ([ən]) or /ɪŋ/. Finally, perhaps the most prominent feature distinguishing Chicano English is its use of certain intonation patterns that often strike speakers of other dialects of American English as uncertain or hesitant.

Chicano English also has characteristic syntactic and lexical patterns. It often lacks the past tense marker on verbs ending in the alveolars /t/, /d/, or /n/; thus "wan" for *wanted* and "wait" for *waited*. At least in Los Angeles, *either . . . or either* instead of *either . . . or,* as in *Either I will go buy one, or either Terry will,* is sometimes heard. Another feature is the use of such prepositions as *out from* for *away from,* as in *They laugh to get out from their problems.* As with African-American Vernacular English and other varieties, Chicano English permits multiple negation *(Us little people don't get nothin').*

It is useful to reemphasize that many (though not all) the customary structures of Chicano English and African-American Vernacular English are also characteristic of varieties of "mainstream" American English (including in some cases the standard varieties), as with consonant cluster simplification and multiple negation. What makes any variety salient is not one but many characteristics, some of which may be shared by other varieties. It is worth stressing that both African-American Vernacular English and Chicano English occur in a number of varieties along a continuum of greater and lesser similarity to varieties of Standard American English.

Socioeconomic Status Varieties

Less striking than regional and ethnic varieties, but equally significant, are the remarkable patterns of speech that characterize different socioeconomic status groups.

New York City   To illustrate this point, we report a well-researched example. New Yorkers sometimes pronounce /r/ and sometimes drop it in words like *car, fourth,* and *beer* (when /r/ follows a vowel either at the end of a word or preceding a consonant). The presence or absence of this post-vocalic /r/ does not change a word's referential meaning. The price of a "beer" and of a "beeah" in a given tavern is the same. A "cah pahked" in a red zone is ticketed as surely as a similarly "parked car." Taxi drivers with day-old "beards" and day-old "beahds" are equally in need of shaves. And whether you live in New York or "New Yoahk," you still have the same mayor (or "maya"). No difference in referential meaning is conveyed by pronunciations with or without /r/.

Still, the occurrence of /r/ in these words is anything but random and anything but meaningless. With a keen ear for variation, linguist William Labov hypothesized that /r/ pronunciations depended on social-class affiliation in New York and that any two socially ranked groups of New Yorkers would differ in their pronunciation of /r/. He predicted that members of higher socioeconomic status groups would pronounce /r/ more frequently than would individuals from lower socioeconomic classes.

To test this hypothesis, Labov investigated the speech of employees in three Manhattan department stores of different social rank: Saks Fifth Avenue, an expensive, upper-middle-class store; Macy's, a medium-priced, middle-class store; and S. Klein, a discount store patronized principally by working-class New Yorkers. He asked supervisors, sales clerks, and stock boys the whereabouts of merchandise he knew to be displayed on the fourth floor of their store. In answer to a question like "Where can I find the lamps?" he elicited a response of *fourth floor.* Then, pretending not to have caught the answer, he said, "Excuse me?" This elicited a repeated—and presumably more careful—utterance of *fourth floor.*

Each employee thus had an opportunity to pronounce post-vocalic /r/ four times (twice each in *fourth* and *floor*) in a natural and realistic setting in which language itself was not the focus of attention.

Employees at Saks, the highest ranked store, pronounced /r/ more often than those at S. Klein, the lowest-ranked store. At Macy's, the middle-ranked store, employees pronounced an intermediate number of /r/s in *fourth floor*. Figure 13-14 presents the results of Labov's survey. The shaded sections represent the percentage of employees who pronounced /r/ four times; the clear sections above the shaded area represent the percentage who pronounced /r/ one, two, or three times (but not four); employees who did not pronounce /r/ at all are not directly represented in the bar graph. As can be seen, 30 percent of the Saks employees pronounced all /r/, and an additional 32 percent pronounced some /r/. At Macy's, 20 percent pronounced /r/ four times, and an additional 31 percent pronounced some. At S. Klein, only 4 percent of the employees pronounced all /r/, with an additional 17 percent pronouncing one, two, or three /r/s. Labov's hypothesis about the social stratification of post-vocalic /r/ seemed strikingly confirmed.

There are other possible explanations for Labov's findings, however. Factors other than socioeconomic status might have influenced the results of his survey, as Labov himself recognized. If he spoke to more men than women in one store, or to more stock boys than sales clerks, or to more African Americans than whites, the difference in pronunciation of /r/ could have been the result of gender, job, or ethnic differences. To rule out the possibility that his findings reflected job, gender, or ethnicity, Labov examined pronunciation among the largest homogeneous group of respondents in his sample. As it happened, there were more white female sales clerks than any other single group, and looking at their pronunciations apart from those of everyone else would eliminate the possibility of findings skewed by gender, job, or ethnicity. The results, given in Figure 13-15, reveal an

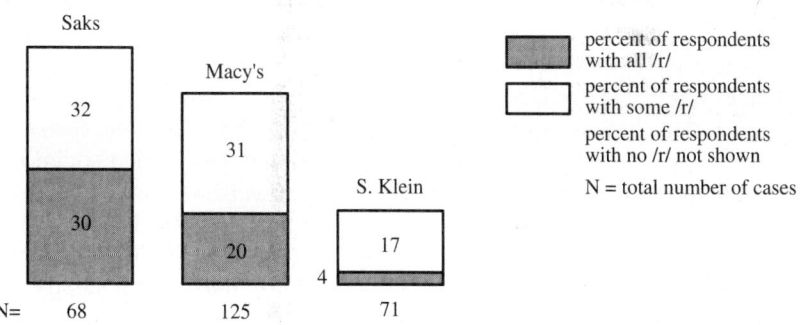

FIGURE 13-14
Overall Stratification of /r/ by Store in New York City

Source: Labov 1966

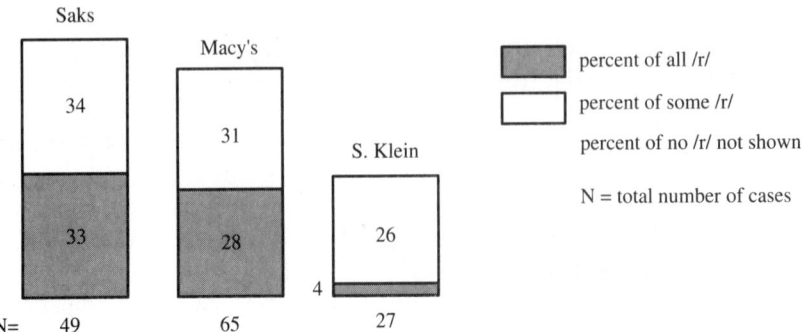

FIGURE 13-15
Stratification of /r/ by Store for Native New York White Saleswomen

Source: Labov 1966

overall pattern of distribution similar to that for the whole sample of respondents. The white female sales clerks at Saks pronounced more /r/ than those at Macy's, who in turn pronounced more than those at S. Klein. Thus Labov ruled out the possibility that his findings reflected ethnic, gender, or in-store job differences.

In a third shuffling of the data, Labov sought to determine whether his hypothesis would hold in an even narrower range of social ranking than that across department stores. This time he examined the pronunciation of /r/ across the three occupational groups working in a single store. (He chose Macy's because it provided his largest sample.) Using the same hypothesis that predicted the ranking across the department stores, Labov now predicted that he would find the highest percentage of /r/ pronunciation among the floorwalkers, least among stock boys, with an intermediate percentage among sales clerks. As Figure 13-16 shows, that is exactly what he found, and he concluded that post-vocalic /r/ pronunciation is indeed socially stratified in New York City—that higher-ranking social groups pronounce more post-vocalic /r/ than lower-ranking groups do.

Using his department store survey as a springboard, Labov undertook a very different kind of investigation. This time, equipped with detailed sociological descriptions of individual residents of Manhattan's Lower East Side, he spent several hours with each of a couple hundred respondents there. As these New Yorkers discussed a variety of topics, Labov tape-recorded the conversations. Labov's interviewing techniques prompted his respondents to use speech samples characteristic of different speech situations, a topic that we addressed in Chapter 12.

Besides post-vocalic /r/, Labov examined *th* in words like *thirty, through,* and *with* (New Yorkers sometimes say *thirty* with /θ/ and sometimes "tirty" with /t/); and the *th* of words like *this, them,* and *breathe* (the infamous "dis," "dat," "dem," and "dose" words, which have the variants /ð/ and /d/). Labov also examined the alternate pronunciation of *-ing* words like *running* versus *runnin'*

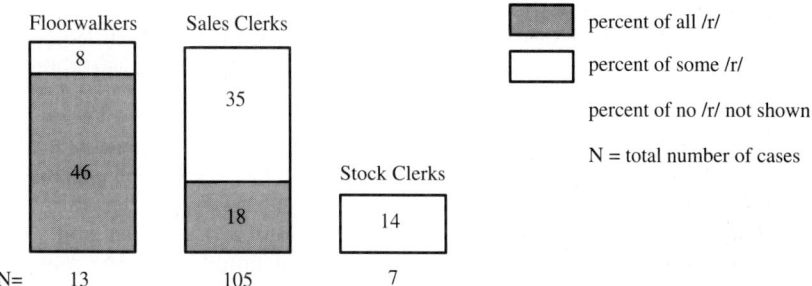

FIGURE 13-16
Stratification of /r/ by Occupational Groups in Macy's

Source: Labov 1966

and *talking* versus *talkin',* which have /ɪŋ/ and /ɪn/ variants.[3] In addition, he examined the pronunciation of the vowels in the two word classes *coffee, soft, caught* and *bad, care, sag.*

In his interviews with residents of the Lower East Side of Manhattan, Labov spoke with women and men, parents and children, African Americans and whites, Jews and Italians—a representative sample of Lower East Side residents. On the basis of extensive information available to him about their education, income, and occupation, he was able to assign each respondent to a socioeconomic status group. Using the education of the respondent, the income of the respondent's household, and the occupation of the principal household breadwinner as criteria, he placed individuals into one of four socioeconomic status categories, which he called lower class, working class, lower-middle class, and upper-middle class. His findings reveal how pronunciation differences reflect aspects of American society in one major city. Such studies can provide the basis for generalizations that can help explain the social basis for linguistic variation.

As expected, upper-middle-class respondents exhibited more /r/ than lower-middle-class respondents, who in turn exhibited more than working-class respondents, who used more than lower-class respondents. Through several graded speech registers—casual style, interview style, and reading style—respondents in all socioeconomic groups increased the percentage of /r/ pronounced (much as you saw in Chapter 12 for the *-ing* variable).

For all variables, each socioeconomic status group had characteristic patterns of pronunciation, and the percentage of pronunciation of the variants was ranked in the same way as the groups themselves. The upper-middle class pronounced

[3] This alternation is often referred to as "dropping the g." But as you know from your study of phonetics in Chapter 2, the alternation is actually between an alveolar nasal /n/ and a velar nasal /ŋ/; there is no *g* to be dropped except in the spelling.

most /θ/ for *th* (as in *thing*), most /ð/ for *th* (as in *then*), most /ɪŋ/ (as in *running*), and most /r/ (as in *car*). The lower-class respondents pronounced fewest of these variants, while the lower-middle class and working class were in between, with the lower-middle class pronouncing more than the working class. Such regular patterns of variation are remarkable, for they suggest that even subtle differences in social stratification can be reflected in language use. While it was common knowledge that differences existed in the language patterns of different social classes, no one had imagined such marked quantitative differences among very closely ranked socioeconomic groups.

The vowels were stratified in a similar way. The predicted difference in the use of vowels had to do with how high they were pronounced in the mouth. New Yorkers have several pronunciations of the first vowel in *coffee*—it ranges from the high back tense vowel [u] through the mid back vowel [ɔ] down to the low back vowel [ɑ] (the last is more characteristic of the speech of much of the western and midwestern United States). The vowel of words in the *bad* class also varies—from low front lax [æ] to high front tense [iᵊ] with an offglide.[4] Higher socioeconomic status groups favored lower vowels in both cases.

Labov sorted the pronunciations into several discrete values depending on vowel height. (Needless to say, this required a very good ear, whose reliability was checked with acoustic phonetics equipment.)

Norwich, England   Curious about how widespread the kind of linguistic differentiation that Labov had found in New York might be among socially stratified groups, British linguist Peter Trudgill investigated the speech patterns of residents of Norwich, England. He found patterns strikingly similar to those of New York. In Norwich, variation in syntactic as well as phonological expression was correlated with the socioeconomic status of speakers. Trudgill divided his subjects into five groups: middle-middle class (MMC), lower-middle class (LMC), upper-working class (UWC), middle-working class (MWC), and lower-working class (LWC). Table 13-1 illustrates the distribution of one phonological feature, the alternation between final /n/ and /ŋ/ in the suffix *-ing*. Data from both the New York City study and the Norwich study are given, as the comparison between the two cities is revealing.

The patterns of distribution for socioeconomic status are strikingly parallel in the two cities. Each successively higher socioeconomic status group pronounces more /ɪŋ/ than the group immediately below it in status. To put it most generally, the higher the socioeconomic status of a group, the less frequently it will pronounce *-ing* as /ɪn/ and the more frequently it will pronounce it as /ɪŋ/.

The patterns of variation found in New York and Norwich are not limited to English-speaking communities. Similar variation across socioeconomic status groups is known to exist for speakers of Continental and Canadian French, Latin

---

[4] A glide is created by movement of the vocal apparatus from the position used for one sound to the position used for a following sound: a transition from a vowel of one quality to the vowel of another quality. In [iᵊ], the superscript schwa represents a glide from the high front position of [i] to the mid central position of [ə]. Glides can be offglides, with the peak being on the first element (as in [iᵊ]), or onglides, with the peak being on the second element (as in certain pronunciations of *spoon* [ᶦu]).

TABLE 13-1
Percent of -ing Suffix Pronounced as /ɪŋ/ for Several Socioeconomic Classes in Norwich and New York City

	Norwich			New York City	
Social class	Casual style	Reading style	Social class	Casual style	Reading style
MMC	72	100	UMC	95	100
LMC	58	90	LMC	68	99
UWC	13	85	WC	51	89
MWC	5	56	LC	20	78
LWC	0	34			

American Spanish, Brazilian Portuguese, and several other languages. We provide illustrations from one French-speaking and one Spanish-speaking community.

Canadian French   In Montreal, French speakers vary the pronunciation of pronouns and definite articles. Except in the word *le,* /l/ is sometimes pronounced and sometimes omitted in personal pronouns, such as *il* 'he' and *elle* 'she,' and articles (and pronouns) like *les* 'the (plural)' and *la* 'the (feminine)' (see Table 4-11, page 96). In the usage of two occupational groups, professionals and laborers, the laborers consistently omitted /l/ more frequently than the professionals did, as shown in Table 13-2 for four such words.

Argentine Spanish   Spanish speakers show similar patterns of phonological variation. In Argentina, to cite one example, speakers sometimes delete /s/ before pauses (as in English, /s/ is a common word-final sound, occurring on plural nouns and on several verb forms). In a study of six Argentinian occupational groups, the percentage of /s/-deletion was greatest in the lowest status occupations and least in the higher status occupations, as shown in Table 13-3, where the highest ranking group is I and the lowest is VI.

   On the basis of evidence from these and other studies, parallel patterns of distribution may be expected for phonological variables wherever comparable social structures are found. Morphological and syntactic variation also exist, though evidence about variation at these levels of the grammar is scanty. What

TABLE 13-2
Percent of /l/-Deletion in Montreal French for Two Occupational Groups

	Professionals	Laborers
il	72	100
elle	30	82
les (pronoun)	19	62
la (pronoun)	13	38

TABLE 13-3
**Percent of Prepausal /s/-Deletion in Argentine
Spanish for Six Occupational Groups**

Group	Percent of Deletion
I (high)	14
II	16
III	19
IV	41
V	63
VI (low)	68

holds true of variation in English, French, and Spanish doubtless holds true of communities speaking other languages as well.

Gender Varieties

It is well known that for many languages, in many speech communities, women and men don't speak identically. In American speech communities, for example, certain words that are closely associated with women may "sound" feminine as a result of that association. Adjectives like *lovely, darling,* and *cute* may carry feminine associations, as do words that describe precise shades of color like *mauve* and *chartreuse.* Likewise (though decreasingly so these days), certain four-letter words may surprise some people when uttered by a woman. Comedian Joan Rivers has capitalized on some of these gender differences, shocking audiences by her use of taboo words generally associated with male rather than female speakers.

In some languages, the differences between women's and men's speech are more dramatic than in English. In Japanese, even the pronoun for 'I' differs for female and male speakers in informal situations: females use *atasi,* males *boku.* In French, *je* is the first person pronoun for males and females alike, but because adjectives are marked for gender agreement, *Je suis heureux* 'I am happy' identifies a male speaker, while *Je suis heureuse* identifies a female speaker. Among the Koasati Indians of Louisiana, women and men use different forms of certain indicative and imperative verbs. For example, men use /s/ instead of the nasalization characteristic of women in some verbs, as in examples 1 and 2 below; and men sometimes add /s/ where the women's form ends in a vowel plus consonant, as in 3 and 4.

Gender Differences in Koasati		
Women	**Men**	
1. lakawwā̃	lakawwás	'he will lift it'
2. kā̃	kás	'he is saying'
3. lakáw	lakáws	'he is lifting it'
4. ĩp	ĩps	'he is eating it'
5. õt	õč	'he is building a fire'

In some cases, the forms used by women are more conservative than those used by men, reflecting older forms of Koasati usage. When the research reported here was conducted fifty years ago, only middle-aged and elderly women used women's forms.[5] Younger women were using forms identical to those of men. (One older man reported that the forms of the older women sounded better to him!) In Koasati culture, both men and women are familiar with the forms used by the other; when stories are told, the characters in the stories speak the forms characteristic of men or women as appropriate, no matter who is telling the story. Moreover, when Koasati parents correct the speech of their children, fathers may correct daughters and mothers may correct sons. Thus there is no taboo on men using women's forms or women using men's forms. Similar striking differences between the language of men and women occur in Creek and Hitchiti (other languages of the Muskogean family), Yana (an extinct Hokan language), Siouan, and certain Eskimo languages, as well as in Carib and other South American Indian languages.

Outside the Americas, reports of striking differences between gender varieties have been made for Chukchee (spoken in Siberia) and for Thai. In polite Thai conversation between men and women of equal rank, women say *dič^hàn* while men say *p^hŏm* for the first person singular pronoun. Thai also has a set of particles used differently by men and women, especially in formulaic questions and responses such as 'thank you' and 'excuse me.' The polite particle used by men is *k^hráp*, while women use *k^há* or *k^hâ*. Because these politeness particles occur frequently in daily interaction, speech differences between men and women can be quite marked in Thai, despite the fact that very few words are so differentiated.

There are also more subtle differences between men's and women's speech, the kinds of quantitative variation between the sexes that we saw between other social groups. For example, in Montreal (where professionals delete /l/ from articles and pronouns less frequently than laborers), there is a systematic difference between men and women in the pronunciation of these same words. As illustrated in Table 13-4, men delete /l/ more frequently than women.

This pattern, where women delete sounds less than men, has been shown also in New York City and Norwich. In these cities, whenever higher social classes behave linguistically in one way to a greater extent than lower social classes, there

TABLE 13-4
Percent of /l/-Deletion in Montreal French for Women and Men

	Women	Men
il (personal)	84	94
elle	60	67
les (pronoun)	41	53
la (pronoun)	23	31

[5] A more recent study of Koasati suggests that socially prominent women also used "male" speech forms; see Kimball (1987).

is a strong tendency for women to behave in that same way to a greater extent than men.

In English, besides the lexical differences between the sexes, there are more subtle differences, some of which go largely unnoticed. One study examined the pronunciations of the *-ing* suffix in words like *running* and *talking*. In a semirural New England village, the speech patterns of 12 boys and 12 girls, aged 3 to 10, were studied. Even in children that young, all but three exhibited both alveolar and velar pronunciations of *-ing*. Interestingly, twice as many girls as boys showed a preference for the /ɪŋ/ forms over the /ɪn/ forms, as shown here.

	Preference for /ɪŋ/	No Preference for /ɪŋ/
Girls	10	2
Boys	5	7

The finding that girls and boys differ in this way may seem surprising, since girls and boys in this New England village (as generally in Western societies) are in frequent face-to-face contact with each other. The separation in communication channels suggested earlier as the motivating factor of great import in the differentiation of speech patterns appears not to be the right explanation in this case. What then is the explanation for such differences between the speech of males and females, even at an early age?

One hypothesis suggested by a number of researchers is the "toughness" characteristic associated with working-class life styles combined with the "masculinity" characteristic associated with the /ɪn/ forms.[6] If using the term "masculinity" to explain gender differences seems to beg the question, it nevertheless hints at an important fact about gender differences in language. Gender differences are not identical to sex differences. Rather, what is important is the cultural fact of gender: what it means in a particular society to be female, what it means to be male. We are aware of gender differences as marked by hair length, clothing, jewelry use, and traditional household duties, to mention just a few. It should not be surprising, then, that language reflects the important social identity of one's gender role.

The Persistence of Stigmatized Dialects

It is no secret that some language varieties carry prestige, while others are stigmatized. Whereas the degree of stigma depends on the group making the judgment, norms of evaluation are often shared throughout a speech community, and

---

[6] Association of /ɪn/ with masculinity may outweigh the associations with prestige and higher socioeconomic status that accompany the /ɪŋ/ variant. In fact, prestigious forms of speech are often more preferred by women than by men. This fact is in accordance with sociologists' findings that women are generally more status conscious than men. If that is so, then the preference for a less prestigious variant may in some cases be a marker of masculinity.

one wonders why stigmatized varieties do not die out. Why don't speakers give them up for more prestigious varieties?

The explanation seems to lie in the fact that one's identity—as a woman or man, as an American or Australian, as a member of a particular ethnic or socioeconomic group—is tied into the speech patterns of that group. Americans talk like other Americans; Australians like Australians; men like men, and women like women. While one's sex is not a matter of choice, one's *gender* is, at least to some extent. What is considered masculine and feminine is a cultural, not a biological, matter, and one can choose to behave in more or less masculine or feminine ways irrespective of one's sex. To change the way you speak is to signal changes in who you are or how you wish to be perceived. For a New Yorker transplanted to California, to start speaking like a Californian is to relinquish some identity as a New Yorker. To give up speaking African-American Vernacular English is to relinquish some identity as an African American. To give up working-class speech patterns acquired in childhood is to take on a new identity. In short, to take on new speech patterns is to reform oneself and present oneself anew.

Language is perhaps the major symbol of our social identity, and we have seen how remarkably fine tuned to that identity it can be. Language is not set apart from social identity and social alliances. If you wish to identify with "nonnative" regional, socioeconomic, or ethnic groups and have sufficient contact with them, your speech will come to resemble theirs. In fact, socially mobile individuals have been shown to exhibit pronunciation patterns more like the group toward which they were heading than like the group of current affiliation; this is true not only of individuals moving up the socioeconomic scale but also of those whose paths are pointing lower.

We can illustrate with a telling investigation of linguistic and social identity on Martha's Vineyard, an island off the coast of Massachusetts. There the vowels /ay/ and /aw/ have two principal variants, with the first element of each diphthong alternating between [a] and [ə]. Words like *night* and *why* are sometimes pronounced with [ay] and sometimes with a more centralized [əy], while words like *shout* and *how* are pronounced with [aw] or the more centralized [əw]. These phonological variants are not typical dialect features; they do not reflect gender, ethnicity, or socioeconomic status. Rather, on Martha's Vineyard, vowel centralization represents identity with traditional island values—with the island and its life. The up-island residents have more centralization than do the residents in sections catering to summer visitors. Most interestingly, young men intending to leave the island and lead their lives on the mainland have the least centralization, while the greatest centralization was shown by a young man who had moved to the mainland but returned to Martha's Vineyard. Thus the centralized diphthongs represent a rejection of mainland values and a positive view of the values of island life.

The important symbolic value of one's language variety cannot be overestimated. In evaluating oral arguments in Britain, speakers of regional varieties rated the *quality* of an argument higher when presented in standard accent, but found the same argument more *persuasive* when it was made using a regional accent.

It is easy for one group of speakers higher on the socioeconomic ladder to ask about a group of speakers lower on the ladder, "Why don't *they* start talking like *us?*" The answer is simple: *Their* social identity is different, and they do not necessarily share the values of the higher socioeconomic groups. Some insight can be gained by thinking about gender dialects, in which the situation is less complicated. Though there have been stirrings of neutrality recently, most people still agree that everyone is entitled to a gender dialect. It is perfectly acceptable for women to speak like women and men to speak like men. Imagine men asking women to speak like them in order to get ahead in "a man's world." Imagine a woman head of a company asking her truck drivers to speak more like women to get ahead in "a woman's world." These are patently unacceptable (though not unimaginable) scenarios. Women's and men's speech patterns are equally acceptable. A nearly similar equality of status is granted to most regional varieties. Imagine a Bostonian moving to Atlanta and being told by the boss to get rid of the New England accent in order to succeed. The employee might rightly infer that the Boston origin, not the Boston accent, was at issue.

When it comes to ethnic and social-class varieties, perceptions are quite different. The widely held view is that African-American Vernacular English and Chicano English and the dialects of lower socioeconomic status groups cannot be employed in the schools or the professional workplace. These views reflect language attitudes; as such, they are social, not linguistic, decisions, and they are partly based on attitudes toward *speakers,* not *speech!*

In study after study, language has been shown to be a central factor in a person's identity. Asking people (asking *you*) to change their (change *your*) customary language patterns is not like asking them (asking *you*) to try on different sweaters; it is asking people to take on a new identity and to espouse the values associated with speakers of a different dialect. The principal reason that nonstandard varieties are so hearty, so resistant to the urgings of education, is that language varieties are deeply entwined with the identities of their speakers and with the values of the groups speaking those varieties.

SUMMARY

With separation and distance—physical or social—people who otherwise would possess shared speechways come to speak differently. Given sufficient time and separation, distinct languages can arise. Conversely, the speech of people talking as members of the same community can develop in unison, even tending to merge in some situations. Still, there are important linguistic differences among social groups within every speech community. Linguistic forms of all sorts can vary greatly from one social group to the next, and social groups may be defined in a number of ways besides regionally. A social group may differ from the rest of the community in ethnicity or in socioeconomic status. Females and males may also be thought of as belonging to different social groups, called gender groups. If we combine these different group distinctions, we obtain a complex picture of the composition of society: Within a particular ethnic group, we find socioeconomic classes, whose members are male or female. Dialect differences support such social identities.

Whatever the social group, its language variety will typically exhibit characteristics that distinguish it from the language varieties of other social groups. The linguistic markers that characterize social varieties may also serve as markers (or symbols) of group membership. When an African-American man wants to stress his membership in his ethnic group, he may exaggerate the African-American Vernacular English features in his speech. If a woman wants to appear particularly feminine, she may choose to exhibit features associated with women's speech and avoid ''masculine-sounding'' expressions. Individuals can thus take advantage of socially marked language characteristics for their own purposes.

EXERCISES

1. Distinguish between an accent and a dialect; between a dialect and a language. What is meant by a language variety? Does it make any sense to say of a language variety that ''it isn't a language, but only a dialect''?

2. Examine a copy of a newspaper or magazine published in Britain (one or more of the following should be available in your library's periodicals room: *The Times, The Economist, Punch, The Spectator, The Listener*) and list as many examples of differences between American and British English as you can notice on two pages. Include examples of words, syntax, spelling, and punctuation.

3. Which of the following words are you familiar with? Make two lists: one comprising words you normally use, and the other comprising words you don't use but have heard others use. With what regional or social group do you associate the words you have heard others use but don't use yourself? Compare your judgments with those of your classmates.

   dragonfly   darning needle, mosquito hawk, spindle, snake feeder, snake doctor

   pancake   fritter, hot cake, flannel cake, batter cake

   cottage cheese   curds, curd cheese, clabber cheese, dutch cheese, pot cheese

   string beans   green beans, snap beans

   earthworm   night crawler, fishing worm, angle worm, rain worm, red worm

   lightning bug   firefly, fire bug

   baby carriage   baby buggy, baby coach, baby cab, pram

4. The following questions are part of the questionnaire used in gathering data for *DARE*. After you answer each question, compare your answers with those of your classmates. Do you and your classmates agree on the regions in which the particular variants are used? (Volume I of *DARE* provides maps for answers to each of the questions.)

   a.   What names are used around here for

      (1)   the part of the house below the ground floor?

      (2)   a container for coal to use in a stove?

      (3)   a small stream of water not big enough to be a river?

      (4)   a round cake of dough, cooked in deep fat, with a hole in the center?

(5)   an oblong cake cooked in deep fat?

(6)   a piece of cloth that a woman folds over her head and ties under her chin?

(7)   the common worm used as bait?

(8)   vehicles for a baby or small child, the kind it can lie down in?

b.   What expressions do you have around here for

(1)   someone who is confused or mixed up, as in "So many things were going on at the same time that he got completely _____"?

(2)   someone who seems to be very stupid—"He doesn't know _____"?

(3)   a very skilled or expert person (for example at woodworking)—"He's a _____"?

How do the answers of your classmates to question (8) in group (a) compare with this map from *DARE* for *baby buggy*?

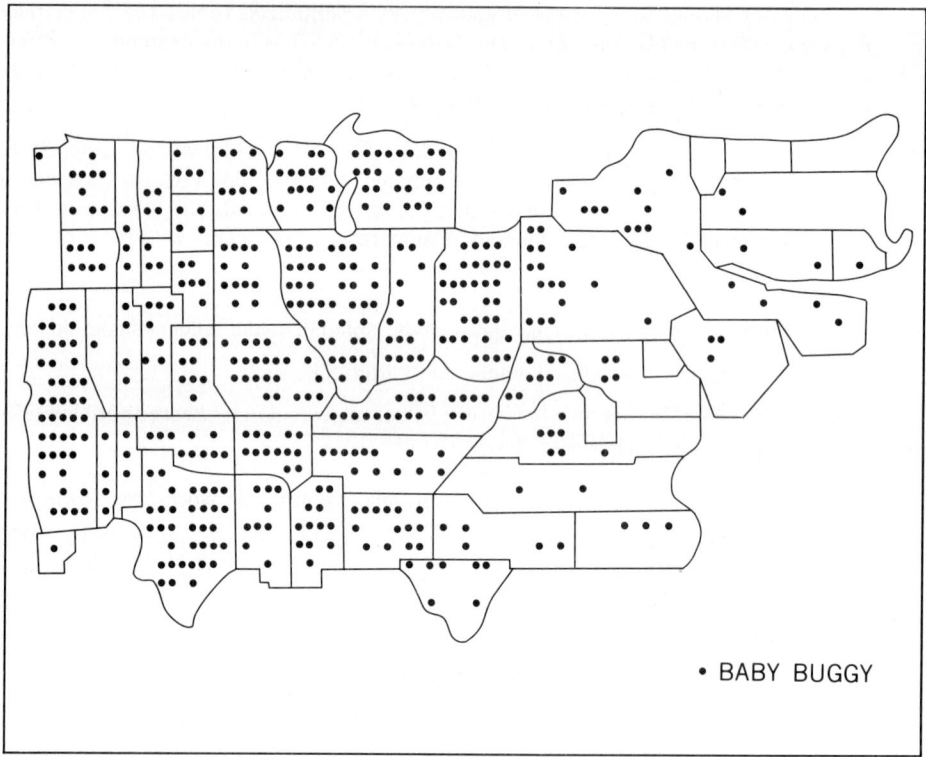

• BABY BUGGY

Source: Dictionary of American Regional English, I, 1985

5.   a.   Below are the opening words of a presentation by a college teacher to a group of southern teachers at a professional meeting (you might wish to imagine it spoken with marked southern pronunciations, as the teacher was born in the south and clearly wished to play upon those affiliations):

Years ago, during my first week in Wisconsin, I was asked by a fellow teacher, "Do you mean they let *you* teach English?" The speaker was a Canadian with what I thought a very peculiar accent. Soon after that, a woman working on a degree in speech asked me with all the kindness and gentleness of which she was capable whether I would let her teach me how to talk right. If I had had her zeal and patience and kindness, I might very well have made the offer first, for I thought her speech highly unsatisfactory.

Provide answers to these six questions, most of which the teacher posed to her audience:

(1) Who should teach whom?

(2) What is the standard pronunciation in American English?

(3) Should education aim to make everybody sound like everybody else?

(4) Could training make everybody sound like everybody else?

(5) How then would everybody sound?

(6) Assuming uniformity could be achieved, how long could it last?

b. The same teacher reports that another southern teacher told her this:

[a: hæv dɪlɪbərɪtlɪ wəkt tu gɛt rɪd av ɪnɪ tresɪz av æksɪnt æz a: θɪŋk ɔwl ɛjəketɪd pipəl šʊd du a: prad masɛf ðæt a: hæv nat wən hwɪt av ɪnɪ tresəbəl æksɪnt ɪn ma spič]

And a southern physician reported this to her:

[mɪnɪ av ma pəyšəns θɪŋk a: æm fram ðə nɔəθ bɪkɔwz æz ən ɛjəketɪd pəsən a: don av coəs hæv ə səðən æksɪnt]

(1) Read the transcribed utterances of the teacher and physician aloud, and write them down using standard orthography.

(2) Make a list of six pronunciation features in these utterances that are characteristic of Southern American speech.

(3) Give the standard orthography for these words as pronounced in the same dialect: /mɔwnɪn/, /kaəd/, /kent/, /hɛp/, /spikɪn/, /həyd/, /mɪnɪ/, /bɪnɪfɪt/.

c. Now answer these questions:

(1) Why do many people believe that they speak *without* an accent?

(2) What would it mean to speak without an accent? (Think globally as well as nationally: What would it mean to speak without an American or British or Australian accent?)

(3) Provide a list of four regional features of *your own* pronunciation that others perhaps have called to your attention.

[Slightly adapted from Jane Appleby, "Is Southern English Good English?" In David L. Shores and Carol P. Hines, eds., *Papers in Language Variation* (University: University of Alabama Press, 1977), p. 225.]

6. What was Labov's hypothesis about the distribution of /r/ in New York City department stores? In your city or town, are there three stores that could be similarly investigated? What two or three phonological features do you think are likely to be socially differentiated in your stores? Design a question for each feature that would uncover the data needed to confirm your hypothesis. (Make the question a natural one for the kind of store you have in mind.) Would you ask your respondents to repeat their answers as Labov did? Explain why or why not.

7. William Labov . . . once said about the use of black English, "It is the goal of most black Americans to acquire full control of the standard language without giving up their own culture." . . . I wonder if the good doctor might also consider the goals of those black Americans who have full control of standard English but who are every now and then troubled by that colorful, grammar-to-the-winds patois that is black English. Case in point—me.

So wrote a twenty-one-year-old African-American college sophomore in *Newsweek* (Dec. 27, 1982, p. 7). The student cites several features of Black (or African-American Vernacular) English such as those described in this chapter.

a. What does *patois* mean and what connotations does it carry in referring to particular language varieties? What does the phrase "grammar-to-the-winds patois" suggest about the writer's attitude toward African-American Vernacular English?

b. What features of African-American Vernacular English do you think the writer means in calling it a "grammar-to-the-winds patois"?

c. To what extend can African-American Vernacular English accurately be called a "grammar-to-the-winds" speech variety? What would be the implications for communication if a speech variety were indeed "grammarless"?

d. What would you assume to be the reason for the writer's judgments about and attitudes toward African-American Vernacular English? What might you explain to the student about patterns of language in every variety and about the status of particular varieties *in terms of their linguistic features?*

8. Comment on the validity of the quotation that follows, and explain your view: "If there were as many oil barons coming up from Mexico as there are farm laborers, the accents of Pancho Villa might sound more musical to American ears." [William F. Mackey, in Juan Cobarrubias and Joshua A. Fishman, eds., *Progress in Language Planning* (Berlin: Mouton, 1983), p. 186]

9. Describe two ways in which the speech of women and men differs in greetings, threats, swearing, and promises. What do you think accounts for these differences? Do you think the differences are increasing or decreasing? Explain the bases for your answers.

SUGGESTIONS FOR FURTHER READING

Francis (1983), Chambers and Trudgill (1980), and Wolfram (1991) focus on dialects. Hudson (1980), Wardhaugh (1991), and Fasold (1984, 1990) also discuss dialects. Trudgill and Chambers (1991) contains twenty-two treatments of grammar in various dialects of America, Australia, Canada, Scotland, and especially England. Scherer and Giles (1979), a collection of essays, treats the linguistic marking of social categories such as gender, social class, and ethnicity. The data and discussion of convergence in Kupwar are based on Gumperz and Wilson (1971). Labov (1972a) is a frequently cited description of African-

American Vernacular English; Penfield and Ornstein-Galicia (1985) treat Chicano English. Other treatments of African-American Vernacular English include Smitherman (1977), from which some of our examples are taken, and Baugh (1985). From Labov (1966, 1972b) come the New York City data, from Trudgill (1983) the Norwich data, from Sankoff and Cedergren (1971) the Montreal French data, from Terrell (1981) the Spanish data. Ferguson and Heath (1981) is a collection of essays describing language use among Native and other Americans: Filipinos, Puerto Ricans, Jews, and Italian, French, German, and African Americans, and others. With its emphasis on British and other European dialects, Petyt (1980) complements the treatment in this chapter. Kurath (1972) is a thorough analysis of the methods and some of the findings of dialect geography, with emphasis on American English (and its roots in England) but with attention to Romance and Germanic languages as well. A brief introduction to American English dialects can be found in Reed (1977), with a number of maps mostly of the Great Lakes states and the Northwest. Carver (1987) is an up-to-date overview of American English dialects, emphasizing their cultural and historical origins. The principal findings of American dialect geographers on the East Coast can be found in Kurath (1949), Atwood (1953), and Kurath and McDavid (1961). See Allen (1973–1976) for the Upper Midwest, Pederson (1986–1991) for the Gulf states, Bright (1971) for California and Nevada, Atwood (1962) for Texas. Cassidy's (1985) *Dictionary of American Regional English* is a comprehensive treatment of American regional vocabulary. An up-to-date treatment of traditional and modern dialects in England can be found in Trudgill (1990), which has thirty-four maps. The relationship between language and the sexes is treated in Smith (1985); Thorne, Kramarae, and Henley (1983) provide an overview of research on this topic in the preceding decade, a number of individual studies, and a lengthy annotated bibliography. Tannen's (1990) treatment of communicative differences between women and men was a national best seller. The data in this chapter on gender differences in Koasati and Thai come from Haas (1940), who also discusses Chukchee. Fischer (1958) reports the New England *-ing* data cited in this chapter. Philips et al. (1987) is a collection of essays examining women's and men's speech in a cross-cultural perspective and gender differences in the language of children. Coates and Cameron (1988) is a collection of eleven provocative perspectives on language and gender. Ochs (1992) relates language and gender through social activities, social stances, and social acts. The relationship between language and social identity is treated in Edwards (1985). The Martha's Vineyard study is reported in Labov (1972b). On the sociolinguistics of French see Ager (1990), on German Barbour and Stevenson (1990) and Clyne (1984).

REFERENCES

Ager, Dennis. 1990. *Sociolinguistics and Contemporary French* (Cambridge: Cambridge University Press).

Allen, Harold B. 1973–1976. *The Linguistic Atlas of the Upper Midwest,* 3 vols. (Minneapolis: University of Minnesota Press).

Atwood, E. Bagby. 1953. *A Survey of Verb Forms in the Eastern United States* (Ann Arbor: University of Michigan Press).

———. 1962. *The Regional Vocabulary of Texas* (Austin: University of Texas Press).

Barbour, Stephen, and Patrick Stevenson. 1990. *Variation in German* (Cambridge: Cambridge University Press).

Baugh, John. 1985. *Black Street Speech: Its History, Structure, and Survival* (Austin: University of Texas Press).

Bright, Elizabeth S. 1971. *A Word Geography of California and Nevada* (Berkeley: University of California Press).

Carver, Craig M. 1987. *American Regional Dialects: A Word Geography* (Ann Arbor: University of Michigan Press).

Cassidy, Frederic G., ed. 1985. *Dictionary of American Regional English* (Cambridge, MA: Belknap Press).

Chambers, J. K., and Peter Trudgill. 1980. *Dialectology* (Cambridge: Cambridge University Press).

Clyne, Michael. 1984. *Language and Society in the German-Speaking Countries* (Cambridge: Cambridge University Press).

Coates, Jennifer, and Deborah Cameron, eds. 1988. *Women in Their Speech Communities* (London: Longman).

Edwards, John. 1985. *Language, Society and Identity* (New York: Blackwell).

Fasold, Ralph W. 1984. *The Sociolinguistics of Society* (New York: Blackwell).

———. 1990. *The Sociolinguistics of Language* (Cambridge, MA: Blackwell).

Ferguson, Charles A., and Shirley Brice Heath, eds. 1981. *Language in the USA* (Cambridge: Cambridge University Press).

Fischer, John L. 1958. "Social Influences on the Choice of a Linguistic Variable," *Word* 14:47–56; repr. in Hymes, ed., 1964, pp. 483–488.

Francis, W. Nelson. 1983. *Dialectology: An Introduction* (New York: Longman).

———. 1961. "Some Dialectal Verb Forms in England," *Orbis* 10:1–14; repr. in Juanita V. Williamson and Virginia M. Burke, eds., *A Various Language: Perspectives on American Dialects* (New York: Holt), pp. 108–120.

Gumperz, John J., and Robert Wilson. 1971. "Convergence and Creolization: A Case from the Indo-Aryan/Dravidian Border in India," in Dell Hymes, ed., *Pidginization and Creolization of Languages* (Cambridge: Cambridge University Press), pp. 151–167.

Haas, Mary R. 1940. "Men's and Women's Speech in Koasati," *Language* 20:142–149; repr. in Hymes, ed., 1964, pp. 228–233.

Hudson, R. A. 1980. *Sociolinguistics* (Cambridge: Cambridge University Press).

Hymes, Dell, ed. 1964. *Language in Culture and Society* (New York: Harper & Row).

Kimball, Geoffrey. 1987. "Men's and Women's Speech in Koasati: A Reappraisal," *International Journal of American Linguistics* 53:30–38.

Kurath, Hans. 1949. *A Word Geography of the Eastern United States* (Ann Arbor: University of Michigan Press).

———. 1972. *Studies in Area Linguistics* (Bloomington: Indiana University Press).

———, and Raven I. McDavid, Jr. 1961. *The Pronunciation of English in the Atlantic States* (Ann Arbor: University of Michigan Press).

Labov, William. 1966. *The Social Stratification of English in New York City* (Washington, D.C.: Center for Applied Linguistics).

———. 1972a. *Language in the Inner City* (Philadelphia: University of Pennsylvania Press).

———. 1972b. *Sociolinguistic Patterns* (Philadelphia: University of Pennsylvania Press).

Marckwardt, Albert H. 1957. "Principal and Subsidiary Dialect Areas in the North-Central States." *Publications of the American Dialect Society,* 27.

Ochs, Elinor. 1992. "Indexing Gender," in A. Duranti and C. Goodwin, eds., *Rethinking Context* (Cambridge: Cambridge University Press), pp. 335–358.

Pederson, Lee. 1986–1991. *Linguistic Atlas of the Gulf States,* 7 vols. (Athens: University of Georgia Press).

Penfield, Joyce, and Jacob L. Ornstein-Galicia. 1985. *Chicano English: An Ethnic Contact Dialect* (Amsterdam: Benjamins).

Petyt, K. M. 1980. *The Study of Dialect: An Introduction to Dialectology* (London: Andre Deutsch).

Philips, Susan U., Susan Steele, and Christine Tanz, eds. 1987. *Language, Gender, and Sex in Comparative Perspective* (Cambridge: Cambridge University Press).

Reed, Carroll E. 1977. *Dialects of American English,* rev. ed. (Amherst: University of Massachusetts Press).

Sankoff, Gillian, and Henrietta Cedergren. 1971. "Some Results of a Sociolinguistic Study of Montreal French," in R. Darnell, ed., *Linguistic Diversity in Canadian Society* (Edmonton: Linguistic Research), pp. 61–87.

Scherer, Klaus R., and Howard Giles, eds. 1979. *Social Markers in Speech* (Cambridge: Cambridge University Press).

Smith, Philip M. 1985. *Language, the Sexes and Society* (Oxford: Blackwell).

Smitherman, Geneva. 1977. *Talkin and Testifyin: The Language of Black America* (Boston: Houghton Mifflin).

Tannen, Deborah. 1990. *You Just Don't Understand: Women and Men in Conversation* (New York: Ballantine).

Terrell, Tracy D. 1981. "Diachronic Reconstruction by Dialect Comparison of Variable Constraints," in David Sankoff and Henrietta Cedergren, eds., *Variation Omnibus* (Edmonton: Linguistic Research), pp. 115–124.

Thorne, Barrie, Cheris Kramarae and Nancy Henley, eds. 1983. *Language, Gender and Society* (Rowley, MA: Newbury House).

Trudgill, Peter. 1983. *Sociolinguistics: An Introduction to Language and Society,* rev. ed. (New York: Penguin).

———. 1990. *The Dialects of England* (Cambridge, MA: Blackwell).

———, and J. K. Chambers, eds. 1991. *Dialects of English: Studies in Grammatical Variation* (New York: Longman).

Wardhaugh, Ronald. 1991. *An Introduction to Sociolinguistics,* 2nd ed. (New York: Blackwell).

Wolfram, Walt. 1991. *Dialects and American English* (Englewood Cliffs, NJ: Prentice-Hall).

14

Language Acquisition

INTRODUCTION

The language of children, even very young ones, is remarkably rich. Early in life children reveal mastery of the phonological, syntactic, and semantic systems described in earlier chapters, as well as a high degree of communicative competence in the appropriate use of language. As early as age five, children playing with hand puppets demonstrate productive control over a range of registers, including aspects of the characteristic talk between doctors and patients and doctors and nurses. Language acquisition seems so natural and effortless that parents, elated with the addition of each successive word, take it for granted that children will acquire their native language without a hitch. It seems obvious to everyone who has interacted with children that the process of acquiring a first language is relatively automatic, although it takes time and is subject to certain predictable missteps. Still, if the apparent ease with which a child accomplishes this magnificent feat titillates parents, it baffles researchers. In this chapter we examine why language acquisition intrigues and puzzles linguists and psychologists and why there is disagreement about the nature of the child's task.

Earlier in this century, it was widely believed that language learning, like other forms of learning, was essentially a process of induction; a child would generalize about linguistic patterns from the language samples it heard in its interactions with parents, siblings, and other caretakers. Rather than resembling such bodily systems as digestion and respiration (which, of course, do *not* require learning), language was thought to be different in nature. Because languages vary from culture to culture, it was thought that children must *induce* the rules and patterns of their language from the speech of those around them. In this respect, language learning appeared to resemble other forms of cultural behavior—like brushing your teeth, tying your shoelaces, or doing addition and subtraction.

In a dramatic shift of perceptions, however, the view of first-language learning as comparable to other forms of learning is now regarded as implausible. In addition, language acquisition is widely viewed as an inductive process only in limited respects. Indeed, rather than focusing on differences in languages, some linguists and psychologists focus on the similarities across languages (the linguistic universals of Chapter 8) and explain their universality as innate structures of the human mind that do not require learning. Other linguists and psychologists view the similarities across languages as the result not so much of uniform mental *structures* as of uniform mental *strategies* or dispositions for analyzing and acquiring language. In either case, there is now intense interest in characterizing what psycholinguists often call the *language-making capacity* and grammarians prefer to call the *language acquisition device*.

Researchers have recently uncovered a good deal about patterns of acquisition in diverse languages, and our understanding of how these patterns can differ from culture to culture while remaining strikingly similar continues to grow. In this chapter we explore certain basic findings about first-language acquisition in children and second-language acquisition among adults. We then briefly examine some animal communication studies.

FIRST-LANGUAGE ACQUISITION

You are aware from previous chapters of this book that acquiring a language entails far more than learning the meaning of various expressions. A child acquiring a language must learn a system that can generate countless sentences (few of which have been heard before) and deploy them appropriately in conversations, stories, inquiries, and the other speech events of everyday life. Language acquisition also entails ability to understand both the new and the familiar utterances of those around us and to interpret them appropriately in their social contexts.

Besides the words of its language and a range of meanings for virtually every word, a child must master all the morphological, phonological, syntactic, semantic, and pragmatic rules of its language. Every child must know when to speak and when to listen; when and how to interrupt and greet; how to recognize teasing from its contextualization cues; and so on. All children must learn how to make utterances achieve their intended objective and how to understand under what circumstances a particular utterance serves different functions—to offer food to someone *(Do you like chocolate?, Have you ever tasted a kumquat?)* or request information *(Do you like chocolate?, Have you ever tasted a kumquat?).* In other words, every child must learn the grammar of its language and the effective and culturally appropriate use of grammatical rules in diverse social situations. Put tersely, acquiring a language entails mastery of the full range of grammatical and communicative competence.

There is evidence to suggest that at least some (and perhaps a good deal) of what children know about language structure could not have been learned from the data surrounding them. To the extent that certain language structures cannot be inferred from the data available to children, it is reasonable to hypothesize that the human language capacity provides those structures at birth or through natural development. The issue can be framed in terms of "nature" versus "nurture," what is inborn versus what must be learned, what is pre-wired into the brain at birth ("hardware," to use a computer analogy) versus what must be programmed by interaction with adult language ("software"). The challenge is to determine the nature and degree of the contributions made by biology and by socialization.

Alternatively, some psychologists and linguists suspect not so much that children share particular language structures as that they share strategies for analyzing language. In Chapter 2, we discussed how difficult it would be for a child to sort out the continuous string of sound that constitutes adult speech into the distinct sounds that constitute the phonological inventory of its language. There is now widespread agreement that children arrive at the task of language learning already in possession of the "knowledge" that language consists of distinct sounds. They are "preprogrammed" to analyze a continuous string of vocal sounds for its individual phonological segments. In the same way, then, children are thought to be naturally endowed with certain strategies for analyzing other aspects of language, and it is this set of *operating principles* for analyzing language that would contribute to the similarity of acquisition patterns across languages. As illustrations of such operating principles, children are thought to pay attention to the order of words in utterances, to the order of morphemes in words, particularly to the ends of words (where inflections are found), and to focus on consistent relationships between expression and content, and look for generalizations.

Operating Principles in First-Language Acquisition

Pay attention to the order of words in utterances.

Pay attention to the order of morphemes in words.

Pay particular attention to word endings (inflections).

Focus on consistent relationships between expression and content.

Look for generalizations.

Many linguists and psychologists are convinced that language is not acquired by imitation—certainly not solely by imitation and probably not principally—although exposure to a particular language is, of course, an essential ingredient in the process of acquiring it. Still, children have an undeniable capacity to be creative with language and certainly do not need to hear a particular sentence before saying it. They often utter sentences they are unlikely to have heard before, and they know intuitively which sentences are possible and which are not, although all children go through periods when they make predictable mistakes. They may say "He eated my candy" or "Oh! Hurt meself" or "Where did you found it?" but not "Mine is candy that" or "Candy my eated he" or countless other conceivable but nonoccurring sentences. In fact, the errors that children make are of a very limited sort. English-speaking children can be heard overgeneralizing that the past tense of all verbs is formed by adding an *-ed* ending and making the other mistakes illustrated above. Because adults do not say *eated* or *did you found* and because even children who lack contact with other children do say such things, these errors cannot arise from pure mimicry. Whatever is involved in language acquisition, it is a robust process that goes beyond inducing the correct generalizations on the basis of forms that have been heard.

Principles of Language Acquisition

Maturation and Symbolization   Two aspects of general maturation are crucial to a child's ability to acquire a language: *the ability to symbolize* and *the ability to use tools.* As a system of symbols, language is an arbitrary representation of other things—other entities, experiences, feelings, thoughts, and so on. In order to acquire language, a child must first be able to hold in mind a symbolic realization of something else. Even if it is no more than a mental picture of an absent object, such symbolization is a prerequisite to language acquisition.

Using Tools   The second ability—wider-ranging than its application to language—is the ability to use tools to accomplish goals. Language is a tool made up entirely of symbols, and among other characterizations it can be seen as a system of symbols that gets work done. From an early age, children routinely use language to get fed, changed, handed a toy, and the many other things they cannot do for themselves. Such purposeful activity is called tool use, and language is a most effective tool for accomplishing work of almost any sort. Given their extremely limited ability to achieve their goals physically, the motivation to develop this powerful symbolic tool must be extraordinarily strong in children (and may be influential in the evolution of the human species).

All Languages Equally Challenging   Every child who is capable of acquiring a particular human language is capable of acquiring *any* human language. There is no biological basis—in the lips or the brain—that disposes any child to learn a particular language. Children apparently find all languages about equally simple to acquire, although particular features of one language may be more difficult to acquire than equivalent aspects of a different language. For example, as we saw in Chapter 4 (see Table 4-10, page 96), German definite articles have several different forms representing three genders, two numbers, and four cases. Children acquiring German take more time to master its definite articles than English-speaking children take to learn the single form *the* that English uses for any gender, number, and case. (English speakers use *the* in the phrases **the** boy, for **the** daughter, and to **the** lions, where the German definite article would have different forms in those phrases: *der, dem,* and *den,* respectively). On balance, though, when considered in their entirety, all languages are about equally easy (or equally challenging) for a child to learn.

Barring severe mental or physical impairments, children the world over have acquired most of what they need to know to speak their language fluently by the age of six. By the time a child arrives in school, perhaps 80 percent of the structures of its language and more than 90 percent of the sound system have been acquired. ''Doubtless the greatest intellectual feat any one of us is ever required to perform,'' Leonard Bloomfield remarked of language acquisition earlier in this century. Fortunately, it is a feat at which all human beings are gifted: Even geniuses have no advantage in acquiring a first language. This universal success has convinced linguists and psycholinguists that infants come to the task of acquiring a language with a genetic predisposition to do so and with certain analytical advantages that facilitate the process of acquisition. There is little doubt that, at the very least, children are born with certain mechanisms or cognitive strategies that help in the task of language acquisition, and many believe that certain structures, or kinds of structure, are innate as well.

Adult Input in Language Acquisition

Stating that language acquisition is not a process of imitation doesn't diminish the crucial importance of exposure to linguistic input in acquiring a language. Acquisition requires interaction with speakers of the language being acquired. As witness to the necessity of adult input, there is the case of ''Genie,'' a child who was not exposed to language while she was growing up. Genie's parents locked her away in an attic for the first thirteen years of her life and seldom spoke to her. When Genie was discovered in 1970, she was unable to speak, and linguist Susan Curtiss tried teaching her English, though without much success. Deprived of linguistic input in the first few years of life, Genie's capacity for language acquisition had become severely impaired.

On the other hand, parents do not generally teach language to young children directly. Instead, children spontaneously acquire language on the basis of the input they receive. Conscious attempts to teach correct linguistic forms to children lead nowhere, because children simply ignore instruction and go on acquiring a native tongue at their own pace. In ordinary settings, parents rarely correct young children's grammatical mistakes, although they do correct utterances that are inaccurate or misleading. A child who says *Kitty's hands are pink* may be told *No, Kitty doesn't have hands; Kitty has PAWS*. But if a child asks *Where Kitty go?* (for 'Where did Kitty go?'), adults are not likely to correct the utterance. To a very great extent, then, children acquire the grammatical rules of their language without direct instruction from adults.

Of course, certain aspects of language use *are* taught to children directly. In cultures around the world, children are engaged in conversation with adults almost from the start. In Western cultures, mothers often treat baby noises as openings to conversations, and not only vocal noises. From their early months children are socialized into interactional routines of turn taking, where even their burps, hiccups, and sneezes are regarded as opening turns to which mothers respond as though they were weighty proclamations. Children are so effectively socialized that the turn-taking patterns of school age children have been pretty much established since age one. Later, when young children go trick-or-treating at Halloween (to take the example of a context in which politeness becomes a salient aspect of interaction), they may not produce the appropriate utterances unless prompted *(Say thank you! What do you say?)*. So children need to learn certain rules of language use consciously, and adults typically provide instruction for these politeness rules.

Baby Talk   Even when adults are not explicitly teaching children the rules of language use, they frequently modify their speech, adapting it to what they think children will readily understand and acquire. You have probably witnessed parents and siblings using *baby talk* (some people call it "motherese") in addressing babies.

> Ooohh, what a biiig smiile! Is Baby smiling at Mommy?
>
> Baby is smiling at her Mommy? Yeess!
>
> Is Baby happy to see Mommy?
>
> Is Baby hungry? Yeess? Oopen wiiide . . .
>
> Hmmmm! Baby likes soup. Yeess!
>
> Wheere's the soup? All gone!

This example, uttered slowly and with exaggerated intonation, is typical of the kind of linguistic input that English-speaking mothers and other caregivers provide to young children.

Baby talk differs from talk between adults in characteristic ways. When addressing babies, adults' voices frequently assume a higher pitch than usual. Adults also exaggerate their intonation and speak slowly and clearly. Repetitions and partial repetitions *(Is Baby smiling at Mommy? Baby is smiling at her Mommy?)* are frequent in baby talk. Sentences are short and simple, with few subordinate clauses and few modifiers. Personal names like *Baby* and *Mommy* are preferred over pronouns like *you* and *I*. Compared to adult talk to other adults, baby talk has more frequent content words (nouns, verbs, and adjectives) and fewer function words (prepositions, determiners). Utterances addressed to very young children frequently include special baby-talk vocabulary—words like *doggie, horsie, tummy,* and *din-din* that are more easily perceived or pronounced but do not normally occur in adult talk—and the choice of baby-talk words is more restricted than in ordinary speech. Baby talk is typically concrete and refers to items and actions in the child's immediate environment and experience. It also includes a high proportion of questions *(Is Baby hungry?)*, particularly for young children, and of imperatives *(Oopen wiiide)*. These modifications may serve to hold a child's attention or to simplify the linguistic input that it hears, possibly making it easier to perceive or analyze. Especially in repetitions and shorter expressions addressed to young children, adults chunk their speech by constituent structure, a practice that could provide useful syntactic insight to learners. Baby talk features are summarized in the table below.

Characteristics of Talk to Babies

Concrete, immediate referents	Higher than usual pitch
Exaggerated intonation contours	Frequent questions
Slow and clear enunciations	Frequent repetitions
Baby talk words (*doggie, tummy*)	Frequent imperatives
Frequent content words (nouns, verbs)	Few modifiers
Personal names instead of pronouns (*Mommy,* not *I*)	Few function words
	Few subordinate clauses

At a somewhat more advanced stage, when children start producing utterances, mothers and other caretakers have been observed to echo those utterances in a fuller form than the child offered. Sometimes the intonation of the caretaker's expansions confirms what the child has said; sometimes a questioning intonation seems to be seeking clarification. The following examples are illustrative.

Adult Expansions of Children's Utterances

Child	Mother
Baby highchair	Baby is in the highchair.
Mommy eggnog	Mommy had her eggnog.
Eve lunch	Eve is having lunch.
Throw Daddy	Throw it to Daddy.

Expansions occur far less frequently when mothers (and other caretakers) are alone with children than when other adults are present (including researchers), and such expansions may be intended as "translations" of the baby's speech, more for the aid of the observer than for the benefit of the child.

Features of baby talk are found in cultures far and wide. When the Berbers of North Africa address babies, they simplify their language in some of the same ways that Americans do, and the same is true of the Japanese. Although not all cultures modify speech to children, modification is widespread. Children themselves acquire baby talk very early in life, and even two-year-olds can be heard using features of this register when addressing younger children and siblings.

The extent to which baby talk helps children in acquiring language is difficult to assess, but in cultures where baby talk is absent (as it is in Samoa and certain parts of Papua New Guinea, for example) children acquire their native language at the same rate as children exposed to baby talk. So we must conclude that baby talk is not essential to successful language acquisition.

Still, baby talk does serve some functions. First, it exposes small children to simple language, and simple language may be helpful in the task of unraveling constituent structures and certain rules of grammar. Since children have to figure out so many different grammatical features, selective input (fewer words, fewer complex sentences, and repetitions) may facilitate their task. In addition, considering English, the unusually high percentage of questions that caregivers address to infants has the effect of exposing them to a greater number of auxiliaries *(Did Baby fall?)* than would the use of declarative sentences *(Baby fell)*. Baby talk may also inculcate certain rules of language *use,* the rules of conversation in particular (see Chapter 11). By asking many questions of small children, adults help socialize them into the question-answer sequences and into the alternating turn-taking patterns of conversation. From the earliest stages, adults alternate their utterances with a baby's babblings, and the implicit message is to alternate your utterances with your interlocutor's. Interactional patterns between caregivers and children can thus provide a framework within which utterances can be situated and acquisition of grammar take place.

Stages of Language Acquisition

Babbling Whatever the nature of the input they receive, children go through several stages in the process of acquiring their native language. At the babbling stage, which starts at about six months, children first utter various series of identical syllables such as "ba-ba-ba" or "ma-ma-ma." A couple of months later, as the vocal apparatus matures, this reduplicated babbling blossoms into a wider range of syllable types such as "bab-bab" and "ab-ab." These early babblings are similar the world over and occur with or without listeners present. When some babbled sounds stabilize for a child and are linked to a consistent referent or appear to be used with a consistent purpose (for example to be handed something), they are called *vocables* or protowords. A child may use a vocable like *baba* to indicate it does not want something while *mama* serves to indicate it does want something.

One-Word Stage Starting around one year old, when children take their first steps, they are also heard uttering words like *mama, dada,* and *up*. These early words have a simple structure and typically refer to familiar people (mother and father), toys and pets (teddy bear and kitty), food and drink (cookie and juice), and social interaction (as in *bye-bye*). By this stage children already use vocal noises to get and hold attention socially and to achieve other objectives.

Often, the same word is used to refer to things that have a similar appearance, as when a child learns the word *doggie* for the family dog and then extends it to all dogs. Children seem inclined to generalize word meanings and even to overgeneralize, as when *doggie* is applied to cats as well as dogs, or even to all animals.

Observation of utterances at the one-word stage suggests that children are not rehearsing simple words but expressing single words to convey whole propositions. For example, a child uses the word *Dada* to mean different things in different contexts: 'Here comes Daddy' (upon hearing a key in the door at the end of the day); 'This is for Daddy' (when handing Daddy a toy); 'That is where Daddy usually sits' (when looking at Daddy's empty chair at the kitchen table); or 'This shoe is Daddy's' (when touching a shoe belonging to Daddy).

One-Word Stage

Expression	Content

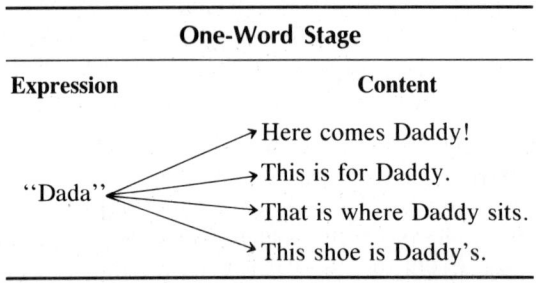

"Dada" → Here comes Daddy!
→ This is for Daddy.
→ That is where Daddy sits.
→ This shoe is Daddy's.

In different contexts, a child may give the same word different intonations. Holding a shoe and uttering *Dada*, a child is not merely naming the object of its focus but is using a relatively simple *expression* to communicate relatively complex *content*.

Two-Word Stage   From the one-word-utterance stage, children move on to utterances like *Daddy come*, *Shoe mine*, and *Apple me*. The transition from the one-word stage to the two-word stage occurs at about twenty months of age, when the child has a vocabulary of about fifty words. At this stage, utterances show a preference for combining a nounlike element with a predicatelike element, and children tend to verbalize in propositions—to name something and then say something about it: *Daddy*, [he is] *com*[ing], *Shoe*, [it's] *mine; Apple*, [give it to] *me*. Other forms also occur, as in *More juice* and *There Daddy*, in which the predicatelike element precedes the noun. One striking fact about the two-word-utterance stage is that children from different cultures appear to express basically similar things in their propositions at this stage.

Two-Word Stage

Expression	Content
"Daddy come"	Daddy, he is coming.
"Shoe mine"	The shoe, it's mine.
"Apple me"	The apple, give it to me.
"More juice"	I want more juice.
"There Daddy"	There is Daddy.

We don't know whether the disposition to verbalize in propositions is a tendency of the language process itself or is tied to aspects of perception. But from the start children seem to be trying to convey propositions, even when the expression is a mere word. If this interpretation is correct, children at the two-word stage are not attempting to communicate more *content* by using two words instead of one but to *express* more of the content than at the one-word stage. In terms of the ideal languages described in the first chapter of this book, the child is progressing on a journey from the "uh" ideal in which a single expression would represent any and all content toward the one-to-one ideal, where each expression would represent unique content. As the child masters its language system, it will learn to balance *expression* and *context* so as to communicate *content* efficiently and effectively.

Beyond Two Words   Beyond the two-word stage, distinct three-word and four-word stages are not recognized. Instead, progress is typically measured by the average number of morphemes (or sometimes words) in a child's utterances. Between about two years (written 2;0) and two and a half years (written 2;6) of age, a child's expressions become considerably more complex. Utterances contain several words representing single clauses.

Consider these single-clause utterances from a boy of two years, five months.

1. Mimo hurt me. [about a past action by his brother]

2. Yeah, that money Neina. (*'Yeah, that money is Zeina's.'*)

3. Me put it back. (*'I'll put it back.'*)

4. No do that again! [to an adult whispering in his ear]

5. Oh! hurt meself. [upon bumping his arm into a door]

6. That's mine, Uncle Ed. [showing a toy to an uncle]

Consider what the child must already know in order to make such utterances. Obviously, he knows some English words: *money, mine, that's*. That entails knowing what sounds they contain and in what order. As the words are used in appropriate contexts, he also knows what they refer to and in what situations they are appropriate. He knows the lexical categories (the parts of speech) of these words and how to combine them with other categories both morphologically (*me, meself, mine*) and syntactically (*Mimo hurt me* and *Me put it back*). Possibly he knows which form of the copula BE agrees with the demonstrative subject *that* and how to contract *is* to *'s* and attach it to *that*, although *that's* may still be an unanalyzed unit for him at this stage. The child has also mastered basic SVO word order, as in *Mimo hurt me* and *Me put it back* (although pronominal subjects are not yet obligatory, as a comparison between *Me put it back* and *Hurt meself* shows). He also shows knowledge of declarative and imperative sentence structures and of negative imperatives.

The phrase *that money* indicates knowledge that *money* belongs to the category of nouns—the category that takes determiners like *that* and *the*. Given the contexts in which the utterances occur, it is also apparent that the child is uttering propositions, although some are incompletely encoded or differ from adult formulations of the same propositions. More noteworthy than the matches between some of these utterances and those of an adult grammar, as with 1 and 6, is the fact that the child is using language in a systematic fashion. The structured utterances are governed by rules of grammar that stay constant from utterance to utterance: Subjects precede verbs; verbs precede objects and other complements; and adverbs (*back* and *again*) follow objects.

Of course, there are many other forms of the adult grammar that the child has not yet fully mastered, and these include syntactic and morphological matters. Syntactically, no subject is expressed in 5, no verb in 2, and no auxiliary in 3, all of which would be required in well-formed adult utterances. Morphologically, the possessive marker is not fully mastered: It appears in *mine* but is lacking in *Neina;* the adult subject form of the first person pronoun *I* and the adult reflexive form *myself* have not yet been acquired.

By around three years of age, utterances containing multiple clauses appear, at first coordinating two clauses as in *There's his face and he's Mister George Happy.* Later, children subordinate one clause to another, with subordinators like *'cause, so,* and *if* in the early stages and then *why* and *what: Me don't know where box is now, Why did you give to her when her been flu?*

Morphological and Grammatical Acquisition

Interestingly, the morphemes and grammatical structures of language are generally acquired by children in a set order, with variation from child to child usually slight. This pattern suggests that there is an internally regulated sequence for grammatical acquisition. Psychologist Roger Brown examined the order in which fourteen morphological and grammatical morphemes were acquired by three English-speaking children and found that they were acquired in the order given below.

Acquisition Order for English Morphemes

1. Present progressive verb (with or without auxiliary): *(is) playing, (was) singing*
2–3. Prepositions *in* and *on*
4. Regular noun plural: *toys, cats, dishes*
5. Irregular past tense verbs: *came, fell, saw, hurt*
6. Possessive noun: *Daddy's, doggie's*
7. Uncontractible copula: *Here I am, Who is it?*
8. Articles: *a* and *the*
9. Regular past tense verbs: *played, washed, wanted*
10. Regular third singular present tense verbs: *sees, wants, washes*
11. Irregular third singular present tense verbs: *does, has*
12. Uncontractible auxiliary: *She isn't crying, He was eating*
13. Contractible copula: *That's mine, What's that?*
14. Contractible auxiliary: *He's crying*

Although the children acquired these forms basically in the same *order,* they did not acquire them *at the same speed.* Between acquisition of the present progressive (the earliest acquired) and the contractible auxiliary (the last), anywhere from six to fourteen months elapsed. One child acquired the contractible auxiliary by 2;3, while another took until 3;6.

The order tracked among Brown's young "consultants" basically replicated the order other linguists and psychologists had tracked with different children, and the slight variations reported probably have to do with the criteria used for judging "acquisition." For example, Brown judged a feature to be acquired only when a child used it correctly in 90 percent of the required cases in three successive sampling sessions. Other researchers used different criteria, such as the first time that a correct use was observed.

Determinants of Acquisition Orders   As to what determines the order of acquisition, it would seem reasonable to suppose that the frequency with which a child hears a form from the adults around it will influence the order of acquisition. In fact, however, Brown was unable to correlate frequency of parental use with the order of acquisition. The most frequent of the fourteen morphemes in the parents' speech was the articles, which appeared eighth in the order of child acquisition. The prepositions, on the other hand, were acquired second by children, although they were used relatively little by parents. In determining the order of acquisition, what seems more influential than frequency is relative complexity. Morphemes that encode several semantic notions and those that are syntactically more complex tend to be acquired later than those that encode a single semantic notion and are syntactically simpler.

Exceptions and Overgeneralizations   No doubt you have observed that children tend to overgeneralize, or overextend, the patterns of inflectional morphology. You've heard children say things like "eated" for *ate* and "foots" for *feet*. There are several dozen irregular verbs in English (not all of them used by children), and among those that get overgeneralized are the ones listed below.

Children's Overgeneralization of Past Tense Verbs

eated	ate	doed	did
maked	made	speaked	spoke
finded	found	breaked	broke
hitted	hit	goed	went
falled	fell	runned	ran

In English there are far fewer common nouns like *foot* that form their plurals irregularly; among those overgeneralized by children are the ones listed next.

Children's Overgeneralization of Noun Plurals

foots	feet	mans	men
tooths	teeth	mouses	mice
childs	children	peoples	people

Evidence from several languages has now been gathered for overgeneralization by children, and it suggests that children tend naturally to overgeneralize or "over-regularize" the morphological rules that they acquire.

Sentence Structure The sentences of the twenty-nine-month-old (2;5) boy (given on page 453) contain single clauses only. Before that boy is five years old, sentences incorporating more than one clause will be commonplace, including imperatives *(Guess who's visiting me)* and interrogatives *(Do you know what I did at school today?).* Even at age five, though, relative clauses will not be fully acquired, although certain kinds of relatives are understood by children even at three years of age. When children first produce relative clauses, they attach them to object noun phrases, as in "You broke the one *that I found.*" Attaching relative clauses to subjects (as in "The one *that I found* is red") represents a later stage of acquisition, and attaching them to other grammatical relations comes later still.

Negation At first, children express negation by the simple utterance *no,* either alone or preceding other expressions: *No, No want, No that, No do that.* At a somewhat later stage, by three years of age, more complex expressions incorporate negations, as in these: *Can't get it off, Don't know, It doesn't go that way, That not go in there.*

Questions As with negations, every language has ways of asking questions. Some do so simply by adding a question word to the end of a statement. English has a relatively complex way of forming questions, and mastery of its question-formation rules takes time. In the early stages, interrogative utterances have the same syntax as declaratives, as in *That mine;* sometimes, though not always, the intonation of questions differs from that of statements. By three years of age, children have mastered most aspects of question formation, as shown in these questions by a three-year old girl named Sophie:

Wh-Questions	Yes/No Questions
What is he called?	Is this a box?
What goes in this hole?	Do it go this side?
Why didn't me get flu?	Can me put it in like that?
Why's he so small?	
Where are you Mummy?	

Acquisition of Vocabulary

At the start of the 2-word stage, around twenty months (1;8) of age, a child knows approximately fifty words. Mostly they are nouns referring to concrete, familiar objects *(shoe, clock, apple, baby, milk, nose)* or expressions for salient notions in the child's environment *(more, no, bye-bye, oh, walk, what's that).* By age 5, the child's vocabulary is increasing by about fifteen or twenty words a day. Estimates of the number of basic words known by schoolchildren of age 6 run about 7,800, even counting a word set like *cat, cats, cat's, cats'* or *walk, walks, walked, walking* as a single word. If you count derived forms like *dollhouse* as a third word besides *doll* and *house,* then 13,000 words would be a reliable figure.

Astonishingly, 2 years later, by age 8, a child's vocabulary has increased to 17,600 basic words (or 28,300 words including derived forms). This represents an average increase of more than thirteen basic words (or twenty-one words and derived forms) *each day*. Of course, a word isn't acquired in its semantic fullness on a single occasion. Instead, a full range of meanings for any word is generally acquired only by stages over a period of time, and this phenomenon, like vocabulary acquisition itself, continues well into adulthood, though at a drastically reduced rate.

Phonological Acquisition

We have all listened to a child uttering words and expressions that we could understand within their context even though the pronunciations did not match our own. "Neina" /nena/ for *Zeina* /zena/ in the speech from the boy of two years five months is one illustration. Other examples might be "poon" or "bude" for *spoon*, "du" for *juice*, and "dis" or "di" [dɪ] for *this*. Such pronunciations suggest that a child masters certain aspects of a word before others. In these cases, the context of use indicates that the child knows the word's lexical category and such semantic information as its referent; it also knows some of its phonological content although mastery of the pronunciation is manifestly incomplete. Here we examine certain patterns of phonological acquisition among English-speaking children and draw some cross-linguistic comparisons.

From as early as two months, infants react differently to different speech sounds, and they can recognize individual voices—their mother's for example. (We know this from changes in the rate of sucking when voices alternate.) Prior to their production of recognizable utterances at about twelve months of age, infants go through a lengthy babbling stage, during which they appear to rehearse a wide range of sounds, extending beyond the ones spoken around them and beyond the inventory needed for their own language.

Early babbling consists of simple syllable-like sequences of a consonant followed by a vowel: "ba-ba-ba." Repetitions of CV syllables are then followed by sequences that juxtapose different CV syllables ("bamama"), first yielding CVCV patterns and then CVC patterns (such as "bam" and "mam," which lack the vowel of the second CVCV syllable). These early babblings reveal a preference for voiced stops [b d g m n] and a dispreference for fricatives [f v θ ð s z] and liquids [l r]. Not surprisingly, sounds that are relatively rare among the world's languages tend to be acquired later than sounds that are common. By eight or nine months of age children are able to mimic adult intonation patterns to a striking degree, and unlike the sounds of babbling, these intonation patterns differ from language to language.

Consonant Sounds of Babbling					
Preferred			**Dispreferred**		
b	d	g	v	ð	z
m	n		f	θ	s
			l/r		

Before the first recognizable words are produced around age one, the list of speech sounds actually shrinks (and a few children even go through a silent period), after which the inventory of sounds belonging to the adult language is gradually and systematically acquired. Full phonological development takes several years, and the last sounds may not be acquired before age six or so.

Between 12 months (1;0) and 18 months (1;6) of age, a child learns to *produce* about 50 words (which is only about one-fourth of those it can recognize). The range of sounds and of syllable types needed to give voice to so small a lexicon is relatively limited (five vowels and ten consonants would generate 50 monosyllabic words of CV type). At about 18 months of age, children typically experience a "word spurt," and for this larger lexicon the previous inventory of sounds and syllables is inadequate: An expansion of the system is necessary.

Around twenty-four months (2;0) of age, an English-speaking child typically has acquired the following consonant sounds, although not all the sounds can be produced in every position in which adults use them.

Inventory of English Consonants at Age Two			
Nasals	m		n	
Stops	b		d	g
	p		t	k
Fricatives		f	s	h
Glides	w			

A year later, at about thirty-six months (3;0), the child has added /y/ and /ŋ/ to its inventory, although [b], [d], [g], and [k] remain elusive in word-final position. Consonant clusters (as in *spilled* [spɪld], *stopped* [stɑpt], and *asked* [æskt]) present children with particular challenges. In fact, of the wide range of clusters that adults use, the three-year-old may have mastered only final /-ŋk/ as in *pink* and *sink*.

By around four years of age, the inventory of consonants has expanded significantly and stands approximately as given here.

Inventory of English Consonants at Age Four			
Nasals	m	n		ŋ
Stops	b	d		g
	p	t		k
Fricatives		f	s	š	h
		v	z		
Affricates				č	
				ǰ	
Glides	w	l/r		y

At this stage the voiced fricatives /v/ and /z/ may be present only in medial position (as in *over* and *dizzy*), but the child may not yet produce them in word-final or word-initial position. Recall that the twenty-nine-month-old (2;5) boy whose utterances we analyzed earlier substituted the nasal [n] for initial [z] in the name *Zeina,* presumably influenced by anticipation of the [n] to follow, as commonly happens with children. The interdental fricative sounds /θ/ and /ð/ (as in *thin* and *then*) have yet to be added to the four-year old's inventory in any position, as has the relatively rare /ž/ (as in *measure*). Thus, between the ages of four and six, an English-speaking child may still lack /ž/, /v/, /θ/, /ð/, and /z/, at least in some positions. And still ahead lies mastery of the morphophonemic rules that account for variation between underlying forms and surface forms (as in the [t]/[D] alternation of *late* [let] and *later* [leDər] or the [d]/[D] alternation of *dad* and *daddy*). Mastery of the more complex syllable structures and consonant clusters also lies ahead.

Substituting Sounds for One Another   One could imagine that until a child mastered the phonological inventory of its language, the sounds not yet learned would be skipped, producing pronunciations like "oo" for *shoe* and *juice*. Of course, that isn't what happens. Instead, children generally attempt to pronounce all the sounds of words, although they do this by various simplifications. The principal simplifications in the early pronunciations of children involve substituting easier sounds for harder ones, as in the following processes:

Stopping: fricatives and affricates pronounced as stops

Devoicing: final obstruents devoiced

Voicing: initial obstruents voiced before vowels

Fronting: velars and palato-alveolars pronounced as alveolars

Gliding: liquids pronounced as glides

Vocalization: liquids replaced by vowels

Denasalization: nasals replaced by oral stops

Processes of Substitution in Child Language

Stopping	v ⟶ b	van ⟶ [bæn]
	ð ⟶ d, n	that ⟶ [dæt], there ⟶ [nɛr]
	ǰ ⟶ d	Jack ⟶ [dæk], jam ⟶ [dæb]
	č ⟶ d	check ⟶ [dɛk]
Devoicing	-b ⟶ p	knob ⟶ [nɑp]
	-d ⟶ t	bad ⟶ [bæt]
	-g ⟶ t	dog ⟶ [dɑt]
	-v ⟶ f	stove ⟶ [duf]
Voicing	p- ⟶ b	pot ⟶ [bɑt]
	t- ⟶ d	toe ⟶ [do]
	k- ⟶ d	kiss ⟶ [dɪ]

(continued)

Processes of Substitution in Child Language (*continued*)		
Fronting	k ⟶ t	duck ⟶ [dɑt]
	g ⟶ d	gate ⟶ [det]
	θ ⟶ f	thumb ⟶ [fʌm]
	š ⟶ z	shoes ⟶ [zus]
	ž ⟶ z	rouge ⟶ [wu:z]
	č ⟶ ts	match ⟶ [mæts]
	ǰ ⟶ dz	cabbage ⟶ [tæ:bədz]
Gliding	r ⟶ w	rock ⟶ [wɑt], sorry ⟶ [sɑwɑ]
Vocalization	l ⟶ u	table ⟶ [dubu]
Denasalization	m ⟶ p, b	lamb ⟶ [bæp], broom ⟶ [bub]
		jam ⟶ [dæb]

(After Ingram, pp. 371–372).

Actually, besides the substitution processes described above, some omission also takes place. For example, as illustrated below, young children typically delete unstressed syllables from trisyllabic words (as in "nana" for *banana*) and sometimes the unstressed syllable of a disyllabic word; they sometimes omit final consonants; and they often reduce consonant clusters.

Processes of Omission in Child Language	
Deletion of Syllable	banana ⟶ [næna], kitchen ⟶ [kɪč], pocket ⟶ [bɑt]
Deletion of Final Consonant	doll ⟶ [dɑ], far ⟶ [fɑ]
Reduction of Consonant Clusters	
stop + liquid ⟶ stop	glass ⟶ [dæs], bread ⟶ [but]
s- + stop ⟶ stop	star ⟶ [dɑ]
s- + nasal ⟶ nasal	snake ⟶ [nek]
nasal + voiced stop ⟶ nasal	hand ⟶ [hæn]

Determinants of Acquisition Order It is not entirely clear what determines the order in which sounds are acquired. If it would seem reasonable to assume that the more frequently a child heard a particular sound, the sooner that sound would be acquired, the facts point elsewhere. Consider that the most frequent English consonant sounds are the fricatives [s], [ð], [z], and [v]. Either [s] or [z] occurs in the plural forms of most nouns, the possessive form of every noun, the third person singular present-tense form of all verbs *(eats, does, is)*, certain common pronouns and possessive determiners *(his, hers, yours)*, and some other common words *(was* and *some)*. In light of such frequency, it is not surprising that [s] is acquired relatively early (by about twenty-four months). But, perplexingly, [z] is not acquired until four years of age and then usually only in medial position. Consider also that [ð], though it occurs in extremely frequent words like *this, that,* and *the,* is acquired very late, while [v], even at four years of age, is produced in medial position but not initially or finally, where it is common in such words as *very, have,* and *of.* Clearly, frequency of occurrence in adult speech cannot be the sole determinant in the order of acquisition.

Of greater influence than frequency is the functional importance of a sound within its phonological system. A sound is said to have a high *functional load* if it serves to differentiate many words (or words that are very frequent), and high functional load seems to promote early acquisition. Thus /č/ is acquired much later by children learning English than by Guatemalan children learning the Mayan language Quiché. The reason appears to be that in Quiché /č/ contrasts with other sounds in many more words than it does in English, and the high functional load of the /č/ sound in Quiché fosters early acquisition. By contrast, the low functional importance of /č/ in English tends to bump it towards the end of the acquisition line.

Phonological Idioms Before acquiring all the sounds in the inventory of its language, a child may be able to produce those sounds as "idioms" in a few words. In much the same way that adults have semantic idioms *(kick the bucket)* and syntactic idioms *(the sooner the better),* so children may produce unanalyzed words containing sounds they have not yet added as units of their phonological inventory. The child makes a lexical contrast without yet having the phonological contrast.

METHODS OF STUDYING CHILD LANGUAGE ACQUISITION

Studies of child language and language acquisition have most commonly been observational studies. Researchers have tape recorded ordinary interactions between adults and children or among children at regular intervals and transcribed those results for analysis. There have also been diary studies (carried out by parents who were themselves linguists or psychologists) that record a child's utterances, the age at which they occur, and the situational context surrounding them. Depending on the focus and goals of the observer, diary studies represent different degrees of detail, from ordinary orthography to a narrow phonetic transcription. Quite naturally, then, observational studies of child language have focused on the *production* of words and sentences.

"FIS" Phenomenon In our discussions so far we haven't said much about a child's *receptive* mastery, or understanding, nor have we drawn a distinction between what a child's grammatical competence might allow but its production apparatus be unable to utter. After all, a child could have the grammatical competence to generate adult pronunciations as far as the phonological processes of the internalized grammar are concerned, but remain unable to utter them because of physiological immaturity in the vocal apparatus. There is an oft repeated story of a child who pronounced *fish* as "fis" [fɪs] but objected to an adult imitating the "fis" pronunciation. "This is your *fis?*" the adult asked. "No," said the child, "my *fis.*" When the adult repeated the question, the child again rejected the "fis" pronunciation. When the adult ultimately said, "Your *fish?*" the child concurred, "Yes, my *fis*"! The child could hear the distinction between *fish* and "fis" and recognized "fis" as an incorrect pronunciation. But in attempting to say *fish* the child produced a word that replicated the "fis" it knew to be wrong. We should be careful interpreting such data, however. While it may seem that the child knows and recognizes the difference between [fɪš] and [fɪs] while being unable to pronounce [fɪš] because of limitations in the vocal apparatus, there are other possible explanations. Consider the case of the child who consistently pronounced *puddle* as "puggle": the obvious hypothesis that the vocal apparatus was not yet capable of pronouncing /d/ intervocalically was belied by the fact that the child systematically pronounced *puzzle* as "puddle."

Consider still another case. In saying a word like *pig* or *tug,* the voicing that is required in pronouncing the *vowels* is anticipated by adults in such a fashion that /p/ and /t/, though they begin without voicing, become voiced just preceding the onset of the vowel. It is almost as if the pronunciation were [pbɪg] and [tdʌg]. The key to an adult's distinguishing initial /p/ and /b/ before vowels is *how long* the voicing is delayed, not whether or not it is present. A child may be perceived as failing to distinguish voiced from voiceless initial stops, pronouncing *tug* and *Doug* alike as [dʌg] or *pig* and *big* alike as [bɪg]. But laboratory analyses indicate that some children systematically distinguish initial /t/ from /d/ and initial /p/ from /b/ by delaying the voicing onset time for the voiceless stops for a longer period than they delay voicing for the voiced stops. The delayed voicing detectable by laboratory instruments, however, cannot be detected by the human ear. This would indicate that the child has heard the voiceless and voiced stops and internalized the differences between them in its lexicon but has not yet learned to delay the onset of voicing long enough to be detected by adults.

There is general agreement that receptive mastery of language outpaces production, but it is not clear that this is so at all stages of language development and in all respects. Still, children generally seem able to understand more than they can produce—that is, their lexical and syntactic repertoire is greater than their production reveals. At about 18 months of age, as we mentioned above, a child understands about 200 words although only about 50 appear in its speech. In an attempt, then, to analyze the language competence of children, naturalistic observation alone may offer an incomplete picture, so researchers have had to invent ingenious ways to get at receptive competence.

One experimental technique elicits from children utterances they would not otherwise have occasion to say. In one study, children were shown drawings of an imaginary bird or animal and told, for example, "This is a wug." The next drawing would depict two such animals, and the child would be suitably prompted to offer a plural form: "Now there is another one. There are two of them. There are two _____?" (See Figure 14-1) This technique can uncover how much morphophonemic variation of the plural morpheme the child has mastered. Alternatively, pictures of people carrying out novel actions such as "ricking" were used to elicit past tenses and progressive forms of verbs. With still another technique, children using hand puppets speak in the voices of their puppets to another puppet given voice by the researcher. In a fourth technique, to trace their progress for repetition of sounds, syllable structures, and grammatical forms, children can also be asked simply to repeat words or sentences. In a fifth technique

THIS IS A WUG.

NOW THERE IS ANOTHER ONE.
THERE ARE TWO OF THEM.
THERE ARE TWO _____.

FIGURE 14-1
A Test for Plural Allomorphs

Source: Jean Berko (Gleason), 1958, "The Child's Learning of English Morphology," *Word,* 14:154.

designed to gauge understanding, children playing with dolls are asked to act out such sentences as "The horse pushed the cow" and "The horse was pushed by the cow."

Although child language and first-language acquisition are important to many aspects of linguistic theory, a great deal about the processes of acquisition remains unclear or uninvestigated. The interaction between physiological and mental limitations, on the one hand, and the nature of the internalized grammar, on the other, makes interpreting child language data challenging. Given the complexities of interpreting child language data, the most reliable findings and theories will be those that emerge from using a variety of investigative methodologies.

SECOND-LANGUAGE ACQUISITION

Comparison of First- and Second-Language Acquisition

Besides their first language, most readers of this book have probably acquired at least the rudiments of a second language, perhaps Russian, Spanish, German,

French, Japanese—or English. The term "first language" refers to the language one acquires in infancy. A second language is *any* language that is acquired after one's first language—it may well be a third or fourth "second language." When we speak of second languages in this chapter, we focus on those acquired as adults.

There are two common situations in which adults learn a "second" language. The one familiar to most of you occurs when someone studies a foreign language in school or in college. As with English taught abroad, such situations often provide relatively little opportunity for experience with the spoken language outside the classroom. In this sense, the study of French in the United States could be called "French as a foreign language," paralleling the "English as a foreign language" studied in Jiddah, Tokyo, Taipei, and elsewhere. Indeed, we talk of "foreign language" requirements for graduation from college, and it is useful to bear in mind that studying a "foreign language" typically involves activities that differ significantly from those surrounding first-language acquisition, as well as from the acquisition of a second language in a community where it is spoken natively and widely. When a language is being acquired in a community in which it is spoken natively, learners can participate in a range of communicative activities in the target language.

When populations of Poles, Italians, Germans, Norwegians, and others migrated to America in the nineteenth and early twentieth centuries, they settled in a land that was largely English speaking, though many initially lived in neighborhoods where their first language could be used with neighbors and shopkeepers as well as family. The migrations of the present day—for example, from Asia and Latin America—represent a similar situation, although the communities in which immigrants now settle often have large enough immigrant populations to maintain the "foreign" language in newspapers and in radio and television broadcasting, as well as in shops, churches, and homes. In some metropolitan areas, dozens of locally broadcast "foreign" languages can be heard on the radio every day, and cable networks broadcast news and entertainment in languages other than English throughout the day. In Los Angeles, television news is broadcast in Korean, Mandarin, and Spanish every day, and there are soap operas and variety shows in these languages and quite a few others. Daily newspapers are also published locally in several languages and sold at newsstands side by side with English-language dailies. For the 1992 presidential election, the sample ballot in Los Angeles included a full-page notice informing registered voters that "Under federal law voter information and sample ballots are available in the following languages," and five brief paragraphs followed, each in a different language, giving telephone numbers for obtaining alternative language ballots in Chinese, Japanese, Vietnamese, Tagalog, and Spanish.

Staff members at many bank branches in Los Angeles are bilingual in English and another language spoken in the neighborhood, and many other commercial and professional establishments routinely provide bilingual service. As a result of such interwoven linguistic networks in some North American communities, and in communities around the globe, the distinction between second language and "foreign" language is not altogether tidy.

Similarities and Differences in Language Acquisition

Typically there are significant differences between first- and second-language learning. To begin with (and by definition), first-language acquisition involves an initial linguistic experience, while a second language is mastered only by someone who already speaks another language. However blank the language slate may be at birth, it is certainly not so after first-language acquisition is completed.

Second, a first language is usually acquired in a home environment by an infant in the care of parents and other caretakers, with many activities—linguistic and otherwise—jointly focused on the child. In such circumstances, language use is closely tied to the immediate surroundings, to the context of language use. Caretakers use language in reference to objects in the immediate environment (objects that can be seen or heard by the infant), and language content reflects ongoing activity in which child and caretaker are participating as actors (as with eating or bathing) or as observers (of activities within sight or earshot). In contrast, second-language learning is seldom so context bound. Ordinarily an adult speaking a second language as in a classroom is using it to discuss imaginary or decontextualized events removed from the learning situation.

A third difference has to do with the adaptability and malleability of learners as a consequence of age and of social identity. Infants have not yet developed strong social identities as to gender, ethnicity, or social status—factors that can be an important part of the social identity and self-awareness of adolescents and adults. Since language use reflects (and helps create) social identity, as you saw in Chapter 13, the social-psychological experiences of first- and second-language acquisition can differ greatly. For many second-language learners, the language variety being studied is emblematic of a different social status or different ethnicity from that represented by their first language, and for nearly all learners it represents new and different cultural values. For infants, this is not the case, of course, so such factors do not come into play in first-language acquisition. Ordinarily, acquisition of a first language and of a social identity go hand in hand and are inseparable.

A fourth difference is that second-language learners ordinarily have linguistic metaknowledge that is lacking at least in the early stages of a first language. That is, with a second language, speakers may already possess a vocabulary for referring to language structures and language uses. They will certainly be aware that words and sounds differ from language to language, that some sounds are more difficult to make than others, that languages differ grammatically, and that speakers can be recognized as native or nonnative by their speech patterns. Naturally, such metaknowledge is lacking for the first-language acquirer, who plays with language spontaneously and unselfconsciously.

Even when second-language learners haven't been exposed to such terms as "noun," "verb," and "sentence," they are aware of certain linguistic phenomena—the existence of words, the notions of regional, social, and foreign accent, the existence of well-formed and ill-formed sentences, and so on. For many other second-language learners, phonological terms like "consonant" and "vowel" and grammatical terms like "verb" and "subject" are familiar. Just what influence knowledge of such categories may have on second-language acquisition is not known. Some investigators believe that conscious knowledge of grammar can facilitate acquisition for some learners, but to what degree and in what ways is not well understood.

Motivation in Second-Language Learning

Among the things that do clearly affect mastery of a second language is the kind of motivation that a learner has. People learn another language for many reasons, from vacationing abroad where you may need to seek directions in the local language to taking up permanent residence in a locale where it is the sole means of communication. For some American students the principal reason for second-language study is to meet a graduation requirement. Motivations for second-language learning can be grouped under the headings of *instrumental* and *integrative*.

Instrumental Motivation   An **instrumental motivation** is one a learner has because knowledge of the target language will help achieve some other goal: reading scientific works, singing or understanding opera, graduation. For such uses, only a narrow range of registers (or even a single register) is necessary, and little or no social integration of the learner into a community using the language is desired.

Integrative Motivation   Integrative motivation is fundamentally different from instrumental motivation. When you take up residence in a community that uses the target language in its social interactions, **integrative motivation** encourages you to learn the new language as a way to integrate yourself socially into the community and become one of its members. Integrative motivation typically underlies successful acquisition of a wide range of registers and a nativelike pronunciation, achievements that usually elude learners with instrumental motivation.

Teaching and Learning Foreign Languages

Of the several methods of foreign language instruction in use, you are probably familiar with pattern drills, translation, composition, listening comprehension, and a few others. Some methods are grounded in the behaviorist assumption that language mastery is a matter of inducing the right habits, much as first-language acquisition was assumed to be earlier in this century. Other methods, aiming to be more "naturalistic," attempt to emulate the kinds of language experience children have when acquiring a first language. With naturalistic methods the emphasis is on interactional use, especially conversation, focused on matters close at hand; noninteractional use aims to provide abundant input that is nearly fully comprehensible to the learner because of its familiarity.

Contrastive Analysis   For many decades, learning a second language was viewed as a matter of knowing and practicing the well-formed utterances of the target language. Learning a second language was approached as a matter of drilling grammatical patterns, and drills focused on patterns that differ from those of the first language. To prepare teaching materials, researchers carried out a **contrastive**

analysis of the phonological and grammatical structures of the native and target languages. Thus they produced a list of morphological, grammatical, and phonological features that could be expected to prove difficult for learners because they differed from those of the first language.

For various reasons, teaching materials based on contrastive analysis have not proven very effective. A number of problems have been uncovered, among them the recognition of an asymmetry between learners acquiring one another's language. Contrastive analysis predicts that when two languages contrast, the difference between them should prove equally challenging for speakers of both languages. In fact, however, difficulties typically prove asymmetrical. Rather than English and Chinese speakers having equivalent difficulties learning one another's language, there are great differences in various parts of the grammar. For example, a distinction that English (and other European languages) makes between masculine and feminine singular pronouns (*he* versus *she*) proves difficult to master for speakers of Chinese, which makes no such distinction, whereas it is easy for English speakers to ignore the distinction. Similarly, Chinese doesn't express the copula BE in many places where English requires it. It is relatively easy for English speakers to omit BE in such sentences but very challenging for Chinese speakers to express it where it is required in English. Likewise, English speakers find it tough to learn the Chinese tone system, while Chinese speakers find it easy to adapt to the absence of a tone system in English. Contrastive analysis also suggests that certain differences in structure should warrant considerable attention, whereas in practice learners avoid the structure altogether, substituting alternative means of expression in the target language.

Interlanguage   Some researchers view second-language learners as developing a series of *interlanguages* in their progression towards mastery of the target language. An **interlanguage** is that form of the target language that a learner has internalized, and the interlanguage grammar underlies the spontaneous utterances of a learner in the target language. The grammar of an interlanguage can differ from the grammar of the target language in various ways: by containing rules borrowed from the native language; by containing overgeneralizations; by lacking certain sounds of the target language; by inappropriately marking certain verbs in the lexicon as requiring (or not requiring) a preposition; by lacking certain rules altogether; and so on. A language learner can be viewed as progressing from one interlanguage to another, each one approximating more closely to the target language.

Fossilization   For various reasons, often related to the kind of motivation a learner has, the language learning process typically slows down or ceases at some point, and the existing interlanguage stabilizes, with further acquisition negligible (leaving aside new vocabulary). When such stabilization occurs, the interlanguage may contain rules or other features that differ from those of the target language. This **fossilization** underlies the nonnative speech characteristics of someone who may have spoken the target language for some time but has stopped the process of learning. In other words, many second-language learners *fossilize* at a stage of acquisition that falls short of nativelike speech. Fossilization then is at the root of a "foreign accent" when, for instance, certain sounds have not been acquired or their allophonic distribution in the fossilized interlanguage does not match that of native speakers of the target language. The pronunciation of English *thin* and *then* as "sin" and "zen" by native speakers of French may reflect fossilization at a stage before the English sounds /θ/ and /ð/ (which do not occur in the French inventory) have been acquired. Likewise, the English speaker who pronounces the French words *pain* 'bread' and *Pierre* with the aspirated [pʰ] that English has in word-initial position (instead of the unaspirated [p] of French) may have fossilized before the distribution of the French allophones was mastered.

Grammatical fossilization is manifest in expressions like those below, which come from a native speaker of Mandarin.

1. I want to see what can I buy.

2. Where I can buy them?

3. What you gonna do on Tuesday?

4. I will cold.

5. Where did you found it?

6. Why you buy it?

7. How you pronounce this word?

8. Oh! Look this.

Such sentences reflect the speaker's current interlanguage grammar; for a speaker whose acquisition of English has ceased to develop, the utterances would represent fossilization.

Attitudes and Second-Language Learning

Language attitudes can have a profound effect on your ability to acquire a second language, especially beyond adolescence. *Studying* a foreign language is parallel to learning math or history; a body of information must be mastered, certainly including much vocabulary and perhaps including terms such as case, tense, (subjunctive) mood, and (subordinate) clause. This kind of foreign language learning differs not only from first-language acquisition but also from second-language acquisition in immersion situations in which you can acquire a language in a fashion approximating (however inadequately) the environment normally surrounding first-language acquisition. Because the language variety you acquire becomes part of your social identity, the acquisition of a second language must be seen not just as an intellectual exercise but as an enterprise that affects or alters your social identity.

Your attitude toward a second language and your motivation can have a profound effect on the success of acquisition. In acquiring a second language, your efforts are mediated by what linguist Stephen Krashen has called an "affective filter"—a psychological disposition that facilitates or inhibits your natural language-acquisition capacities. Krashen maintains that if there is sufficient comprehensible language use surrounding a learner, the acquisition of a second language, even by an adult, can proceed as effortlessly and efficiently as first-language acquisition, provided that the affective filter is not blocking the operation of these capacities.

The learning of a second language in school is increasingly viewed not as an intellectual or educational phenomenon but as a social-psychological phenomenon. One social psychologist describes this view as follows:

> In the acquisition of a second language, the student is faced with the task of not simply learning new information . . . which is part of his *own* culture but rather of *acquiring* symbolic elements of a different ethnolinguistic community. The new words are not simply new words for old concepts, the new grammar is not simply a new way of ordering words, the new pronunciations are not merely 'different' ways of saying things. They are characteristics of another ethnolinguistic community. Furthermore, the student is not being asked to learn about them; he is being asked to acquire them, to make them part of his own language reservoir. This involves imposing elements of another culture into one's own lifespace. As a result, the student's harmony with his own cultural community and his willingness or ability to identify with other cultural communities become important considerations in the process of second language acquisition.[1]

Harmony with a cultural community, then, is one of the things at the heart of second- as well as first-language acquisition, and it would appear to make language acquisition a peculiarly human experience. Indeed, human language is thought by many to be unique to the human species, but others judge it to differ only in degree from forms of animal communication. The comparison between human and animal communication systems has occupied researchers for some time, and a few enterprising researchers have even attempted to teach modes of human language to animals. We now turn to a brief review of some of that research.

ANIMAL COMMUNICATION

When we observe animals in groups, it doesn't take long to realize that they too interact: Dogs display their fangs to communicate displeasure or aggression; bees appear to tell each other where they have found flowers; male frogs croak in order to attract female frogs. It is only natural to ask, How do the forms of communication used by animals differ from human language?

People sometimes speak of porpoises, chimpanzees, gorillas, dolphins, whales, bees, and other animals as though they had language systems similar to those of humans. Almost any week, television programs show people trying to communicate through music with apes, alligators, or turkeys (turkeys gobble when a particular note is played on a wind instrument). There is no doubt that most, and presumably all, species of animals have developed systems of communication with which they can signal such things as danger and fear, hunger and the whereabouts of food, rutting instincts and sexual access. We now know a good deal about what, why, and how bees communicate. More recently, chimpanzees, with

---

[1] R. C. Gardner, "Social Psychological Aspects of Second Language Acquisition," in Howard Giles and Robert St. Clair, eds., *Language and Social Psychology* (Oxford: Blackwell, 1979), pp. 193–194.

their extremely limited vocal apparatus, have been raised as human infants and taught sign language so as to skirt the difficulties or impossibility of their vocalizing.

Communication among Animals in Their Natural Environments

People had wondered for a long time how bees were able to communicate to one another the exact location of a nectar source, and there was speculation about a "language" that bees must possess. After years of careful observation and hypothesizing, Karl von Frisch claimed that honeybees have an elaborate system of dancing by which they communicate the whereabouts of a honey supply. Various aspects of the dance of a bee returning to a hive indicate the distance and the direction of a nectar source. The quality of the source can be gauged by sniffing the discovering bee. Although some of his interpretations have been questioned, von Frisch's careful analysis demonstrated that the kind of creativity characteristic of a child's speech is lacking in the bee's dance. Bees do not use their communicative system to convey anything beyond a limited range of meanings (such as 'There is a pretty good source of nectar in this direction'). Analogies between bee dancing and child language are therefore farfetched and misleading.

The same lack of creativity characterizes the communication that takes place between other animals. Beyond a limited repertoire of meanings, even intelligent mammals like dogs do not have the mental capacity to be communicatively creative.

Furthermore, much of the communication that occurs between animals relies on signs rather than symbols. When gazelles sense potential danger, they flee and thereby signal to other gazelles in the vicinity that danger is lurking. The communicative function of the act is incidental to its more pressing survival function. Similarly, a dog signals the possibility that it might bite momentarily by displaying its fangs. These acts are not arbitrary symbols; rather, they are signs that accompany desires and possibilities.

Vocalizations that might be construed as symbols of various sorts in different animals are usually accompanied by gestures. One study found that only 3 percent of the signals among rhesus monkeys were not accompanied by gestures. Whatever animals express through sounds seems to reflect not a logical sequence of thoughts but a sequence accompanying a series of emotional states. Animals' communicative activities thus differ from human language in that they consist essentially of signs, not arbitrary symbols.

Teaching Human Language to Chimpanzees

The situation with chimpanzees is more complicated and more interesting. In the wild, chimps use a limited nonlinguistic communicative system similar to that of other mammals, though more sophisticated. However, because the intelligence of chimps comes closest to that of humans, there have been several attempts to teach chimps human language in laboratory settings. There is disagreement among researchers as to whether and to what degree chimps can achieve humanlike linguistic competence.

The earliest chimp to gain some notoriety for her communicative prowess was named Vicki. After being raised for about seven years by psychologists Keith and Catherine Hayes, Vicki could utter only four words—*mama, papa, up,* and *cup*—and she managed these only with considerable physical strain. Chimps are simply not equipped with suitable mouth and throat organs to enable them to speak.

Though chimps do not have the *physiological* capacity to speak, the question remains: Do they have the *mental* capacity to learn language? After viewing a film of Vicki trying to vocalize human language with her limited vocal apparatus, psychologists Allan and Beatrice Gardner began their own research on chimp language. In 1966 they gave a home to ten-month-old Washoe, a chimpanzee whom they raised as a human child in as many ways as possible. Eventually, Washoe came to eat with a fork and spoon, to sit at a table and drink from a cup, and even to wash dishes after a fashion. She wore diapers and became toilet trained; she played with dolls and showed affection toward them. Like human children of her age, Washoe was fond of picture books and enjoyed having her human friends tell her stories about the pictures in them.

Ingeniously, the Gardners arranged to conduct all communication with Washoe in American Sign Language (also known as ASL or Ameslan), which they also used to communicate between themselves and with members of their research team whenever Washoe was present. ASL consists of both representational and arbitrary gestural symbols—called signs—that can be combined in accordance with rules that resemble the grammar rules of ordinary spoken language.

The Gardners were keen observers of the kinds of simplified communication that human parents commonly provide for children, and, like parents talking to human babies, they used repetition and simplified signing in talking with Washoe. The results? In the first 7 months in her very human environment, Washoe learned 4 signs. I the next 14 months, she mastered an additional 30 signs. After 51 months, Washoe had acquired 132 signs that describe objects and thoughts, and she understood about three times that many. Washoe used the signs not only for particular objects but also for classes of objects. She used the sign for 'shoe' to mean shoes in general; she used the 'flower' sign for flowers in general, and even for aromas like the smell of tobacco. Washoe signed to everyone, even to dogs and trees. She asked questions about the world of objects and events around her. After mastering the use of only 8 signs, Washoe started combining signs to make complex utterances: YOU ME HIDE; YOU ME GO OUT HURRY LISTEN DOG (when a dog barked); BABY MINE (referring to her doll); and so on. After just 10 months in her foster home, Washoe made scores of combinations of 3 or more signs, such as ROGER WASHOE TICKLE and YOU TICKLE ME WASHOE.

In subsequent work with four other chimps (Moja, Pili, Tatu, and Dar) who arrived at the Gardners' laboratory within days of birth, the Gardners demonstrated that chimps who are cross-fostered by human adults replicate many of the basic aspects of language acquisition characteristic of hearing and hearing-impaired human children, including the use of signs to refer to natural language categories such as DOG, FLOWER, and SHOE. Remarkably, when these chimps subsequently took up residence in another laboratory, an infant chimp named Loulis acquired at least 47 signs that had no other source than the signing of his fellow chimps.

In cross-fostering Washoe and her chimpanzee playmates, the Gardners had made the simple but crucial assumptions that human language is acquired by children in a rich social and intellectual environment and that such richness contributes to the cognitive and linguistic life of a child. The Gardners are convinced—and have convinced some other observers by their research with cross-fostered chimpanzees—that there is no absolute difference between human language and the communicative system that chimps can learn. They believe there is a continuum between human and nonhuman communication, albeit a continuum about which a great deal remains to be learned.

The language activities of other celebrity chimps were neither vocal like Vicki's nor gestural like Washoe's, but visual. Sarah used plastic chips as symbols for words and showed considerable ability to put them in sequence. Lana used an appropriately marked computer terminal to create series of symbols similar to the plastic ones used by Sarah.

The Failure of Project Nim

Certain psychologists have voiced skepticism about the various projects to teach chimps human-style language. Some critics believe that the individual words that the chimps select in the various modes could have been triggered in some instances by inadvertent clues from the researchers. As a result, they claim, the sequences of strings produced by chimps are not productive sentences parallel to those that human children create. Other critics doubt that chimps have the ability to use language to make comments, ask questions, and express feelings as humans do.

In an attempt to provide more control on the effort to teach language to a chimp, a rigorous experiment sought to avoid many of the objections to previous research (though, inevitably, it introduced new problems of its own). The chimp in this instance was named Nim Chimpsky, after the well-known linguist Noam Chomsky of the Massachusetts Institute of Technology, a proponent of the hypothesis that the nature of human language is very different from that of animal communication. In the course of his education Nim had several linguistic accomplishments, reflecting in part repetitions of the achievements of his predecessors. However, after five years of work with Nim, psychologist Herbert Terrace concluded that chimpanzees are not in fact capable of learning language as children do. Even with elaborate training, Nim produced very few longer utterances and displayed little creativity and spontaneity in his use of signs. *Unlike* Washoe, Nim would sign only when researchers prompted him and would never initiate interactions. These characteristics, Terrace contends, clearly distinguish between what Nim was able to learn and what children can do with language.

Critics of Project Nim note that Terrace employed some sixty-odd research assistants over the five years and believe that fact may have contributed importantly to the limitations in Nim's linguistic achievements. Moreover, the assistants were instructed to treat Nim not like a human baby but in a detached fashion. They were forbidden, for example, to comfort Nim even if he cried during the night. The question arises as to how similar Nim's learning environment was to the environment in which a normal human child acquires language. Critics maintain that the research conditions of Project Nim had a crippling impact on Nim's emotional and linguistic education.

Conclusions and Implications

What sense can we make of the seemingly contradictory conclusions of these researchers? What is clear is that chimps can learn to symbolize and to use such symbolization as a tool for achieving other ends. It is also clear that chimpanzees are more intelligent than had previously been suspected and that their intelligence may be only quantitatively different from that of human children. With respect to chimps' acquisition of language, it would appear that the exceptional success of the Gardners' cross-fostering may be due in large part to their efforts to encourage the acquisition of signing in heavily contextualized circumstances approximating those ordinarily provided for infant children. The Gardners have in fact been critical of researchers who attempt to teach language to chimps in essentially laboratory training sessions. Similar exercises and drills have proved woefully inadequate in teaching foreign languages to human beings in schools and colleges and would presumably fail equally to foster first-language acquisition in children in the absence of a rich, natural, and socially and emotionally interactive home life.

We have described several attempts to teach language to chimps, thought to be the most likely candidates to demonstrate that animals could acquire something akin to human language. Research with porpoises and monkeys has rather consistently failed to provide convincing evidence that animals could develop anything closely resembling human language, although some success with a gorilla named Koko has aroused renewed interest in this perennial question. The consensus of opinion at present seems to be that animal expression is usually tied directly to the animal's emotional state at the time of utterance, but that the evidence produced by the Gardners and other psychologists working with chimpanzees raises serious questions about the extent of this generalization. Many observers believe that Washoe and her chimpanzee companions learned to communicate in ASL about as well linguistically as human children two to three years old. Others remain skeptical. Research in the future will unravel the mysteries of child language acquisition and of animal communication. Probably some readers of this book, perhaps you, will be among the contributors to this enterprise.

SUMMARY

Children do not acquire their native language through instruction by adults or through mere imitation of what they hear adults say. While a child must receive some linguistic input in order to acquire language, input is not the sole factor and may not be the chief factor that accounts for the development of grammatical competence and the ability to produce and understand language. Rather, there is considerable evidence that children are born with the mental capacity to acquire language, probably with a disposition to acquire certain kinds of structures, and perhaps with additional specifications as to the kinds of grammar that are eligible for acquisition. Various stages of language acquisition can be identified, distinguished by the amount of content a child is able to express in an utterance vis a vis an adult's expression in equivalent circumstances. Even before children utter their first interpretable words, they use language socially, for example by engaging in turn-taking expressions with caregivers.

One's views of oneself are intimately linked to one's language patterns, especially the language of one's childhood. Adopting a second-language variety—whether a standard variety of one's first language or a "foreign" language—is not merely an intellectual exercise but an experience fraught with emotional overtones. The study of a foreign language cannot be equated with the study of history or math because, more than understanding, it involves adapting to certain customs, or mores, of a distinct ethnolinguistic group.

Human language is primarily a system of arbitrary symbols rather than a system of nonarbitrary signs, and this fact distinguishes human language from the communicative systems that animals use in their natural environment. Animal communication is more akin to a system of signs. While humans are the only species that has evolved an innate ability to use language, it is unclear to what extent animals (chimpanzees in particular) are able to learn human language in experimental settings. Some researchers have claimed that chimps are capable of learning and using sophisticated systems of symbols, while others have concluded that language is the exclusive property of human beings.

EXERCISES

1. Provide a list of baby talk vocabulary in your language. Identify the kinds of referents baby talk vocabulary has, the lexical categories most frequently represented, and the phonological form of such vocabulary. If there are different first languages represented in your class, compare the characteristics of baby talk terms cross linguistically as to kinds of referents, lexical categories, and phonological form.

2. a. Explain in what ways the use of personal names like *Baby* and *Mommy* could be easier for a young child to perceive and analyze than personal pronouns like *I* and *you*.

   b. Explain in what ways the use of content words (nouns, verbs, adjectives) could make baby talk easier for a child to analyze and understand than function words such as prepositions and articles.

3. Tape record a brief passage of talk between an adult or older child and a young child. Transcribe forty-five seconds of the recorded talk, and identify an example of each feature of baby talk discussed in this chapter; organize your list into features of phonology, lexicon, syntax, and discourse. (Hint: Television shows for children may provide the readiest access to such samples).

4. On the basis of what you know about overgeneralizations of morphological rules, what forms might you predict children to use for each of the adult words below? In each case identify the rule that is being overgeneralized.

threw	told	took	hurt	geese	good
spat	came	bled	rode	sheep (pl.)	myself

5. The utterances below (taken, slightly adapted, from Fletcher (1985)) were spoken by an English child named Sophie on three separate days over the course of about a year. Examine them closely and characterize the progress of Sophie's language acquisition across the three occasions with respect to the following features:

possessive determiners *(my, your)*	yes-no questions
the copula BE *(is, are)*	prepositions
adverbs *(down, there)*	interrogative word order
declarative word order	negative sentences
clauses per utterance	wh-questions
auxiliary DO	auxiliaries other than DO
contractible copula	regular noun plurals

Example: Personal pronouns. Based on this sample, Sophie, at 2;4, displays second-person *you* and first-person singular *me; me* is used for both subject and oblique grammatical relations. At 3;0 *her* is used for subjects and oblique relations. At 3;5, the adult forms *I, you,* and *we* occur as subjects, *me* as object, and *it* as subject and object, but *her* appears as the subject form instead of *she.*

Age 2 Years, 4 Months

(1) Me want your tea.

(2) Mary come me.

(3) That your turn.

(4) You play "Snakes and Ladders" me?

(5) Where's the doll house?

(6) Me want Daddy come down.

(7) That's a mess.

Age 3 Years

(8) Shall me sit mon my legs?

(9) That not go in there.

(10) What this one called?

(11) What is that one called?

(12) Can me put it in like that?

(13) Why did Hester be fast asleep?

(14) What did her have wrong with her?

(15) Daddy didn't give me two in the end.

Age 3 Years, 5 Months

(16) This isn't a piano book.

(17) Where my corder?

(18) How did that broke?

(19) If you do it like this, it won't come down.

(20) While Hester at school we can buy some sweets.

(21) When her's at school I'll buy some sweeties.

(22) I want to ring up somebody and her won't be there tomorrow.

(23) I don't know what to do.

(24) Can you take off my shoes?

(25) You won't let me play a guitar.

6. List four reasons that make it more difficult to gather language data from preschoolers than from adults, and identify several technological advances (such as the tape recorder) that can help overcome those difficulties and increase the data on which first-language acquisition research can be carried out.

7. Compare the nonnative adult English sentences on p. 468 with the native English sentences of the child Sophie given in exercise 5. List as many features as you can that are shared by both sets of data; list as many features as you can that belong only to one set or the other. Which features seem easier for the young Sophie to learn than for the adult nonnative speaker, and which seem easier for the nonnative speaker than for Sophie? What explanation can you offer for why certain features might be harder for Sophie or harder for the nonnative speaker to learn?

8. Most linguists would claim that animal languages are fundamentally different from human languages. Identify three significant ways in which animal language and human language differ, and give an argument for each that supports (or denies) its status as a fundamental difference.

SUGGESTIONS FOR FURTHER READING

Baby Talk, an interesting and informative video about first-language acquisition, produced by NOVA for public television in 1985, can be rented in video stores. Another video, called *English Speaking World,* part of the series *The Story of English,* with host Robert MacNeil, discusses English around the world and offers insight into instrumental motivations for second-language acquisition.

About first-language acquisition, a good next step after this chapter would be Gleason (1989), with separate chapters on phonology, syntax, semantics, pragmatics, and so on. Also highly accessible are Elliot (1981) and Chapter 4 of Slobin (1979), as well as the books by de Villiers and de Villiers (1978; 1979). Goodluck (1991) provides a clear introduction to aspects of child language acquisition that bear closely on current grammatical theory.

Curtiss (1977) is a thorough account of Genie, the child who received virtually no language input. On the role of input in language acquisition, see Ferguson and Snow (1977). Schieffelin and Ochs (1986) contains fascinating descriptions of socialization into linguistic and social roles in diverse cultures, including Samoa, Papua New Guinea, Lesotho (in southern Africa), and Japan. Andersen (1990) describes the mastery of preschoolers over the registers associated with such social roles as father, mother, and child in middle-class American homes, as well as teacher and doctor. The socialization of children into gender roles is explored in Swann (1992). Gleason (1980) describes observations of adults teaching children politeness rules for Halloween trick-or-treating, an example of consciously prescriptive input. Slobin (1985) is a wealth of information on language acquisition around the globe. Peters (1983) investigates the strategies that children use to analyze linguistic input and ways in which baby talk may help that process.

Wanner and Gleitman (1982) lay out the state of knowledge in language acquisition from diverse vantage points; we have relied for some of our discussion on the overview chapter by the editors and on Slobin's chapter, "Universal and Particular in the Acquisition of Language." Ingram (1989), on which we have relied for the stages of phonological acquisition, offers detailed discussion of the research on first-language acquisition and is a useful reference work. Brown (1973) remains a valuable treatment of first-language acquisition and provided our examples of mother's expansions of children's utterances and the list of fourteen morphemes ordered by sequence of acquisition. Fletcher (1985) contains four substantial samples of Sophie's language at six-month intervals between 2;6 and 4;0; we have borrowed quite a few examples of child language from these transcriptions. Our discussion of vocabulary acquisition follows M. C. Templin's *Certain Language Skills,* as reported in Miller (1977).

For second-language acquisition, Krashen and Terrell (1983) present an integrated approach that emphasizes naturalistic ways of experiencing comprehensible input. Ellis (1986) and Klein (1986) offer comprehensive and accessible treatments of second-language learning. Ryan and Giles (1982) discuss the empirical study of language attitudes and address the role of attitudes in second-language acquisition. Gardner and Lambert (1972) discuss attitudes and motivation in second-language acquisition.

Ranging from the popular to the technical, sources on animal communication abound. A useful survey can be found in Premack (1985), in which the chimpanzee Sarah is discussed. Von Frisch (1967) reports his findings on the "language" of bees. The Gardners (1971; 1974; 1978) compare Washoe's acquisition patterns to those of children. Vicki's attempts to speak are described in Hayes and Hayes (1952), while Terrace (1979) gives an account of the Nim Chimpsky project. Relevant to the study of animal language are Lieberman (1975; 1984), which present fascinating hypotheses about how the ability to speak evolved in humans; Chapter 10 ("Apes and Children") of the 1984 work provides a good summary of research on chimpanzees.

REFERENCES

Andersen, Elaine Slosberg. 1990. *Speaking With Style: The Sociolinguistic Skills of Children* (London: Routledge).

Brown, Roger. 1973. *A First Language: The Early Stages* (Cambridge, MA: Harvard University Press).

Curtiss, Susan. 1977. *Genie: A Psycholinguistic Study of a Modern-day "Wild Child"* (New York: Academic).

De Villiers, Jill G., and Peter A. de Villiers. 1978. *Language Acquisition* (Cambridge, MA: Harvard University Press).

De Villiers, Peter A., and Jill G. de Villiers. 1979. *Early Language* (Cambridge, MA: Harvard University Press).

Elliot, Alison J. 1981. *Child Language* (Cambridge: Cambridge University Press).

Ellis, Rod. 1986. *Understanding Second Language Acquisition* (Oxford: Oxford University Press).

Ferguson, Charles A., and Catherine Snow, eds. 1977. *Talking to Children: Language Input and Aquisition* (Cambridge: Cambridge University Press).

Fletcher, Paul. 1985. *A Child's Learning of English* (London: Blackwell).

Gardner, Beatrice T., and R. Allan Gardner. 1971. "Two-Way Communication with an Infant Chimpanzee," in A. M. Shrier and F. Stollnitz, eds., *Behavior of Non-human Primates,* vol. 4 (New York: Academic), pp. 118–184.

————. 1974. "Comparing the Early Utterances of Child and Chimpanzee," in Anne D. Pick, ed., *Minnesota Symposia on Child Language,* vol. 8 (Minneapolis: University of Minnesota Press), pp. 3–23.

Gardner, R. Allan, and Beatrice T. Gardner. 1978. "Comparative Psychology and Language Acquisition," *Annals of the New York Academy of Science,* 309:37–76.

Gardner, Robert C., and Wallace E. Lambert. 1972. *Attitudes and Motivation in Second-Language Learning* (Rowley, MA: Newbury House).

Gleason, Jean Berko. 1980. "The Acquisition of Social Speech: Routines and Politeness Formulas," in Howard Giles, W. Peter Robinson, and Philip M. Smith, eds., *Language: Social Psychological Perspectives* (New York: Academic).

————, ed. 1989. *The Development of Language,* 2nd ed. (Columbus, OH: Merrill).

Goodluck, Helen. 1991. *Language Acquisition: A Linguistic Introduction* (Oxford: Blackwell).

Hayes, Keith, and Catherine Hayes. 1952. "Imitation in a Home-Raised Chimpanzee," *Journal of Comparative and Physiological Psychology,* 45:450–459.

Ingram, David. 1989. *First Language Acquisition: Method, Description, and Explanation* (Cambridge: Cambridge University Press).

Klein, Wolfgang. 1986. *Second Language Acquisition* (Cambridge: Cambridge University Press).

Krashen, Stephen D., and Tracy D. Terrell. 1983. *The Natural Approach: Language Acquisition in the Classroom* (Hayward, CA: Alemany).

Lieberman, Philip. 1975. *On the Origins of Language: An Introduction to the Evolution of Human Speech* (New York: Macmillan).

————. 1984. *The Biology and Evolution of Language* (Cambridge, MA: Harvard University Press).

Miller, George A. 1977. *Spontaneous Apprentices: Children and Language* (New York: Seabury).

Peters, Ann M. 1983. *The Units of Language Acquisition* (Cambridge: Cambridge University Press).

Premack, David. 1985. *Gavagai! On the Future History of the Animal Language Controversy* (Cambridge, MA: MIT Press).

Ryan, Ellen Bouchard, and Howard Giles, eds. 1982. *Attitudes Towards Language Variation: Social and Applied Contexts* (London: Edward Arnold).

Schieffelin, Bambi B., and Elinor Ochs, eds. 1986. *Language Socialization Across Cultures* (Cambridge: Cambridge University Press).

Slobin, Dan I. 1979. *Psycholinguistics,* 2nd ed. (Glenview, IL: Scott Foresman).

————, ed. 1985. *The Crosslinguistic Study of Language Acquisition.* 2 vols. (Hillsdale, NJ: Erlbaum).

Swann, Joan. 1992. *Girls, Boys and Language* (Oxford: Blackwell).

Terrace, Herbert S. 1979. *Nim: A Chimpanzee Who Learned Sign Language* (The Hague: Mouton).

von Frisch, Karl. 1967. *The Dance Language and Orientation of Bees,* trans. Leigh E. Chadwick (Cambridge, MA: Harvard University Press).

Wanner, Eric, and Lila R. Gleitman, eds. 1982. *Language Acquisition: The State of the Art* (Cambridge: Cambridge University Press).

15

Writing

INTRODUCTION

"Writing is the single most important sign system ever invented on our planet," a linguist has recently claimed. Whereas the ability to speak arose hundreds of thousands of years ago as part of our intellectual developments during evolution, writing was invented quite recently. Humans have been able to represent language in written form for a mere five or six thousand years. Though language underlies both spoken and written communication, the two modes are fundamentally different in nature. For one thing, speaking developed in human beings naturally, but we had to invent writing. For another, speaking has been with us for hundreds of millennia, writing for only a few. In every society, every ordinarily healthy human being knows how to speak; writing, on the other hand, is an advanced technology, even a luxury, and it is not a luxury possessed by everyone.

Writing has become second nature to most members of literate societies, so much so that it colors much of the thinking about language itself. Elementary school graduates, asked how many vowels there are, commonly respond five, and cite ⟨a⟩, ⟨e⟩, ⟨i⟩, ⟨o⟩, ⟨u⟩, and, some will add, sometimes ⟨y⟩. In terms of speech, this reply misses the mark, but it demonstrates that when we talk of *vowels* (or consonants) it is almost second nature to think of *letters* of the alphabet or (in other cultures) characters or syllabaries. It is common in literate societies to find that people ostensibly speaking of "language" say things that are appropriate only to written language, not to spoken language. This is perhaps not surprising in most Western societies, where language is first discussed objectively in schools, whose primary linguistic goal is to teach children literacy, to teach children to read and write—to master the *written* word. Because the spoken word often plays only an incidental role in education, from an early age it is writing that comes to be the salient focus of our linguistic analysis.

In Chapter 12 we examined the grammatical relationships between spoken and written registers. In this chapter we examine the history of writing and the development of different types of writing. As will become apparent, our knowledge about the history of writing is uneven. While we have a reasonably good understanding of how writing has evolved over the centuries, just how it was invented, and how many times, remains uncertain. While we understand how spoken language and written language differ, just how such differences arise is open to discussion. Such unanswered questions, however, do not prevent us from marveling at the extraordinary human achievement that writing represents. More than being the single most important *sign system* ever invented on our planet, there are those who would claim that writing is the single most important invention in human history.

THE HISTORICAL EVOLUTION OF WRITING

Long before we developed writing, humans were producing graphic representations of the objects that surrounded us. The prehistoric records in the extraordinary cave paintings of Spain, France, and the Sahara Desert, which are between twelve thousand and forty thousand years old, bear witness to an age-old fascination with animals, hunters, and deities. In that they represent concepts rather than words, these paintings are very different from writing. They are representations of real-life objects, not of the words that represent these objects. Writing, by contrast, is a system of visual symbols representing audible symbols.

Of course the drawings and paintings that prehistoric people produced contained the seeds of writing. At first, people would communicate by using drawings. In time, certain stylized representations of objects like the sun came to be associated with the words for those objects. Thus, to imagine an example, the drawing ☼, which originally represented the sun as an object or concept, could have come to be associated with the sound of the word *sun*—with [sʌn]. This association—between ☼ and the sound [sʌn]—was the first symptom of the birth of a writing system, in which a drawn representation did not directly evoke a concept but evoked the spoken word for the concept. The stage was set for using such a visual symbol to represent other words that sounded the same. If we think of English, the symbol ☼ as a representation of the sun could be extended to represent the word *son* or the first part of *Sunday*. From a picture of an object, a written symbol of a *sound* is born.

The Leap from Pictures to Writing

To use a *written* symbol to represent a sound is an extraordinary achievement (comparable to using a spoken symbol to represent a concept). To use one symbol to represent another symbol required a stunning leap of the imagination.

For all that, writing appears to have been invented several times in the course of human history. It is not surprising, though, that not all the world's great civilizations made the leap. The Aztecs, for example, technological geniuses of pre-Columbian Central America, developed intricate systems of drawings and symbols for calendars, geneaologies, and history. An illustration of these **pictograms** (from the Latin root *pictus* 'painted' and the Greek root *graphein* 'to write') is provided in Figure 15-1. But the Aztecs may not have thought of using these pictograms to represent the sounds of spoken language; in any case, the Aztec pictograms did not evolve into writing.

Today, the same impetus that gave rise to the first writing systems recurs so commonly that it is difficult to appreciate the magnitude of the original imaginative leap that used a visual mark—a written symbol—not to represent an object itself but to represent another symbol, an oral symbol of the object. Writing thus involved a leap from primary to secondary symbolization.

A modest modern example of creative secondary symbolization occurs when automobile owners design their own license plates. The space limitations of license

FIGURE 15-1
Aztec Inscription

Source: Gelb 1963 (from Eduard Seler, *Gesammelte Abhandlungen zur amerikanischen Sprach- und Alterthumskunde*)

plates invite such secondary symbolization as "GR8" and "GR8FUL," "SK8ING" and "4GET IT," along with such inventive items as "C-SIDE," "7T YRS," and "PLEN-T," some of which have arisen because the traditional spellings of the words are too long or have been preempted by other license plates. The ingenuity now expressed in license plates (as well as in advertising) originally sparked what is arguably humanity's greatest invention, for once a visual symbol like ⟨8⟩ came to stand for an auditory symbol (the sound [et]), and not for the notion 'eight,' an alphabetic writing system was birthing.

In what was perhaps the first instance, the leap of imagination that gave rise to writing took place around 3500 B.C. in Mesopotamia between the Tigris and Euphrates rivers in modern-day Iraq. Sometimes referred to as "the cradle of Western civilization," Mesopotamia (meaning 'between the rivers') was inhabited at the time by the Sumerians and the Akkadians. These peoples were city dwellers with a sophisticated economic system based on agriculture, cattle, and commerce. Exactly how the Sumerians and Akkadians invented writing will never be known, but we can surmise that the potential for secondary symbolization was discovered fortuitously as someone struggled to formulate a visible message for which no agreed-upon visual symbols existed.

As early as 3000 B.C., the Egyptians had developed a writing system of their own, and writing also appeared in the valley of the Indus (now in Pakistan and India) around 2500 B.C. Around 2000 B.C. the Chinese began using pictograms as symbols for words rather than concepts. By 1500 B.C. several of the world's most technologically complex civilizations had developed systems to commit spoken language to visual representation.

The most ancient inscribed stone tablets that have been found talk of cattle, sales, and exchanges. Thus the most extraordinary invention in human history may have arisen as an answer to the mundane task of recording commercial transactions. Gradually, over the centuries, our ancestors began exploring the world of possibilities opened by the invention of writing. Writing could be used to record important events in a way that was less likely to be forgotten or distorted than oral accounts. Dwellers of the ancient world also found that writing could be exploited to communicate across distances: One could write a letter and entrust it to a messenger, who would deliver it to its addressee. Letters can be more confidential and more secure than oral messages sent by messenger; they often could not be read by the messenger, and they could be sealed. The uses of literacy as a recording tool and as a means to communicate at a distance could also be combined, as the Mesopotamians and the ancient Chinese discovered, to build and maintain large states ruled by a central government: Laws could be recorded by those in command; orders could be transmitted to lower-echelon executives in faraway provinces; data on the citizenry could be stored and retrieved whenever needed. In short, a literate bureaucracy could function with an efficiency that could never been attained in a preliterate culture.

Of course, it took centuries for early societies to explore the avenues opened by the invention of writing. The ability to read and write does not automatically make a society more technologically developed, better equipped to become a bureaucratic state, or otherwise superior to a preliterate society. As recently as the Middle Ages, for example, the English had a basic suspicion of written land-sale contracts, which could be tampered with, and the courts gave more credence to oral testimony if a land dispute arose. It took centuries for Europeans to discover that sentence boundaries could be marked with punctuation to ease reading and that book pages could be numbered to ease the task of retrieving information. Obviously, the fact that a particular society is literate does not necessarily mean that its members will exploit all the possibilities literacy offers. Sometimes strong social pressures prohibit the writing down of certain materials. For example, the Warm Springs Indians of Oregon regard any attempt to make written records of their traditional religious songs and prayers as very offensive. For them, writing down these texts would violate their sacredness. Literacy opens novel ways of communicating and recording language, but whether or not these possibilities will be exploited depends in large part on a society's norms.

WRITING SYSTEMS

The writing systems that developed in ancient Mesopotamia, India, and China were fundamentally different from the writing system now used in Western societies. Ours is an *alphabetic* system based on the premise that one graphic symbol—a letter—should correspond to one significant sound—a phoneme—in the language to be represented. The writing systems originally developed in the Middle East and Asia were based not on a relationship between graphs and individual sounds but on a relationship between graphs and words or syllables. Though they developed at different times in history, all three types of writing—alphabetic, syllabic, and word writing—are still in use today.

Syllabic Writing

When the dwellers of the ancient Middle East and Asia began developing their writing systems, they had at their disposal the earlier pictograms, which were symbols for objects and concepts. Rather than create an entirely new system of symbols, the inventors of writing modified these pictograms and used them to develop writing systems. The pictograms were not, of course, modified overnight; their shapes gradually became more and more stylized in the process of becoming written symbols. Table 15-1 illustrates the evolution of a number of symbols over time. The table's left-hand column shows the original pictograms, which become more like writing as we proceed to the right. After many centuries of gradual evolution, the symbols illustrated in the right-hand column had become so stylized that they no longer bore any resemblance to the pictograms from which they originated.

The written symbols that the Sumerians and Akkadians had developed at that stage are called **cuneiform** symbols. *Cuneiform* means 'in the shape of a wedge' and refers to the peculiar form the symbols had taken. The ancient Mesopotamians were not familiar with paper, but clay from the Tigris-Euphrates river basin was readily available as a writing material. From the beginning, writing consisted of engraving marks pressed into soft clay tablets with a hard, sharp, pointed object called a *stylus,* typically a cut reed. Since it is difficult to draw curved strokes on

TABLE 15-1

The Evolution of Cuneiform Writing from Pictograms

| PICTOGRAMS | | 'CLASSICAL' SUMERIAN | | OLD-AKKADIAN | OLD-ASSYRIAN | OLD-BABYLONIAN | NEO-ASSYRIAN | NEO-BABYLONIAN | Picture | Meaning |
URUK c.3100 BC UPRIGHT	JEMDET NASR c.2800 BC TURNED 90° TO LEFT	c.2400 BC LINEAR	CUNEIFORM	c.2200 BC	c.1900 BC	c.1700 BC	c.700 BC	c.600 BC		
									NECK + HEAD	HEAD FRONT
									NECK+HEAD + BEARD or TEETH	MOUTH NOSE TOOTH VOICE SPEAK WORD
									SHROUDED BODY (?)	MAN
									SITTING BIRD	BIRD
									BULL'S HEAD	OX
									STAR	SKY HEAVEN-GOD GOD
									STREAM or WATER	WATER SEED FATHER SON
									LAND-PLOT + TREES	ORCHARD GREENERY TO GROW TO WRITE

Source: Gaur 1984

clay with a stylus, the first written symbols consisted of various combinations of straight strokes.

Not only the shape but also the meaning of cuneiform symbols evolved from early pictograms. The pictogram that represented an arrow evolved into this cuneiform symbol for the Sumerian word /ši/ 'arrow.'

Sumerian scribes had difficulty finding appropriate symbols for more abstract notions. There was no modified pictogram for the word 'life,' for example. But the word for 'life' happened to be homophonous with the word for 'arrow' (as the *bank* of a river and a financial *bank* are homophonous in English)[1]. Since finding a symbol for the concept 'life' was not an easy task, why not use the symbol for

[1] Homophonous means 'having the same sound.' Thus we can speak of homophonous syllables, morphemes, and words (as well as letters and groups of letters). *Homonymous* means 'having the same name.' *Homonymous* and *homophonous* are sometimes used interchangeably.

'arrow'—seeing that 'arrow' and 'life' are both pronounced /ši/? It was through this extension of a symbol's representing a thing to its representing a sound that writing as we know it was invented.

Having solved that problem, the Sumerians recognized that the same symbol could also be used to represent the syllable /ši/ whenever it occurred in a word. For example, they started using it to represent the first syllable of the word /šibira/ 'blacksmith.' In due course, the cuneiform symbol lost its original association with the concept 'arrow' and became a symbol for the syllable /ši/ wherever that syllable occurred. Cuneiform writing is thus a **syllabic writing** system, in which graphic symbols represent whole syllables, not individual sounds as in an alphabet.

The process through which early pictograms evolved from being graphic symbols for concepts to being graphic symbols for syllables was a long and arduous one. Archaeological remains found in Mesopotamia indicate that for many centuries the Sumerians and the Akkadians used an extremely complex system in which some symbols were "ideograms," representing objects and concepts, while others were true phonetic writing, representing syllables. Even when all graphic symbols had come to represent syllables, the system was imperfect, because certain graphs could represent different syllables, depending on the word in which they were used, and several different graphs might represent the same syllable. Despite its imperfections, this system appears to have been used for centuries.

The Mesopotamian syllabic system may have been the model for several other systems. The ancient Egyptians, who had their own ideographic system, may have borrowed from the Sumerians and Akkadians the idea of representing spoken syllables with graphic symbols; in any case, around 3000 B.C., they began using their ideograms to represent different sound combinations. These Egyptian written symbols are the famous *hieroglyphics* (see Figure 15-2). Like cuneiform writing, hieroglyphic writing was basically syllabic, and it had the same complexity and shortcomings as cuneiforms. Thus the hieroglyphic symbol for 'house' ⊏⊐ (third symbol from the left in the thirteenth line of Figure 15-2) stood for several syllables in which the consonants /p/ and /r/ were coupled with any permitted vowel such as /per/ and /par/.

There is nothing inherently cumbersome in syllabic systems of writing. The difficulties of the Mesopotamian and Egyptian systems can be attributed to the fact that they continued to bear traces of their ideographic origins. Much later in history, an efficient syllabic system was devised by a Cherokee Indian named Sequoya. Its eighty-four symbols, shown in Figure 15-3, are based on the Latin alphabet, and they were used in the early part of the nineteenth century by both missionaries and Cherokee for writing the Cherokee language.

Another syllabic system devised around the same time by the Vai, an ethnic group today numbering about twelve thousand people in western Liberia, is still in use. The Vai system has one graph for each of the approximately two hundred syllables in the language. This system is particularly well-adapted to the Vai language, which has a relatively small number of possible syllables. The Vai syllabary is given in Table 15-2, page 488.

Syllabic writing is also used to represent various languages of India. Tamil, spoken in the southern tip of the subcontinent, is written with a syllabic system

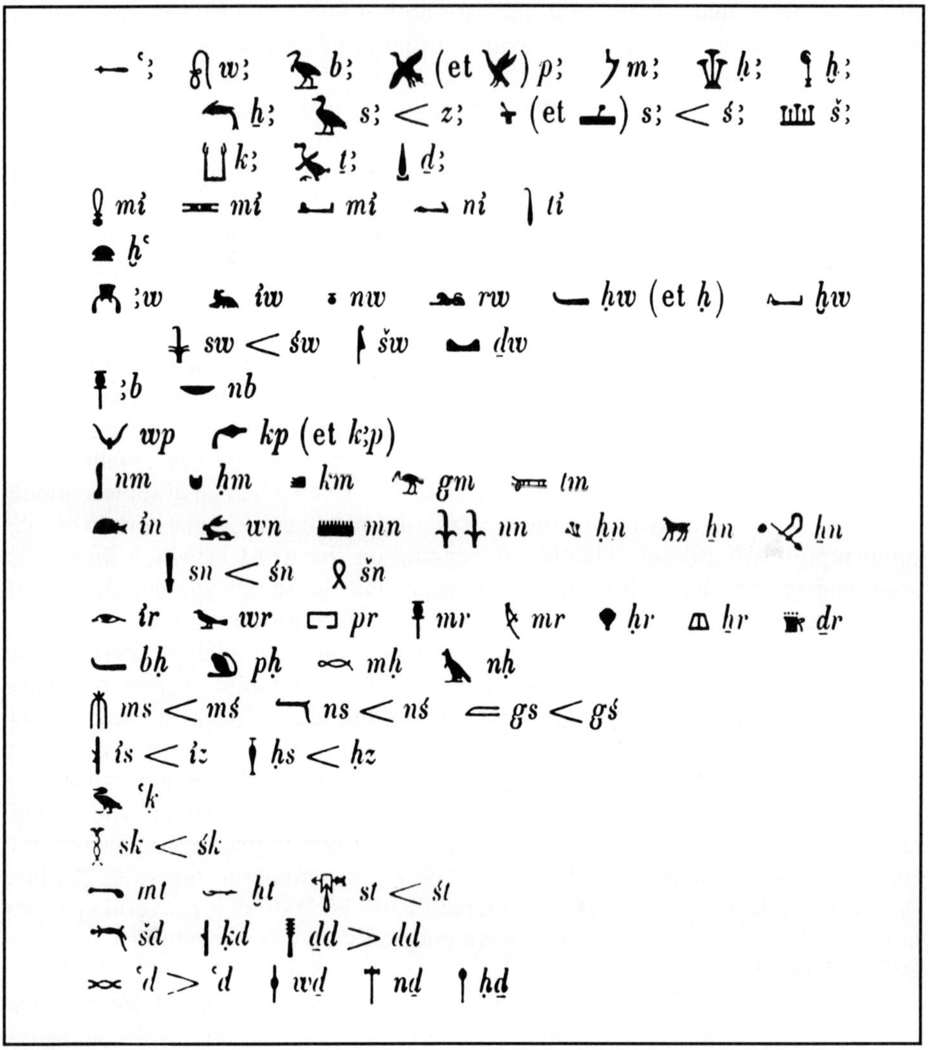

FIGURE 15-2
Egyptian Hieroglyphics*

* Because this figure comes originally from a French language source, the French word *et* 'and' appears in several lines.

Source: Gelb 1963

of 246 graphic symbols, given in Table 15-3. The Tamil syllabic system is highly regular. Each vowel has two graphic representations in the syllabary. One is an independent graph used at the beginning of a word; the other is used when the vowel combines with a consonant elsewhere in a word. Thus, in initial position, /a:/ is represented by ⟨ᴈ⟩ but appears as ⟨ா⟩ when it combines with consonants

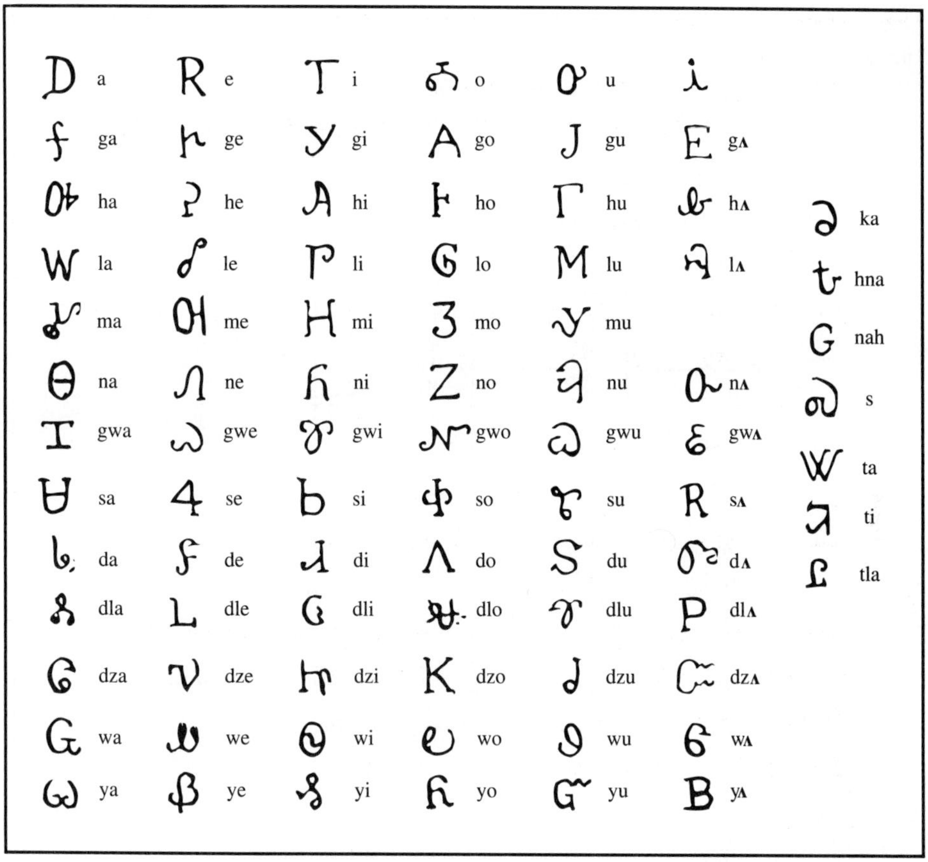

The Cherokee Syllabary (Figure 15-3):

a	e	i	o	u	v
ga	ge	gi	go	gu	gʌ
ha	he	hi	ho	hu	hʌ
la	le	li	lo	lu	lʌ
ma	me	mi	mo	mu	
na	ne	ni	no	nu	nʌ
gwa	gwe	gwi	gwo	gwu	gwʌ
sa	se	si	so	su	sʌ
da	de	di	do	du	dʌ
dla	dle	dli	dlo	dlu	dlʌ
dza	dze	dzi	dzo	dzu	dzʌ
wa	we	wi	wo	wu	wʌ
ya	ye	yi	yo	yu	yʌ

Additional graphs (right margin): ka, hna, nah, s, ta, ti, tla

FIGURE 15-3
The Cherokee Syllabary

Source: H. A. Gleason, *An Introduction to Descriptive Linguistics,* rev. ed. (New York: Holt, Rinehart and Winston, 1961), p. 414.

as in /ka:/ கா , /ḍa:/ டா , /ta:/ தா . To represent a consonant sound alone, the graph representing that consonant as it appears with /a/ is used, but a dot is placed above the symbol to mute the vowel. Thus, except for the dots, the graphs of the first column are identical to those of the second column. In the first row across the top of the syllabary are the written vowel symbols and their phonemic value; next to each graph of the first column is given its phonemic value. You can readily see that one part of the symbol represents the consonant, the other part the vowel. Learning this system thus amounts to learning the different parts of symbols and the possible combinations between these different parts. One of the attractive features of the Tamil system is that its simplicity and regularity make it easy to learn.

Syllabic systems thus have the potential of being highly regular, with a one-to-one correspondence between syllables and graphs. Furthermore, the shape of

TABLE 15-2
The Vai Syllabary

	i	a	u	e	ɛ	ɔ	o
p							
b							
ɓ							
mɓ							
kp							
mgb							
gb							
f							
v							
t							
d							
l							
ɖ							
nɖ							
s							
z							
c							
j							
nj							
y							
k							
ŋg							
g							
h							
w							
–							

ɤ Syllabic nasal

Nasal syllables

	ĩ	ã	ũ	ɛ̃	ɔ̃
ɦ					
m					
n					
ny					
ŋ					

Source: Sylvia Scribner and Michael Cole, *The Psychology of Literacy* (Cambridge: Harvard University Press, 1981).

cow   river   below

FIGURE 15-4

the graphic symbols can be such that their pronunciation is retrievable from a decomposition of the graph into different parts. A regular syllabary like the Vai or Tamil systems is easily learned and simple to handle. Such a writing system is best adapted to languages that have a limited number of possible syllables. Syllabic systems can be economical, needing only as many symbols in a word as there are syllables.

Logographic Writing

Around four thousand years ago, a new writing system was developed in China that used visual symbols to represent *words*, not *syllables*. Such a **logographic writing** system differed fundamentally from the Sumerian-Akkadian syllabic system; partly for this reason, it is believed that the Chinese did not borrow the idea of writing from the Mesopotamians but developed it on their own.

Like the ancient Middle Eastern syllabic writing, the Chinese logographic system originated in ideograms. From archaeological records, we know that ideograms like those in Figure 15-4 were used to represent objects and ideas such as 'cow,' 'river,' and 'below.'

Toward the end of the Bronze Age (around 1700–500 B.C.), these ideograms came to represent not concepts but words. Today, in the three characters (or logographic symbols) that denote the Modern Chinese words *niú* 'cow,' *chuān* 'river' and *xià* 'below' (see Figure 15-5), we can recognize the ideograms that originally represented these three notions.

From a very early stage, ideograms were combined to represent abstract ideas and other notions that are difficult to represent graphically. Figure 15-6(a), for example, is made up of two ideograms placed one on top of the other. The lower part represents a type of dish used in divination ceremonies; the upper part represents a tree, upon which the divination dish was suspended. This complex ideogram was modified over the centuries to become a character that in Modern Chinese represents the word *gào*, which means 'to announce, to proclaim.' As Figure 15-6(b) shows, the modern character with this meaning bears a striking

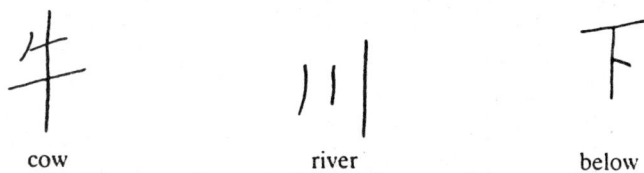

cow   river   below

FIGURE 15-5

TABLE 15-3
The Tamil Syllabary*

		அ a	ஆ ā	இ i	ஈ ī	உ u	ஊ ū
க்	k	க ka	கா	கி	கீ	கு	கூ
ங்	ŋ	ங ŋa	ஙா	ஙி	ஙீ	ஙு	ஙூ
ச்	ç	ச ça	சா	சி	சீ	சு	சூ
ஞ்	ɲ	ஞ ɲa	ஞா	ஞி	ஞீ	ஞு	ஞூ
ட்	ḍ	ட ḍa	டா	டி	டீ	டு	டூ
ண்	ṇ	ண ṇa	ணா	ணி	ணீ	ணு	ணூ
த்	t	த ta	தா	தி	தீ	து	தூ
ந்	n	ந na	நா	நி	நீ	நு	நூ
ப்	p	ப pa	பா	பி	பீ	பு	பூ
ம்	m	ம ma	மா	மி	மீ	மு	மூ
ய்	y	ய ya	யா	யி	யீ	யு	யூ
ர்	r	ர ra	ரா	ரி	ரீ	ரு	ரூ
ல்	l	ல la	லா	லி	லீ	லு	லூ
வ்	v	வ va	வா	வி	வீ	வு	வூ
ழ்	ṛ	ழ ṛa	ழா	ழி	ழீ	ழு	ழூ
ள்	ḷ	ள ḷa	ளா	ளி	ளீ	ளு	ளூ
ற்	r	ற ra	றா	றி	றீ	று	றூ
ன்	n	ன na	னா	னி	னீ	னு	னூ

* A dot beneath the phonetic representation indicates a retroflex sound (one in which the tip of the tongue is curled up and back, just behind the alveolar ridge). Note that there are two graphic symbols for /r/ and two for /n/.

resemblance to the ideogram from which it originates. Such similarities between modern-day characters and ancient ideograms are few and far between. The shapes of most modern Chinese characters have lost all traces of the original ideograms from which they developed some three or four thousand years ago.

Modern Chinese Characters   In an ideal logographic system, each word of the spoken language would be represented by a different graphic symbol. To a certain extent, the Modern Chinese system has this characteristic, in that a portion of its vocabulary is represented by individual characters, as illustrated in Figure 15-7.

Most modern Chinese characters can be decomposed into two elements. The one is called the *radical* (or *signific*) and can sometimes hint at meaning. The other, of which there are many types, can sometimes give a clue to pronunciation and is known as the *phonetic*. Most radicals can also be used alone as characters, and some dictionaries are organized according to radicals, of which there are

எ e	ஏ ē	ஜ ai	ஒ o	ஓ ō	ஒள au
கெ	கே	கை	கொ	கோ	கௌ
ஙெ	ஙே	ஙை	ஙொ	ஙோ	ஙௌ
செ	சே	சை	சொ	சோ	சௌ
ஞெ	ஞே	ஞை	ஞொ	ஞோ	ஞௌ
டெ	டே	டை	டொ	டோ	டௌ
ணெ	ணே	ணை	ணொ	ணோ	ணௌ
தெ	தே	தை	தொ	தோ	தௌ
நெ	நே	நை	நொ	நோ	நௌ
பெ	பே	பை	பொ	போ	பௌ
மெ	மே	மை	மொ	மோ	மௌ
யெ	யே	யை	யொ	யோ	யௌ
ரெ	ரே	ரை	ரொ	ரோ	ரௌ
லெ	லே	லை	லொ	லோ	லௌ
வெ	வே	வை	வொ	வோ	வௌ
ழெ	ழே	ழை	ழொ	ழோ	ழௌ
ளெ	ளே	ளை	ளொ	ளோ	ளௌ
றெ	றே	றை	றொ	றோ	றௌ
னெ	னே	னை	னொ	னோ	னௌ

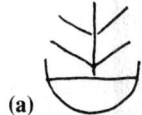

(a) **(b)** 告

FIGURE 15-6

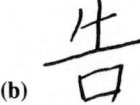

國	我	法
guó	wǒ	fǎ
'country'	'I, me'	'way'

FIGURE 15-7

FIGURE 15-8

214. The signific that traditionally corresponds to the character for the word *wéi* 'enclosure' occurs as the radical of many characters, some of which have a meaning related to 'enclosure' and some of which have little to do with the meaning of the radical (see Figure 15-8). In Modern Chinese, the radical for 'enclosure' is in disuse as an independent character and has been replaced by the more complex

character 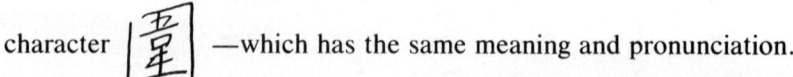 —which has the same meaning and pronunciation.

It is difficult to know exactly how many different characters the Chinese logographic system contains, just as it is virtually impossible to know how many words are in the lexicon of any language. It is thought that one must be able to recognize about five thousand characters (and have a good command of spoken Chinese) in order to read a Chinese newspaper. To read a learned piece of literature, a reader would need to be familiar with up to thirty thousand characters. Compared to the number of words needed for similar tasks in English, these numbers are relatively modest. The reason can be found in the morphological structure of Chinese. In Chinese, morphemes (which are always one syllable long) can combine with each other to form compounds that together denote a new idea whose meaning is more or less clearly related to the meaning of the parts. Of course, this is reflected by corresponding compounds in writing. The word for 'bicycle,' for example, is made up of three morphemes that together mean 'self-propelled vehicle'; the three characters corresponding to these three morphemes are used to represent 'bicycle' in writing. Similarly, the word for 'grammar' is a compound that means 'language rule' (see Figure 15-9).

Though compounding greatly reduces the number of characters needed in common use, learning to read and write the Chinese logographic system is still a

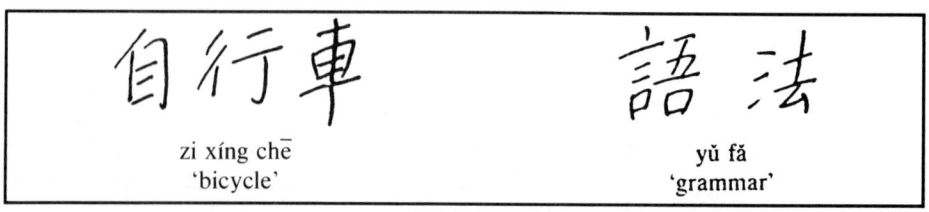

FIGURE 15-9

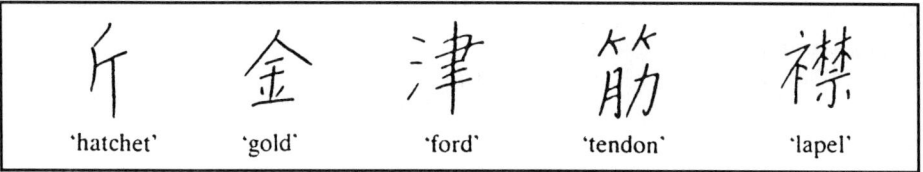

'hatchet'   'gold'   'ford'   'tendon'   'lapel'

FIGURE 15-10

formidable task, considerably more difficult and time consuming than learning the Vai or Tamil syllabary or the English alphabet. Bear in mind that since modern characters provide a reader little information as to the pronunciation or meaning of the words they represent, learning to read and write Chinese involves learning the shape of characters as well as their meaning and pronunciation. Though several transcription systems have been devised for Chinese (some of which use the Roman alphabet, some a type of syllabary), the logographic system continues to survive after nearly four thousand years.

Why would such a seemingly impractical and complex system endure for so long, you might wonder. Well, not surprisingly, the Chinese logographic system has a number of important advantages. The first stems from the fact that though there are many homophonous words in Chinese, they usually have different written representations—as illustrated by the five characters in Figure 15-10, each of which represents a word that is pronounced [jīn]. Thus the Chinese character system provides a way of distinguishing visually among different words that a syllabic system or an alphabet could not provide. (Compare the unusual distinction in English of a pair of homophones like *cite* and *sight* or *read* and *reed* with the more common orthographic confusion between a river *bank* and a savings *bank*). A logographic system enables writers to compensate for homophony. This feature is especially advantageous for a language with as many homophonous words as Chinese.

The second major advantage of the Chinese logographic system is peculiar to the Chinese situation. The language that is called Chinese is a set of numerous spoken dialects, some of which are mutually intelligible, some not. Fortunately, for written communication all these dialects use the same set of characters. A character may be pronounced one way in one region of China and another way in another region, making spoken communication complicated, but the *meaning* of the character remains the same throughout that vast country. For example, the character 我 is read [wǒ] in the Beijing dialect, [gòa] in the Taiwan dialect, [wà] in the Minnan dialect (spoken in south China), [ŋə̀] in the northwestern dialect of Shanxi, [ŋō] in the southern dialect of Hunan, and [ŋú] in the Shanghai dialect. In all dialects, it means 'I' or 'me.' Furthermore, since the syntax of most Chinese dialects is similar, any dialect can be more or less understood *in writing* (though not in speech) by speakers of a wide variety of dialects. The character system thus has a unifying force for a nation that comprises many ethnicities speaking so many different language varieties.

The Chinese logographic system thus meets two important objectives: the need to distinguish between homophones and the need to communicate across dialect boundaries. It is a system well-equipped for the situation it serves, despite the difficulties involved in learning it and in managing the enormous variety of characters in arenas like computer processing and telegraphic communication.

In the course of history, many nations of the Far East have borrowed the Chinese logographic system. The Vietnamese modified certain Chinese characters to create their own writing system, which was essentially logographic as well. (Today the Vietnamese no longer use this system.) The Koreans and the Japanese borrowed the Chinese character system very early, and in due time each developed several subsidiary systems. Koreans now write their language with the help of an alphabet and the original Chinese characters. Similarly, several systems are combined for use in modern Japan: Two syllabic systems known as *hiragana* and *katakana* are used alongside Chinese characters, called *kanji* (a word borrowed from the Chinese compound *hànzì* 'character'). Both written Korean and written Japanese are curious in that symbols from different systems can appear within the same sentence and even within the same word. Today the Chinese remain the only people to make exclusive use of a logographic system.

Alphabetic Writing and Orthography

An **alphabet** is a set of graphic symbols each of which represents a distinctive sound. Alphabetic writing thus differs from syllabic writing (whose graphs represent syllables) and from logographic writing (whose graphs represent words). In the view of some scholars, the first true alphabet was developed by the ancient Greeks from a North Semitic writing system that they had borrowed, probably from the Phoenicians, probably about 900 B.C. The claim that credits the Greeks with inventing the first true alphabet rests on one interpretation of how to evaluate the so-called consonantal alphabets, which had been in use since about 1700 B.C. Consonantal alphabets are writing systems that represent only the consonants, not the vowels, of a language, and it was just such an alphabet that the Greeks borrowed from the Phoenicians.

It is not surprising that a consonantal alphabet should have been developed to represent the Semitic languages. Recall from Chapter 4 that Semitic morphology builds upon tri-consonantal roots such as Arabic /k-t-b/. In languages like Arabic and Hebrew, vowels are interdigitated with tri-consonantal roots to produce words such as *kita:b* 'book,' *kutub* 'books,' *ka:tib* 'writer,' and *kita:ba* 'writing'—all of which contain the same tri-consonantal root. The paramount role of consonants in such a system led, perhaps inevitably, to a consonantal alphabet. Now, the graphs used for writing Semitic languages can be viewed in one of two ways: as representing *only* the consonants (which would be a true alphabet, though lacking in vowel graphs) or as representing the consonants plus any vowel (which would be a kind of syllabary, albeit an unusual one). On the first view, a graph would represent a single consonant, say /k/; on the second view, the

TABLE 15-4
The Cyrillic Alphabet as Used in Modern Russian (Only printed lowercase letters are shown.)

Cyrillic letter	Russian phoneme represented	Cyrillic letter	Russian phoneme represented
а	a	п	p
б	b	р	r
в	v	с	s
г	g	т	t
д	d	у	u
е	yɛ	ф	f
ё	yo	х	x
ж	ž	ц	ts
з	z	ч	č
и	i	ш	š
й	y	щ	šč
к	k	ы	i̇
л	l	ь	(y)
м	m	э	ɛ
н	n	ю	yu
о	o	я	ya

same graph would represent /k/ plus any permissible vowel: /ka/, /ki/, /ku/, and so on. The first view of consonantal writing would incline one to credit a Semitic origin of the alphabet. The second view would incline one to credit a Greek origin, for it was the Greeks then who viewed graphs as representing a single sound and therefore designated specific symbols (those not needed to represent Greek consonants) for representing vowels. Whatever interpretation one is inclined to, it is clear that the Greeks definitely had a true alphabet and that around 600 B.C. the Romans borrowed it (via the Etruscans) and developed the basis of today's familiar Roman alphabet.

The Roman alphabet is not the only alphabet currently in use. The Greeks still use an alphabet of their own, as do the Russians, Ukrainians, Bulgarians, and Serbs. These alphabets are based on the same principles as the Roman alphabet, differing only in the shape of certain letters. The alphabet currently in use for Russian, called Cyrillic in honor of Saint Cyril who devised it in the ninth century, is partly given in Table 15-4.

An alphabet is matched as closely as possible to the sound system of the language it must represent. The system used to achieve this match is the **orthography,** or spelling system. In an ideal orthography, each phoneme of the spoken language would be represented by a different graph, and each graph would represent only one phoneme. Spanish orthography comes close to this ideal: There is a virtual one-to-one correspondence between letters of the Roman alphabet and the phonemes of the language, and it is this match that students of Spanish have in mind when they say that in Spanish "every letter is pronounced." In contrast, English and French do not have anything close to a perfect match. As you saw in Chapter 2, the number of distinctive sounds in English includes twenty-four consonants and between fourteen and sixteen vowels and diphthongs. With only twenty-six letters of the alphabet, English orthography falls definitively short of an ideal one-sound/one-graph model. Because there are not enough letters to provide a symbol for each phoneme, some phonemes must be represented by a combination of letters (for example, the phoneme /i/ is often represented by a double ⟨e⟩ as in *meet;* the phoneme /θ/ is represented by the two letters ⟨th⟩ as in *thin*). In addition, English pronunciation and orthography have not kept pace with one another over time, so that some words contain letters that no longer represent any sounds (like the ⟨k⟩ and ⟨gh⟩ in *knight*). On the other side of the coin, a particular sequence of letters can represent a diverse spectrum of sounds, as ⟨ough⟩ does in the words *cough, tough, through, trough, though, thorough, bough,* and *hiccough.*

A common response to the chaos of the English orthography is to call for spelling reform, as George Bernard Shaw did early in this century. But for an international lingua franca like English, an orthography that genuinely attempted to represent pronunciation would have to sacrifice the uniformity that exists across national varieties. Spelling reform would raise other serious problems as well, having to do with the considerable morphophonemic variation of the language (which was treated in the final section of Chapter 4). Recall that a word such as *photograph* in its normal phonological contexts has different stress patterns: [fótəgræf] versus [fətʰágrəfər]. Compare the three vowels in *photograph* [o ə æ] with the first three in *photographer* [ə ɑ ə]. An orthography that attempted to represent actual sounds would be forced to represent the vowels of *photograph* and *photographer* differently, perhaps as "photagraeph" and "phataagraphar."

Because English has such complex morphophonemic alternations the differences in the pronunciation of a given morpheme can be considerable, as with *photograph* and *photographer*. If an orthography were devised in which sounds and symbols were closely matched, the task of reading would be greatly complicated. While English does have a few words whose morphophonemic variants are represented orthographically (the [f]/[v] sounds of *wife* and *wives* are distinguished orthographically, but the contrast between [θ]/[ð] in *breath* and *breathe* is not), we would have many more pairs and trios in which the spelling system would better represent pronunciations. Given their different pronunciations, we would even have to spell the plural inflection of *dogs* and *cats* differently, perhaps as ⟨dogz⟩ and ⟨kats⟩, obscuring the fact that ⟨z⟩ and ⟨s⟩ represent the same morpheme. (Notice, of course, that English does not ignore the difference between /z/ and /s/ in general.) Similarly, the morpheme MUSIC would sometimes be spelled ⟨muzak⟩ (as in *musical*) and sometimes ⟨muzish⟩ (as in *musician*). By the same token, all homophonous words would be spelled alike, so that *wood/would, balm/bomb, sea/ see, to/too/two,* and *quaffed/coifed* could not be distinguished.

Advocates of English spelling reform thus tend to overlook the valuable advantages of the current spelling system, which places a premium on morphological resemblance. Just as the Chinese logographic system is well adapted to the situation in which it functions, the Roman alphabet and English orthography are remarkably well adapted to English.

Developing Writing Systems in Newly Literate Societies

The twentieth century has witnessed an enormous increase in communications among regions, countries, and continents. Oceans and mountains, challenging obstacles only a hundred years ago, are now easily overflown. There is probably not a single inhabited area of the world that has had no contact with the outside. This is a remarkable fact, given that as recently as the 1950s large inhabited areas of Papua New Guinea, Amazonia, and the Philippines were still completely isolated from the rest of the world.

The consequence of this communications boom is that many people who had never seen writing a few decades ago are now literate. When a language is written down for the first time, a number of important questions arise: What kind of writing system should be used? How should the system be modified or adapted to fit the shape of the language and the needs of its speakers? Who makes these decisions?

Literacy has often been introduced to a people along with a new religion. For example, literacy was first imported into Tibet from India in the seventh century, the same time the Tibetans converted to Buddhism. Today literacy is commonly introduced to preliterate societies by Christian missionaries. What links religion and literacy is the fact that the reading of religious texts is an important doctrinal element of many religions. Because literacy is commonly introduced by missionaries, their foreign writing system is usually adopted by the incipiently literate society to write its language. Today, newly literate societies commonly adopt the Roman alphabet because English-speaking and other Western missionaries are the most active promoters of literacy in many regions of the world.

At times a society will change from one writing system to another. Vietnam, for example, was colonized by the Chinese around 200 B.C. and remained colonized for about twelve centuries. During that time, Chinese was used in writing, while Vietnamese remained unwritten. After the end of Chinese domination, the Vietnamese began to use a syllabic writing system adapted from Chinese logographic writing for their own language. Then, at the beginning of the seventeenth century, Jesuit missionaries devised an alphabetic system for Vietnamese, which the Vietnamese gradually adopted, partly under pressure from the French colonial government. Today the system devised by the Jesuits is the only one in use for Vietnamese.

One thorny problem that newly literate societies face is developing a standard orthography that everyone will agree to use. Ideally, an orthography must be regular, so that native writers will be able to spell a word they have never before seen in writing. The orthography must also be easy to learn and to use. Finally, it must be well-adapted to the phonological and morphological structure of the language. As we saw in our discussion of English orthography, satisfying all these requirements can be challenging. A system that looks complex at first blush can have hidden advantages. Devising a standard orthography can be such a difficult task that a few Western nations (including Norway) have not yet done so, even after centuries of literacy.

Language-related concerns are not the only factors involved in devising orthographies. One extremely important factor is social acceptance. An orthography that, for one reason or another, rubs users the wrong way is not likely to be successful. If the orthography is imposed by an outside political or religious body, it may carry negative associations and never succeed. For several decades, the United States Bureau of Indian Affairs hired linguists and anthropologists to devise orthographies for American Indian languages. The orthographies were never really accepted, however, because the Indians viewed the bureau and its activities with suspicion.

Likewise, at the end of the last century, Methodist and Catholic missionaries devised different orthographies to transcribe Rotuman, the language of the South Pacific island of Rotuma. Since then, because relations between Methodist Rotumans and Catholic Rotumans have been strained, both orthographies have survived, and there is no prospect of either group adopting the other's orthography. Similar situations can involve not only orthographies but writing systems. In Serbia and Croatia, a single language is used, but the Serbs use a Cyrillic alphabet similar to that used for Russian, while Croats use the Roman alphabet. Even when they were united in a single country, both groups adamantly kept their alphabet as a symbol of social identity. Social acceptance is thus extremely important to the development of a standard orthography.

SUMMARY

Writing is a relatively recent invention that developed from pictograms, which became writing when they began representing sounds rather than objects and concepts. There are several types of writing systems in use today. In *syllabic* writing, symbols represent syllables; in *logographic* writing, symbols represent morphemes or words; and in *alphabetic* writing, symbols represent phonemes. The writing system used for English utilizes the Roman alphabet, and English orthography is strongly influenced by morphological considerations. The system that dictates how the letters of the alphabet are used to represent the phonemes of a language is called its *orthography*. Devising orthographies for hitherto unwritten languages is a complicated task, which must take into account both linguistic and social factors.

EXERCISES

1. a. Identify two invented sign systems besides writing, and briefly evaluate their importance relative to writing.
   b. Identify what you judge to be two of the most important human inventions of all time, and evaluate their importance with respect to writing.
   c. Specify two or three of the central criteria you used in evaluating "importance" in (a) and (b).

2. Discuss the relative merits and disadvantages of logographic, syllabic, and alphabetic writing systems. In your discussion of each type of system, address the following questions.

   a. How easy is it to learn the system?
   b. How easy is it to write the individual graphs?
   c. How efficiently can one read the graphs?
   d. What kinds of problems does the system present for printing?
   e. How adaptable is it to computer technology such as word processing?
   f. How easy is it to represent foreign names and new borrowings from other languages?
   g. What sociological and historical factors might interact with the preceding questions in evaluating the appropriateness of each system to particular situations? (Be concrete by considering a particular situation you are familiar with.)

3. English is often said to have a phonemic orthography (approximating one graph for each distinct sound). To some extent this is true in that English orthography distinguishes between, say, [b] and [p] but not among [p], [pʰ], and [pˡ]. In light of this claim, examine the following typical sets of words and compare their orthographic representation with their pronunciation: *cats/dogs/judges; history/historical; life/lives*.

   a. Is English orthography phonemic? Explain.
   b. In what sense would it be more accurate to describe the English orthographic system as morphophonemic?
   c. To what extent would it be fair to say that English is logographic in representing such sets of homonyms as the following: *meet/meat/mete; leaf/lief; seize/sees/seas?*
   d. What is the nature of such graphic symbols as ⟨&⟩, ⟨301⟩, ⟨$⟩, and ⟨%⟩? Can they be called logographic? Explain.

4. a. Using the Tamil syllabic symbols given in Table 15-3 (pp. 490–91) transcribe the following Tamil words into Roman script.

தொழில்	'work'	ஏழு	'seven'
மூக்கு	'nose'	புலி	'tiger'
அவன்	'he'	ஆடு	'goat'
வாழைப்பழம்	'banana'	மரம்	'tree'

   b. Briefly describe the general patterns that are used in forming syllabic characters in this script. For example how is the symbol for /ke/ formed from the symbols for /k/ and /e/? How are word-final consonants and word-initial vowels represented?

5. The following table (adapted from Sampson 1985) is a partial representation of the inventory of graphs used in writing Korean consonants. "Tense" means (in part) that the sound is held for a longer period of time than normal, and "lax" means that the sound is held for the normal duration. (The tenseness is represented in phonetic symbols with an apostrophe as in [p'].)

   a. What principles govern the shape of graphs in this system?
   b. What are the advantages of such a system over an alphabetic system like the Roman system, in which the shape of graphs is completely arbitrary?

	Bilabial	Dental	Palatal	Velar
Lax nasals	ㅁ m	ㄴ n		
Lax fricatives		ㅅ s		
Lax stops/affricate	ㅂ p	ㄷ t	ㅈ c	ㄱ k
Tense aspirated stops/affricate	ㅍ p^h	ㅌ t^h	ㅊ c^h	ㅋ k^h
Tense fricative		ㅆ s		
Tense unaspirated stops/affricate	ㅃ p'	ㄸ t'	ㅉ c'	ㄲ k'

6. Suppose that you were devising a syllabic writing system for English. What steps would you take to make such a system as simple to learn as possible? To what extent does the phonological and morphological structure of English present problems for syllabic writing?

7. Hebrew and Arabic are usually written from right to left, using a type of alphabetic writing called "consonantal" writing. Here is an example of a Classical Hebrew sentence from the Old Testament (adapted from Comrie (1987)).

וְאֵינָם מַכִּירִים לְדַבֵּר יְהוּדִית

Transliteration: W$^{\partial}$YNM MKYRYM LDBR YHWDYT

Pronunciation: wə$^{\partial}$ē^{y}nä̃m makkī^{y}rī^{y}m ləðabber yəhū^{w}ðī^{y}θ

[*Note*: ä represents a low round back vowel]

'And they do not know how to speak Judean.'

   a. On the basis of this sample, describe precisely how consonantal writing differs from straightforward alphabetic writing.
   b. Write out an English sentence in Roman script using the principle of consonantal writing; then ask (at least) two people to figure out what you have written. In light of which syllable structures your readers found easy and which tough to decipher, assess how practical such a system would be for use with the English language.
   c. Recall (or review) what you read about the morphological structure of Hebrew and Arabic in Chapter 4. What makes consonantal writing better adapted to these languages than to English?

SUGGESTIONS FOR FURTHER READING

Gelb (1963) is a classic study of the development of different writing systems in antiquity. Linguistically oriented surveys of writing systems can be found in Sampson (1985) and Coulmas (1989); the quotation at the opening of our chapter is from Coulmas. Gaur (1984) is a readable and lavishly illustrated history of writing. The story of the decipherment of ancient scripts is narrated in Gordon (1982). Diringer (1968) discusses the discovery and development of alphabetic writing through the centuries. Six excellent booklets, each by a distinguished author, have been gathered into a handsome book introduced by Hooker (1990); among other topics, it covers cuneiform, Egyptian hieroglyphs, and the early alphabet. Comrie (1987) provides illustration and discussion of orthography for some of the world's major languages. Interesting hypotheses about the influence of literacy on thinking and on culture are advanced in Goody (1977) and in Ong (1982). These hypotheses are constructively criticized by Street (1983).

REFERENCES

Comrie, Bernard, ed. 1987. *The World's Major Languages* (New York: Oxford University Press).

Coulmas, Florian. 1989. *The Writing Systems of the World* (Cambridge, MA: Blackwell).

Diringer, David. 1968. *The Alphabet* (London: Hutchinson).

Gaur, Albertine. 1984. *The Story of Writing* (London: The British Library).

Gelb, I. J. 1963. *A Study of Writing,* 2nd ed. (Chicago: University of Chicago Press).

Goody, Jack. 1977. *The Domestication of the Savage Mind* (Cambridge: Cambridge University Press).

Gordon, Cyrus H. 1982. *Forgotten Scripts: Their Ongoing Discovery and Evolution,* 2nd ed. (New York: Basic Books).

Hooker, J. T., ed. 1990. *Reading the Past: Ancient Writing from Cuneiform to the Alphabet* (Berkeley: University of California Press/British Museum).

Ong, Walter. 1982. *Orality and Literacy* (London: Methuen).

Sampson, Geoffrey. 1985. *Writing: A Linguistic Introduction* (Stanford: Stanford University Press).

Street, Brian V. 1983. *Literacy in Theory and Practice* (Cambridge: Cambridge University Press).

GLOSSARY

This Glossary defines and explains many important terms used in this book. When first discussed within the text, such terms have been printed in **boldface** to indicate that they are defined in the Glossary for ease of reference. Within the Glossary that follows, any **boldface** term has its own entry in the Glossary. To locate still further discussion of a term or concept, consult the Index on page 517.

Absolute universal   A linguistic pattern at play in all languages of the world without exception. Example: "Any language with voiced stops also has voiceless stops."

Accent   The pronunciation features of a **dialect.**

Adjacency pair   A set of two consecutive, ordered turns that "go together" in a conversation, such as question/answer sequences and greeting/greeting exchanges.

Adjective   A lexical category of words that serve semantically to specify the attributes of nouns *(tall ships)* and that can be morphologically or syntactically marked to represent degrees of comparison *(taller, most beautiful);* adjectives can occur in **attributive** position *(The steep hills)* or **predicative** position *(The hills are steep).*

Adposition   A lexical category of **function words** that serve syntactically as heads of prepositional (or postpositional) phrases and semantically to indicate a relationship between two entities; adpositions are called *prepositions* when they precede their noun phrase complements *(to school, with liberty, in the spring)* and *postpositions* when they follow them (as in Japanese *Taroo no* 'of Taro' and *hasi de* 'with chopsticks').

Affective meaning   The information conveyed by an expression about the attitudes and emotions of the producer toward the content or the context of expression; together with social meaning, affective meaning is sometimes called *connotation.*

Affix   A **bound morpheme** that occurs attached to a root or stem **morpheme.** *Prefixes* (attached to the beginning of the root or stem) and *suffixes* (attached to the end) are the most common types of affixes. Less common in the world's languages are *infixes* (inserted within the root or stem) and *circumfixes* (a part of which is attached at each end of the root or stem).

Affricate   Also called *stop fricative,* a sound produced when air is built up by a complete closure of the oral tract at some **place of articulation** and then released and continued like a **fricative.** Examples: English /č/ (as in *chin*) and /ǰ/ (as in *gin*); German /ts/ (as in *Zeit* 'time').

Agreement   The marking of a word (as with an **affix**) to indicate a particular grammatical relationship to another word in the sentence; a verb that *agrees* with its **subject** in **person** and **number** has a form that indicates that relationship; an adjective may agree with its head noun in **gender, number,** and **case.**

Allomorph   The alternate phonetic forms of a morpheme in particular linguistic environments. For example, the English plural morpheme has three allomorphs: [əz] (as in *buses*), [z] *(twigs),* and [s] *(cats).*

Allophone   A phonetic manifestation of a **phoneme** in a particular phonological environment. Example: In English, unaspirated [p] and **aspirated** [pʰ] are allophones of the phoneme /p/, and they occur in **complementary distribution.**

Alphabet   A writing system in which, at least ideally, each graphic symbol represents a distinctive sound of the language.

Alveolar   A sound articulated at the alveolar ridge, the bony ridge just behind and above the upper teeth.

Ambiguous   A term used to characterize an expression that can be interpreted in more than one way as a consequence of having more than one **constituent structure** *(John or Jack and Bill)* or more than one **referential meaning** (*river bank* and *savings bank*).

Antonymy   A term used in **semantics** to denote opposite meanings; words with opposite meanings are said to be *antonymous.*

Appropriateness conditions   Conventions that regulate the interpretation under which an **utterance** serves as a particular **speech act,** for example as a question, a promise, an invitation.

Approximant   A sound produced when one articulator is close to another but the vocal tract is not sufficiently narrowed to create the audible friction that typically characterizes **consonants;** thus, *approximant* refers to a **manner of articulation.** Examples: [w], [y], [r], [l].

Argument   A noun phrase that occurs in a verb phrase as part of a proposition. For example, the verb *wash* has one argument, a **direct object,** in *Alice washed the car.* (Some books would also treat the **subject** as an argument.)

Aspect   A grammatical category of verbs used to mark the way in which a situation described by a verb takes place in time, for example as continuous, repetitive, or instantaneous.

Aspirated   The term applied to sounds produced accompanied by a puff of air; represented in phonetic transcription by a following raised [ʰ].

Assimilation   A phonological process whereby a sound becomes phonetically similar (or identical) to a neighboring sound. Examples: In Korean, underlying

/p/ is pronounced as [b] between vowels; that is, /p/ assimilates to the voicing of the neighboring vowels. In English, /z/ (the underlying form of the plural morpheme) is realized as [s] following voiceless consonants other than sibilants.

Attributive adjective   An adjective that is syntactically part of the noun phrase whose head it modifies *(a spooky house);* distinguished from a **predicative adjective** *(The house is spooky).*

Auxiliary verb   A verb used with (or instead of) the main verb to carry certain kinds of grammatical information such as **tense** and **aspect.** In English, it is the auxiliary verb that is inverted with the **subject** in yes/no questions *(Will Lou fail?)* and that carries the negative element in contractions *(Lou can't sing).*

Bilabial   A **place of articulation** involving both lips.

Bilingualism   The state of having **competence** in more than one language.

Bound morpheme   A **morpheme** that functions as part of a word but cannot stand alone as a word. Examples: -MENT (as in *establishment*), -ER *(painter),* and 'PLURAL' *(zebras).*

Case   A grammatical category associated with nouns and pronouns that indicates their grammatical relationship to other elements in the clause, often the verb. Example: The pronoun *I* is marked for common case, *me* for objective case, and *mine* for possessive case; in the phrase *John's book, John's* is marked for possessive case, while *book* is said to be unmarked or to be marked for common case.

Circumfix   See **Affix.**

Clause   A constituent unit of syntax consisting of a verb with its subject and **argument** noun phrases; clauses can function as **constituents** of a sentence or can stand by themselves as simple sentences.

Click   A **stop consonant** defined by its **manner of articulation** and pronounced at various **places of articulation;** clicks such as the alveolar click used in English to express disapproval as in *tsk-tsk* or *tut-tut* function as phonemes in languages of the Khoisan family, such as Zulu.

Cognates   Words or morphemes that have developed from a single, historically earlier source. Example: English *father,* German *Vater,* Spanish *padre,* and Gothic *fadar* are cognates because all have developed from the same reconstructed Proto–Indo-European word *(pəter).* The term *cognates* is also used of languages that have a common historical ancestor. Example: English, Russian, German, Persian, and all the other **Indo-European** languages.

Communicative competence   See **Competence.**

Comparative reconstruction   A method used in historical linguistics to uncover the structures and vocabulary of an ancestor language by drawing inferences from the evidence that remains in several daughter languages.

Competence   The ability to produce and understand grammatical sentences in a language is called *grammatical competence,* and the ability to produce and interpret utterances appropriate to their context of use is called *communicative competence.*

Complementary distribution   A pattern of distribution of two or more sounds that do not occur in the same position within a word in a given language. Example: In English, [pʰ] does not occur where [p] occurs (and vice versa).

Complex sentence   A sentence that consists of a matrix **clause** and one or more embedded (or subordinate) clauses.

Conjugation   See **Paradigm.**

Consonant   A speech sound produced by partial or complete closure of part of the vocal tract, thus obstructing the airflow and creating audible friction. Consonants are described in terms of **voicing, place of articulation,** and **manner of articulation.** Abbreviated *C.*

Constituent   A syntactic unit that functions as part of a larger unit within a sentence; typical constituent types are verb phrase, noun phrase, prepositional phrase, and **clause.**

Constituent structure   The linear and hierarchical organization of the words of a sentence into syntactic units.

Content   Information that is conveyed or communicated by linguistic **expression.**

Content word   A word whose primary function is to describe entities, ideas, qualities, and states of being in the world; **nouns, verbs, adjectives,** and adverbs are content words; contrasted with **function words.**

Context   The social situation in which words, phrases, and sentences are uttered and which helps determine their interpretation.

Contrastive   A term used in **semantics** of a noun phrase that is marked as being in opposition to another noun phrase in a **discourse.**

Contrastive analysis   A method of analyzing languages for instructional purposes whereby a native language and target language are compared with a view to establishing points of difference likely to cause difficulties to learners.

Converseness   The term used to characterize a reciprocal relationship between pairs of words, as in *husband* and *wife.*

Cooperative principle   The set of four maxims that describe how language users cooperate in producing and understanding utterances in context: maxim of quantity, maxim of quality, maxim of relevance, and maxim of manner.

Coordinate sentence   A sentence that contains two (or more) **clauses,** neither of which functions as a grammatical constituent of the other; the clauses of a coordinate sentence are usually joined by a coordinating conjunction such as *and* or *but* (*John went to England, and Mary went to France*).

Correspondence set   A set of sounds in different languages all of which derive from a common earlier sound.

Creole   A contact language, a former pidgin, that has "acquired" native speakers.

Cuneiform   A written symbol developed by the Sumerians and Akkadians in the Middle East around 3000 B.C.; characterized by the wedgelike shape that results from its being written on clay with a stylus.

Declension   See **Paradigm.**

Deep structure   See **Underlying structure.**

Definite   A term used of a noun phrase that is marked to indicate that the speaker assumes that the addressee is able to identify its referent; opposed to *indefinite.* In English, definiteness and indefiniteness are marked by the choice of article (*the* versus *a*).

Reference   A semantic category through which language provides information about the relationship between noun phrases and their **referents.**

Referent   The entity (person, object, notion, or situation) in the world referred to by a linguistic expression. Example: The referent of *John's dog* is the four-legged canine belonging to John.

Referential   Said of a noun phrase that refers to a particular entity; *a good piano teacher* is referential in *Tom knows a good piano teacher* but not referential in *Tom wants to find a good piano teacher.*

Referential meaning   The meaning that an expression has by virtue of its ability to refer to an entity; referential meaning is contrasted with **social meaning** and **affective meaning,** and is sometimes called *denotation.*

Referring expression   An expression that refers to an entity or situation.

Reflex   A term used in historical linguistics for a linguistic form that derives from an earlier form called its **etymon;** reflexes of the same etymon are referred to as **cognates.**

Register   A language **variety** associated with a particular situation of use. Examples: baby talk, legalese.

Relative clause   A **clause** syntactically embedded in a noun phrase and semantically serving to modify a noun. The modified noun is the *head* of the relative clause. Example: In *This is the book that I told you about,* the relative clause *that I told you about* modifies the head *book.*

Repair   A sequence of turns in a conversation during which a previous **utterance** is edited, corrected, or clarified.

Repertoire   See **Linguistic repertoire.**

Representational   See **Iconic symbol.**

Semantic role   The way in which the **referent** of a noun phrase is involved in the situation described or represented by a **clause**—for example, as agent, patient, or cause.

Semantics   The study of the systematic ways in which languages structure meaning, especially in words and in sentences.

Sibilant   A member of a set of **fricative** sounds made by passing a continuous stream of air through a narrowed passage in the vocal tract thereby causing hissing, such as that created between the blade of the tongue and the back of the **alveolar** ridge in the production of [s] and [š].

Sign   A nonarbitrary indicator of an object or event, as smoke is a sign of fire; often contrasted with **symbol.**

Simple sentence   A sentence that contains only one **clause.**

Social dialect   A language **variety** characteristic of a social group, typically socio-economic groups, gender groups, or ethnic groups, as distinct from regional groups.

Social meaning   Information that words and sentences convey about the social characteristics of their producers and of the situation in which they are produced; together with **affective meaning,** social meaning is sometimes called *connotation.*

Sonorant   A class of **consonant** sounds comprising **nasals** and liquids.

Speech act   An action carried out through language, such as promising, lying, and greeting.

Stop   A speech sound created when air is built up at a **place of articulation** in the vocal tract and suddenly released through the mouth; sometimes called *oral stops* when **nasals** are excluded.

Subcategorization   Information about the types of **clause** structure that each **verb** permits in the verb phrase; for example, a verb may permit one or two noun phrases or none, as in *He burned the rice, She sold him the book,* and *He fell,* respectively.

Subgroup   The term used to refer to a set of languages that belong to the same **language family** and that developed as a single language for a period of time after other subgroups had developed into separate languages; thus, Romance and Germanic are subgroups of **Indo-European;** West Germanic is the subgroup of Germanic to which English belongs; also called *branch.*

Subject   A noun phrase immediately dominated by S in a phrase structure.

Subordinator   A word that marks the boundary between an embedded clause and its matrix clause; *that* is a subordinator in *I think that he fell.*

Suffix   See **Affix.**

Surface form   A word's actual pronunciation; generated by the application of the **phonological rules** of a language to the **underlying form;** sometimes also said of sentences (see **Underlying structure**).

Surface structure   The **constituent structure** of a sentence after all applicable **transformations** have applied.

Syllabic writing   Writing in which each graphic **symbol** represents a **syllable** rather than a word or a sound.

Syllable   A phonological unit consisting of one or more sounds, including a peak (or nucleus) that is usually a **vowel** or **diphthong;** frequent syllable types are CV and CVC.

Symbol   An arbitrary representation of an event or entity.

Synonymous   The term used to refer to words or sentences that mean the same thing.

Syntax   The structure of sentences and the study of sentence structure.

Tense   A category of the **verb** that marks time reference—for example, as past *(walked)* or present *(walk).*

Terminal string   The string of syntactic symbols (such as DET, N, V) generated by application of all applicable syntactic rules of a grammar; it is a string to which no further **transformations** can apply.

Topic   The main center of attention in an **utterance.**

Transformation   A syntactic rule that alters **constituent structure** in a systematic way; also called *transformational rule.*

Transitive verb   A verb such as *find* that takes a **direct object:** *She found the book.*

Trill   A **manner of articulation** characterized by the rapid (20 to 30 times per second) vibrating of an articulator caused by air passing rapidly over it; does not include vocal cord vibration.

Typology   A field of inquiry that seeks to classify the languages of the world into different types according to particular structural characteristics.

Underlying form   The form of a **morpheme** that is stored in the internalized **lexicon;** sometimes also said of sentences (see **Underlying structure**).

Underlying structure   The abstract structure of a sentence before any **transformations** have applied, specified by **phrase-structure rules;** also called *deep structure.*

Universal   A linguistic pattern at play in most or all of the world's languages; see also **Absolute universal** and **Universal tendency.**

Universal tendency   A linguistic pattern at play in most, but not all, of the world's languages; also called *relative universal.* Example: Most (but not all) verb-final languages place adjectives before the nouns they modify.

Utterance   An **expression** produced in a particular context with a particular intention.

Variety   Any language, **dialect,** or **register.**

Velar   A **consonant** sound whose **place of articulation** is the velum—that is, a consonant produced by the tongue approaching or touching the roof of the mouth at the velum.

Verb   A lexical category of words that syntactically determine the structure of a clause especially with respect to noun phrases, that semantically express the action or state of being represented by a clause, and that morphologically can be marked for certain categories (not all of which are realized in English): **tense** (present:*walk*/past:*walked*), **modality, aspect** *(walk/walking),* **person** (first:*walk*/third:*walks*), and **number** (singular:*walks*/plural:*walk*).

Voicing   The vibration in the **larynx** caused by air from the lungs passing through the vocal cords when they are partly closed; speech sounds are said to be *voiced* or *voiceless.*

Vowels   One of two major classes of sounds (the other being **consonants**); vowels are articulated *without* complete closure in the oral cavity and *without* sufficient narrowing to create the friction characteristic of consonants. Abbreviated *V.*

I N D E X

A separate Language Index follows this general index.
Terms followed by an asterisk (*) are defined in the Glossary, on pages, 503–15. The abbreviation "ex" following a number refers to an exercise.

LANGUAGE INDEX